D1083323

Under the editorship of Leonard Carmichael

New Directions in Client-Centered Therapy

Edited by

J. T. Hart

and

T. M. Tomlinson

BRIAR CLIFF COLLEGE
LIBRARY

SIOUX CITY, IOWA

HOUGHTON MIFFLIN COMPANY · BOSTON

New York   Atlanta   Geneva, Ill.   Dallas   Palo Alto

Copyright © 1970 by J. T. Hart and T. M. Tomlinson. The selections in this book are used by permission of and special arrangement with the proprietors of their respective copyrights. All rights reserved. No part of this work may be reproduced or transmitted in any form or by any means, electronic or mechanical, including photocopying and recording, or by any information storage or retrieval system, without permission in writing from the publisher.

Printed in the U.S.A.

RC
481
.H3x

Contents

58923

Foreword

Since this book points primarily toward the future trends which are growing out of the present currents in client-centered therapy, let me introduce it by taking a quick look at the past.

In the 1930's, I was developing a way of working with individuals which was influenced by my Freudian training at the Institute for Child Guidance in New York, by my own continuing experience with children and adults; and by the Rankian thinking to which I had been exposed through members of my staff and through a brief conference led by Rank. It seemed to me my way of working was simply that of the main current of therapeutic effort. It was not until I was invited to give a talk at the University of Minnesota in December, 1940, on "Newer concepts in psychotherapy," that I discovered these ways of working and thinking were regarded as new, controversial, radical, and threatening. I was forced to realize that I was saying something which came from *me,* that I was not simply summarizing a general trend, and that I was developing a viewpoint which was my *own.*

Thus what started for me in the 30's as a changing but supposedly well-accepted way of working therapeutically with individuals, was clumsily articulated as my own view in the early 1940's. During the next two decades it was found by an increasing number of individuals to be a congenial point of view. It was seized upon and developed (by them and by me) and enriched and given a firmer base through research. A theory was formulated out of the growing amount of experience with more and more diversified clients. In the 60's it continued to reach into new areas, to blossom and bear fruit in previously unimagined ways. This book is testimony to that fact.

Thus one might say that a "technique" of counseling became a practice of psychotherapy. This in turn brought into being a theory of therapy and of personality. The theory supplied the hypotheses which opened a whole new field of research. Out of this grew an approach to all interpersonal relationships. Now it reaches into education as a way of facilitating learning at all levels. It is a way of conducting intensive group experiences, and has influenced the theory of group dynamics. It has infiltrated industrial management, student personnel work, and the pastoral counseling of the religious worker in various faiths. It has had significance in the area of community development, both here and abroad. It has been a prime force in the trend toward a new science of man, toward a new philosophy of the behavioral sciences. And still its delicate branches, like the tender shoots of a spreading vine, continue to reach further in new directions which continually surprise me.

It has been an exciting thing to have been a part of the core of this whole development throughout more than three decades. It has been even more exciting to see younger colleagues — and students of colleagues — pushing out into areas new and strange to me, and to learn from their efforts. One of the facts that has always given me great satisfaction is that client-centered therapy, by its very nature, has always provided a congenial home for the development of creative hunches. Many of the chapters of this book provide ample evidence of this fact.

Lest I leave the impression that the fluidity and change in the client-centered field leave nothing that is constant or stable, let me quote four statements from my Minnesota talk of December, 1940, which still have, I believe, relevance for the present and future of this whole trend.

At that time I said that this newer approach "relies much more heavily on the individual drive toward growth, health, and adjustment. [Therapy] is a matter of freeing [the client] for normal growth and development." This emphasis on unused human potential, on the urge toward self-actualization, upon the release of individual capacities, has continued to be a theme of much that has followed.

Another statement was that "this therapy places greater stress upon . . . the feeling aspects of the situation than upon the intellectual aspects." The incredible hunger of individuals for this emphasis has been evident in recent years in developments as diverse as encounter groups (T-groups, sensitivity groups), the "flower children," and task-oriented industrial executives who deal *first* with the feelings involved in their relationships, and second with the intellectual and operational problems they face. Even in education, that bastion of conservatism, students are refusing to attend educational institutions simply as disembodied intellects — impersonal, information-absorbing computers. They are insisting that feelings have a place, too, in the educational system.

A third statement was that "this newer therapy places greater stress upon the immediate situation than upon the individual's past." This has become so widely accepted that it scarcely needs comment. Field theory has won out over theories rooted in the sequential past. An existenial thrust pervades every field of our endeavor. Life is lived *now*, not simply in the past or future. The belief that an interpretation of the past is of significant help to the person in his current behavior has so diminished that it has almost disappeared.

Finally, "this approach lays stress upon the therapeutic relationship itself as a growth experience." From the vantage point of 1940 it would hardly have been possible to envisage the ways in which teachers, executives, religious workers, group leaders, as well as therapists, would come to operate on this basis — providing a personal relationship which is a growth-promoting psychological climate. Nor could we have foreseen the development of a theory of experiencing which helps to describe the way in which the relationship is used by the person to enhance and enrich and clarify the life he is living.

In addition to these four elements which were expressed, even in 1940, as a part of the client-centered approach, there are at least four others which have been implicit from the outset and deserve to be mentioned.

The willingness to change, the openness to experiential and research data, has been one of the most distinctive features of client-centered therapy. It has never, I believe, been an orientation founded on dogma. The incorporation of this element of openness, of changingness, has helped to set it apart from most other therapeutic orientations. The confidence of the client-centered worker is not a confidence in truth already known or formulated. It is a confidence in the *process* by which truth is dimly perceived, tested, and approximated.

Another implicit feature is that the client-centered therapist has seen the unique, subjective, inner person as the honored and valued core of human life. In taking this perspective, the client-centered orientation has taken a stance profoundly at variance with the major trend of American psychology which sees human beings as measurable objects, to be viewed through an atomistic, mechanistic, deterministic frame of reference. The client-centered view has no apologies for having taken an opposing stance.

Another element, perhaps clearer only in more recent years, is the recognition that the affluent person of today is literally crying out with hunger for a human relationship which is deep, real, nondefensive — a truly person-to-person relation. This I believe we have helped to provide from the first, but we are now more aware of that profound need.

One final implicit assumption should be stated. It is that training for a person who desires to engage in a helping relationship cannot be cognitive only, but, in fact, must be primarily *experiential.* Little did we realize that this simple conviction, aimed at training successful therapists, would eventually throw out a significant challenge to the whole educational system, with its belief that learning exists only "from the neck up." We have attempted to help potential therapists sense their attitudes, their feelings, their changing personal reactions, and in doing so we have underscored the value of educating the whole person, and the sterility of much that passes for education.

Thus it is out of such a past, out of some simple but far-reaching assumptions and convictions, that the client-centered orientation has continued to grow and flower, and to reach into the most unlikely areas of modern life. The diversity of that flowering, the outreach into process research, phenomenological and existential theory, self-directed encounter groups, family therapy, and new points of view on a philosophy of values — all of these and more are demonstrated in the contributions made by many people in the following chapters. I hope the excitement of this spreading impact will be caught by the reader.

Carl R. Rogers
La Jolla, California

Preface

The book first planned is not always the book that is finally written. When we began to discuss doing a book on client-centered therapy about five years ago, our plan was to write a primer that could provide an introduction to the orientation's basic ideas and techniques. A primer seemed like a good idea then, and it still does. Introductions are available for the systems of Freud, Jung, Adler, Frankl, and other therapists, but there is nothing comparable to introduce the student and general reader to the therapy of Carl Rogers. This book, the result of our earlier discussions, is not the primer we'd planned; rather it presents new findings and new ideas and was written for the specialist rather than the general reader.

One reason we did not carry out our original writing project was that we soon found ourselves more interested in surveying recent developments than in summarizing and explaining familiar concepts. Our little book quickly became a big book, and the collaboration between the two of us became an editorial collaboration involving many contributors.

Still, in one respect our original motivation for writing a primer was maintained and fulfilled. We thought such an introduction was needed because client-centered therapy is not simple and cannot be quickly understood; it needs a book to itself. Too frequently we found that the textbook versions of client-centered therapy in the heads of students and colleagues were grossly oversimplified. Throughout the planning and writing of this book we tried to demonstrate that client-centered therapy is much more than a simple "uh huh" therapy. We think that the chapters of this book show the Rogerian orientation to be a many-sided, theoretically sophisticated, and experientially complex system of therapy.

Another reason the book changed is that we changed. When we began to plan the book, one of us (J.H.) had just completed a series of laboratory experiments on the feeling-of-knowing experience and was primarily interested in connecting this laboratory research to the experiential theory of client-centered therapy. But this research soon led to broader concerns about the psychology of awareness and into research on meditation and the autoregulation of brain waves. These concerns are described and related to psychotherapy in the final chapter "Beyond psychotherapy." As for the second editor (T.T.), he was involved in studying the effect of role modeling on small group interaction and attempting to develop laboratory analogues to psychotherapy process. Then the Watts riot occurred, a research project (Los Angeles Riot Study) on the causes and consequences of the riot was initiated, and soon after this editor changed his address from UCLA to the Office of Economic Opportunity in Washington. Perhaps these fragments of personal history will explain why our interest shifted from doing a primer to surveying, and developing, new directions.

Some of the chapters included here are reprints while others were commissioned especially for this book. Several of the authors (Rogers, Gordon, Gendlin, and Shlien) have long been associated with the client-centered orientation; the others are newer names. All the authors have a common background of practice in client-centered therapy and have done research related to therapy. We thank the contributors for their tolerance of the delays that inevitably accompany the preparation of a multi-author book.

Our selection of chapters was guided by two criteria: one, the *significance* of the individual contributions; and two, *coverage* of new developments. We sought to survey most of the important new developments in client-centered theory, research, and practice. Unfortunately, there are omissions; for example, the new and very promising institutional treatment techniques for children worked out by Nicholas Hobbs are not reported in this volume. Even so, the coverage we did achieve makes for a diversity of content that does not facilitate rapid transitions from chapter to chapter. Simplicity and coherence, our original criteria for the primer, have been sacrificed in order to present the real diversity that is found in contemporary client-centered therapy. This means that this is not a book many readers will want to read from cover to cover. Our advice is like that of a smorgasbord to its customers: sample, don't gobble.

Before closing this preface we want to express our special gratitude to Carl Rogers. He has contributed to this work from its inception, but our indebtedness to him extends beyond the book. Of course, any statement about client-centered therapy must owe a debt to the originator of the orientation, but our indebtedness is more personal than that. Both of us were graduate students at the University of Wisconsin where we worked with Dr. Rogers as therapists and research colleagues. He is a teacher who believes students should be encouraged to do their own work; we have attempted to do so, with the result that some of the ideas expressed in this book are not ones with which Dr. Rogers fully agrees. Nonetheless, he has urged us to develop and publish these ideas, whether as possible extensions of or departures from client-centered therapy.

This book is dedicated to Carl Rogers is grateful acknowledgment of the man and his thought. We learned from the ideas and the person.

Acknowledgments

We thank the following publishers for permission to reprint articles and chapters from their publications: Aldine Publishing Company, American Journal of Psychotherapy, the American Psychological Association, Appleton-Century-Crofts, Association for Supervision and Curriculum Development, Australian Journal of Psychology, Basic Books, Inc., Charles E. Merrill Publishing Company, Houghton Mifflin Company, John Wiley & Sons, Inc., Journal of Humanistic Psychology, McGraw-Hill Book Co., and Yale Scientific.

We are grateful to Mr. Robert Rooney, Miss Jacqueline Pourciau, and Mrs. Nancy Bergman of Houghton Mifflin for the editorial assistance they provided and to Miss Lorna Haworth for the typing and other secretarial services she so skillfully rendered.

PART ONE

Introduction

Newspaper journalism reports the events of the day, magazine journalism discusses the events of the week and the month, and history examines the events we cannot remember but feel we should. Within this classification, the chapters of Part I are neither journalism nor history. They resemble historical studies in that ideas and techniques and research are re-examined that are not current in modern client-centered therapy. They are, if such bastard entities may be permitted a name, chapters of journalistic history.

Of course, some critics may wonder whether an orientation as young as the client-centered one can have a history. Others will doubt that it has a present. And perhaps a few critics will charitably grant a past and a present to client-centered therapy but will be loathe to wish it a future. We believe it has all three.

For a scientific orientation to have a history it must have done more than exist; it must have discovered and formulated something of continuing significance. Each of the three chapters in this introductory section discusses the significant advances made by client-centered therapy during its thirty-year history. The chapters differ in the kinds of advances they emphasize.

Chapter 1 stresses the changes that have occurred in the ways client-centered therapists do therapy. The chapter emphasizes that what client-centered therapists do and do not do has changed. Dr. Hart argues that these changes are so pronounced that client-centered therapy must really be divided into three: nondirective, reflective, and experiential therapy. Each corresponds to a different period in the development of client-centered therapy. For a vivid illustration of the differences between the three periods, the author provides many therapy excerpts, especially for the most recent version, experiential therapy.

The first chapter is complemented and supplemented by van der Veen's

Chapter 2 on "Recent trends in the client-centered framework." He also emphasizes advances in the practice of the therapy but, unlike Hart, organizes his presentation around research findings rather than examples. He focuses particularly on the recent client-centered thinking about processes that unfold during therapeutic change and on conditions the therapist must create to promote them. These processes and conditions are thought to be necessary for effective therapy with any client, whether student, soldier, housewife, or hospitalized schizophrenic. In van der Veen's chapter the special difficulties of creating the necessary conditions for therapy with hospitalized schizophrenics are emphasized; this emphasis is itself historically interesting because older versions of client-centered therapy were thought to be inapplicable to hospital patients.

Chapter 3 continues and expands the emphasis on research findings begun by van der Veen; Shlien and Zimring examine the full scope of client-centered research. No doubt we should avoid missing the forest for the trees when acres of research findings are surveyed, but we need a few pathways so that we can get in and out of the forest of results and retain a map of the journey. In their carefully organized chapter, the authors notch many trees and carve many paths, so that the reader who carefully follows their survey will be well prepared to understand the context of the more recent research findings presented in later sections of this book.

Shlien and Zimring's grouping of client-centered developments in research and theory into four *stages* corresponds to the three *periods* discussed by Hart if Stages III and IV are collapsed into one period, Period III, which Hart calls the "Period of Experiential Therapy." The contents of the remaining parts of this book are expositions of recent developments in experiential therapy.

We believe that these introductory chapters demonstrate that client-centered therapy has a meaningful and interesting past. While doing so they develop an historical frame into which the jigsaw of details discussed in succeeding parts of the book can be fitted. As for client-centered therapy's future, we believe it has one. What that future is likely to be is foretold in Part Six. In Part One the authors review central ideas, general trends, and overall perspectives in the style of journalistic history. In Part Six they also take a long view to gain perspective rather than a close view to scrutinize details; the chapters in Part Six might be considered histories in the future tense. It would not be bad advice to recommend that *New directions in client-centered therapy* be read as some people read novels — begin at the beginning, jump to the ending, ease into the details of the middle, and then read the ending again.

1

The Development of

Client-Centered Therapy*

JOSEPH HART

Client-centered therapy has changed strikingly in the last three decades. The changes are important, since they express new insights gained through countable hours of therapy and research. Unfortunately, many of these changes are comparatively unknown; the client-centered orientation of the 1940's is widely known but the developed orientation of the late 1960's is not.

The professional therapist who knows only early versions of client-centered therapy has seen the seeds but not the pumpkins. It is understandable, of course, since so much is happening in the world, even in the small world of psychotherapy, that we frequently and conveniently assume that therapies we have not studied recently remain the same. Crowded professional lives are thereby eased, but stereotypes substitute for information and pumpkin seeds are mistaken for pumpkins.

The usual sterotype of the client-centered therapist is one who is passive, innocuous and addicted to uh-huhs. Such a stereotype has never been accurate, but it does convey, in a distorted way, one of the main features of the early client-centered approach, nondirectiveness. As a caricature of modern client-centered therapy, however, it misses the mark. By how much and for what reasons it will be the task of this chapter to demonstrate.

Today the field of psychotherapy is in a state of healthy, if not happy, eclecticism. Few therapists believe that a single technique or a single theory can encompass the entire range of problems and applications they must

* This chapter was developed from a paper that appeared in the Wisconsin Psychiatric Institute Bulletin (Hart, 1961).

3

meet. Nonetheless, despite this tolerant eclecticism, there is a tendency on the part of most professionals to attend only to the newest and flashiest developments in the field. We develop a journalistic sensitivity to proclamations of revolution and a corresponding insensitivity to re-formulations of familiar ideas and techniques. Although the conceptual and technical changes reviewed in this chapter do not provide the revolution or breakthrough in psychotherapy that journalists, politicians, and proselytizers demand; they do add new ingredients and new blendings to the eclectic pot. These changes may contribute to the eventual development of a general theory of therapeutic change. Consistent with this aim, it should be stressed that it is not the purpose of this chapter (nor of this book) to persuade Freudians, Jungians, Adlerians, Skinnerians, or devotees of other persuasions to become Rogerians. (There is only one Rogerian, and sometimes I am not so sure about him.)

An Overview of Change

Understanding of the ideas and techniques of client-centered therapy will be aided if its thirty year span of development, from 1940 to 1970, is divided into three periods: the period of nondirective therapy, 1940-1950; the period of reflective therapy, 1950-1957; and the period of experiential therapy, 1957-1970. These periods are displayed in Table 1.1.

TABLE 1.1

Periods in the Development of
Client-Centered Psychotherapy

	Functions of the Therapist	Personality Changes
Period I Nondirective Psychotherapy 1940-1950	Creation of a permissive, noninterventive atmosphere; *acceptance* and *clarification*.	Gradual achievement of *insight* into one's self and one's situation.
Period II Reflective Psychotherapy 1950-1957	*Reflection* of feelings, avoiding threat in the relationship.	Development of congruence of self-concept and the phenomenological field.
Period III Experiential Psychotherapy 1957-1970	Wide range of behaviors to express basic attitudes. Focus on the client's experiencing. Expression of the therapist's experiencing.	Growth in the process continuum of inter- and intra-personal living by learning to use direct experiencing.

The table and this chapter are organized around the evolving answers offered by the client-centered orientation to the general questions:

(1) What behaviors and attitudes of the therapist facilitate the client's growth?

(2) What basic personality changes occur in the client during successful psychotherapy?

As these questions indicate, the focus of this chapter is on the therapy-specific concepts that developed in client-centered therapy. *How* can therapeutic personality change be effected and *what* changes occur? Questions about *why* personality can change, involving more abstract concepts such as Rogers' idea (1957b) of an innate actualizing tendency, are not considered in detail here. This is a legitimate restriction; many therapists interested in the client-centered orientation are unsure about the Rogerian assumptions concerning the basic nature of man — they are simply interested in anything that works. Undeniably, ethical assumptions are significant since they influence what one tries to make work, but they will be considered in Parts Five and Six.

Each period will be linked to a major book by the founder of nondirective psychotherapy, Carl Rogers. When nondirective therapy became widely known in the 1940's, Rogers attracted many students and colleagues. This meant that the number of contributors to the theory and practice of the therapy increased. Nevertheless, it is reasonable to represent each historical period by one of Rogers' books because he is certainly the best known articulator of the client-centered position.[1]

Using Table 1.1 as a guide, we can now consider the ideas and practices that emerged in each period. The presentation of experiential therapy will be more detailed than those of the nondirective and reflective periods. I am most concerned with presenting modern client-centered therapy, not the earlier therapies for which plenty of sources are already available to the reader.

Nondirective Psychotherapy

As described in Rogers' book *Counseling and psychotherapy* (1942), non-directive therapy placed central importance on the client's gradual achievement of insight into himself and his situation. The therapist attempted to facilitate this insight by creating a permissive, nonauthoritarian setting in which the client was free to proceed at his own pace and in his own directions. By his accepting and noninterventive manner the therapist tried to free the client from the necessity of binding and blinding defensiveness. The thera-

---

[1] See Part Six, for Rogers' reflections on the development of client-centered therapy.

pist's activity was mainly that of helping the client clarify his feelings and perceptions.

> Effective counseling consists of a definitely structured, permissive relationship which allows the client to gain an understanding of himself to a degree which enables him to take positive steps in the light of his new orientation. This hypothesis has a natural corollary, that all techniques used should aim toward developing this free and permissive relationship, this understanding of self in the counseling and other relationships and this tendency towards positive self-initiated action (Rogers, 1942, p. 18).

Even in this early stage, client-centered psychotherapy exhibited a characteristic that has distinctively defined its position among therapeutic approaches. A definite effort was made by Rogers and his colleagues to collect and make available for scientific analysis the raw material of psychotherapy. Empiricism has remained an integral part of the client-centered orientation and is, in large measure, responsible for the ever-developing, ever-tentative nature of this approach. Theories and constructs that do not yield testable and general hypotheses have been discarded in favor of those that do. Rogers' book *Counseling and psychotherapy* contained, when published in 1942, what was then a unique feature — a complete transcript of phonographically recorded therapy case. Here is an excerpt from that case that directly presents the style of nondirective psychotherapy.[2]

> C: I don't know how, though — I think they'll work out pretty well. Darned if I can make it out (looking at his notes). (Pause.) Oh, that had to do with a girl I got to talking to! She said she hoped that there would not be a strip-tease to the floor show, and I was trying to analyze why she objected to it. I guess maybe she didn't want any competition. Either she would feel that the girl would be superior to her, or she had secret desires in that direction which she could condemn in someone else but not in herself.
>
> T: Doing a little evaluating of others' motives as well as your own, hmm?
>
> C: Oh, yes. I've always done that. Well, I've always analyzed others perhaps a little bit more than myself. (Pause.) Well, then, to sum all this up: I think that I should seek out every and all healthy situations and enter into them. I noticed a curious thing. When I made a resolve that I would take the hard way, and even though it might be the long way too, although I made the resolve in a vacuum, I got a release (laugh), so that way back in the last analysis, one experiences only one's own nervous system, so that it seems to be the resolve that counts, but at the same time that resolve does have to be nourished by the outward situations. And I suppose once in a while a person can resolve in a vacuum when they really sincerely mean it, but it's too hard to keep meaning it in a vacuum.

[2] For other examples of nondirective psychotherapy, see Combs (1946), Snyder (1947), Raskin (1948), and Curran (1945).

T: And also, as you pointed out before, perhaps your earlier notion of doing something in a vacuum was really not too much a desire to make a resolve, but more a desire to get away from making a resolve.

C: M-hm. Well, there's all sorts of masks. (Pause.) What do you think of my prescription? Do you care to add anything to that?

T: No, I think that — well, we might be able to add details to it, but I think that that is the prescription that really will count toward more long-time satisfactions. I think you're right — it may be a hard road, may be a long road. But — at least it's the only road.

T: It's a road that you feel pretty well convinced now offers more satisfactions in the long run than in the other direction (Rogers, 1942, pp. 411-412).

The conditions in the United States at the time Rogers' book on nondirective therapy was published were just right for its acceptance. Despite doubts on the part of the publisher and the author, *Counseling and psychotherapy* sold very well and is still selling. Clinical psychologists and counselors had found psychoanalysis not fully appropriate to American needs. Besides, the analysts in the United States had formed a medical guild that effectively excluded nonphysicians. A therapist might practice psychoanalytic therapy but he could not be an analyst — he remained a layman, a second-class practitioner. Directive psychotherapy, the other major alternative open to therapists, was equally unappealing. Giving information to people about how they should and could change didn't seem to change them.

We can see why American psychologists were ready to respond favorably to a psychotherapy that emphasized helping relationships, a psychotherapy that rejected both the medical model of the analysts and the vocational model of the directive therapists. Nondirective therapy filled a gap.[3]

The orientation was enthusiastically accepted by many therapists even though nondirective concepts such as "permissiveness," "clarification," and "insight" were given meaning mainly by examples rather than by systematic integration into a well-developed theoretical structure or by research. Therapists of the nondirective orientation were identified almost more clearly by what they did not do than by what they did do. During this period, therapist responses such as giving advice, expressing opinions or feelings, interpretations, offering plans, and other interventive activities were eschewed. Considerable emphasis was placed upon using the individual's self-initiated drive toward growth, health, and adjustment. The therapist was a psychological midwife, whose function it was to aid in bringing forth the client's own insights and positive actions.

---

[3] An excellent panoramic history of the people, events, and ideas influential in the early growth of clinical psychology is available in Reisman's *The development of clinical psychology* (1966).

Reflective Psychotherapy

As we pass from Period I to Period II the orientation is noticeably more mature. In Period II we find that many of the concepts and practices of client-centered therapy have been systematized and supported by extensive research. The most striking change in the actual practice of psychotherapy was the therapist's emphasis on responding sensitively to the affective rather than the semantic meaning of the client's expressions. "Shallow" and "content" responses, sometimes characteristic of nondirective clarification, were avoided. This period is best represented by Rogers' book, *Client-centered therapy* (1951).

As mentioned previously, from the beginning client-centered therapy committed itself to a scientific approach to the phenomena of psychotherapy. This commitment and its effects are clearly illustrated in passing from Period I to Period II. Considering quantity alone, the second period is characterized by a decided increase in the amount of research available on many aspects of psychotherapy. (See Hobbs, 1955; Cartwright, 1957; and Seeman, 1948, 1956.)

In Period II the therapist's role was reformulated and elaborated, with new emphasis placed on his sensitive responsiveness to the client's feelings. Reflection of feelings was substituted for clarification, and cognitive features of the interaction were de-emphasized. To implement the client's reorganization and reintegration of his self-concepts the therapist's basic task was to remove sources of threat from the relationship and to mirror the client's phenomenological world to him. The technique available to the therapist in achieving this implementation was reflection of feelings. Raskin described the technique in these words:

> . . . counselor participation becomes an active experiencing with the client of the feelings to which he gives expression. The counselor makes a maximum effort to get under the skin of the person with whom he is communicating, he tries to get *within* and to live the attitudes expressed instead of observing them, to catch every nuance of their changing nature; in a word, to absorb himself completely in the attitudes of the client. And in struggling to do this, there is simply no room for any other counselor activity or attitude; if he is attempting to live the attitudes of the other, he cannot be diagnosing them, he cannot be thinking of making the process go faster. Because he is another, and not the client, the understanding is not spontaneous but must be acquired, and this through the most intense, continuous and active attention to the feelings of the other, to the exclusion of other types of attention (as quoted in Rogers, 1951, p. 29).

Raskin's description clearly portrays the reflection of feeling response as a more focused and intense means of clarification.

To convey the style of this stage of therapy, I again quote briefly from a therapy transcript:

T: That catches a little more of the flavor of the feeling, that is, it's almost as if you're really weeping for yourself . . .

C: And then of course, I've come . . . to see and to feel that over this, see, I've covered it up. (Weepy.) But . . . and . . . I've covered it up with so much *bitterness,* which in turn I had to cover up. (Weeps.) That's what I want to get rid of! I almost don't *care* if I hurt.

T: (Gently.) You feel that here at the basis of it, as you experienced it, is a feeling of real tears for yourself. But that you *can't* show, mustn't show, so that's been covered by bitterness that you don't like, that you'd like to be rid of. You almost feel you'd rather absorb the hurt than to . . .than to feel the bitterness. (Pause.) And what you seem to be saying quite strongly is "I do *hurt* and I've tried to cover it up."

C: I didn't *know* it.

T: M-hm. Like a new discovery really.

C: (Speaking at the same time.) I never really did know. But it's . . . you know, it's almost a physical thing. It's . . . it's sort of as though I — I — I were looking within myself at all kinds of nerve endings and — and bits of, of . . . things that have been sort of mashed. (Weepy.)

T: As though some of the most delicate aspects of you — physically almost — have been crushed or hurt.

C: Yes, And you know, I do get the feeling, oh, you poor thing. (Pause.)

T: Just can't but feel very deeply sorry for the person that is you (Rogers and Dymond, 1954, pp. 326-327).

Without delay we will now shift into a discussion of experiential psychotherapy. The coverage of the first two periods has been brief, but my intent was to provide a background, not a history. The reader who wants more information may consult the original sources already cited or the secondary sources: Hall & Lindzey (1957) and Ford & Urban (1963).

Experiential Psychotherapy

Experiential psychotherapy, although clearly an outgrowth of the nondirective and reflective psychotherapies, is more difficult to characterize. It is still taking shape; yet because of its relative maturity, it is a broader, more general development in the practice and theory of psychotherapy. Some of the viewpoint's early ideas can be found in Rogers' book *On becoming a person* (1961).

One impetus for the evolution of reflective psychotherapy into experiential psychotherapy was provided by the attempts of a group of client-centered therapists to offer psychotherapy to hospitalized psychotics and well-adjusted normals. In working with these people, the therapists encountered new problems and difficulties and, consequently, were forced to seek new ways to implement and understand their efforts. (See Shlien, 1961; Gendlin, 1966b; and Rogers, 1967b.) However, even before the application of client-centered therapy to new client populations, the emphasis within this group had begun to shift from specific therapeutic techniques (such as reflecting feelings) to a focus on general therapist attitudes and abilities that could be communicated via a wide range of therapist behaviors. Rogers, in his paper on "The necessary and sufficient conditions of therapeutic personality change" (1957b), introduced the idea that, given certain basic conditions of therapy, among them the therapist attitudes of positive regard, empathic understanding, and genuineness, positive personality change would occur.[4] Personality change was hypothesized to occur regardless of the specific techniques used by the therapists or the particular psychological problems of the clients.

Worthy of special mention is the condition of genuineness. As client-centered therapists began to move farther and farther from prescriptions for what-to-do and when-to-do-it the ramifications of this concept for their daily practice of therapy became more apparent. They found themselves being more expressive and active in communicating their own concerns and feelings to their clients. This greater expressiveness and outgoingness was found to be essential later in working with regressed and recalcitrant schizophrenic patients (Gendlin, 1966b).

In the significant paper, "A process conception of psychotherapy" (1958), which forecast another trend in the evolution of client-centered therapy, Rogers discussed client changes during therapy in broad terms, encompassing many aspects and levels of the client's interpersonal and intrapersonal relationships. The significance of this paper lies not only in the specific process conception it outlined, but also in the overall emphasis of the argument on a *pervasive process of personality change* embracing all significant aspects of the client's changing inner life and its effects on his personal relationships and life situation.

Psychotherapy can be investigated and conceptualized at many levels — physiological, verbal, behavioral, and existential. Yet when therapists discuss therapy they most often talk in experiential (existential, subjective, phenomenological) terms. Client-centered therapy in its research endeavors has embraced all levels, but its theorizing has most often been formulated in phenomenological terms. In nondirective psychotherapy central emphasis was placed on the phenomenological event, insight. For reflective psychotherapy, self-concepts were central. In his "Process" paper, Rogers laid the groundwork for the broadest and potentially most productive phenomenological conception, that of experiencing.

The concept of experiencing as applied to psychotherapy originated with Gendlin and Zimring (1955), and in recent writings Gendlin (1961b, 1966a) has extended the theory. The word "experiencing" refers both to the theory of experiencing and to the phenomena of experiencing. Briefly described, it refers to the apperceptive mass of the individual's subjective life, the im-

[4] Consult Ellis (1959) for a critique of Rogers' paper.

plicity felt and directly known inner sense that is the source of personal meanings.

Experiencing is an everyday phenomenon; for example, experiencing occurs whenever we try to explain something to another person and can't quite express our meaning. We say something like, "No, that's not quite it. Just a moment. Let me see if I can put it another way." The inner sense that our words do not quite match our meanings is an example of experiencing. If we did not have this inner sense of discrepancy between words and meanings, we would not pause, we would have no reference for evaluating our verbalizations. In fact, we do search for the right words and finally, if successful in our inner focusing, say (or feel), "yes, that's it, that's what I mean." Experiencing is a subjective process of inner referring. Gendlin's theory of the effectiveness of client and therapist in-therapy activities is formulated in terms of the phenomena of experiencing.

> An effective therapeutic response refers to what the individual is now aware of. However, it does not refer simply to his words or thoughts. Rather, it refers to the present felt datum, his present experiencing . . . An effective therapeutic response thus aims to do three closely related things: (1) to refer directly and help the individual refer directly, to his present experiencing, (2) to allow him to feel this present experiencing more intensely, to grapple with it, face it, tolerate it, work it through, and (3) to help him put its implicit meaning into concepts which accurately state it (Gendlin, 1961b, p. 245).

Because psychology for many years outlawed subjective experiences from the domain of proper scientific investigation (unless they masqueraded as contentless verbal reports) it must be emphasized that the phenomena of experiencing are not unamenable to scientific research (Gendlin and Berlin, 1961; Tomlinson and Hart, 1962; Hart, 1965). However, it is likely that the traditional procedures of rat psychology and agricultural statistics cannot be applied with power to the investigation of experiencing. One of the most pressing needs of contemporary psychology is the development of adequate methodologies and instruments to study subjective processes (Bergin, 1964).

One caution: the phenomena of "experiencing" are not synonymous with those of consciousness or subjective experience. Experiencing refers to a demarcated subjective process (or processes) that is known but not always conscious in the sense that it can be put into words. A complete psychology must of course deal with all significant subjective processes but, in psychotherapy, many of the simple events of conscious life are comparatively irrelevant and insignificant as objects for the client's and therapist's attention. The process of experiencing refers to the individual's sense of personal meanings; it is a process of internal sensing rather than a something.

Examples of the application of the theory of experiencing to phenomena of psychotherapy will be given later. Let us first complete this sketch of the transition from reflective psychotherapy to experiential psychotherapy.

With the application of the client-centered psychotherapy to hospitalized schizophrenics the shift, among client-centered therapists, from reflection of the *client's* feelings to active communication of warmth and the *therapist's* feelings was accelerated. Client-centered therapy, after more than a decade of research and practice, has been rightly established as an effective technique for aiding maladjusted out-patients. Relying upon the attitude of basic respect for the individual client and his potentialities for self-direction, client-centered therapists successfully employed the technique of reflecting feelings to communicate their vital and close understanding of the client's moment-to-moment feelings. The early, research-attested accomplishments should not be ignored.

However, when faced with nonverbal, nonexploring and, nonmotivated schizophrenic patients, the client-centered therapist was bound to be frustrated in his attempts to respond to the patient's verbalized feelings. Therapists were impelled to seek new modes of expressing and fulfilling their therapeutic aims. Building upon the face-to-face attempts to do therapy with recalcitrant patients and the concepts of Rogers, Shlien, Gendlin, and others, modes of responding and new conceptualizations of psychotherapy were developed. This new therapy, experiential psychotherapy, although initially fashioned to deal with resistive psychotic patients, also applies to other client and patient groups.[5]

Let us now try to picture the changing features of experiential psychotherapy, without forgetting that they are changing. First, a few therapy excerpts provide a starting point for discussing the ways experiential psychotherapy resembles and differs from reflective psychotherapy. Notice especially, when reading these excerpts, how the experiential therapists are more responsive in communicating their feelings to the clients. Although reflection of feeling is used, the feelings to which the therapists respond are often the nonexpressed or vaguely expressed preconceptual feelings — responses are directed at the clients' experiencing. These excerpts were selected from the files of a research project that investigated the processes of psychotherapy with schizophrenic patients. (The research is reported in Rogers, 1967b.)

HUT

    C: (Has been talking about her husband's job.) And that's about all the news I know. This other fellow is finally going . . .

    T: (Interrupts.) Don't have to tell me the news.

    C: Finally going into . . .

    T: (Interrupts.) That's one thing . . .

[5] Kirtner & Cartwright (1958) provide a detailed analysis of the failures among counseling center out-patients; it is probable that experiential therapy will prove effective with some of these clients.

C: (Interrupts.) . . . business for himself.

T: . . . One thing I feel which I . . . do want to say (C: mhm.) that I have enjoyed sharing the news with you, and yet, looking back, I wonder whether I shouldn't have said more often somehow that I knew that some way it was hard for you to do anything else . . . with me sometimes but share the news. You know what I mean?

C: Not too well.

T: I felt that was true in this moment, that, well, I really would like to hear how it came out (C: mhm.) with these guys but, uh, then I felt like saying (C: mhm.) maybe we could, I don't know, stand the embarrassment of not knowing how to fill up the . . .

GET

(Long pause.)

T: Am I right that in some ways you're in your kind — in your kind of tent right now and don't want to be bothered about coming out.

(Long pause.)

T: You look awfully sad —

C: Mhm (sigh) — I was just thinking — I sometimes wonder — (laugh) — it sounds crazy though — it seems I'm married to two guys (laugh) — been married to two guys (quiet wondering echo).

T: (Pause.) You mean it bothers you that you're not sure whether you were or not, or the idea bothers you?

C: (Quiet mm-m.) Not being sure — (long pause) — it seems though it was just for during the summer but it seems so crazy — just the summer. (Laugh.)

T: Sounds as though you missed them.

C: Mm-mm — one especially . . . (Long pause.)

T: It would be awfully nice to find out you were married or are married, to the one you miss, wouldn't it?

C: Hm-hm (quiet, yes). (Long pause.)

T: I hope you're not still married to both at once. That would be rather complicated! (Said in a joking way.)

C: Mm-mm (quiet, trailing). (Long pause.) What time is it getting to be? (With a sigh.)

T: Twenty to twelve. (Long pause.) No wonder you feel like going off in your tent where you can think about it without being bothered.

C: Mm-hm. (Quiet, in agreement.)

T: Even though it makes you sad . . . (Long pause.) I hope that along with the sadness maybe there's a touch of (pause) him, — and hope to find him again, or somebody as nice or and that all is going well with him. I mean, isn't that —

C: Hm-hm (quietly and agreeably).

T: Or wondering if he knows how rough things have been for you. It can set off all kinds of things you want to go off into your tent and think about . . . (pause and sigh). So I'll stop talking.

WED .
(Long silence.)

    T: Sometimes when you're very quiet and feel lousy and so on, I just feel as though I don't understand what it's all about.

    C: You think —

    T: Last time and this time I have a strong feeling that I do understand what it's all about. I could be mistaken, but — I feel I do have some understanding about it. (Pause.) I guess one way I've found my-self wondering about it is whether — (long pause) — whether in some ways maybe you feel more upset about us, the possibility of going out than you did when you felt nobody would let you out. (Pause.) But I don't know. (Long pause.) I guess the way I understand some of your feelings is that there's a possibility you might actually be out — meeting the world. (Long pause.) Perhaps, and here I'm just sort of guessing, perhaps it's a little bit more comfortable to try to put all thought of such things out of mind and just, and to pull back into yourself than it is to — take a look at them. Perhaps it's something like that or am I way off the beam? (Long pause.)

    C: Naw. Naw, I'm not afraid that the world is terrible, I don't know, I was wondering the other day, because the people I do know here and like, I wish would go out there with me.

    T: Uh, hum. But the way it shapes up in your feelings is not that you're afraid of going out but that you do wish very much that some of the people here that you care about could go out with you. I mean so you'd have some companionship in it, huh? (Long pause.) I just wish you could take them with you when you go. (Long pause.) I expect that you feel it'd be pretty lonesome if you couldn't take them with you. (Long pause.)

    C: Yeah. Especially the ones that they, I play cards with everyday.

    T: Uh, hum.

    C: I feel just like a part of them.

    T: Huh?

    C: Feel like now I guess, like a part of them.

    T: They feel like a part of you, would you say?

    C: Of me.

GET

I found GET in the dayroom and she joined me with such dejected heavi-ness that I found myself having to pull within myself to dig for some reserve strength. Neither of us talked as we went down the stairs and through the tunnel. GET walked with what seemed like sagging hopelessness. I walked with dread of the hour ahead because my own loneliness now seemed small compared to hers and I felt inadequate to help or comfort her.

. . . I sat with all these feelings and found the silence soothing. My fear lessened as I let in the quietness, but my pain grew with a new wanting to reach out somehow to GET who sat so close and yet seemed so far off and shut away inside her loneliness. I felt so *unalone* in my loneliness and I wanted to share that unaloneness with her somehow. I looked at her downcast face and hoped that she would look up. I don't know how long I sat there looking at her before I broke the silence . . .

(After 15 minutes of silence.)

T: You look as though you felt very much alone . . .

C: (No response.)

(After several minutes of silence.)

T: When I say *alone* rather than *lonely* I mean more than lonely . . . as though you were so lonely that you can't bear to tell anybody how lonely you are . . .

C: Hm-mn.

T: So it makes you all alone in it.

C: Course it don't help it any either.

T: It's awfully hard to reach out of loneliness sometimes . . . I don't quite know what you meant but . . . if you feel as though people don't want to hear or don't care . . .

C: No . . . Nn-nn . . . It seems like everybody has got an ear but I don't have no words to say . . . nothing to say . . .

T: You mean you feel you don't have anything to *offer* anyone?

C: Hm-nn . . .

(Silence for 2-3 minutes.)

T: I guess what I'm trying to say is you don't have to offer or be able to give anything . . . just sit with it and it may feel less alone . . . I think sometimes it's awfully hard to find words to say how . . . I guess I'll put it: *I* sometimes find it hard to find words to say how low *I* feel when I'm low . . . so that I can't reach out to somebody who might be able to understand . . . but . . . sometimes it helps just to sit with somebody I know would understand if I could talk about it . . . especially somebody who doesn't ask *"What's* the matter? *How* do you feel? *What* do you . . ."* when I just plain feel like crying for no reason . . . just sit. . . . So I'll shut up. . . . All I'm trying to say is *I care* . . . I care and I'm sorry everything is so hard for you now.

C: It isn't so bad . . . it's better than it used to be.

T: The sun isn't exactly shining though, is it? (This is a reference to an earlier interview when GET told me that her mother once complained that she, GET, always expected the sun to shine on her.)

C: Last week it just seemed that I had something to say every minute we were down here . . . and today . . . nothing . . . I'm trying to find . . . can't remember what we talked about . . .

T: I do. . . . You were thinking about the future. . . . What you'd like to do. . . . You were doing some very realistic, very honest thinking about what you might be able to do . . . and ended up getting yourself pretty discouraged.

C: I still think that I'd kinda like to be a lady boxer . . . because I've got the temper for it I think. . . . It seems like I'm always angry . . .

(Silence for 3-4 minutes.)

T: "It seems to me like I'm always angry." . . . It seem to *me* like *I'm* angry when everything seems too hard . . . when I can't find sunlight

> . . . when I wish somebody would take care of me . . . when everything
> seems to go wrong . . . and when I get feeling very *alone* with that
> whole dark picture . . . I think *you've* felt alone for some 20 years. . . .

I have included more examples of experiential psychotherapy than of reflective and nondirective psychotherapy. Few sources are presently available
that present experiential cases and examples are necessary to illustrate
stylistic changes. Of course, the several examples provided do not convey
the full range of therapy behaviors used by the experiential therapists, e.g.,
those involving physical contact and nonverbal communication. Below are
listed a few comments, made by some of the therapists associated with the
research project investigating the process of psychotherapy with hospitalized
schizophrenics. These comments concern incidents in their relationships with
the patients. The descriptions are vignettes, not case presentations.[6]

> Patient did not wish to be seen after first two contacts, I told him "that's okay
> with me" only to find that "that isn't okay with me." I called him back and
> asked him to come in ten times, then decide. Since we had already decided to
> play cards since he refused to sit in silence, he then provided a cribbage
> board. After five hours he indicated that he would like to come in as long as
> he is here. Now I have a cribbage partner who cheats, or tries to.

> I felt bored and angry with Mr. SAF, with myself, and with the relationship.
> When I was finally able to partially express these feelings (about the thirtieth
> interview) the relationship seemed to improve. At present I am not sure
> where it will go.

> Initially Mrs. FIN was very resistant to therapy and, after four interviews,
> refused to come again. At this point the therapist insisted that Mrs. FIN
> continue but gave her more freedom within the therapeutic hour by explain-
> ing that she could leave when overly uncomfortable. A turning point in the
> relationship occurred when, under the stress of moving to a new ward, Mrs.
> FIN cried and expressed her feelings of aloneness and helplessness to the
> therapist. Possibly the most meaningful elements of the relationship with
> Mrs. FIN were my nonverbal expressions of concern and caring (seeing her
> on the ward, loaning my coat to her, etc.).

> He comes (I feel at my implicit request, although I feel he also wants, on
> some level, to come); he talks constantly (I have to interrupt to make a
> response). For the first ten interviews or so, I felt that it made no difference
> to him whether it was me he talked to or anybody else. I feel now that he is
> beginning to be aware of *me*, and the relationship *begins* to develop. With
> this is coming slowly some show of embarrassment before me in regard to

---

[6] The author expresses his gratitude to the therapists who provided these comments. The
comments were originally intended as personal communications and are presented in the
informal style in which they were written. The research on psychotherapy with schizophrenics is fully reported in Rogers (1967b).

past and present extratherapy feelings he discussed, as well as rare but meaningful spontaneous and felt interchanges between us.

The patient refused right from the start to meet with me. To every mention of "next time" and to every invitation to enter a room with me he reacted with explicit anger and demands that I leave him alone. Over some weeks I accepted his feelings, anger, dislike of me; I let him leave; I had him brought by attendants; I argued with him; I was both honest and dishonest; I could not help but react negatively to his rejection and I felt he cut the ground out from under my right to be with him. Because of these feelings in me I decided that he should not be further coerced to see me, since he would only discover a threatened and threatening person in me. How to make the contacts continue — and yet without the sort of coercion which brought his rejection and altered my inward climate? I could do nothing else, so I visited the patient on the ward. I made my meetings brief since I did not want to inflict too much of my then very determined and tense feelings. When I stayed longer, standing next to where the patient stood, I soon found that he did not walk away, nor did he ask me to leave. I discovered here a dimension of free choice for him and an unavowed, subverbal way of developing a relationship. He reacts very totally, smiles, is furious, moves three steps away suddenly, at something I have said, or a motion I have made. Whenever I get such reactions, I look inside myself and talk till I have described just how I feel at the moment. I experience that this withdrawn man is in one sense the very opposite of withdrawn . . . so skinless and sensitive that my presence next to him was almost too intense for him to bear. And his many and seemingly deep reactions to me, as we stood in long silences, made me uncertain, tense, nakedly and doggedly present, getting from him such strong and minutely sensitive feedback to myself that I, too, felt thoroughly non-withdrawn.

A colleague who read the manuscript of this chapter said of the therapy excerpts and comments, "Why these sound like everyone from Albert Ellis to John Rosen and Freida Fromm-Reichman! You can't use these as examples of client-centered therapy. People will say that client-centered therapists are merely doing what others have done for a long time." He's right and he's wrong; because of the diversity of the problems they encounter and the variety of temperaments brought to those problems, experiential therapists such as those quoted do respond to silence and resistiveness in different ways. Some ask questions of the patient, some try to express their own inner feelings, some try to respond to the patient's nonverbal communications — most do all these at one time or another. Their style of approach varies, but their aims and their touchstone of responsiveness are the same. This touchstone is experiencing — the central phenomenon of experiential psychotherapy. And it is the theory of experiencing which provides the framework for evaluating the effectiveness and meaningfulness of the therapists' responses.

The theory of experiencing provides a theoretical network within which the client-centered constructs and activities are elaborated. For example, a reflection of feeling response is effective when it focuses on the client's inner experience. A mere repetition of the client's verbalizations is inadequate and not therapeutic. In the same line, an interpretation, to be a useful response, must be a verbalization by the therapist of the client's *experiencing* that has not yet reached the verbal level. An interpretation that is not directed at the client's experiencing does not facilitate but provokes defensiveness. By responding to a client's experiencing we can see that experiential therapists have maintained and given fuller meaning to a characteristic of Periods I and II — a respect for the client as an independent person with human capabilities and potentialities. By responding to the client's experiencing the therapist recognizes and conveys his responsiveness to the client's essential humanness. Despite the bizarreness of patients' symptoms and the furor of their rejections, it is possible to respond to them as subjective, experiencing persons.

Similarly, when the therapist responds to the client or patient by openly conveying his (the therapist's) in-the-moment experiencing, he has responded to the person as a person. The patient or client is free to accept or reject the therapist's communications, but he may eventually be touched and changed by them.

The preceeding paragraphs should have made clear why my friend's evaluation of the therapy excerpts and comments was both right and wrong. Client-centered therapy is not a hodge-podge, but it has expanded both its techniques and its concepts. Concepts about essential therapist attributes and the process of experiencing are intended to encompass many styles of therapy. Gendlin has commented about the generality of the modern client-centered approach, ". . . for a number of reasons, it is likely that the positive patient process is the same in all orientations. If so, some grounds for a universal theory of psychotherapy may be extrapolated" (1966b). In another paper he extends these claims:

> Current developments in psychotherapy have obscured the lines between different orientations. For example, contrast psychoanalysis and client-centered therapy. What a sharp difference that once seemed to be! Today, looking back, we see the similarity: both were highly formal denials of a real relationship. One role-played a relationship of transference; the other role-played a perfectly neutral acceptance. We see two of a kind — artificial, formalistic avoidances of genuine interaction between two people. The patient's real feelings were considered invalid (transference). The analyst's feelings were also considered invalid (counter-transference). Similarly, in client-centered therapy, it was a mistake for the therapist to interject his own feelings into the therapeutic situation. Today, client-centered therapists make "genuineness" the first condition for therapy and therapist-expressivity and spontaneity main therapeutic factors. Psychoanalysts are also moving toward real involvement and commitment as persons, with less reliance on technique (1966a, pp. 210-211).

The therapist "attitudes" Rogers discussed in his "Necessary and sufficient conditions" paper (1957b) can be viewed as prerequisite abilities or interpersonal skills the therapist must possess before he can establish a relationship and respond to the client in a therapeutic way. A therapist cannot facilitate the client's learning to refer to and rely on his own (the client's) inner feelings unless the therapist is (1) genuinely, outgoingly positive toward the client (unconditional positive regard); (2) sincerely attempting to share the client's inner world and communicating his accurate understanding (empathic understanding); and (3) able to reveal his own inner feelings (congruence or genuineness).

Some therapists object to this formulation of the therapist's role. To them the emphasis on congruence, positive regard, and empathy seems unprofessional, it is merely "playing pals" with patients. In one respect their objections are certainly correct; client-centered therapy is not compatible with the kind of professional training program that, after a number of years of irrelevant training, sends its accredited professionals out to heal the sick. Recent research has shown very clearly that nonprofessionals can do psychotherapy and do it well. These nonprofessional therapists might be said to "play pals" with the people they help, but this activity should not be derided. Very few people encounter friends or pals who are able and willing to manifest the understanding, sympathy, and sincerity that will help them to cope with problems of living and the search for a meaningful identity. Empathy, positive regard, and congruence should be viewed as interpersonal skills; they are just as real and just as complex as the cognitive skills that are usually emphasized in our schools for professional therapists.[7]

Period II emphasized the client's integration of his self-concepts. This idea can be encompassed within the framework of experiential psychotherapy. The increasing integration of self-concepts is viewed as one aspect of the client's increasing access to his experiencing. As his process of experiencing becomes more directly available and usable, his self-concepts, which are a product of the experiencing, change, because he incorporates new inner sources for self-concept checking.

It is important to reiterate that experiential psychotherapy is still developing; as a theory of therapy it will need many more modifications. Hebb (1958, p. 465) has said, "What we need from a theory is that it should hold together long enough to give us a better one." Through research and clinical applications, experiential psychotherapy will alter and improve, and will itself be encompassed by more general and more detailed formulations. Rogers' comments (1959) about the meaning of research for the future of psychotherapy are pertinent here.

> Its major significance, it seems to me, is that a growing body of objectively verified knowledge of psychotherapy will bring about the gradual demise of "schools" of psychotherapy including this one. As solid knowledge

---

[7] See Goodman, Chapter 18, for a discussion of how these skills can be assessed.

increases as to the conditions which facilitate therapeutic change, the nature of the therapeutic process, the conditions which block or inhibit therapy, the characteristic outcomes of therapy in terms of personality or behavioral change, there will be less and less emphasis upon dogmatic and purely theoretical formulations. Differences of opinion, different procedures in therapy, different judgments as to outcome, will be put to empirical test rather than being simply a matter of debate or argument (pp. 29-30).

In this discussion of Period III, I have tried to sketch the basic trends in experiential psychotherapy. The basic ideas will be discussed, expanded, applied, and related to research findings in the following chapters. For review, here is a summary of the basic features:

(1) A wide range of therapist behaviors are encompassed. This includes some interventive activities (such as expressing opinions and feelings or asking questions) that, in Periods I and II, were considered undesirable.

(2) The orientation postulates certain therapist attitudes (congruence, empathic understanding, and unconditional positive regard) as necessary for the initiation and continuance of an effective therapeutic relationship.

(3) The flexibility of therapist behavior mentioned in (1) is structured within the phenomena of experiencing. The therapist's responsiveness within the therapy relationship is based upon his own immediate experiencing of the interaction and is directed toward the client's subjective processes. This focus on experiencing leads the therapist to express, at times, many of *his* immediate and momentary feelings to the client.

(4) Although experiential psychotherapy centralizes the basic raw material with which therapists deal — their own experiencing — it views the client as an integrated, biosocial person. Research and theory construction in experiential psychotherapy attempt to identify and interelate the relevant physiological, behavioral, social, and phenomenological events of psychotherapy. The continuity of therapy phenomena and other interpersonal and intrapersonal events is stressed.

This chapter gave an overview of important changes in client-centered therapy,[8] with a concentration on the most recent period, experiential therapy. Many examples were provided so that readers could judge for themselves whether client-centered therapy has changed. In the succeeding chapters, less emphasis will be given to examples and more to research and therapy.

---

[8] For other accounts of the history of client-centered therapy, see Rogers (1967a) and Seeman (1966).

REFERENCES

BERGIN, A. E. Psychology as a science of inner experience. *Journal of Humanistic Psychology,* 1964, 4, 95-103.

CARTWRIGHT, D. S. Annotated bibliography of research and theory construction in client-centered therapy. *Journal of Counseling Psychology,* 1957, 4, 82-100.

COMBS, A. W. Basic aspects of non-directive therapy. *American Journal of Orthopsychiatry,* 1946, 16, 589-605.

CURRAN, C. A. *Personality factors in counseling.* New York: Grune and Stratton, 1945.

ELLIS, A. Requisite conditions for basic personality change. *Journal of Consulting Psychology,* 1959, 23, 538-540.

FORD, D. H. and URBAN, H. B. *Systems of psychotherapy.* New York: Wiley, 1963. Ch. 11, pp. 396-444.

GENDLIN, E. T. Initiating psychotherapy with "unmotivated" patients. *Psychiatric Quarterly,* 1961a, 35, 134-139.

GENDLIN, E. T. Experiencing: A variable in the process of therapeutic change. *American Journal of Psychotherapy,* 1961b, 15, 233-245.

GENDLIN, E. T. *Experiencing and the creation of meaning.* Glencoe, Ill.: Free Press, 1962.

GENDLIN, E. T. Existentialism and experiential psychotherapy. In C. Moustakas (Ed.), *Existential child therapy.* New York: Basic Books, 1966a, pp. 206-246.

GENDLIN, E. T. Research in psychotherapy with schizophrenic patients and the nature of that "illness." *American Journal of Psychotherapy,* 1966b, 20, 4-16.

GENDLIN, E. T. and BERLIN, J. I. Galvanic skin response correlates of different modes of experiencing. *Journal of Clinical Psychology,* 1961, 17, 73-77.

GENDLIN, E. T. and ZIMRING, F. The qualities or dimensions of experiencing and their change. *Counseling Center Discussion Papers,* 1955, (1, Whole No. 3).

HALL, C. S. and LINDZEY, G. *Theories of personality.* New York: Wiley, 1957, Ch. XII. Pp. 467-502.

HART, J. T. The evolution of client-centered therapy. *Psychiatric Institute Bulletin,* 1961, 1 (Whole No. 2).

HART, J. T. Memory and the feeling of knowing experience. *Journal of Educational Psychology,* 1965, 56, 208-216.

HEBB, D. O. Alice in wonderland, or, psychology among the biological sciences. In H. F. Harlow and C. N. Woolsey (Eds.), *Biological biochemical bases of behavior.* Madison: University of Wisconsin Press, 1958. Pp. 457-467.

HOBBS, N. Client-centered psychotherapy. In J. L. McCary and D. E. Shear (Eds.), *Six approaches to psychotherapy.* New York: Dryden, 1955. Ch. 1.

KIRTNER, W. and CARTWRIGHT, D. Success and failure in client-centered therapy as a function of initial in-therapy behavior. *Journal of Consulting Psychology,* 1958, 22, 329-333.

RASKIN, M. M. The development of non-directive therapy. *Journal of Consulting Psychology,* 1948, 12, 92-110.

REISMAN, J. M. *The development of clinical psychology.* New York: Appleton-Century-Crofts, 1966.

ROGERS, C. R. *Counseling and psychotherapy.* Boston: Houghton Mifflin, 1942.

ROGERS, C. R. *Client-centered therapy.* Boston: Houghton Mifflin, 1951.

ROGERS, C. R. A note on the nature of man. *Journal of Counseling Psychology,* 1957a, 4, 199-203.

ROGERS, C. R. The necessary and sufficient conditions of therapeutic personality change. *Journal of Consulting Psychology,* 1957b, 21, 95-103.

ROGERS, C. R. A process conception of psychotherapy. *American Psychologist,* 1958, 13, 142-149.

ROGERS, C. R. Client-centered therapy in its context of research. English version of Ch. XII in C. R. Rogers and Marian Kinget, *Psychotherapie en menselyke verhoudingen: Theore en praktyk von de non-directive therapie.* Utrecht, Holland: Ultgeverijket Spectrum, 1959.

ROGERS, C. R. *On becoming a person.* Boston: Houghon Mifflin, 1961.

ROGERS, C. R. Client-centered therapy. In S. Arieti (Ed.), *American handbook of psychiatry.* New York: Basic Books, 1967a. Vol. III.

ROGERS, C. R. (Ed.) *The therapeutic relationship and its impact: A study of psychotherapy with schizophrenics.* Madison: University of Wisconsin Press, 1967b.

ROGERS, C. R. and DYMOND, ROSALIN (Eds.) *Psychotherapy and personality change.* Chicago: University of Chicago Press, 1954.

SEEMAN, J. Research perspectives in client-centered psychotherapy. In O. H. Mowrer (Ed.), *Psychotherapy theory and research.* New York: Ronald, 1948.

SEEMAN, J. Client-centered therapy. In D. Brower and L. Abt (Eds.), *Progress in clinical psychology.* New York: Grune & Stratton, 1956.

SEEMAN, J. Perspectives in client-centered therapy. In B. J. Wolman (Ed.), *Handbook of clinical psychology.* New York: McGraw Hill, 1966. Pp. 1215-1229.

SHLIEN, J. A. A client-centered approach to schizophrenia: First approximation. In A. Burton (Ed.), *Psychotherapy of the psychoses.* New York: Basic Books, 1961. Ch. XI, pp. 285-317.

SNYDER, W. U., et al. *Casebook of non-directive counseling.* Boston: Houghton Mifflin, 1947.

TOMLINSON, T. M. and HART, J. T. A validation study of the process scale. *Journal of Consulting Psychology,* 1962, 26, 74-78.

2

Recent Trends in the

Client-Centered Framework*

FERDINAND VAN DER VEEN

Introduction and Historical Overview

Since its inception, client-centered therapy and research has sought to
specify as accurately as possible the basic elements of psychotherapy. This
chapter presents some theoretical developments and the results of a research
program which have taken some large steps toward furthering our understanding of the therapy process. Some early characteristics of client-centered
work will first be reviewed to help place these developments in proper perspective.

Client-centered therapy became a coherent approach in the early 1940's.
Carl Rogers, the originator and central figure in this approach, came to Ohio
State University after more than a decade of work in a community guidance
clinic in Rochester, New York. The early theoretical and research development of client-centered work took place at Ohio State University. Central
ideas, such as the role of the self-concept and the concept of defensiveness,
were developed by Rogers and a very active group of staff and students.
A major technical innovation was the use of the wire recorder (tape re-
corders had not been invented yet) to record therapy interviews for training
and research.

At this point, the approach was termed "nondirective" by its founders.
This label emphasized their belief in the inherent capacity of the person in

* This chapter is adapted from a paper presented at the Veterans Administration Center,
Wichita, Kansas, August, 1966.

treatment to guide his own growth when given the opportunity. "Nondirective" also helped to characterize the use of the reflection of feeling as the primary technique in therapy, strongly rejecting "directive" or controlling therapist activities as helpful for personal growth. The term "nondirective" was later dropped in favor of "client-centered." "Nondirective" focused too narrowly on one aspect of the relationship, namely, not controlling the client; while "client-centered" better characterized the therapist's consistent attempt to understand the client and respect his inner resources.

It was Carl Rogers who discovered that major personality change could occur in therapy if the therapist listened closely to the client and then phrased as carefully and simply as he could what he thought the client was feeling at that moment, from the client's frame of reference. For a time this was called reflecting the client's feelings, but now it is called empathically understanding the client. While this discovery was initially overworked as a technique, it is still the foundation on which all the subsequent developments have been built.

Some curiosity has been expressed about the choice of the term "client" rather than "patient," to designate the person seeking help. No doubt the nonmedical university setting played a part in this choice. But more central was the belief that anything in either the therapist or the client that promoted the dependent, "directive," qualities typical of the doctor-patient relationship would be detrimental. The capacity of the client for taking an active responsible role in his therapy has always been considered crucial to its success.

Client-centered therapy came on the clinical scene as somewhat of a maverick, and with good reason. In several ways it went counter to prevailing schools of thought. First it avoided esoteric language and attempted to use concepts that were directly observable in experience. Second, it avoided professionalism, maintaining that what made a good therapist was not the degree he held nor his professional identity but rather his personal qualities and attitudes in the relationship with the client. And third, it avoided the diagnostic point of view, in terms of both testing and categorizing disorders. From the very beginning its focus was that the client needed to be understood from his own point of view, and that diagnosis would only rarely be of help in therapy and could often be harmful through delay and through thinking in terms of labels rather than the client's experience.

In place of these three objections — to esoteric language, to professionalism, and to the diagnostic point of view — client-centered therapy focused on the here and now, the immediate present moment in the experience of the client; on the basic attitudes of the therapist toward the client and on his ability to listen; and on the careful recording and measurement of client and therapist variables in research and training.

As could be expected, the acceptance of client-centered technique and theory has varied tremendously. In some professional fields, such as psychiatry and social work, it has had a limited impact, while in others, such as counseling and pastoral psychology, it has become a dominant force.

Recent Developments

Rather than give a detailed review of the changes in client-centered thought over the past two decades, I will sketch briefly some of the more recent theoretical developments, developments which have gone a long way toward identifying the ingredients in the process of therapy.[1]

The framework for the theory is essentially one of a scientific hypothesis: *if* certain conditions are present, *then* certain changes will follow. This is in contrast to most other therapy approaches, which are concerned with the "why" of behavior — why persons do what they do. Client-centered theory is also concerned with the "why," but strictly to help understand the "how" of personality change. The theory is not limited to therapy but is also applicable to helping relationships in any interpersonal area, be it psychiatry, education, religion, business, industry, or government. While each of these areas has its special skills and demands, the success of their endeavors to help others through the medium of the personal relationship depends upon similar factors as are found in successful psychotherapy.

The "if-then" hypothesis of client-centered theory is that *if* certain conditions are present in the therapist and the client, *then* certain predictable changes will take place in the client. It states further that *only* these conditions are necessary, no others are needed. What are these essential ingredients? For the therapist, they all concern his personal attitudes in relation to the client, how he acts and feels toward the client. There are three of these personal attitudes: the therapist's *genuineness* or *congruence,* his *empathic understanding,* and his *acceptance* or *unconditional positive regard. Genuinenss* or *congruence* means being yourself, not putting on a front, not being defensive with the client. Congruence is defined more technically as a condition within the person in which his feelings, his awareness of his feelings, and his expression of them to the other person, all correspond or are congruent with one another. An example of low congruence would be where the therapist feels angry or disgusted· but denies it and pretends to like the client.

The second therapist condition, *emphathic understanding,* refers to the accurate moment-to-moment awareness of the client's present experience, as the client sees it. Like a good interpretation, a good empathic understanding is put in such a way that the patient can understand and accept it as an accurate statement of his present experience. A great deal of selectivity is required of the therapist to know what in the client's expression is most important to him. In this area, perhaps more than any other, technical training

---

[1] The substance of these developments is presented in Rogers (1957, 1959a, and 1959b). Also relevant is the work of Gendlin (1961, 1964), Barrett-Lennard (1962), Standal (1954), and Krause (1964).

is of vital importance. Most of us just do not have the opportunity in our everyday social experience to test our empathic skills. It is surprising how few attempts are made, even within the family unit, at empathic understanding of another person's feelings.

The third condition, *acceptance,* means valuing or prizing all aspects of the client, including the parts that are hateful to himself or that appear wrong in the eyes of society. The more technical term for this condition is *unconditional positive regard,* which means that the therapist does not attach "conditions of worth" to the client and does not manipulate the client into behaving in a way the therapist values, but instead, that he cares for the client without strings attached.

While these conditions are stated in a somewhat all-or-none way, they are meant to represent end points on a continuum. No therapist is expected to be 100 per cent genuine or acceptant, not if he is human, but if he is 60 per cent, more progress will occur than if he is only 30 per cent.

An essential quality of the therapist conditions is that each is important to us in all our personal relationships. While we may not always put it into words, we immediately sense and respond differently to someone who is being formal and socially "correct" with us, than to someone who is being direct and open. When we are trying to get something across, we usually know right away whether we are getting an understanding ear or a preoccupied one. We very easily have a sense of being liked or not, even in quite casual contacts. The point of the technical labels is not to make these attitudes or conditions seem remote from our everyday experience, for they are not, but to define as clearly as possible the relationship dimensions that are of special importance to the process of psychological growth.

Given these therapist conditions, and given some psychological contact between therapist and client, what qualities in the client are necessary for change? Client-centered theory holds that the therapist conditions are so central for change that only two, relatively simple, client conditions are necessary. One is that the client is *anxious or vulnerable.* He has some sense that he wants something about his present condition changed. The other element is that he *perceives the therapist conditions* to a minimal degree. He needs to have a minimal sense that the therapist is genuine, empathic, and has positive regard for him in order to risk changing.

To the degree to which the therapist conditions (genuiness, empathy, and acceptance) and the client conditions (vulnerability and some awareness of the therapist's attitudes) are present, a predictable change will take place in the client. Speaking very generally, this change has the usual aspects of successful outcome, for example, the traditional triad of adequacy at love, work, and play. However, the concern with what goes on in the interview itself, with the kind of change process that can be detected in the client *during* the interview, has led to the formulation of a process conception of therapeutic change.

The Process Conception

The process idea is a somewhat radical change from earlier thinking about psychological health. It holds that psychological functioning can be located on a continuum, which at one end is rigid, fixed, and static, and at the other end is flexible, flowing, and changing. This dimension applies to our inner experience and to the meanings that experience has for us. If our experience is *in process,* changing, flowing, and continually meaningful, we are psychologically healthy. When our experience is not in process, when it is static, repetitive, and unresponsive, we are psychologically maladjusted.

The general conception of process was derived from a number of specific dimensions of change observed in the therapy behavior of clients. Specific scales have been developed for these dimensions, which make it possible to measure a client's stage of process at a particular time in therapy. Examples of these scales are the client's Manner of Problem Expression, his Degree of Intrapersonal Exploration, and his Manner of Relating to the Therapist. At the low end on the *Manner of Problem Expression* scale the client does not see problems, or sees them as completely outside himself. In the middle, he recognizes his own contribution to the problem. At the high end, he is resolving the problem through self-exploration and understanding. On the *Intrapersonal Exploration* scale no personally relevant material is discussed at the low end. In the middle, the client is attempting to understand what is going on inside of him. At the upper end, he is expressing himself fully in a spontaneous and open fashion. On the *Manner of Relating* scale the client moves from a distrustful, closed, and impersonal relationship with the therapist, to a trustful, open, and personal one. In each example, the low end represents a fixed way of viewing events, a way that is distant from the person's feelings, while the high end describes a creatively changing response involving the person's inner experience.

The scientific equation now reads that if the therapist conditions of genuineness, empathic understanding, and unconditional positive regard are present, and if the client perceives these to a minimal degree and also experiences some vulnerability, then the client will move from a rigid mode of experiencing, with fixed meanings, to a flexible mode, with a flow of experience and new meanings. With this psychological change process, improvement will occur in the client's social and work activities and in his sense of personal fulfillment.

Some Research Findings

While these ideas and terms may sound good, can we reduce them to actual observations and put them to the test? There has been a great deal of research on client-centered therapy, too much to outline here. A bibliography of client-centered work compiled in 1957 listed more than one hundred titles (Cartwright, 1957). The chapter by Shlien and Zimring in this book reviews client-centered research in detail. However, it is possible to present some recent findings and implications from a comprehensive research program that attempted to measure all aspects of the scientific equation on one sample of cases. Measures were obtained of the conditions provided by the therapist, their perception by the client, process scale changes by the client, and client changes on personality tests.

The research program involved a significant new application of the client-centered approach. During its history client-centered therapy has been identified with the university out-patient setting, evolving its practices and theory around experiences with community and student cases. Partly to overcome this limitation, partly to provide a critical test of the present theory, but most of all because of the therapeutic challenge it involved, the step was taken several years ago to work intensively with the hospitalized patient, primarily those diagnosed as schizophrenic. This coincided with the appointment of Rogers to the Psychiatry and Psychology Departments at the University of Wisconsin in 1957.

A comprehensive research design was formulated, based upon the experience of earlier therapy studies with counseling center clients and exploratory work at a local mental hospital. In several ways this was a unique research undertaking. First, experimental work with the psychotherapy of schizophrenics was almost nonexistent. Also, the research involved collecting data on a large test battery from severely disturbed patients and their controls, from the therapists, and from ward personnel over a long period of time. But perhaps most significantly, it involved the tape recording of more than two thousand hours of therapy.

Therapy researchers have consistently been handicapped by the sheer abundance of material that needs analysis. A unique method for dealing with the vast array of taped interview material was the use of two or three brief segments, each four minutes long, randomly selected from an interview. Obtaining reliable indices of interaction on the basis of brief samples of behavior proved to be an important breakthrough in the methodology of studying the therapy process.

What kinds of findings were obtained from these segments and the comprehensive test data? I will describe here some major findings of one study in the program (van der Veen, 1967). A detailed report of a number of studies and of clinical findings can be found in Rogers, et al. (1967).

The subjects in the study were fifteen schizophrenic therapy cases. They had had from twenty-five to one hundred and seventy-five therapy interviews at the time the later test data were collected. The cases were randomly selected from the hospital population and were not necessarily motivated for therapy. In fact, many were not.

The test battery contained standard psychological tests — the MMPI, Rorschach, TAT, and others — that were used to arrive at an outcome criterion of the degree of improvement over therapy. Ratings of the tape-recorded segments were obtained for both the therapist condition variables and the client process variables. The segments were rated, with moderate reliability, on three therapist scales: degree of congruence; empathic understanding; and positive regard. The patients were rated on the manner in which they expressed problems, their exploration of personal material, and their manner of relating to the therapist.[2] These are the same therapist and patient scales described earlier in the chapter. A third set of data, an inventory which the client filled out to indicate the degree to which he perceived the therapist conditions, completed the picture. Thus we could see whether clients changed more on the process scales when therapist conditions were higher; whether test outcomes were better when therapist conditions were higher; and whether the client perceived higher conditions when his test outcome and movement on the process scales were greater. These three hypothesized relationships are central to the scientific equation of the theory.

One of our major findings turned out to be essentially negative. It was that the patient's process movement from early to late therapy was not related to either the level of therapist conditions or to pre- to post-test change by the client. In other words, the degree of therapist congruence, empathy, and regard did not affect the change from early to late in the client's exploration of himself and his problems, nor in his way of relating to the therapist. Several possibilities suggest themselves. One is that the theory may be wrong. Another is that our rating scales and sampling methods are not sufficiently sensitive. Or, we may need to look for the isolated breakthrough rather than a steady upward movement by the client. Also, it may be that psychological movement takes place in a more subverbal or subvocal way than we have heretofore thought. The patient may talk in a similar vein yet experience his situation quite differently after a particularly significant therapy episode.

This last possibility is supported by the second major finding, which was that the patient's pre- to post-test changes are clearly related to his *level* of process behavior throughout therapy. Those patients who were more open to their personal experience and difficulties *throughout* therapy showed more positive *change* on the personality test measures. The process scale may reflect a change process that is occurring in a more general way throughout the patient's personality. If the process conception of psychological health is valid, this means that at a high level of psychological health considerable personality change still continues to take place. This notion would be quite discrepant from the more usual static image of the mature person.

A third major result was that therapist conditions, like patient process

[2] Credit is due the following authors for the respective instruments: J. T. Hart, the Congruence Scale; C. B. Truax, Accurate Empathy and Intrapersonal Exploration Scales; J. Spotts and W. P. Wharton, Positive Regard Scale; F. van der Veen and T. M. Tomlinson, Manner of Problem Expression Scale; and E. T. Gendlin and M. Geist, Manner of Relating Scale. (See Rogers, et al., 1967.) G. T. Barrett-Lennard (1962) constructed the inventory for perceived therapist conditions.

variables, were higher when there was greater pre- to post-test change by the patient. This result directly supports the theory, which predicts a better outcome of therapy when the therapist is more congruent, empathic, and positive in his regard. It could mean, of course, either that the better outcome is caused by a more therapeutic therapist, or that a therapist functions better with cases who are in more of a process of change. It is likely that both of these are true. Several studies have shown that the therapist and patient affect each other's behavior (van der Veen, 1965a; Matarazzo et al., 1965; Moos and Clemes, 1967). Therapy is a two-way street; when it is not, it is likely to be a dead end. Therefore, the therapist is not as omnipotent as he might like. But he *can* use his awareness of his own attitudes as a guide. For example, when he is not congruent or is having difficulty liking or understanding the client, he can infer that the client is probably gaining little from therapy at that point and that some special effort is necessary.

Are there any guides in the data that might help to understand what kind of behavior is *critical* for personality growth in the client? What kind of behavior, as described by the scale ratings, is needed before positive change can occur? We have some clear-cut results for our sample of cases. Those cases in which the therapist was rated in at least one interview (of the five that were sampled) as expressing an accurate sense of both his own experience and that of the client, in a way that encouraged the client toward further self-exploration, were the more successful cases. In failure cases, on the other hand, the therapist was rated as withholding himself and not clearly pointing the client toward self-exploration. Two elements appear critical for successful therapist behavior: that he come across as a genuine person, and not in a distant or removed fashion; and that he actively help the client toward a deeper exploration of himself. For the client's behavior, successful clients were rated in at least one interview as expressing personally relevant material with spontaneity and feeling, and as focusing on personal reactions in relation to problems. Clients who did not show these behaviors were, on the whole, not able to profit from therapy. While these results are necessarily tentative and in need of further study on larger samples, they suggest that we can delineate with surprising precision the qualities in the therapist and patient that foster the patient's personality growth.

One other question posed by the findings deserves attention, particularly because it means that some important additions may need to be made to a theory of therapeutic change. In this study as well as in others (Tomlinson and Hart, 1962; Kirtner and Cartwright, 1958), it has been found that the individual who is more disturbed and who is lower on the process scale is less likely to profit from psychotherapy. Why is this? What about personality disturbance makes the therapy relationship less effective? There is a clue in the results of one study, in which it was found that more disturbed cases perceive distinctly lower therapist conditions, with the exception of empathic understanding, than less disturbed ones (van der Veen, 1965b). The perception of lower conditions was also related to a lower level of process, to a more rigid mode of experiencing in the interview, for the schizophrenic sample of cases (van der Veen, 1967). The client's inability to *perceive others* as genuine, empathic, and accepting may be a major stumbling block on his path to psychological change. This can be especially true when the age, background, or social class of the client and therapist differ greatly.

This leads to a final thought. Innovations involving the environment, particularly social relationships, are often necessary before significant personality progress can take place. Present-day interests in such diverse areas as community mental health, the therapeutic community, operant conditioning, family therapy, and experiential groups have a common element of concern to try to reach those individuals whom psychotherapy has failed to reach or help. In the case of community mental health, the effort is to inject mental health principles into ongoing social institutions or to provide new organizations that directly meet a social health need. The therapeutic community is an attempt to bring therapeutic experiences, which would fail to reach him through formal psychotherapy, into the ongoing milieu of the hospital patient. The recent interest in operant conditioning for behavior and learning problems lies to a significant extent in its potential for reaching the socially or organically retarded child, and providing for positive change in a largely nonverbal way. Family therapy is receiving increased emphasis, based on the recognition that today the family is the only group in our society in which close intimate relationships are sanctioned. Family members are likely to influence one another a great deal more than a therapist can. Experiential groups (basic encounter groups, T-groups, sensitivity groups) offer a group process to persons seeking to live more effectively in their social relationships. These diverse methods all provide opportunities for increased exposure and sensitivity to positive interpersonal attitudes. There seems to be little question that the door to new opportunities and approaches needs to be thrown wide open. The knowledge we now have about the conditions that promote psychological growth can benefit many more people than it has so far.

REFERENCES

BARRETT-LENNARD, G. T. Dimensions of therapist response as causal factors in therapeutic change. *Psychological Monographs,* 1962, 76 (7, Whole No. 562).

CARTWRIGHT, D. S. Annotated bibliography of research and theory construction in client-centered therapy. *Journal of Counseling Psychology,* 1957, 4, 82-100.

GENDLIN, E. T. Experiencing: A variable in the process of therapeutic change. *American Journal of Psychotherapy,* 1961, No. 15.

GENDLIN, E. T. A theory of personality change. In P. Worchel and D. Byrne (Eds.), *Personality change.* New York: Wiley, 1964. Ch. 4.

KIRTNER, W. L. and CARTWRIGHT, D. S. Success and failure in client-centered therapy as a function of initial in-therapy behavior. *Journal of Consulting Psychology,* 1958, 22, 329-333.

KRAUSE, M. S. An analysis of Carl R. Rogers' theory of personality. *Genetic Psychology Monographs,* 1964, 69, 49-99.

MATARAZZO, R. G., PHILLIPS, J. S., WIENS, A. N., & SASLOW, G. Learning the art of interviewing: A study of what beginning students do and their pattern of change. *Psychotherapy: Theory, Research and Practice,* 1965, 2, 49-60.

MOOS, R. H. and CLEMES, S. R. Multi-variate study of the patient-therapist system. *Journal of Consulting Psychology,* 1967, 31, 119-130.

ROGERS, C. R. The necessary and sufficient conditions for personality change. *Journal of Consulting Psychology,* 1957, 21, 95-103.

ROGERS, C. R. A theory of therapy, personality, and interpersonal relationships as developed in the client-centered framework. In S. Koch (Ed.), *Psychology: A study of a science. Vol. 3.* New York: McGraw-Hill, 1959a.

ROGERS, C. R. A tentative scale for the measurement of process in psychotherapy. In E. A. Rubinstein and M. R. Parloff (Eds.), *Research in psychotherapy.* Washington, D. C.: American Psychological Association, 1959b. Pp. 96-107.

ROGERS, C. R. (Ed.), GENDLIN, E. T., KIESLER, D. J. and TRUAX, C. B. *The therapeutic relationship and its impact: A study of psychotherapy with schizophrenics.* Madison, Wisconsin: University of Wisconsin Press, 1967.

STANDAL, S. The need for positive regard: A contribution to client-centered theory. Unpublished doctoral dissertation, University of Chicago, 1954.

TOMLINSON, T. M. and HART, J. T., JR. A validation study of the Process Scale. *Journal of Consulting Psychology,* 1962, 26, 74-78.

VAN DER VEEN, F. Effects of the therapist and the patient on each other's therapeutic behavior. *Journal of Consulting Psychology,* 1965a, 29, 19-26.

VAN DER VEEN, F. Perceived therapist conditions and degree of disturbance. Unpublished manuscript, University of Kansas, 1965b.

VAN DER VEEN, F. Basic elements in the process of psychotherapy: A research study. *Journal of Consulting Psychology,* 1967, 31, 295-303. Summarized in "Dimensions of client and therapist behavior in relation to outcome," *Proceedings of the 1965 Annual Convention of the American Psychological Association.* Washington, D. C.: American Psychological Association, 279-280.

3

Research Directives and

Methods in

Client-Centered Therapy*

JOHN M. SHLIEN   FRED M. ZIMRING

Introduction

Methodology

As a method of research in psychotherapy, we take a school of thought as a subject, examining four stages of development to point out the way in which changing theory leads to particular foci and emphases of investigation. It is our general purpose to present and illustrate a functional-historical outline in research methodology. This consists of the *interplay* of (1) developing stages of theory, (2) empirical lines of investigation stemming from and feeding into theory, (3) instruments and sources of data. This chapter is essentially a study of methodology rather than of methods alone. We believe that only the combination of theory and method as it comes out of a program of thought qualifies as research. A technique is not a method, and a method is not by itself a research. Thinking is research. The rest is isolated fact-finding and dilettantism. It is this program of thought, the life-style of a direction of search and

* Adapted from "Research directives and methods in client-centered therapy" by John M. Shlien and Fred M. Zimring in *Methods of research in psychotherapy* by Louis A. Gottschalk and Arthur H. Auerback. Copyright © 1966 by Meredith Publishing Company. Reprinted by permission of Appleton-Century-Crofts.

a system of research which we have in mind, not as dry bones of methodology but as living interests of people. The portrayal requires a slice of actual history in which we have a unique opportunity to observe a 25-year period covering the life span to date of one school of therapy. We mean to demonstrate the main line of descent and variation in one program of thought and the inter-adaptation of associated specimen researches.

Intending to throw only main elements into relief, and within the limits of a single chapter, we cannot present all theories conceived throughout this span. The reader can turn to Standal (1954) and Gendlin (1962) for their extensions. We cannot report more than a fraction of the findings, but many of these are available in the notable landmark in outcome studies, *Psychotherapy and personality change* (1954). Nor can we catalogue the scores of research efforts but this has been admirably done by Cartwright in his "Annotated Bibliography" (1957). We will not try to characterize the whole effort by presenting only the most sophisticated and complex products; a book such as Butler, Rice and Wagstaff, *Quantitative naturalistic observation* (1963) is a methodological study in itself which does not bear reduction to a resumé. Seeman and Raskin (1953) provide excellent coverage of the first dozen years of development. It is beyond our scope to cover, much less do justice to, many researchers who have made weighty contributions to this school. We are working from a narrow perspective which does not admit the whole field of influence but only deals with a *functional microcosm* — a group working so closely in time and space as to be immediately influenced by the shift in theory, or immediately influencing it. These will be primary groups, of which Carl Rogers is an influential and influenced member, working in the Universities of Ohio State, Chicago, and Wisconsin. Because of the immediate functional effect, we will use a dating system which corresponds to the actual schedule of circulation and effect, not publication dates. What we call the "1940 theory" both took effect and was published in 1940, but what we call the "1955 theory" was not published until 1959, with private circulation in the years between. The "1947-51 theory" drew heavily upon the work of Raimy, circa 1943, but was not published until 1948, and upon ideas in Snygg and Combs which were not published until 1949.

Substance

It is then our main intent to present the *natural history* of a set of ideas and methods. First, a digression to relate some actual history and to place this school of thought. Few approaches have such an intense research orientation, or such extensive research production covering so wide a range of methods, as this one. The reasons are worth noting. Client-centered therapy has had an exceptional growth rate, and has grown almost entirely within an academic setting. Most therapies have developed outside universities, and influenced research indirectly and later. Rogers too spent a period of intensive clinical practice during which his views evolved (from an essentially diagnostic base), but when he took his first academic post, he brought with him the new directions of his therapy in a systematic statement already cast in terms which made it a ready research vehicle. When this coincided with the experimental necessities of scholarly careers, many climbed aboard to set off a tradition of hypothesis-and-test which linked research to the therapy from its inception.

Although the new therapy was under pressure to prove itself, both as an upstart going against the main stream and to fit the laboratory atmosphere of American psychology, research was not simply response to the environment. It was rather a consonant expression of one basic thrust of this school of thought: toward a more literal, nonesoteric, fact-based understanding of behavior. Rogers (1960) commented on this in his 1960 review, saying:

> There has always been a strong push on the part of those associated with the client-centered orientation to "take a look" at the raw data of psychotherapy. They have not been content with high-flying abstractions, nor descriptions of therapy remote from the actual personal interaction.

The value he places on this thrust is evident as he continues,

> It seems probably that whatever memories of different schools of psychotherapy remain 50 years from now, client-centered therapy will at least be remembered for its willingness to take a square look at the facts, at the actual ways in which therapy is conducted, and the operational differences which divide therapists.

Also worth mentioning is the shift from *nondirective* to *clientcentered.* This is not incidental revision of nomenclature. It signifies the clarification of a perspective. The reader will see that the therapy and research has always been client-centered. In the second decade of development, it became increasingly clear that *nondirective* is a negative term, a protest contra to *directive,* and misleading in that it suggests merely the absence of direction. Worse, it was not to the main point of the operating theory, which was to stay within the client's complex, shifting, and internal frame of reference. In this shift the image of the therapist changes from that of the mirror-like, passively non-influencing listener[1] to that of the sensitive, actively understanding human respondent. What is relevant to research is the way in which this shift in terminology is related to changing assumptions about the therapist's *activity,* with

---

[1] The apparent passivity and homogeneity seemed entirely characteristic to outsiders. Hoch, in an amusing review of *Psychotherapy and personality change* spoke of a "type of treatment that consists of saying nothing to a patient, or at most repeating what he says, acting warmly the while." Of the reported changes, he says "Doubtless many will take heart at such results. They will feel that if such homeopathic psychiatry has measurable effects, other stronger, 'deeper' methods will have correspondingly larger effects" (1954).

corresponding changes in research interests. When the therapist was viewed as essentially neutral, passive, self-effacing, all therapists would be assumed to be equal, i.e., homogeneous by virtue of their inactivity. When the therapist image changes, the research and theory tend to focus somewhat upon him, though still largely on the client.

Four Stages: The Line of Theoretical Development Taken as Research Directives

Throughout, the focus of theory is upon *operations* rather than *personality*. This style makes the research orientation. The focus is not upon the static categorical state — an individual's obsessional characteristics, narcissism, introversion, submissiveness, or personality type. Focus is upon the behavioral change, and usually on an *if-then* basis. Given certain conditions (if the therapist, then the client — ; or if the client inside therapy, then he will outside — ; or if an individual shifts perception, then his behavior, etc.) predictable consequences will follow. The processes are generally examined within the client, often inside therapy itself, but sometimes in the outside world, then called *global*.

Relative Emphasis of Themes and Contexts. Figure 3.1 is designed to show the relative emphasis of three elements during four periods of time. The elements (therapy, phenomenology, and process theory) interact throughout; but some are more prominent at one time or another. The times, here called *stages* (on the left vertical), are periods in which one or another element takes precedence and directs new phases of research effort. Whether the focus is primarily on one element or another, the emphasis may turn in the direction of therapist or client, as indicated by the center verticle line of the figure. In Stage I, the context is therapy, with emphasis on the client. This is the beginning, in 1940. A thin thread of the phenomenological line begins as an expression of the assumption that there are forces in the client which the therapist needs only to release. In Stage II the line of phenomenology expands to cover developments in the theory of perception and personality which become broader than the shrinking context of therapy. This emphasis changes from one element to another but remains in the client's field. In Stage III, the emphasis shifts for the first time to the therapist, temporarily, while *conditions of therapy* are specified. At this point, the therapist continues to act as a releaser, but his activities expand, while in the client, perception of the therapist's intent is required. In Stage IV, the emphasis returns to the client. Phenomenology again expands, this time in relation to an explanation of experiential processes *within* the client, *in* therapy. Thus all three elements merge. This figure is an approximate visual statement of time spans and the contained research and theoretical emphasis, to help outline what the following text will cover.

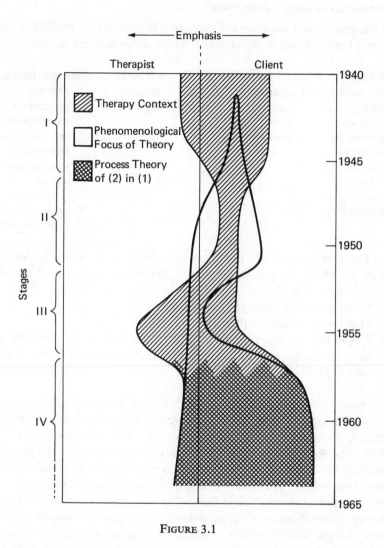

FIGURE 3.1

It should be understood that currents of influence run back and forth between stages. Researchers may reach back in time for prior directives, and leading theoretical statements were often stimulated by research previously completed. Further, the interaction between stages is additive; not I, II, III, IV, but I, I-II, I-II-III, etc. This is nicely illustrated by the titles of the papers as the stages gather momentum. I was called "The Process of Therapy;" II, "A Theory of Personality and Behavior;" III, "Therapy, Personality, and Interpersonal Relationships."

Characteristics of Stage I (circa 1940)[2]

This (Rogers, 1940) is a theory of therapy restricted almost entirely to operations and consequences *in the client*. It states, as we segment it, that:

If the *client*	and if the *therapist*	and if *both*	then the *client* will
1. feels need of help,	1. operates so as to release rather than intervene,	1. establish rapport,	4. own his expressions,
2. has at least minimal intelligence,			5. recognize and accept his spontaneous self,
3. is not faced by overwhelming environment,			6. make responsible choice,
			7. gain insight,
			8. grow toward independence.

A. The *conditions* reside mainly in the client. This is the beginning of *trust in the organism,* and the source of the phenomenological bent which carries through all the stages.

B. *Consequences* are discrete, nonordered.

C. *Focus* is the context of therapy.

D. *Emphasis* is on client behavior. The only activity of the therapist, aside from his contribution to rapport, is to release the assumed potential of the client, and to avoid intervention.

Associated Research. This stage led to what has been called *molecular* research. Though relatively little was specified as to the therapist's behavior in Stage I, the therapy was called *nondirective.* This alone introduced a distinction to be studied, and much of the early research attended the questions: What does the therapist actually do? Can nondirective behavior be distinguished from other? The source of the data was verbatim, transcribed interviews, an important innovation in itself. The first study was by Porter (1943). He set up a classification of verbal behavior on a directive-nondirective continuum. Judges found it possible to reliably differentiate between counselors on this continuum, and also to measure the consistency of individual counselor's behavior. The same method was applied a year later by Gump (1944) to Rogerian and psychoanalytic recordings, with the distinctions showing in the predicted directions.

Snyder (1945) studied both client and therapist, again using content analysis. He found nondirective therapists to be consistently so (which seemed to end the matter and to leave the therapist as an "assumed' quantity for some

---

[2] For an easier grasp of the history, each stage is characterized in the same outline of terms: A. Conditions; B. Consequences; C. Focus; and D. Emphasis.

time to come). He developed categories for judged analysis of client behavior which showed movement from early to late interviews in emergence of insight, increased planning activity, positive feelings following negative expressions — all fitting the postulated consequences of Stage I theory. In a replication of Snyder's study, Seeman (1949) used the same categories and found that non-directive behavior had increased to 85 per cent in the later counselors as compared with 63 per cent for those in Snyder's cases.

Curran (1945) charted the course of single interviews, carefully inventorying the problems and solutions of the client. He found that problems reduced in number, fell into relationship, and were eventually related to causes. He was dealing with the learning process, and his method of intensive individual study somewhat presaged the later *Q*-technique.

Bergman (1950) studied the interaction of client and counselor responses. This differs from the earlier studies in that it does not simply tabulate proportions of types of client or counselor behavior in earlier and later phases of therapy, but relates the two as cause and effect. Using category systems similar to those of early studies, it was found that directive (structuring or interpreting) counselor statements were followed by abandonment of self-exploration while counselor's responses classified as nondirective (reflection of feeling) were followed by continued self-exploration or insight. It is interesting to see this later research, carried out in 1950, reaching back to Stage I but executing a more complex study.

The nature of Stage I research contributions may be summarized (except for Raimy's conceptualizing of self-theory) by Raskin's (1952) five steps:

1. The *electrical* recording of cases.
2. The definition of *concepts* which provides an understanding of these cases.
3. The development of objective *measures* of these concepts.
4. The *application* of these measures to the same or similar case material.
5. The interrelating of the results of this application in order to (a) establish the relationships existing between the concepts, and (b) obtain a well-rounded picture of individual cases.

Before moving into the next stage, we note that Stage I, conditions 2 and 3, regarding the client, fade from view. They were not productive of research and did not appear in later theory. Only condition I for the client remains, his *felt need,* a phenomenal quality which will reappear. The condition for the therapist is a somewhat negative statement; it implies much of what is to come in later theory, but for the moment simply says that the therapist will be warm, supportive, but essentially "stay out of the way." He is not powerful, assertive, but *releasing,* so he may be assumed to be an unvarying element. No research is likely to find him a fascinating subject. The vectors of attraction would turn in other directions. But there is the implication of a powerful, highly charged force in the *other* person, the client. This leads to the next stage.

Characteristics of Stage II (circa 1947-51)

This is a phenomenological *theory of personality,* a theory of self and of change. The first statement in 1947 was "Some observations on the organization of personality" (1950). A complete statement is given in the 1951 edition of Rogers' book, *Client-centered therapy,* as the last chapter, "A theory of personality and behavior." It is headed "Implications for Psychological Theory" and, although in a book about therapy, could stand apart from the context. The concepts of personality have little to do with genesis of personality, or personality types. There is only a clear-cut general theory of mechanisms of *how* personality changes, and a theory of adjustment on a continuum of congruence between self and experience. Nothing is stated as to the operations of the therapist. He is assumed, and his conditions are still general prescriptions of nonintervention (though in the book itself, the therapist is beginning to show emotional overtones, and there is emphasis on attitudes vs. technique, which emerges fully in Stage III). Stage II is the "bulge" of the phenomenological thread running through all stages. A special era of research follows from it. Part *A* concerns *if-then* changes, Part *B* concerns general outcomes.

The theory of personality and behavior makes certain assumptions prior to its conditions. These concern the uniqueness of phenomenal reality; the growth motive of the organism; the nature of the self as construct made up of perceptions and experiences. From the 1951 statement of nineteen propositions, we extract the following representative conditions, the first of which is the main basis of this section, and the others of which are derivative:

If	*Then*
1. there is perceptual organization	behavioral change
2. need	the organism will seek satisfaction
3. threatened	perceptions & behavior will be rigid
*4. not threatened	open to experience
5. perceptions are consistent with self-concept	will be accurate, accepted, incorporated
6. perceptions are not consistent with self-concept	will be denied, distorted, or ignored
7. perceptions are congruent with experience	psychological adjustment
8. perceptions are not congruent with experience	psychological maladjustment
9. adjustment	more accepting of others

* It is suggested in the accompanying text that the function of the therapist is to remove threat by his acceptant behavior, but we repeat therapy is *not* the focus of this theory.

A. *Conditions*   are   perceptual change
B. *Consequences*   are   behavioral change
C. *Focus*   is   largely outside of and separate from therapy
D. *Emphasis*   is   the individual person, may be client

Associated Research. One series of coordinated researches (Raskin, 1949) applied several methods and questions to ten recorded complete cases. Some have a particular bearing on Stage II theory. Sheerer (1949) devised categories to measure acceptance of self and of others. Judges reliably rated clients' statements on a 5-point scale, and tested for an increase over therapy of acceptance of self, and subsequent acceptance of others. Stock (1949) analyzed these cases by denoting each client statement in terms of its referent and its affect, and found a correlation between the way a person feels about himself and feels about others. Haigh (1949), using the same ten recorded cases, studied the first and second half of therapy and judged the amount of defensiveness reported by the client, and exhibited by the client. Decreasing reported defensiveness correlated with improvement according to other process measures. Most of these researches, as well as those in Stage I, used raw uncoded units of verbatim interviews, ordered by time in therapy, measured by ratings on category systems applied by judges with sufficiently established reliability. In the ten-case coordinated study, these were supplemented by counselor ratings and by Rorschach evaluation. The latter, in a study by Carr (1949), showed no consistent or reliable changes.

Cartwright (1954) looked for evidence relating to the proposition that experiences not consistent with the self would be repressed or less assimilated. A group of subjects were exposed to a set of items and objects with which they differentially identified. In a later test of memory, he found that stimuli which are consistent with self-structure are better recalled.

The other phase of Stage II produced more research than any other period, with one main topic: *outcomes.* It was timely, almost necessary to prove that therapy, the subject of so much internal investigation, had demonstrable effects. The previously final *then* terms (the client will express himself more openly, etc.) become intermediate *if* terms (and then as a result of more open expression, he will). Since the phenomenological theory of Stage II did not predict consequences for a client inside therapy (as in Stage I) so much as for a person in general, and since there were as yet only general assumptions about the operations of the therapist, the study of outside *global* changes was in order.

Psychotherapy and personality change (Rogers and Dymond, 1954) is the basic book reporting this period. In it, a fairly large number of clients and controls (roughly 25 of each) were tested with several measures at various points pre-, post-, and follow-up, with complete recording and transcription of all cases (a very large and expensive procedure), Many variables were examined, the instruments including self-reports, counselor ratings, projective tests (scored 'blind" by a diagnostician), judgments of outside individuals, and the problem of experimental controls was attacked. The overall design of this pioneer effort will be depicted in our section on the *Q*-sort.

A second major outcome study, known as the *change project,* was conducted and is being reported by Cartwright, Fiske, and Kirtner (1963). In the analysis of the first large outcome study, it was observed that there was a low, sometimes negative correlation between observers using the same instrument, or between different instruments. For example, two TAT diagnosticians from differing orientations disagreed on blind interpretations of the same client's stories (Rogers and Dymond, 1954), and there was a low correlation btween the perception of client, diagnostician, and client's friend, though all exhibit a fairy high degree of self-consistency. This raises the problem of *perceptual vantage points,* a problem to be expected in criterion research. To attack this problem, these researchers chose the tools of factor analysis. They reasoned that the criteria and vantage points could not be so fragmented as to be entirely independent, and sought the factor or factors representing change. They asked, do all criteria change together, and if not, in what relation to one another?

To begin with, this was not solely a study of client-centered outcomes, but a study of change factors for therapy in general. It commenced with a review of the literature for psychotherapy at large (Cartwright, et al., 1963) and fourteen conceptions of possible change were extracted to cover as completely as feasible the range of previous research variables, ratings, test scores, clinical judgments, self-reports. To carry out this study required a large sample (the N was 100) of clients to which all fourteen conceptions of change were applied, at pre-, post-therapy and follow-up through the use of a ten-point evaluative rating scale for each concept. The concepts were represented by such instruments as MMPI, TAT, sentence completion test, self-sort, counselor ratings, and diagnostician's evaluation. These and all scales such as *adequacy of contentedness of relationships with others, energy deployment over courses of actions,* were intercorrelated. It was found that no single factor or global scale would adequately represent the outcome of therapy, but that factors depended upon instrument-observer combinations. This is surely one of the largest, most energetic and complex studies in the field, and it warns the future researcher that "measures of therapeutic change are highly specific to the observer's role and to the instrument he uses." In a subsidiary research, Kirtner and Cartwright (1962) found that classification of the client's behavior in the first two interviews made differential prognosis possible. Prediction of length of therapy and of success or failure were achieved by observing the manner of experiencing and relating to his problems during this early therapy period. This is an important advance, and could enable future researchers to control outcome studies with much more assurance, since they can relate the power of the treatment effects to the ease with which those effects might be obtained from the particular client involved.

The overall result of the outcome studies points up the very complicated problems of research in psychotherapy.

Characteristics of Stage III (circa 1955)

A second version of a theory of therapy, this one is surrounded by a larger body of theory which subsumes all previous ones. The main new element is the statement of conditions, "The necessary and sufficient conditions of therapy (1957)." Here the emphasis is much upon the therapist (whereas it was upon the client in 1940). The role of the therapist was limited, in Stage I, to that of nonintervening releaser. Now the therapist is given main responsibility for the "If" conditions. The theory requires that:

1. Two persons are in contact.
2. The client is vulnerable or anxious.
3. The therapist is congruent.
4. The therapist is experiencing positive regard.
5. The therapist is experiencing emphatic understanding.
6. The client perceives (4) and (5).

Conditions 1 and 2 restate the 1947 requirements of *rapport,* and *felt need.* Conditions, 3, 4, and 5 are all *positive* specifications of therapist operations. Whereas before he was adjured not to intervene in order to release, he might now intervene, if necessary, in order to be congruent in order to release. If he continues to fulfill conditions 4 and 5, he has made his contribution to the activity of therapy and the process to follow. The larger body of theory in this stage has not stimulated research in interpersonal relationship, for instance, but drew upon previous research for footing. The theory of therapy did have an impact on further research.

A. *Conditions: if* the six stated necessary and sufficient conditions
B. *Consequences: then* a process is set up in the client
C. *Focus:* on the therapist in therapy
D. *Emphasis:* on the therapist's attitude

Associated Research. Halkides (1958) studied the relationship of conditions 3, 4, and 5 to success in therapy. When she had judges blindly rate the degree of these conditions in the recordings of interviews of ten cases found to be successful on multiple criteria, and ten unsuccessful cases, she found that all three of these conditions were significantly associated with the more successful cases.

Barrett-Lennard (1959) investigated the effect of the client's experience of these three conditions by having the clients themselves (not judges) complete a Relationship Inventory incorporating statements representing these conditions after their fifth interview, and after the completion of therapy. He found that clients improve in their adjustment according to the extent they perceive their therapist (after five interviews) as understanding, congruent, positive, and unconditional in his regard for them.

Goodman (1962) investigated the congruence of inner feelings and outer expression of both client and therapist. Each used a (same) variant of the Semantic Differential after every third interview until the twenty-first. On separate sheets of an adjective list, the client scaled the inner feelings he experienced and his outer expression of them. The therapist followed the same procedure for himself. Difference scores showed the distance between each one's self-perceived feelings and expression, thus his *self-disclosure.* For the therapist, this score measured condition 3, his congruence. Each person then predicted the other's self-description. To the extent that the therapist's prediction agrees with the client's self-description, the therapist shows understanding, a fulfillment of condition 5 (understanding). To the extent that the client's prediction agrees with the therapist's self-description, he fulfills half the condition 6, by perceiving condition 5. Goodman found that the match between the two parties increased as therapy progressed. This is a keen example of research following theory.

Stage IV: A Process Conception of Psychotherapy (1957 to present)

Interest in a particular sort of process is the fourth major theme, from which Rogers' paper (1958) emerged. The word *process* has been so much used as to become somewhat confusing. There have been at least three different methodological aspects. We will try to specify our use of the terms.

The first is the *sequential* or *series* meaning. In this use process refers to a variable examined in segmented sequences over time. For example, one might measure statements of successful clients in terms of self-reference, find an increase from first to last interviews, and discuss the "process of increasing self-reference."

A second aspect is the *cause and effect relationship,* or *interaction.* A study investigating the connections between behaviors of therapist and client might refer to this as the process of therapy.

The third and present meaning of process has reference to the *type of variable involved.* If one examines the position of a physical object at one moment, then at a second moment, and again at a third, the variable *position at a given time* is not of the same nature as a variable such as *motion.* Variables having to do with *movement* or *flow* of the client are now referred to as process variables and should, we think, have a special claim on the term. Rogers is concerned with process in this third meaning.

There has been continuing interest in some type of *process* starting with Snyder's 1943 study and continuing with Porter, Seeman, *et al.* These Stage I studies investigated process in the sequential sense, measuring the change in behavior over therapy.

A substantial methodological advance in the study of sequence was made with Butler's qualitative factor analysis for use in naturalistic observation. The method may be described as a variant of factor analysis in which the basic data are the behaviors of client and therapist rather than scores. This provides a statistical technique for describing sequences of observable events (1962).

There has been little investigation of process in the interaction sense. Comparison of client-therapist behaviors when done in the same study was carried out in either summary fashion, by relating the therapist scores for the first third of therapy to the client's scores in that segment of therapy, or else by comparing a single client response to a single therapist response. Rogers' concern was not with process in the interactive sense. In Stage IV, he assumes that the therapist's conditions are met, and is interested in the change in the *client*.

Gendlin and Zimring (1955) and Gendlin (1962) defined and focused upon a variable which referred to the underlying substrata in the individual as central core in process of change. This variable, called *experiencing*, referred to the ongoing flow of events in the individual. Rogers (1959) used this and a few of the discrete variables investigated in earlier studies as some aspects of what he saw to be the underlying continuum: fixity to changingness, from rigid structure to flow, from static to process. This underlying continuum was conceptualized in terms of seven strands of flow: (1) relationship to feeling and personal meaning, (2) manner of experience, (3) degree of incongruence, (4) communication of self, (5) manner in which experience is constructed, (6) relationship to problems, and (7) manner of relating. The strands are predicted to co-vary within the client. That is, a client judged as being near the fixity end of one strand was likely to be near the fixity end of whatever other strands he exhibited. It should be emphasized that each strand was a particular manifestation of a single underlying continuum of change.

This continuum is divided into seven stages. To illustrate the content of these stages we list the characteristics of the first and seventh stages.

First Stage	*Seventh Stage*
Personal constructs are extremely rigid.	Personal constructs are tentatively reformulated, to be validated against further experience, but even then, to be held loosely.
There is much blockage of internal communication.	Internal communication is clear, with feelings and symbols well matched, and fresh terms for new feelings.
	New feelings are experienced with immediacy and richness of detail, both in the therapeutic relationship and outside.
Feelings and personal meanings are neither recognized nor owned.	The experiencing of such feelings is used as a clear referent.

There is an unwillingness to communicate self. Communication is only about externals.

No problems are recognized or perceived.

There is no desire to change.
Ex. "I think I'm practically healthy."

Close and communicative relationships are dangerous.

There is a growing and continuing sense of acceptant ownership of these changing feelings, a basic trust in his own process.

Experiencing has lost almost completely its structure-bound aspects and becomes process experiencing — that is, the situation is experienced and interpreted in this moment, not as in the past.

The self becomes increasingly simply the subjective and reflexive awareness of experiencing. The self is much less frequently a perceived object, and much more frequently something confidently felt in process.

It is of more than passing interest to note that Rogers arrived at the conception of an underlying continuum by listening, with as little bias as possible, to many therapy recordings. The power of this system of naturalistic observation is little recognized by the average researcher, yet it is the basic method of scientists who make history.

A. *Conditions: if* the client perceives himself as fully received
B. *Consequences: then* he will change as described by a continuum from fixity to fluidity
C. *Focus:* movement *in therapy*
D. *Emphasis:* client

Associated Research. Tomlinson and Hart (1962) started with a recording of an early and a late interview from each of ten cases chosen as representative of Counseling Center clients. Nine two-minute segments were chosen from each of these 20 tapes and these 180 segments were then coded and randomized. Two raters with previous experience of the scale then individually decided in what scale portion each of these segments belonged. For this purpose they used typescripts and tape recordings. Since five of these ten clients were successful clients and five unsuccessful, this design enabled them to compare the stages of process of early interview to late as well as success to failure.

Research here returns to old types of operations, i.e., categories of behavior, rated by judges using interview material. There is nothing new in that, except for some advance in showing that scales involving subtle conceptions can be reliably applied to complex interview material. But the real contribution, since the system of analysis is old, lies in the invention of new theory. From this, it seems that if new theory leads to new research with old techniques, theory constitutes a method in itself.

"Q-Sort" — The Case History of a Method and Its Modification

The history of psychology has been said to rest upon available instrumentation. In the *practice* of psychotherapy, where the instruments are people, this is certainly true. In clinical *research,* theory has wandered like an apparition looking for tools with which to make itself visible. Often something is lost in the process. Rich and complicated experience, when phrased in researchable terms, is reduced to the limitations of instruments. The self-concept is somewhat ephemeral, for all its commonness in our language and its brilliant history in social-psychological theory. It was pre-eminent in Stage II of Rogerian theory. But how is one to get at it most directly? The most empathic judges, watching through screens and reading dials connected to all known physiological measures are still once removed from the inner experience of the client's *phenomenal* self. And how is one to quantify the client's own report?

The answer seemed to come from the work of W. Stephenson (1953), fortunately at the University of Chicago when self-theory was burgeoning. His *Q*-technique offered an idiosyncratic quantitative method in which an individual is applied to a set of statements over time; the correlation between the person arrays is then subjected to factor analysis. Intra-individual rather than inter-individual differences are the issue. This makes it most appealing to the clinical researcher. The technique was applied to single cases in early studies by Hartley (1951) and Nunnally (1955). They had clients describe themselves in terms of a *Q*-sort at various points over therapy. The result showed details of the movement through therapy in terms of changing factor loadings in the descriptive statements. Exposition of the case in quantitative, hypothesis-testing terms was clearly achieved, but the results, though objective, were still somewhat unwieldy, as in any single case analysis. This first application was genuinely *Q*-technique.

The next study was a milestone which will be used to represent the major outcome studies mentioned in Stage II and reported in full in *Psychotherapy and personality change.* From *Q*-technique, it took only the *Q*-sort, aimed at the instrumentation of the self-concept but also adjusted to inter-individual differences. To help the reader visualize the procedure, we shall describe it in some detail. The *Q*-sort can be considered as essentially an inventory, consisting of a number (usually between 50 and 150) of descriptive statements. This is called the *Q-sort,* and the person describing himself is said to be *sorting.* Typically, the procedure begins with devising or selection of *trait universe.* In this case, the Butler-Haigh study (1954), 100 statements were taken from recordings of clients in different stages of therapy. The items may be phrased positively ("People always like me"), or negatively ("I'm no damned good to anyone"); they may consist of long sentences or single adjectives such as "cheerful." The subject is asked to distribute these items on a continuum of "like me" to "not like me." Instructions under which he sorts vary widely, according to the researcher's interests. One may describe himself in the present, the past, the future, as he wishes he were, as his friends see him, as he sees himself in relation to them, or he may describe others with the same items in equally varying ways.

The technology of *Q*-sorting is quite advanced. Each item is printed on a card, the cards are placed on a *Q*-board which holds them up for view so that the sorter can change their placement at will (on a paired comparison basis). The desired distribution is outlined on the board, usually of a forced-normal approximation, so that the number of cards in each pile on the continuum is controlled and thus weighted. Any two distributions may be correlated by recording the differences in placement of each card, squaring and summing the differences, and reading an extrapolation table from which the sum gives an .r, a procedure which takes about two minutes. For nonsymmetrical distributions, Cartwright (1956a) devised a rapid computational procedure.

In this illustrative study, the researchers used two instructions: "Sort these cards to describe yourself as you are," and then, "now sort these cards to describe the ideal, the person you want to be." The result provided the widely quoted *self-ideal correlation,* which these authors call a measure of self-esteem. The person who has a large discrepancy between self and ideal is not likely to be acceptant of himself, and probably experiences tension. This is all based on the concept of the phenomenal self, and relates to Stage II, yet it should be noted that congruence of self and *ideal* does not represent the *Congruence* between Self-Structure and *Experience* which Rogers in Stage II postulates as the basis of adjustment. This is an example of the instrumental limitation (*experience* is not as easily encompassed as *ideal*) and also of the way in which individual researchers veer off in their own directions (though Butler and Haigh see the self and ideal coming closer together "on the basis of a broader awareness of experience").

Results demonstrated outcome effects which appear to be desirable, stable, and to have occurred as a consequence of therapy rather than mere passage of time. This is depicted on the chart (Figure 3.2) which shows mean S-I correlations at pre-, post-, and follow-up points. (These data are essentially the material from the Butler-Haigh study.)

Two *experimental* or *treated* groups are shown. One is the total research population, which moves from a zero-order correlation to a significant .34 at post therapy, and shows no significant change in follow-up. On the assumption that more improved clients should show greater increase in this measure, a subpopulation was selected as improved on the combined basis of two other measures, TAT diagnostic rating and counselor judgments. The "improved" population does indeed show less self-ideal discrepancy, and also shows stability in follow-up. All figures are *averages,* for the groups.

How can this be attributed to therapy? The complicated problem of controls was attacked in two ways. First (line *X*) there is the conventional *matched normal,* equivalent on the basis of age, sex, and socioeconomic status (gross variables which have little meaning, as it turns out) to the matching individuals in the therapy group. As each client is tested, so is his matched control person. Those controls are "normal' in the sense that they volunteered to participate in research for payment, and had not requested therapy. Their status on the measure is significantly higher than other groups at pre-therapy, and does not change, on the average, over time without therapy. However, the matching is incomplete, does not cover the relevant psychological variables, and leaves much to be desired. How does one match for these relevant variables (when not even sure what they are)? Make each person his *own* control. Then he is perfectly matched for himself. This was done by asking half of those who applied for therapy to take the tests, waiting for 60 days, and then beginning therapy (line Z). This group, self-declared as in need of therapy, shows zero-order S-I correlation at time of application for therapy and no change over time until the pre-therapy point. (The *own control* line should actually be outside the chart and to the left, since its position on the follow-up axis really represents the pre-therapy test point and its position at pre-therapy really represents "pre-wait.") These two

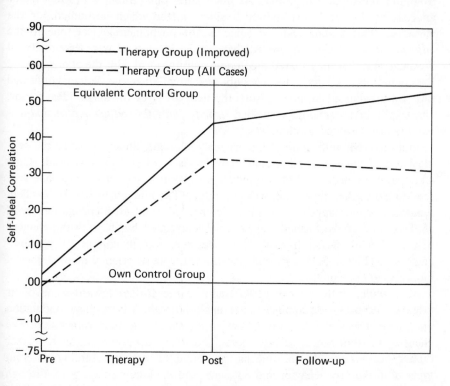

FIGURE 3.2
Mean Correlation Chart

control groups help to prove the efficacy of treatment vs. no treatment, but they are open to criticism. When people are told that their therapy has yet to begin, there is the complication of possible suggestion (a negative *placebo* effect) in the evidence of no change during the wait period. There is also the need to control for individual growth potential in relation to initial status. That is, study of diet K for children requires not only initial height and weight, but some estimate of likely adult height, such as mean of parents' size, before matching is valid. Differential prognosis is required, and this is a problem only now being attacked in designs. Beside the development of adequate controls, another method with convincing power is that of replication, a method all too rare in clinical research. Shlien (1960) repeated the S-I outcome study with two other groups in a time-limited therapy study and found very similar results.

In a further study of this population, Dymond further separated the Q-sort from Q-technique. Using only the *self-sort* she asked clinicians to divide the items into those describing good and poor adjustment. From this, she was able to make an *adjustment score* of the Q-sort self-description which was framed in terms of the values of outside observers, though the data still came from the self-report. (1954b) At about this time Butler's (1956) factor analysis of the ideal sort showed a single factor which accounted for the variance. This finding restored some of the phenomenological tone to the *adjustment score,* since it proved that clients' ideal sorts were essentially all the same and that they shared a common cultural ideal with the clinicians and the counselors. A later study (unpublished) by Shlien and Jenney confirmed this: on a balanced 80-item Q-sort, the item array of the single ideal factor, when split in the middle coincided *exactly* with the *adjustment-maladjustment* items as judged by clinicians.

In a further modification of the original technique, Shlien removed the self-ideal ratio from any explicit content whatever. No Q-deck was used. Only an apparatus constructed of two moveable semi-transparent spheres, one representing self, the other ideal, was presented. The amount to which the client separated or overlapped these spheres composed a self-ideal correlation (read as the cosine of the formed angle) which correlated highly with the conventional Q-sort-derived self-ideal. This measure, though completely phenomenological (Figure 3.3) was totally abstracted from its original methodological moorings in Q-technique.

Meanwhile, Butler's work (1960) moved the Q-data toward some of its original purposes. He applied factor analysis to the whole client population (i.e., to matrices of inter-correlations of clients at one time rather than one client at different times) at pre-, post-, and follow-up points, in an R- rather than Q-technique. By this means, he found factors representing different types of in-therapy behavior and outcome, and the factor arrays gave, through each client's factor estimation, a description of the clients with high loadings on those factors. These clients were differentiated in terms of self-concept,

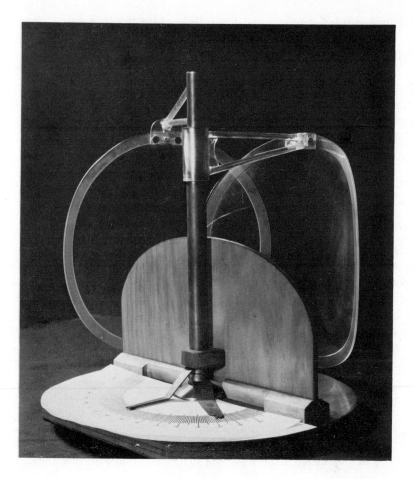

FIGURE 3.3
What ever happened to the Q-sort? Abstract Apparatus, Rear View

described in terms of Q-items, and related as types to other outcome measures such as TAT change, ratings by friends of the client, and ratings by the therapist. This method does not follow the single case, but follows and describes groups of cases which cluster as factorial types.

Our effort here has been to illustrate a common event in research activity, and in so doing, to detail some of the design of a research and the viscissitudes of an instrument. All approaches search for methods compatible with their theories, and it so happens that compatible techniques give more favorable results. (When one study found that S-I correlations showed positive results while the TAT showed negative results on the same population, Henry, a leading TAT analyst and theoretician, considered the possibility that "the TAT is unfriendly to client-centered therapy.") Stage II theory seized upon

Q-technique, used it in classical form, then converted it to meet contemporary research needs, somewhat departing from the original technique and original clinical theory, as so often happens because usable instruments do not directly express or lend themselves to exact representations of the theory. The modifications moved to a point of complete abstraction from the original technique, then finally back to a more workable reconciliation of method adapted to the actual research situation.[3]

Summary

In this chapter, we have tried to display cross sections of the architecture in a school of therapy built of research-shaped bricks. One can hardly think of research methods that have not been used here. There are actuarial studies, intensive clinical studies, counselor rating scales, hypothesis dictated studies and hypothesis-generating studies, physiological measures, projective techniques, semantic differentials and *Q*-sorts, prognosis and diagnosis, self-reports and judges' evaluations, uses of diaries, films, sound recordings, longer therapy, shorter therapy, and published research on all of them. Yet it is not these methods which give a research program its character and force. Methods do not tell one what to do with them. Theory does. We have tried to throw into relief four stages of development with associated researches, each stage leading in some line to those behind and ahead. The basic necessities of a foundation have been achieved in the way of theories of therapy and personality. A point of maturity has been reached such that main theoretical directives for research may now come from persons other than Rogers. In any event, we venture to predict the next stage, not from advance information but because our reading of history points that way. The next theory will be a theory of knowledge. And what will that have to do with research? Absolutely everything.

REFERENCES

AIDMAN, T. Changes in self-perception as related to changes in perception of one's environment. *American Psychologist*, 1948, 3, 286.

ANDERSON, R. P. An investigation of the relationship between physiological and verbal behavior during client-centered psychotherapy. Unpub. Ph.D. thesis, Univ. of Chicago, 1955. (Also *Journal of Counseling Psychology*, 1956, 3, 174-184.)

ASSUM, A. L., and LEVY, S. J. Analysis of a non-directive case with follow-up interview. *Journal of Abnormal and Social Psychology*, 1948, 43, 78-89.

[3] See Tomlinson and Whitney (Ch. 24) for an expanded analysis of the relationship between method and theory.

BARRETT-LENNARD, G. T. Dimensions of the client's experience of his therapist associated with personality change. Unpublished Ph.D. thesis, University of Chicago, 1959.

BERGER, E. M. Relationships among acceptance of self-acceptance of others, and MMPI scores. *Journal of Counseling Psychology,* 1955, 2, 279-284.

BERGMAN, D. V. The relationship between counseling method and client self-exploration. Unpublished M.A. thesis, University of Chicago, 1950.

BUTLER, J. M. Factorial studies of client-centered psychotherapy. *Counseling Center Discussion Papers,* 1956, II, No. 9.

BUTLER, J. M. Self-concept change in psychotherapy. *Counseling Center Discussion Papers,* 1960, VI, No. 13.

BUTLER, J. M. and HAIGH, G. V. Changes in the relation between self-concepts and ideal concepts consequent upon client-centered counseling. In C. R. Rogers and R. F. Dymond (Eds.), *Psychotherapy and personality change.* Chicago: Univ. of Chicago Press, 1954. Pp. 55-75.

BUTLER, J. M., RICE, L. N., and WAGSTAFF, A. K. *Quantitative naturalistic research.* Englewood Cliffs, N. J.: Prentice-Hall, 1963.

CARR, A. C. An evaluation of nine non-directive psychotherapy cases, by means of the Rorschach. *Journal of Consulting Psychology,* 1949, 13, 196-205.

CARTWRIGHT, D. S. A study of imbalance in immediate memory. Unpublished Ph.D. thesis, University of Chicago, 1954.

CARTWRIGHT, D. S. A computational procedure for tau correlations. *Psychometrika,* 1956a, 22.

CARTWRIGHT, D. S. A rapid non-parametric estimate of multijudge reliability. *Psychometrika,* 1956b, 21, 17-29.

CARTWRIGHT, D. S. Self-consistency as a factor affecting immediate recall. *Journal of Abnormal and Social Psychology,* 1956c, 52, 212-218.

CARTWRIGHT, D. S. Annotated bibliography of research and theory construction in client-centered therapy. *Journal of Counseling Psychology,* 1957, 4, 82-100.

CARTWRIGHT, D. S., KIRTNER, W. L., and FISKE, D. W. Method factors in changes associated with psychotherapy. *Journal of Abnormal and Social Psychology,* 1963, 66, 164-175.

CARTWRIGHT, D. S., ROBERTSON, R. J., FISKE, D. W., and KIRTNER, W. L. Length of therapy in relation to outcome and change in personal integration. *Journal of Consulting Psychology,* 1961, 25, 84-88.

CARTWRIGHT, D. S. and ROTH, I. Success and satisfaction in psychotherapy. *Journal of Clinical Psychology,* 1957, 13, 20-26.

CHODORKOFF, B. Adjustment and the discrepancy between perceived and ideal self. *Journal of Clinical Psychology,* 1954a, 10, 266-268.

CHODORKOFF, B. Self-perception, perceptual defense, and adjustment. *Journal of Abnormal and Social Psychology,* 1954b, 49, 508-512.

CURRAN, C. A. *Personality factors in counseling.* New York: Grune & Stratton, 1945.

DYMOND, R. F. Adjustment changes over therapy from self-sorts. In C. R. Rogers and R. F. Dymond (Eds.), *Psychotherapy and personality change.* Chicago: Univ. of Chicago Press, 1954a. Pp. 76-84.

DYMOND, R. F. Adjustment changes over therapy from Thematic Apperception Test ratings. In C. R. Rogers and R. F. Dymond (Eds.), *Psychotherapy and personality change.* Chicago: University of Chicago Press, 1954b. Pp. 109-120.

DYMOND, R. F. Effects of psychotherapy on self-consistency. *Journal of Counseling Psychology,* 1957, 4, 1.

FISKE, D. W., CARTWRIGHT, D. S., and KIRTNER, W. L. Are psychotherapeutic changes predictable. *Counseling Center Discussion Papers,* Chicago, 1962, VIII, No. 4.

GENDLIN, E. T. *Experiencing and the creation of meaning.* New York: Free Press, 1962.

GENDLIN, E. T., and ZIMRING, F. The qualities or dimensions of experiencing and their change. *Counseling Center Discussion Papers,* Chicago, 1955, I, No. 3.

GOODMAN, G. Emotional disclosure of therapists and clients over the course of psychotherapy. Unpublished Ph.D. thesis, University of Chicago, 1962.

GORDON, T. and CARTWRIGHT, D. S. The effect of psychotherapy upon certain attitudes toward others. In C. R. Rogers and R. F. Dymond (Eds.), *Psychotherapy and personality change.* Chicago: University of Chicago Press, 1954. Pp. 167-195.

GRUMMON, D. L. An investigation into the use of grammatical and psychogrammatical categories of language for the study of personality and psychotherapy. Unpublished Ph.D. thesis, University of Chicago, 1950.

GRUMMON, D. L. Personality changes as a function of time in persons motivated for therapy. In C. R. Rogers and R. F. Dymond (Eds.), *Psychotherapy and personality change.* Chicago: University of Chicago Press, 1954. Pp. 238-255.

GRUMMON, D. L. and JOHN, E. S. Changes over client-centered therapy evaluated on psychoanalytically based thematic apperception test scales. In C. R. Rogers and R. F. Dymond (Eds.), *Psychotherapy and personality change.* Chicago: University of Chicago Press, 1954. Pp. 121-144.

GUMP, P. V. A statistical investigation of one psychoanalytic approach and a comparison of it with nondirective therapy. Unpublished M. A. thesis, Ohio State University, 1944.

HAIGH, G. Defensive behavior in client-centered therapy. *Journal of Consulting Psychology,* 1949, 13, 181-189.

HALKIDES, G. An experimental study of four conditions necessary for therapeutic change. Unpublished Ph.D. thesis, University of Chicago, 1958.

HARTLEY, M. W. Q-technique: its methodology and application. Unpublished manuscript, Counseling Center, University of Chicago, 1950.

HARTLEY, M. W. A Q-technique study of changes in the self-concepts during psychotherapy. Unpublished Ph.D. thesis, University of Chicago, 1951.

HENRY, W. E., and SHLIEN, J. M. Affective complexity and psychotherapy; Some comparisons of time-limited and unlimited treatment. *Journal of Projective Techniques and Personality Assessment*, 1958, 22, 153-162.

HOCH, P. Book review of *Psychotherapy and personality change*, C. R. Rogers and R. F. Dymond (Eds.). *Journal of the American Medical Association*, 1955, 175, 690.

HOGAN, R. A. A theory of threat and defense. *Journal of Consulting Psychology*, 1952, 16, 417-425.

JAMES, W. *Principles of psychology*. New York: Dover, 1950.

KIRTNER, W. L. and CARTWRIGHT, D. S. Success and failure in client-centered therapy as a function of client personality variables. *Journal of Consulting Psychology*, 1958, 22, 259-264.

LECKY, P. *Self-consistency: A theory of personality*. New York: Island Press, 1945.

MOWRER, O. H. "Q Technique" — Description, history and critique. In O. H. Mowrer (Ed.), *Psychotherapy: Theory and research*. New York: Ronald, 1953. Pp. 316-375.

MEUNCH, G. A. An evaluation of non-directive psychotherapy by means of the Rorschach and other tests. *Applied Psychology Monographs*, No. 13, Stanford, California: Stanford University Press, 1947.

NUNNALLY, J. C. An investigation of some propositions of self-conception: the case of Miss Sun. *Journal of Abnormal and Social Psychology*, 1955a, 50, 87-92.

NUNNALLY, J. C. A systematic approach to the construction of hypotheses about the process of psychotherapy. *Journal of Consulting Psychology*, 1955b, 19, 17-20.

PORTER, E. H. The development and evaluation of a measure of counseling interview procedures. *Educational and Psychological Measurement*, 1943, 3, 105-126, 215-238.

RAIMY, V. C. Self-reference in counseling interviews. *Journal of Consulting Psychology*, 1948, 12, 153-163.

RASKIN, N. J. An analysis of six parallel studies of the therapeutic process. *Journal of Consulting Psychology*, 1949, 13, 206-220.

RASKIN, N. J. An objective study of the locus-of-evaluation factor in psychotherapy. In W. Wolff and J. A. Precker (Eds.), *Success in psychotherapy*. New York: Grune & Stratton, 1952. Ch. 6.

ROGERS, C. R. The processes of therapy. *Journal of Consulting Psychology*, 1940, 4, 161-164.

ROGERS, C. R. *Client-centered therapy: Its current practice, implications, and theory*. Boston: Houghton Mifflin, 1951.

ROGERS, C. R. Changes in the maturity of behavior as related to therapy. In C. R. Rogers and R. F. Dymond (Eds.), *Psychotherapy and personality change*. Chicago: University of Chicago Press, 1954, Pp. 215-237.

ROGERS, C. R. A theory of therapy, personality, and interpersonal relationships. *Counseling Center Discussion Papers,* 1955, I, 5. (Also in, S. Koch (Ed.), *Psychology: A study of a science,* 1961, III.)

ROGERS, C. R. The necessary and sufficient conditions of therapeutic personality change. *Journal of Consulting Psychology,* 1957, 21, 95-103.

ROGERS, C. R. A process conception of psychotherapy. *American Psychologist,* 1958, 13, 142-159.

ROGERS, C. R. A tentative scale for the measurement of progress in psychotherapy. In E. A. Rubinstein and M. B. Parloff (Eds.), *Research in psychotherapy.* Washington, D. C.: American Psychological Association, 1959. Pp. 96-107.

ROGERS, C. R. Significant trends in the client-centered orientation. *Progress in Clinical Psychology,* 1960, 4, 85-99.

ROGERS, C. R., and DYMOND, R. F. *Psychotherapy and personality change: Coordinated studies in the client-centered approach.* Chicago: Univ. of Chicago Press, 1954.

SEEMAN, J. A study of the process of non-directive therapy. *Journal of Consulting Psychology,* 1949, 13, 157-168.

SEEMAN, J. Counselor judgments of therapeutic process and outcome. In C. R. Rogers and R. F. Dymond (Eds.). *Psychology and personality change.* Chicago: University of Chicago Press, 1954. Pp. 99-108.

SEEMAN, J., and RASKIN, N. J. Research perspectives in client-centered therapy. In O. H. Mowrer (Ed.), *Psychotherapy: Theory and research.* New York: Ronald, 1953, Pp. 205-234.

SHEERER, E. Analysis of the relationship between acceptance of and respect for self and acceptance of and respect for others. *Journal of Consulting Psychology,* 1949, 13, 169-175.

SHLIEN, J. M. Toward what level of abstraction in criteria? In H. H. Strupp and L. Luborsky (Eds.), *Second research conference in psychotherapy.* Washington, D. C.: American Psychological Association, 1961.

SHLIEN, J. M., MOSAK, H. H., and DREIKURS, R. Effect of time limits: A comparison of client-centered and Adlerian psychotherapy. *Counseling Center Discusion Papers,* 1960, VI, No. 8.

SNYDER, W. U. An investigation of the nature of non-directive psychotherapy. *Journal of Genetic Psychology,* 1945, 33, 193-223.

SNYGG, D., and COMBS, A. W. *Individual behavior.* New York: Harper & Row, 1949.

STANDAL, S. W. The need for positive regard: A contribution to client-centered theory. Unpublished Ph.D. thesis, University of Chicago, 1954.

STEPHENSON, W. *The study of behavior.* Chicago: University of Chicago Press, 1953.

STOCK, D. An investigation into the interrelationships between the self-concept and feelings directed toward other persons and groups. *Journal of Consulting Psychology,* 1949, 13, 176-180.

THETFORD, W. N. The measurement of physiological responses to frustration before and after non-directive psychotherapy. Unpublished Ph.D. thesis, University of Chicago. 1949.

TOMLINSON, T. M., and HART, JR., J. T. A validation study of the Process Scale. *Journal of Consulting Psychology,* 1962, 26, 74-78.

WALKER, A. M., RABLEM, R. S., and ROGERS, C. R. Development of a scale to measure process changes in psychotherapy. *Journal of Clinical Psychology,* 1960, 16, 79-85.

PART TWO

Theory

Theorizing is much like shadowboxing; done correctly, with zest, it can be invigorating, but if done ploddingly nothing is more dull. And it is easy to plod because a theorist never really encounters anything. The propositions and issues and questions he considers are all of his own making. Reality does not intrude upon his shadows until he begins to test hypotheses through research and practical work.

The seven chapters that comprise this section on theory and basic research are not easy to read. We believe they were written with proper zest but following them closely will be fatiguing. This fatigue is unavoidable. To read theories closely we must shadowbox with the theorist; we cannot merely spectate. Most of us are willing to exercise for a few minutes now and then, but to get into the theoretical problems of psychotherapy and personality we must keep at it for hours.

The organization of the chapters is designed to keep the reader's fatigue within tolerable bounds. This is done by providing chapters that take different theoretical vantage points, by including chapters that have different mixes of abstraction and empiricism, and by varying the complexity with which the theories are extended.

We begin with Bergin's chapter on "Psychology as a science of inner experience," which is something of a warmup exercise. He argues that theories of psychotherapy have been of significant service to psychology as a whole through their concern with inner experience. He urges psychologists to accept as a starting point for theory and experimentation that "the data of psychology can consist of experience . . . they are primary phenomena."

In the next chapter, Gendlin moves from Bergin's starting point by discussing the contributions of existentialism to experiential psychotherapy. The author is uniquely qualified to write about this subject. He is a professor of

59

philosophy and psychology at the University of Chicago; since his days as a graduate student at that institution, he has become accustomed to living two professional lives, one at the Department of Philosophy and one at the University Counseling Center. He attempts to show how diverse psychotherapies can be integrated within the conceptualizations of experiential therapy. Although Gendlin takes his examples from reports of therapy with children, the analyses apply equally well to adult psychotherapy — this is the generality of experiential theory. Much has been written about the contributions of existentialism to psychotherapy, but Gendlin also considers the contributions of psychotherapy to existentialism, "Felt concreteness is difficult to describe philosophically, whereas in therapy we are continually working with it and familiar with it. The work of Jung, Rank, Allen, Rogers, and others (coming directly from psychotherapy) joins with the philosophical existential trend. Both streams are going to make up a new philosophy and psychotherapy."

Shlien's chapter continues the discussion of phenomenology begun by Gendlin but emphasizes the interweavings of general psychological theory, personality theory, psychotherapy theory, and phenomenology. In this wide-ranging discussion the author manages to move intelligibly from physiology to relativity theory, from methodology to ethology, and from Husserl to Rogers. All this is done with an adroitness that reveals the underlying connections of these diverse subjects. Psychotherapists are apt to feel insular, alone as they frequently are with their clients in private offices. Shlien's chapter is a pleasant corrective to this feeling since he demonstrates that, in theory at least, the whole conceptual world spins inside those small offices.

Returning to the metaphor about shadowboxing, we can say that Gendlin's theory of personality change presented in Chapter 7 is definitely the heavyweight exercise of this section on Theory. He provides twenty-six carefully defined terms as an analytic language for theorizing about personality change. The definitions are preceded by a careful critique of other personality theories. In the critique Gendlin argues that most personality theories focus on *content* and *structure,* to the exclusion of ideas about personality *change.* For this reason, personality theories have been of no essential relevance for psychotherapy, which must of course center on the practical problems of bringing about changes in personality. Personality theories are almost always complicated, because personalities are complicated. Gendlin's experiential theory of personalty change will repay the therapist who makes the necessary effort to follow the complications. His theory explains what makes a difference in therapy and what does not, and why — a kind of shadowboxing any therapist will find valuable.

4

Psychology as a Science

of Inner Experience*[1]

ALLEN E. BERGIN

The field of psychology originally grew out of concerns with intimately human and ultimately philosophical issues. The natural history of its development from philosophy and theology (Boring, 1950) hardly requires further documentation, but central to the present thesis is the assumption that psychology, indeed, came into being partly in response to the desire to explain and guide the most profound and practical qualities of human experience.

There has been a significant period of estrangement from such involvements which is indelibly marked in our history by the behavioristic revolution against the subjective and experiential (Hebb, 1960). No matter how the future may evaluate it, behaviorism and its descendants have been the lifeblood of American psychology. Regardless of our current preoccupations or our investments in new pathways, it is this fact that has made the following facetious remark such a poignant commentary upon our scientific past:

* From *Journal of Humanistic Psychology*, 4, 1964, pp. 95-103. Reproduced by permission.

[1] An earlier version appeared in the *Discussion Papers* of the Wisconsin Psychiatric Institute (Volume 1, No. 4, 1961) and was presented at a symposium on "Mythology and methodology in psychological research," New Jersey Psychological Assn. meetings, December, 1961. It was written during the tenure of a postdoctoral research fellowship at the University of Wisconsin sponsored by the National Institute of Mental Health, U.S. Public Health Service. I am deeply indebted to Carl Rogers for stimulating much of the thought that has gone into this paper. I am also grateful to Charles B. Truax and Edward J. Shoben, Jr. for helpful criticism and encouragement.

"American psychology first lost its soul, then its mind, and finally its consciousness, but it still behaved" (Waters, 1958).

Because of a continuing commitment to the essentials of this behavioristic trend, academic American psychology has had a tendency to turn away from issues of significance for a comprehensive science of man. It seems that the field moved away from those issues perhaps with due cause, but like the prodigal son is now returning with its hard won independence and sophistication to the basic issues of human living it once left. While an estrangement from the weightier dimensions of human experience may have been a temporary necessity during the operational-behavioristic revolution, it is unacceptable as an enduring trait if we are to treat systematically the basic problems which have been spurned as mentalistic and, therefore, misleading for an objective science. Fortunately, the repercussions of the behavioristic revolt have settled and their positive contributions have been absorbed into the main stream of psychological science. Psychology now seems able, and has shown some evidence of being willing, to move on from quarrels about proper subject matter to become a more comprehensive science of human functioning.

There is no intention here of minimizing the great contributions made by S-R psychology but it is important to clarify their basic qualities. The primary contributions of the behavioristic and logical-positivistic traditions have been the bringing of objective, operational, and fertile theoretical *methods* into psychology. The tools of inquiry thus provided can now be applied to the problem areas long ago staked out as the province of psychology. Earlier attempts to attain objectivity by emphasis upon physiology, motor movements, or animal research has produced an objective psychology which has had great difficulty coming to terms with the major problems of a comprehensive science. Evidence is now accumulating, though not often recognized, that it is possible to have both the kind of objectivity that behavior theory strived for *and* significance at the same time *if* we accept the inner life of man as not only personally real but as subject to adequate observational methods.

The Return to the Great Issues

While an important minority within psychology (Allport, 1961; Murray, 1959; Rogers, 1959) have stressed, for decades, the significance of subjective, inner experience, it is only recently that psychology, as a science, has begun to move again in that direction. It appears that we are on the frontier of a new breakthrough in the measurement, manipulation, and conceptualization of intrapsychic phenomena. The natural history of the field reveals periods of peak activity in areas where significant change is occurring and where the potential energy for a sustained impact is being accumulated. The rise of behaviorism and subsequent theories of learning is an obvious example. The *Zeitgeist* appears to be again on the march — toward the re-inclusion of the subjective within the explicit framework of psychology.

An even cursory review of recent theoretical statements in the areas of motivation and personality reveals an impressive contingent of proponents favoring both the elimination of methodological codes for scientific endeavors and the bringing of significant human experience within the realm of objective analysis. Unambiguous commitments to these purposes are salient features of the first three volumes of the monumental *Psychology: A study of a science:*

> The results of Study I set up a vast attrition against virtually all elements of the Age of Theory Code . . . for the first time in its history, psychology seems ready . . . or almost ready . . . to assess its goals and instrumentalities with primary reference to its own indigenous problems . . . the more adventurous ranges of our illimitable subject matter so effectively repressed or bypassed during recent decades, are no longer proscribed. (Koch, 1959, p. 783; also quoted in Jessor, 1961.)

Independently of the Study I authors, many others have voiced serious concern that psychology has not attended sufficiently to its basic subject matter and that its problems demand new methods generating from its own soil. Jessor argues compellingly for an objective study of experience, an avoidance of traditional reductionism and definitions of S and R in psychological and meaningful terms (1961). Colby (1960) proclaims with equal assertion the irrelevance of most behavior-laboratory derived methods for analyzing the psychoanalytic process. Blum's (1961) substantive and conceptual work provides a stimulating example of the objectification of the subjective. It is not often that an experimentalist offers a concepual model of the *mind* and research which stresses ". . . mental functions occurring *between* stimulus and response . . ." studied, in part, by means of *introspection*. Tomkins (1962) has creatively reformulated vast domains of psychological data and theory via a conceptual framework centered significantly upon "private" experience. His opening statement that "The empirical analysis of consciousness has been delayed by two historical developments, Behaviorism and Psychoanalysis," could not have been more timely nor, perhaps, more significant. Holt's recent interpretation of the history of research on imagery (1962) gives strong reinforcement to this position as does Arnold's creative review of the field of emotion (1960). The mind, consciousness, imagery, emotion, all of these are the subject of renewed and vigorous attack which is depending largely upon objective operations for obtaining reports of inner, subjective experiences. All of the foregoing and more are considered by Koch (1961) in his bold recipe for a future psychology which would unify the sciences and humanities by coming to terms with the great issues of human concern within an objective framework.

The Need for a Methodology of Introspection

Perhaps the most important and at the same time most difficult problem of this increasing trend in psychological science concerns the objective study of what a person privately experiences. Thus far, it appears that there is no way of approaching this problem psychologically save via some type of introspective report. However, the most immediate association one is likely to have to this is: "Look what happened to introspection!" But what did happen to introspection? Ordinarily we think of Titchenerian introspection in this context and we must recognize that the failure of this method, its unreliability, was due more to the way in which it was used than to the method itself. The fatal assumption was that correct observation produced immediate experiences which did not differ from individual to individual. It seems clear that the re-introduction of introspection need not bring with it the attendant fallacies of the older method as we apply it to new problems. Personality inventories are a good example of such a modern application.

Historically, the quest for objectivity coupled with the unreliability of introspective reports of the Titchenerian variety served to focus attention away from direct experiencing and upon phenomena correlated or concomitant with the internal, subjectively sensed processes. This eventually led to the development of more reliable, but external, measures based upon physiological changes or motor movements which are indirect approaches to the old problem of inner experience. The failure of these methods to adequately solve the problems they were devised to attack is becoming increasingly obvious (Lacey, 1958) and is representative of the more general failure of behavioristic techniques to cope with the subjective.

Other approaches have emphasized methods similar to introspection but without acknowledging the fact. This is indicated by Boring (1953) when he asserts that the basic principle of introspection remains with us today under various aliases which range from psychophysical perceptual responses to patients' protocols. If he is correct, we might assume that it is so because the principle deals with phenomena of essential concern to a science of man and because it yields data thus far unobtainable in any other way.

The importance of reconsidering the value of introspection is attested to not only by Boring but by a great variety and an increasing number of psychologists. This can be illustrated specifically at a research level, but first let us consider the more sweeping observations being made of this particular issue. Koch (1959) notes in his Epilogue to the three volumes of the APA's Study I that "an important and quite general trend of the essays is an increased recognition of the role of direct experential analysis in psychological science." These are psychology's systematists speaking. Carnap (1956) evaluates the method by asserting that while ". . . many of the alleged results of introspection were indeed questionable, a person's awareness of his own state of imagining, feeling, etc., must be recognized as a kind of observation in principle not different from external observation, and, therefore, as a legitimate source of knowledge." Feigl, in his comments upon the philosophical embarrassments of psychology notes this new trend with optimism if not with delight:

The reintroduction of introspection, the new concern with the phenomenal field, the clinical attention to subjective experience, the studies in social perception, etc., seem to me to indicate, not indeed a regression to an obsolete psychology, but rather an advance along the spiral . . . of the evolution of the scientific outlook (1959, p. 123).

Thus, an historical view reveals how the early philosophical psychology was concerned with the problems of inner experience but that it lacked empirical precision. It also reveals how the introspectionists retained formal interest in the problem but did not deal with meaningful material and did not obtain objective reliability; and finally how the behavioristic reform brought objectivity but left out the historically meaningful content. Now that objectivism is soldly part of our discipline the possibility of moving on to a fruitful psychology of experience via a modernized introspective methodology seems feasible, if we but attend to it.

The problem of measuring and manipulating experiential phenomena is not simple, however, and we must recognize, as Skinner does, the exceptional difficulty involved in coming to terms with this problem:

> Behaviorism has been at least to most behaviorists nothing more than a thoroughgoing operational analysis of traditional mentalistic concepts . . . but behaviorism too stopped short of a decisive positive contribution . . . and for the same reason: it never finished an acceptable formulation of the verbal report. The conception of behavior which it developed could not convincingly embrace the use of subjective terms (1945, p. 271).

Skinner's own contribution to this problem (1957) does not, however, convincingly account for subjective experience either, but in fact avoids it by focussing upon verbal behavior as behavior without reference to the experience associated with it. Acting as though the inner processes do not exist does yield substantially different approaches to research and theory than if one assumes their existence and that verbal behavior has direct reference to them.

It is perhaps at this juncture that the crucial issue of this paper stands out. We do not disagree with the conviction that the only things a science can use are overt observables. Our point is a matter of emphasis, an emphasis stressing the notion that verbal behavior refers to actual phenomena and that centralizing our concern on these referred-to phenomena is more crucial than centralizing our concern on the verbal behavior, or any other reporting behavior, per se. The significance of that emphasis should not be underestimated with regard to its potential impact upon the entire domain of psychological work.

As an example, a currently important research area deriving from Skinner's position concerns the manipulation or shaping of verbal responses by selectively reinforcing them. In some research contexts, the changes in verbal behavior thus produced have been considered psychotherapeutic (Bandura,

1961; Lindsley, 1962). Let us contrast this for a moment with the research by Rogers (1960), Truax (1961; 1963), and others at Wisconsin. They have been concerned with the relationship between a number of therapist attitudes or feelings and associated therapeutic change in Schizophrenic clients. They have found significant relationships between variables such as therapist genuineness (or congruence), understanding, liking, etc., and therapeutic change as measured by indices of inner experience in the patients. Their approach utilizes both ratings which infer inner feeling states from verbal behavior and measures of the relationship as subjectively perceived by client and therapist (Truax, 1963; van der Veen, 1961). The procedures involved and the functional relationships arrived at differ markedly from a verbal behavior analysis of the Skinnerian variety simply by virtue of acting as though inner experiences do exist and that they have a significant effect upon the functioning of both participants in an interaction. This clearly suggests that intrapsychically oriented research can add significantly to the variance accounted for in personality functioning.

It should be noted here that the therapeutic interaction is somewhat unique in that the most significant human experiencings are most salient and the need for such an analysis is thus most apparent. In fact, it should be noted that clinical psychology in general has had a significant role in the changing orientation of the whole science (Bakan, 1956). *It is possible, however, that behavior theory has been able to thrive without including inner experiences within its framework precisely because the research problems selected have been ones where such variables are not salient.*

Osgood's contribution to the measurement of subjective meaning via the semantic differential (1957) is a further illustration of the explanatory power which can be generated by applying a rigorously objective approach to the analysis of inner experience. His has been a boldly imaginative and scientifically fertile grappling with the difficulties of adequately operationalizing introspective report, an unexpected but gratifyingly fruitful response from one identified with an S-R tradition.

Psychology's New Look

The extent to which introspective reports such as those just specified are utilized in psychology is not often fully recognized. It is common practice in studies of stress, attitude change, and inter-personal perception to demonstrate that the experimental manipulation was successful by obaining a report of whether the subject actually experienced the intended antecedent condition. It would not do, for example, to test the effects of differing levels of communicator prestige upon the amount of attitude change on communicatees without being certain that subjects would actually perceive the prestige differences as intended. This amounts to no less than a perceptual or experiential definition of the stimulus condition. Interestingly, in many of these studies the criterion or dependent variable is equally experiential and its measurement equally dependent upon introspective reports. Reports by subjects of their attitudes is just this kind of a procedure. On this basis, it is easy to see that a great portion of social psychology consists simply of the analysis of experential factors.

The entire range of personality tests from the MMPI to the Rorschach represents attempts to sample inner experience in the hope of developing adquate predictive equations for complex behavior. Most studies of achievement motivation and of anxiety are similarly crucially dependent upon overt indices of inner referents. The entire field of perception from psychophysics to "new look" perception is related to the same problem. The objective measurement of physical stimulus intensities does not, in principle, differ from the reliable estimation of the *meaning* of social stimuli as it pertains to personal predispositions, and, in both instances, the crucial dependent variables are indexed by overt responses that refer directly to private experiences. Many other existing areas of study focus more explicitly on analyses of experience: Studies of the self, of feelings and emotions, and many experimental explorations of psychoanalytic concepts (Klein, 1958; Rapaport, 1959) can all be conceived within this framework. Self-related Q sorts are indeed, like the semantic differential, nothing more than an objectified approach to the subjective and private in one's experience.

It is not difficult to see that much of psychology has addressed itself to and is dependent upon the study of personal phenomenology. The incongruous and surprising thing is that this research is not seen in that light. If it were, it is very likely that, as the psychotherapy research cited or in the recent work of Blum (1962), some new dimensions of investigation would be added and some new concepts developed. It is conceivable, in fact, to envision much of psychology becoming re-oriented around the task of a science of inner experience simply by a change in emphasis. The groundwork is already laid in the vast research enterprises just cited.

The Need for Further Change

As psychologists have addressed themselves to basically phenomenological subject matters, even though they have been behavioristically oriented, the subject matter they have been dealing with has forced them to utilize methods dependent upon subjective reports and has forced the stretching of old theories or the developing of new concepts that are indeed very similar to the tradition of phenomenological theory building. Unfortunately most researchers have continued implicitly to operate within a behavioristic theory which is inappropriate to what is really a phenomenological subject matter.

An important re-orientation could easily come about (a) by a further attenuation of the behavioristic influence upon psychological thinking which has made it so difficult to fully realize just what we have in actuality been doing, and (b) by the explicit recognition that the data of psychology can consist of experiences, that they are primary phenomena and that overt observables can be a means of measuring them rather than that the overt observables are the only subject of study in and of themselves.

The imminent possibility of such a consummation is overwhelmingly testified to by the numerous contributions to theory and research noted above. That this is so and that it is desirable should in no way minimize or undermine the distinctive contributions of behavioristic and neo-behavioristic approaches to human and animal phenomena.

Whether one considers the rising status of concerns with inner experience in terms of developing a two-factor theory of behavior or in terms of an integration of the neo-behavioristic and phenomenological traditions, it is stimulating to realize that the acknowledgement of either as an important and substantively feasible alternative casts psychology, as a science, in a modified perspective, one which may indeed signify a movement towards increasing comprehensiveness and social significance.

REFERENCES

ALLPORT, G. W. *Pattern and growth in personality.* New York: Holt, Rinehart & Winston, 1961.

ARNOLD, MAGDA. *Emotion and personality.* New York: Columbia Univ. Press, 1960. 2 Vols.

BAKAN, D. Clinical psychology and logic. *American Psychologist,* 1956, 11, 655-662.

BANDURA, A. Psychotherapy as a learning process. *Psychological Bulletin,* 1961, 58, 143-159.

BLUM, G. S. *A model of the mind.* New York: Wiley, 1961.

BORING, E. G. *A history of experimental psychology.* New York: Appleton-Century-Crofts, 1950.

BORING, E. G. A history of introspection. *Psychological Bulletin,* 1953, 50, 169-189.

CARNAP, R. The methodological character of theoretical concepts. In H. Feigl & M. Scriven (Eds.), *Minnesota studies in the philosophy of science.* Vol. II. Minneapolis: University of Minnesota Press, 1956, 38-76.

COLBY, K. M. The viewpoint of the psychoanalyst. Paper presented at the American Association for the Advancement of Science meetings. New York, December, 1960.

FIEGL, H. Philosophical embarrassments of psychology. *American Psychologist,* 1959, 14, 115-128.

HEBB, D. O. The American revolution. *American Psychologist,* 1960, 15, 735-745.

HOLT, R. R. Imagery — The return of the ostracized. Presidential address presented to Division 12 at the meetings of the *American Psychological Association,* St. Louis, August, 1962.

JESSOR, R. Issues in the phenomenological approach to personality. *Journal of Individual Psychology,* 1961 (Spring).

KLEIN, G. S. Cognitive control and motivation. In G. Lindzey (Ed.), *Assessment of human motives.* New York: Rinehart & Co., 1958. Pp. 87-118.

KOCH, S. Epilogue. In S. Koch (Ed.), *Psychology: A study of a science.* New York: McGraw-Hill, Vol. III, 1959. Pp. 729-788.

KOCH, S. Psychological science versus the science-humanism antimony: Intimations of a significant science of man. *American Psychologist* 1961, 16, 629-639.

LACEY, J. I. Psychophysiological approaches to the evaluation of psychotherapeutic processes and outcome. In E. A. Rubinstein & M. B. Parloff (Eds.), *Research in psychotherapy.* Washington, D.C.: *American Psychological Association,* 1958. Pp. 160-208.

LINDSLEY, O. R. Direct behavioral analysis of psychotherapy sessions by conjugately closed-circuit television. Paper presented at the meetings of the American Psychological Association, St. Louis, September, 1962.

MURRAY, H. A. Preparations for the scaffold of a comprehensive system. In S. Koch (Ed.), *Psychology: A study of a science,* New York: McGraw-Hill, Vol. III, 1959. Pp. 7-54.

OSGOOD, C. E., SUCI, G. J. and TANNEBAUM, P. H. *The measurement of meaning.* Urbana, Ill.: Univ. of Illinois Press, 1957.

RAPAPORT, D. The structure of psychoanalytic theory: A systematizing attempt. In S. Koch (Ed.), *Psychology: A study of a science.* New York: McGraw-Hill, Vol. III, 1959. Pp. 55-183.

ROGERS, C. R. A theory of therapy, personality, and interpersonal relationships, as developed in the client centered framework. In S. Koch (Ed.), *Psychology: A study of a science.* New York: McGraw-Hill, Vol. III, 1959. Pp. 184-256.

ROGERS, C. R. Significant trends in the client-centered orientation. In D. Brower & L. E. Abt (Eds.), *Progress in clinical Psychology.* New York: Grune & Stratton, Vol. IV, 1960.

SKINNER, B. F. The operational analysis of psychological terms. *Psychological Review,* 1945, 52, 270-277.

SKINNER, B. F. *Verbal behavior.* New York: Appleton-Century-Crofts, 1957.

TOMKINS, S. S. *Affect, imagery, consciousness.* New York: Springer, Vol. 1, 1962.

TRUAX, C. B. Effective ingredients in psychotherapy: An approach to unraveling the patient-therapist interaction. *Journal of Counseling Psychology,* 1963.

TRUAX, C. B. The process of group psychotherapy: Relationships between hypothesized therapeutic conditions and intrapersonal exploration. *Psychological Monographs,* 1961, 75, No. 7 (Whole No. 511).

VAN DER VEEN, F. The perception by clients and by judges of the conditions offered by the therapist in the therapy relationship. Paper read in a symposium on "Therapeutic and research progress in a program of psychotherapy with hospitalized schizophrenics" at the meetings of the *American Psychological Association Convention.* New York City, September, 1961.

WATERS, R. H. Behavior: Datum or abstraction. *American Psychologist,* 1958, 13, 278-282.

5

Existentialism and

Experiential Psychotherapy*

EUGENE T. GENDLIN

In this chapter, I want to introduce the new formulations of existential and experimental theory. I shall try to state what existentialism has contributed to psychotherapy and to outline and illustrate experiential therapy.

Experiential Theory

In the new thinking, human experiencing is approached directly rather than studied after it has been translated into theoretical machinery. Therefore, theory for the new therapies is different in kind. It not only involves different concepts but a new way of using concepts. Both concepts and experiences enter into this theory in a very special kind of interplay.

The existential approaches use concepts as "pointers" that refer directly[1] to felt experience. That sounds very modest, and it is. Yet, the use of concepts as pointers to felt experience is the steppingstone to a new theoretical outlook.

For example, the articles in existential child therapy share a common outlook. Yet, they employ a huge range of different theoretical concepts. The

---

* Chapter 11 of *Existential child therapy* edited by Clark Moustakas © 1966 by Clark Moustakas, Basic Books, Inc., Publishers, New York.

[1] Eugene T. Gendlin, *Experiencing and the creation of meaning* (New York: The Free Press of Glencoe, 1962); Eugene T. Gendlin, A theory of personality change. In Worchel and Byrne (Eds.), *Personality change.* New York: John Wiley, 1964. (See Chapter 7.)

authors themselves come from radically diverse theoretical orientations. A few phrases from the articles illustrate this diversity: "existential moment," "pattern of neurotic interaction," "acceptance," "alienation," "explore analytically," "separation anxiety," "the Great Mother." Clearly, what these authors have in common is not their theoretical vocabulary!

If you take any of these phrases as well-defined concepts (and each is a well-defined concept in the context of its proper theory), then, of course, they are highly inconsistent with each other. The implications which follow by theoretical logic from one of these concepts are very different from those which follow from another. Since these authors share a common approach to psychotherapy, they are not using their concepts in accordance with original definitions. This divergence accounts for the impression that existentialism in psychotherapy is no more than a protest movement against theory and that it combines under its aegis a diversity of views united only by the refusal to think clearly — thinking clearly (logically, theoretically, that is) would reveal definite inconsistencies.

This confusing picture is altered when we see that these therapists employ concepts, not chiefly via their logical-theoretical implications, but in a different way. I can illustrate this new way by means of the gentle example of the articles in existential child therapy.

These authors do not reason from concept to concept through logical chains. Their reasoning is not based on theoretical concepts as such. Rather, they use concepts to point to and differentiate directly felt experiencing. This new use of concepts turns theoretical orientations into mere vocabularies. A few decades ago, these concepts were not "vocabulary," but fundamental forces, entities, or constituents of personality. Each theory viewed the nature of man differently, with different practical applications. Yet, today, something is the same in all these different theoretical writings. Something transcends the differing vocabularies (indeed, makes them merely "vocabularies"). It is the direct reference by each concept to specific differentiations of felt experiencing.

Let me say more exactly what I mean: Frederick H. Allen in *Existential child therapy* tells of a little girl who did not want to go to school or even separate from her mother because she feared that great harm would come to her mother. In one of the interviews, the child told Allen that her mother was really her twin. Allen writes. "The feeling of separation aroused a feeling of being nobody, at best a twin, but with no adequate confidence of being a unique and distinct person." Here is an "interpretation" via the theory of separation anxiety and birth trauma. It seems to be a totally different interpretation than that of Eve Lewis (1966).

Discussing a little boy's insistence on sleeping in his mother's bed, this therapist, Lewis, interprets the behavior as a difficulty in "facing the problem of the Great Mother." We recognize the Jungian interpretation. Yet, throughout these experiences, we know what both therapists are talking about;

it is the same thing! We are unconcerned about their theoretical differences. We do not relate separation anxiety to birth trauma, as the theory would. We do not ask: Is it realy birth trauma or is it an archetype? Notice, as I now cite two more statements from these same therapists, that it is difficult to know which expression is Jungian and which is Rankian. "I pointed out . . . that being alone is sometimes inevitable, that it was a requirement of living . . . the fear that mother might be killed was actually . . . a wish to escape once and forever the imprisoning mother." "To be brighter, keener, more aware, more in touch with life was a frightening thought . . . to transcend mother was equivalent to killing her."

Our direct words about experiencing, our direct differentiations of experiencing, do not depend upon conceptual definitions. As we differentiate experiencing directly, and, rather finely, we may occasionally use theoretical terms, newly invented words and old words that have differentiating power when referring to feelings.

Articles by therapists use case reports and are naturally full of descriptive detail. But descriptive detail is really meant, and the concepts have meaning only in terms of descriptive life. The meaning of the concepts is precisely what they point to; it is not based on theoretical definitions. Existential thinking does not move from concept to concept through logical implications. Rather, it moves through experiential detail, through differentiations that make experiential sense and that enable further experience. In existential child therapy, the steps of discussion are steps of experiencing, not steps of conceptual derivation. The experiences are not defined by the concepts, but, on the contrary, the concepts are defined by the steps of experiencing.

The descriptive detail is not merely an "application" or "manifestation" of conceptually defined entities. At one time, the detailed texture of experience was considered "epiphenomena," manifestations of conceptually defined forces, entities, psychologic factors. In the newer use, you might say the concepts are the "epiphenomena," pointers whose sole meaning consists of the experiential texture at which they point, and which help us to differentiate so that we may directly feel and know the experiential steps in therapy as the therapist discusses them.

This method, of course, requires concepts. It is a use of concepts, but a different use than the chain which moves: concept — implication — concept — implication — concept. It is a chain which moves: experiential step — concept — experiential step — concept.

These steps of experiencing (of differentiating and moving from feeling to feeling) must make direct experiential sense to us. They are always much more specific than any theoretical concept. Therefore, we could not possibly gain the sense of these steps by means of a theoretical concept. On the contrary, the theoretical concept, as used, gets its meaning from the detailed steps we must first directly feel.

Current developments in psychotherapy have obscured the lines between different orientations. For example, contrast psychoanalysis and client-centered therapy. What a sharp difference that once seemed to be! Today, looking back, we see the similarity: Both were highly formal denials of a real relationship. One role-played a relationship of transference; the other roll-played a perfectly neutral acceptance. We see two of a kind — artificial, formalistic avoidances of genuine interaction between two people. The patient's real feelings were considered invalid (transference). The analyst's feelings were also considered invalid (counter-transference). Similarly in client-centered therapy, it was a mistake for the therapist to interject his own feelings into the therapeutic situation. Today, client-centered therapists make "genuineness" the first condition[2] for therapy and therapist-expressivity[3] and spontaneity[4] main therapeutic factors. Psychoanalysts are also moving toward real involvement and commitment as persons, with less reliance on technique.

A second main trend that cuts across orientations is emphasis on directly felt experience instead of insistence on certain special contents. For example, in classical analysis all difficulties had to lead back to Oedipal sexual conflicts. Few analysts today would construe psychotherapy so narrowly. The other orientations also place less emphasis on contents once held as necessary for successful therapy. Concepts, such as self-perception, power drive, separation anxiety, archetype, sexual conflict, and interpersonal reactions no longer fix the direction and movement of therapy. Today, there are many different "orientations," but they do not differ along really essential lines. What appeared to be major differences in the essential personality determinants now seem more differences in vocabulary. Today, whatever the theory, the directly felt process in the patient is basic. The patient can oblige his therapist and express his felt experiences in any one of the content languages.

The present explorations in psychotherapy reflect a period of transition. The new essential dimensions, shared very broadly by some therapists in all orientations, are *the relationship process between two humans and the therapeutic feeling process.* Both of these dimensions are experiential in character. For this reason, I am calling the new therapy "experiential therapy." In every orientation, today, we find discussion for and against the new emphasis, in contrast to the technique forms on which we once concentrated so heavily.

I have already mentioned the direct experiential way of talking about and proceeding in therapy. Let me now emphasize the experiential relationship and the individual's feeling process. The concrete living personal relationship is much more than two people and their individual patterns, more than what

[2] Carl R. Rogers, *On becoming a person.* Boston: Houghton Mifflin, 1961.
[3] Eugene T. Gendlin, Subverbal communication and therapist expressivity trends in client-centered therapy with schizophrenics. *Journal of Existential Psychiatry,* IV (1963), No. 14; Eugene T. Gendlin, Schizophrenia, problems and methods of psychotherapy, *Review of Existential Psychology and Psychiatry,* IV (1964), No. 2.
[4] J. M. Butler, "Client-centered counseling and psychotherapy," in D. Brower and L. E. Abt, Eds., *Progress in clinical psychology* (New York: Grune & Stratton, 1958), Vol. III, *Changing conceptions in psychotherapy.*

each thinks of the other or how each sees the other, more than units of meaning communicated from one to the other. Martin Buber says of the therapist that "if he has really gathered the child into his life then that subterranean dialogic . . . is established and endures." This is no mere professional relationship to a patient; it is a life relationship of two humans. They both live really there, in the "reality *between* them." And this reality is a "subterranean" connection and interaction. It isn't merely something perceived and communicated, or specific reactions of one to the other. It involves one's whole ongoing aliveness. Poetic language — but we have no well-established technical terms for it. We all know, for example, the concrete sense of being looked at by another human being, when someone looks *at* us. That is not what he really thinks or what we wish he would think, or how we wish he had seen us. It isn't this or that perception he may be getting. It is the live, direct sense of existing in the "reality between" ourselves and him, of being seen by him, and of meeting him in his seeing.

I believe that successful psychotherapy of any type has always centrally involved this concrete type of encounter. Yet, there has also been a great deal of artificiality, of therapists limiting their involvement as persons (as if it were an error betraying the therapist's weaknesses, needs, or softness), much painfully distant dealing with patients as though with forceps. Therapists have often felt they had to sit behind screens of various kinds — fully seeing the patient, but themselves neither visible nor visibly involved in an encounter.

But the fully real relationship involves the therapist's own person and hence his weaknesses and fears. Therefore, case reports of such relationships are quite personal. Both therapist and child are fully rounded and fully human persons. Only recently have case reports reflected this kind of human encounter. After all, one use of the word "clinical" and "case" is as a cliché for impersonal oblivion of humanness. No one likes to be treated "as a case" or to be looked at "clinically" — as if we all knew that, when the therapist looks at us "clinically," he is in some way violating our person! There is no longer such inhuman formalism here: a theme running through content and manner of these papers is the directly felt encounter and the concrete way in which it involves the therapist as a person.

But why call it "subterranean"? Only because it involves our total, live, ongoing being rather than this or that message or analytic tool? More than that: because this concrete encounter easily and constantly transcends words. "The physician tried to convince him that the needle would hurt him only a little. . . . He screamed repeatedly. . . ." "During this time, I held his hand. . . . I did not talk about the realities involved." So much action, without words, all of it direct living connections, specific, eventful, concrete.

Or, there is Jerry, a supposedly retarded boy who "struggled through almost the entire . . . Wechsler-Bellevue with little or no response. Everything I said, everything I showed him, seemed beyond his comprehension. . . ." "Yet,

I could not stop. But this time there was a difference; he was able to copy the third demonstration. Then . . . he was able to complete the next five designs. . . . Jerry appeared to be a different boy. He seemed to relax."

What is happening here? A relationship: a concrete interaction, a different boy. What is being said — how was it achieved? What technique was used? What of the facts shown in the Wechsler-Bellevue? What kind of facts are such facts, and what kind of facts are "he was able to copy the third demonstration" and "the next five designs . . ."? What is a person? What kind of facts? And, again, what different thing is a person-in-relationship, and what kind of facts are these different ones that grow out of a relationship?

In these relationships the individual is already, in these moments, ongoingly, a different person differently involved and differently alive than he was as a lone set of facts.

Here is one author's clear tracing of how the individual is what he is in interaction, and how he changes in the moments in which the interaction is concretely different. Colm (1966) describes the older brother Bobby and the little Gavin:

> And I saw Gavin slowly, slowly moving his foot closer against the big, complicated building that Bobby had just erected for an army barracks. Bang! It collapsed by "accident." Bobby instantly became the monster and threw a stone. Gavin cried out *desperately* and ran to me for protection.

If the therapist is temporarily drawn into the child's pattern of provoking unreal acceptance, pity, or protection, he must catch this in himself, and make it a useful experience for the child, and for himself.

> I said, "Oh shucks. . . . Poor little Gavin (*pause*) or (*pause*) really like superman? . . . could wreck even big Bobby's building *and* could make Mom come and scold Bobby and comfort *him*." . . . An embarrassed . . . smile came from Gavin. At this point, I gave him a short hug — not before, when he had tried to force me into protecting him.

Sometimes therapists know and describe moments when it is clear and self-explanatory by just what steps the relationship changes the individual. At other times therapists equally well know these moments and describe them in finely caught detail, yet only the child's unfolding is visible — the why is mysterious. The *general* explanation is the same: it isn't that the interaction affects the individual and then makes him different. In the very ongoing of that interaction, he is already different.

The therapists sometimes know and can say just what kind of change they bring, in what way they make the interaction (and the changed person in that interaction) into something more positive, more alive, more free and lifeworthy. At other times such "making positive" is not specific nor known to the therapist. It happens nevertheless. It is a function of the nature of two people connected, open, honest, and struggling. To be helpless, hopeless, isolated, unloved, lost in weirdness — we call these things negative; but no "value judgment" is required of the therapist in order to alter these negatives in the patient. The very nature of finding oneself concretely seen, felt, connected, and one's every feeling and motion responded to constitutes finding oneself no longer helpless, hopeless, no longer isolated, unloved, lost in weirdness. The concrete mode of living is already different. The words with which to perceive and say what has changed, these can come later. For example, Allen (1966) writes: "I reflected the side of her that wanted to live, helping her to recognize her own fear of growing up, but, at the same time, her desire to be connected with life and to emerge as a distinct and independent person. . . . Once she remarked, . . . when I come here I know I want to live."

That is what a relationship does! Always the *positive* being of the person is concretely extended and made real. But this is no "value choice" of accentuating the positive. It does not mean at all that one welcomes positive feelings and plays down negative ones. In the case above, it was just as important to respond to "her own fear of growing up." The making real of the person's positive being lies in the concrete relating, in the response and welcome to every shade of feeling, in the kind of ongoing person-process made by such responding. Precisely "the side of her that wants to live" is made real and alive as *she* is responded to in whatever she may be up against. A responded-to person is already a more positively alive one, than the dulled, life-blocked, hardly ongoing, lone facts of the person were.

Concrete existential encounters make the positive ongoingly real, and it hardly matters whether a therapist's design is quite conscious and clear, or whether he has no design at all — except precisely to relate responsively and connectedly. That subterraneously includes all possible positive designs. For example: ". . . I responded to him in ways which told him that a strong adult who knew the realities of life was his honest ally . . ." (Kogl, 1966); or "I give myself to you without fear of losing myself" (Baruch, 1966); or "The therapist never loses touch with himself as a person . . . (and brings) to the child the full resources of a real self . . ." (Moustakas, 1966). The experiential relationship, the existential encounter then, is fully and mutually personal and not just professional; it is much more than verbal, it is a concrete interplay and connectedness; and in the very ongoing of this kind of interaction the individual is already different and more fully and positively alive.

And, literally as a corollary of concrete relating, another pervasive theme concerns the experiencing process in the individual. The concrete relationship involves humans as experiencing and feeling persons. And so, the individual is ongoing as a new and different process of experiencing, of feeling. Not this or that content, but the type of process determines illness or health.

The very contents of an individual are different depending upon what kind of feeling process he is — and the relationship determines that. Baruch (1966) speaks of children's "preposterous giant imaginings." "A child must pathetically hide inside him the monstrous things." Yet, these are normal!

Baruch pleads with us as parents and therapists to give "attention, more hearing, more understanding that goes forth in quiet peace to meet our children's feelings." In this way, she tells us, "the normal problems of childhood remain normal." These "monsters" of childhood, as such, don't create trouble. Rather, it is the way in which the child is responded to, and allowed to exist as an ongoing being — that determines sickness or health.

Similarly, Colm's (1966) Bobby and his "monster" dreams. As the little Gavin goads him, "Bobby instantly became the monster. . . ." And, when Bobby experiences himself in a different interaction, no longer as unwanted and goaded, "the monster dreams disappeared."

These concrete relationships change the individual just because an individual isn't these or those facts inside, but always an ongoing feeling process in interaction. The monsters aren't "psychotic contents." They are as human as having your block building kicked over by your sneaky little brother who competes for your mother's love. They are the consequence of being isolated and unresponded to as children. They "disappear" in a relationship as a distinct person emerges. Or, as Wenkart (1966) states "By being responded to lovingly, by being nourished and valued he [the child] develops responsiveness in kind; he builds bridges to objects and to people."

What is the individual? Not these or those factual contents but the felt, ongoing process. Moustakas (1966) describes it in "The Existential Moment" as "an entirely unique and particular substance which is his own . . . an essence which can be recognized and called forth in the encounter." The encounter calls it forth, it brings it about that "the person feels his feelings . . . ," is more fully alive as his own unique substance, and is just thereby and just in that way changed from how he was before!

Insight plays a great role in this feeling process which transcends content. But, in these chapters, it is not an insight brought up dead, like a long-drowned fact from the bottom of the unconscious sea. As Allen puts it, "the child's inner life is revealed in such a way that the child participates directly and actively in the resolution of his own conflicts and problems." Throughout these chapters, recognition, "helping him to see . . . ," this is insight that stems from the concretely felt flow of ongoing inner life. The payoff and truth directly bring an immediately experienced release, a more fully being alive, concretely. This is insight which emerges out of felt experiencing and leads right into a movement of that experiencing.

The Theoretical Questions

How, now, shall we formulate these themes more exactly? There is great promise but also danger in the new experiential psychotherapy. *The promise is for genuine therapy and a genuinely human science of man.* The danger is a therapy without theoretical perspectives and trainable principles. Existential psychotherapy can look like a mere rejection of theory and precise thought. No such rejection is implied here — only that the main concerns and the very method of thought are still in the process of being formulated, and they are different from older theories.

Having pointed to some of the main themes as exemplified in these chapters, let us formulate these more exactly. We must develop a theory of experiential process and experiential steps. Experiential process plays a central role in at least three related respects: in the function of experiential steps, in the interpersonal relationship, and in the individual during psychotherapy.

The individual during psychotherapy could not change in personality if he did not engage in directly felt experiential steps. If we thing of his experiential steps as merely an experiental version of conceptual steps, then we cannot explain how he changes. Suppose he and we describe accurately how it is with him now, the what and why of his painful, self-defeating patterns, the factors which have made it so and keep it so. Suppose he remains only within what logically follows, what is logically consistent with this way of being. He would never change. To remain consistent with — that means precisely not to change. Any account of how someone changes and resolves difficulties must involve a process that moves beyond what can follow consistently from how the individual is.

For this reason, the older theories failed to define the change process in the individual. Freudian theory, for example, calls the change process "working through," an admittedly chaotic, little-understood struggle in which the individual "somehow" overcomes what the theoretical diagnosis represented. The theoretical diagnosis explains why and how the individual came to be and had to remain as he is. If the experiential process of the individual did not move through steps other than those which could be deduced from the diagnosis, the diagnosis would continue to fit him. He would not have changed. The experiential steps cannot possibly be only concrete versions of consistent conceptual steps. Thus, our theory must not portray experiential steps and resolution as if they were logical steps. Patients and therapists employ not only concepts, but also experiential steps. We do not want merely to "intellectualize" or "rationalize" — neither *in,* nor *about* psychotherapy.

I call this reliance on experiential as well as conceptual steps the "experiential use" of concepts. In "experiential use," concepts, words, or other symbols have a vital function, but a different one than that of leading directly (by logical implication) to other words or concepts. Steps of experiential differentiation intervene between one concept or set of words and the next. Rather than leading by implication directly to other words or concepts, there is first a directly experienced effect. Something directly felt is newly noticeable. That newly noticeable experiencing then leads to further concepts. The new conceptualization "makes sense"; it follows understandably *from* the preceding concepts, yet one could not have gotten to it by any conceptual implications *of* the preceding step.

One can, and often does, move directly from concept to concept by conceptual implication. But therapeutic change and resolution occur because of those times when one moves via intervening experiential steps.

An experiential use of concepts still requires that concepts retain their logical precision and meaning — for that is what has the power to refer to experiencing. It is an error to drop logic, language, definition, and logical precision. That leads to arbitrary emotionalism, not to experiential steps. It is true that there is here a difficult philosophic problem,[5] just how to know what aspects of a conceptual construct one employs to refer to experiencing, as against those aspects one ignores for the moment, as being experientially irrelevant. To so use concepts systematically involves a systematic method. For the moment I want only to point out that a glorification of "ambiguity" and "inexpressibility" is not in order. Concepts and intellectual differentiations play a vital role both in psychotherapy and in civilized man generally. We cannot differentiate experiencing and move along experiential steps unless we are willing to grant concepts even more precise and specific power than when we use them abstractly. For example, recall how often in psychotherapy the client struggles for the exactly right way of stating something he feels. Many statements may be rejected as "not quite it," even though conceptually they seem to be the same as what he finally asserts is "exactly it." That exactly right statement has a powerful experiential effect. The person may visibly relax, exhale deeply, and feel released and deeply relieved, often despite the fact that the statement asserts something awful. The "felt rightness" (as we usually call it) of such a statement is obviously not at all arbitrary. Not any and all concepts or words will do. Only just exactly these words have this effect of experiential movement. We experience this effect as "the words are exactly right; they feel true"; just this is a deeply felt experiential movement and change. A few minutes or days later, it thereby becomes possible to conceptualize quite a different experiential step. That new conceptualization may well now contradict the one that felt so true, and just because of the change made by this "feeling true." Thus the process of felt experiential steps is involved not only in our own experiential use of concepts, but also in the client's change process in therapy.

This process of felt steps helps to explain the value of the personal relationship in psychotherapy.

Again, the old method of conceptual machinery fell short. Just as the change process within the individual is a mystery if only constructs and their implications are considered, so also, without the experiential process, it is a mystery how the interpersonal relationship creates its powerful change-effects.

Freud explained how the patient repeats his self-defeating patterns (the "transference"), but he did not explain why the patient ever ceases this repetition, how he ever becomes different, how the transference is "handled" or

[5] Eugene T. Gendlin, *Experiencing and the creation of meaning.* New York: The Free Press of Glencoe, 1962.

"overcome." More basically, it was said that the presence of the therapist in a close transference relationship "changes the libidinal cathexes" or "alters the dynamic balance." Today, with our new experiential way of using concepts, we need not object to these terms. The personal relationship indeed changes the "dynamic balance," we may agree. We say "of course it does." We aren't even thinking of "dynamic balance" as the theoretical construct it is, with all its conceptual implications of bound forces and hydraulic economic complexes. We are not using the definition of "dynamic balance" when we easily assent that, indeed, a personal relationship of a certain sort can alter the dynamic balance. We can let this phrase stand as a pointer to what we feel directly: the way in which one's whole manner of being alive feels and is different, depending upon toward whom and with whom we live, feel, and express.

The therapeutic change, resolution, working through, overcoming of repetitive and limiting patterns, occurs not from more exact revelation of how the patient is and came to be as he is, not from more and more fully showing him that he must be as he is, and must react as he does. It comes from making this now ongoing relationship into a new and different concrete life experience for him, a kind of experiencing he could not be, and was not, until now. Thus, the effects of a personal relationship must be understood as the new and different experiential process that a genuine relationship makes possible.

Existentialism

Previous theories looked upon the interpersonal relationship second; they considered the individual first. The individual was explained (his behavior, personality, feelings, and so forth). Then, when two individuals met, they "communicated," or "interacted." Such interaction was explained in terms of basically individual entites. Behavior was explained out of individual motives, drives, patterns, or tendencies. Outside "stimuli" set off patterns or forces in the individual, and these determined his behavior. The individual was regarded as a self-contained box, and his internal machinery determined his feelings and acts. Existentialism overthrows these kinds of perceptions and interpretations.

Being in the world and being with others is the first consideration of existentialism; the individual as a separate entity is explainable only in the second place. In America, Sullivan[6] effected a similar theoretical revolution, although in different terms and not quite as thoroughly.

For existentialism there is no "subject" within, separate from the "objects" outside. Our language and habits of thought have been guided so long by British Empiricism that even existentialists sometimes fall back into just those modes of thought which existentialism most opposes. For Husserl, and phe-

---

[6] Harry Stack Sullivan, *The interpersonal theory of psychiatry.* New York: Norton, 1953.

nomenology since then, the basic term is "intentionality." This word means that experience as we have it is always about something, toward something, in reaction to something, of something, with something, never *just* an entity inside our heads or bodies. Phenomenology rejects the theory that we see "percepts" that we think "images" and "sensory traces" or "nervous simula-tions." Husserl, in examining directly-given experience, found that he just never saw a percept. No one has ever seen a percept. We always see a tree or a person or a room. We always see something outside us (even dream images are like that), never a percept in our heads. We always feel angry at what someone did because of what happened to us and what we must now do. We never feel anger as just something subjective, an entity within, unrelated to the world we live in. What we actually experience eliminates the old barrier between the objective (geometrically conceived atoms and physical forces out-side) and the subjective (entities or forces inside). Husserl found that the whole human world was really implicit in our experience and that the supposed entities within were mere theoretical constructs.

The individual's gut-felt experience (for example, "I am all tense and tied-up") is no mere internal entity (like a swallowed rock) but implicitly contains a whole texture of concerns about situations, reactions to others, perceptions of things and people. The following speech illustrates the many situational conditions and perceptions implicit in what may seem to be purely internal entities, being tense or afraid or ashamed:

> Oh, I'm so tense because I know I am going to have a talk about X and I don't want to because of what you'll think of me . . . and what I'll think of myself, I guess I am ashamed, really, because I did this awful thing, but really that isn't the main of it, it's that I had to do it not out of meanness but because I was afraid to stand up to him because I'd have to fight and so it was really out of fear I got pushed into it, and having to admit that is worse than just what I did, and I was afraid to admit that. Boy, *was* I tense.

In the old theory, we talked as though "affects" (internal entities) were "attached" to situational stimuli. The formula we used is "I am tense because of X" and the "because" bridged the artificial gap between the subjective and the objective. But, this "attached affect" hides the real way it is. Notice, in the few lines above, first tension was "attached," then "fear," then "shame." These different emotional colorings did indeed come and go, but the individual was really explicating one felt chain of experience. As he told why he felt tense, he no longer felt tense, but instead, ashamed. Nor was he merely "tense" as an entity within. He was tense at the prospect of having to discuss some-thing with someone. He did not merely have shame as an entity within. He was ashamed at being pushed into certain things through fear. His "fear" was not an entity within but a being afraid of having to fight.

It is an essential character of felt experience, that it is internally differentiable,[7] that it may, after moments, turn into a long chain of complex situational and interpersonal aspects. Experience is not something "within," but something interactive, implicitly containing many aspects of the situations one lives in.

Existentialism defines human beings as being "in the world." It defines subjective or individual experience not as something within, but as "in the world." It defines the individual human as a being here (Dasein). This means he is concretely sentient. Existence is always yours, mine, his. It is the concrete ongoing living we feel and are. It implicitly contains how we are alive and geared into our situations.

Other persons are perhaps the most important aspect of the world and the situations we live in. Human beings are always a "being-with."[8] (Loneliness is no exception; in fact we can feel lonely only because being-with is an essential aspect of human beings.)

Being-with and being-in (situations, the world) are not mere "traits" of humans. They are what it is to be human, they are human "being." Much as Sullivan had altered theory from individualized entities to "dynamisms" (ongoing exchanges between people), so also existentialism portrays human nature as first and essentially an ongoing living in and with. What we feel and do stems not from inner self-contained machinery, but rather from what is felt toward and done toward people and things, to bring about situations, to alter them, to realize possibilities we foresee and avoid possibilities we fear. If you take away from human beings, this aspect of a "projected" world (of fearing, caring, worrying, planning, arranging, being glad at, or avoiding), nothing is left, since all feeling, thought, and behavior is being in the world. The past is nothing but a texture of feelings and behaviors that were once fears, cares, concerns, and alterations of situations, avoidances and acceptances of conditions we lived in. True, all that is over and settled, and we can recall it as though it were fact, but it is still this peculiar type of being which, unlike a thing on the table, is never just what it is but always something else, something worried about or desired or cared for or done because of.

One false version of existenialism makes it into the subjectivism that existentialism opposes. Another false version makes it into an emphasis on the present, as though there were a present that did not consist of creating and being concerned about a future. Indeed, existentialism holds that the past does not make us what we are, but this is because the kind of "are" applicable to human beings is fundamentally the way we are in the world, always a possible way of being about to act or be affected. Human beings "are" never just here, in the room, but they "are" writing a paper about —— because —— and for ——; they are getting something in order to do something with, waiting for someone, or avoiding someone, or resting from, or being lonely for. Of

---

[7] Gendlin, Experiencing: A variable in the process of therapeutic change. *American Journal of Psychotherapy*, 1961, 15, 2.
[8] A. Burton, Beyond the transference. *Psychotherapy: Theory, research and practice*, 1 (1964), No. 2; M. Heidegger, *Being and time*. New York: Harper & Row, 1962.

course, humans have their factual aspect (facticity). A human in a room is just here and cannot, without transportation, suddenly be in England. As a factual "thing" he can be shot, hit, or transported. But as a human kind of being, he is thinking about, feeling affected by, angry at, glad in, lonely for, close to, concerned about, and happy with.

It is therefore not the case that I know only myself (as an entity within) and can know you only via my analogous inner entities. Rather, there is no entity-self within but only the ongoing self in the world. I know directly how you affect me because the kind of being I am is a being affected in the world, a being-in and a being-with. I know myself secondarily from out of relationships, from out of my ongoing being-in and being-with.

When you communicate to me, existentialism implies, you do not rearrange some old entities within me; you affect me in ways in which I have never been alive before. What you stir in me are not entities that sit waiting in me like marbles or rocks or pictures or pathways. I do not first have a given machinery-like nature and am then affected by what happens. I am always, only, a being affected by what happens. It is not the case that you act, and then I perceive your act, and then I react to your act out of my own constitution. Rather, as soon as you act, I am already this being affected by you. There is much to be said about how individuals have differing perceptions and reactions, how they remain within certain limitations and repetitious structures, how they avoid aspects of their human ongoing — indeed Heidegger makes such avoidance the most common mode of being human — but just as loneliness is possible only for a "being-with" type of being, so also avoidance and inauthenticity are possible only for a being-in type of being.

Individuals are not boxes full of entities into which a therapist tries to put new entities (information, example, insight, values). We have no way to get such entities into somebody. Personality change is just this shift of a person from being unable to learn, to take in, or to perceive accurately to being able to do so. Hence, even if information, example, insight, and values are "communicated" from therapist to patient, the question of change is: What happens in psychotherapy so that the patient "becomes aware," "learns," "accepts," "takes in" from his living what, at first, he was unable to be aware of, or learn; what happens to alter his self-defeating patterns?

If the essential nature of human beings is conceived of as a being-with and a being-in, then it is most easily explainable that people change when their surroundings change, that people are different when they are with someone different. If there is a puzzle, it is how we avoid being alive in new ways, how we repeat patterns that are not a being affected by the situation or person, here, now. (For this reason existentialists discuss at such length the avoidant "bad faith" or "inauthentic" modes of being.)

This is not to say that there is no separate, individual, self-based personality, but only that personality is not a thing. We have our separate being as selves — but only as we carry it forward by our actions, thoughts, gestures, and moves (all of them *at, in,* or *toward* situations). When we think or say what we feel or are, we do not "dig up" contents of self that were lying down under there but, rather, we have this ongoing being this or being that only as we complete it in action, in process, in symbolizing, in feeling. To the extent we are able to so carry forward our own process, to that extent we are separate and independent selves. Conversely, in those respects in which another person carries our experiencing forward in ways we alone cannot, in those regards we are not separate persons.

But, we cannot conclude from this that an optimal person would be able to carry his own experiencing forward in *every* respect in which it *could* be carried forward with others in a relationship! Every new individual who relates with me may carry my experiencing forward in ways that then seem terribly valuable and essential to what I (then) feelingly am. There is no set, limited, exhaustive list of what I am or could be in all respects! Again, humans are not set things! They have no exhaustive table of contents. But, an optimal person does carry forward his own experiencing (responds to himself with action and thought) sufficiently to constitute a broad ongoing process of experiencing, even when alone in his room, or for years in a lonely forest.

The view of human beings as entities or containers of entities comes from physics, from Galilean science, from the absurd (but highly fruitful) assumption that nothing is real except mathematically behaving masses and energies. But should we really accept as basic the type of construct that inherently assumes that people are not part of reality? Aren't we once and for all here, and part of reality? For some sciences it may be fruitful to assume that humans do not exist, but that is not a fruitful assumption for a science of man. Yet it is the assumption implied in a type of construct still often employed in studying human behavior.

Philosophy often sounds very arid and abstract because it is a discipline of discussing *types* of constructs. No one asserts that people do not exist. But many will persist in a type of construct that fits physical reality only if the humans who live in it, and study it, are first abstracted away. Existentialism poses the possibility of types of construct based on human modes of being, rather than on subsistence apart from human living.

Thus humans should not be conceived as containers with thinglike entities within (like a box full of individualized forces, energies, contents, experiences, drives or motives, wishes or needs, archetypes or repetition compulsions, instincts or nerve patterns, anxiety bonds or repressions, power drives or conflict equilibria, laws of thought or firing synapses, representations, images, percepts, or sensory traces). This is not to say that one or another of these construct systems might not generate fruitful hypotheses or lead to behavior predictions. But a more fruitful science of man must adopt more human-fitting types of constructs than that of the thing in the container.

Existentialist philosophers are giving us alternative types of constructs.

Sartre,[9] for example, states that "thirst' is not a thing inside. It is my "drinking from a glass" which "haunts" how I am now (it isn't actual, yet it isn't unreal either) . . . a possibility that I *feel* and call thirst. Another example: "A belief" is not an entity, a content. It is just as much the "believing," an ongoing process. The process can never be separated off, so that entity-like contents exist as such. The process always "surpasses" whatever seem to be the entities, the beliefs, the emotions, the thoughts. Contents are "made to be" by the process and sustained by it.

We "interrogate" ourselves inwardly to discover what we feel, wish, are. This "self" we interrogate is not an "inhabitant" inside. In one respect it is "present" (our directly-felt bodily concreteness), in another respect it is "absent." (We must ask ourselves, dig, project questions "down there.") Sartre calls it the "absent-present," deliberately portraying it as one process, rather than as two separately existing things (like the Freudian down under, and the Freudian ego). There are no contents or "laws of consciousness" (there is only consciousness of laws and contents). The process as concretely ongoing is always more basic. The type of construct that fits such phenomena always needs hyphens in English, because it combines what had previously been split into two thinglike entities, and because it presents this combination, not as a tying together of two things, but as an ongoing process.

When we conceptualize or express how we are, what we feel, what our feelings imply, we are not digging up things which were down under there in just the same shapes as they now have, when we express them. Rather, to "dig up," to "express," these are ongoing life processes. They make meaning, rather than simply finding meaning already there. This may be expressed by the hyphenated pair "facticity-surpassing." There is always a given situation I factually find myself in, but to think, feel, interpret, react, explicate, perceive it, there is a process that alters what the situation is for me. Situations do not exist apart from me. A situation is not purely physical attributes, but human relational factors, what I can and cannot do, need, expect, achieve, use, avoid, and so forth. All the "attributes" of the facts as "situation" are in terms of someone's living, doing, using, and avoiding, altering, or failing to alter. But this means that there are not already given finished facts in us, or around us. Rather, to say how I feel is a living process that "surpasses" what was given when I began to talk. And, to tell you how I feel is, of course, a different being-in-the-world, than to say it to myself or some other person.

Existentialism is phenomenological; that means it aims to explicate directly what we concretely are, live and experience. Often, very abstruse constructs are coined, and these make existentialism seem like any other abstract conceptual-assumption system. Existentialists struggle to emphasize that they do not impose or assume their schemes to be in experience as such. Everything we say, both in theory and in personal self-expression, is a "lifting out," a "mak-

[9] J. P. Sartre, *Being and nothingness,* New York: Philosophical Library, 1956.

ing be" of order, meaning, pattern, and situation, a "surpassing" in the very process of concrete living and doing, speaking, and thinking.

Thus they use words like 'preontological" (that is to say, before ontology or philosophy is formulated), "prereflective" (before one reflects upon it and fashions a content that is reflected on), "preobjective" (before given objects are precisioned out, fashioned as objects) to convey the concrete flow of sentient living. All philosophic assertions are an explicating, a precisioning, "based on" the concrete ongoing living and feeling process.

Yet, this seemingly complicated way of describing concrete experience can be misleading. Many readers of existentialism do not realize the simple, obvious, concrete reference to their own "gut sentience," which these technical phrases attempt. Then it seems that existentialism is simply vague, "ambiguous," and one is invited to glorify the ephemeral as something described only by negative phrases (like God's negative attributes): It cannot be reduced to analysis; it cannot be reduced to words; it cannot be presented as lawful; it cannot be predicted; it is ever new, unique, unexpected, irreducible and hence incapable of being thought about clearly. This is an error. What is intended is the directly experienced, felt sentience which you are all the time, and out of which you live and look through your eyes. Nothing is more ordinary and known to you than your concrete sentient "being here" — in its "preontological," "predefined" concreteness. Only from out of it do you genuinely express yourself or genuinely make the specific contents and patterns, emotions and chains of explication, experiential steps and reactions that you find as you explicate phenomenologically (and these are always about the world, others, situations, what you want, fear, might do, hoped to avoid, and are affected by). Thus the crux of existentialism is this formula that humans exist without defined essence. Humans have as their being just their existence (ancient philosophic words for that alive felt sentience you are).

The crux of existentialism, however, is not merely to assert that concretely felt experiencing is basic, but to put all concepts and thoughts into direct interplay with it. Phenomenological assertions are "based on" direct concrete existent living. What does "based on" mean? What is this peculiar interplay of the patient's living-and-formulating that we call genuine psychotherapy? How is it different from the mere mongering of verbalizations or concepts that we call intellectualizing? The difference lies in a peculiar relationship between directly felt sentience and words or concepts.

"Being-in-the-world" is *concrete*. It isn't something general; it is always your existence, or mine, or his. "It is my 'here,'" says Heidegger. He explains: it isn't this or that mood, but the very possibility of mood or quality of feeling. Feelings are our ways of being affected in the world, more exactly, the very possibility of being affected. What we are is feeling — an "openness to being affected" (Heidegger). Similarly, Sartre points out that our feelings are "possibilities," possible actions in the world. We interrogate what seems like ourself, down under there (the "absent-present"), but these possibilities are really the stuff of the body. We *feel* our possibilities before we shape them and verbalize them.

Experiential Psychotherapy

In the last section I presented what the philosophy called existentialism contributes to psychotherapy. But, it is also true that psychotherapy contributes greatly to existential philosophy. Felt concreteness is difficult to describe philosophically, whereas in therapy we are continually working with it and familiar with it. The work of Jung, Rank, Allen, Rogers and others (coming directly from psychotherapy) joins with the philosophical existential trend. Both streams are going to make up a new philosophy and psychotherapy.

In psychotherapy, the concretely felt is so familiar that we define therapy as just this. We call it "rationalizing" or "intellectualizing" or "externalizing" (not therapy) if an individual talks and explains without the direct participation of his ongoing experiencing. We call it genuine therapy only when he freshly phrases his ongoing feelings, or otherwise symbolizes them, reacts to us from out of them, and lets his feeling process evolve and move in relation to us. As practicing therapists, we do not merely intellectualize, and we wish our clients to do more than that. Why, then, as theorists, should we remain on a merely intellectualized plane? Existentialism succeeds if we equate "existence" with "experiencing." For the client, the ongoing sentience is the basis of what he says and does in therapy, and it is what we try to respond to interactively, it is what we try to maximize, to free, to permit its fuller ongoing.[10]

Those who work with children (and with adult schizophrenics too) have always emphasized the experiential, and have always looked at words, gestures, play activity, and all symbolic activity generally as growing out of concretely ongoing sentient experiencing. It is not what is said or what is painted that does the effective changing of the personality, but rather it is the living experiential process of so speaking to someone and of so painting.

When an individual expresses accurately for the first time how he is, just then and precisely in so doing he is no longer that way. The accuracy which he feels so deeply — the physically sensed release of the words which feel exactly right — this very feeling is the feeling of change, or resolution, of experiencing moving a step forward.

From this carried-forward experiencing, from this new step, everything now looks somewhat different. Solutions may not be in sight. What was said earlier (perhaps with deep-felt rightness) may now be false or irrelevant. The whole scene may have changed. The issues and questions may be different, they may be worse than one had thought yet it always feels good and enlivening to have the experiential process carried forward.

To say how it is does not simply represent, but it creates, it moves, it carries forward; it is a process of living.

[10] Gendlin, "A theory of personality change," *loc. cit.*

No wonder, then, that a similar process is possible with nonverbal symbolizations. Therapists of children have always been ahead of others (for example, Allen or Rogers) in pointing out that psychotherapy is an experiential process.

Not only can playthings and dramatized situations symbolize experiencing and carry it forward; the other person's responses, too, can be considered as symbolizing and carrying forward the patient's experiencing. We are using the word "symbolizing" here in an odd but true way. Symbolize here does not mean represent in symbols. Symbolize means for external events (words, acts, others) to so fit the individual's implicit preconceptual feelings that the process is carried forward.[11]

I prefer to call this view of psychotherapy "experiential," since the "concrete existence" existentialists speak of is really experiencing.

I have described three closely related contributions of existentialism to the current developments of psychotherapy: (1) the relational being-in-the-world and being-with character of human beings as the primary type of construct with which to study human behavior; (2) the concrete sentient life process of an individual as not reducible to entities, pictures, contents (supposedly within), but rather as a feeling process; (3) a mode of thinking in which concepts and words are "based on" felt experiencing directly, precisioned or lifted out, creatively fashioned, not merely represented conceptually, but directly felt as a result of being thought about and differentiated in this way.

To discuss these three points I have already had to add a good deal of more therapeutically-oriented experiential theory. Let me make my own further steps clearer by discussing them separately:

As I mentioned earlier, in the United States existentialism came late upon the therapeutic scene. The contributions of Otto Rank, J. Taft, Frederick Allen, George H. Mead, Harry Stack Sullivan, Frieda Fromm-Reichmann, Carl G. Jung, Carl A. Whitaker, John Warkentin and Thomas P. Malone (they first coined the term "experiential psychotherapy"), Paul Federn, Abraham H. Maslow, Carl R. Rogers, and many others had already created a major movement in the experiential direction.

I will quote now from just a few sources to illustrate earlier trends toward what we have been discussing. First, Jung:

> According to this definition, the self . . . transcends the powers of imagination to form a clear picture of what we are as a self. . . . Thus we can, for example, see ourselves as a *persona* without to much difficulty . . . [but] the self remains a superordinate quantity. [The self is] . . . an actual, living something, poised between [conscious and unconscious]. . . . I have used the word "sensing" in order to indicate the apperceptive character of the relation between ego and self.[12]

[11] Gendlin, *Experiencing and the creation of meaning, loc. cit.;* Gendlin, A theory of personality change," *loc. cit.*
[12] Carl G. Jung, *Two essays on analytical psychology.* New York: Meridian, 1956.

Thus Jung points both to the concretely sentient, felt nature of experiencing and to its noncontent character, the way contens (ego, persona) are only aspects of the concretely "sensed" process. Similarly, Rank says:

> As long as one makes the feeling experience as such, in which the whole individuality is revealed, the sole object of the explanation and understanding, one finds one's self on sure ground, and also, in my opinion, insures the only therapeutic value, that is, to allow the patient to understand himself in an immediate experience which, as I strive for it in the therapeutic process, permits living and understanding to become one.[13]

Only in recent years are these views really understood by most therapists. To cite one of those who moved developments in this direction, Rogers wrote:

> As the individual perceives and accepts . . . more of his organismic experiences, he finds that he is replacing his present value *system* . . . with a continuing organismic valuing *process* . . . (the individual) examines . . . in terms of a more basic criterion — namely, his own sensory and visceral experiences.[14]

Rogers developed a method of responding to "feeling" (this word is not yet in the index of the 1951 edition, however). The "reflection of attitudes" he discusses soon became known informally as "reflection of feeling." In client-centered parlance a "feeling" was always something like "You resent her criticism" (p. 28), something which the client *feels* viscerally as he speaks, but which he probably does not know conceptually, or say. Client-centered therapy is a method of doing regularly and systematically at every step what Rank described in more general terms in the sentence above. It depends upon the therapist using all his words to phrase and point at the client's ongoing, not fully formulated experiencing, something directly felt, yet upon explication always about living in situations, reacting to, feeling about, worrying over, fear of, and so forth.

Even when the therapist is not at all clear about just what the client directly senses and feels (and when the client is not at all clear about it), both persons can point their words at it. It is concretely felt. Both people's attention and symbolizing "carries forward" this experiencing process, as I formulate it today.[15]

Words, acts, other people's reactions . . . all "carry forward" the experiencing process, and that is what man in: a sentient, interactive organism. Like the oxygen and food we take in, like the CO_2 and feces we give off, the life process is inherently an interaction. Even the animal's physical structure dies and disintegrates when it ceases to inhale and exhale, to push against the ground and bury feces in it, to ingest food and circulate blood whose very in-

[13] Rank, *Will therapy.* New York: Knopf, 1950.
[14] Rogers, *On becoming a person.* Boston: Houghton Mifflin, 1961.
[15] Gendlin, *Experiencing and the creation of meaning; loc. cit.;* Gendlin, "A theory of personality change," *loc. cit.*

ternal content consists of external oxygen and food particles. The sentience of this live body is its complex ongoing (not "in" the environment like a thing lying in a container, but "as" ongoing process, much like the water is not "in" the river, but is the river). Our experiences are not "in" us. We are our felt experiencing. Whatever we bodily feel is already highly organized. To put words or points or action to it "carries it forward" further, "surpasses it," so that words do not render it, but are "based on" it, in relation to it, explicative of it, in a direct interplay with it.

No all words and responses have this effect of "carrying forward." Only very few do, everything else affects us, to be sure, but not in a way of making the ongoing experiencing move forward more fully and broadly. When that happens, there is a release and relief, a powerful bodily felt effect which convinces us of the accuracy of what was said, or the rightness of what was done, even just as we change by this very movement, being carried forward.

That the words or symbols "fit" or "feel right" means that what is said or symbolized or done was already *implicit* in experiencing earlier. But "implicit" does not mean "in the same form as explicit, only hidden." Rather, it means not yet formed, not yet ongoing fully, and therefore amenable to many different ways of being formed (though these many ways are still few, compared to all the possible words, deeds, and responses which do not fit, and would leave the aspect implicit and unlived).

When even one experiential step occurs (when some words, gestures, symbols, responses, actions, or events have carried experiencing forward in some respect), then there is a felt change, a shift. One feels at least a slight release, a "give" in the felt referent, and thereafter new aspects arise and can be referred to. True explanations which do not carry experiencing forward are worthless when compared to one even slight *referent movement,* that felt sense of "give" in what we feel, after which arise new facets and changed aspects of our feelings and situation.

A feelingly accurate statement or symbol (even if it makes little conceptual sense, or seems awfully obvious, like "I don't know what to do, that's what I feel now") can have this effect of referent movement. As a result of referent movement, there is *content mutation,* that characteristic way in which the contents shift in the therapeutic process. Often, even one slight, felt referent movement takes the process in a totally unpredicted direction, all the parameters of the discussion change, the decision at which the client seemed about to arrive is now irrelevant or different, the whole scene changes.

Experiencing never consists of sheer emotions (the affect-tonality reified into a thing): joy, fear, anger, etc. Rather, *experiencing is always internally differentiable and explicable.*

We should not confuse intensity of emotion with experiencing. Anxiety can double one up, shame or guilt can make one weird and intensely pained. Schizophrenics whose self-processes have largely stopped feel intense and weird discomforts. Primitively structured sounds and pictures occur. In dreams (where interactive experiencing is also curtailed by sleep) the same sort of static imagery occurs. Whenever the process of felt ongoing living-in-the-world is narrowed and inhibited (sleep, hypnosis, poisons of all sorts, stimulus deprivation, isolation), these peculiar phenomena occur: instead of functioning as the apperceptive sensing of ongoing living, the shape of feeling and sensing becomes weird and frightening, psychotic and primitive, the body's own life process without full interaction in the human world.

When the apperceptive flow of differentiable felt experience is narrowed, then words and events are not interpreted by an ongoing feeling process. Reactions and interpretations are no longer modifications of this felt sentience, as we are accustomed to have it. Rather, it is all dark and dank, swampy and silent stuck and dully painful. Passively, with only little ongoing sentient flow, an individual still watches the rampant specters. But these are weird childlike imagery. Such imagery is very, very much akin to the small child's imagery when he is left alone at night for a long time. His interactive process ceases, his capacity to respond to himself in human in-the-world ways is not great enough to carry his own experiencing forward and, instead, very psychoticlike imagery appears. Respond to the person (or the "psychotic contents") in an adult way but similarly to the way you would respond to a weirdly frightened child, and an ongoing human process will replace the psychotic material. That "material" is not "contents" in him, but a manner, a mode, that mode in which there is too little ongoing *inter*action-with.

For the same reason we should not turn away from someone who is "latently psychotic" because we fear (as the contents-in-people theory implies) that the psychosis will "erupt." Psychosis is not an entity in people that erupts. Whether psychosis occurs or not depends on whether one helps or fails to help carry experiencing forward.

The fear of incipient psychotic material arose because so many therapists employed methods in which psychological entities were "dug up" and symbolized without response to the individual, his feeling process, his personal relating to the therapist. Many patients did become psychotic as a result of *such* therapy. They felt their effort to relate warded off and defeated, their ongoing experiencing further deadened inside themselves.

We should never avoid what an individual *implicitly* feels because we fear he cannot take it. He is already taking it! The question is: "Will you enable him to live it with you or only alone (two entirely different sorts of experiential processes)?" But, this principle applies only if we respond personally, if we refer concretely to exactly what the individual feels and if we go with him the steps in which — with our help — he explicates it.

But we must make responses not only to what he seems to say and do, but also the sort of responses which first make personality, the picking up of a child, the touching gently on the shoulder, the expression of some of our feelings to him, the spontaneity of having another person be with one. Therapy too often consists only of clarifying conceptually the admittedly inadequate and undeveloped machinery he has. In contrast, to respond to what another feels carries experiencing forward because experiencing (feeling) *is* an interactive ongoing-in and with.

Similarly, at times we express our own feelings toward him (the content seems different — it seems to be about us), and the carrying forward effect occurs. Expressing our feelings does not just tell about entities in us. Rather, expressing our feelings toward him is an interactive process and constitutes what occurs in him as much as in us.

Therapist expressivity and carrying forward concerns *the individual's* ongoing process. It is a carrying forward and reconstituting of his life process that cannot be done without a genuine other person genuinely responding with the whole gamut of his feelings to the patient's whole gamut of feelings. We know best with children that this is a personality development process. With children we do not expect everything to be "in there" already. However, such a relationship requires that the therapist's feelings be expressed as clearly his own, and the child's as clearly the childs' own. To protect another's freedom we do not need to paralyze ourselves. That would give him only a useless emptiness instead of a full relationship in which he is free. We need to express our feeling reactions and then still let him be free — by virtue of the fact that these reactions are our own. They don't preempt *his*. We point again and again at his, ask about them, make room for them, refer to them — even at a time when, perhaps, he remains totally silent and neither expresses anything of his own feeling life, nor has it at all clearly.

Today, the main parameters of therapy are the experiential process in the patient, and our carrying it forward directly by living as people toward him. In ourselves as therapists (our loud, when possible) we must do with our own ongoing experiencing what we try to help the client do with his: we must differentiate it, we must explicate it. We must not just blurt out: "You bore me," or "Why do you never say anything important?" Instead, we must ourselves carry forward our own experiencing for a few moments in a chain of content mutation and explication. For example, "I am bored. . . . This isn't helping him. . . . I wish I could help. . . . I'd like to hear something more personal. . . . I really would welcome him. . . . I have more welcome on my hands for him than he lets me use . . . but I don't want to push away what he does express. . . ." The resulting therapist expression now will make a personal interaction, even if the client says nothing in return. The therapist will say something like: "You know, I've been thinking the last few minutes, I wish I'd hear more from you, more of how you really feel inside. I know you might not want to say, but whenever you can or want, I would like it." Or, to the silent, unwilling schizophrenic: "I don't know how you felt when the aids pushed you in here so roughly, but I felt bad about it. I hate seeing you pushed and shoved." Or, "I know *I* am going to feel a lot better when you're out of the hospital and we can meet in town, but I guess it's no simple thing to you. You haven't said how *you* feel about it." Or, "Gee, am I glad to see that they gave you back your shoes. How I have hated seeing you in those rags they had you wear instead. Are you glad too?"

If there is one rule which encompasses the many we are still formulating, it may be: Let us conceive of the individual as not fully formed sentient experiencing, and pay attention to it, respond to it, refer to it, and make room for it, even when silent and without shape. Then let us respond from our own persons in whatever way is immediate and plainly real for us, but quickly again make room for attention to the newly moving experiencing in him which we thereby create. For no one can predict what will come next and can be referred to next by him, in this newly ongoing further process.

How radical this sounds for adult therapy, how obvious it sounds for therapy with children! It is what each illustration in this volume exemplifies. Those who work with children know instinctively to respond to children with a real self, know to pick them up rather than only talk at them; know to make positive what seems negative (we hug the child that cries and pounds at us with fists). We respond to experiencing if the child lacks the words; we respond to fashion positive interaction rather than only explaining what is lacking.

In summary: Therapy must be "experiential," experiencing is always internally differentiable (never just this or that set of contents, always a moving directly felt process). Change comes through directly felt experiential steps. Interpersonal relationships carry the experiencing process forward, if the therapist expresses his own actual reactions (as clearly his own) and at the same time gives room, attention, and reference to the client's felt reactions as the client's own. Our words (in theory and practice) must refer to this felt, as yet not carried forward sentience of experiencing. Words, in practice, and in theoretical statements must refer to what we directly feel. We can call that "experiential theory" and "experiential psychotherapy."

REFERENCES

ALLEN, F. Therapy as a living experience. In C. Moustakas (Ed.), *Existential child therapy.* New York: Basic Books, 1966. Ch. 7.

BARUCH, D. Little mocking bird. In C. Moustakas (Ed.), *Existential child therapy.* New York: Basic Books, 1966. Ch. 2.

BURTON, A. Beyond the transference. *Psychotherapy, Theory, Research and Practice,* 1964, 1, 2.

BUTLER, J. M. Client-centered counseling and psychotherapy. In D. Brower and L. D. Abt (Eds.), *Progress in clinical psychology,* Vol. III. *Changing conceptions in psychotherapy.* New York: Grune & Stratton, 1958.

COLM, H. The self-defeating search for love. In C. Moustakas (Ed.), *Existential child therapy.* New York: Basic Books, 1966. Ch. 4.

GENDLIN, E. T. *Experiencing and the creation of meaning.* New York: Free Press of Glencoe, 1962.

GENDLIN, E. T. A theory of personality change. In P. Worchel and D. Byrne (Eds.), *Personality change.* New York: John Wiley, 1964. (See Chapter 7.)

GENDLIN, E. T. Experiencing: A variable in the process of therapeutic change. *American Journal of Psychotherapy,* 1961, 15, 2.

GENDLIN, E. T. Subverbal communication and therapist expressivity trends in client-centered therapy with schizophrenics. *Journal of Existential Psychiatry,* 1963, 4, 14.

GENDLIN, E. T. Schizophrenia: Problems and methods of psychotherapy. *Review of Existential Psychology and Psychiatry,* 1964, 4, 2.

GENDLIN, E. T. Values and the process of experiencing. In A. Mahrer (Ed.), *The goals of psychotherapy.* New York: Appleton-Century-Crofts, 1967.

HEIDEGGER, M. *Being and time.* New York: Harper & Row, 1962.

JUNG, C. G. *Two essays on analytical psychology.* New York: Meridian, 1956.

KOGL, R. C. Just a stupid little boy. In C. Moustakas (Ed), *Existential child therapy.* New York: Basic Books, 1966. Ch. 3.

LEWIS, E. Initiation of an obsessional adolescent. In C. Moustakas (Ed.), *Existential child therapy.* New York: Basic Books, 1966. Ch. 8.

MOUSTAKAS, C. (Ed.) *Existential child therapy.* New York: Basic Books, 1966.

RANK, O. *Will therapy.* New York: Knopf, 1950.

ROGERS, C. R. *Client-centered therapy.* Boston: Houghton Mifflin, 1951.

ROGERS, C. R. *On becoming a person.* Boston: Houghton Mifflin, 1961.

SARTRE, J. P. *Being and nothingness.* New York: Philosophical Library, 1956.

SULLIVAN, H. S. *The interpersonal theory of psychiatry.* New York: Norton, 1963.

WENKART, A. The child meets the world. In C. Moustakas (Ed.), *Existential child therapy.* New York: Basic Books, 1966. Ch. 10.

6

Phenomenology and Personality*

JOHN M. SHLIEN

Introduction

What makes another approach to personality necessary, particularly one which stresses the very subjectivity which others have tried to avoid? Is it just one more reflection of the "clash of temperaments" in the history of a developing field, or does the answer really depend upon what one considers to be the raw material, and the avenues of access to it, in the study of personality?

At the heart of the need for a phenomenological psychology lies a fact which Kluver (1936) has expressed as follows:

> Whether or not behavior takes this or that direction is, generally speaking, dependent on whether or not this or that *phenomenal* property exists. The facts that something appears phenomenally as "red," "larger than," cannot be deduced from the properties of the atom but only from studies of reacting organisms.

To this must be added the generally accepted observation that apparent phenomena differ in their appearances. Since we learn so many of our meanings from our culture — i.e., each other (Blake & Ramsey, 1951) the first fact of inscrutability plays a large part in causing those differing perceptions. It makes communication of meanings weak and uncertain. If the mind could not think silently; if there were outwardly audible and visible signs directly indicating specific mental activities, we would all be rank behaviorists, and the history of psychology, to say the least, would have hinged on a very different

* Reprinted from Joseph M. Wepman and Ralph W. Heine, editors, *Concepts of personality* (Chicago: Aldine Publishing Company, 1963); copyright © 1963 by Aldine Publishing Company.

95

set of data. But this is not the case. As things stand, we have both internal and external events *experienced* by the total organism; experienced, recorded at some level of awareness, and in some cases, given meaning. The phenomenologist is convinced that much goes on "inside," and that the behavioristic concept of the "empty organism" is narrow, and largely spurious. Most of our experience and its meanings exist in "private worlds," not expressed on pointer readings. Nor is this to say that phenomenology is only here on borrowed time.

Instruments have been and will be developed to probe the silent and private world of inner experience, but men are not likely to become transparent. Much will remain hidden; meanings will differ from person to person; modes of experience and interpretation will change over time for each individual. Physiological indexes of internal states will have immense value for the study of experience, but heart rate, brain waves, pupil size, endocrine output, or whatever comes will only measure increase or decrease without meaning unless the identifying code is first given and then continually validated by the wise and willing knower. As Kohler (1938, p. vii) says,

> Never, I believe, shall we be able to solve any problems of ultimate principle until we go back to the source of our concepts — in other words, until we use the phenomenological method, the qualitative analysis of experience.

And, the more the knower is wise and willing, the better the accuracy of his information and verification. Thus the approach may be applied to animals and infants, but reaches its more productive stage in the study of language-using humans.[1]

It is not always constructive to haggle over terminology, but neither is it fair to introduce the problem with a term which, if accepted, envelops the reader in a biased frame of reference. We have referred to activity of the human "mind." Use of this word, to the behaviorist, is at least a concession and, to the phenomenologist, a minor victory. J. B. Watson abhorred the word, and Pavlov is said to have levied fines upon students using such mentalistic terms in his laboratory. As recently as 1943, Clark Hull warned against the use of "mind" saying, "Even when fully aware of the nature of anthropomorphic subjectivism and its dangers, the most careful and experienced thinker is likely to find himself a victim of its seductions." (Hull, 1943.) He suggests that this powerful effect be warded off by observing all behavior as if it were produced by a dog, rat, or robot. Gordon Allport, in a vein typical

---

[1] Zener (1958) advised psychologists to recognize limitations and capabilities which vary both with the phenomena to be observed and the motivation, intelligence, etc. *of the observer*. Not all are equal in this respect. A striking example of possibilities in the upper ranges of observation by a psychologist is to be seen in a brilliant analysis of the "psychology of secrets" by Bakan (1954). While anyone may make a satisfactory "naive" subject for certain kinds of experiments, phenomenology can best thrive through investment in sophisticated informants.

of the "personalistic" phenomenologist, objects to Hull's precaution as an affront to human dignity and an avoidance of human realities because it represents "an addiction to machines, rats, or infants which leads us to overplay those features of human behavior that are peripheral, signal-oriented, and genetic,[2] and to underplay those features that are central, future oriented, and symoblic" (Allport, 1947).

The quarrel exposed by this conflict over a mere word really revolves around these major issues: (1) Is the human being active or only reactive? (2) Is activity only external or also internal? (3) If it is internal, can "subjectivity" be reconciled with "science" (the latter in quotes because it has its fashions too)? We could brush aside the question of terminology by saying simply, "When you 'make up your mind' to read this chapter, we are talking about whatever you made up." That is true enough, but the phenomenologist characteristically uses mentalistic terms such as "mind." "Mind" is clearly returning as acceptable scientific language in the literature (Scher, 1962); and its use or non-use implies a decision about the legitimacy of inner life as proper subject matter. As Kurt Lewin (1951) says,

> Arguments about attributing "existence" to an item may seem metaphysical in nature and may therefore not be expected to be brought up in empirical sciences. Actually, opinions about existence or non-existence are quite common in the empirical sciences and have greatly influenced scientific development in a positive and a negative way. Labeling something as "non-existing" is equivalent to declaring it "out of bounds" for the scientist. Attributing "existence" to an item automatically makes it a duty of the scientist to consider this item as an object of research; it includes the necessity of considering its properties as "facts" which cannot be neglected in a total system of theories; finaly, it implies that the terms with which one refers to the items are acceptable as scientific "concepts" (rather than as "mere words").

It matters, then, that we acknowledge the existence of each person's *faculty for knowing*. This is a basic assumption, expressed in an extreme and unabashed statement by a French phenomenologist, Merleau-Ponty (1945), "I am the absolute source." We do experience — we sense, perceive, think. Though silent and invisible, thought precedes and attends all of our behavior not accomplished through the reflex arc. Precedings are called determinants, attendings are called interpretations, and there is even evidence that thought should not be distinguished from behavior but may actually *constitute* behavior. A dozen years ago, when "transfer of training" experiments were popular, Beattie used a dart board with a graded target as a performance measure. As usual in such experiments, subjects practiced with one hand, rested, were retested with the other hand in various combinations of practice periods, hands, and rest periods. Longer rest periods seemed related to im-

---

[2] Genetic here refers to history, not biology.

proved scores. We have long been given to think of this effect in terms of "spaced versus massed practice." But it also suggested "rehearsal" effects. Finally, some subjects were given imaginary practice, i.e., were instructed to simply sit at throwing distance from the target (after a base line performance had been established) and to "think about" throwing for a practice period. These "merely" rehearsing subjects often improved their performance as much as those who had "actual" practice trials (Beattie, 1949)! This reminds us that in the behavioristic strategy of focusing upon specifics of input and output, whatever was unseen was considered as undone (a strange and arrogant subjectivity on the part of the experimenter).

Tolman puts our unobserved learning back into proper behavioral perspective with his statement: "What [the organism] learns is, in short, a *performance* (and each such performance can be carried out by a number of different motor skill)" (Tolman, 1959, p. 133). The phenomenologist is vitally interested in that internal performance, the process of experiencing. Whether or not the performance is also evident, he believes in the reality of the internal state as a mode of behavior. This mode consists of sensations, perceptions, thoughts, and feelings, all of which constitute experiencing that can only be approached through the standpoint of the experiencer.

The nature of this approach raises some fundamental questions. Is there really a field of study such as psychology, separate from the biological or electro-chemical basis of behavior? What is its subject matter, where to find it, and how to deal with it? To illustrate some of these points, here is an accurate report of a true event in a human transaction:

A 28-year-old graduate student in sociology finished his mid-year examinations. He wearily packed a bag and boarded a bus for a vacation journey to visit his family several hundred miles away. Choosing a seat next to the window, he stretched out as well as he could, hoping to sleep through the night since he felt quite exhausted. In his own words, the report continues:

> After an hour or so, the bus stopped in a small town, and a few passengers got on. One of them was a blonde girl, very good looking in a fresh but sort of sleazy way. I thought that she was probably a farm girl, and I wished she'd sit by me. By God, she did. She was really comely, if you know what I mean, and she smiled a bit so I felt sure she'd be approachable. Oh boy, what luck. I didn't want to be too eager, and I was still exhausted, so we just smiled and talked for a minute. I made sure that she was comfortable, and then sort of dozed off for a little while, hoping to recuperate by the time the driver turned out the lights and meanwhile enjoying my fantasies about the prospects for the rest of the trip. The last thing I remember was smiling at her and noticing that when her skirt slipped up on her knee as she reached up to the back of the seat, she didn't pull it down. Wow! About four hours later we were pounding along the road in complete darkness when I opened my eyes. Her leg, the outside of it, was against mine, and the way it pressed and moved with the motion of the bus woke me up. This was more than I'd

dreamed of. I was terribly excited, and when I stirred a little the steady pressure of her leg didn't move away. By this time, I had a terrific erection, and the more I thought about this cute little babe pressing against me, the worse it got. I was just about to reach out and touch her when we pulled into a gas station for a stop, and when the light came through the window, *she* wasn't there at all She must have left while I was asleep. A fat man with a growth of beard and a dead cigar dropping ash on his vest was sprawled next to me, sound asleep. It was *his* leg pressing against me, and he was so fat and slovenly that even when I drew myself away, his sloppy flesh stayed against me. I was so dumbfounded — disappointed too, and the funny thing — I lost that erection almost immediately, got up and moved to another seat. What a let down.

From this event in someone's private life, we can draw several conclusions which bear an introduction to phenomenological thought.

First, there is such a thing as psychology. It operates in such a way as to influence behavior, and it cannot be accounted for simply in terms of physics or biology. Again quoting the extremist Merleau-Ponty, "The body is not a fact, it is a situation." An erection is a signal of a notable reaction to something in the environment — what? Not, in this case, the pressure of so many p.s.i., nor that in combination with body temperature of a certain degree, nor both those in combination with motion and friction of a specifiable sort. Those elements remained. The erection-behavior did not. Something interior changed when a certain group of stable physical sensations were given a different meaning as the perception of the experiencer was alerted. What had been exciting became revolting.

Second, it tells us that if we are to study that which is peculiarly psychological, the primary subject matter must be *experience*. Experience is subjective, i.e., it takes place within the opaque organism of the experiencer, and *may* not be public or even repeatable.

Third, from this it seems clear that the approach to this subject matter is to learn the secrets of individual perception, and sometimes of hidden consequent behavior. Whether the secrets are intended to be so, or are merely screened from view by the normal separatedness of people, they are private.

Thus, fourth, is implied a methodology which must be largely dependent upon our ability to obtain the hidden and private data, via some part of the family of introspective methods, or to deduce via such comparative experimental methods as "stimulus equivalence" those discriminant perceptions which lend themselves to this technique. Most of the investigations will have to rely on some form of self-report; this would seem a special weakness to some, but as William James (1950, p. 191) points out, "Introspection is what we have to rely on first and foremost and always" and as for its weakness, *"introspection is difficult and fallible; and the difficulty is simply that of all observation of whatever kind."*

Fifth, there is implied in this illustration a definition of pathology according to the phenomenologist's approach. Pathology would consist of a lack of awareness of one's own experience; of not knowing or understanding it; of being in a state of self-deception. Putting it more simply in perceptual terms, to see clearly is the greatest good — the blind spots are evil.

Sixth, we see in this example the "real life" nature of the context in which this approach can operate and from which it typically draws its data. The world and any part of it is a laboratory for the naturalistic observation. Its characteristic problems are the major attitudinal states which move men mightily — for example, pride, shame, grief, love, passion, loneliness, hatred, freedom, boredom, anxiety, despair, being and well-being, death, pain.[3]

Background and Characteristics

Toward a Definition — Field and Streams

What is phenomenology, exactly? Exactly, no one can say. It is an old term, now stewing in its own liberal metaphysical juice, which has to allow such scope for change and individuality that during the first phases there could be almost as many phenomenologies as there are phenomenologists.[4] This is simply because the essential concern is *meaning,* and meanings can vary extensively. At the moment the term is a large envelope containing a confusing mixture of philosophies, psychology, science, myth, and fad. There is, as Boring (1950, p. 408) says, "room in phenomenology for acts as well as content; it is a tolerant discipline."

This tolerance is to its credit, and is also its peril. Always there is precaution against premature formulation of hypotheses, allowing for the "unprejudiced" naturalistic observation of events. MacLeod (1951) speaks of "a disciplined naivete"; Gibson (1959, p. 461) of "cultivated naivete." European phrasing is more extreme: French psychologist Merleau-Ponty says, "The whole effort is to recover naive contact with the world," while the German philosopher Eugene Fink speaks of the "shock of amazement at the fact of the world . . . a stunned amazement to which he assigned the function of

---

[3] Pain is a particularly interesting and ephemeral quality, in spite of its pervasiveness. As such, it is a striking illustration of the need for a phenomenology. Everyone "knows" what pain is, but no one can feel another's pain (though the closer the involvement between people, the more a loved one's pain causes behavior in the observer; this comes close to being the behaviorist nightmare, "the interaction of two 'minds.' "). For all its ubiquity, and its frequent use in experiments, no one can "objectively" measure pain, or even accurately localize it or its source in many instances! The same stimulus, such as an electric shock of given intensity, by no means causes the same response in two subjects. Finally, outward behavior, ranging from stoicism to malingering, may or may not express inner experience of pain.

[4] In practice — in the practice of classifying, anyway — this lack of organized principles does not seem to hold. It is possible to group types of phenomenologies, usually in three or four categories ranging through "classical," "existential," "pure philosophical," "eidetic," "transcendental," "psychological," etc. (Spiegelberg, 1960, p. 642; Landsman, 1958).

converting the trivial into what is worth questioning" (Spiegelberg, 1960, p. 600). But which trivia are worth the conversion? *The Place of Value in a World of Facts* (Kohler, 1938) demonstrates the unavoidable subjectivity which makes phenomenology liable to the same criticism it has leveled at behaviorism. The only advantage lies in awareness of the prejudice and the possibility of deliberately suspending or reversing it, or "bracketing" it, to use Husserl's term. The bigger problem is to find the correct balance of discipline and naivete, of course. The fresh eyes of innocence and the free curiosity of the fascinated naturalist need to be combined with the sophistication of the practiced researcher — combined with, but not subdued by. That is part of the thrust of reviving phenomenology.

The word to which so many lay claim derives from the Greek *phainesthai*, "to appear," or "to appear so," or "as it appears." It is instructive to note that in the original usage, the phenomenal was "that which is known through the senses and immediate experience" rather than deduction. This is still the case. One binding theme running through all variants of phenomenology is the preoccupation and fascination with the facts (or the data) of immediate experience. This characteristic of both the original and present usage is often taken to pit "common sense" against "deduction," thus supposedly making phenomenology a hopeless anachronism in the realm of science. Kimble (1953) points out, for example, how "common sense" tells us that the world is flat; science that it is round. The method of direct intuition, or that which is known through the senses, then, would be basically a source of error. But even on the level of description, it is not common sense which fails; it is our constricted scope of vision which feeds in limited information. If one can look at the ocean from a mountain top, or take a picture of its surface with a wide angle lens, the application of a straight edge will tell us via "common sense"[5] that the world has a curved surface. If common sense could not confirm the shape of the earth's surface in just this way, there would indeed be a conflict, and "phenomenology" would have to disavow and separate itself from "science."

The important point is that what we see tells us *our* truth — the "world-for-us" rather than *the* truth — the "world-as-is," but that the distinctions are not necessarily opposed or impossible of reconciliation. The original Greek philosophies separated the *Phenomenal World* from the *Ontal World* of permanent being and the *Ideal World* of permanent truth, with the Phenomenal World containing changeable and developing aspects, dealt with as perceptible aspects or appearances rather than their "true," ideal, fixed or substantial natures. We have inherited the idea that these worlds are all orthogonal to each other as a matter of fact, rather than as a matter of logical convenience or preference.

---

[5] Anyone who has read Piaget's studies of intelligence will realize that it is a mistake to identify "common sense" at only the lowest level of development.

Phenomenology has a prejudice. It clearly holds that, psychologically speaking, man is the measure of all things, each man the measure of all his things, and that the reality to which he responds is his own. The frequent accusation of solipsism does not apply. Neither does Hume's philosophy that no matter exists independent of mind, the mind being nothing but representations. Kant is more to the liking of the phenomenologist with the notion that there are phenomena, and they are all we know, but there is more beyond.

The current general philosophy in American personality study would probably run to this effect: there is external reality, which we more or less distort, though it exists absolutely while its appearances are relative. But, to the purely phenomenological psychologist, does "real reality" matter? Is there anything in psychology to study except the perceptions of individuals? Psychologically, "real" things have only a relative existence. *Phenomena* are absolute (not permanent, but for the moment absolute); *they* control behavior since it is predicated upon *them;* when *they* change, behavior changes. (Behavior, not things, concerns the psychologist. If this makes "behaviorists" of all of us, so be it, only with the reservation that behavior is covert as well as overt.)

There is a limit to the profit one can take from philosophical speculations in this field. Neither the historical or functional connections between European philosophies and American psychologies are clear or prominent. MacLeod suggests that on might read Kuenzli's (1958) collection *The phenomenological problem* and conclude that phenomenology is an indigenous American product. But the German philsopher, Edmund Husserl, is generally credited as the main instigator of the movement. Whether he had a direct effect on modern personality theory as it developed in the group identified with Rogerian practices is a moot question. It may well be that here the spectacle of independent invention rather thean cultural diffusion, and that the current preoccupation with Husserl is a retrospective tracing of geneology by a successful native development.

Rogers already displayed a phenomenological, almost ethological attitude when he published his first book on *Counseling and psychotherapy* in 1942. Although the idea of the "internal frame of reference" was not yet featured, the remarkably phenomenological technique of "reflection," as a "natural" non-controlling environment was, and the book shows unmistakable signs of intention to comprehend the inner world of the client without disturbing the natural course of events — a "disciplined naivete," that is. At this time, Rogers had not heard of Husserl, nor had he yet read him when the second book, *Client-centered therapy,* with its phenomenology showing loud and clear, was published in 1951.[6] Snygg and Combs, whose 1949 book, *Individual behavior,* is an outstanding demonstration of a personality theory based on the concept of the phenomenal field, had certainly influenced Rogers, but there is no reference to Husserl in their work. (The up-dated edition of 1959, how-

[6] Personal communication.

ever, contains four references to Husserl.) Their work has been called, "A remarkably independent new type of phenomenological psychology" (Spiegelberg, 1960, p. 638). He adds, "Rogers' own approach also shows its phenomenological ingredients without any commitment to its philosophical ancestry." (What ancestry? It is very hard for a historian to accept the notion of independent invention.) These American developments lean heavily on Syngg's earlier article (1941), the import of which is expressed in its title, "The need for a phenomenological system of psychology." Snygg, originally a behaviorist, is reported by Spiegelberg as having been influenced toward phenomenology by his contact with Kurt Lewin and Wolfgang Kohler. Certainly both of these men knew Husserl's work, but Lewin is said by Spiegelberg to have been influenced "much more prominently" by the phenomenology of Carl Stumpf than by Husserl. As for Kohler, he discusses Husserl extensively, critically, and is one of those who interprets Husserl's first principle of "logical requiredness" as having "little to do with psychology" (Kohler, 1938, p. 48). Husserl was often considered anti-psychological, and his major translator and interpreter, Farber (1943, p. 567), tries to heal this "misunderstanding"[7] which had been nourished by "Husserl's own repeated efforts" to distinguish phenomenology from psychology. Husserl does have a demonstrable connection with the existential form of phenomenology[8] through his student Heidegger, and thus to Sartre, Camus, Rollo May, Tillich, and others prominent in this stream of the movement.

As a final note, it is worth comment that Van Kaam (1959) finds William James a source of the stream. He quotes J. Linscohten ("one of Europe's leading existential phenomenologists"), who in turn quotes the diary of Husserl for proof that "the father of European phenomenology admits the influence of the thought of the great American, James, on his own thinking" (May, 1961, p. 14). James, we may be sure, had a direct and deep influence

---

[7] It is well worthwhile to quote his summary of Husserl's position:

"(c) There are a number of things which phenomenology conspicuously does not do or mean. (1) It does not 'tear the meaning loose from the act.' (2) It does not deny or reject the external world. (3) It does not try to answer all questions, and is not intended to be all-inclusive as a method for all purposes. (4) It is also not intended to be a substitute for other methods, and above all, for those involving factual and hypothetical elements. (5) It does not deny inductive truth, nor does it fail to distinguish between different types of 'truth.' (6) It is not a trap for metaphysical purposes. . . .

"(d) In contrast to these misunderstandings there are a number of things that phenomenology does do or mean. (1) It is the first method of knowledge because it begins with 'the things themselves' which are the final court of appeal for all knowledge. . . . (2) It views everything factual as an exemplification of essential structures and is not concerned with matters of fact as such. (3) It deals with not only 'real essences' but also with 'possible essences.' (4) Direct insight, evidence in the sense of the self-giveness of the objectivity is the ultimate test for it. (5) Despite the 'reduction' the phenomenologist still has a brain (an 'evolutionary' brain) in the same sense that he breathes. That statement is as true as it is irrelevant to the method."

[8] An embarrassment to some "respectable" phenomenologists as it is embarrassed itself by the Beatnik or Left Bank Existentialists, who also cherish immediacy of experience, self-consciously examine their own despair, etc.

on all of the American "self psychologies." (His writings on the subject have not been surpassed. They are the best single source available yet.)

The intent of this review is not to chauvinistically plant a flag on new territory. For one thing, it is very old territory which has been crossed by many travelers. The point is rather to free us of philosophical domination where those philosophies have little or no real connection with the psychologies bearing the same name, especially since "the very vaguest speculation has sometimes found shelter under the roof of phenomenology" (Kohler, 1938, p. 68). Husserl's philosophy bears to clinical phenomenological psychology about the same order of relation as does Wundt's (or Titchner's) classical introspection to the modern forms of self-report. To understand phenomenology, it is more illuminating, and more in keeping with the very style of this approach, to look at its characteristics rather than to trace its history.

Further Toward a Definition — Some Common Characteristics

Since phenomenology is not yet gathered together in a sufficiently homogeneous body to be identified, it is composed of like-minded people,[9] with similar attitudes, objectives, and methods, working rather independently in a gathering "third force," as Maslow sometimes calls it (May, 1961, p. 52). To help delineate this gathering, we turn to some characteristic interests or attitudes on which there has occasionally been some issue.

The Scientific Posture

In relation to science, there is a position which demands redefinition of what "sciencing" means. Phenomenology calls for intensive descriptive analysis — a description that often leads to an impatient demand for its supposed opposite, explanation via the "definitive" experiment. Science cannot be confined to the experimental alone, but must include exploration and discovery. This "naturalistic observation" is being reintroduced with a new power as "the foundation of all science" (Butler, 1962, p. 178). Zener reminds us that science consists of far more than confirming already observed relationships. A science not reviewing its problem area is dying, and he suggests "that twentieth-century psychophysics has exploited the capital of phenomenological distinctions made in the nineteenth century — and [I] am apprehensive that no new comparable wealth of phenomenal distinctions relevant to more complex perceptions is presently being accumulated" (Zener, 1958, p. 364).

Science is subject to such change in fashion over time and even in locality

---

[9] One wonders who to name by way of illustration: Lewin, Rogers, G. Allport and perhaps F. Allport, Maslow, R. May, Bruner, Cantril, Patterson, Snygg, Jessor, as well as many others mentioned elsewhere in this chapter. And Freud, before "hardening of the categories" set in. Since these independent types seldom declare themselves, especially when the movement is still so ill-defined, others will appear more clearly in the future, as association does not imply guilt.

that its objectives can always be questioned. Buytendijk quotes Cantril in this regard:

> The aim of science is often defined as the attempt to increase the accuracy of our predictions. While the accuracy of predictions is clearly a most important criterion of progress in scientific formulation, emphasis on prediction alone can easily obscure the more fundamental aim of science covered by the word *understanding* (David & von Bracken, 1957, p. 198).

Prediction and control are often found linked together in the literature. The phenomenologist gives second place to prediction, as just indicated, and may reject control altogether. First, control is not science — it is just politics, or management. Second, if exercised in experimentation it is limiting and unfair, since it makes the task of the scientist all too easy, and too meaningless. The isolated reaction of the eye blink to the air puff is controlled, specific, but insignificant. The limited behavior of the man in a six by four cell is more predictable but less valuable to human beings because he is less human as he is more controlled.[10] Wellek says, "It is the task of psychology to teach men to understand themselves and each other better. Understanding presupposes phenomenology. It is itself a phenomenological act, an experience" (David and von Bracken, 1957, p. 293). It is this understanding (*Verstehen*) of fully human beings which constitutes the aim of this branch of science.

Understanding comes about through description, or is a concurrent process. Must description be opposed to explanation? What better explanation could there be than a complete description? If one really understands, if the description is fine enough, this reveals the mechanism, and explains *how* — but not *why*. "How" is the scientific question. "Why" belongs to the child or the theologian. A fine grained description of the digestive process tells us everything about the process from input (*subjectively* called "food") to output (*subjectively* called "waste"). Any explanation of "why" beyond that means "purpose of this process." That could be "because the person needs fuel," or "the food wants to be transformed into another state," or "God orders this process between person and food for the sake of either, both or neither but a third purpose to which they are incidental." Thus it is quite reasonable for MacLeod to put the question of science simply as "what is there" without regard to "why," "whence," or "wherefore" (Kuenzli, 1959, p. 156).

Reductionism

There is a strong anti-reductionistic bias characteristic of this movement. One finds objections to "reductionism" to biological drives (hunger, etc.), to simpler mechanisms, to lower forms, of things to each other. Jessor (1961) believes that the banishment of experience took place as psychologists sought safety in a "methodological objectivity" which forced a three-pronged reduc-

---

[10] The "control group" as a comparison technique, or the "control" of variables to hold some steady while others vary is not the control referred to here.

tionism: "(a) behavioral — the employment of arbitrary (physical) micro units of stimulus and response, unlikely to enable meaningful constitution by the human organism; (b) physiological — employment of units logically remote from experiential significance for the human organism; (c) phylogenetic — the use of lower organisms for whom language is, of course, unavailable."

The general view is that man must be understood *as a totality*. To understand parts separately does not describe the totality they would form. Man has a special nature (his "being," currently called) which defies atomistic understanding in the way we have understood inanimate things and some lower forms of life. Half a piece of chalk is still a piece of chalk, only smaller; half a planarian worm is half of one worm, but still a worm in itself; half a man is not a man at all.

R. May (1961, p. 18) argues that man cannot be reduced to "drives" since "the more you formulate the forces or drives, the more you are talking about abstractions and not the existing, living human being." Opposition to simple stimulus-response reductionism has been steady since Dewey first wrote his objections to the reflex arc concept as the basis of all behavior. The phenomenologist is sure that between the physical properties of S and the R stands a whole system of potential choices in the prepared and evaluating, not passive organism, not at all likely to be moved on a simply stimulus receptor basis.[11] Responses may have multiple determinants, or single stimuli may have differential responses, or the organism may be downright selective about what stimulus it perceives, or even seeks out (Fiske and Maddi, 1961).

Also opposed is the genetic reductionism which tries to reduce not only complex forms to simple ones, but later states to earlier ones (Kuenzli, 1959, p. 153). The phenomenologist tries to take the fact as it is given, and to let it be as big as it is, rather than to cut it down to his size, or to the size of his measuring instruments.

The existence of this anti-reductionist bias as it applies to the genesis of behavior points to another closely related characteristic. So far as time orientation and determinism, the phenomenologist tends to be a historical. Their position is simply stated as, "the past is relevant only as it lives in the present." This refers only to the *psychological* past, of course. "The behavior's field at any given instant contains also the views of the individual about his past and future. . . . The psychological past and the psychological future are simultaneous parts of the psychological field existing at a given time" (Lewin, 1943,

[11] For the reader who is not acquainted with an actual statement of the contrasting view, the statement by Kimble (1953, p. 158) is quoted here.

"For all practical purposes, it is possible to construct a science of psychology in which the organism is considered as empty. For my own part, I can conceive of a psychology based on stimulus and response events entirely, one in which the existence of the organism is a completely unimportant fact. The scientific account will, after all, deal with behavior in the abstract."

To the "experientialist" this statement must sound incredible, but in fairness, the whole of his article should be read.

pp. 292-310). While it is not true that "the past is a bucket of ashes," neither is man a prisoner of the past — indeed, besides heavy emphasis on present and immediate functioning without historical reconstruction, there is some inclination to see behavior as future-oriented more than past-restrained. Ideals, goals, striving, "self realization" figure prominently in the literature of this group.

Anti-Statistical?

Is there an anti-statistical character to phenomenology? There has been, and may still be. Quantitative methods are not worshipped in the qualitative temple. The phenomenologist works on problems of *individual* behavior. He focuses on the unique, the atypical, but not the average, since groups do not perceive through a mass sensorium. By and large, group correlational methods will not tell the phenomenologist exactly what he wants to know either, since he wants to know *exactly*. There are statistical methods now developed for individual cases, and they are used with keen appreciation (Stephenson, 1953; Rogers and Dymond, 1954). Still, what the phenomenologist seeks is absolute certainty about individual circumstances, not probabilities about groups of non-identical units. In a symposium on "Clinical vs. Statistical Methods in Prediction," Meehl, representing statistical theory, described two six-shot revolvers, one containing five bullets and one empty chamber, the other one bullet and five empty chambers. Which would you choose to hold to your temple? Snygg, representing the clinical view, is not interested in the safety of numbers or the advantage of chance, therefore offered to choose the more heavily loaded gun with only one empty chamber, if he could know this particular gun to his clinical satisfaction and on that basis judge that the empty chamber was next to be fired. Wellek (1957, p. 291) put his relation of qualitative to quantitative analysis this way:

> The assertion that description cannot yield any generally valid results is itself something subjective, an untenable dogma. If somebody can count correctly or incorrectly, he can also describe something rightly or wrongly. If a correct calculation is universally recognized, then a true description should be similarly accepted.

Mind-Body?

In relation to the biological, phenomenology holds a somewhat tenuous position. If "the body is not a fact but a situation," it cannot be considered separate from its environment. As a biological substrate, it is the object of much thought in phenomenological work, especially among the perceptual specialties where neuro-anatomical structures are sought. But even there, the structures are pointed out by the functions — apparent phenomena. At the same time, it is well recognized that different structures "create" for the animal different environments — and thus different phenomenal worlds — as with simple or compound eyes, to mention an elementary example. Many phenomenologists are of the opinion that man does not live merely in order to survive, but rather to achieve some human value — "self realization" or some form of spiritual development. Part of the reservation in regard to biological "bedrock" stems from an emphasis on the social and cultural forces in shaping of behavior (for example, in the behavior of the person who starves to death in a "hunger strike"), but another comes from the anti-reductionistic bias applied to the reasoning about humans from lower and simpler forms of life. This will undoubtedly continue, but meanwhile, keen biological research is demonstrating that the simple forms are not so simple as often thought. Best (1963) mentions the example of the half-blinded (one-eyed) bee, flying in a circle, therefore thought to be an "autonomous" governed by asymmetric stimulation to its one remaining "photoelectric cell." Yet the bee has been shown to have a language "for communicating precise navigational information." The primitive worms which he trained in a Y maze showed signs of wanting freedom more than food at certain points, leading to the postulation of bio-phenomenological concepts such as "protoboredom," "protointerest," "protorebellion."[112] However, until self-consciousness is demonstrated in lower forms, the clinical and social psychologist will probably maintain the concept of unique capacity for experience in the human being and may continue to consider it superorganic.

Freedom and Human Values

In the continuing debate between freedom and control, the phenomenologist is always found to be favoring some aspect of choice, will, decision, responsibility, as opposed to unadulterated determinism (Rogers and Skinner, 1956). This is not a stand based on punitive moralizing about blame, but an emphasis on the qualities of emergence, or "becoming" as well as "being." Freedom of action is considered to have more than political tones — it is a psychologically healthy condition for growth, i.e., the man most free has the widest scope of

---

[12] In connection with new findings in "protopsychology" and old thoughts on freedom, it is especially interesting to add Hebb's comments on the increasing autonomy of the "higher" evolutionary levels:

"I hope I do not shock biological scientists by saying that one feature of the phylogenetic development is an increasing evidence of what is known in some circles as free will; in my student days also referred to as the Harvard Law, which asserts that any well-trained experimental animal, on controlled stimulation, will do as he damn well pleases. A more scholarly formulation is that the higher animal is less stimulus-bound.

Brain action is less fully controlled by afferent input, behavior therefore less fully predictable from the situation in which the animal is put. A greater role of ideational activity is recognizable in the animal's ability to "hold" a variety of stimulations for some time before acting on them and in the phenomenon of purposive behavior. There is more autonomous activity in the higher brain, and more selectivity as to *which* afferent activity will be integrated with the "stream of thought," the dominant, ongoing activity in control of behavior. Traditionally, we say that the subject is "interested" in this part of the environment, not interested in that; in these terms, the higher animal has a wider variety of interests and the interest of the moment plays a greater part in behavior, which means a greater unpredictability as to what stimulus will be responded to and as to the form of the response" (Hebb, quoted in Scher, 1962, p. 726).

choice, therefore he (and his free culture) is in the best position to make adaptive responses to changing conditions. That conditions will change is also a conviction of the typical phenomenologist. Novelty is considered to be a feature of the environment, and evidence is rapidly accumulating to indicate that the organism will actively search for new experience (Fiske and Maddi, 1961). Man as a free and active agent is vividly described by Merleau-Ponty (1956), again expressing the extreme view:

> I am not a "living being" or even a "man" or even a "consciousness" with all the characteristics which zoology, social anatomy or inductive psychology attributes to these products of nature or history. I am the absolute source. My existence does not come from my antecedents or my physical or social entourage, but rather goes toward them and sustains them.

Lest that seem too strident or distant a view to take seriously, here is a statement of equally assertive force from Rogers' (1963) most recent comments:

> . . . man does not simply have the characteristics of a machine, he is not simply in the grip of unconscious motives, he is a person in the process of creating himself, a person who creates meaning in life, a person who embodies a dimension of subjective freedom.

Humanists tend to gather in this movement. They are interested in human beings as persons, albeit sometimes sensitive to accusations of "softness" (as if it referred to heads as well as hearts). Words such a "prizing" and "respect" commonly appear in the literature dealing with their conduct of human observations. The attitude is similar to that displayed by naturalists toward birds, deer, or other species which fascinate them. Out of this desire to let the object of study be free, methods develop as set by the problem rather than to suit available instrumentation — a slow and difficult process.

Behaviorism

The position with regard to behaviorism is somewhat in flux at the moment, with the bare possibility of areas of reconciliation or synthesis, but there has been basic tension and mutual antagonism for decades. This fundamental opposition has already been mentioned. It is common opinion that the "behavioral tide is ebbing." Jessor points to a shift in the literature on motivation as one sign (White, 1959) and to reconstruction in the philosophy of science (Feigl, 1959) as another. Not only has behavioristic learning theory and research proved to be largely sterile but "behaviorism and its canons of scientific procedure have failed in what must be considered the primary task of psychology — the scientific reconstruction of the person as we know him in ordinary life" (Jessor, 1961). One of the main logical criticisms of behaviorism's "false objectivity" is that it always assumed the stimulus to have a peculiarly independent status — physical, invariant, and stable in its meaning, almost as if it had chosen itself to engage in the experiment (and *then* frozen).

This notion is not the straw man invention of the phenomenologist. It has been suggested, for instance, by Davis (1953, p. 10), for physiological psychology:

> For a "stimulus" (external event) to qualify under the proposed canon, it would have to be something which an experimenter could ascertain without there being any organism for it to work on.

But such a system would require that the experimenter himself were not an oragnism. For, as Koch (1959, pp. 768-769) points out:

> If stimuli and responses are acknowledged to depend for their identification on the perceptual sensitivities of human observers, then the demand for something tantamount to a language of pointer readings . . . must be given up. . . . If, further, the requirement is asserted that S be specified in a way which includes its inferred meaning for the organism, then *any* basis for a difference in epistemological status between an S-R language and what has been called "subjectivistic" language is eliminated.

Those who wishfully think that "behaviorism is dead" are mistaken. Phenomenology may have a chance to come alive in a climate no longer dominated by pseudo-physics in psychology, but behaviorism is now moving into significant areas of human behavior (Krasner, 1962), and even reformulating a "subjective behaviorism" (Pribham, 1963). (Of those earlier behaviorists who are being discarded, Hebb (1954, p. 101) says, "These men were narrow — they were wrong, and without them, without the simplification they achieved, modern psychology would not exist.") What is very likely to remain is the strong opposition of internal and external views of the subject. Even when the same event is under discussion, these two views remain in conflict. For example, when the "externalist" describes the *reinforcement* of the operant conditioning process (conducted by the outside observer), the "internalist" claims that the significant part of the process is the invention of the operant[13] (which emerges from within through the effort of the actor). (See Shlien and Krasner, in Strupp and Luborsky, 1962, p. 109.)

The "Essential Structure"

One final characteristic formulated by most writers on phenomenological theory is that it should be the study of essences, or essential structures. This has to do with the notion that when one describes acts of meaning, there should be a definitive reference to the meant things. These meant things or their representations in awareness (ideal concepts) are thought to have cores, or centers of stratified structures, which centers are *irreducible categories*. These are the "things in themselves," not translatable into any other perception

---

[13] In this regard it is of interest to note that in studies of "imprinting," ducklings *must* be permited to waddle after the decoy, from which Hess concluded that: "the strength of the imprinting appeared to be dependent not on the duration of the imprinting period but *on the effort exerted by the duckling*" (Hess, 1958). (My italics.)

(Tymieniecka, 1962, Ch. II). For the most part, the stratified structure model is applied by European phenomenologists. Wellek applies this notion to studies of hypnosis. A subject is asked, during deep trance, to do something in conflict with his values. Refusal to execute the command in a post-hypnotic state is taken as evidence of a core region which cannot be overcome (David and von Bracken, 1957, p. 290). Piaget is interpreted as illustrative of this model in his studies of intelligence, finding higher mental adaptations (stages) not reducible to lower ones. Anthropologist Lévi-Strauss is likewise interpreted as having made use of the stratification model in kinship studies (Tymieniecka, 1962, pp. 38-44). With few exceptions (Gendlin, 1962), American phenomenologists have not understood or used Husserl, and this aspect of stratification or essential structures has not been followed in any deliberate way. It may be making an appearance in the factor analytic studies by Butler and others (Butler, Rice and Wagstaff, 1962; Butler, 1963) or in descriptive statements about the core of the phenomenal self (Snygg and Combs, 1949, p. 126), but is mentioned here chiefly because "essences" have figured in most theoretical descriptions of phenomenology, and may yet turn out to be a genuine part of the empirical system.

Characteristics in Method

Any system depends for its progress on methods. Phenomenology, like the rest of psychology, has been somewhat ill equipped in this regard, although some truly ingenious thinking has gone into Gestalt studies of phenomena, into studies of perceptual constancies, stimulus equivalence, the family of introspective and projective methods, empathic techniques, and some statistical methods applicable to individual percepts.

The overall problem is that of subjectivity. All methods in this approach depend more or less on the response of the experiencer, and often on his own report (admission or assertion) of it. Quantitative analysis does not take the curse off, nor does the controlled experiment. Subjectivity has hung like an albatross around the neck of the phenomenologist, since it has been almost synonomous with "unscientific."[14]

Much has been said about the subjective-objective axis. It is based on a dualistic philosophy of separation between the knower and the known. "Subjective" is thought to mean the representing experience; "objective" refers to what is represented. But one person's experience can be the object of another's representation (or we can experience our own experience) so that experience itself is not subjective beyond rescue, nor the known object so separate from experience that it has a life of its own. It is not necessary to continue the "history of philosophy [in which] the subject and its object have been treated as absolutely discontinuous entities" (James, 1947, p. 52). It seems much more

Excellent references are Jessor, 1956; Bakan, 1954; Zener, 1958. What has passed for "scientific" has been concensus, stated in numbers and fortified by apparatus.

reasonable (to the phenomenologist) to assume that subjective/objective is a matter of degree, not of kind. (This holds with the understanding that he is not trying to study the physical world, or a class of things, but the psychological individual.)

A curious line of thinking led to what now appears to be a false division, deeply imbedded in our ideology. Cantril and others who have developed a "transactional" point of view have shown that most of the behavior we analyze takes place in an *intersubjective* situation. So-called objective stimulus and so-called subjective response hardly deserve to be seen on two different levels since the latter defines the former. Further, the observer of the "subject" is himself a responding reactor: he is subjective about his "object" toward whom he was to be "objective" by simple virtue of the other *being* an object. What we really have, then, is a situation composed of two subjective viewers, either of whom might be called more objective *when viewing the other*. ("There is the objective — mind as it may be seen by others — and the subjective — mind as he the [cyberneticist] experiences it in himself.") (Ashby, 1962, p. 305.) Some scientific virtue was supposed to reside in distance from the observed according to a formula which seems to run: (a) distance makes the observer impersonal; (b) impersonal attitudes make the other an object; (c) thus, distance and impersonality contribute to "objectivity." Is this true?

It seems quite possible that distance could make for less objectivity, if by that we mean reliable and accurate representation of the phenomenon being observed. Too much distance could only lead to "projectivity," since the original object would be out of sight. Should the observer then better be the one in the very center of the experience? Is there some optimum distance? This leads to a rephrasing of the question, which should really be "who can be the most distant?" or "who can make the other more an object?" but simply "who is the best knower?" That person is closest to the truth. The problems then become: (1) Does he know? (2) Will he tell? (3) Has he the capacity to describe? If we are to have a science of experience, it will come mainly through the efforts of the skillful, intelligent, nondefensive and/or courageous persons who can know experience well and communicate knowledge, for verification and general comparisons, if possible. The current methods are approximations of that possibility.

Introspection

Introspection is supposed to have ended, with a whimper, when behaviorism outlawed it. That was one special, classical form. Bakan, as already noted, has revived the deliberate use of the method, by name, in a promising approximation which demonstrates the possibilities mentioned above. But also, Boring has pointed out that "introspection is still with us, doing business under various aliases, of which the *verbal report* is one." This verbal report is so ever-present and of such unavoidable significance that everyone must find some sort of accommodation to it. Spence (1944, p. 57) is willing to say that, "the phenomenological approach has its advantages, particularly in the complex field of social behavior of the human adult. It is obviously easier to gain some notion as to the relevant variables by asking the individual to verbalize them than it is to employ the procedure of trying to hypothesize them from knowledge of past history." At any rate, this shows some trust in the possibilities of communication, at least for convenience. Hilgard (1957, p. 4) goes farther:

> Some extremists believe that private experiences have no place in science; they believe that such experiences belong to the province of the artist or poet. But most psychologists hold that these private experiences are just as much a part of the real world as more observable activities, and they accept the *verbal report* of these experiences as data for science.

Skinner (1953, p. 282) who stands guard more sternly, is only willing to allow for some linguistic clues, as he writes by the light of the burning straw-man:

> The verbal report is a response to a private event, and may be used as a source of information about it. A critical analysis of the validity of this practice is of first importance. But we may avoid the dubious conclusion that, so far as science is concerned, the verbal report or some other discriminative response is the sensation.

True, the verbal report is not the sensation.[15] Neither is the pointer reading. But then, neither is Skinner's observation of behavior the behavior itself! Nor is his report of it his observation! The verbal report is not alone in its failure to *be* the experience it attempts to signify, and the *questions about its validity apply to all types of observations.* No sign is its referent — even the knowing is not the known, nor is the process of experiencing the experience, but it is as close as one can get, and quite close enough, I assert, for psychological study. Under certain conditions, I trust my thoughts, feelings, and even expressions of them, quite as much or more than I trust my (or your) observations of the direction of a pigeon's head, or a tennis ball's behavior in flight. (Remember, these things do not speak for themselves.)

All agree, some reluctantly, that there are private events. Most agree that there is private awareness of them. Can these events be considered as behavior? Not by the behaviorist, unless external signals are considered sufficiently representative to be accepted in the local and current framework of science, or "ways of knowing." Why such lack of trust in the verbal report? There are good reasons. One is that we have multiple thoughts for one voice, so that not all internal behaviors can be simultaneously expressed. Another is that we know, from our own experience, that the verbal report can be false. We have accidentally or deliberately made it so, and observed this. However, cannot

---

[15] We dislike being limited to "sensation," the least of our concerns — and to the term "verbal report" — a slighting and pseudo-scientific reference to the full potency of language in communication, but for the moment, it is sufficient to accept the behaviorist's terminology.

the verbal report be true? It can, and can be more true than our outward behavior, and this we know from our experience also. It is more difficult (except in simple sensations and expression such as "ouch") to report the truth, if only because mistakes are easier to make than to avoid, but the verbal report cannot be said to have *by its nature* a low or negative correlation with the private event it represents. (It is odd that the determinists who rule out "free will" also distrust the verbal report, as if the behaver does have the capacity to falsify at will, if he is not merely stupid.)

Whatever stance one takes toward it, the verbal report is fundamental, and the latest technical advances are simply elegant extensions of it. This includes such excellent tools as the semantic differential (Osgood, 1960) and the Q-sort (Stephenson, 1953; Butler and Haigh, 1954; Shlien, 1962a). Introspection means, according to James, "looking into our minds, and reporting what we there discover," and these techniques are manipulatible data language for "reporting what we there discover."

Another problem in the verbal report, somewhat neutralized by tools such as those above which provide the semantic frame of reference, is the difficulty in overcoming the lack of precision in even the extensive vocabulary. It is partly for this reason (that we are only semi-articulate) that the poet in Hilgard's statement seems to have special access to private experience. What we lack is not so much the experience, or access, but the poet's refined and heightened imagery and his very hard work to formulate it. Our failure to have *le mot juste* ready at hand seems to put experience beyond accurate description. We only see the nature of our ordinary failure when we look at its exaggeration, in aphasia. It is next to impossible for one to describe the exact shade of feeling, meaning, color tone and intensity, etc., to another, especially in complex experience. There are, for simplification, yes/no answers, but then the phrasing of the question becomes complex. There is also the possibility of matching techniques, such as color matching, or with words, to match judge's perceptions of the speaker's meaning.

Kluver (1936) offered an experimental technique based on matching of response values (stimulus equivalence and nonequivalence), for the study of personality. It has been little used, though it would seem to hold some promise still. Interestingly enough, many of his early observations were drawn from the field of ethology, which has a clear but little recognized connection with phenomenological principles.

F. J. J. Buytendijk, whose early work with toads is cited by Kluver, has moved from animal observation into some of the most elusive human qualities, in his "Femininity and Existential Psychology," for example (David and van Bracken, 1957, pp. 197-211). Von Uexkull, one of the founders of ethological method, is often quoted in the literature of phenomenology, since his concept of "private worlds" or environments for each species and even each animal is very much to the phenomenological point (Tymieniecka, 1962, pp. 121-123). McKellar (1962, p. 636) in his chapter on introspection remarks,

"To some extent, the ethologists like Tinbergen and Lorenz have reintroduced the methods of the naturalist into psychology." Principles of ethology as described by Hess (1962, p. 160) are highly compatible with those of phenomenology:

> Study of [animal] behavior must begin by obtaining as complete a knowledge as possible of the behavior of the species during the entire life cycle . . . because *all facts on behavior must be acquired before any hypotheses are formulated.* . . . [Ethologists] have come to this conclusion because behavior is so multiform that a wealth of evidence can always be compiled in support of any theory, no matter how capriciously constructed." (My italics.)

Though the "entire life cycle" is beyond the reach of the study immediate experience, the other ideas, including the intent to study the animals in states which most closely resemble the natural habitat, without fear of the observer, fits phenomenology well.

Empathy

It was noted earlier that the Rogerian technique of "reflection" is almost ethological in its effort to preserve just such conditions as are described above. This technique was a remarkable invention, though it has been maligned by caricature and wooden application. It not only aims toward allowing free emergence of the dynamics of interaction without interference, but expresses perhaps better than any other form of interaction that much used and discussed quality, "empathy." Empathic understanding is described as one of the primary modes of knowing another and as a method in promoting personality change and development. According to Rogers,

> A second necessary condition of psychotherapy, as I see it, is the experiencing by the therapist of an accurate and empathic understanding of the client. This means that he senses and comprehends the client's immediate awareness of his own private world. It involves sensing the cognitive, perceptual, and effective components of the client's experiential field, as they exist in the client. Where the therapist is adequately sensitive, it means not only recognizing those aspects of experience which the client has already been able to verbalize, but also those unsymbolized aspects of his experience which have somehow been comprehended through subtle non-verbal clues by the delicate psychological radar of the therapist. The skilful therapist senses the client's world — no matter, how hallucinated or bizzare or deluded or chaotic — as if it were his own, but without ever losing the "as if" quality (Shlien, 1961, p. 304).

Van Kaam (1959, p. 70) calls this "co-experiencing":

> The understanding person shares at an emotional level the experience of the subject understood. The prefix "co-" represents the awareness of the subject that the person understanding still remains another.

Rogers defines the act precisely in Koch (1959):

> *Empathy.* The state of empathy, or being empathic, is to perceive the internal frame of reference of another with accuracy, and with the emotional components and meanings which pertain thereto, as if one were the other person, but without ever losing the "as if" condition. Thus it means to sense the hurt or the pleasure of another as he senses it, and to perceive the causes thereof as he perceives them, but without ever losing the recognition that is *as if* I were hurt or pleased, etc. If this "as if" quality is lost, then the state is one of identification.

Empathy, or co-experiencing, has not been thoroughly described or researched, but it is well known *as an experience*. It may be put in terms such as those already quoted, or in what we are given to call "mystical" (though this seems to refer more to our ignorance or sheepishness than to its quality) ways such as those described by Buber (1925):

> A man belabours another, who remains quite still. Then let us assume that the striker suddenly receives in his soul the blow which he strikes; the same blow; that he receives it as the other who remains still. For the space of a moment he experiences the situation from the other side. Reality imposes itself on him. What will he do? Either he will overwhelm the voice of the soul, or his impulse will be reversed.
>
> A man caresses a woman, who lets herself be caressed. Then let us assume that he feels the contact from two sides — with the palm of his hand still, and also with the woman's skin. The twofold nature of the gesture, as one that takes place between two persons, thrills through the depth of enjoyment in his heart and stirs it. If he does not deafen his heart he will have — not to renounce the enjoyment but — to love.
>
> I do not in the least mean that the man who has had such an experience would from then on have this two-sided sensation in every such meeting — that would perhaps destroy his instinct. But the one extreme experience makes the other person present to him for all time. A transfusion has taken place after which a mere elaboration of subjectivity is never again possible or tolerable to him.

Not everyone will recognize or remember this quality of experience, and still fewer admit it, but some would vouch for it as an actuality (Shlien 1961, p. 316). At least we realize that we hesitate to cause pain (or else enjoy causing pain) because we believe that the pain of others resembles our own. At least, that.

If this type of description gives uneasiness, one can find more solid comfort in recent physiological studies (Greenblatt, 1959; Dimascio, *et al.,* 1955, 1957; Dittes, 1957) which suggests physiological evidence of "co-experiencing":

> Studies of different doctor-patient dyads have shown us that the doctor is quite as reactive as the patient. [Findings] . . . suggest physiological rapport at least for *some* of the emotions experienced by the patient. It is further worth noting that the *rapport phenomenon was most striking when*

the doctor was "actively listening" and less striking when he was distracted or "not listening" . . . (Our italics.) (Bebout & Clayton, 1962.)

Lacy (1959) in his review, comments that "these are surprising data, and . . . may imply, as the authors [Coleman, Greenblatt and Solomon] seem to feel, a "physiological relationship" between the therapist and patient revealing a process of 'empathy.' "

To Rogers, empathy is not just *a* way of knowing but perhaps *the* primary method in comprehension of all phenomena. He speaks of empathy as a way of knowing both the other, and also oneself, via empathy turned inward. While objects (stones and trees) have no experience to share, even "objective" knowledge is related to empathy. Empathic understanding in that case is directed toward the reference group which objectifies, by consensus, one's experimentally derived information. Empathy, then, is the fundamental way of knowing, and its direction may turn inward or outward (Rogers, 1959, 1963). It is of singular importance in this methodology. There are two elements of knowing: (1) feeling, or the pathic way (from *pathetos,* able to suffer or subject to suffering) which is the process of *understanding,* and (2) seeing, (from *spectore,* to look at) which is the process of spection, intro or extro, or *perceiving.* Together, these two are ways of knowing for phenomenology, if not for all of science.

Perception and Personality

Perception

This is often called a perceptual approach to personality.[16] Rogers (1951, p. 307), for instance, writes of the actual "reorganization of visual perception" during therapy in contrast to the loose descriptive analogy implied by such phrases as "seeing things differently." Combs and Snygg (1959, p. 20) base an absolute law of behavior on perceptual experience: *"All behavior, without exception, is completely determined by, and pertinent to, the perceptual field of the behaving organism."* Does this sound like S-R theory writ large, with "perceptual field" standing for "stimulus"? For clarification, they add, *"By the perceptual field, we mean the entire universe, including himself, as if it is experienced by the individual at the instance of action."* So, to the extent that the entire universe can be reduced to an identifiable stimulus in a given moment of experience, we are in bed with the enemy. Should we simply acquiesce to the inevitable and say "good night," or try to avoid the scandal?

No scientist, looking for lawful descriptions of behavior, wants to turn away from cause and effect. But by now, many phenomenological reservations have appeared; indeed these are precisely what and all that distinguish

---

[16] Basic references for the interested student are Combs & Snygg (1949); Rogers (1951, 1957, 1959); Patterson (1959); and Gendlin (1962).

phenomenology and S-R theory. We come to the perceiving situation with differing needs. These are well known to affect the perception of the stimulus. We also come with a different history of experience. We may even bring different perceptual structures, either in physiological capacity or psychological expectancy. What we react to is not someone else's stimulus, but *our* total perception of *our* phenomenal world. In elegantly contrived visual demonstrations, Ames has shown that "what is perceived is not what exists but what one believes exists" (Combs & Snygg, 1959, p. 84). "Seeing is believing," if one can see, but "believing is seeing," too. We construct our phenomenal world to fit expectations. Reik (1962) working with college "drop-out" students finds it the rule that they "describe mothers as being in delicate health, liable to become ill at any moment. What is important here is not what the parents are like in actuality, but that the student's conception of them produces a very real upset in his inner world."

It might seem that all of these individual differences in perception are the result of the variations in need, structure, past experience, and aim or expectation, thus all "distortions." Many are, but we do not derive all differences from parataxic errors, like the blind men describing the elephant. It is worthwhile to note Bronowski's description of the "clock paradox" based on relativity theory, which proves that two clocks, moving with respect to one another, run at different speeds. It is demonstrated that two observers of a moving light, one moving with it and the other standing still, will have time pass *at different speeds for them*. If time did not, then the speed of light would have to vary (Bronowski, 1963). In the field of perception, then, it is not just cultural relativity or egocentrism which causes differences (though these factors must account for most of the variance) but also unavoidable physical relativity.

Because of these relativites, the perceptual system organizes on the basis of what are called "perceptual constancies." These constancies are assumptions to the effect that actions will take place as we have become accustomed to them in the past. Thus we tend to judge depth or distance by apparent size of a familiar object, or we catch a baseball that we did not see after it arrived at a point two feet from our glove. "Constancies" make us subject to optical illusions, but for the most part they make it possible to carry out relatively stable operations in a constantly active and changing environment (Ittleson & Cantril, 1954).

Before turning to a definition of personality, something should be said in the way of a definition of perception. Definitions are only opinions, of course. One opinion would be that all impingement of stimuli (such as light or sound, upon receptive nerve cells) is perception. A distinction made by J. J. Gibson (1963, p. 1) is important. *"Perception involves meaning; sensation does not."* (Our italics.) To clarify this a bit more, we would say: radar reflects; a phototropic cell senses; and a mind perceives. Ours is a perceptual theory of personality in that it: deals with *meanings,* and requires cognitive apparatus.

Personality

Now a definition of personality is in order. While these definitions are not sheer snares and delusions, neither are they scientific revelations. They are only a part of the system. In this system, personality must have some relation to the subjective, and to the perceptual. It reflects the very shift which has taken place in psychology as described by Bruner, Goodnow and Austin (1956, p. 106) who note that,

> The past few years have witnessed a notable increase in interest in an investigation of the cognitive process. . . . Partly, it has resulted from a recognition of the complex processes that mediate between the classical "stimuli" and "responses" out of which stimulus-response learning theories hoped to fashion a psychology that would bypass anything smacking of the "mental." The impeccable peripheralism of such theories could not last long. As "S-R" theories came to be modified to take into account the subtle events that may occur between the input of a physical stimulus and the emission of an observable response, the old image of the "stimulus-response bond" began to dissolve, its place being taken by a mediation model. As Edward Tolman so felicitously put it some years ago, in place of a telephone switchboard connecting stimuli and responses it might be more profitable to think of a map room where stimuli were sorted out and arranged before every response occurred, and one might do well to have a closer look at these intervening "cognitive maps."

This well describes what has been developing throughout the chapter. Phenomenology could never have adopted a "switchboard" model. It could and did adopt the image of a map. That is how the "self-concept" or "self-structure" is often described — as a map to which the person refers when he is about to make a move. This map is, in fact, one of those "perceptual constancies" which helps to stabilize behavior, and it is also one of the reasons for the emphasis on self-consistency (Lecky, 1945). Personality is one's view of himself, the self-concept, by which he tends to order and interpret his internal and external experiences.

Rogers (1951, Ch. 11) developed theory of personality and behavior based on the phenomenal self, stated in a set of nineteen propositions which are abstracted in a summary by Shlien (1962a). Some of these fundamentals have already been mentioned in the earlier discussion.

(1) Each person is unique. No one else can ever completely know his experience. Since each person's neurological capacities and life history combine in unique ways, the closest approach to another's experience is to see it through his own eyes, insofar as possible. Some of his experience is consciously symbolized. Some is at lower levels of awareness, where it has a lesser influence, perhaps a less controllable influence, on behavior.

(2) Behavior is a consequence of perception. The organism reacts to reality as it is perceived and defined *by that organism*. The "objective evidence" of the thermometer notwithstanding, he who thinks the room hot

opens the window; who thinks it cold closes the same window. Who see a light red, stops; sees the same light green, goes; sees an object as delicious eats it; the same object as refuse, avoids it or sickens from it. Whatever "it" may be — by consensus, physical measurement, or philosophical proof, the way in which "it" is perceived will determine behavior toward it.

(3) From this, it follows that if one wants to promote a stable change in behavior, one must change the *perception* of the one who is behaving. (Unstable changes can be forced from outside, but enduring alterations motivated by internal shifts depend on new perceptions.)

(4) The perception of threat is always followed by defense. Defense may take many forms — aggression, withdrawal, submission, etc. — but it is the general and categorical response to danger.

(5) Perception is narrowed and rigidified by threat. (Experimentally, the phenomenon of "tunnel vision" can be evoked by threat.) Narrowed and rigidified perception blocks change in behavior. Threat, therefore, does not permanently change behavior. It only arouses defenses. Attacking the defense system is likely to complicate it, causing more of the psychological economy to be devoted to defense, still further restricting perception and inhibiting change.

(6) Of the whole perceptual field, a portion becomes differentiated as the self. *This is the self-concept.* The self-concept has dimensions, and the dimensions have values. Thus the self-concept may be one of weakness or strength, for instance. Lovable — hateful, lucky — unlucky, worthy or contemptible, are other examples of dimensions which influence behavior. They influence behavior because the interpretation of the self leads to a reactive interpretation of the external object. For instance, if one feels strong, a boulder is a weapon to push into the treads of an armored tank; if weak, the same boulder is a refuge to hide behind. If one feels sick and helpless, the nurse is a creature of mercy, appealed to for comfort. The same nurse may be seen as a temptress, to be sexually pursued, if the patient sees himself as well and sturdy. All experience is evaluated as friendly or dangerous, interesting or boring, possible or impossible, etc. depending *not* upon the nature of the experience so much as upon the *self-concept of the experience.*

(7) As experiences occur, they are related to the self structure, and depending on it, each experience will be (a) symbolized accurately, perceived consciously, and organized into the self structure, (b) ignored, though sensed (as a sensation) because it has no significance to the self, or (c) denied or distorted when symbolized because it is threatening to the self.

"Conscious and Unconscious" Aspects

Throughout this chapter, we have been thinking primarily about ways of knowing. The statement in 7c (above) leads us to consider also remembering and forgetting, and selective attention and inattention.

The issue of the "unconscious" tends to distinguish two clinical divisions — the psychoanalytic and the phenomenal — though not all Freudian concepts are completely foreign to phenomenology, and not all phenomenologists reject the unconscious. Those few who do not are mainly proponents of projective techniques, who rest their *interpretations* heavily upon psycho-analytic dynamics, though they rest their operational *assumptions* upon phenomenology. Thus L. K. Frank, writing (in the company of phenom-enologists) about the "private world of personal meanings" (Kuenzli, 1959, p. 96), would readily agree that "we see things not as they are, but as we are." However, he expresses doubts, held by most adherents of projec-tive techniques, that the individual either has a clear understanding of him-self, or would reveal such understanding in the face of social pressure. Or, H. A. Murray puts it, "the most important things about an individual are what he cannot or will not say." This succinctly states the problem — is it a matter of cannot, or is it will not? There is no doubt that Murray values the interior experience. But the phenomenologist will more readily depend on the face value of the testimony or self report of the individual. Is this his strength or his weakness? It depends in part as to whether he can create conditions that do not force concealment but favor revelation. It also depends on whether or not he postulates an inaccessible unconscious. Patterson, for in-stance, "sees no need to postulate an unconscious" and finds support in studies and opinions which conclude "that a man's expressed opinions and values are more indicative when it comes to prediction than are projective techniques" (Patterson, 1959, p. 255). A similar finding is reported in a study of the "role of self-understanding in prediction of behavior" (Rogers, Kell, & Mc-Neil, 1948).

It may be that the dimension of rational-irrational is the great divide be-tween those, like Murray and Frank, who are generally phenomenologists, and those otherwise like minded theorists who do not adopt the unconscious. Allport, for instance, considers humans to be "characteristically rational. Ir-rational aspects appear in the undeveloped personality of the child, or the mentally ill" (Maddi, 1963). Rogers believes that man, as a healthy, fully functioning person, is "exquisitely rational" — even his defenses have a cer-tain wisdom about them.

In the main, then, the phenomenological position is in some opposition to the concept of "the unconscious." There are knotty problems involved, which may be analyzed in terms of learning, differentiation, remembering, or forgetting, with self-consistency and Sullivan's concept of "selective inatten-tion" brought into play — but which are beyond the scope of this chapter.

From the standpoint of the existential phenomenologist such as Sartre (1953), the unconscious is a rejected concept, representing "bad faith." As such, it is simply an avoidance of responsibility, via suppression rather than repression, "playing the game" of mental illness. The ideas of Rogers, Syngg and Combs, and others of their school can probably be expressed in this way: two elements, "span of attention" and "level of awareness," operate within an energy system in which energy levels are raised and lowered, and attention directed and focused, by emotions. A favorite example in the perceptual analogies commonly used is that of angle of vision as affected by threat. Normally, under relaxed conditions, the angle of vision is wide enough to permit peripheral perceptions at 80+ degrees to either side when the viewer looks straight ahead. Under conditions of intense emotion (of which threat is one) the phenomenon of "tunnel vision" can be induced. The view becomes narrow, as if the viewer were looking through a tube. In that event, the peripheral scene, which is no longer perceived, is not "inaccessible." It is simply out of sight until normal vision is restored.

Span of attention and level of awareness are thought to enlarge and constrict, or rise and fall, according to the energy available at a given time. If sensation is distinguished from perception according to Gibson's previously noted idea, then sensation registers at a very low level of awareness. There are many sensations which, depending on energy available, we do not immediately or perhaps ever (the process can be delayed) turn into perceptions. To the extent that sensations enter awareness at all, they vaguely influence behavior. A soldier on watch in a jungle slaps only those mosquitos actually noticed. The remainder contribute to some general impression of feeling tone of uneasiness,[17] much less significant than his fear for his life. As he is pinned down by enemy fire, the mosquitos may become ferocious, but fade as perceptions. Long after, at rest in his lawn chair, he may viciously swat and spray, vowing to kill all mosquitos, hating them for sensations caused years ago, now raised to perceptions in a different situation.

The idea of an energy level model is perhaps especially appropriate to a neurological system, but that is not its justification. Its value is in the distinct and important difference between it and the so-called "hydraulic" model as Freud's concept of the unconscious is often described (MacIntyre, 1958, p. 22). If, as Freud thought, the "sum of excitations" in the nervous system is constant (like the volume of blood in the circulatory system, for instance), then an experience, when forgotten, must go some place — some place "out of consciousness." The hydraulic model makes a "reservoir" an absolute necessity. In an energy model, where the sum of excitations is *not* constant but varies according to variation of intake and metabolic rate, forgetting and remembering are functions of a variable process. Once perceived, an experience moves in and out of consciousness *in time,* not in space. The forgotten does not move to an inaccessible location. It stays where it is, and the amount of light cast upon it grows dim, as it were.

---

[17] William James (1950, p. 607) observed that "if you make a real red cross (say) on a sheet of white paper invisible to an hypnotic subject, and yet cause him to look fixedly at a dot on the paper on or near the cross, he will, on transferring his eye to a blank sheet, see a bluish-green after image of a cross. This proves that it has impressed his sensibility. He has *felt* it, but not *perceived* it." Some sensations, such as the weight of this book on your finger tips, may become perceptions if attention is so directed, or if the amount of available energy varies in such a way as to increase sensitivity. Obviously, in social situations which are often complex and fast moving, many high level sensations or low level perceptions are experienced and forgotten in the rush of events on the fluctuations of energy levels.

Theoretically, given complete absence of threat, and a resultant complete freedom of energy from defensive activities, memory would be as complete as the needs of the moment dictated, limited only by the levels of awareness permitted by energy available at that moment. Such conditions are seldom if ever achieved, and then only temporarily, since the press of new experience and changing social environment alters the situation, recreating "normal" levels of stress. Perhaps just to the extent that these ideal conditions are approximated, the phenomenologist is justified in taking at face value the self reports toward which his methodology points and which others so distrust.

Motivation

Unconscious or not, motivation is one remaining problem. Presumably the definition of motivation does not differ much throughout these chapters — it has to do with what the person is trying to accomplish through his behaviors. There is only one basic motive to which all behaviors are ascribed in this system. It is called "growth," or "self-enhancement," "self-realization" (Butler & Rice, 1963). Combs and Snygg (1959, p. 46) put it as *"that great driving, striving force in each of us by which we are continually seeking to make ourselves ever more adequate to cope with life."* Rogers (1963) adds, "Whether the stimulus arises from within or without, whether the environment is favorable or unfavorable, the behaviors of an organism can be counted on to be in the direction of maintaining, enhancing, and reproducing life. That is the very nature of the process we call life."

Conclusion

There is, by way of summary, a story about a psychologist which is somewhat legendary in the Chicago area. It is a commentary upon many elements which have been discussed: language, personal meanings, frames of reference, motives, private worlds, methods of observation, etc. And it points out that it is not always true that the human mind thinks silently. It can, but it sometimes thinks out loud, from which we can learn if we listen.

The upper class parents of a small boy were worried. Their son was quiet, sensitive, lonely, nervous, afraid of and highly excited by other children. He stammered in the presence of strangers, and was becoming more shy and withdrawn. The parents were embarrassed and did not want to expose their fears, but wanted some professional advice before the child entered school. The father solved their dilemma by calling a college friend whom he had not seen for years, and who had become in those years a well known clinical psychologist. For "old times' sake" an invitation for a weekend in their suburban home was extended, and with some curiosity, accepted. After dinner, the mother "casually" mentioned their concern about the child; the father amplified this and suggested that after lunch the next day, the boy might be observed at play for a psychological appraisal. The visitor understood now the purpose of his visit, asked appropriate questions about history and behavior, and prepared to take up his assignment. He watched, unseen, from a balcony above the garden where the boy played by himself. The boy sat pensively in the sun, listening to neighboring children shout. He frowned, rolled over on his stomach, kicked the toes of his white shoes against the grass, sat up and looked at the stains. Then he saw an earthworm. He stretched it out on the flagstone, found a sharp edged chip, and began to saw the worm in half. At this point, impressions were forming in the psychologist's mind, and he made some tentative notes to the effect: "Seems isolated and angry, perhaps over-aggressive, or sadistic, should be watched carefully when playing with other children, not have knives or pets." Then he noticed that the boy was talking to himself. He leaned forward and strained to catch the words. The boy finished the separation of the worm. His frown disappeared, and he said, "There. Now you have a friend."

REFERENCES

ALLPORT, G. W. The personalistic psychology of William Stern. *Character and Personality,* 1936, 5, 231-246.

ALLPORT, G. W. Scientific models and human morals. *Psychological Review,* 1947, 54, 182-192.

ASCH, S. E. *Social psychology.* New York: Prentice-Hall, 1953.

ASHBY, C. What is mind? Objective and subjective aspects in cybernetics. In J. Scher (Ed.), *Theories of the mind.* Glencoe, Ill.: Free Press, 1962.

BAKAN, D. A reconsideration of the problem of introspection. *Psychological Bulletin,* 1954, 51 (2), 105-118.

BEATTLE, D. M. The effect of imaginary practice on the acquisition of a motor skill. Unpublished M. A. dissertation, University of Toronto, 1949.

BEBOUT, J. E. & CLAYTON, MARTHA. Toward a concept of shared experiencing in psychotherapy. *Counseling Center Discussion Papers,* Vol. 8, No. 10, 1962.

BECK, S. J. & MOLISH, B. (Eds.) *Reflexes to intelligence: A reader in clinical psychology.* Glencoe, Ill.: Free Press, 1959.

BERENDA, C. W. Is clinical psychology a science? *American Psychologist,* 1957, 12, 725-729.

BEST, J. Protopsychology. *Scientific American,* 1963, 208 (2), 54-75.

BORING, E. G. *A history of experimental psychology.* New York: Appleton-Century-Crofts, 1950.

BORING, E. G. A history of introspection. *Psychological Bulletin,* 1953, 50, 169-189.

BLAKE, R. & RAMSEY, G. (Eds.) *Perception: An approach to personality.* New York: Ronald Press, 1951.

BRONOWSKI, J. The clock paradox. *Scientific American,* 1963, 208 (2), 134-148.

BRUNER, J. S. GOODNOW, JACQUELINE J., & AUSTIN, G. A. *A study of thinking.* New York: Wiley, 1956.

BUBER, M. *Between man and man.* London: Kegan Paul, 1947.

BUTLER, J. M. *Quantitative naturalistic research.* New York: Prentice-Hall, 1962.

BUTLER, J. M. & HAIGH, G. V. Changes in the relation between self-concepts and ideal-concepts. In C. R. Rogers & Rosalind F. Dymond (Eds.), *Psychotherapy and personality change.* Chicago: University of Chicago Press, 1954.

BUTLER, J. M. & RICE, LAURA. Adience, self-actualization, and drive theory. In Joseph Wepman and Ralph W. Heine (Eds.), *Concepts of personality.* Chicago: Aldine, 1963. Ch. 4.

BUTLER, J. M., RICE, LAURA N., & WAGSTAFF, ALICE. On the naturalistic definition of variables: An analogue of clinical analysis. In H. Strupp & Luborsky (Eds.), *Research in psychotherapy,* Vol. II. Washington, D.C.: American Psychological Association, 1962.

COLEMAN, R., GREENBLATT, M., & SOLOMON, H. C. Physiological evidence of rapport during psychotherapeutic interviews. *Diseases of the Nervous System,* 1956, 17, 2-8.

COMBS, A. W. & SYNGG, D. *Individual behavior: A perceptual approach to behavior.* New York: Macmillan, 1959.

DAVID, H. & VON BRACKEN, K. *Perspectives in personality theory.* New York: Basic Books, 1957.

DAVIS, R. Physiological psychology. *Psychological Review,* 1953, 60, 7-14.

DiMASCIO, A., BOYD, R. W., & GREENBLATT, M. Physiological correlates of tension and antagonism during psychotherapy. A study of "interpersonal physiology." *Pyschosomatic Medicine,* 1957, 19, 99-104.

DiMASCIO, A., BOYD, R. W., GREENBLATT, M., & SOLOMON, H. C. The psychiatric interview: A sociophysiological study. *Diseases of the Nervous System,* 1955, 16, 2-7.

DITTES, J. E. Galvanic skin response as a measure of patient's reaction to therapist's permissiveness. *Journal of Abnormal Social Psychology,* 1957, 55, 295-303.

FARBER, M. *The foundation of phenomenology.* Cambridge: Harvard University Press, 1943.

FEIGL, H. Philosophical embarrassments of psychology. *American Psychologist,* 1959, 14, 115-128.

FISKE, D. & MADDI, S. *Functions of varied experience.* Homewood, Ill.: Dorsey Press, 1961.

FRANK, L. K. Projective methods in the study of personality. In A. Kuenzli (Ed.), *The phenomenological problem.* New York: Harper, 1959.

GENDLIN, E. *Experiencing and the creation of meaning.* Glencoe, Ill.: Free Press, 1962.

GIBSON, J. J. Perception as a function of stimulation. In S. Koch (Ed.), *Psychology: A study of a science,* Vol. I. New York: McGraw-Hill, 1959.

GREENBLATT, M. Discussion of papers by Saslow and Matarazzo, and Lacey. In E. A. Rubinstein & M. B. Parloff (Eds.), *Research in psychotherapy.* Washington, D.C.: American Psychological Association, 1959.

HEBB, D. O. The problem of consciousness and introspection. In E. Adrian (Ed.), *Brain mechanics and consciousness,* Oxford: Blackwell Scientific Publications, 1954.

HESS, E. H. Imprinting in animals. *Scientific American,* 1958, 198:81.

HESS, E. H. Ethology: An approach to the complete analysis of behavior. In *New directions in psychology.* New York: Holt, Rinehart & Winston, 1962.

HILGARD, E. R. *Introduction to psychology* (2nd ed.). New York: Harcourt, Brace, 1957.

HULL, C. *Principles of behavior.* New York: Appleton-Century, 1943.

ITTLESON, W. & CANTRIL, H. *Perception: A transactional approach.* Garden City: Doubleday, 1954.

JAMES, W. *Essays in radical empiricism: A pluralistic universe.* New York: Longmans, 1947.

JAMES, W. *Principles of psychology.* New York: Dover Press, 1950 edition.

JESSOR, R. Phenomenological personality theories and the data language of psychology. *Psychological Review,* 1956, 63 (3), 173-180.

JESSOR, R. Issues in the phenomenological approach to personality. *Journal of Individual Psychology,* 1961, 17, 27-38.

KIMBLE, G. Psychology as a science. *Scientific Monthly,* 1953, LXXVII (3).

KLUVER, H. *Behavior mechanisms in monkeys.* Chicago: University of Chicago Press, 1933.

KLUVER, H. The study of personality and the method of equivalent and nonequivalent stimuli. *Character and Personality,* 1936, 5, 91-112.

KOCH, S. (Ed.) *Psychology: A study of a science,* Vol. III. New York: McGraw-Hill, 1959.

KOHLER, W. *The place of value in a world of facts.* New York: Liveright, 1938.

KRASNER, L. The therapist as a social reinforcement machine. In H. Strupp & Luborsky (Eds.), *Research in psychotherapy,* Vol. II. Washington, D.C.: American Psychological Association, 1962.

KUENZLI, A. E. (Ed.) *The phenomenological problem.* New York: Harper, 1959.

LACEY, J. I. Psychophysiological approaches to the evaluation of psychotherapeutic process and outcome. In E. A. Rubinstein & M. B. Parloff (Eds.), *Research in psychotherapy.* Washington, D.C.: American Psychological Association, 1959.

LANDSMAN, T. Four phenomenologies. *Journal of Individual Psychology,* 1958, 14, 29-37.

LECKY, P. *Self-consistency: A theory of personality.* New York: Island Press, 1945.

LEWIN, K. *Field theory in social science: Selected theoretical papers.* D. Cartwright (Ed.), New York: Harper, 1951.

MACINTYRE, A. C. *The unconscious.* London: Routledge & Kegan Paul, 1958.

MACLEOD, R. B. The place of phenomenological analysis in social psychological theory. In J. H. Rohrer & M. Sherif (Eds.), *Social psychology at the crossroads.* New York: Harper, 1951.

MADDI, SALVATORE R. Humanistic psychology: Allport and Murray. In Joseph M. Wepman and Ralph W. Heine (Eds.), *Concepts of personality.* Chicago: Aldine, 1963. Pp. 162-205.

MAY, R. *Existential psychology.* New York: Random House, 1961.

MCKELLAR, P. The method of introspection. In J. Scher (Ed.), *Theories of the mind.* Glencoe, Ill.: Free Press, 1962.

MERLEAU-PONTY, M. *La phenomenologie de la perception.* Paris: Gallimard, 1945.

MERLEAU-PONTY, M. What is phenomenology? *Cross Currents,* 1956, 6, 59-70.

OSGOOD, C., SUCI, G., & TANNENBAUM, P. *The measurement of meaning.* Urbana: University of Illinois Press, 1957.

PATTERSON, C. H. *Counseling and psychotherapy: Theory and practice.* New York: Harper, 1959.

POLANYI, M. *Personal knowledge.* Chicago: University of Chicago Press, 1958.

PRIBHAM, K. H. Interrelations of psychology and the neurological disciplines. In S. Koch (Ed.), *Psychology: A study of a science,* Vol. IV, New York: McGraw-Hill, 1963.

REIK, L. The drop-out problem. *The Nation,* 1962, 194 (20).

ROGERS, C. R. *Counseling and psychotherapy.* Boston: Houghton Mifflin, 1942.

ROGERS, C. R. *Client-centered therapy: Its current practice, implications and theory.* Boston: Houghton Mifflin, 1951.

ROGERS, C. R. The necessary and sufficient conditions of therapeutic personality change. *Journal of Consulting Psychology,* 1957, 21, 95-103.

ROGERS, C. R. *On becoming a person.* Boston: Houghton Mifflin, 1961a.

ROGERS, C. R. Two divergent trends. In R. May (Ed.), *Existential psychology.* New York: London House, 1961b.

ROGERS, C. R. The actualizing tendency in relation to "motives" and to consciousness. Nebraska Symposium on Motivation, 1963.

ROGERS, C. R., & DYMOND, ROSALIND. *Psychotherapy and personality change.* Chicago: University of Chicago Press, 1954.

ROGERS, C. R., KELL, B. L., & MCNEILL, H. The role of self understanding in prediction of behavior. *Journal of Consulting Psychology,* 1948, 12, 174-186.

ROGERS, C. R. & SKINNER, B. F. Some issues concerning the control of human behavior. *Science,* 1956, No. 3231, 1057-1066.

SARTRE, J. *Existential psychoanalysis.* New York: Philosophical Library, Inc., 1953.

SCHER, J. (Ed.) *Theories of the mind.* Glencoe, Ill.: Free Press, 1962.

SHLIEN, J. M. A client-centered approach to schizophrenia. In A. Burton (Ed.), *Psychotherapy of the psychoses.* New York: Basic Books, 1961.

SHLIEN, J. M. The self concept in relation to behavior: Theoretical and empirical research. In Stuart W. Cook (Ed.), *Research Supplement to Religious Education,* July-August, 1962a.

SHLIEN, J. M. Toward what level of abstraction of criteria. In H. Strupp & Luborsky (Eds.). *Research in psychotherapy,* Vol. II. Washington, D.C.: Amer. Psychol. Assoc., 1962b.

SKINNER, B. F. *Science and human behavior.* New York: Macmillan, 1953.

SPENCE, K. The nature of theory construction in contemporary psychology. *Psychological Review,* 1944, 51, 49-68.

SPIEGLEBERG, H. *The phenomenological movement: An historical introduction.* Hague: Martinus Nyhoff, 1960.

SNYGG, D. The need for a phenomenological system of psychology. *Psychological Review,* 1941. 48, 404-424.

SNYGG, D. & COMBS, A. W. *Individual behavior.* New York: Harper, 1949.

STEPHENSON, W. *The study of behavior.* Chicago: University of Chicago Press, 1953.

TOLMAN, E. Principles of purposive behavior. In S. Koch (Ed.), *Psychology: A study of a science,* Vol. II. New York: McGraw-Hill, 1959.

TYMIENIECKA, ANNA-TERESA. *Phenomenology and science in contemporary European thought.* New York: Farrar, Straus & Cudahy, 1962.

VAN KAAM, A. L. Phenomenal analysis: Exemplified by a study of the experience of "really feeling understood." *Journal of Individual Psychology,* 1959, 15, 66-72.

WALLEK, A. The phenomenological and experimental approach to psychology and characterology. In H. P. David & H. von Bracken (Eds.), *Perspectives in personality theory.* New York: Basic Books, 1957.

WHITE, R. Motivation reconsidered: The concept of competence. *Psychological Review,* 1959, 66, 297-333.

ZENER, K. The significance of experience of the individual for the science of psychology. In *Minnesota studies in the philosophy of science,* Vol. II. Minneapolis: University of Minnesota Press, 1958.

7

A Theory of Personality Change*[1]

EUGENE T. GENDLIN

After a few pages which state two main problems and two observations, a theory of personality change will be presented. The theory is another step in the continuing work on "experiencing" (Gendlin, 1957, 1962a; Gendlin and Zimring, 1955). The theory of experiencing provides a frame of reference in which theoretical considerations are viewed in a new way.

A theory requires terms, defined words with which to specify observations, and a formulation of a chain of theoretical hypotheses. The theory presented here is developed within this basic structure, and special notice should be given to the new terms which are introduced and defined. These terms are pointed out and numbered. (We can have a genuine theory only with carefully defined terms, and only by using defined terms can we later modify, improve, and extend theory.)

Problems and Observations

In most theories, the static content-and-structure aspects of personality are primary, and therefore personality change is an especially difficult problem. The present theoretical frame of reference is especially suited to account for change, since it employs concepts that apply to the experiencing process, and to the relationships between that process and content aspects of personality.

* Chapter 4 from *Personality Change* edited by P. Worchel and D. Byrne (New York: John Wiley and Sons, 1964). Reprinted by permission.

[1] *I am grateful to Malcolm A. Brown for many helpful and clarifying discussions, which greatly aided the process of writing this chapter, and to Dr. Sidney M. Jourard, Marilyn Geist, Dr. William Wharton, Joe T. Hart, David Le Roy, and Ruth Nielsen for their valuable comments and editorial help.*

Personality Theory and Personality Change

Personality theories have chiefly been concerned with the factors that determine and explain different individuals' personalities as they are, and the factors which have brought about the given personality. What is called personality maintains its character despite circumstances. Aspects of an individual fail to puzzle us if his current situation explains them. We do not even attribute it to his personality when an individual shows all sorts of undesirable behavior under overwhelmingly bad circumstances, or when he becomes likable and secure under the influence of events which (as we say) would make almost anybody likable and secure. What we do attribute to personality is the reverse: when an individual remains likable and secure under overwhelmingly bad circumstances, and when an individual remains afraid and in pain despite apparent opportunities and good luck. Thus, it could be said that, far from explaining personality change, our theories have been endeavoring to explain and define personality as that which tends not to change when one would expect change.

To some extent this view of personality as factors which resist change is justified. We usually think of a person as involving identity and continuity through time. However, the contents and patterns in the theories are a *type of explanatory concept* which renders change impossible by definition. The structure of personality (in theories) is formulated in such a way that it is said to maintain itself against all new experience which might alter it. The individual is viewed as a structured entity with defined contents. These explanatory concepts can explain only why an individual cannot change.

Personality theory, then, has concentrated upon the factors which explain why an individual is as he is, how he has become so, and how these factors maintain him so, despite circumstances, fortunes, and opportunities. Such explanatory concepts of content and structure tell us what prevents an individual from being changed by experience, what factors will force him forever (by definition) to miss or distort everything that might change him unless (as we commonly say) his personality (somehow) changes first.

Since structure and content do tend to maintain themselves and distort present experience, we can account for personality change only if we can show exactly how this change resistance yields to change.

Theories in the past have not wanted to portray personality change as impossible. On the contrary, the theories assert that change does actually occur. The chief personality theories have sprung from psychotherapy — that is to say (when psychotherapy is successful), from ongoing personality change.

Quite paradoxically, as personality change occurs before their eyes and with their participation, therapists find their minds formulating what has been wrong. Even the individual, himself, as he searches into his feelings and expresses these, speaks as if the whole endeavor were to investigate what has been wrong — what has constituted the aspects of his personality which have prevented ordinary adaptation and change. And, usually, such an individual becomes aware of much which, he then says, has been true all along but of which he has not been aware.

Thus, psychotherapy regularly gives us this observation of an individual "uncovering" or "becoming aware" of these stubborn contents and his previous inability to be aware of them. So well have the various personality theories formulated these contents and this self-maintaining and censoring structure that, while we have concepts to explain what makes an individual as he is, we cannot formulate how he can change. Yet all the time the individual has been changing just these "uncovered" factors which we formulate in terms of static explanatory contents.[2]

I will now present in more detail the two main ways in which much current formulation of personality makes change appear theoretically impossible. I call these two impossibilities "the repression paradigm," and "the content paradigm."[3]

Since these theories, nevertheless, also assert that change does occur, I will then take up the two main ways in which theories attempt to account for change. I will try to show that theories usually cite two observations: a *feeling process;* and a certain *personal relationship.*

Two Problems

The "Repression Paradigm"

Most personality theories (in different words and with somewhat different meanings) share what I call the "repression paradigm." They agree that in an individual's early family relations he introjected certain values, according to which he was loved only if he felt and behaved in certain ways. Experiences which contradicted these demands on him came to be "repressed" (Freud), or "denied to awareness" (Rogers), or "not me" (Sullivan). Later, when the individual encounters experiences of this contradicting sort, he must either distort them or remain totally unaware of them. For, were he to notice the contradictory experiences, he would become intolerably anxious. The ego (Freud), or self-concept (Rogers), or self-dynamism (Sullivan), thus basically influences awareness and perception. This influence is termed "resistance" (Freud), or "defensiveness" (Rogers), or "security operation"

---

[2] This tendency to view ongoing change in terms of the static contents it reveals can be seen also in the very many research projects which have employed psychotherapy and hospital situations to study diagnostic and classificatory aspects of people as compared with the very few researches which have employed these treatment settings to study change. Our psychometric instruments do not as yet have standardized or even defined indices of personality change, having been used so rarely before and after psychotherapy. This is another example of the way we tend to think most about the change-resistant contents of personality, even in treatment situations.

[3] "Paradigm," or model, refers to the *theoretical* models used in these theories, regardless of whether they use the words "repression" and "content" or not.

(Sullivan), and a great deal of behavior is thereby explainable. A personality is as it is, and remains as it is, because it cannot take account of these experiences. Or if, somehow, repression is forcefully lifted and the individual is made to become aware of these experiences, the ego will "lose control," the self will "disintegrate," and intolerable "uncanny emotions" will occur. In psychosis, it is said, the individual is aware of such experiences and the ego or self-organization has indeed broken down.

If the individual needed merely to be reminded, or to have the "repressed" factors called to his notice, he would soon be straightened out. There are always helpful or angry people who attempt this, and many situations grossly demand attention to these factors. The individual, however, represses not only the given factors within him but also anything outside him which would relate to these factors and remind him of them.[4] He misunderstands or reinterprets so as to prevent himself from noticing the aspects of events and persons which would bring these factors to his awareness.

Thus, the specific personality structure maintains itself and change is theoretically impossible. Whatever would change the individual in the necessary respects is distorted or goes unnoticed just to that extent and in those respects in which it could lift the repression and change him.

Now, this explanation (shared in some way, as I have tried to indicate, by the major personality theories of the day) is based on the striking way in which the individual during psychotherapy becomes aware of what (so he new says) he has long felt but has not known that he felt. Moreover, the individual realizes how powerfully these previously unaware experiences have affected his feelings and behavior. So many individuals have now reported this that there is no longer much doubt that it is a valid observation. The open question is how we are to formulate it theoretically.

Once we formulate theory along the lines of the repression paradigm, we cannot then blithely turn around and "explain" personality change as a "becoming aware" of the previously repressed. Once we have shown how anything will be distorted which tends to bring these experiences to awareness, we cannot then consider it an explanation to simply assert that personality change is (by definition supposedly impossible) a becoming aware. Change happens. But, to say that is not to offer an explanation — it is only to state the problem. We may take the "repression paradigm" to be one basic aspect of personality change — one of the two basic factors with which this chapter will be concerned. To account for personality change, we will have to account for how this crucial becoming aware really does occur, and then we will have to go back and reformulate our theory of repression and the unconscious.

---

[4] The repression paradigm in its most oversimplified form can be noticed in use when person A insists that person B has some content he cannot be aware of, because it is "unconscious." B's own experiences and feelings are, by definition, undercut and "thrown out of court." No way to the supposed content exists which B can use.

The "Content Paradigm"

The second basic aspect of personality change (and the second way in which current modes of formulating make change theoretically impossible) concerns the view of personality as made up of various "contents." By "contents" I mean any *defined* entities, whether they are called "experiences," "factors," "S-R bonds," "needs," "drives," "motives," "appraisals," "traits," "self-concepts," "anxieties," "motivational systems," "infantile fixations," "developmental failures," or whatever.

If we are to understand personality change, we must understand how these personality constituents can change in nature.

To account for this change in the nature of contents, we need a type of definition (explanatory constructs) which also can change. We cannot explain *change* in the nature of the *content* when our theory specifically defines personality only as content. Such theory can formulate what needs to be changed, and later it can also formulate what has changed, and into what it has changed; but it will remain theoretically unexplained how such change is possible, so long as all our explanations are in terms of concepts of this or that defined content.

We require some kind of more basic personality variable to formulate an account of how, under what conditions, and through what process, change in the nature of contents can occur.

Thus, for example, chemistry defines the elements in terms of more basic activities of electrons and protons, and thereby we can account for the subatomic processes by which elements engage in chemical change reactions and through which an element can be bombarded with subatomic particles and turned into a different element. Without these concepts, which view elements as motions of something more basic, we could not explain the chemical and atomic *change* we observe, nor operationally study and define the conditions under which it occurs. We could state only that at t_1 the test tube had certain contents, A, B, while at t_2 the contents were C, D. Only if A, B, C, D, are not themselves the *ultimate* explanatory concepts can we expect to explain changes from one to another. And so it is with personality change. If our ultimate explanatory constructs are "contents," we cannot explain the change in the nature of just these contents.

Our conclusion here is not simply that defined contents of personality do not exist. Rather, it is that if we define personality as contents and in no further, more basic way, then we cannot expect to use the same concepts to explain just how these contents change. And, inasmuch as it will have been just these contents which define the personality (and the respects in which change must occur if it is to be important personality change), exactly this theoretically impossible task is posed when personality theories come to explain change.

For example, during psychotherapy the patient finally comes to realize these essential contents (they will be conceptualized in whatever the vocabulary of the particular theory the psychotherapist uses). He realizes now that he has been full of "hostility," or that he has felt and acted from "partial, fixated sexual desires," or that he "hates his father," or that he is "passive-dependent," or was "never loved as a child." "Now what?" he asks. How do you change such contents? No way is given. The fact that these contents actually do change is our good fortune. The theories explain the personality in terms of these defined contents, these "experiences," or "needs," or "lacks." The theories cannot explain how these contents melt and lose their character to become something of a different character. Yet they do.

Our second basic problem of personality change, then, is this "content paradigm." The question is, "In what way should the nature of personality definitions change so that we can arrive at a means of defining that will fit the process of change in personality contents?" In answering this, we will describe something more basic or ultimate than defined contents. Then we will consider how defined contents arise in this more ultimate personality process.

Two Universal Observations of Personality Change

Now that two basic *problems* of personality change have been stated (becoming aware and change in the nature of contents), we will turn next to two basic *observations* of personality change. In contrast to the aforementioned *theoretical* impossibilities, most theories of personality cite two *observations,* which they assert are nearly always involved in personality change.

(1) Major personality change involves some sort of intense affective or feeling process occurring in the individual.

(2) Major personality change occurs nearly always in the context of an ongoing personal relationship.

The Feeling Process

When major personality change occurs, intense, emotional, inwardly felt events are usually observed. I would like to give the name "feeling process" to this affective dimension of personality change. The word "feeling" is preferable to "affective," because "feeling" usually refers to something concretely sensed by an individual. In personality change the individual directly feels an inward reworking. His own concepts and constructs become partly unstructured and his felt experiencing at times exceeds his intellectual grasp.

In various contexts it has been noted that major personality change requires not only intellectual or actional operations, but also this felt process. For instance, psychotherapists (of whatever orientation) often discuss the presence or absence of this feeling process in a particular case. They discuss whether the individual, in a given psychotherapy hour, is engaged in "merely" intellectualizing, or whether (as they phrase it) he is "really" engaged in psychotherapy. The former they consider a waste of time or a defense, and they predict[5] that no major personality change will result from it. The latter they consider promising of personality change.

Now, although this difference is universally discussed, it is most often phrased so unclearly, and the words following "merely" ("merely" intellectualizing, defending, avoiding, externalizing, etc.), and the words following "really" ("really" engaged, facing, dealing with) are so undefined that we may as well simply refer to this difference as the difference between "merely" and "really." Although it may not be phrased well, what is always meant or referred to by "really" is a *feeling process* which is absent when something is termed "merely."

A similar distinction between "merely" and "really" is talked about in education: There has always been much concern with the contrast between "mere" rote learnings of facts and "really" learning something (making it one's own, becoming able to "integrate," "apply," and "creatively elaborate" it).

"Really" learning is predicted to result in observable behavior changes, while "mere" rote learning is predicted to result in little (or different) behavior change. The learning process is said to differ in the two instances, depending upon the degree of the individual's "internal motivation," his way of "taking the new material in," his "application of himself to what he learns," his genuine grasp of meanings. These metaphoric phrases indicate that, here again during learning, the difference between "really" and "merely" refers to a certain participation of the individual's feelings in the learning process.

Let me give some further aspects of this observation from psychotherapy.

An Adlerian therapist some years ago told me: "Of course interpretation is not enough. Of course the person doesn't change only because of the wisdoms which the theraptist tells him. But no technique really expresses what makes the change itself. The change comes through some kind of emotional ligesting; but then you must admit that none of us understand what *that* is."

Therapists often miss this fact. They labor at helping the individual to a better explanation of what is wrong with him, yet, when asked how the individual is to *change* this now clearly explained maladaption, nothing very clear is said. Somehow, knowing his problem, the individual should change, yet *knowing* is not the process of changing.

---

[5] Throughout, the new concepts and words defined here are intended to lead to new and more effective operational variables. Where research is cited, the theory has already led to some operational variables. One must distinguish *theoretical concepts* from *operational variables*. For example, above, "feeling process" is a theoretical concept. The operational variables (and there will be many specific ones) which a theoretical concept lads us to isolate and define are indices of behavior and exactly repeatable procedures hereby these can be reliably measured.

When it is held that the difference above between "really" and "merely" is a "subjective" difference, this only means that we have *not yet* defined the observable variables which enable a common-sense observer to predict differential behavioral results.

A good diagnostician, perhaps with the aid of a few psychometric tests, can often give a very accurate and detailed description and explanation of an individual's personality. Therapist and client often both *know,* after such testing and a few interviews, a good deal of what is wrong and what needs to be changed. Quite often, after two years of therapeutic interviews, the description and explanation which was (or could have been) given at the outset appears in retrospect to have been quite accurate. Yet it is clear that there is a major difference between knowing the *conceptual* explanation of personality (which one can devise in a few hours) and the actual *feeling process* of changing (which often requires years). Relatively little has been said about this process,[6] how one may observe and measure it, and just in

[6] Rogers discovered how, in practice, the individual can be helped to overcome the repression paradigm.

His discovery is that defensiveness and resistance are obviated when one responds to an individual "within his own internal frame of reference." This phrase means that the psychotherapist's response always refers to something which is directly present in the individual's own momentary awareness.

Rogers at first found that even if the therapist did nothing more than to rephrase the client's communication — that is to say, if the therapist clearly showed that he was receiving and exactly understanding the client's moment-by-moment communications — a very deep and self-propelled change process began and continued in the client. Something happens in an individual when he is understood in this way. Some change takes place in what he momentarily confronts. Something releases. He then has something else, further, to say; and if this, again, is received and understood, something still further emerges which the individual would not even have thought of (nor was capable of thinking), had not such a sequence of expressions and responses taken place.

Rogers next found that if he aimed to conceptualize exactly what the client now wished to communicate, and if he kept this aim visible and known to the client, he could formulate the client's present message much more deeply and accurately than the client had done. Perhaps the client gave a long series of externalized reports of incidents and his generally angry reactions. The therapist, after listening, could sense what I now call the felt meaning. Thus, in response to some long situational reports the therapist might say, "It frightens you to think that you are helpless when that sort of thing happens."

Rogers found that, while interpretations, deductions, and conceptual explanations were useless and usually resisted, the *exact* referring to the client's own momentarily felt meaning was almost always *welcome* to the client and seemed to release him into deeper and further self-expression and awareness.

I like to think of this diagrammatically, as two dimensions of a communication. Along one, say the horizontal dimension, one may deduce or adduce from what an individual says quite a lot of other things about him — his background, his usual behavior, his probable emotional patterns, traits, etc. One does this by moving away from what he now feels, through concepts and generalizations, *to other* things, which he does *not now feel.* In contrast, what I call the vertical dimension depends on the fact that any such communication refers inwardly to a mass of feelings, perceptions, intentions, judgements, wishes, etc., which *are now felt.* While a communication says only a little in verbal form, it arises from a great deal that is felt now in the speaker's awareness. I call it "felt meaning": Experiencing is *implicitly* complex and felt as such, even when what is explicitly said is very little. This implicit complexity is the individual's body life interaction in his situations. Therefore one can respond very deeply and yet remain continuous with what he now feels. The present theory will define "implicit" and "continuous with." I will show how interpersonal responses can be continuous with and carry forward, what is now felt, into new experiential process.

what theoretical way this feeling process functions to permit personality change.

The Personal Relationship

Just as the feeling process is observed as essential in personality change — while little is said to delineate, observably define, or theoretically account for it — so also the personal relationship is always cited. Can theory define this enormous and critical difference which it makes to the individual to live in relation to another person?

We observe that when the individual thinks about his experiences and emotions by himself, there is often little change. We observe that when he speaks about these things to *some* other people, equally little change occurs. However, when we come to the "therapeutic" or "effective" personal relationship, we say that "suggestion," or "libidinal support," or "approval and reinforcement," or the other person's "therapeutic attitudes," or the "conversation between the two unconsciousnesses," somehow obviates the factors which otherwise shape all his experiences and personal relations to keep the individual as he is. Somehow, now, he is said to "become aware" of what he previously could not be aware of, he is "influenced" by suggestions, he "overcomes" the transference, his "libidinal balance" is altered, he somehow now "perceives the attitudes" of the therapist, where he has always distorted and anticipated the attitudes of others. This is really the problem, not the explanation, of personality change.

But we do *observe* that almost always these changes occur in the context of a personal relationship. Some definitions of the kind of relationship which does (and the kind which does not) effect personality change have been offered (Rogers, 1957, 1959b). Very little has been said about how relationship events affect the conditions making for repression and the nature of contents, so that these alter.

So far we have formulated two problems of personality change and we have then cited *two observations*; the feeling process in the individual; and the personal relationship.

Our two observations and our two problems are related: simply, we may say that, while it is *theoretically* impossible for the individual to become aware of what he must *repress* and to change his personality *contents* into other *contents,* we *observe* that both occur *when* the individual is engaged in a deep and intense *feeling process* and in the context of a *personal relationship.* We need a theoretical account of this observed possibility, and we need to reformulate the theory of repression and the definitions of personality constituents, so that observed changes can be theoretically formulated.

The Theory

Basic Concepts — What Are Psychological Events?

(1) Experiencing

(*a*) The "ing" in the term "experiencing" indicates that experience is considered as a *process*. (We will have to define the theoretical conceptions which go to make up a process framework.)

Now, of course, the above is not really a definition, since the usage of the word "experience" is currently confused and various. The field of psychology lacks a theory of experience. However, the theory of experiencing (Gendlin, 1962b) attempts to provide a process for determining a theory of experience.

Since the term "experiencing" is extremely broad, more specific terms will be defined for specific aspects of experiencing. Anything in particular which we may consider will be a particular *manner* or *mode* of experiencing, or a particular *function* of it, or a particular logical pattern we choose to impose. The term "experiencing," then, denotes all "experience" viewed in terms of the process framework.

(*b*) The word "experience" in psychology, wherever employed, means concrete psychological events. The same is the case here. Experiencing is a process of concrete, ongoing events.

(*c*) Finally, by experiencing we mean a *felt* process. We mean inwardly sensed, bodily felt events, and we hold that the concrete "stuff" of personality or of psychological events is this flow of bodily sensing or feeling.

Experiencing is the process of concrete, bodily feeling, which constitutes the basic matter of psychological and personality phenomena.

(2) The Direct Referent

Both in social talk and in theory we so largely emphasize external events and logical meaning that it almost seems as if it were difficult to notice that, in addition to external objects and logic, we also have an inward bodily feeling or sensing. This is, of course, a commonplace that can be readily checked by anyone.

At any moment he wishes, one can refer directly to an inwardly felt datum. Experiencing, in the mode of being directly referred to in this way, I term the "direct referent."

Of course, there are other modes of experiencing. Situations and external events, symbols, and actions may interact with our feeling process quite without any reflexive attention paid to the direct referent. We are aware and feel without this direct attention as well as with it.

One can always refer directly to experiencing.

(3) Implicit

It is less apparent, but still easily checked by anyone, that this direct referent contains meaning. At first it may seem that experiencing is simply the inward sense of our body, its tension, or its well-being. Yet, upon further reflection, we can notice that only in this direct sensing do we have the meanings of what we say and think. For, without our "feel" of the meaning, verbal symbols are only noises (or sound images of noises).

For example, someone listens to you speak, and then says: "Pardon me, but I don't grasp what you mean." If you would like to restate what you meant in different words, you will notice that you must inwardly attend to your direct referent, your *felt* meaning. Only in this way can you arrive at different words with which to restate it.

In fact, we employ explicit symbols only for very small portions of what we think. We have most of it in the form of *felt* meanings.

For example, when we think about a problem, we must think about quite a number of considerations together. We cannot do so *verbally*. In fact, we could not think about the meaning of these considerations at all if we had to keep reviewing the verbal symbols over and over. We may review them verbally. However, to think upon the problem we must use the *felt* meanings — we must think of how "this" (which we previously verbalized) relates to "that" (which we also previously verbalized). To think "this" and "that," we employ their *felt* meanings.

When felt meanings occur in interaction with verbal symbols and we feel what the symbols mean, we term such meanings "explicit" or "explicitly known." On the other hand, quite often we have just such felt meanings without a verbal symbolization. Instead we have an event, a perception, or some word such as the word "this" (which represents nothing, but only points). When this is the case, we can term the meaning "implicit" or "implicitly felt, but not explicitly known."

Please note that "explicit" and "implicit" meanings are both *in awareness*. What we concretely feel and can inwardly refer to is certainly "in awareness" (though the term "awareness" will later require some reformulations). "Implicit" meaning is often confusingly discussed as if it were "unconscious" or "not in awareness." It should be quite clear that, since the direct referent is felt and is a direct datum of attention, it is "in awareness." *Anything termed "implicit" is felt in awareness.*

Furthermore, we may now add that even when a meaning is explicit (when we say "exactly what we mean") the felt meaning we have always contains a great deal more implicit meaning than we have made explicit. When we define the words we have just used, or when we "elaborate" what we "meant," we notice that the felt meanings we have been employing always contain implicitly many, many meanings — always many more than those to which we gave explicit formulation. We find that we employed these meanings. We find they were central to what we did make explicit, that they made up what we actually meant, yet they were only felt. They were implicit.

(4) Implicit Function (in Perception and Behavior)

So far we have thought of implicit meanings as existing only in the direct referent; that is to say, only if and when we directly refer to our experiencing as a felt datum. However, quite without such direct reference to experiencing, most of life and behavior proceed on implicit meanings. (Explicit meanings serve only a few special purposes.) We say, for example, that our interpretation of and reactions to present situations are determined by our "past" experiences. But in which way are our past experiences here *now*? For instance, if I am to observe an immediate situation and then describe it, in what way are there present my knowledge and experiences of past events, my knowledge of language, and my memories of this situation which I have just observed so that they function now? To describe the situation I just observed, my words will arise for me from a felt sense of what I have observed, reacted to, and now mean to say. Rarely, if at all, do I think *in words* what I now observe. Nor do I think each of the past experiences which function in this observing. Rarely do I think in explicit words what I will say. All these meanings *function implicitly as my present, concretely felt* experiencing.

(5) Completion; Carrying Forward

(6) Interaction

Implicit meanings are *incomplete.* Symbolic *completion* — or *carrying forward* — is a bodily felt process. There is an *interacting,* not an equation, between implicit meaning and symbols.

I must now make it quite clear that "implicit" and "explicit" meanings are different in nature. We may feel that some verbal statement says exactly what we mean; nevertheless, to feel the meaning is not the same kind of thing as verbal symbols. As we have shown, a felt meaning can contain very many meanings and can be further and further elaborated. Thus, the felt meaning is not the same in kind as the precise symbolized explicit meaning. The reason the difference in kind is so important is because if we ignore it we assume that explicit meanings are (or were) already in the implicit felt meaning. We are led to make the felt, implicit meaning a kind of dark place in which countless explicit meanings are hidden. We then wrongly assume that these meanings are "implicit" and felt only in that they are "hidden." I must emphasize that the "implicit" or "felt" datum of experiencing is a sensing of body life. As such it may have countless organized aspects, but this does not mean that they are conceptually formed, explicit, and hidden. Rather, we *complete* and form them when we explicate.

Before symbolization, the "felt" meanings are *incomplete.* They are analogous, let us say, to the muscle movement in my stomach which I can call "hunger." This sensation certainly "means" something about eating, but it does not "contain" eating. To be even more graphic, the feeling of hunger is not a repressed eating. It does not contain within itself the search for an animal, the killing and roasting of this animal, the eating, digesting, and absorbing of food particles, and the excretion and burying of wastes. Now just as all these steps (some of them patterned in the newborn organism, some of them learned) do not exist within the hunger sensation of muscle movement, so also the symbolic meaning "hunger" does not exist within it. Symbols must interact with the feeling before we have a meaning. The verbal symbol "hunger," just as "food," must interact with it before we carry forward the digestive process. The symbol "hunger," like other aspects of the search for food or my sitting down at a table, is a learned step of the digestive process and carries that process forward. Before that occurs, the feeling of the muscle movement implicitly contains the body's patterned readiness for organized interaction but not the formed conceptual units. Implicit bodily feeling is *preconceptual.* Only when *interaction* with verbal symbols (or events) actually occurs, is the process actually carried forward and the explicit meaning formed.[7] So long as it is implicit, it is *incomplete,* awaiting symbols (or events) with which it can interact in preorganized ways.

Thus, to explicate is to *carry forward* a bodily felt process. Implicit meanings are *incomplete.* They are not hidden conceptual units. They are not the same in nature as explicitly known meanings. There is no equation possible between implicit meanings and "their" explicit symbolization. Rather than an equation, there is an *interaction* between felt experiencing and symbols (or events).[8]

The Feeling Process — How Change Takes Place in the Individual

7) Focusing

"Focusing" (or, more exactly, "continuous focusing") will be defined in terms of four more specific definitions (8 — 11) below. "Focusing" is the whole process which ensues when the individual attends to the direct referent of experiencing.

We noted earlier that direct reference is one mode of experiencing. The feeling process we term "experiencing" also occurs in an individual's awareness without direct reference to it as a felt datum. In these other modes, also, experiencing has important functions in personality change. We will discuss them later.

Experiencing is essentially an *interaction* between feeling and "symbols" (attention, words, events), just as body life is an *interaction* between body and environment. In its basic nature, the physical life process is interaction. (This is an application of Sullivan's basic concepts.) For example, the body consists of cells which are interaction processes involving the environment (oxygen and food particles). If we apply this concept of interaction to experiencing, we can view it as an interaction of feeling and events ("events" here includes verbal noises, others' behaviors, external occurrences — anything that can interact with feeling).
For the full theory of affect and meaning see Gendlin (1962a). As will be seen later (definitions 15 — 18 and 26), the discussion here lays the ground for a view of personality which avoids the "content paradigm"; i.e., the erroneous assumption that psychological events involve conceptually formed static units.

"Focusing" refers to how one mode of experiencing, the direct referent, functions in ongoing personality change.

The foregoing definitions (1—6) will be employed in the following discussion and four more definitions concerning focusing will be formulated.

Focusing will be analyzed in four phases. The division into these phases is more a result of my way of formulation than of any inherent four-step divisibility in the process. Although it may occur in these clearly separable phases, more often it does not.

(8) Direct Reference in Psychotherapy (Phase One of Focusing)

A definitely felt, but conceptually vague referent is directly referred to by the individual. Let us say he has been discussing some troublesome situation or personal trait. He has described various events, emotions, opinions, and interpretations. Perhaps he has called himself "foolish," "unrealistic," and assured his listener that he really "knows better" than to react in the way he does. He is puzzled by his own reactions, and he disapproves of them. Or, what amounts to the same thing, he strongly defends his reactions against some real or imaginary critic who would say that the reactions make no sense, are self-defeating, unrealistic, and foolish. If he is understandingly listened to and responded to, he may be able to refer directly to the felt meaning which the matter has for him. He may then lay aside, for a moment, all his better judgment or bad feeling about the fact that he is as he is, and he may refer directly to the felt meaning of what he is talking about. He may then say something like: "Well, I know it makes no sense, but in some way it does." Or: "It's awfully vague to me what this is with me, but I feel it pretty definitely." It may seem as if language and logic are insufficient, but the trouble is merely that we are not used to talking about something which is conceptually vague, but definitely and distinctly *felt*.

If the individual continues to focus his attention on this direct referent (if he does not break off attending to it because it seems too foolish, or too bad, or too doubtful whether he isn't just coddling himself, etc.), he may become able to conceptualize some rough aspects of it. For example, he may find: "I feel that way whenever anyone does such-and-such to me." Or: "I think there is something about that kind of thing which could make something completely terrible and frightening happen to me, but that's silly. You have to accept things like that. That's life. But that's the way it feels, kind of a terror."

Having conceptualized some such rough aspect of "it," the individual usually feels the felt meaning more strongly and vividly, becomes more excited and hopeful about the process of focusing within himself, and is less likely now to settle for the conceptual explanations, accusations, and apologies. It is a profound discovery for most people when they find it possible to continue direct reference. It comes to be deeply valued as "I am in touch with myself."

As the individual continues to focus on such a direct referent, he may puzzle over what a funny kind of a "this" he is talking about. He may call it "this feeling," or "this whole thing," or "this is the way I am when such-and-such occurs." Very clearly it is an inwardly sensed referent in his present experiencing. Nothing is vague about the definite way he *feels* it. He can turn to it with his inward attention. Only *conceptually* is it vague.

A very important and surprising fact about direct reference to felt meanings is that if the matter under consideration is anxiety producing or highly uncomfortable, this felt discomfort *decreases* as the individual directly refers to the felt meaning. One would have expected the opposite. Certainly the opposite is true, for example, when the individual chooses between various topics for discussion. The prospect of talking about this difficult, anxiety-provoking matter certainly makes the person more anxious than the prospect of talking about some neutral or pleasant subject. Thus, he may be in quite a lot of inward pain as he decides to bring the matter up at all. However, once into the topic, the more directly he attends to the direct referent, the felt meaning, the less his discomfort and anxiety. If he momentarily loses track of it, the anxiety flares up again, and the diffuse discomfort of the topic returns.

As the individual symbolizes some aspects of the felt meaning, he senses its rightness partly by the degree of *easing* of the anxiety which he feels.

In contrast to the anxiety or discomfort, the felt meaning itself becomes sharper, more distinctly felt, as he refers to and correctly symbolizes what it is. In fact, his sense of whether or not he has "correctly" symbolized is partly just his sense of increased intensity of the felt meaning.[9]

This decreased anxiety is a very surprising fact, much against the general assumptions about anxiety-provoking material. We generally assume that to focus directly on the experiencing makes us more anxious. My observations indicate that increased anxiety comes from topic choice, and it is this which we generally expect. On the other hand, given the topic, the more we focus directly upon the felt meaning, and the more of it we symbolize correctly, the more relief we feel. Even a little error in symbolizing ("no, what I just said isn't quite it") again increases the anxiety.

We may theoretically interpret this observation in terms of definitions 5 and and our use of the work of Mead and Sullivan. To symbolize a directly felt implicit meaning carries the organismic process a step forward. It is felt so. It also appears from this that we should consider the direct reference (or the giving of attention), as itself, already a kind of symbolizing. Direct reference,

The word "correctly" here really refers just to this interaction between the felt referent and the symbols which we are describing. The fact that, a few minutes later, the same type of interaction with further symbols can again produce a very different, yet now "correct" further conceptualization shows that "correctness" does not imply that a given set of symbols means what the felt referent alone means. Rather, "correctness" refers to the experienced effect which certain symbols produce and which is described above, and in definitions 5 and 6.

as well as the resulting symbolizations, involves bodily felt tension relief.[10]

There are other ways of describing the individual's focusing on a direct referent of experiencing. We may say that, at such moments, his experiencing is "ahead of his concepts." It "guides" his concepts. He forms concepts and "checks them against" his directly felt meaning and, on this basis, decides their correctness.

As he continues to refer directly to the felt meaning (he is probably calling it "this"), he may find that his previous formulation which felt correct must be replaced by another which now feels more correct. The listener can help by pointing his words also at "this" and by helping to find words and concepts that might fit it.[11] The listener, of course, cannot judge the correctness. Not even the individual himself judges it but, we might say somewhat poetically, his direct referent does the judging. Both persons may thus be surprised by the direction which the symbolizing takes.

The above has been a description of how an individual may directly refer to or "focus on" a direct referent of experiencing which, for him, constitutes the felt meaning of some topic, situation, behavior, or personality aspect.

(9) Unfolding (Phase Two of Focusing)

Sometimes, in focusing on a directly felt referent, there is a gradual step-by-step process of coming to know explicitly what it is. Yet, it may "open up" in one dramatic instant. Most often there is both a gradual coming to know it better and some instants during which there is a very noticeable "opening up." With a great physical relief and sudden dawning, the individual suddenly knows. He may sit there, nodding to himself, thinking only words such as "yes, I've got it" quite without as yet finding concepts to tell himself what it is he "has got." However, he knows that now he *can* say. It is possible that, if he is now suddenly interrupted, he may "lose it," so that later he can only say, "I really felt I knew what it was at that moment, but I've lost it now." Usually, however, he will as swiftly as possible find concepts and words to say what has opened up. It is almost always a number of things. For example:

[10] Research (Gendlin and Berlin, 1961) employing autonomic correlates has borne out this observation operationally. Individuals were given tape-recorded instructions to engage in various processes. After each instruction there was a period of silence in which to carry it out. It was found that galvanic skin resistance (also skin temperature and heart rate) indicated tension reduction during the period when individuals were instructed to (and reported later that they did) focus inwardly on the felt meanings of troublesome personal problem. It has continued to be difficult to define and check individuals' performances after this and other instructions. Therefore, this research remains tentative. Nevertheless, several replications have supported the observation that while threatening topics in general raise tension, direct inward focusing involves tension reduction.

[11] It is extremely important that the listener refers his words to "this" felt datum in the individual and that he shares the sense that the datum itself decides what is correct and what is not. It is much less important whether or not the listener's words turn out be accurate.

Yes, *of course* he is afraid, he realizes. He has not permitted himself even to think about dealing with *this* and *this* aspect of the situation, and this has been because he has not believed that these aspects really existed. Well, yes, he did realize they existed, but he also felt compelled to blame himself for them as if he merely imagined them. And if they do exist (and they do), he does not know how he could possibly live with them. He has not allowed himself to try to deal with them (he now realizes) or even to consider them anything other than merely his imagination, because, my God, if they are really there, then he is helpless. Then there is *nothing* he can do! But they are there. Well, it is a relief to know at least that.

This example illustrates the multiplicity one generally finds in an implicit meaning which was felt as one "this." It may, as in the example, be a multiplicity which can still be thought of as "one thing." Experiencing has no given definite unit experiences.

The example also illustrates that, often, the meanings one finds with such great relief are not at all pleasant or good. The problem is not at all resolved. Quite the contrary, now it *really* looks impossible. Now it seems clear why one has been so anxious. It *does* seem hopeless. Yet it is a great and physically experienced tension reduction when the directly felt referent "unfolds" in this way.

The unfolding of a direct referent always involves a surprising and deeply emotional recognition of the good sense of our own (previously so seemingly irksome) feelings. *"Of course,"* we say over and over, "Of course!" Or, we say "Well, what do you know, that's what that was!"

Because what was previously felt now actually "makes sense," problem resolutions can occur at this stage. For, we may see that given *this or that judgment,* or perception, or event, or situation, "of course" we felt as we did, but we do not now judge it in the same way. However, my example illustrated that even when the solution seems further away than ever, still the physiological tension reduction occurs, and a genuine change takes place. I believe that this change is really more basic than the resolution of specific problems.

A whole vast multiplicity of implicit aspects in the person's functioning and dysfunctioning is always involved. For, when a direct referent of experiencing "opens up," much more change has occurred than the cognitive realization of this or that. This is most dramatically evident when, after the "unfolding," the individual still sees no way out. He says, "At least I know what it is now, but how will I ever change it or deal with it?" Yet, during the following days and in the next therapy hour, it turns out that he is already different, that the quality of the problem has changed and his behavior has been different. And, as for a good explanation of all this resolution . . . "well, it just seems all right now." There is a global change in the whole manner of experiencing in this regard. From this *felt change,* with its lack of logical description, come some of our simple-minded notions: "Just accept it," we tell ourselves and others.

We can recall that we have observed individuals, such as I just described, *report* a basic change in such a simplistic way:

"How is everything different?"

"Well, it just seems OK now!"

"Do you still feel that such-and-such might happen and you couldn't deal with it?"

"Yes, but now I kind of feel, well, that's life. That's the way it is, you have to accept things like that."

And that is just what he had said to himself over and over again, *without any effect,* before the process in which he focused on the felt meaning and it unfolded!

Thus, as I have said, only sometimes does *what* is unfolded lead to a solution in an explicable way. More often, deep global feeling change occurs as one unfolds the direct referent, even when it seems to open into something which sounds worse and more hopeless than one had expected. Whether or not some specific resolution is noticeable, the change appears to be broad and global. It is not just this problem resolved, or that trait changed, but a change in many areas and respects. We can say that the broad multiplicity of aspects which are implicit in any felt meaning are all of them changed — thus the global change. Or we can say that meanings are aspects of the experiencing process and that the very *manner of* experiencing changes, hence also the quality of all of its meanings.

As one client put it: "Until now I always saw this problem in black and white terms, and I struggled for a solution that would be gray. But now, this new way isn't black or white, *or* gray. It's in color!" Thus the unfolding of a felt referent does not just inform one about what was involved but, rather, it changes the whole manner in which one experiences.

(10) Global Application (Phase Three of Focusing)

This global way in which the process of direct reference and unfolding affects many aspects of the person is noticeable not only in his later reports of the resulting difference, but also in the moments which immediately follow the unfolding of a felt referent. The individual is flooded by many different associations, memories, situations, and circumstances, all in relation to the felt referent. Although conceptually they can be very different, they share the same felt meaning with which he has been dealing. Except for this they may concern quite different and unrelated matters.[12] "Oh, and that's also why I can't get up any enthusiasm for this-and-this." "Yes, and another thing about it is, this comes in every time somebody tells me what to do or think. I can't

---

[12] We can always apply logic after the process and formulate the relationships implied but we can almost never choose correctly ahead of time which of the thousands of possible relations between various problems and topics will function in a concretely felt process as described above.

say, well, what *I* think is more important, because, see, this way of making myself wrong comes in there." "Oh, and also, back when this and this happened, I did the *same* thing."

During this "wide application" period which often follows the unfolding of a felt referent, the individual may sit in silence, only occasionally voicing some of the pieces from this flood.

I realize that some of the foregoing observations have been termed by others as "insight." I believe that is a misnomer. First, the global application is in no way a figuring out, nor is it chiefly a better understanding. Rather, insight and better understanding are the results, the by-products, of this process, as a few of its very many changed aspects call attention to themselves. One can be sure that for every relation or application the individual here explicitly thinks, there are thousands which he does not think of, but which have, nevertheless, just changed. Not his thinking about the difference which the unfolding has made, but the unfolding itself, changes him in all these thousands of respects. The change occurs whether or not he thinks of any such applications, and whether or not he considers the unfolding to be a resolving. For, as I emphasized, he may well walk out saying, "I have no idea what I can do with this, or how I change it." But, it has already changed, and the great multiplicity of respects in which "it" *implicitly functions* have all changed.

(11) Referent Movement (Phase Four of Focusing)

A definite alteration or movement in the direct referent is felt. This "referent movement" often occurs after the three phases just described. When there has been *direct reference*, dramatic *unfolding* occurs, and when the flood of *global application* subsides, the individual finds that he now refers to a direct referent which feels different. The *implicit* meanings which he can symbolize from this direct reference are now quite different ones. It is a new direct reference; and so the four-phase process begins again.

But focusing is not always such a neatly divisible four-phase process. As noted before, *unfolding* can occur with or without a noticeable flood of *global application*. Unfolding can also occur quite undramatically, in very small steps of successive symbolization. And, even without unfolding, even without any symbolization which feels "correct," the individual's direct reference can *carry forward* the feeling process and is experienced with bodily tension relief. What we are here calling the fourth phase of focusing, the *referent movement,* can occur at any of these times. Usually, direct reference alone does not change or move the direct referent, but does make it stronger, sharper, and more distinctly felt. It increases its intensity as a feeling and diminishes the diffuse tension, discomfort, and anxiety. However, sometimes the mere process of continuous direct reference will change or "move" the direct referent. More often, such a movement occurs after at least some unfolding and symbolizing, and especially after the felt flooding of global application.

The individual distinctly feels a change in the quality of the felt referent. It is not only a change but a directly experienced "give" or "movement" which feels right and welcome. Its tremendous importance lies in the fact that after such a referent movement (even very small), the implicit meanings are now different. The "scenery," as it were, which one confronts, changes.

It is just this referent movement which is usually missing when one *talks at* oneself, when one has recited all the good reasons, considerations, and ways one should feel and would be more sensible to feel, etc. Most often, thereafter, the *same unchanged* felt referent is still there, and the same diffuse anxiety as well. From this lack of referent movement, one knows that nothing has really changed.

Conversely, after referent movement, the meanings and symbolizations one formulates are different. The relevant considerations are different. The whole scene is different. Of course, most often in one such step one does not find "solutions." The individual may say: "Well, that doesn't help me either, because now this helpless feeling, it just seems like the worst crime in the world to be helpless, weak, just let everything happen to you. I can't stand that either. I don't know what is so bad about it. I mean, if actually, in reality, I can't do anything about it anyhow." Here we see that there is no hint of anything like a solution, but the relevant surrounding considerations have now changed. What he looks at and symbolizes is different as the felt referent to which he directly refers is different.

Reference movement gives direction to the focusing process. The individual's attention and symbolizing tends to follow that direction which produces referent movement.

Without reference movement, what is said is "merely" talk, "merely" intellectualization, "merely" hair splitting, or "merely" reporting.

Reference movement is the direct experience that something more than logic and verbalization has occurred. The movement can often be logically analyzed (that is to say, logical relationships can be formulated between what he said earlier and what he says now). However, such logical analysis can be made between any verbalizations, whether or not there has been reference movement. And, often, for a small bit of reference movement the logical or conceptual shift is extremely large. Even a *slight* reference movement can make for what conceptually looks like a totally different vantage point.

Reference movement is a change in the felt meaning which functions in symbolizing.

I hope I have conveyed something of the overlapping characters of what call the four phases of focusing. To summarize them: phase one, *direct refer ence* to a felt meaning which is conceptually vague but definite as felt; phase two, *unfolding* and the symbolizing of some aspects; phase three, a flooding o *global application;* phase four, *referent movement,* and the process can begi again with phase one.

These four definitions (8—11) define "focusing."[13]

[13] I must now describe some common sorts of so-called "internal" attention which do not involve direct reference and thus are not *focusing*.

Since the term "experiencing" includes any kind of experience at all, so long as we consider it as inwardly *felt* and apply to it the theoretical formulation of *process*, misunderstandings have arisen concerning the mode of experiencing called the *direct referent*. By this latter, more specific term we do not at all mean just anything at all which can be called inward attention.

Especially since the direct referent is "felt," it has been confused with emotions. (Emotions are also said to be "felt.") But the direct referent is internally complex and an individual feels "in touch with himself" when he refers to it, while emotions are internally all one quality . . . they are "sheer." They often keep him from sensing that in himself which is the complex ground of the emotion.

This and other distinctions will become clearer in the following list of kinds of occurrences in an individual which are not direct reference and thus are not focusing.

Direct reference is not:

(1) *Sheer emotions.* The emotions of guilt, shame, embarrassment, or feeling that I am "bad" are *about* me or this aspect of my experience and its meaning to me. These emotions are not themselves the experience and its meaning to me. The emotions as such are not a direct reference to the felt experiencing. I must, at least momentarily, *get by* these emotions *about it* (or about myself) in order to refer directly to what all this means to me, why and what makes me feel ashamed. For example, I must say to myself: "All right, yes, I *am* very ashamed; but for a minute now, although it makes me feel very ashamed, I want to sense *what* this is in me."

For example: One client spent many sleepless hours each night with anxiety, shame, and resentment. He blamed himself for his reactions to a certain situation. He felt foolish and ashamed of the whole thing. As he tried to resolve it, he alternately felt resentful (he would decide to confront them, fight it out, not back down, etc.), and alternately he felt ashamed (he was a fool, and humiliatingly so, etc.). Only in the psychotherapy hour did it become possible for him to focus directly on "this," what it was, how it felt, and where it "lived" in him. In "this" he found a good many valid perceptions concerning the other people and the situation which he had not been able to specify before, and a good many personal aspects of himself. During a number of hours he directly referred to successive direct referents and felt meanings. Yet between hours he was unable to do this alone, but felt only shame or resentment. Only by moving temporarily "on by" these emotions could he refer directly to "this," "what I feel," about which, granted, I also have these emotions.

It seems quite striking and universal that we feel guilt, shame, and badness, *instead* of feeling that concerning which we feel shame, guilt, and badness. It is almost as if these emotions themselves preclude our feeling what it all is to us — not so much because they are so unpleasant, as because they skip the point at which we might complete, symbolize, respond or attend to that which centrally we feel. I am inclined to hypothesize that guilt, shame, and badness are emotions which occur as responses instead of the response which, by action or symbolizing, we would otherwise give our felt referent. These emotions seem to complete but actually "skip" the incomplete implicit meanings. It is like an animal whose response to hunger is to bite itself in the leg. Instead of responding with a behavior which in some way "symbolizes" the hunger and carries forward the organismic digestion process, such an animal would be most aware of the pain in its leg and would behave accordingly. At any rate, the preoccupation with these emotions is not to be confused with the felt meaning which, though connected to these emotions, needs the focusing.

One client describes it in terms of a hurricane: "If you only go so far into something, it's like going into a hurricane and getting terribly blown around. You have to go into it and then keep going further and further *in* till you get to the eye of the hurricane. There it's quiet and you can see where you are." This beautifully expresses the fact that the direction of focusing is definitely into the emotions, not away from them, yet also that focusing involves something qualitatively very different than merely "being blown around" by the emotions. The illustration also captures something of the centrality, depth, and quiet which one finds — the quality which others have called "being in touch with myself." The felt referent, for the moment, *is* "me." It *unfolds* and is a thousand things. In comparison, the emotional tone which attaches to it and precedes it is not itself a thousand things. To remain with it merely feeds it. There is always a "breath-held," tense, tight quality about most of these emotional tones. Yet to turn away from the emotion is to turn away also from the direction in which one "finds oneself." Thus, one must "move into" and "through," or "on by," these emotional tones to the direct referent which is the *felt meaning* of it all.

The difference between focusing and "wallowing" or "being trapped in" certain emotions is most dramatically evident when one compares the usual experiences of an individual when he works on a personality difficulty alone and when he does so in the presence of an understanding other person. The difference is dramatic, because during many hours he has gone round and round, feeling the same series of emotions and lacking any *referent movement*. In contrast, often even just saying to the other person a little of what one has been feeling and thinking produces direct reference and referent movement. Later I will discuss this role of the other person in making focusing and other therapeutic processes possible. Another person's responses to the emotions, for instance, can make it possible to "grant them," "let them," and "get by" them, so as to refer directly to the felt meanings. It is often possible, though always unsteady and difficult, for the individual to focus by himself.

(2) *Circumstantial orbit.* Just as one may get lost in the sheer emotions of guilt, shame, or badness, so one may also get lost in an inward recitation of circumstances, such as: what one ought to have done or did do; what others did, or might have done, or can be imagined to have done, etc. Such circumstantial play and replay, the inward repetitions of conversations, and dramatic re-enactings are clearly different from the felt meaning all this has and on which the individual could (perhaps, with help) focus. Often the client arrives for the therapy hour after sleepless night and tired days of this kind of circumstantial "runaround" and finds, with a few responses to the felt meaning of "all this," that with great relief he now directly refers to and unfolds the felt meaning. No matter what a bad look it turns out to have, the physically felt and verbalized steps of focusing are clearly and relievingly different from the circumstantial orbit.

(3) *Explanatory orbit.* Attempts at explanations are different from direct *reference*: "Is it just that I'm so hostile?" "It must mean that I'm projecting some latent homosexuality." "This means I have a need to fail." "It's just that I'm trying to be right." "I'm just trying to get the love I didn't get as a child." "This is paranoid." "Other people don't get upset at this, so it must be that I'm not grateful for what I have."

Whether the explanatory concepts are simple and foolish, or sophisticated and quite correct, they are useless unless one employs them as pointers to momentarily name and hold onto a directly felt meaning. Without that, our cogitates in a vacuum and gets "no further." The explanatory "runaround" races the mental engine, disengaged from the wheels. It make one tired and confused, and it is quite different from focusing on the felt meaning. Even one small step of the focusing process can change the inner scene so that one's whole set of explanatory concepts suddenly becomes irrelevant. In comparison with the felt meaning, explanatory concepts are so gross, so general, so empty, that even when they are accurate they are helpless abstractions.

(4) *Self-engineering.* A fourth runaround consists in something that might be called self-engineering." In this also one does not attend to one's felt meaning. Instead, one "talks at" oneself, inwardly. One is very active and constructive, arranging and rearranging one's feelings without stopping to sense quite what they are. This self-engineering i clearly different from focusing on a felt referent and the sensing and symbolizing of it implicit meaning.

Self-engineering is not always futile. In fact, it can succeed exactly to the extent to which one's experiencing in the given regard functions implicity. The trouble with will power and enginering is not, as Sullivan held and Rogers sometimes seems to assume that there is no such thing. There is. One is not always automatically "wafted" into

(12) The Self-Propelled Feeling Process

As the individual engages in focusing, and as *referent movement* occurs, he finds himself pulled along in a direction he neither chose nor predicted. There is a very strong impelling force exerted by the direct referent just then felt. The individual may "get off the track," "talk about something else," or put up with considerable distracting comments and useless deductions by his listener; and still the given felt, direct referent remains strikingly as the "next thing" with which he must deal.

If the listener's responsiveness makes it possible, the individual finds himself moving from one referent movement and unfolding to another and another. Each time the inward scene changes, new felt meanings are there for him. The cyles of the four phases set into motion an overall feeling process. This feeling process has a very striking, concretely felt, self-propelled quality.

As a psychotherapist I have learned that I must depend on this self-propelled feeling process in the client. This is an important principle, because I have the power to distract him. When I do so (by too many explanations or insights of my own into what he says), then this feeling process does not occur. On the other hand, I have also learned that my questions and self-expressions can be useful, provided I always intend what I say to refer to the individual's felt referent and I show that I would like him to continue to focus on it.

In order to permit the feeling process to arise, we must sometimes remain silent, at least for some brief periods. If either he or I talk all the time, little direct reference can take place. Therefore, when he has stopped talking and I have stopped responding, I am glad if there is a little silence in which he can feel the meaning of what we have been saying. I am especially glad if the next thing he then says follows not simply and logically from what we have said, but shows that he has been immersed in something felt. In this way I can notice that a felt referent has provided the transition from what he did say to what he now says. This "descent" into himself, this focusing, and the overall feeling process which arises, give verbalization to the underlying flow of events

---

action or self-control. Willpower, decision, and self-engineering are often necessary. However, they cannot be effectively exerted at points where experiencing does not implicity function. In such regards self-responses or the responses of others are required first, so that the process can be carried forward and experiencing then does implicity function.

This focusing may be what has always been meant in religious terms by "listening to the still small voice." This has more recently been confused with conscience (and, only in very well-adjusted people can one identify conscience with direct reference). All but a few people have been puzzled as to where inside to "listen" and "hear" this "voice." The above indicates that to "listen" really means to keep quiet, to stop "talking at" yourself, and to sense just what is there, bodily felt, meaningful, and about to become clearer and then verbalizable.

The rule for focusing — a rule to be applied inwardly to oneself — is "Keep quiet and listen!" Then, by referring to the concretely felt referent, it will unfold; the sense of its meaning, and then the words, will come into focus.

of personality change. This self-propelled feeling process is the essential motor of personality change.

Once this feeling process has arisen, it continues even between the times the individual engages in the four-phase focusing process I have outlined. Thus, during the several days between two psychotherapy hours, the client may find important thoughts, feelings, memories, and insights "coming" to him. He may find a generalized "stirring," an inward "eventfulness," even without a specific symbolized content. Thus the overall *feeling process* comes to be self-propelled and broader than just the four phases of focusing I have described.

The Role of the Personal Relationship — How Another Person's Responses Affect the Individual's Experiencing, and How Personality "Contents" Are Inherently Changeable Thereby

We tend to be so concerned with content (symbolized meanings) that we sometimes discuss psychological questions as if personality were nothing but contents. We forget the obvious differences which exist not only in *what* an individual's experience is at a given moment, but also in *how* he experiences. Thus we ask a question such as this: What difference does the personal relationship make, since the individual can think and feel the same contents when he is alone as he can when he talks to another person?

Often a psychotherapist (or any listener who wants to be helpful) will feel that he must "do something," "add something," bring in some new content or insight, so that he will be helpful and make a difference.

Yet, there is already all the difference between *how* one thinks and feels *alone* and *how* one thinks and feels *with another person*. The conceptual content may (for a time) be the same as the individual can think and feel by himself; but, the *manner* of experiencing will be totally different. Consider, for example, the type of listener who interrupts with his own concerns and is inclined to be annoyed and critical long before he understands what is said. With him, my manner of experiencing will be quite constricted. I will think of less and feel less than I do when I am alone. I will tend to say what I must in round, general, swiftly finished terms. I will *not* tend to feel deeply, or intensely, or richly. Certain things will never occur to me when I am with him or, if they do occur to me, I will save them for the time when I am alone, and can feel them through without the constricting effects of his responses. We all know this difference between the manner of our experiencing with certain persons as compared with when we are alone.

Similarly, there are others (we are fortunate to know one) with whom we feel more intensely and freely whatever we feel. We think of more things, we have the patience and the ability to go more deeply into the details, we bear better our own inward strain when we are speaking to this person. If we are sad and dry-eyed alone, then with this person we cry. If we are stopped by our guilt, shame, and anxiety, then with this person we come to life again, inwardly, as being more than these emotions. If we have showered disgust and annoyance on ourselves to the point of becoming silent and deadened inside, then with this person we "come alive" again. As we tell this person some old, familiar, many times repeated story, we find it richer and freshly meaningful, and we may not get all the way through it for the many facets of personal meaning which now unfold.

How shall we theoretically explain these differences in the *manner* in which we experience in different relationships and alone?

(13) Manner of Experiencing

Whatever the content which we are said to experience, there is also the manner in which we experience. Few terms in our formal psychological language denote differences in *manner of experiencing*. Let us, therefore, define some more terms. (These terms overlap, so that fully explicating one of them would give us the others.)

Immediacy of Experiencing. Immediacy can be contrasted with disassociation or postponement of affect. Descriptive and poetic terms are usually invented by individuals to describe immediacy and its opposites: "I do everything right, but I'm not in it"; or "I am a spectator of my own behavior"; or "What it means to me so occupies me that I don't feel what is going on at all"; "Life is going on all right, but I'm in some back room. I merely hear about it, I'm not living it."

Presentness. Am I reacting to the present situation? Am I feeling a *now,* or is the present situation merely an occasion, a cue for a familiar, repetitious structured pattern of feeling?

Richness of Fresh Detail. Any moment's experience has a host of fresh details that I experience implicitly, some of which I could symbolize and differentiate. In contrast, the structured feeling pattern consists of only a few emotions and meanings. Sometimes, however, I have none of the richness of the present, only the same old, stale feeling pattern. In such instances psychologists are inclined to notice chiefly the content of the stale pattern. We say: "This is a protesting reaction against authority," or "this is a need to dominate," or a "partial" infantile sex drive such as "voyeurism," or "exhibitionism," or a "passive-aggressive need." We tend to neglect the fact that such feeling patterns are also different in *manner* from an immediate, present, and richly detailed experiencing. It is not only that I react poorly to authority. Rather, I react this way to *every* person whom I perceive as an authority. And, more important, I react *only* to his being an authority, not to him as a person, and to the very many present facets of him and our situation which are different from any other situation. The "authority pattern," or any similar pattern, is really only a bare outline. My experiencing is *structure-bound* in manner, when I experience only this bare outline and feel only this bare set of emotions, lacking the myriad of fresh detail of the present. I might resent my boss's behaviors even if my manner of experiencing were optimal. Too much time and attention is wasted in deciding whether my reaction to him is to be blamed on me or on him. It does not matter. What does matter is the *manner* of my experiencing. No matter how obnoxious he may really be, if my experiencing is structure bound, I do not even experience *his* obnoxiousness except as mere cues for the experience of my old bare structure.

Frozen Wholes. We often speak of contents or "experiences" as if they were set, shaped units with their own set structure. But this is the case only to the extent that my experiencing is structure bound in its manner. For example, when I listen as you tell me something of your feelings I may occasionally think of my own experiences. I need the feelings and meanings of my own experiences in order to understand yours. However, if I must keep thinking of my experiences explicitly as such, then I cannot grasp the meanings yours have to you. I will then insist that your experiences are the same as mine (or, if I am wise, I will know that I am not understanding you). Unless *my* experiences *implicitly function* so that I can newly understand *you,* I cannot really understand you at all. Insofar as my experiencing is structure bound, it does not implicitly function. It is not "seamlessly" felt by me with its thousands of implicit aspects functioning so that I arrive at some fresh meaning, something you are trying to convey to me. Rather, in this regard, my experience is a "frozen whole" and will not give up its structure. Whatever requires the implicit function of experiencing in these regards makes me feel my whole frozen structure and nothing new.

Repetitive versus Modifiable. Since within the bare structured *frozen whole* experiencing does not function in interaction with present details, the structure is not *modified* by the present. Hence, it remains the same, it repeats itself in many situations without ever changing. So long as the manner of experiencing remains structure bound, the structures themselves are not *modifiable* by present occurrences.

Optimal Implicit Functioning. It is clear from the above that, to the extent the manner of experiencing is structure bound, the implicit functioning of experiencing cannot occur. Instead of the many, many implicit meanings of experiencing which must interact with present detail to interpret and react, the individual has a structured feeling pattern.

These terms define *manner of experiencing.*

(14) In Process Versus Structure Bound

Experiencing is always in process and always functions implicitly. The respects in which it is *structure bound* are not experiencing. The conceptual content *in an abstract way* can *appear* to be the same with different manners of experiencing. However, in the structure-bound manner the experiencing process is, in given respects, missing. By "missing" we mean that from an external viewpoint we may notice that the implicit functioning of experiencing ought to be there, but there is only the process-skipping structure, *and the experiencing surrounding it and leading up to it.* Thus we say that *structure-bound* aspects are not *in process*.

(15) Reconstituting

Earlier we said that symbols, or events can *carry forward* the process of experiencing. Experiencing is essentially an *interaction* between feeling and "symbols" (attention, words, events), just as body life is an *interaction* between body and environment. In its basic nature, the physical life process is interaction. It requires not only the body's respiratory machinery but also oxygen. And the body's respiratory machinery itself consists of cells which again are chemical processes involving oxygen and food particles. If we apply this conceptual model of interaction process to experiencing, we can consider it an *interaction* of *feeling* and events ("events" here includes verbal noises, others' behaviors, external occurrences — anything that can interact with feeling).

If we formulate the theory of experiencing in this way, we can formulate why the other person's responses so basically affect the individual's manner of experiencing.[14] For, *if there is a response, there will be an ongoing interaction process.* Certain aspects of the personality will be *in process*. However, without the response, there will not (in these respects) be a process at all.

Subjectively, phenomenologically, people describe this as "coming alive inside," or as "feeling many more facets" of oneself. *Responses* can *reconstitute* the experiencing process in respects in which, before the response, there was no process (no interaction between feeling and something else and hence no *ongoing* interaction process).

The peculiar condition of "experience" which is not *in process* has puzzled psychology for many years. It has been called "unconscious,"[15] "repressed," "covert," "inhibited," "denied," etc. The fact is that we observe individuals awarely and actively feeling (in ways which were missing before) when they are responded to in certain ways. The individual feels that the feelings "have always been there in some sense, but were not felt." Psychology cannot deny this common observation. One way of formulating it is as the *reconstituting* of the experiencing process.

(16) Contents Are Process Aspects

What is a "content" of experience (or "*an* experience," when that is meant to

---

[14] Our formulation here may be seen as an extension of Sullivan's basic concepts referred to earlier at the beginning of our discussion of Sullivan.
[15] Recall our earlier discussion of the repression paradigm. Also see later discussion of the unconscious, definition 24.

refer to a given content)? We noted (definitions 3 and 5) that the felt implicit meanings of experiencing can be put into interaction with verbal symbols. We then say that the symbols "mean" or "represent" what the experience is "of" or, more simply, that the symbols symbolize the experience. Such a *symbolized unit is a content.*[16]

Thus, in order for there to be a content, some aspect of *implicit function* (see definition 4) must be ongoing in interaction with symbols.

But what if there are not, as yet, any *verbal* symbols? Is there then no ongoing experiencing either? The answer is that verbal symbols are not the only events with which feelings can be in an interaction process. External occurrences, other people's responses, even our own attention, can interact with feeling so as to constitute a process.

Therefore, it is often the case that there is an ongoing experiencing process without verbal symbols. In fact, most situations and behaviors involve feeling in interaction with nonverbal events. Experiencing *functions implicitly* with countless meanings which, as felt (without verbal symbolization), are aspects of the ongoing interaction.

The respects in which experiencing is ongoing are also those in which we *can* verbally symbolize contents. The respects in which it is not ongoing (no matter how it may appear externally) cannot be verbally symbolized. Only pale, useless, general meaning can be given to concepts of the supposed contents which are not at this instant process aspects. Contents are aspects of ongoing felt process. That is to say, contents are *process aspects*.

(17) The Law of Reconstitution of the Experiencing Process

An individual can symbolize only those aspects which are *already* implicitly functioning in ongoing experiencing.

In any experiencing (that is to say, in any ongoing interaction of feeling and events) a great many implicit meanings are process aspects (so-called "contents"). Thus, for any moment's ongoing experiencing one can symbolize a great many contents. These are *incomplete* (definition 5) until some symbols (or events) *carry forward* the process in these respects.

Thus there are two different definitions: to *carry forward,* and to *reconstitute.* To "carry forward" means that symbols (or events) occur to interact with *already* implicitly functioning aspects of ongoing experiencing. To "reconstitute" means that the process has become ongoing and implicitly functions in respects in which it previously was not ongoing.

We can now state a *law of the reconstitution of experiencing process:* When certain *implicitly functioning* aspects of experiencing are *carried forward* by symbols or events, the resulting experiencing always involves *other* sometimes newly *reconstituted* aspects which thereby come to be *in process* and *function implicitly* in that experiencing.

---

[16] Compare our earlier discussion of the "content paradigm."

(18) Hierarchy of Process Aspects

If contents are viewed as process aspects — that is to say, as implicitly functioning aspects of ongoing experiencing — then *the law of reconstitution* implies that *certain* contents (process aspects) must be symbolized before certain *other contents* (process aspects) can thereby become process aspects that are capable of being symbolized.

This fact gives the individual's self-exploration an ordered or hierarchical character. It is as if he can "get to" certain things only via certain other things. We must let him travel his "own road," not because we believe in democracy, and not because we like self-reliance, but because *only* when the experiencing process has been reconstituted, so that certain aspects become implicit in it, can he symbolize these.

(19) Self-Process

To the extent that experiencing does *implicitly function,* the individual may respond to himself and may *carry forward* his own experiencing. This interaction of the individual's feelings with his own (symbolic or actual) behavior,[17] we term "self." A more exact term: *self-process.*

To the extent that experiencing does not implicitly function, the individual cannot respond to himself and carry forward his experiencing. In whatever respects it does not function (is structure bound), responses are needed first to *reconstitute* the interaction process of experiencing in these respects.

Why is it that the individual himself does not *carry forward* his already *implicitly functioning* experiencing in ways which would newly reconstitute *structure-bound* aspects of it? Of course, he cannot respond to the structure-bound aspects, as such (they are not implicitly functioning), but neither can the psychotherapist. The psychotherapeutic response can be defined as one which responds to aspects of experiencing which *are* implicitly functioning, but to which the individual himself tends not to respond. More precisely, his own response is a whole frozen structure which does not carry forward the felt experiencing process in these respects.

(20) The Reconstituting Response Is Implicitly Indicated

The response which will *reconstitute* the experiencing process (in some now *structure-bound* respect) is already implied[18] in the individual's experiencing.

---

[17] Compare George Herbert Mead (1938, p. 445): "The self ... grown out of the more primitive attitude of indicating to others, and later arousing in the organism the response of the other, because this response is native to the organism, so that the stimulation which calls it out in another trends to call it out in the individual himself."

[18] This point has been made by others. Freud said that the energy of the defense comes from the repressed — i.e., that the *concrete force* which motivates the behavior is the *real* one, despite the opposite and *unreal* nature of the *structure that determines the behavior*. Rogers said that the most therapeutic response is to take the basic, intended felt meaning of the individual's self-expression at face value, no matter how obvious the defensiveness and rationalization. But we may add specificity to these more general statements.

One must respond *to the functioning experiencing, not to the structure.* In practice this means that one must take at face value and give a personal response to the *functioning* aspect of the person. No one is greatly changed by responses and analyses of how he does not function (though we are often tempted in this direction). We see that the individual's work behavior actually defeats his desire to work, that his sexual behavior turns away opportunities for genuine sexuality, that his desire to please makes him annoy people, that his way of reaching out to people actually turns people away, that his self-expression is dramatized and hollow. Yet these structures are his responses *to* his *actually functioning* desire to work, his actually functioning sexuality, his actually functioning desire to relate to people and be close to them, and his actual self-expressive urge. Only if we respond to these actually functioning aspects of his experiencing (despite the obviously opposite character of his behavior and symbolic self-responding) can we carry forward what is now actual and reconstitute the process where he himself had (symbolically and actually) responded only with structure.

(21) Primacy of Process

We tend to neglect the fact that contents are process aspects. We pay the most attention to contents as symbolized meanings with specific logical implications (which they also are). Hence we often discuss self-exploration as if it were purely a logical inquiry in search of conceptual answers. However, in psychotherapy (and in one's private self-exploration as well) the logical contents and insights are secondary. Process has primacy. We must attend and symbolize in order to carry forward the process and thereby reconstitute it in certain new aspects. *Only then,* as new contents come to function implicitly in feeling, can we symbolize them.

In definition 9 we noted that "unfolding" can occur as a felt "now I've got it," quite without symbolization. This is a direct experience of *reconstituting.* The process is felt as ongoing in newly reconstituted respects. Reconstituting occurs when one symbolizes meanings which, in the previous moments, have already been implicit. The carrying forward of these implicit meanings turns out to involve the wider process which reconstitutes the new aspects.

In psychotherapy, therefore, the situation is not that first we figure out what is wrong with an individual and how he must change — and then, somehow, he does it. Rather, his experiencing with us is *already* vitally different with us than it previously could be. From this different experiencing arise the solutions of his problems. The changes are already occurring as he speaks. *Our* responses (as verbal symbols *and as events*) interact and carry forward *his* experiencing. Our gestures and attitude, the very fact that he is talking *to* us, the differences which each moment he makes to us — all of this interacts concretely with what implicitly functions in him, his felt experiencing. Conceptually it may look like a futile statement and restatement of problems. Or, conceptually, we may arrive at *the* most basic causes and factors — the ways in which an individual ought to change, the reasons and lacks which prevent him from so changing — but no genuine *solution* is *conceptually* arrived at. The conceptual search ends by shrugging and attaching some blameful label to the individual who, through bad will or constitution, is said to lack these or those basic essentials. Yet, *given certain interpersonal responses, he is already different.*

By *primacy of process* over conceptual content, we mean this fact:[19] The presently ongoing experiencing process must be *carried forward* concretely. Thereby it is in many respects reconstituted, made more immediate in its manner of experiencing, more full of differentiable detail. Thereby new process aspects (contents), "solutions," and personality changes arise. Most often these solutions seem terribly simple,[20] conceptually (see definition 9), and cannot possibly be the reason for the change. Rather, they are rough conceptualizations of a few aspects of a broadly different process.

(22) Process Unity

There is a *single* process which involves all of the following: environmental interaction, body life, feeling, cognitive meanings, interpersonal relations, and self. The concretely occurring process is one, although we can isolate and emphasize these various aspects of it. Our "thing language" tends to present whatever we discuss as if it were a separable object in space. In this way we artificially separate environment, body, feeling, meanings, other people, and self.[21] When they are discussed as separable things, their obvious interrelations become puzzling: How can *feelings* be involved in (psychosomatic) body illnesses? How can *cognitive* thought be influenced by *felt* needs? How is it that expressing ourselves *interpersonally* results in changes in the *self*? At every juncture the "separate thing" view of these phenomena builds these puzzles into our discussions. Instead we can employ a frame of reference which considers the *one* process which concretely occurs. I want to give the

[19] I call it a fact, because in psychotherapy we observe it. In the above context it is a matter of theoretical formulation, not of fact.

Some observable research variables have been defined: Assents to one set of descriptions of "immediacy" were found to increase significantly in successful psychotherapy (Gendlin and Shlien, 1961). One group of therapists observed significantly more of the above described new experiencing during the hour in success cases (Gendlin, Jenny, and Shlien, 1960). Successful clients were judged significantly higher on scale-defined variables called immediate manner of experiencing and expression (concerning self, personal meanings, the therapist, problems . . . any content), as compared with failure clients.

[20] This is a trouble with most concepts about personality change and psychotherapy, as well as with most concepts of ideals, moral values, and life wisdom: The concepts tell a little something of how it seems when one has arrived at the aim, but they tell nothing of the process of getting there. Such concepts make all sorts of mischief because we tend to try to fit them without allowing ourselves the very different process of getting there. Better concepts about the process of getting there can remedy this age-old problem.

[21] Many contemporary writers point to the essential interpersonal relatedness of the human individual. Daseinsanalyse, Sullivan, Mead, and Buber point out that individual personality is not a self-contained piece of machinery with its own primary characteristics which is *then* placed into interaction. Rather, *personality is an interacting.*

name *process unity* to the way in which the one concrete process is basic to these various aspects.

We have tried to show that *feeling* is a bodily affair, an aspect of physiological process. We have shown that *cognitive meanings* consist not only of verbal or pictorial symbols, but also of a *felt* sense which is implicitly meaningful and must function in interaction with symbols. *Interpersonal responses* (like other types of events) can interact with *feeling* and carry forward the concrete process. Now we will try to show that the *self* (the individual's own responses to his implicitly functioning experiencing) is also an aspect of the one concretely felt process, continuous with body, feeling, meanings, and interpersonal relations.

(23) The Self Process and its Interpersonal Continuity

Throughout this discussion we have been dealing with one concretely occurring interaction process between *feeling* and *events*. Interpersonal events occur before there is a self. Others respond to us before we come to respond to ourselves. If these responses were not in interaction with feeling — if there were nothing but other people's responses as such — the self could become nothing but the learned responses of others. But interpersonal responses are not merely external events. They are events *in interaction with the individual's feeling*. The individual then develops a capacity *to respond to* his feeling. The self is not merely a learned repertoire of responses, but a response process *to* feeling.

If feeling did not have implicit meaning, then all meaning would depend totally on the events or responses which occur. Again then, the self could never become anything but the repetition of the responses of others. The individual would always have to interpret himself and shape his personal meanings just as others had interpreted him.

But feeling has implicit meanings. Therefore, to the extent that a feeling process is ongoing, we can *further* respond to it differently than others have. However, to the extent to which we respond to our own feeling so as to skip or stop the process rather than carry it forward, to that extent we need others to help us be ourselves. Not only the genesis, but the adult development of the self also may require interpersonal responses. Such responses are required not because of their appraisal or content, but because we need them concretely to reconstitute the feeling process. If in certain respects the process is not ongoing when we are alone, it does not help to recite to ourselves some content or happy appraisal which we may remember from a person with whom we felt "more ourselves"; that person's effect on us was brought about not by his appraisal or evaluation, which we can recite to ourselves. Rather, the effect occurred through his responses to our concrete feeling process and, in some respects, reconstituted it and carried it forward. If we can do *that* alone, we are independent selves in that respect.

Thus, personality change in us is not a result of our perceiving another's positive appraisals of us or attitudes toward us. It is true that rejecting attitudes toward us are unlikely to carry forward our implicit meanings. However, that is not because of the negative appraisal as such, but because rejection usually ignores the implicit meanings of my feeling. To reject is to turn away or push away. In contrast, someone's "unconditional positive regard" toward us is not only an appraisal or attitude. They respond and carry forward the concretely ongoing process with their responses.

We must, therefore, reformulate Rogers' (1959b) view that personality change depends on the client's *perception* of the therapist's attitude. The present theory implies that the client may perceive the therapist's attitudes correctly, or he may not. He may be convinced that the therapist must dislike him and cannot possibly understand him. Not these *perceptions,* but the *manner of process which is actually occurring,* will determine whether personality change results. In many cases, the client can perceive positive therapist attitudes only after the concrete personality change process has already occurred.

The change-effective factor is not the perception of a content, an appraisal, an evaluation, or an attitude, considered apart from the concrete process.

Personality change is the difference made by *your* responses in *carrying forward my* concrete experiencing. To be myself I need your responses, to the extent to which my own responses fail to *carry* my feelings *forward.* At first, in these respects, I am "really myself" *only when I am with you.*

For a time, the individual can have this fuller *self-process* only in just this *relationship.*[22] That is not "dependence." It should not lead one to back away,

---

[22] Only in verbal and conceptual content is "self-exploration" in psychotherapy distinguishable from the personal "relationship." As an ongoing experience process they are the same. The individual may say "only here am I myself" (showing the process to include both self and relationship), or he may speak mostly about the *relationship,* or mostly about *himself.* It is the same process whether the content seems to be mostly about self or mostly about the relationship.

One research finding (Gendlin, Jenny, and Shlien, 1960) employed some operational variables related to this point. Psychotherapists were asked to make ratings of the extent to which "therapy, for this client, focuses chiefly on his problems, or . . . on his relationship with you." These ratings were *not* associated with outcome.

On the other hand, outcome did correlate with the following two scales: "How important to the client is the relationship as a source of new experience? Examples: 'I've never been able to let go and just feel dependent and helpless as I do now'; or, 'This is the first time I've ever really gotten angry at someone.' " Another scale which also correlated with outcome was: "To what extent does the client *express* his feelings, and to what extent does he rather talk *about* them?" These findings indicate that outcome is not affected by whether the *content* (*topic*) is the self or the relationship. Rather, it matters whether the individual is engaged in a *manner* of ongoing interaction process which involves newly reconstituted aspects of experiencing.

This research illustrates the usefulness of process concepts as compared to content concepts to generate operational research variables. Earlier research (Seeman, 1954) had posed the problem by finding no significant association between success in psychotherapy and discussion of the relationship with the therapist. The finding seemed to contradict the importance of the relationship. New research replicated that finding and added scales concerning the ongoing interaction *process.*

We need theory to create operational definitions. The most effective kind of theory for that purpose is one which employs process concepts in reference to experiencing. We must carefully distinguish from theory the operational terms (to which it leads) that are then defined by procedure and observation, not by theory.

but to fuller and deeper responses carrying forward the experiencing, which, for the time being, the individual says he can feel "only here." The continued *carrying forward* into *ongoing interaction process* is necessary to *reconstitute* the experiencing long enough for the individual himself to obtain the ability to carry it forward as *self-process*.

Repression and Content Definitions Reformulated

(24) The Unconscious as Incomplete Process

When "ego" or "self-system" are said to "exclude" some experiences from awareness, usually it is assumed that these experiences nevertheless exist "in the unconscious" or "in the organism." Our discussion, however, leads us to the conclusion that they do not. *Something* exists, to be sure, but it is not the experiences as they would be if they were optimally ongoing. Rather, what exists is a felt and physiological condition which results when, in some regards, the body interaction process is stopped — i.e., is not occurring. What kind of condition is that?

We have shown how the resulting dysfunction will be such that something is "missing," but we should not place what is missing into the unconscious (any more than we should place *eating* into the unconscious when someone is *hungry*). Rather, the unconscious consists of the body's stopped processes, the muscular and visceral blockage — just as a stopped electric current does not consist of a current that is going on under cover, but rather of certain electric potentials which build up in various parts (not only at the interruption) of the circuit. When a conductor re-establishes the electric current, different events occur than were occurring in its interrupted condition — yet, of course, the two are related. We say that this is the electrical energy which existed (in static form) before the current was reconstituted. This is "the unconscious."

When we say that certain experiences, perceptions, motives, feelings, etc. are "missing" from our awareness, it is not that *they* exist "below" awareness (somewhere under there in the body or in an unconscious). Rather there is a narrowed, or in some respects blocked, interaction and experiencing. The manner of experiencing which we have described is one in which, in a good many regards, the experiencing and body life process is *not* "completed" or fully ongoing.

Does this mean that there is no "unconscious"? Only what we are aware of exists? To put the matter in that too simple way ignores important observations. The present theory must be able to account for these observations.[23] Therefore, we are basically reformulating the theory of the unconscious rather

---

[23] I will choose two observations and show how the reformulation accounts for them:

(1) A sequence of words is flashed, each for fractions of a second, on a screen by means of a tachistoscope. When the individual is unable to read the word it is flashed again and again. Now, for example, an individual may be able to read the words "grass,"

"democracy," "table," "independence," with an average number of repetitions, but for the word "sex" he requires twice as many repetitions. The theories of the unconscious explain this as follows:

The organism can discriminate a stimulus and its meaning for the organism without utilizing the higher nerve centers involved in awareness.

The current theories have this assumption in common: Words such as "unconscious," "repression," "covert," "not me," "denial to awareness," "subception," all involve the uncomfortable but seemingly necessary assumption that there is a discrimination before an aware discrimination takes place, and that the experience or *content* which the individual misses in awareness actually exists somewhere in him. How else can one account for the above example and the many other observations just like it?

But we need not assume that something in the individual first reads the word sex, then becomes anxious about it, and then forces it to remain outside of awareness. Rather let us try to interpret this observation as a case where the individual does not ever read it until he does so in awareness. Why then does he take so long to read just that word when he could read the others in half the time? We have tried to show earlier (definitions 4 and 16) that, in order to read a word and to say what it is, the function of *felt* experiencing is necessary. We read without *explicitly* thinking the meanings of what we read. We have the sound images and *we have the felt meaning*. Now if for some reason our felt process cannot interact with the words, our eyes may continue, but we cannot say what we have read.

To explain the matter, process theory must take the place of content theory. The process of interacting with the symbols, of "reading them," requires the function of experiencing (the inwardly felt body process). If this felt process is not functioning in some regards, then the expected discriminating will not occur in these regards. Aspects which ought to be "implicit" will not function and, therefore, cannot interact and interpret the present situation. Hence, in these regards, the individual may misconstrue or simply miss (be unable to complete) the process, without this implying that he first interpreted these fully and then keeps them out of awareness.

The difference can be put simply: content theories assume that one completes the process of knowing, experiencing, interpreting, reacting, but that some of this process does not reach awareness. The present theory holds that the process does not completely occur.

(2) A second observation:

An individual leaves a certain situation feeling quite happy. Four days later he becomes aware that really he has been quite angry about what happened. He feels that he "has been" angry all along but "wasn't aware of it."

Now, our theory denies that what he now calls anger was in his body all along, without awareness. Rather, *there was something, but not the process of being angry.* He calls it being angry *now,* because *now* he is engaged in that process, and he clearly feels the releasing (see definition 8) quality which physiologically lets him know that his present anger "satisfies," "discharges," "releases," "symbolizes," "completes" — in short, *has some deeply felt relation to* — the condition he physically felt during the four preceding days. The process *was not* occurring, and that made for a physiological condition which is *only now* altered. When "structure bound" experience "goes to completion," we feel that we *now* know what it was *then;* we did not know it then, because the ongoing process of now is different from the stopped condition of then.

Only by *completing* the process by response to the feeling or felt meaning that is there (and is *not* anger) does the individual then "become aware" of anger. If we view this in terms of content, it is all very puzzling. First the content is not there, and then, later on, it is said to have been there all along (hidden in there, somewhere). But in terms of process it is precisely this deeply felt relationship of the later anger to the previously felt condition that tells us that a previously stopped process has only now been completed.

We, therefore, need not assume that there are two minds in the individual — one being an unconscious mind that first perceives a content and then permits or prohibits the aware mind to perceive it. Rather, the aware feeling (whatever it is — let us say it is a tension or a dissatisfaction, not at all anger) must be responded to and carried forward. Only thereby does the process go to completion and anger (or whatever supposed content) come to be an aspect of the reconstituted process.

than in any simple way throwing it out. The unconscious is redefined as *incomplete process.*

Since there is no sharp distinction between *carrying forward* what is implicitly felt, and *reconstituting* experiencing in previously stopped respects (the former will involve the latter),[24] the felt datum which *is* there, in a sense contains everything. In what sense does it? In the sense that, *given fully carrying forward responses* to it, everything will be here as aspects of ongoing process.

Therefore, in practice the rule is: "Never mind what is not being felt. Respond to what is being felt."

(25) Extreme Structure-Bound Manner of Experiencing (Psychoses, Dreams, Hypnosis, CO₂, LSD, Stimulus Deprivation)

Throughout, we have been discussing the *felt, implicit functioning* of the interaction process we term "experiencing." We have been pointing out that all appropriate behavior and interpretations of present situations depend on this *felt* functioning. It constitutes the thousands of meanings and past experiences which determine appropriate present behavior. In addition, it is this felt functioning to which we can respond ourselves, and this is the *self-process.* The functioning I am discussing is *felt,* meaning that we can refer to it ourselves. For example, as we read this page the words are sound images for us. These sound images are all we explicitly have in mind. However, we also have the *meanings* of the sound images. How? We do not *say* to ourselves what it all means. We *feel* the meanings of what we read as we go along. They function implicitly. This feeling process is an interaction between the symbols on the page and our feeling. This felt *interaction* process is now *ongoing* and gives us appropriate feelings and meanings.

When the *interaction process* is greatly curtailed (as in sleep, hypnosis, psychosis, and isolation experiments), the inwardly felt experiencing is thereby curtailed. The individual then lacks the implicit function of felt experiencing and loses both his sense of "self" and his capacity to respond to and interpret present events appropriately. Both require the felt process just illustrated.

The peculiar phenomena which occur under these circumstances are somewhat more understandable when they are considered in terms of curtailment or stoppage of the *interaction* process and *implicit function* of *felt* experiencing.

I would like now to state some of the characteristics of this (hallucinatory or dreamlike) *extreme structure-bound manner of experiencing.*

Structures are Perceived as Such. Ordinarily, past experiences and learnings function implicitly in felt experiencing, so that we interpret and perceive the present, not the past experiences themselves. Yet under hypnosis, in dreams, and in hallucinations, we may perceive rigid structures and past events as such. Characteristically, we do not then have the relevant aspects

---

[24] See definition 17, the law of reconstitution.

of felt process which usually function. Thus hallucinations and dreams are not understandable to the present individual. He is puzzled or aghast at them. They often seem to him "not his." The felt experiencing that would give him a sense of their being "his," and would let him know their meaning, is not ongoing. Dreams and hallucinations are, so to speak, decomposed pieces of what would otherwise be a functioning, felt process. This interaction process with the present is not ongoing, and hence the felt meanings are not functioning.

Let me now trace through these several different kinds of circumstances how in each the interaction process is first curtailed, and how in each the function of felt experiencing is then missing.

Extreme Structure-Bound Manner Occurs Whenever the Interaction Process is Greatly Curtailed. Dreams, hypnosis, psychosis, CO_2 and LSD, and stimulus deprivation share at least one factor, the curtailment of ongoing interaction.

In sleep there is a great reduction of external stimuli. Dreams occur with this curtailment of the usually ongoing interaction process with the environment.

In hypnosis, too, the subject must shut off his interaction with present stimuli, and must cease his own self-responsivenes. He must concentrate on a point.

Psychosis, as has often been remarked (for example, Shlien, 1960), involves both in its genesis and later, an "isolation," a curtailment of interaction between feeling and events. Also, physical isolation from people can, in some individuals, bring on hallucinations.

Certain poisons (CO_2, LSD) are inimical to the physiological interaction process of body life. CO_2 narrows (and eventually stops) the process of respiration.

Experiments in which individuals are placed in soundproof and lightproof suits that also prevent touch stimuli result (after a few hours) in psychotic-like hallucinations.

The peculiarly similar experiences which arise under these widely different conditions hint at something similar. At least one factor they all share is the curtailment of the ongoing interaction process which, as felt, is experiencing. We would thus expect a lack of the implicit functioning which ongoing experiencing usually provides.

And indeed this is shared by the phenomena which occur in all these circumstances. The peculiar character of these phenomena is understandable as a rigidity or lack of this *felt functioning* which usually interprets every present situation for us, and to which we respond in *self-process*. Thus appropriate interpreting of situations and sense of self are lost.

Lack of Implicit Function. This implicit function (see definition 4) of felt experiencing becomes rigid (not *in process*) or "literal" in all these conditions.

In hypnosis, for example, when the individual is told to "raise your hand," he will lift the palm of his hand up by his wrist. He will not, as when awake, interpret the idiomatic phrase appropriately (it means, of course, to raise one's whole arm up into the air). The same "literal" quality occurs in dreams and in psychosis. Much of what has been called "primary process," "schizophrenic thinking," or the schizophrenics inability to "abstract" his "concrete" thinking, his "taking the part for the whole" (Goodstein, 1954), really consists of this *literal* and rigid manner in which experiencing functions. As in dreams and hypnosis, the *felt* process of experiencing is curtailed and does not provide its implicit functioning.

The many implicit *felt* meanings that are needed for appropriate interpretations and reactions do not function, since the *felt* process (of which they are process aspects) is not ongoing. That is exactly what "literal" means: the lack of functioning of *other* meanings which should inform our interpretation of a given set of words or events.

"Loss of Self." Another characteristic shared by dreams, hypnosis, psychosis, and the phenomena obtained in stimulus-deprivation and LSD, is the loss of a sense of self. In dreams what we perceive is beyond the control, interpretation, ownership, of the self (or ego). In hypnosis the individual specifically accepts another's suggestions for his own and totally permits them to replace his own self-responding. And in psychosis so often the patient complains: "I didn't do that. Something made me do it"; or "I'm not myself"; or "These voices are not mine"; or, "Inside me I'm nothing at all." The hallucinations, voices, and things in his head are not *felt* to be his own. He lacks the sense of self. If he does have a sense of self (an "intact ego"), this felt sense does not inform the hallucinatory phenomena. In regard to these, he has no sense of self that implicitly contains their meaning.

This loss of self is due to the missing felt functioning of experiencing. Just as outward events (to the extent of psychosis) are not interpreted and interacted with on the basis of felt experiencing, so also this felt experiencing is missing for self-responses.

We have defined the self as *self-process*. The self exists to the extent that the individual can carry his felt process forward by means of his own symbols, behaviors, or attention. Experiments with stimulus deprivation have found that individuals who develop psychosis more slowly have a greater capacity to respond to themselves (the most "imagination" and "creativity," it was called). The finding would corroborate our views since, to the extent the individual can carry forward his own experiencing, he will be maintaining (by symbols and attention) his interaction process. When the interaction process is greatly narrowed, not only do psychotic-like experiences occur, but the sense of "self" is lost. The felt process to which there can be self-response becomes static and the individual has *unowned* perceptions.

Static, Repetitious, Unmodifiable Manner. Insofar as the implicit function of felt experiencing is rigid, there is no way for present situations to interact with it, and to modify it so that it becomes an interpretation of the present situation. Instead we perceive a repetitious pattern that is not modified by the present situation. The sequence may "go off" as a result of being "cued" by present events, but it is not an interpretation of, or response to, present events.

The University of Psychotic "Contents." Experiences in the extreme structure-bound manner are not *process aspects*. They occur precisely to the extent that the felt process is not ongoing. It is striking how certain themes universally recur — usually the familiar "oral, anal, and genital" themes. It seems that this is the stuff of which we are all composed . . . and into which the usually ongoing process decomposes, insofar as it is not ongoing.

Psychotic Experiences Are Not "the Repressed." It is fallacious to consider these structure-bound manifestations as repressed experiences which have now "emerged" or "erupted." To so consider them raises the puzzling question: On the one hand many theories hold that adjustment requires awareness, and that repression makes maladjustment, but on the other hand they hold that the psychotic is "too aware" and needs to "rerepress" all these experiences.

A better formulation, I think, would be to interpret this observation as follows: Optimally these universal past experiences function implicitly in felt experiencing. When that ongoing process ceases, decomposed static patterns occupy the center of the sensorium.

The implications of this reformulation can be seen, for example, in the following. "The psychosis," in this view, is *not* these supposedly underlying contents (in that sense everyone is "psychotic"). Rather, *"the psychosis" is the curtailment or cessation of the interaction process of feeling and events.* When, therefore, we label an individual "borderline psychotic," this does *not* mean that certain dangerous *contents* lie down there in him. Rather, he is "isolated," "uninvolved," "not quite there," "withdrawn," or "out of touch with himself"; i.e., his *manner* of experiencing is highly structure bound. To prevent "the psychosis" from occurring, one must respond as much as possible to such feelings as do implicitly function, so as to carry forward and reconstitute ongoing interaction and experiencing.

The view of *"latent psychotic contents"* leads to two dangerous errors: either one decides that the individual's feelings of difficulty and trouble had better be ignored (lest they "blossom into" full psychosis), or one "interprets" them and "digs" them "out." Either decision denies and pushes away the personal interaction and the individual's *implicitly functioning* feelings. Either decision will result in psychosis — they involve the same self-verifying misconception that "contents" are psychotic.

There is nothing "psychotic" about any "underlying contents." What is psychotic is the structure-bound manner of experiencing, the absence or literal rigidity of felt experiencing and interaction.

Whether "borderline" or seemingly "gone," the person will "come alive" if interaction and experiencing[25] is reconstituted by personal responses which carry forward what does still function.[26]

[25] In the large research (Rogers, 1960, p. 93) into psychotherapy with schizophrenics in which I am now engaged, we are applying process variables to the behavior changes of psychotics. The findings so far (Rogers et al., 1961) indicate that improvement on diagnostic tests is associated with operational behavior variables of a less rigid, less repetitive, less structure-bound manner of experiencing, and a greater use of felt experiencing as a direct referent and as a basis for behavior, expression, and relating. These tentative findings are defined in terms of rating scale variables and rating procedures.

[26] Therapist's self-expression used to reconstitute process:

When the client's varbalization or behavior gives us a sense of the implicit, felt meanings from which he speaks, then responding to that (even if it is not at all clear) carries the process forward and reconstitutes it as well. However, when the client is silent or speaks only of external matters, then *the therapist's* voicing his own feelings is an important mode of response which can reconstitute *the client's* experiencing process.

There are several other kinds of difficulties. Sometimes the client's talk is bizarre and hard to understand. If there are bits which do make sense, one must repeat these carefully, checking one's understanding. This gives the isolated individual a moment-by-moment sense of contact — something like the pier is for a drowning man. I do not want to be merely poetic in saying that. I want to point up the need for a concretely felt sense of the interacting listener which, where welcome to the client, should be given every few moments during talk that is hard to follow.

Sometimes there is no understandable *logical* content, but the symbolic images do add up to a feeling. (Client: "The Austrian army took all my possessions. They're going to pay me a million dollars." Therapist: "Somebody did you dirt? Took everything away from you? You want to make them pay back?").

Sometimes even less is understandable, but one can be sure the individual is suffering, lonely, hurt, having a rough time. The therapist can talk about any of these without needing any confirming response from the client.

Sometimes the therapist must simply *imagine* what *might* be going on in the client. If the therapist says he does not know, would like to know but need not be told, and imagines so-and-so, the therapist can speak about what he imagines and thereby an interaction process is restored.

The client may not say a word, but what is occurring is a felt interaction process in which articulation and symbolization is given his feelings. One person's behavior can *reconstitute* the interaction and experiencing process of the other person (see definition 23).

During silent hours the therapist can express what might go on in a troubled person uncomfortably sitting there; or, what goes on in the therapist as he wishes to help, wishes to hear, wishes not to pressure, hates to be useless, would be glad if he knew the silent time was useful, or imagines many feelings and perhaps painful ones going through the client's mind which he is not ready to talk about yet.

These therapist self-expressions require four specifications:

(1) They are expressed explicitly *as the therapist's own*. If they imply anything about the client, then the therapist says he is not sure it is so, he imagines it, has this impression, etc. It needs no affirmation or denial from the client. It is the therapist, speaking for himself.

(2) The therapist spends a few moments *focusing* on the feeling he might express. He seeks some aspect from all he feels, some bit which he can safely and simply say. No one can say all of the thousand *implicit* meanings he feels at one moment. One or two — especially those which, at the moment, seem too personal or bad or embarrassing —

(26) Content Mutation

As *implicitly functioning* felt meanings are *carried forward* and the process is *reconstituted* and made more immediate in *manner,* there is a constant change in "content." As *referent movement* occurs, both symbolization and direct referent change. There is a sequence of successive "contents." Sometimes these successive contents are said to "emerge" as if they had always been there, or as if the final basic content is now finally revealed. But I prefer to call this *content mutation.* It is not a change only in how one interprets but, rather a change both in feeling and in symbols. The contents change because the process is being newly completed and reconstituted by responses. What the contents will be depends greatly on the responses.

An example of *content mutation* has already been given (definitions 8—9). Here are more examples of content mutation:

The client is in terror. She says there will be "doom." The world will fly to pieces. Something awful will happen. There is a monster.

---

become, after a moment's *focusing,* an intimate and personal expression of present interaction.

Perhaps it is hard for me that we are silent and I am perhaps useless ·to him. There! That is something I can tell him. Or, I wonder if in this silence he is doing anything at all. I find that I am glad to be silent if that gives him time and peace to think and feel. I can express that. Such expressions are a warmly personal interaction. But they require a few moments of self-attention during which I *focus* on and *unfold* my present experiencing in this interaction.

(3) The phrasings and meanings which arise in us are very strongly influenced by our overall feeling toward the person to whom we speak. The therapeutic attitude toward the client as a person is an attitude of being totally for him — Rogers' (1957) "unconditional regard." Whitehorn (1959) terms it being like the patient's "lawyer." It is an attitude that whatever we both dislike about this trouble, *the individual as a person is "up against" that in himself.* I can always truly assume that. (This attitude has nothing to do with an overall approval or agreement or liking for this or that behavior, trait, attitude, or peculiarity.) Often I must imagine the person inside, who is "up against" all this. Only months later do I come to love and know that person.

It is amazing what a definable and concrete attitude this is. One can depend on it. There is always a person *"up against"* anything dislikable in him.

(4) When the client expresses himself, a response to *that* is needed. At such times therapist self-expression can get in the way.

When one has an opportunity to respond to the client's feeling, to *his* specific felt meaning, and the exact way of perceiving and interpreting something, responding exactly to that is the best and most powerful response. The self-expressive modes of responding fit those clients who give little to which one can respond.

Therapist self-expression as a mode of responding is important with those among the people labeled psychotic, who express little feeling, only externalized situational descriptions, or who sit in pure silence. However, there are many well-functioning persons with whom it is difficult to form a deep interaction because they do not express themselves. Kirtner and Cartwright (1958) found that individuals can be predicted to fail in therapy if their *first* interview shows little inward attention. Recently we are learning that therapist self-expression can help reconstitute the interaction and experiencing process of such individuals.

Here is "the psychosis" someone might say. At any rate, a common enough psychotic *content*.

She is awfully afraid, she says. I respond that she is afraid and that I want to keep company and be with her, since she is afraid. She repeats that she *is* afraid. No matter how much or little meaningful symbology there is to the "doom," she is *afraid now*.

Minutes or months later she can say:

"I'm afraid of being lost. I'm lost. I'm *so* lost!"

"For years I have had to know exactly what to do every moment. I'd plan to know exactly what to do so I'd be distracted. It's like blinders. I'd be afraid to look up, sort of. I need someone or something to hold on to, or I'll disappear."

This is more understandable than world doom. The *content* seems now to be "object-loss" or "passive-dependent needs." Whatever it is, the response needed must provide contact: I grasp her hand; or I talk gently, saying something, pertinent or not — something from me to maintain contact and not to talk away the fear of being lost. In terms of *process unity* such talking and such touching are really the same, in that they both *reestablish interaction*. To do so it must be personal and it must convert the *need* to "hold on" into a successfully *ongoing* contact, real or symbolic.

"I need to hold on, but I'm a monster. No one can love me. You must be sick of me. I need so much, all I do is need. I'm just selfish and evil. I'll suck you dry if I can. I'm just a horrible mouth."

Oral needs, oral incorporation, are now the contents that might be proposed.

But her need *does feel* endless, infinite, hungry. "Sure," I say, "It feels endless, bottomless, and awful to you. It's like you want to be fed and held forever."

Then, or some other time, she may say: "I'm just a baby. I hate that child. An ugly child. I *was* an ugly child. Nobody could like me the way I am."

But we have come a long way when the monster is now a child! A child is quite a nice thing. What became of the monster? A child is quite a human, every day, daylight thing. What became of the terror? *The psychosis?*

Such *content mutation* can occur within a few minutes or over months. It may occur in such words and symbols as above or in purely socially acceptable language, or with bizarre incoherent words, or in silence. The point I am trying to make is that *the content changes as one responds* and thereby carries forward and reconstitutes an interaction process. Such interaction constitutes felt experiencing, and contents are always aspects thereof. As the process changes, the contents change. I term it *content mutation*.

Content mutation occurs strikingly with so-called "psychotic contents." The monsters, weird fears, infinite hungers, and doom-expectant terrors are so often aspects of isolation, loss of self and interaction. They are not psychotic "things" in a person, but a narrowed or stopped interaction process. As the interaction process is restored the contents change and, also, they become more understandable and commonly human.

But *content mutation* occurs not only with quite dramatic expressions, such as in the above example. It occurs equally with the often silent, unexpressive, and "unmotivated" individuals with whom we have so largely been working in the current research on psychotherapy with schizophrenics (Shlien, 1960; Gendlin, 1961), although these individuals often conceptualize so little of what they are feeling. The following is a further example of *content mutation:*

An individual talks about a chain of circumstances which disturb him. Numerous patterns, characteristics, and personality "contents," seem noticeable in his report of these circumstances.

Perhaps with the aid of responses, he goes on to find that this chain of circumstances really makes him very *angry*. That's it! He is furious. He wishes he could harm and destroy the people involved. He is afraid he will attack them when he next sees them. He hopes he will be able to control this destructive desire. He is amazed at his own *hostility* and his own fear of it. He hardly needs further to report the circumstances, so deeply true is his experience of this anger and destructive need. Again, now, we are tempted to consider personality "contents." Our first deductions now seem too broad. Here, really, we have some contents of this man's personality. We are familiar with this fear of one's own hostility and what some of the bases of the hostility probably are.

But let us say the man continues (and I continue to respond to his *felt meanings*). He imagines himself attempting to vent his anger at these people. He finds now that he is not afraid he will uncontrollably attack and harm them. It is more likely (of all things!) that he will not be able even to yell at them, because perhaps he will cry. His voice would choke up, he is sure. In fact, it is somewhat choked up right now. This thing is not really hostility, it now appears. It is rather that he feels so *hurt!* They should not have done this to him! They hurt him, and . . . what can he do? And now he feels, with some relief, that he finally is in touch with what all this really means to him. (We may now propose a third group of personality contents, again different.)

But, as he continues, it turns out that the circumstances as such do not really matter. No wonder! It seemed all along quite a petty thing to be so upset about. The content is really something else and that is what hurts. And he finds now it is not a hurt after all. Rather, it brought home to him that he feels weak and helpless. "I'm not really hurt" (he now finds), "it's more that it points up to me how I can't make it in the world" (passively, castration, we may now say).

The term "content mutation" can be applied to this sequential shifting of what seems to be the "content." Contents are process aspects of ongoing feeling process. They can be symbolized because they function implicitly in that feeling process. As it is carried forward, there is referent movement and change in what can be symbolized. It is not merely a shifting of interpretation. There is *referent movement* — that is to say, *that which is being symbolized* is changing.

Content mutation does not imply that all our concepts are simply inapplicable. Often they are correct in terms of predicting the individual's other behaviors, and often they enable us to guess or be sensitively ready for a next content mutation. However, the concepts of personality contents are static and much too general[27] and empty. They are never a substitute for *direct reference, referent movement,* and *content mutation.*

REFERENCES

GENDLIN, E. T. A process concept of relationship. *Counseling Center Discussion Papers*, III, 2. Chicago: University of Chicago Library, 1957.

GENDLIN, E. T. Initiating psychotherapy with "unmotivated" patients. *Psychiatric Quarterly*, 1961, 35, 134-139.

GENDLIN, E. T. *Experiencing and the creation of meaning.* New York: The Free Press of Glencoe, 1962a.

GENDLIN, E. T. Need for a new type of concept: Current trends and needs in psychotherapy research on schizophrenia. *Review of Existential Psychology and Psychiatry*, 1962b, 2, 37-46.

GENDLIN, E. T., and BERLIN, J. I. Galvanic skin response correlates of different modes of experiencing. *Journal of Clinical Psychology*, 1961, 17, 73-77.

GENDLIN, E. T., JENNY, R. H., and SHLIEN, J. M. Counselor ratings of process and outcome in client-centered therapy. *Journal of Clinical Psychology*, 1960, 16, 210-213.

GENDLIN, E. T., and SHLIEN, J. M. Immediacy in time attitudes before and after time-limited psychotherapy. *Journal of Clinical Psychology*, 1961, 17, 69-72.

GENDLIN, E. T., and ZIMRING, F. M. The qualities or dimensions of experiencing and their change. *Counseling Center Discussion Papers*, 1, 3. Chicago: University of Chicago Library, 1955.

GOODSTEIN, L. D. Interrelationships among several measures of anxiety and hostility. *Journal of Consulting Psychology*, 1954, 18, 35-39.

[27] A note on the many new terms:

In the realm of personality *change* we largely lack sufficiently specific concepts to discuss and define observations. The present theory attempts to offer such concepts. It is hoped that with these concepts (and others) our thinking and discussing will be advanced and our ability to isolate and define observations sharpened.

There may be some difficulty in holding fast to new definitions such as *direct referent, referent movement, carrying forward, reconstituting, manner of experiencing, implicit function.* It cannot be hoped that all twenty-six definitions will succeed in entering the language. Nevertheless, we need these (or better) terms to discuss personality change.

KIRTNER, W., and CARTWRIGHT, D. Success and failure in client-centered therapy as a function of initial in-therapy behavior. *Journal of Consulting Psychology*, 1958, 22, 329-333.

MEAD, G. H. *The philosophy of the act.* Chicago: University of Chicago Press, 1938.

ROGERS, C. R. The necessary and sufficient conditions for therapeutic personality change. *Journal of Consulting Psychology*, 1957, 21, 95-103.

ROGERS, C. R. A process conception of pychotherapy. *American Psychologist*, 1958, 13, 142-149.

ROGERS, C. R. A tentative scale for the measurement of process in psychotherapy. In E. Rubinstein (Ed.), *Research in psychotherapy*. Washington, D. C.: American Psychological Association, 1959a. Pp. 96-107.

ROGERS, C. R. A theory of therapy, personality, and interpersonal relationships as developed in the client-centered framework. In S. Koch (Ed.), *Psychology: A study of a science*, Vol. III. *Formulations of the person and the social context*. New York: McGraw-Hill, 1959b. Pp. 184-256.

ROGERS, C. R. Significant trends in the client-centered orientation. In D. Brower and L. E. Abt (Eds.), *Progress in clinical psychology*, Vol. IV. New York: Grune & Stratton, 1960. Pp. 85-99.

ROGERS, C. R. The process equation of psychotherapy. *American Journal of Psychotherapy*, 1961, 15, 27-45.

SEEMAN, J. Counselor judgments of therapeutic process and outcome. In C. Rogers and R. F. Dymond (Eds.), *Psychotherapy and personality change*. Chicago: University of Chicago Press, 1954. Pp. 99-108.

SHLIEN, J. M. A client-centered approach to schizophrenia: First approximation. In A. Burton (Ed.), *Psychotherapy of the psychoses*. New York: Basic Books, Inc., 1960. Chapter 11.

WHITEHORN, J. C. Studies of the doctor as a crucial factor for the prognosis of schizophrenic patients. Paper from the Henry Phipps Psychiatric Clinic of the Johns Hopkins Hospital, 1959.

PART THREE

Research on the
Processes and Conditions
of Psychotherapy

The last decade (1958-1968) of research in client-centered therapy has been principally an outgrowth of the conditions-process equation generated in two papers by Carl Rogers. In essence, the equation stated that if certain therapist behavioral conditions obtained (empathy, positive regard, unconditionality, congruence), then certain other responses would be observed in the client (increased self-awareness, autonomy, movement from rigidity to flow, etc.). The theory held that the conditions were necessary and sufficient to produce productive personality change (process movement) in the client, and that the amount of process change was proportional to the degree to which the therapist provided the conditions *and* the degree to which the client was aware of their presence. If the client perceived the presence of conditions of empathy, etc. and those conditions were present in optimum degree then the client should grow along predicted lines. To the degree the client failed to perceive the conditions, or if they were not optimally provided, the client's progress would be proportionately retarded.

Validating research has been carried out on both the conditions and process dimensions of the equation, and there have been several attempts to examine the interaction between conditions and process in the same group of clients. The major work to date on the conditions-process hypothesis appeared in C. R. Rogers (Ed.) *The therapeutic relationship and its impact: A study of psychotherapy with schizophrenics.* The research reported in this section

175

both antedates and moves beyond the work with schizophrenics and will spell out the research foundations for the conditions-process theory.

The development of the theory has been discussed in Part One. Upon publication of the two central papers, "The necessary and sufficient conditions of therapeutic personality change" and "The process equation of psychotherapy" (Chapter 9), the groundwork was laid for a major theoretical-methodological advance in client-centered therapy research.[1] However, there have been several papers that provided preliminary research support for the conditions and process conceptualization. One is the first paper in this section (Chapter 8), in which Kirtner and Cartwright lay out the empirical foundations for one of the central strands of behavior in the process model, "client approach to problems." The results of this paper provided evidence that success in psychotherapy, in both the long and short run, was related to the manner in which the client treats his problems. Groups of clients judged to be therapeutic successes were distinguished from those judged to be failures by a stronger tendency among the successes to "seek internally for the cause and resolution of felt discomfort," to seek after people to relate to in order to feel worthwhile, and to be intropunitive in their evaluations of self.

Using this evidence in combination with his own perceptivity, Rogers identified seven different strands of behavior, and several of them, most notably "manner of experiencing," have been given considerable theoretical and research attention (e.g., Chapter 7). One of the first major efforts to provide validation to the process concept was Tomlinson and Hart's "A validation study of the process scale" (Chapter 10). This paper indicated that measures derived from the process scale distinguished between more-successful and less-successful neurotic clients, and showed greater fluctuation in the more-successful than in the less-successful cases. From this study it seemed apparent that Rogers' conceptualization of the process of personality change was valid, and that the change was reflected in and could be measured by alterations in the client's expressive style.

The next two chapters, 11 and 12, develop further the empirical foundations of the conditions-process equation by studying the relationship between the two sets of formulations. Van der Veen presents data that indicates that client personality is related to the perception of the offered conditions, and that movement in process (personality change) is positively related to the client's perception of the conditions. But most important, client movement was found to be more closely related to the degree to which the conditions of therapy were actually offered than it was to the degree to which the client perceived the conditions. Thus it helps in the production of positive personality change if the client is aware of the offered conditions; but even if he isn't, their presence has positive impact on his therapeutic outcome. The op-

---

[1] The paper "The necessary and sufficient conditions of therapeutic personality change" (*Journal of Consulting Psychology,* 21, 95-103, 1957) was omitted because it receives extensive discussion in several papers in this book, e.g., Chapters 2, 3, and 24.

timal situation results when the client is sharply aware of a high level of presence of therapeutic conditions, but the central point is that the conditions themselves are the principle vehicle by which constructive change takes place.

Bergin and Solomon, in Chapter 12, develop the theme of the relationship between ability to offer the conditions and the therapeutic outcome. Taking empathy as the variable for investigation, they relate a measure of it to several indices of therapist personality and behavior. Their data indicate that, while empathic ability is a uniformly valued aspect of therapist behavior, it is by no means characteristically found in "raw" form. Therapists, while desiring to be empathic, often have to learn by observation of others who possess this ability in high degree. Nevertheless, it also seems clear that a variety of personality variables are related to the capabilities of the therapists to learn to be empathic, and that, in turn, empathy itself is closely related to therapeutic success. Thus Bergin and Solomon have further validated a necessary (if not sufficient) condition for positive therapeutic effect, and identified some of the therapist personality variables that inhibit or enhance its effect. In the authors' words, "The simple fact of finding significant correlations between personal variables and therapeutic behavior known to produce personality change provides a beginning toward isolating the most potent therapeutic agents while at the same time eliminating factors that interfere with the power of those agents to produce positive change."

In Chapter 13 Kiesler summarizes the research to date with both the process and conditions method, and then spells out areas in need of further research. Speaking to the methodological problems inherent in this type of psychotherapy research, Kiesler underscores the detailed and painstaking labor necessary to develop the scales to an operational point. It is easy enough to say that the process-conditions scales are used to rate client-therapist interaction, but it is quite another thing to specify exactly how and under what circumstances such ratings may be validly made. For example, the simple questions of what part and how much of an interview should be rated before a reliable fix can be made on the general level of process-conditions involved several years of systematic variation of segment length, segment position in the interview, presentation media, segment content (should it include therapist response when client process is being rated, and vice versa) and optimal rating combinations of all of the foregoing. The main point is that sources of variance in the rating of therapy interaction are very extensive, and go far beyond the utterances of the therapist and client. Kiesler's position is that failure to control these method variables is in large part responsible for the generation of much invalid information from psychotherapy research. In the general perspective, however, the willingness of client-centered researchers to devote the time and energy to the pursuit of these important but tedious problems buttresses the assertion Bergin makes in the next chapter, namely, that client-centered therapy is the only traditional therapy that has clear research validation.

In Chapter 14 Bergin spells out the essentials of the data that bear on today's issues in psychotherapy and psychotherapy research. In his review he makes clear that the best available evidence indicates that clients may get better *or* worse in psychotherapy, that client progress in therapy is associated with therapist warmth, empathy, adjustment, and experience, that client-centered therapy is the only "talking" therapy that has received clear research validation, that time-honored talking therapies are limited in their effect and relevance for the universe of psychological disorders, and, in the scholarly tradition of dispassion, that behavior therapies show sufficient promise to warrant continued utilization and experimentation.

Bergin's position is clearly consistent with the purpose of this book, namely, to assess the extant data and to indicate desirable new directions for research and action. Bergin's paper and the papers in the next two parts indicate an awareness that psychotherapy of the traditional variety is no panacea; in fact, they indicate that traditional therapy has been found to be seriously wanting, though perhaps "all right in its place." Bergin underscores once again the findings that, given the presence of the therapeutic conditions, positive things happen to the client, and that these things have been identified and examined more systematically and effectively in the context of the client-centered method than in any other. Nonetheless, given that traditional therapies, including client-centered therapy, are severely limited in the effectiveness with which they meet their task, Bergin's paper is a clear, if implicit, call to expand the horizons of investigation and implementation of change-producing agents.

8

Success and Failure in

Client-Centered Therapy as a

Function of Client Personality

Variables*[1]

WILLIAM L. KIRTNER   DESMOND S. CARTWRIGHT

Cartwright (1955) has presented evidence for the existence of a "failure-one," ranging between 13 and 21 interviews, in client-centered therapy. In a subsequent paper, Taylor (1956) presented closely comparable evidence with respect to psychoanalytically oriented psychotherapy.

Cartwright demonstrated that therapeutic outcomes were divided by the failure-zone and suggested that there may be two forms of therapeutic process, identifying these processes as "short" (1 — 12 interviews) and "long" (13 — 77 or more interviews). He further hypothesized (1955, p. 362) "that certain individual differences between clients give rise to different kinds of therapeutic process."

From William L. Kirtner and Desmond S. Cartwright, "Success and Failure in Client-entered Therapy as a Function of Client Personality Variables," *Journal of Consulting Psychology,* Vol. 22, No. 4, 1958, pp. 259-264. Copyright 1958 by the American Psychological Association, and reproduced by permission.

This investigation is based upon a dissertation submitted by the senior author to the University of Chicago in partial fulfillment of the requirements for the degree of master of arts. It was supported in part by research grants from the National Institute of Mental Health, National Institutes of Health, U.S. Public Health Service, and from the Ford Foundation.

On the basis of these results and hypotheses, five client groups were distinguished: short success, 1 — 12 interviews; short failure, 1 — 12 interviews; failure-zone, 13 — 21 interviews; long success, more than 21 interviews; and long failure, more than 21 interviews. Utilizing this schema, Kirtner (1955) hypothesized that therapy length-by-outcome is related to the personality structures of clients at the beginning of therapy. The present paper reports an investigation of this hypothesis.

Method and Procedure

Subjects

From the research files of the Counseling Center, University of Chicago, all clients were selected for whom the following four conditions held: (a) the therapists' rating of outcome on a 9-point success rating scale (Seeman, 1954) fell either between 7 and 9 inclusive ("success") or between 1 and 4 inclusive ("failure"); (b) the exact number of interviews was recorded; (c) a pretherapy Thematic Apperception Test (TAT) protocol was available; and (d) a recorded or transcribed first therapy interview was available. Twenty-four clients fulfilled all conditions. Two clients who fulfilled conditions (a) (b), and (c), but not (d), were also included, yielding $n = 26$ for this study All clients were seen by experienced therapists (25 male and 1 female) between 1949 and 1954. The sample included 12 males, 14 females; 10 students, 16 nonstudents; the mean age was 27.5 years and the range 19 to 41 years.

Instruments

Rating scales were developed to measure twelve personality variables These variables were selected to comprehend: (a) some of those variable widely referred to as designating level of pattern of personality integration e.g., sex role and identification, motivation, impulse life; (b) some of thos variables particularly relevant to the phenomenological basis of client-centere therapy, e.g., decision-making, rule usage, sense of self as a causative ager (Rogers, 1951; Rogers, et al., 1954, pp. 4-5); and (c) some of those variable especially associated with previous research in client-centered therapy, e.g sensitivity to others (Sheerer, 1949; Stock, 1949; Tougas, 1954); intrapun tive feelings (Haimowitz, 1952). Upon analysis of the results derived fro the application of the 12 scales, 6 scales were eliminated due to function overlap with the remainder. Numerical ratings made by an independent judg on the 12 scales were intercorrelated. The resulting matrix was inspected f clusters from each of which one scale was selected, yielding four relatively i dependent scales, numbered I, IV, X, and XI. Scale VIII, while substantial correlated with Scale I, was uncorrelated with the other three selected scal and is therefore reported upon. Scale XII, highly correlated with Scale X on numerical ratings, is also reported upon because of its distinctive qual tative differentiation between clients. Over the six scales, the range of inter-correlations was — .24 to .77. The median correlation was .29.

Following are brief descriptions of the six scales reported in this study. In complete form, all are 5-point, fully anchored scales.[2] A rating of 1 indicates minimal disturbance (optimal adjustment), and a rating of 5 indicates maximal disturbance.

Scale I — Impulse Life

From free flow and expression of generative impulses and ideas, to extreme:
   a. fright about impulses but with expression;
   b. control or repression;
   c. distortion of impulses.

Scale IV — Sense of Capability

From a sense of felt capacity to cope adequately with situations, to a sense of helplessness and lack of internal resources to cope with situations.

Scale VIII — Sex-role and Identification

From direct and open expression of sexuality with good control of feelings, to extreme conflict, uncertainty, and confusion about sex.

Scale X — People — Object Orientation

From the ability to relate deeply both to people and in activities, to:
   a. a desperate need for people;
   b. avoidance of relating to people with concomitant desperate need for activities;
   c. immobilization.

Scale XI — Sense of Comfort and Satisfaction

From a sense of self-comfort and satisfaction with the ability to locate problem sources both internally and externally in good balance, to:
   a. intensely driven to search himself for causes of discomfort and dissatisfaction;
   b. intensely driven to search outward for causes of discomfort and dissatisfaction;
   c. intense hopelessness to locate causes.

Copies of the complete scales and of the raw data from both judges may be obtained without charge from William L. Kirtner, Counseling Center, University of Chicago, 5737 Drexel Avenue, Chicago, Illinois or for a fee from the American Documentation Institute. Order Document No. 5585, remitting $1.75 for microfilm or $2.50 for photocopies.

Scale XII — Punitive Feelings

From a self-appraising person who is not self-reproachful, to:
   a. extremely self-punishing person;
   b. extreme anticipation of punishment from external source;
   c. vacillation between *"a"* and *"b."*

It will be noted that some of the scales include alternate descriptive anchors, indicated by letters *a, b, c.* Such letter ratings occur only in connection with numerical ratings of 3 or more. As the level of disturbance increases in a given area (as the numerical rating is higher on these scales), the behavior displayed may take on one of several modal characteristics. Salient non-reactive, explosive, or other features of behavior become usual and representatively distinguishing attributes of the person rated. Such salient characteristics or modal patterns of behavior must be discretely described in order to obtain a fully anchored scale of levels of disturbance. As the level of disturbance decreases (as the numerical rating is lower on these scales), the behaviors displayed do not require multiple discrete descriptions; salient non-reactive, explosive, or other features of behavior are neither usual nor representatively distinguishing attributes of the person rated.

While the foregoing paragraph presents the descriptive (i.e., scale-making) problem, the existence of the problem invites explanation. The authors hold the working hypothesis that the individual adopts certain specifiable modes or techniques of behavior in order to control his internal disturbance or anxiety with respect to a given segment of his experience. As anxiety or disturbance intensifies, the techniques required for control of the disturbance, or for maintenance of personality organization, become more drastic and more representatively typical of the individual.

Ratings

Ratings of each client, on each of the six scales, were made on the basis of the pretherapy TAT protocol in conjunction with the recorded or transcribed first therapy interview. In two cases, the recorded first interview was not available, and the TAT protocol alone was used.

Ratings were made independently by the senior author and by another judge. The latter ("Judge II") knew neither the length nor the success rating of any case.

Reliability

Reliability of the therapist rating of outcome on the 9-point scale has been previously reported (Cartwright, 1955; Seeman, 1954) as slightly better than $r = .80$. To determine reliability for the numerical ratings on the six scales, all ratings by the two independent judges were correlated using Kendall's tau for ties in both rankings (1948). The computational procedure employed was that developed by Cartwright (1957a). Corrections for continuity were made using Schaeffer and Levitt's (1956) modification of Whitefield's correction (1947). The routine for computing corrections for continuity and *p* values was that described by Cartwright (1957b). Table 8.1 presents these reliability data, which were considered adequate throughout.

TABLE 8.1

Reliability Coefficients (Tau) for Numerical Ratings on Six Scales

Scale	Tau	*p*
I. Impulse life	.65	.01
IV. Sense of capability	.62	.01
VIII. Sex-role and identification	.53	.01
V. People-object orientation	.73	.01
XI. Sense of comfort and satisfaction	.85	.01
XII. Punitive feelings	.83	.01

Letter ratings occurred on four out of the six scales. Since such ratings are associated only with numerical ratings of 3 or more on these scales, a long and tedious problem in combinatorics would have to be solved to obtain an exact estimate of reliability, which did not seem justifiable. A fortiori, it did not seem justifiable to work on a solution for the reliability of joint numerical-plus-letter ratings. Instead, simple percentages of agreement were computed for all cases where both judges employed a letter rating, and regardless of numerical rating. Table 8.2 presents these data and includes, for the reader's information, the number of cases where neither judge used a letter rating.

TABLE 8.2

Percentages of Agreement for Letter Ratings on Four Scales

	Number of cases for which letter ratings were used by			
Scale	Neither judge	Both judges	Agreements Number	%
I.	3	22	20	91
X.	0	26	23	88
XI.	0	26	25	96
XII.	1	25	22	88

No statistical analysis of results from letter ratings was made. However, the authors judge the data of Table 8.2 to warrant descriptive characterization of modal behaviors displayed by subjects rated on the four scales referred to.

Analysis

The sample of 26 cases was divided into length-by-outcome groups according to the schema given. Table 8.3 summarizes descriptions of the resulting groups.

TABLE 8.3

Summary Description of Groups

Group	Number of interviews	Range of outcome ratings	N	Male	Female	Student	Non-student
Short failures	<13	1-4	10	4	6	4	6
Short success	<13	7-9	4	0	4	3	1
Failure-zone	13-21	1-4	7	5	2	1	6
Long failure	>21	1-4	1	1	0	1	0
Long success	>21	7-9	4	2	2	2	2

Regrettably for the research, only one long-failure case was among those available. This group was therefore eliminated from subsequent analysis. The remaining groups were examined in all possible pairs on each of the six scales as numerically rated by Judge II. All comparisons were made using tau for a dichotomy in one ranking as described by Kendall (1948, pp. 32-34). The significance of differences between groups was computed in the manner previously indicated for the reliability analysis. In order to show the direction of differences between pairs of groups, mean values for each group on each scale were also computed.

Results

Numerical Ratings

Table 8.4 presents means for groups on each of the six scales and the p values of the differences between groups.[3]

Rejecting the null hypothesis if $p < .05$, each success group shows a lesser degree of disturbance than either failure group on Scale I. Also, the short success groups shows a lesser degree of disturbance than either failure group on Scale VIII.

[3] See footnote 2.

TABLE 8.4

*Significance Levels of Differences Between Groups on Six Scales,
and Means Indicating Direction of Differences*

	Means of Groups [b]				*p* of Differences [a]					
Scale	SS	LS	SF	FZ	SS vs. LS	SS vs. SF	SS vs. FZ	LS vs. SF	LS vs. FZ	SF vs. FZ
I.	2.00	3.00	4.10	4.43	<.10	<.01	<.01	<.01	<.01	>.20
IV.	3.00	3.25	4.30	3.71	>.20	<.02	>.20	<.03	>.20	<.07
VIII.	2.50	3.75	3.80	4.57	<.07	<.02	<.02	>.20	<.10	<.02
X.	3.50	3.75	4.10	4.00	>.20	>.20	>.20	>.20	>.20	>.20
XI.	3.75	4.50	3.90	3.57	<.15	>.20	>.20	>.20	<.08	>.20
XII.	3.25	4.25	3.80	3.85	<.19	>.20	>.20	>.20	>.20	>.20

Two-tailed tests throughout.
SS — short success; LS — long success; SF — short failure; FZ — Failure-zone.

Of special interest are results setting a given group apart from the other three groups. We reject sets of three null hypotheses if in each instance *p* < .10. On this basis, Table 8.4 contains the following results: the short-success group shows less disturbance than any other group on Scales I and VIII; the short-failure group shows more disturbance than any other group on Scale IV; and the failure-zone group shows more disturbance than any other group on Scale VIII.

Letter Ratings

Table 8.5 presents the number of letter ratings agreed upon by both judges for four scales with respect to the four groups.

TABLE 8.5

Letter Ratings Agreed on by Both Judges

	Short success			Long success			Short failure			Failure zone		
Scale	*a*	*b*	*c*	*a*	*b*	*c*	*a*	*b*	*c*	*a*	*b*	*c*
I.					4		2	3	4		5	1
X.	4				4		1	4	4	2	1	2
XI.	3				4			8	2		6	1
XII.	3				4			8	1		4	1

The most interesting feature of Table 8.5 is that success groups appear to differ from failure groups on Scales X, XI, and XII. While there were no differences on these scales as numerically rated for degree of disturbance, differences in typical mode of controlling inner disturbance were observed by both judges.

Distinguishing Descriptions

The results and observations mentioned in connection with Tables 8.4 and 8.5 are given embodiment in descriptions distinguishing the groups. Descriptions employ the language of those scales, and only those scales, for which either statistically significant differences or clear qualitative observations have been made.

The short-success group shows a generally higher level of personality integration than that descriptive of other groups. In particular, they are rather open to their impulse life (I), and, while showing some distortion and uncertainty, they are a good deal less confused about their sex role than other groups (VIII).

Though similar to the short-success group in many respects, the long success group shows a somewhat lower level of personality integration in general. In particular, they are rather anxious about their impulse life (I) and rather confused about the meaning and place of sex in their identity (VIII)

Both success groups differ from each failure group in showing less disturbance in their impulse life (I). Letter ratings show the success groups typically displaying a strong need for people to relate to in order to feel worthwhile (X), seeking internally for the cause and resolution of felt discomfort (XI), and rather strongly condemning, berating, and disvaluing themselves (XII).

The short-failure group shows a generally low level of personality integration. Especially distinguishing is their extreme underlying sense of incapacity to deal with their life situations (IV).

The failure-zone group also shows a generally low level of personality integration. Especially distinguishing is their extreme conflictedness about and rejection of their sex role (VIII).

Both failure groups show greater disturbance than either success group on several scales. They are extremely disturbed in their impulse life (I), with expressions frequently occurring in over-controlled or distorted modalities as indicated by letter ratings. Over-control seems somewhat more typical for the failure-zone group. Letter ratings show the failure groups typically looking outward for the cause and resolution of their discomfort (XI), and typically anticipating punishment from external sources (XII).

Discussion

The foregoing results seem unambiguously consistent with the general hypothesis motivating the study: that therapy length-by-outcome is related to the personality structure of clients at the beginning of therapy. While cautio must be invoked due to the small sizes of the groups studied, the results add to the growing body of knowledge about factors which favor or limit therapeutic change in client-centered therapy. Earlier work in this area has been summarized by Rogers (1954, pp. 423-424, 427-428).

It may be noted that the present approach constitutes a synthesis of two trends in previous work on the general problem. One trend has dealt with the relations between pretherapy characteristics of clients and eventual ratings of improvement or outcome (e.g., Barron, 1953a, b; Gallagher, 1954; Kirtner, et al., 1953; Mindess, 1953; Rosenberg, 1954; Tougas, 1954). The other trend has dealt with the relations between pretherapy characteristics of clients and their length of stay in treatment (e.g., Gallagher, 1953; Kotkov and Meadow, 1953; Lutes, 1952; Rogers, et al., 1951; Rubinstein and Lorr, 1956). To our knowledge, only one previous investigator, Dana (6), has attempted to predict improvement and length of treatment jointly. Due to the findings of Cartwright (1955) and Taylor (1956), a fusion of the two main trends into systematic emphasis upon length-by-outcome groupings now seems necessary. More generally, it is necessary to predict both amount and rate of change constituting improvement. While something of a beginning has been made in this direction by Dana's results and by those of the present study, much more needs to be done.

Summary

Twenty-six clients, who had completed a course of client-centered therapy at the Counseling Center, University of Chicago, were divided into five groups on the basis of length-by-outcome:

Short success (1 — 12 interviews) — *N* equals 4
Short failure (1 — 12 interviews) — *N* equals 10
Failure-zone (13 — 21 interviews) — *N* equals 7
Long success (more than 21 interviews) — *N* equals 4
Long failure (more than 21 interviews) — *N* equals 1

Twelve personality variables were selected, and 5-point rating scales were constructed to describe both intensity and mode of behavior with respect to each of the 12 variables. These scales were applied independently by two judges to the pretherapy Thematic Apperception Test protocol in conjunction with the recorded or transcribed first therapy interview in each case. Interjudge agreement was deemed adequate throughout.

The ratings made by an independent judge were intercorrelated, and the resulting matrix was inspected for clusters from each of which one scale was selected, yielding four relatively independent scales. Two further scales were reported upon because, though substantially correlated with one of the four

selected scales, they are uncorrelated with the others and point up interesting
and distinctive differences between client personality structure.

It was thus found that therapy length-by-outcome is related to the personality structure of clients at the beginning of therapy. The most marked differences found on these scales were those between success groups and the
failure groups.

REFERENCES

BARRON, F. An ego-strength scale which predicts response to psychotherapy
Journal of Consulting Psychology, 1953a, 17, 327-333.

BARRON, F. Some test correlates of response to psychotherapy. *Journal of Psy
chology*, 1953b, 17, 235-241.

CARTWRIGHT, D. S. Success in psychotherapy as a function of certain actuaria
variables. *Journal of Consulting Psychology*, 1955, 19, 357-363.

CARTWRIGHT, D. S. A computational procedure for tau correlation. *Psychometrika*
1957a, 22, 97-104.

CARTWRIGHT, D. S. A note concerning Kendall's tau. *Psychological Bulletin*
1957b, 54, 423-425.

DANA, R. H. The effects of attitudes towards authority on psychotherapy. *Journa
of Clinical Psychology*, 1954, 10, 350-353.

GALLAGHER, J. J. A comparison of clients who continue with clients who discon
tinue client-centered therapy. In Psychotherapy Research Group (Ed.), *Grou
report of a program of research in psychotherapy*. State College, Pa.: Pennsy
vania State College, 1953. Pp. 21-38.

GALLAGHER, J.J. Test indicators for therapy prognosis. *Journal of Consulting Psy
chology*, 1954, 18, 409-413.

HAIMOWITZ, NATALIE R., and HAIMOWITZ, M. L. Personality changes in clien
centered therapy. In Werner Wolff (Ed.), *Success in psychotherapy*. Ne
York: Grune & Stratton, 1952. Pp. 63-94.

KENDALL, M. G. *Rank correlation methods*. London: Griffin, 1948.

KIRKNER, F. J., WISHAM, W. W., and GIEDT, F. H. A report on the validity of th
Rorschach Prognostic Rating Scale. *Journal of Proj. Tech.*, 1953, 17, 465-47

KIRTNER, W. L. Success and failure in client-centered therapy as a function
personality variables. Unpublished master's thesis, University of Chicago, 195

KOTKOV, B., and MEADOW, A. Rorschach criteria for predicting continuation
individual psychotherapy. *Journal of Consulting Psychology*, 1953, 17, 16-20.

LUTES, B. C. A factorial study of an attrition group in client-centered therap
Unpublished master's thesis, University of Chicago, 1952.

MINDESS, H. Predicting patients' responses to psychotherapy: A preliminary stu
designed to investigate the validity of the Rorschach Prognostic Rating Scal
Journal of Proj. Tech., 1953, 17, 327-334.

ROGERS, C. R. *Client-centered therapy*. Boston: Houghton Mifflin, 1951.

Rogers, C. R., and Dymond, Rosalind F. (Eds.), *Psychotherapy and personality change*. Chicago: University of Chicago Press, 1954.

Rogers, L. S., Krauss, Joanne, and Hammond, K. R. Predicting continuation in therapy by means of the Rorschach test. *Journal of Consulting Psychology,* 1951, 15, 368-371.

Rosenberg, S. The relationship of certain personality factors to prognosis in psychotherapy. *Journal of Clinical Psychology,* 1954, 19, 341-345.

Rubinstein, E. A., and Lorr, M. A comparison of terminators and remainers in outpatient psychotherapy. *Journal of Clinical Psychology,* 1956, 12, 345-349.

Schaeffer, M. S., and Levitt, E. E. Concerning Kendall's tau, a nonparametric correlation coefficient. *Psychological Bulletin,* 1956, 53, 338-346.

Seeman, J. Counselor judgments of therapeutic process and outcome. In C. R. Rogers and Rosalind F. Dymond (Eds.), *Psychotherapy and personality change.* Chicago: University of Chicago Press, 1954. Pp. 99-108.

Sheerer, E. T. An analysis of the relationship between acceptance of and respect for self and acceptance of and respect for others in ten counseling cases. *Journal of Consulting Psychology,* 1949, 13, 169-175.

Stock, D. An investigation into the interrelations between the self-concept and feelings directed toward other persons and groups. *Journal of Consulting Psychology,* 1949, 13, 176-180.

Taylor, J. W. Relationship of success and length in psychotherapy. *Journal of Consulting Psychology,* 1956, 20, 332.

Tougas, R. R. Ethnocentrism as a limiting factor in verbal therapy. In C. R. Rogers and Rosalind F. Dymond (Eds.), *Psychotherapy and personality change.* Chicago: University of Chicago Press, 1954. Pp. 196-214.

Whitfield, J. W. Rank correlation between two variables, one of which is ranked, the other dichotomous. *Biometrika,* 1947, 34, 292-296.

9

The Process Equation of

Psychotherapy*

CARL R. ROGERS

For many years now I have been trying to formulate for myself the process by which change in personality and behavior is achieved in psychotherapy. These formulations change in various ways as my experience as a therapist increases. They continue to change as little by little we gain a more exact knowledge of the process through research. Sometimes I feel that our progress in gaining understanding is discouragingly slow. At other times, when I look back to what was known about psychotherapy thirty years ago, when I first became a therapist, then I feel that we have made very considerable strides.

I have been encouraged in recent years by our ability to write some crude equations. We can formulate statements which are comparable to crude chemical equations. We can say that given a person desiring help, and a second person providing a relationship with elements a, b, and c, then a process of change occurs which involves elements x, y, and z. We can specify rather definitely the nature of each of these elements. We have acquired, in other words, more objective knowledge of cause and effect in psychotherapy.

I would like in this paper, to present my current formulation of the process of therapy which incorporates some of this more recently acquired knowledge.

* From *American Journal of Psychotherapy*, Vol. 15, No. 1, 1961, pp. 27-45. Reproduced by permission.

The Effective Relationship

There are two recent studies in which the findings excite me because they represent a considerable step forward in defining objectively the effective elements which bring about therapeutic change.

The Relationship as Perceived by "Judges"

The first study I wish to report is one completed by Halkides (1958). She began with a theoretical formulation of mine regarding the necessary and sufficient conditions for therapeutic change (Rogers, 1957). She hypothesized a significant relationship between the extent of constructive personality change in the client and four therapist variables, four subtle attitudinal characteristics: (a) the degree of empathic understanding of the client manifested by the therapist; (b) the degree of positive affective attitude (unconditional positive regard) manifested by the therapist toward the client; (c) the extent to which the therapist is genuine or congruent, his words matching his own internal feeling; and (d) the extent to which the therapist's response matches the client's statement in the intensity of affective expression.

To investigate these hypotheses she first selected, by multiple objective criteria, a group of 10 cases which could be classed as "most successful" and a group of 10 "least successful" cases. She then took an earlier and a later recorded interview from each of these cases. On a random basis she picked nine client-counselor interaction units — a client statement and a counselor response — from each of these interviews. She thus had nine early interaction units and nine late interaction units from each case. This gave her several hundred units in these interview samples, which were now placed in random order. The units from an early interview of an unsuccessful case might be followed by the units from a late interview of a successful case, etc.

Three judges, who did not know the cases, or their degree of success, or the source of any given unit, now listened to this material four different times. They rated each unit on a seven-point scale, first as to the degree of empathy, second as to the degree of the counselor's positive attitude toward the client, third as to the counselor's congruence or genuineness, and fourth as to the degree to which the counselor's response matched the emotional intensity of the client's expression.

I think all of us who knew of the study regarded it as a very bold venture. Could judges listening to single units of interaction possibly make any rating of such subtle qualities as I have mentioned? And even if suitable reliability could be obtained, could 18 counselor-client interchanges from each case — a minute sampling of the hundreds or thousands of such interchanges which occurred in each case — possibly bear any relationship to the therapeutic outcome? The chance seemed slim.

The findings are surprising. It proved possible to achieve high reliability between the judges, most of the inter-judge correlations being in the .90's except on the last variable. It was found that a high degree of empathic understanding was significantly associated, at an .001 level, with the more successful cases. A high degree of unconditional positive regard was likewise associated with the more successful cases, at the .001 level. Even the rating of the therapist's genuineness or congruence — the extent to which his words matched his feelings — was associated with the successful outcome of the case, and again at the .001 level of significance. Only in the investigation of the matching intensity of affective expression were the results equivocal and inconclusive.

It is of interest, too, that high ratings of these variables were not associated more significantly with units from later interviews than with units from earlier interviews. This means that the counselor's attitudes were quite constant throughout the interviews. If he was highly empathic, he tended to be so from first to last. If he was lacking in genuineness, this tended to be true in both the earlier and later interviews.

Another finding of interest is that three of the four variables investigated show a high degree of relatedness. The measures of empathy, unconditional positive regard, and genuineness or congruence correlate highly, from .72 to .89. Evidently all of these three are very much tied together, or may represent three measures of one more underlying factor. The matching of the client's affective intensity by the therapist did not correlate significantly with the other three, any more than it did with success.

Halkides findings may be expressed very simply. The quality of the therapist's interaction with his client may be reliably judged on the basis of a very small sampling of his behavior. There is a strong probability of an effective helping relationship if the therapist is congruent, his words matching his feelings; if the therapist likes and accepts the client, unconditionally; and if the therapist understands the feelings of the client as they seem to the client, communicating this understanding.

The Relationship as Perceived by Clients

A second study of the therapeutic relationship has been completed by Barrett-Lennard (1959). He too wished to investigate the theory I had proposed as to the essential qualities in a relationship which produces therapeutic change. Instead of using objective judges, however, he studied the manner in which the relationship was perceived by the client and by the therapist. He developed a Relationship Inventory which had different forms for client and therapist, and which was designed to study five dimensions of the relationships. Thus far he has analyzed only the data from the client's perceptions of the relationship, and it is these findings which I shall report. Barrett-Lennard studied a fresh series of cases, in which he knew that he would have various objective measures of degree of change. He gave his Relationship

Inventory to each client after the fifth interview. In order to give more of the flavor of his study, I will elaborate with regard to each variable.

He was interested, first, in measuring the extent to which the client felt himself to be emphatically understood. He therefore included items pertaining to the therapist which were evaluated by the client on a 6-point scale which ranged from very true to very strongly not true. It will be evident that these represent different degrees of empathic understanding.

> He appreciates what my experience feels like to *me*.
> He understands what I say from a detached, objective point of view.
> He understands my words but not the way I feel.

Second, he wished to measure the *level* of regard, the degree of liking of the client by the therapist. To measure this there were items such as those listed below, each one again rated from strongly true to strongly not true.

> He cares about me.
> He is indifferent to me.
> He disapproves of me.

To measure the unconditionality of the regard, the extent to which there were "no strings attached" to the counselor's liking, items of this sort were included.

> Whether I am expressing "good" feelings or "bad" ones seems to make no difference to the way he feels toward me.
> His interest in me depends on what I am talking to him about.

In order to measure the congruence or genuineness of the therapist in the relationship, items of this sort were used.

> He behaves just the way that he *is*, in our relationship.
> He pretends that he likes me or understands me more than he really does.
> He is playing a role with me.

He also wished to measure another variable which he regarded as important — the counselor's psychologic availability, or willingness to be known. To measure this, items of this sort were used.

> He will freely tell me his own thoughts and feelings, when I want to know them.
> He is uncomfortable when I ask him something about himself.
> He is unwilling to tell me how feels about me.

Barrett-Lennard's findings are of interest. The more experienced of his therapists were perceived as having more of the first four qualities than the less experienced therapists. In "willingness to be known," however, the reverse was true.

In the more disturbed clients in his sample, the first four measures all correlated significantly with the degree of personality change as objectively measured, and with the degree of change as rated by the therapist. Emphatic understanding was most significantly associated with change, but genuineness, level of regard, and unconditionality of regard were also associated with successful therapy. Willingness to be known was not significantly associated.

Thus we can say, with some assurance, that a relationship characterized by a high degree of congruence or genuineness in the therapist; by a sensitive and accurate empathy on the part of the therapist; by a high degree of regard, respect, liking for the client by the therapist; and by an absence of conditionality in this regard, will have a high probabability of being an effective therapeutic relationship. These qualities appear to be primary change-producing influences on personality and behavior. This statement holds whether these elements are rated by an impartial observer who listens to the recorded interviews, or whether they are evaluated by the client as he perceives them. It seems clear from both studies that these qualities can be measured or observed in small samples of the interaction, relatively early in the relationship, and can be used to predict the outcome of that relationship.

These elements appear necessary to successful therapy of a client-centered type. Whether they are necessary for *any* constructive personality change is unknown, but I would hypothesize that this is true. Whether they represent *all* the necessary conditions is likewise unknown, but it is of interest that two other relationship qualities which were measured proved *not* to be related to degree of change in therapy.

A Tentative Equation

Thus we can phrase our crude equation in several ways. Given a relationship between therapist and client we can say:

> Genuineness plus empathy and unconditional positive regard for the client equals successful therapy for the client.

More accurately we can phrase it this way:

> Perception by the client of genuineness, empathic understanding and unconditional positive regard in the therapist equals successful therapy for the client.

Or perhaps still better:

> The more the therapist is perceived by the client as being genuine, as having an empathic understanding, and an unconditional regard for him, the greater will be the degree of constructive personality change in the client.

I am sure that this question will be modified and rewritten as we are better informed through further study. That we have enough empirical knowledge to write it at all is to me a striking advance.

The Process in the Client

I have tried to spell out the left hand or causal side of the equation of therapy. Is it possible to give, in equally factual detail, the right hand or effect side of the equation? What happens in the client? What is this process of change, of learning, of therapy, which is set in motion? Here it seems to me the formulations have been even more varied, and our knowledge is even more tentative. Yet beginnings have been made. We are identifying various types of learnings which occur, the sequential events which characterize the process.

During the past three years I have especially concerned myself with the process of sequential events which occur in the client (Rogers, 1958). I have immersed myself in recordings of psychotherapeutic sessions. In these I have tried to discern the characteristic changes or learnings which occur when therapy is helpful. From this experience has come a somewhat different formulation of a continuum of psychologic functioning. I should like to present it in a very tentative form. I see it as a long, uphill pathway of change and development. A given client begins therapy at some point on this pathway and, if he is helped, moves a variable distance up the slope.

I hope that the nature of this pathway will become more clear in what follows. It should be sufficient for the present to say that it commences at one end with a rigid, static, undifferentiated, unfeeling, impersonal type of psychologic functioning. It evolves through various stages to, at the other end, a level of functioning marked by changingness, fluidity, richly differentiated reactions, by immediate experiencing of personal feelings, which are felt as deeply owned and accepted. In any successful therapy, I would hypothesize, the client moves upward on this pathway from whatever point he initially finds himself.

A group of us at Wisconsin have tried to take the observations of this sequential process and turn them into an operational scale (Rogers, 1958; Walker, et al., 1959). We have at least succeeded to the point where, given a segment of a recorded interview we can say, with satisfactory objectivity and reliability, that it is characteristic of a given point on the continuum. I would like to try to give you some feeling for the qualities of personal expression which are characteristic of different stages in the process, and also for the different strands out of which the process appears to be woven.

The Change in Relationship to Feelings

Let me speak first of the manner in which the client relates to the feelings and personal meanings which exist within himself. Brief examples may help. In these excerpts, it is not the content but rather the quality of expression which is important for our present purposes. A patient in a state hospital says, "Voices keep bothering me all the time, saying filthy things, and I can't stop them." Notice that these are not owned as her feelings at all. They are completely unowned, out of her control, unrecognized as being related to her. If she were able to say, "I am troubled by my sexual feelings," she would be much further along on the continuum.

Or take another example, characteristic of a somewhat higher point on the scale. A man says "It discourages me to feel dependent because it means I'm kind of helpless about myself." Here he is freely describing his feelings as objects existing in the present, and to some degree owned by himself. He is not expressing them, but he is describing them. He determines the meaning and significance of his feeling by an intellectual process rather than by sensing the meaning in himself.

Still further up the scale, we find statements of this sort. The client is quite perplexed as to what she is feeling and finally voices it this way, "It feels like I sort of have — I don't know — I have a feeling of *strength,* and yet I have a feeling of realizing it's so sort of fearful, of fright." Here it is clear that she is expressing the feelings she is having in the moment, living them, sensing them, differentiating them and owning them at the same time that she is expressing them.

Thus if I were to try to describe briefly the way in which this strand changes from the lowest point on the continuum to the highest, it would go something like this. At the lowest end the individual does not recognize or own his feelings. This changes to a description of feelings as remote, unowned objects not now present, usually existing in the past. Then they are described as present objects, with some sense of ownership. Then feelings are fearfully expressed — not described — in the immediate present. Feelings which have been denied in the past now bubble painfully through into awareness. Finally the person comes to live in the process of experiencing a continually changing flow of feelings. He is no longer remote from the feelings and personal meanings which are continually occurring in him. He is freely and acceptantly living them.

Change in the Manner of Experiencing

What I have been saying can be formulated in a different way, with reference to the client's manner of experiencing, as that concept has been developed by Gendlin and Zimring (1958, 1955). The client moves toward living in his experiencing, and using it as the referent for guiding himself in his encounter with life. He is no longer characterized by remoteness from his experiencing nor does he discover its meaning only long after it is past. Thus typical of a low point on the continuum is a client who, trying to tell of the problem which brought him to the therapist, says, "The symptom was — it was just being very depressed." We may assume that at some point he experienced deep depression, but the closest he can come to this experiencing is to conceptualize it in the past, and to remove it from himself. It is not he who was depressed. It was simply a symptom which existed.

As clients move in therapy they come closer to their own experiencing, become less fearful of it. They recognize that it may have value as a referent, as a basis for discovering meanings. Thus a client says, in regard to something going on within him, "I really don't have my finger on it. I'm just kinda describing it." Here he realizes that he is not entirely *in* his experiencing but he wishes that he were. Still further up the continuum a client says "I feel stopped right now. Why is my mind blank right now? I feel as if I'm hanging on to something, though I've been letting go of other things; and something in me is saying, "What more do I have to give up?" In this bit he is acceptantly living in his immediate experiencing. He recognizes that if he can symbolize what is going on in him at the moment, it will provide meaning for him, will serve as a useful guide. This is the kind of reaction characteristic of the person who has moved far toward the upper end of the continuum.

Change in Personal Constructs

Another strand of learning which is woven into this continuum is a change in the way the client construes his experience. At the lower end of the continuum his personal constructs, to use Kelly's term, are rigid, and are unrecognized as constructs, but are thought of as facts. Thus a client says "I can't *ever* do anything right — can't ever finish it." Here this seems to be a description of a fact — this is the way things are. As he learns, in the safety of therapy, he begins to question this rigid construct. A client at this higher stage says "I don't know how I got this impression that being ashamed of myself was such an *appropriate* way to feel." Here he is doubting and changing a personal construct which has always seemed to him unchangeable. At the upper end of the continuum experience is never given more than a tentative construction, and the construing is recognized as something "I" am doing, not a quality inherent in the situation. The client learns that meaning is something he gives to an experience. It is not a fact inevitably fastened to the experience.

Change in Communication of Self

Still another strand of learning in this total continuum is the client's learning of the satisfaction involved in communicating himself. In the lower portion of the pathway there is a real unwillingness to communicate self. We find clients making statements like this: "Well, I'll tell you, it always seems a little bit nonsensical to talk about one's self except in times of dire necessity." Communication is only about externals and nonself material. Gradually the client learns that it is safe and satisfying to talk about himself as an object. Then he learns to own and express his self feelings. An example from the upper half of the continuum: "The real truth of the matter is that I'm not the sweet, forebearing guy that I try to make out I am. I get irritated at things. I feel like snapping at people, and I feel like being selfish at times; and I don't know why I should pretend I'm *not* that way." At the upper end of the continuum self, as an object, tends to disappear. The individual loses consciousness of self.

He finds satisfaction in being and expressing the complexity of his feelings of the moment. He is continually in process of discovering himself.

Braaten (1958) has provided corroboration of this kind of movement in therapy. He finds that when early and late interviews from more successful cases are compared with early and late interviews from less successful cases, the more successful cases show a significantly greater increase in the amount of self-reference. Even more interesting they show a greater increase in expression of the immediately present self. Further, when one compares the expression of the private self — the internal communication within the individual, his awareness of being and functioning — this too increases significantly more in the successful than in the less successful cases.

Change in Relationship to Problems

There are at least two more strands in this continuum which I would like to describe briefly. The first has to do with the client's relationship to his problems. Kirtner (1958) was the first to observe this and to formulate the different ways in which clients present and approach their problems, and the correlation of these approaches with outcome. Put in my own terms, we might say that at the lowest point on the continuum the client recognizes no problems, or perceives them as entirely external to himself. A state hospital patient summarizes his problems this way. "I sleep here a little too much. I have a bad tooth problem and a couple of others like that." Here we find no recognition of the real problem nor any involvement in it. As the client loosens up in therapy, there is more recognition of problems and more feeling of self responsibility for problems. Gradually the client is able to face the fact that the most pressing issues are problems of feeling-in-relationship-to-others, and there is a desire to examine the inner reactions which may be contributing to these difficulties. Gradually he learns to live these problem feelings in the relationship with the therapist, and comes, through accepting them, to utilize them more constructively.

Change in Interpersonal Relationships

Finally, there is the strand of relating to others. At a lower point on the continuum the person is fearful of close personal contact, and avoids it through many devices, including intellectualization. He asks questions of the therapist. He wants to play the proper role. But he does not wish to enter, as a person, this dangerous and unknown world of relating. Gradually he learns that it is safe to risk himself occasionally on a feeling basis. Thus one client dares to say to his therapist, "Oh, all right, I *don't* trust you." Increasingly he dares to live openly in relationship to the therapist, as an ever-changing but integrated flow of feelings. He can express freely his fear of the therapist, his love for the therapist, his anger also. He finds he can live a relationship on the basis of his feelings.

Example of the Upper Portion of the Continuum

In the upper ranges of the scale, all these different strands which I have described tend to merge together and become one. Here is a very brief example of one of the "moments of movement" in therapy which illustrate this. Notice the qualities in his excerpt. The client is experiencing something right now, in this moment, and trying to sense the meaning of what is going on within him. He is changing a personal construct which he has always held — "I am not likable." He is communicating himself deeply, not withholding himself or talking about himself but *being* the internal communication going on within himself. Finally he is doing all this in a very open and fluid relationship with the therapist. Here is the excerpt:

> I could even conceive of it as a possibility that I could have a kind of tender concern for me — but how could *I* be tender, be concerned for *myself*, when they're one and the same thing? But yet I can *feel* it so clearly. You know, like taking care of a child. You want to give it this and give it that. I can kind of clearly see the purposes for somebody else, but I can never see them for myself — that I could do this for me, you know. Is it possible that I can really want to take care of myself, and make that a major purpose of my life? That means I'd have to deal with the whole world as if I were guardian of a most cherished and most wanted possession, that this *I* was between this precious *me* that I want to take care of, and the whole world. It's almost as if I *loved* myself — you know — that's strange — but it's true.

This is a good example of a higher stage on the continuum.

The Process Summarized

Let me summarize these learnings which I see as involved in the process of therapy, using a segment of an earlier paper. "I have tried to sketch, in a crude and preliminary manner, the flow of a process of change which occurs when a client experiences himself as being received, welcomed, understood as he is. This process involves several threads, separable at first, becoming more of a unity as the process continues.

"This process involves a loosening of feelings. From feelings which are unrecognized, unowned, unexpressed, the client moves toward a flow in which everchanging feelings are experienced in the moment, knowingly and acceptingly, and may be accurately expressed.

"The process involves a change in the manner of experiencing. From experiencing which is remote in time from the organic event, which is bound by the structure of experience in the past, the client moves toward a manner of experiencing which is immediate, in which he senses and conceptualizes meaning in terms of what *is*, not what was.

"The process involves a loosening of the cognitive maps of experience. From construing experience in rigid ways which are perceived as external facts, the client moves toward developing changing, loosely held construings of meaning in experience, constructions which are modifiable by each new experience.

"The process involves a change in the self. From being a self which is not congruent with experience, the client moves through the phase of perceiving self as an object, to a self which is synonymous with experience, being the subjective awareness of that experience.

"There are other elements, too, involved in the process: movement from ineffective to effective choice, from fear of relationships to freely living in relationship, from inadequate differentiation of feelings and meanings to sharp differentiation.

"In general, the process moves from a point characterized by fixity, where all these elements and threads are separately discernible and separately understandable, to the flowing peak moments of therapy in which all these threads become inseparably woven together. In the new experiencing with immediacy which occurs at such moments, feeling and cognition interpenetrate, self is subjectively present in the experience, volition is simply the subjective following of a harmonious balance of organismic direction. Thus, as the process reaches this point, the person becomes a unity of flow, of motion. He has changed; but, what seems most significant, he has become an integrated process of changingness" (Rogers, 1958, p. 149).

Empirical Corroboration

Is the foregoing description simply another speculative, unverifiable, clinical formulation? I believe not. We have, as mentioned earlier, built an operational "Scale of Process in Psychotherapy" out of these ideas. Several investigations have been made, using this Scale and others are in process. Some of the current findings of an investigation being conducted by Hart and Tomlinson (1962) may be reported.

These investigators took cases unknown to themselves or the judges who helped them, cases in which various criteria of success were available. Nine two-minute samples were taken from the recordings of the second and next to last interview in each case. These samples were randomized and presented to three judges who worked independently. The task of the judges was to rate each interview segment on a 70-point continuum as outlined in the Scale. When their ratings were completed they were compared with the case outcome, the cases having been divided into more and less successful cases on the basis of objective criteria.

They found the Scale of Process in Psychotherapy to be a reasonably reliable instrument. Interjudge correlations range from about .60 to .85 depending upon the experience of the raters and the auditory or visual presentation of the material.

Two studies (Walker, et al., 1959; Hart and Tomlinson) have shown that the Scale distinguishes sharply between more and less successful cases in early interviews. The less successful cases begin and end at a significantly lower point on the Scale than do the more successful cases. This was an unexpected finding.

This tends to confirm the earlier study by Kirtner and Cartwright (1958), and shows that we have little success in helping, through psychotherapy, those clients who initially rate low on this Process Scale. This means that with further refinement of the instrument, we may be able to predict which clients we are going to be able to help, and which we are not, given the present state of our knowledge.

The studies indicate a sobering fact. The change in the direction of fluidity is modest, even in the more successful cases. Thus the average change in the more successful cases in terms of the Process Scale, is usually less than the difference which we found between the less and more successful cases. Perhaps the changes due to therapeutic learning are always relatively small, even though important. At least this is suggested by these findings.

Probably the major finding of these studies is that we have uncovered another dimension of the process of therapy. Some of our earlier research indicated that change in the concept of self was one such dimension (Rogers, 1954). Now we can say with some assurance that in therapy which by objective measures is shown to be successful, there is a significant degree of movement away from fixity and rigidity and toward a quality of changingness. This movement is not found in unsuccessful cases (Walker et al., 1959; Hart and Tomlinson).

The Whole Equation

From what I have described as the process of therapy, I think I can now spell out the whole equation as it stands today in its crude and tentative form.

The more the client perceives the therapist as real or genuine, as empathic, as having an unconditional regard for him, the more the client will move away from a static, unfeeling, fixed, impersonal type of functioning and the more he will move toward a way of functioning which is marked by a fluid, changing, acceptant experiencing of differentiated personal feelings.

Implications

I have presented some of the knowledge we have recently gained about the causal aspect of psychotherapy, the relationship. I have presented some recent knowledge of the sequence of events which the relationship sets in motion. I have tried to formulate the equation. What are the implications of what I have been saying? I should like to spell out a few.

It seems to me that we are making a solid beginning on cause and effect in psychotherapy. This knowledge, as it is refined and improved, can have vast importance. It will mean that we answer questions regarding psychotherapy by recourse to factual studies, rather than on the basis of theoretical dogma or clinical hunch.

We are acquiring more detailed knowledge of one process of constructive personality change, of one equation which we can write in this field. We may learn that there are many processes of change, each with its antecedent conditions. Perhaps each therapeutic orientation produces its own distinctive changes. We do not know. This makes it imperative to discover the equation in other therapies.

The facts seem to suggest that personality change is initiated by *attitudes* which exist in the therapist, rather than primarily by his knowledge, his theories, or his techniques.

It seems to be clear that very small samples of our interaction with our clients can reveal the quality of the relationship we have established, and the likelihood of its being therapeutic.

It appears probable from our findings that we can soon identify, very early in the relationship, the individuals whom we are not likely to help by means of psychotherapy as it is today. This constitutes a tremendous challenge to all of us to develop new approaches which will help these individuals.

The studies suggest that it may be a new way of experiencing, experiencing in a more immediate, more fluid way, with more acceptance, which is the essential characteristic of therapeutic change, rather than, for example, the gaining of insight or the working through of the transference relationship, or the change in the self-concept.

The studies suggest a clearer picture of the goal or end-point of therapy. Therapy seems to be moving toward a full living in the moment — and away from a rigid intellectualized conforming to built-in expectations. It is a harmonious actualizing of all the sensitivities which the organism possesses, so that the individual can be fully alive to what is going on in him at this moment, and equally alive to all of the demands and realities of his environment, personal and impersonal. Behavior is then the sensitive and harmonious adaptation to all of the inner and outer stimuli.

This clearer picture of the end-point, of the right hand side of the equation, gives society the right to accept or reject this way of living as a suitable goal. Certainly many people would be frightened by the fluidity and changingness which I have pictured, and would not choose to move in this direction.

Finally these findings mean to me that therapy is a relationship which challenges the therapist to *be,* as sensitively as he is able, the person he is in this moment, knowing that it is his transparent realness, together with the liking and empathic understanding which are fostered by that realness, which can be of help to his client. To the extent that he can be a person in this moment, he can relate to the person, and the potential person, in his client. This I believe is the healing, growth-promoting, essence of psychotherapy.

Epilogue

So then what is the process of counseling and therapy? I have spoken of it objectively, marshalling the facts we have, writing it as a crude equation in which we can at least tentatively put down the specific terms. But let me now try to approach it from the inside, and without ignoring this factual knowledge, present this equation as it occurs subjectively in both therapist and client.

To the therapist, it is a new venture in relating. He feels, "Here is this other person, my client. I'm a little afraid of him, afraid of the depths in him as I am a little afraid of the depths of myself. Yet as he speaks, I begin to feel a respect for him, to feel my kinship to him. I sense how frightening his world is for him, how tightly he tries to hold it in place. I would like to sense his feelings, and I would like him to know that I understand his feelings. I would like him to know that I stand with him in his tight, constricted little world, and that I can look upon it unafraid. Perhaps I can make it a safer world for him. I would like my feelings in this relationship with him to be as clear and transparent as possible, so that they are a discernible reality for him, to which he can return again and again. I would like to go with him on the fearful journey into himself, into the buried fear, and hate, and love which he has never been able to let flow in him. I recognize that this is a very human and unpredictable journey for me, as well as for him, and that I may, without even knowing my fear, shrink away within myself, from some of the feelings he discovers. To this extent I know I will be limited in my ability to help him. I realize that at times his own fears may make him perceive me as uncaring, as rejecting, as an intruder, as one who does not understand. I want fully to accept these feelings in him, and yet I hope also that my own real feelings will show through so clearly that in time he cannot fail to perceive them. Most of all I want him to encounter in me a real person. I do not need to be uneasy as to whether my own feelings are 'therapeutic.' What I am and what I feel are good enough to be a basis for therapy, if I can transparently *be* what I am and what I feel in relationship to him. Then perhaps he can be what he is, openly and without fear."

And the client, for his part, goes through far more complex sequences which can only be suggested. Perhaps schematically his feelings change in some of these ways. "I'm afraid of him. I want help, but I don't know whether to trust him. He might see things which I don't know in myself — frightening and bad elements. He seems not to be judging me, but I'm sure he is. I can't tell him what really concerns me, but I can tell him about some past experiences which are related to my concern. He seems to understand those, so I can reveal a bit more of myself.

"But now that I've shared with him some of this bad side of me, he despises me. I'm sure of it, but it's strange I can find little evidence of it. Do you suppose that what I've told him isn't so bad? Is it possible that I need not be ashamed of it as a part of me? I no longer feel that he despises me. It makes me feel that I want to go further, exploring *me,* perhaps expressing more of myself. I find him a sort of companion as I do this — he seems really to understand.

"But now I'm getting frightened again, and this time deeply frightened. I didn't realize that exploring the unknown recesses of myself would make me feel feelings I've never experienced before. It's very strange because in one way these aren't new feelings. I sense that they've always been there. But they seem so bad and disturbing I've never dared to let them flow in me. And now as I live these feelings in the hours with him, I feel terribly shaky, as though my world is falling apart. It used to be sure and firm. Now it is loose, permeable and vulnerable. It isn't pleasant to feel things I've always been frightened of before. It's his fault. Yet curiously I'm eager to see him and I feel more safe when I'm with him.

"I don't know who I am any more, but sometimes when I *feel* things I seem solid and real for a moment. I'm troubled by the contradictions I find in myself — I act one way and feel another — I think one thing and feel another. It is very disconcerting. It's also sometimes adventurous and exhilarating to be trying to discover who I am. Sometimes I catch myself feeling that perhaps the person I am is worth being, whatever that means.

"I'm beginning to find it very satisfying, though often painful, to share just what it is I'm feeling at this moment. You know, it is really helpful to try to listen to myself, to hear what is going on in me. I'm not so frightened any more of what *is* going on in me. It seems pretty trustworthy. I use some of my hours with him to dig deep into myself to know what I *am* feeling. It's scary work, but I want to *know.* And I do trust him most of the time, and that helps. I feel pretty vulnerable and raw, but I know he doesn't want to hurt me, and I even believe he cares. It occurs to me as I try to let myself down and down, deep into myself, that maybe if I could sense what is going on in me, and could realize its meaning, I would know who I am, and I would also know what to do. At least I feel this knowing sometimes with him.

"I can even tell him just how I'm feeling toward him at any given moment and instead of this killing the relationship, as I used to fear, it seems to deepen it. Do you suppose I could be my feelings with other people also? Perhaps that wouldn't be too dangerous either.

"You know, I feel as if I'm floating along on the current of life, very adventurously, being me. I get defeated sometimes, I get hurt sometimes, but I'm learning that those experiences are not fatal. I don't know exactly *who* I am, but I can feel my reactions at any given moment, and they seem to work out pretty well as a basis for my behavior from moment to moment. Maybe this is what it *means* to be *me.* But of course I can only do this because I feel safe in the relationship with my therapist. Or could I be myself this way outside of this relationship? I wonder. I wonder. Perhaps I could."

What I have just presented does not happen rapidly. It may take years.

It may not, for reasons we do not understand very well, happen at all. But at least this may suggest an inside view of the factual picture I have tried to present of the process of psychotherapy as it occurs in both the therapist and his client.

REFERENCES

BARRETT-LENNARD, G. T. *Dimensions of perceived therapist response related to therapeutic change.* Unpublished Ph.D. dissertation, University of Chicago, 1959.

BRAATEN, L. J. *The movement from non-self to self in client-centered psychotherapy.* Unpublished Ph.D. dissertation, University of Chicago, 1958.

GENDLIN, E. T. *The function of experiencing in symbolization.* Unpublished Ph.D. dissertation, University of Chicago, 1958.

GENDLIN, E. T. and ZIMRING, F. *The qualities or dimensions of experiencing and their change.* Counseling Center Discussion Papers, University of Chicago Counseling Center, 1, No. 3, 1955.

HALKIDES, GALATIA. *An experimental study of four conditions necessary for therapeutic change.* Unpublished Ph.D. dissertation, University of Chicago, 1958.

HART, J. T. and TOMLINSON, T. M. A validation study of the process scale. *Journal of Consulting Psychology,* 26, 1, 74-78, 1962. (See Chapter 10.)

KIRTNER, W. L. and CARTWRIGHT, D. S. Success and failure in client-centered therapy as a function of initial in-therapy behavior. *Journal of Consulting Psychology,* 22, 329-333, 1958.

ROGERS, C. R. The necessary and sufficient conditions of therapeutic personality change. *Journal of Consulting Psychology,* 21, 95-103, 1957.

ROGERS, C. R. A process conception of psychotherapy. *American Psychologist,* 13, 142-149, 1958.

ROGERS, C. R. and DYMOND, ROSALIND F. (Eds.). *Psychotherapy and personality change.* University of Chicago Press, 1954.

ROGERS, C. R. and RABLEN, R. A. *A scale of process in psychotherapy.* Unpublished manual, University of Wisconsin, 1958.

WALKER, A., RABLEN, R. A., and ROGERS, C. R. Development of a scale to measure process changes in psychotherapy. *Journal of Clinical Psychology,* 16, 79-85, 1959.

10

A Validation Study of

the Process Scale*[1]

T. M. TOMLINSON   J. T. HART

In a 1958 article Rogers presented a theoretical and descriptive formulation of some of the process changes in personality and personal expression which occur during successful psychotherapy. Since the publication of that article a number of investigations have been conducted to empirically elucidate and operationalize Rogers' formulation (Hart, 1961; Rogers, 1959; Tomlinson, 1959; van der Veen, 1961; Walker, Rablen, and Rogers, 1960).

The first step in this line of research was the development by Rogers and Rablen (1958) of a scale to quantify the process conception of personality. As described by Rogers (1959), the rating scale portrays aspects of client functioning in therapy along a general continuum extending from "rigidity and fixity of psychological functioning on the one hand to psychological flow and changingness on the other."

For a detailed description of the Process Scale the reader should consult the article by Walker, Rablen, and Rogers (1960). The measure can be briefly characterized, for the purposes of this paper, as a seven-stage standard scale for the rating of typescript and/or tape excerpts from therapy interviews.

* From T. M. Tomlinson and J. T. Hart, Jr., "A Validation Study of the Process Scale, *Journal of Consulting Psychology,* Vol. 26, No. 1, 1962, pp. 74-78. Copyright 1962 by the American Psychological Association, and reproduced by permission.

[1] This investigation was supported (in part) by research fellowship awards from the United States Office of Vocational Rehabilitation, Washington, D.C. and by a research grant from the National Institute of Mental Health (as part of a larger project), Grant No. M-3496.

The scale as a whole is divided into seven vertical subcategories or strands — Feelings and Personal Meanings, Experiencing, Incongruence, Communication of Self, Construing of Experience, Relationship to Problems, and Manner of Relating. When rating, the raters take each strand or subscale into account and arrive at a global rating of the client's process level which may range from 1.0 to 7.0.

This paper reports the latest investigation in the series of studies which have been carried out to determine the reliability and validity of the Process Scale.

Hypotheses

For the Process Scale to be a useful instrument for research and assessment it must, in the hands of competent judges, yield the following kinds of information. First, a scale should be able to discriminate, by means of obtained ratings, a more successful case from a less successful case.

Secondly, and possibly most important, there should be a difference between the obtained ratings for early as opposed to late interviews. These differences should be in the direction of later interviews yielding a higher process rating than earlier interviews. Further, the differences should be more pronounced for interviews from a successful case than for interviews from a less successful case.

Carrying the above one step further, if the scale is sensitive to the hypothesized changes which occur as a function of psychotherapy, and if psychotherapy is a reasonably continuous phenomenon, then there should be differences, though small, between first and second halves of an interview. Again the differences should be greater for a more successful case than for a less successful case.

The above can be summarized in the form of hypotheses as follows:

(1) Process ratings for more successful cases, hereafter abbreviated m.s., as rated by multiple criteria of outcome, should be significantly higher than process ratings for less successful cases, hereafter abbreviated l.s.

(2) Process ratings should be significantly higher for later interviews than for early interviews.

Corollary (2a) Process ratings should show more pronounced differences between early and later interviews of a m.s. case than between early-late interviews for a l.s. case.

(3) Process scores will be higher for the second half than for the first half of a given interview, although this intrainterview difference will be smaller than the interinterview difference.

Corollary (3a) Process ratings should show more pronounced differences between first and second halves of interviews in a m.s. case than between halves of a l.s. case.

Method

Cases and Rating Segments

A sample of 10 cases, considered representative of the University of Chicago Counseling Center clients, was selected. For each of the 10 cases an early interview and a late interview tape recording was obtained; the second interview from the beginning and the next to the last interview. Nine 2-minute samples of therapy were systematically selected from each of the 20 tapes. The sampling units were arbitrarily chosen at every 3-minute interval within the interview, e.g., 3'interval-2'unit-3'interval-2'unit-3'interval-2'unit, and so on until nine units had been selected from each tape. After selection these 180 units were coded to disguise their origin from the raters, and in addition, the 180 units were randomly assigned to 18 rating groups with 10 rating units per group. For every 2-minute unit a tape recording and a typescript of the tape recording were given to the judges for ratings.

Raters

Two raters were used both of whom had participated in previous studies of the Process Scale. These two experienced raters rated all 180 units — assigning one rating to each 2-minute sample. The rating period extended over 18 days since each rater rated 10 of the 180 units per day. The raters made the ratings at separate times and were not allowed to discuss their ratings with one another — or with others. Both raters had previous experience in psychotherapy and were considered sensitive to intherapy events.

Procedure

The raters used both tape recordings and typescripts to make their ratings of the 2-minute units. Typescripts were necessary because of the poor fidelity of some of the tape units. Tape recordings were used in addition to the typescripts to provide such cues as tone quality, rate of speech, emphasis, etc.

Of the 10 cases selected, 5 were considered more successful cases and 5 were considered less successful cases on the basis of a multicriteria success score. The criteria included therapist ratings of outcome, patient ratings of outcome, and a self-concept Q sort. The m.s. and l.s. cases were randomly assigned to rating groups and all cues in the tape segments concerning the number of the interview or the satisfaction of the client with the therapy were eliminated.

The judges were instructed to rate each unit as a separate entity and to try not to relate an earlier rating to a later rating. The judges reported no influence in their rating due to hearing previous segments from the same case, however this was impossible to assess objectively within the present design.

Results and Discussion

Using the Pearson method of correlation, a coefficient of .65 was obtained between the two judges. Considering the complexity of the judgmental task this figure was accepted as adequate. However, it is not a high reliability figure and the results presented hereafter should be interpreted accordingly.

Before presenting the main body of results and discussion it should be pointed out that the variable "Interviews" and "Halves" were not independent, and the reader should interpret the findings within this limitation.

The results then, which are summarized in Table 10.1 are as follows:

(1) Success: The variable success is significant beyond the .01 level in the direction of the m.s. cases having a higher process rating than the l.s. cases and thus supports Hypothesis 1. This highly significant difference between success groups supports previous results by Walter et al. (1960) and Tomlinson (1959), and has proven to be the most stable finding in this series of studies. This means that the Process Scale is able to discriminate, in a highly reliable way, cases rated m.s. from those rated l.s.

(2) Interviews: The scale was able to detect differences between early and later interviews at beyond the .05 level thus supporting Hypothesis 2. Process ratings were, on the average, higher for the later interview than for the early interview.

(3) Interview $\times$ Success: Corollary 2a is not statistically supported ($p >$ .05), however, the result is in the predicted direction. Tentatively, process ratings increase in magnitude as a function of success and time of occurrence, e.g., the late, m.s. group received the highest mean rating. Table 10.2 illustrates this statement more clearly.

(4) Halves: This is no statistical support ($p > .05$) for the contention that process scores will be higher for second than for first half of an interview. However, Table 10.2 shows that all means are in the predicted direction with one exception, and it can hardly be called a major reversal of prediction.

(5) Halves $\times$ Success: Corollary 3a is not statistically supported ($p > .05$), but the trend seems clearly supportive of the prediction. Table 10.2 shows that the differences between m.s. halves are relatively clear as compared to the differences between l.s. halves of interviews.

(6) Judges: The differences between judges is highly significant, ($p < .01$). When considered in light of the interjudge reliability, this result indicates that although judges appear to be able to rate up and down the scale in a fairly reliable way, they are subect to error which makes them consistently different in the rating they assign to a given segment. It is believed that this differential bias is the reason for the significant second and third order interactions. Plotting the mean process ratings for both judges indicates that there is a generally increasing linear trend in process ratings as a function of time and success, but the magnitude of the interaction depends on which judge makes the rating.

It is not surprising that the difference between halves of interviews is not significant. Successful psychotherapy is at least in part a function of the number of interviews (Standal & van der Veen, 1957) and it would be unusual if within any single interview there was a sudden, perceptible personality change. For this reason no significant difference in mean scores for halves was expected. However, if the process of psychotherapy is a fairly continuous phenomenon, it would be reasonable to expect consistent differences between halves, in the direction of the second half being higher in process rating than the first half. To test this notion a nonparametric statistical procedure (sign test) was used. The differences, holding Success and Judges constant, are in the predicted direction 13 of 19 times ($p = .084$) for the early interviews and 15 of 19 times ($p = .010$) for the late interviews. Holding Judges and Time constant, 16 of the 20 ($p = .006$) interviews are in the hypothesized direction for the more successful cases while 12 of 18 ($p = .119$) are in the positive direction for the less successful cases. Thus it seems that movement within the interview is both a function of time and success. From these results it would seem that the process of personality change within an interview is directly analogous to that which occurs between interviews, i.e., during the course of therapy. The only difference is in the magnitude of the change. Further, the results suggest that the change is a cumulative one whose direction and possibly magnitude varies positively as a function of success and time.

If personality change is a function of psychotherapy and if the Process Scale is sensitive to the behavioral differences that occur concomitantly with this change, then one would expect these changes to be most noticeably reflected in the differnces between early and late successful interviews. Table 10.1 shows this to be the case statistically, but the magnitude (See Table 10.2) of the differences is hardly of practical value, being on the average only .7 of a stage for Judge 1 and .3 of a stage for Judge 2. Yet Walker, et al., were able to detect mean change scores of 1.93 stages in the marked success group ($N = 3$) using the same scale. However, Walker used cases chosen for the purpose of representing end-points of a success-failure continuum. The cases used in this study cover the entire continuum of success-failure. As such it is reasonable to expect overlap between m.s. and l.s. cases in the middle of the continuum. Further, in analyzing the results in terms of means the differences within the individual success and/or failure cases are washed out. Difference scores were computed for each case between early and late interview ratings and the results suggest that the Process Scale detects differences between early and late interviews at least in part as a function of a success-failure continuum. For Judge 1 the differences betwen early and late, m.s. interviews range from 1.5 to .0 stages, while for Judge 2 the range is .8 to − .1 stages. For the l.s. group the range for Judge 1 is .6 to − .3 stages and for Judge 2, .2 to − .1 stages. Thus it appears that the Process Scale is sensitive to change as a function of success-failure.

One final comment: This study is the latest in a series which have attempted to validate the Process Scale. Out of these studies one clear finding has always resulted, namely that the m.s. case almost invariably starts therapy at a higher stage of process than the l.s. case. In this study, using the Mann-Whitney U test to test the significance of the difference between early, m.s. and early, l.s. cases, the differences were significant in the expected direction at about the .02 level ($U = 20.5$; $N_1 = 10$, $N_2 = 10$). Here as in the previous studies, the m.s. clients seem to enter therapy at a higher stage of process than the l.s. ones. This suggests at least two things: (a) there may be some personality characteristics which each client must possess in some minimal degree to profit from psychotherapy, and (b) those clients below this minimum will not progress in psychotherapy. This conjecture is similar to and supports Kirtner's (1955) finding that the successful client is characterized by different personality attributes than the client who fails to profit from psychotherapy. If this approach continues to be fruitful then perhaps more light can be shed on the nature of and the reasons for the failure case.

TABLE 10.1

Analysis of Variance of Process Ratings

Source	df	SS	MS	F
Success (S)	1	11.55	11.55	40.10**
Judges (J)	1	7.08	7.08	26.04**
Interviews (I)	1	1.57	1.57	6.00*
Halves (H)	1	.14	.14	.53
S × J	1	.11	.11	.42
S × I	1	.80	.80	3.05
S × H	1	.12	.12	.46
I × J	1	.228	.22	.84
H × J	1	.05	.05	.19
H × I	1	.01	.01	.04
H × S × J	1	1.44	1.44	4.75*
I × S × J	1	.28	.28	1.07
H × I × S	1	.97	.97	3.70
H × I × J	1	.30	.30	1.15
H × I × J × S	1	1.52	1.52	5.81*
SS/Success	8	2.30	.288	1.10
Residual	56	14.70	.262	

* $p < .05$.
** $p < .01$.

Summary

The steps which have been taken to objectify and validate Rogers' conception of the process of psychotherapy have been summarized. The study

TABLE 10.2

*Mean Process Ratings, Number of Interviews, and Counselor Ratings
of Outcome for Each of Ten Cases and Two Judges*

	No. of inter- views	Coun- selor rating	Judge 1				Judge 2			
			Early		Late		Early		Late	
Case			1/2	2/2	1/2	2/2	1/2	2/2	1/2	2/2
1	45	7	3.6	4.1	4.0	4.0	2.5	2.6	2.4	2.6
2	46	8	2.8	3.2	2.9	3.1	2.6	2.7	2.4	2.6
3	21	8	3.5	3.8	5.2	5.0	3.9	4.1	4.6	4.8
4	25	8	3.4	3.1	4.4	4.8	2.7	2.4	3.4	3.5
5	14	6	3.7	3.8	3.8	4.0	3.5	3.2	3.1	3.7
Mean			3.4	3.6	4.1	4.3	3.0	3.0	3.2	3.4
6	28	3	3.2	3.3	3.8	3.9	2.9	2.6	2.8	2.9
7	27	2	2.7	2.8	2.4	2.6	2.2	2.2	2.4	2.1
8	27	5	3.4	3.2	3.4	3.5	2.6	2.4	2.5	2.6
9	26	3	2.7	2.8	2.7	2.4	2.2	2.4	2.5	2.5
10	38	5	2.5	2.8	2.8	3.0	2.4	2.6	2.5	2.2
Mean			2.9	3.0	3.0	3.1	2.5	2.4	2.5	2.5

currently reported, and the previous studies justify the following conclusions
in regard to the Process Scale and its operational meaning.

(1) Interjudge agreement is always adequate and significantly better than
chance, as estimated by parametric and nonparametric statistics. Interjudge
reliability appears to have a minimum of about .60.

(2) It distinguishes between more successful and less successful cases at
a high level of statistical significance.

(3) It indicates that more successful cases begin as well as end at a significantly higher level of process.

(4) There is evidence that there is greater movement (process change)
on the Process Scale during the period of therapy in more successful than
in less successful cases. The difference is only modestly significant and its
utility is yet to be determined.

(5) There is a tendency for the second half of each interview to be rated
higher on the Process Scale than the first half. This tendency toward intrainterview change is definitely significant in the more successful group of cases.

REFERENCES

HART, J. T. A reliability study of the process scale. Unpublished M.S. thesis, University of Wisconsin, 1961.

KIRTNER, W. H. Success and failure in cilent-centered therapy as a function of personality variables. Unpublished M.A. thesis, University of Chicago, 1955.

ROGERS, C. R. A process conception of psychotherapy. *American Psychologist,* 1958, 13, 142-149.

ROGERS, C. R. A tentative scale for the measurement of process in psychotherapy. In E. A. Rubinstein and M. B. Parloff (Eds.), *Research in psychotherapy.* Washington, D. C.: American Psychological Association, 1959. Pp. 96-107.

ROGERS, C. R., and RABLEN, R. A. A scale of process in psychotherapy. Unpublished manual, University of Wisconsin, 1958. (Mimeo.)

STANDAL, S. W., and VAN DER VEEN, F. Length of therapy in relation to counselor estimates of personal integration and other case variables. *Journal of Consulting Psychology,* 1957, 21, 1-9.

TOMLINSON, T. M. A validation study of a scale for the measurement of the process of personality change in psychotherapy. Unpublished M.S. thesis, University of Wisconsin, 1959.

VAN DER VEEN, F. Strand scale analysis of the psychotherapy process scale. *Psychiatry Institute Bulletin,* 1961, 1, No. 1.

WALKER, A., RABLEN, R. A., and ROGERS, C. R. Development of a scale to measure process change in psychotherapy. *Journal of Clinical Psychology,* 1960, 1, 79-85.

11

Client Perception of Therapist
Conditions as a Factor in
Psychotherapy*

FERDINAND VAN DER VEEN

The client's perception of the basic therapeutic conditions offered by the therapist has been accepted as an important part of client-centered theory for a number of years. Recently both theory and experimental method have become sufficiently developed to permit intensive research on the function of this variable in the process of therapy. Rogers (1957) has developed a concise theoretical statement describing the necessary and sufficient conditions of therapeutic personality change. Stated simply, the theory holds that the client grows more as a person when the therapist can fully understand the client's feelings, can accept all aspects of the client, and can be genuinely himself with him, *and* when the client perceives the therapist as having these attitudes. The theory maintains that these conditions are essential for

* The studies reported here were carried out at the Wisconsin Psychiatric Institute, University of Wisconsin, as part of a program of research under the direction of Carl R. Rogers and supported by grants from the Human Ecology Fund, the Wisconsin Alumni Research Foundation, and the National Institute of Mental Health (No. M-3496). An abbreviated version of the paper was presented at the Annual Meeting of the American Psychological Association in New York City, September 1961. It has been distributed informally as issue No. 10 (e), Vol. 1, 1961, of the Wisconsin Psychiatric Institute Bulletin: "The perception by clients and by judges of the conditions offered by the therapist in the therapy relationship."

The author wants to express his gratitude to Norton Stoler, Philippa Mathieu, Charles Truax, Jules Spotts, and Marylin Geist for the use of data and findings, as indicated in the report.

the growth of personality in the therapy relationship. The theoretical statement was followed by Barrett-Lennard's (1962) construction of an inventory to measure the client's perception of these therapist attitudes. This instrument, called the Relationship Inventory, consists of sets of specific itemized descriptions for four theoretical variables: the therapist's empathic understanding of the client, his degree of positive regard for the client, the degree to which his regard is unconditional or unqualified, and the extent to which the therapist is congruent in the relationship. These variables are probably familiar to you except possibly for unconditionality of regard. This is one-half of the theoretical variable of "unconditional positive regard" (Standal, 1954; Rogers, 1957). Barrett-Lennard divided this theoretical variable into two components: positiveness of regard and unconditionality of regard, the latter referring to a uniform level of prizing all the client's aspects, without specific disapproval or approval for particular client expressions.

The entire Inventory consists of 72 items, 18 for each of the four variables. For the variable, *empathic understanding* of the client by the therapist, there are items such as "He is interested in knowing what my experiences mean to *me*," and "He nearly always knows exactly what I mean." For *degree of positive regard,* there are items such as "He is friendly and warm toward me," and "He feels that I am dull and uninteresting." For *unconditionality of regard,* "He likes me in some ways, and dislikes me in others," and "Sometimes he is warmly responsive to me, at other times cold or disapproving." And for the *genuineness* or *congruence* of the therapist, "He responds to me mechanically," and "I feel I can trust him to be honest with me." Each item is rated for the degree to which it is felt to be true or not true of the therapist and scored according to whether it shows the attitude to be present or absent.

Barrett-Lennard has since sponsored research using the Relationship Inventory in widely varying areas, including teacher-student and parent-child relationships. The results have been encouraging. In the initial study of the Relationship Inventory with a sample of counseling center clients, Barrett-Lennard found that success in psychotherapy was positively related to the client's perception of the therapist conditions. The Inventory was included in our research to test the hypothesis that this variable is also an essential aspect of the therapeutic process in hospitalized schizophrenic patients and to study further its relationship to personality change. Using it, we have obtained some interesting and promising findings.

Perceived Conditions and Client Personality Variables

Data obtained in the analyses of the initial battery and the sampling interviews by Stoler permitted us to investigate partially three questions regarding the factors that influence perception of the conditions. *The first question is whether, in fact, therapists are perceived as offering more of the conditions hypothesized to be essential for psychotherapy than other significantly helpful persons.* We predicted that they would be. In our sample we had Relationship Inventory ratings of therapists by the clients and by each control nontherapy subject of the person he felt had been of most help to him.

Figure 11.1 shows that the therapists were perceived more highly on all the conditions than were significant nontherapist persons. Not all the conditions contributed equally to the difference between the two groups. The difference for unconditionality of regard was significant at the 1 per cent level; the differences for empathy and congruence were significant at the 5 per cent level; while for positive regard the difference was significant at only the 10 per cent level. Therefore, for three of the four therapist conditions and for the total score, the hypothesis that therapists are perceived as having more of these conditions than other important and significantly helpful persons was supported.

The next question concerns the relationship of the perception of the conditions in the therapist to the client's personality. The hypothesis was that there is a positive relationship between psychological adjustment and the perception of the conditions. Stoler found that the total score on the Relationship Inventory had a significant negative relationship with many of the MMPI clinical scales for the entire group of normal and hospitalized subjects.

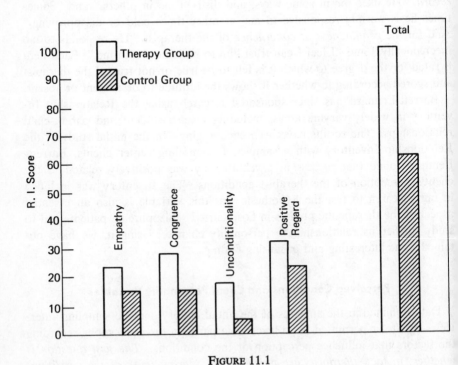

FIGURE 11.1

Mean Conditions Perceived by Therapy and Control Groups

Among the outstanding ones were the Psychastenia scale, the Schizophrenia scale, the Social Introversion scale, and the Welsch Anxiety Index. There was also a positive relationship between the perception of the conditions and the Barron Ego Strength scale. These relationships were all in the direction of the perception of lower conditions with more evidence of clinical problems. The range of these correlations was from .34 to .44. The results suggest that the perception of therapist conditions is moderately related to the degree of psychological adjustment of the perceiver.

The important question arose as to whether the perception of conditions was a function of behavioral personality variables as well as ones that depended upon self-report instruments. Ratings were available of client behavior on two process scales, the Problem Expression scale and the Experiencing scale (cf. Rogers, 1959). The Problem Expression scale concerns a client's orientation to his problems and gives an estimate of the extent to which he talks about problems and relates them to himself and his situation. The Experiencing scale provides an estimate of the extent to which the client talks about and refers to his personal experience. For ratings of the client's behavior in the sampling interviews, Stoler found no significant relationships for the Experiencing Scale, but highly significant positive relationships for the Problem Expression Scale. These correlations ranged from .45 to .60 for the different Relationship Inventory scores for the hospital group of therapy and control subjects.

For the ratings of client behavior in the therapy interviews on the same two scales, obtained in a study by Mathieu, we found significant positive relationships between the total score on the Relationship Inventory and the process ratings for the therapy interview closest in time to the administration of the Inventory. The rank-order correlations were .79 for the Problem Expression Scale and .58 for the Experiencing Scale. Therefore we can say with some degree of confidence that the hospital client perceives higher therapist conditions if he functions at a higher level of process in the therapy situation.

Perceived Conditions and the Effect of Therapy

Following is a presentation of the findings on the basic hypothesis of the project regarding the relationship between the perception of conditions and change over therapy in the client.

Truax hypothesized that clients showing more test improvement will initially perceive greater therapist conditions and, since perception of the conditions was found to be related to the client's adjustment, that clients showing more test improvement will show a greater increase over therapy in their perception of the conditions than clients showing less improvement.

To test these hypotheses a group of ten schizophrenic patients for whom more than one Relationship Inventory was available was divided into two equal groups of five clients showing more test improvement and five showing less. A Q-sort adjustment score, an anxiety measure, and the MMPI were used to determine the degree of test change over therapy. Changes on the tests were from the pretherapy battery to the latest one available for each client. The initial Relationship Inventory was obtained three months after the initiation of therapy and the later Relationship Inventory was the last one available for each case. At the time of the later inventory, the test improved group had an average of 93.2 interviews of therapy and the test deteriorated group had 99.0 interviews, so that both groups had received approximately the same amount of therapy when the early and late inventories were obtained.

Truax found the hypothesis of higher initial perception of conditions for the more improved group to be unsupported except for the condition of positive regard, which was significantly higher for the more improved group at the 1 per cent level. On the other hand, empathic understanding was significantly lower for this group than for the less improved clients.

For the hypothesis of change in the perception of conditions over therapy he found that for the total score, as well as for three of the four separate conditions (excepting only unconditionality of regard), the more improved group showed a significantly greater increase in the perception of conditions than did the less improved group, at the 1 per cent level of significance using the *t* test. As a group, the less improved clients perceived very slightly lower conditions later in therapy than earlier (73.8 vs. 78.2, for the total score) while the more improved group perceived higher conditions later in therapy than earlier (107.8 vs. 84.0, for the total score). Thus it was found that clients who showed more test improvement over therapy showed a greater increase in their perception of therapist conditions than did clients showing less test improvement. This finding supports the earlier ones concerning the positive relationship between psychological adjustment and the perception of therapist conditions, and it extends them to include change shown by the client over therapy.

So far I have presented our findings regarding the client's perception of conditions and personality variables, interview behavior, and test improvement. Two questions remain for which we have beginning answers. Is the client's perception of conditions related to his process movement over therapy, and is movement over therapy related to the conditions as perceived by objective judges?

A study by the writer investigated the hypothesis *that the degree of client movement is positively related to the client's perception of the conditions in the therapist.* Estimates of in-therapy client process behavior were provided by data from Mathieu's study on the relationship between client process and therapist conditions, for the second, fifth, fifteenth, and thirtieth interviews, on the Problem Expression scale and the Experiencing scale. The sample consisted of thirteen hospitalized clients with the diagnosis of schizophrenia, as supported by the initial battery analysis, for whom both process ratings and

Relationship Inventories were available. The analyses presented here will be limited to the total inventory score, which gives an estimate of the presence of all four of the therapist conditions.

Table 11.1 presents the results of the analysis. Three movement scores were derived for the process rating scales, based on mean interview ratings for each client. The first movement score is the difference between the thirtieth interview and the second interview, the second score is the difference between the average of the thirtieth and fifteenth interviews and the average of the second and fifth interviews, and the last is the average of these two scores. For the difference in movement between clients who perceived higher conditions and those who perceived lower ones, the group of thirteen was divided at the middle, with seven clients in the higher group and six in the lower group.

TABLE 11.1

*PE and EXP Movement Over the First 30 Therapy Interviews
and Client Relationship Inventory Scores*

| | Mean Movement | | | | |
	Higher C.R.I. (n = 7)	Lower C.R.I. (n = 6)	U sig.	rho (n = 13)	sig.
PE Scale Movement Score:					
30-2	1.13	.43	.09	.28	n.s.
Av. L.I. — Av. E.I.	.97	.06	.05	.62	.05
Combined Average	1.05	.25	.01	.57	.05
EXP Scale Movement Score:					
30-2	1.14	.30	n.s.	.37	n.s.
Av. L.I. — Av. E.I.	.83	.02	.02	.64	.05
Combined Average	.99	.16	.05	.59	.05

The mean movement for the higher perceivers was about one stage for both he Problem Expression and the Experiencing scales, while for the lower group t varied from no movement to about .4 of a stage. The differences between he two groups were significant at less than the 5 per cent point for two of he three movement scores for each scale, using the Mann-Whitney U Test. Rank-order correlations between the Inventory scores and the different movement scores yielded two moderately high correlations for each scale, .62 ind .57 for the Problem Scale and .64 and .59 for the Experiencing Scale, all ignificant at less than the 5 per cent point. These results clearly supported the hypothesis that movement in the first thirty interviews of therapy for schizophrenic clients is positively related to the extent to which the therapist conditions are perceived by the client at the three-month point.

The preceding findings depend upon the extent to which the client is able to perceive the conditions offered by the therapist. *Is movement in therapy also related to the degree to which the conditions of therapy are actually offered by the therapist, regardless of how these are perceived by the client?*

To investigate this question, the writer and Spotts and Geist undertook a study of therapist conditions, using Relationship Inventory ratings of the therapists by judges after they listened to a tape recording of a therapy interview. The Relationship Inventory was slightly modified to make the items appropriate for persons not participating in the interview. Each of six judges rated one interview for each case.[1] The interview was selected to be closest to the time of administration of the client's Relationship Inventory. One judge failed to correlate significantly with any other judge and was omitted from the analysis. The remaining five judges had a median intercorrelation of .50 for eighteen cases. The mean total inventory score of the five judges for each case was used in the analysis. The sample consisted of ten of the eighteen cases for whom therapy process ratings were available. The process data consisted of the ratings obtained by Mathieu for the second, fifth, fifteenth and thirtieth interviews, as in the previous analysis.

Table 11.2 presents the results for the three process movement scores and the total scores on the Judge Relationship Inventory. The mean movement for the clients whose therapists were rated higher on the Inventory varied from about .6 to 1.1 stages for the two scales, while the movement for clients whose therapists were rated lower varied from 0 to .3 stages. The differences were significant for one movement score for the PE scale and for two scores for the EXP scale, beyond the 5 per cent point. The significant rank-order correlations between judge estimates and movement were .56 for the Problem Scale and .55 and .62 for the Experiencing Scale.

To find out if the judges' ratings may have been contaminated by the level of the client on the process scales, the Judge Relationship Inventory scores were correlated with the process scores for the interview closest to the one rated by the judge. For the PE Scale the correlation was $-.07$ and for the EXP Scale it was .04. Therefore there was no indication that the judges were influenced in their ratings of the therapists by the process level of the clients. These findings supported the hypothesis that movement in therapy is positively related to the level of conditions offered by the therapist for our population of hospitalized schizophrenic clients.

To see if this association was actually independent of the client's perception of the conditions, the judges' Inventory ratings were correlated with the

[1] The authors of this study want to express their gratitude to Shirley Epstein, Margaret Evans, R. Smith, and Wendy Spotts for their generous participation as judges.

TABLE 11.2

PE and EXP Movement Over the First 30 Therapy Interviews and Judge Relationship Inventory Scores

	Mean Movement				
	Higher J.R.I. (n = 5)	Lower J.R.I. (n = 5)	U sig.	rho (n = 10)	sig.
PE Scale Movement Score:					
30-2	1.00	.16	.03	.56	0.5
Av. L.I. — Av. E.I.	.63	.06	n.s.	.16	n.s.
Combined Average	.82	.11	.06	.34	n.s.
EXP Scale Movement Score:					
30-2	1.14	.28	.10	.38	n.s.
Av. L.I. — Av. E.I.	.65	.02	.03	.55	.05
Combined Average	.90	.15	.02	.62	.05

clients' inventory scores for the ten cases. The correlation was essentially zero (.09), indicating that the two sets of scores were unrelated and that the amount of movement in therapy was a function of the actual conditions provided by the therapist over and above the extent to which they were perceived by the client.

Conclusion

In conclusion I would like to summarize what I believe these initial analyses of our data have shown. First, they show that therapists are perceived as providing more of the conditions client-centered theory postulates as essential for personality growth than are other significantly helpful persons. They also indicate that the perception of these conditions is dependent upon important psychological variables related to adjustment and to therapy behavior, and that change in the perception of conditions is related to change in adjustment over therapy. With respect to the basic hypothesis of our research, we have several important conclusions. One is negative: for the data presently available, there is no relationship between test improvement and the client's perception of conditions early in therapy. On the other hand, for process movement in therapy the hypothesis was clearly supported. Our findings show that (1) hospitalized schizophrenic clients who perceive higher therapist conditions show greater process movement over the first thirty interviews of therapy; (2) clients of therapists who are judged to provide more of the conditions in the therapy interview show greater process movement than do clients of therapists who provide lower conditions; and (3) amount of movement in therapy is a function of *both* perceived and actual therapist conditions.

These results, if they are borne out by further research, have several implications for our understanding of the treatment of the schizophrenic patient. If it is true that the patient's adjustment and his improvement are a function of the attitudes he perceives toward him, this could be used as a central therapeutic principle in the procedures used to help him. In other words, the hospital procedures with the patient could have as one of their main therapeutic elements the objective of increasing the patient's perception of these attitudes toward him. Besides individual therapy, this can occur in a variety of other procedures, in fact in any that involve relationships within the hospital. The patient's perception of being accepted, understood, and related to in a genuine way is a therapeutic factor which can be widely utilized in treatment, training, and research.

One final comment concerns the possible ways in which these attitudes can be communicated to the patient. If it is the patient's *perception* of them that is an essential element in therapy, then the therapist can behave in any way that is likely to communicate them to a particular patient. Therefore, it is possible for therapists to vary widely in their behavior in order to convey these basic attitudes. How they can best be conveyed remains a question for further study.

REFERENCES

BARRETT-LENNARD, G. T. Dimensions of therapist response as causal factors in therapeutic change. *Psychological Monographs,* 1962, 76, No. 43 (Whole No. 562).

ROGERS, C. R. The necessary and sufficient conditions for personality change. *Journal of Consulting Psychology,* 1957, 21, 95-103.

ROGERS, C. R. A tentative scale for the measurement of process in psychotherapy. In E. A. Rubinstein and M. B. Parloff (Eds.), *Research in psychotherapy.* Washington, D.C.: American Psychological Association, 1959. Pp. 96-107.

STANDAL, S. W. The need for positive regard: A contribution to client-centered theory. Unpublished doctoral dissertation, University of Chicago, 1954.

12

Personality and Performance Correlates of Empathic Understanding in Psychotherapy*[1]

ALLEN E. BERGIN   SANDRA SOLOMON

Only a few short years ago it was accurately stated that the bulk of psychotherapy research had been up to that time patient-oriented (Bandura, 1956). At a theoretical level, the idea of the therapist as a neutral catalyst was rapidly breaking down (Rogers, 1957), but there was as yet little that could be definitively asserted on empirical grounds regarding the unique contributions of therapists *as persons* to the treatment process.

The intervening years have witnessed a dramatic focusing of attention upon the therapist as a human being who inevitably reacts personally and significantly in the clinical interaction. The impact of his personal attributes upon the patient are now known to be of such importance that it is impossible to further maintain the notion of therapist neutrality (Bandura, 1956, 1960; Betz, 1962; Cutler, 1958; McNair, Callahan, and Lorr, 1962; Krasner, 1962; Murray, 1956; Rosenthal, 1955). As a result, the hypothesis that the more potent therapeutic and antitherapeutic factors have to do with the therapist's personality (Fiedler, 1950a, 1950b) has become more fully accepted, even though debate continues as to whether positive personality factors are simply

* Paper presented at the American Psychological Association Convention, Philadelphia, September, 1963.

[1] We express our appreciation to the therapists who contributed considerable time to this project and to the faculty supervisors whose cooperation was also essential. The study was supported by the Bailey K. Howard Faculty Research Fund, Teachers College.

necessary preconditions or whether they are sufficient conditions in and of themselves for producing client personality change (Ellis, 1959; Rogers, 1957).

The present study is an attempt to delineate further therapeutically relevant therapist qualities by specifying sources of individual differences in empathic understanding as measured by the Truax Accurate Empathy Scale (Truax, 1961a). Empathy was selected for study because it is almost universally considered an essential attitudinal condition for producing positive therapeutic change and because recent evidence indicates that it is significantly related to process measures of client change and to several independent measures of outcome (Truax, 1963). The reliable measurement of this ubiquitous variable and the subsequent demonstration of its relationship to practical criteria has been a signal achievement in and of itself. The importance of this attainment for selection, training, and practice is attested to not only by the wide acceptance of empathy as an important variable in psychotherapy but also by empirical evidence indicating that low empathic ability is, alas, associated with personality deterioration in patients (Truax, 1963; Bergin, 1963). The specification of therapist trait dimensions having relevance to variation in empathic behavior during actual treatment interviews should close even further the gap between the general hypothesis of personal therapist influence and its application to practical realities such as therapist selection.

Hypotheses

(1) Since both clinical and research evidence suggest that personality disturbance in the therapist interferes with therapeutic efficacy, it was hypothesized that scores on the clinical scales of the Minnesota Multiphasic Personality Inventory (MMPI) would correlate negatively with empathy as measured during the psychotherapy process. The D, Hy, Pd, and Pt scales were assumed to be of particular relevance, *D* and *Pt* as indicators of subjective discomfort, *Hy* as an index of repressive tendencies, and *Pd* representing unconcern for others.

(2) It was hypothesized that enduring "normal" qualities of personality as measured by the Edwards Personal Preference Schedule (EPPS) should be related to empathy. The Intraception and Nurturance Scales were specifically predicted, on the basis of face validity, to be positively related to empathy.

(3) Davitz' (1964) recently developed laboratory method for measuring accuracy in perceiving emotional meanings was introduced in order to test the measure's validity with regard to empathic sensitivity in psychotherapy. It was hypothesized that accuracy of perception would be positively related to empathic understanding.

(4) On the assumption that theoretical ability and academic knowledge are unlike the elements of clinical skill, it was further hypothesized that grade

point averages in practicum courses would be positively related to empathic ability, whereas grade point averages in academic courses would not.

(5) Since empathic ability is presumed to be one essential quality of therapeutic proficiency, it was hypothesized that empathy would be positively related to supervisors' ratings of therapeutic competence.

(6) Since it has been assumed by some clinicians that high intelligence is necessary for accurately developing empathic responses, and since vocabulary scores were shown by Davitz (1964) to correlate with perceptivity of emotional meaning, it was hypothesized that GRE verbal scores would correlate significantly with empathy.

Method

Subjects

Eighteen post-internship students in clinical and counseling psychology provided a total of fifty-three hours of tape-recorded therapy interviews for analysis. Ten Ss provided two hours separated by at least one week for each of two clients, a total of four hours per therapist, except in a few instances. The remaining eight Ss provided recordings for one client only. Recordings were selected from the sixth and seventh months of an eight-month period of therapy during the 1961-62 academic year. Clients were adolescent and adult neurotics who were seen at the Teachers College Guidance Laboratory in an intensive psychotherapy practicum. Three of the eighteen Ss were unable to participate in the testing portions of the study, an additional S turned in an invalid MMPI and EPPS, another did not turn in his test protocols at all, and still another was already familiar with the construction of the Davitz measure. For these reasons it will be noted that the sample N's vary from variable to variable in the date analysis. It should be noted here that these Ss were, with rare exceptions, rather unfamiliar with the details of MMPI and EPPS scoring, a reflection in part of the eastern (New York?) bias favoring projective tests. A check of individual profiles indicated only one that was clearly invalid.

Empathy Ratings

Before any other data were analyzed, the authors independently rated the middle one-third of each therapy hour for eight therapists on the Truax Scale of Accurate Empathy. After establishing that adequate reliability had been attained in these ratings, the remaining recordings were divided and rated by one rater only. Accurate empathy is defined by Truax (1961a) as a modification of Rogers' earlier description (1957):

> It involves both a sensitivity to current feelings and a verbal facility to communicate this understanding in a language attuned to the client's current

feelings. The therapist's responses . . . serve to clarify and expand the client's awareness of his own feelings or experiences. This is communicated . . . by the total voice qualities which reflect the seriousness, the intentness, and the depth of feeling . . . the therapist may be accurately describing psychodynamics to the patient but a lack of empathy would be indicated by such description being in a language not that of the client or by being presented at a time when these dynamics are far removed from the current feelings of the client, so that the therapist is "pulling" the client along rather than being "with" the client in his own self-exploration (Truax, 1961a, pp. 2-3).

The scale itself consists of nine points, each being defined by a descriptive statement and a series of verbatim examples from recorded interviews. For our purposes the scale was expanded to ten points by inserting an additional point between empathy levels 2 and 3. Other liberties of definition were taken with the scale, and copies of the revised version are available from the authors.

Supervisor Ratings

Therapists were supervised in groups of three or four by individual clinical or counseling psychology faculty members. The supervisors were instructed to rate the general therapeutic competence of each student on a grading scale, utilized for all practicum courses, which varies from: A+: very outstanding and rarely given, to C: unsatisfactory and judged not likely to improve, a signal that the faculty should consider whether the student should be dropped from the program. Since only one supervisor was intimately acquainted with each student's performance, interrater reliability of these ratings was impossible to determine; however, supervisors did have approximately 120 hours of intensive small group contact with their supervisees in addition to weekly sessions in a large case seminar. Weekly supervisors' meetings where student progress was discussed also operated to minimize the possible distortions in these ratings.

Perception of Emotional Meaning

Davitz' work (1964) in the communication of emotional meaning has resulted in the design of an instrument for measuring perceptual accuracy in response to eight reliable differentiable emotions. Emotions are communicated nondiscursively by standard communicators who use identical verbal content for expressing them. The communications are recorded and presented in counterbalanced order so that each emotion is presented five times. Scores consist of the total number of correct designations by the subject. Since the measure samples sensitivity to subtle fluctuations in tone quality as indicators of feeling, it was assumed to estimate qualities essential in empathic ability.

Therapist Goals

As a check on whether level of empathy might be in part a function of therapist orientation, Ss were asked to rate their goals or intentions with each client on a set of five-point rating scales. The scales indicated the degree to which the therapist attempted to be Interpretive, Warm, Empathic, Supportive, and Advising. The scale for Empathy was as follows: "Characterize the procedures you are attempting to use and the goals you had in mind as you conducted therapy with client _____: Tried to communicate to the client my empathic understanding of his feelings: most important, very important, moderately important, slightly important, unimportant." The Empathy rating was the critical one desired, and the others served to guise this fact. *S*s were not informed until after the collection of the data as to the purpose of the study.

Results

Reliability

Interrater reliability on the accurate empathy scale was .79 for the 28 therapy hours which were rated by both judges.

TABLE 12.1

Correlates of Empathy

Variable	r	N	Variable	r	N
Supervisor Rating	.41**	18	MMPI (cont.)		
Davitz Tape	.14	15	Si	−.18	12
Anxiety Rating	−.13	15	Es	.08	13
Grade Ave. (Diag. pract.)	−.17	18	EPPS		
Grade Ave. (Acad.)	−.16	18	Con	−.54**	13
GRE (Psych.)	−.18	17	Aff	−.18	13
GRE (Q)	.21	18	Def	−.23	13
GRE (V)	−.30	18	Ach	−.15	13
Age (23-38)	.15	17	Ord	−.41*	13
Age (23-29)	.50*	11	Exh	−.12	13
MMPI			Aut	.37	13
K	.15	12	Int	−.53**	13
Hs	−.31	12	Suc	.00	13
D	−.41[a]	12	Dom	.54**	13
Hy	−.30	12	Aba	−.12	13
Pd	.10	12	Nur	−.19	13
Mf	.37	12	Chg	.55**	13
Pa	−.05	12	End	.08	13
Pt	−.54**	12	Het	−.05	13
Sc	−.05	12	Agg	.04	13
Ma	.32	12			

[a] $p < .06$ * $p < .05$ ** $p < .01$

Intercorrelations of Variables

It may be seen from Table 12.1 that the Depression and Psychasthenia Scales of the MMPI correlate negatively with empathic understanding in therapy, as hypothesized. Although none of the other scales provide significant correlations, it is of interest to note that in every case the positive correlations are with those variables which indicate personality strength when not extreme (K, Ma, Es), whereas the negative relationships occur exclusively with variables indicative of personality disturbances.

The Consistency, Order, and Intraception Scales of the Edwards Personal Preference Schedule were all negatively related to empathy (E) while the Dominance and Change variables correlated positively. Intraception, one of the two Edwards variables about which a specific prediction was made, correlated in the opposite direction predicted. The other postulated relationship, between Nurturance and Empathy, did not occur. The Davitz measure correlated significantly with Autonomy, Aggression, *Sc,* and *Si,* although it did not correlate with any of the other variables used in the study including E.

None of the indicators of intelligence or academic achievement correlated significantly with E. The practicum grade average based upon two years work in diagnostic testing and interviewing was also unrelated to E.

The supervisor ratings (SR) of therapeutic competence correlated significantly with E, further indicating the validity of the Truax Scale and suggesting that the measured empathy is something which diversely oriented supervisors value. The relationship of SR to the variables that correlated significantly with E are given in Table 12.2.

Although the relationship between the EPPS and the MMPI has been previously studied (Merrill, 1956), it was thought worthwhile to explore the relationships among those measures that correlated significantly with E in our

TABLE 12.2

Correlates of Supervisor Rating

Variable	r	N
Pt	−.36	12
D	−.39	12
Ord	−.23	13
Int	−.04	13
Dom	.46*	13
Chg	−.02	13
Age (23-29)	.66**	11
Davitz	−.03	15
Anx. Ratg.	−.69**	15
Grades (acad.)	−.04	18
Grades (pract.)	−.22	18

* p <.05   ** p <.01

selected sample. The correlations were mostly quite low and nonsignificant, as has been reported in previous work (Table 12.3).

The distributions of the various scores are given in Table 12.4. The most noticeable evidence contained there is that regarding the restricted ranges of

TABLE 12.3

Intercorrelations of Variables Related to Empathy

	SR	Pt	D	Ord	Int	Dom	Chg	Age (23-29)	Age (23-38)
E	.41**	−.54**	−.41ᵃ	−.41*	−.53**	.54**	.55**	.50*	−.15
SR		−.36	−.39	−.23	−.04	.46*	−.02	.66**	−2.2
Pt			.67**	−.30	.15	−.28	−.36	−.24	.15
D				−.17	−.23	−.45*	−.41*	−.23	−.20

** $p < .01$ * $p < .05$ ᵃ $p < .06$

TABLE 12.4

Means and Standard Deviations for Therapist Variables

Variable	Mean	SD	Variable	Mean	SD
Empathy Ratings	2.51	1.01	EPPS		
Davitz Score	24.33	4.53	Con	50.36	7.14
Anxiety Rating	3.20	1.12	Aff	46.29	11.02
Supervisor Rating	4.05	1.39	Def	43.43	10.81
Grade Ave. (Pract.)	7.20	0.77	Ach	56.93	10.78
Grade Ave. (Acad.)	7.07	0.86	Ord	45.79	10.77
GRE (V)	652.22	61.96	Exh	50.93	9.25
GRE (Q)	527.22	85.69	Aut	51.64	8.67
GRE (P)	604.71	78.82	Int	57.29	7.60
MMPI			Suc	54.71	13.10
K	58.46	6.72	Dom	44.00	12.26
Hs	49.77	6.77	Aba	42.00	5.92
D	52.62	7.80	Nur	49.36	6.51
Hy	58.69	7.12	Chg	46.36	10.50
Pd	60.00	8.05	End	49.36	10.90
Mf	57.31	19.54	Het	56.50	9.63
Pa	55.00	7.16	Agg	53.64	6.95
Pt	55.00	5.51			
Sc	57.23	4.32			
Ma	58.38	7.79			
Si	49.92	7.01			
Es	50.38	3.75			

many variables and the small N's for our sample. In light of this observation, we optimistically surmised that larger and more diverse samples would yield a greater number of significant relationships and increased clarity.

Influence of Therapist Orientation

There was no relationship between the therapists' self-reported desire to be empathic and their interview-rated empathy as indicated by a nonsignificant *Chi* Square. The desire to be interpretive was similarly unrelated to amount of empathy.

Supervisor Influence on Empathy

Since it is likely that supervisors differ in their emphasis on empathic behavior in psychotherapy, Ss were divided according to supervisor and mean empathy scores were computed for each supervisory group to test whether supervisors differentially affected level of therapist empathy. As can be seen from Table 12.5, the mean for one of the groups is substantially above that of the others. Informal interviews indicated that the supervisor of this group was the only one who explicitly attempted to teach his students specific empathic behaviors and was the only one who valued empathy above other types of therapist responses. Since the analysis of the supervisory process was not a purpose of the present research, we cannot offer more than these suggested indications of supervisor effect. It should be noted, however, that if supervisors significantly influenced the degree of therapist empathy the influence was not great enough to attenuate seriously the impact of the personal factors indicated by the correlations between personality measures and empathy. If supervisor effect had been controlled, it is likely that these latter correlations would have been even higher. Supervisor effects certainly could not have spuriously inflated them.

Anxiety Ratings

Two faculty members independently rated the manifest anxiety of fifteen therapists on a five-point rating scale from "high" to "low." This was done

TABLE 12.5

Mean Empathy Ratings for Supervisory Groups

Supervisor	A	B	C	D	E	F
No. Supervisees Participating	4	4	1	3	3	3
Mean Empathy	2.14	3.84	3.20	2.02	1.91	2.08

The Mean for group B is larger than that of all groups except C. t < .05, two-tailed test.

after the other data had been collected and analyzed, and is presented here because of interesting comparisons that can be made with the results published by Bandura (1956). These ratings did not correlate with Empathy ($r = -.13$), but they did relate significantly to Pt ($r = .41$) and Supervisor ratings ($r = -.69$). The latter correlation is interesting in light of the fact that Liking ratings made by one faculty member who was not a supervisor correlated $-.78$ with the anxiety ratings.

Discussion

The small and inexperienced sample of therapists in this study and the lack of direct outcome measures prohibits us from making very broad generalizations about the relationship of personal factors to therapeutic competence. Keeping this limitation in mind, it is of interest to note that hypotheses which have been postulated about therapists in general are empirically valid for our sample. The most significant present illustration is the negative relationship between measures of subjective discomfort (*Pt* and *D*) and empathic understanding. The idea that therapist personality disturbance interferes with the quality of a therapeutic relationship is not new. Our present advantage over previous notions, however, is that we can empirically specify personal disturbance factors related to variation in empathic responses to clients, even though we cannot assert that those therapists who were low in empathy were indeed "disturbed" in some absolute sense.

The failure of faculty anxiety ratings to correlate with *E* is difficult to comprehend, especially since they correlated negatively with SR and positively with *Pt*. Since these variables are far from completely overlapping (see Tables 12.2, 12.3), it is conceivable that overt anxiety as perceived by faculty members is different from the self-reported discomfort sampled by the MMPI. If so, then it appears that the internally experienced disturbance is associated with Empathy scores whereas the overt symptomatic type is not. An alternative suggestion discussed among clinicians is that one's "social self" differs from one's "therapeutic self" due to the very different structures and demands in the two situations.

A final point regarding the anxiety ratings concerns the Bandura study (1956) in which it was found that rated anxiety was negatively related to ratings of therapeutic competence. Bandura's r of $-.69$ is identical with that found in the present study between similar ratings. The point to be noted here is that rated anxiety is *not* related to actual in-therapy behavior as measured by the *E* scale; therefore, it cannot be argued, as Bandura did, that such ratings are necessarily related to therapeutic efficacy. The two studies also differ in that Bandura found no relationship between self-reported anxiety and ratings of competence. This could have resulted partly from the use of an unvalidated self-reporting technique.

The negative relationship of intraception to empathy is, at first, a puzzle.

The defining qualities of the need for intraception (interest in analyzing one's own and others' motives) seem very similar to those essential in the therapeutic flow of empathic responses. It is conceivable, however, that what *Int* measures is a cognitive-analytic interpersonal orientation which may be more akin to interpretive rather than to empathic therapeutic behavior. Its lack of relationship with MMPI scales (Merrill, 1956) suggests that it does not measure the pathological type of self-preoccupation indicated by the *D* or *Pt* scales which might, at first, be supposed because of its high negative relationship with *E*.

Apparently n Order's negative relationship with *E* is like that of intraception in the sense that it is manifestly loaded with cognitive-planning oriented responses, is unrelated to the MMPI, and may have more to do with interpretive-directive behavior than empathic behavior.

The high positive correlation between Dominance and Change and *E* were unanticipated, but can be readily rationalized. Dominance appears to be essentially an indicator of psychological health. It ". . . is probably most closely related to a normal MMPI profile, has positive relationships with the 'healthy' MMPI experimental scales and negative correlations with the 'sick' scales" (Merrill, 1956, p. 313). Smith (1958) also found that Dominance was negatively related to instability of ideal self-concept. It appears that high dominance preferences have to do with freedom from subjective discomfort and perhaps with feelings of interpersonal confidence, both of which may permit the emotional freedom necessary to enter freely and empathically into another person's frame of reference. It seems, therefore, that the term "Dominance" should not be taken as an adequate description of the personality construct which the scale implies. This seems particularly reasonable since the Edwards Scales continue to require construct validation and since literal dominance is incompatible with the Client-centered empathy measure used in this study. It may be that the correlation between Age and Empathy, like the one between Dominance and *E*, represents the development of an assurance and freedom with age which permits more complete focusing on the client rather than upon one's own needs. That this correlation does not reflect amount of clinical experience is evidenced by the fact that all therapists were at the same level in training and did not differ in amount of pretraining clinical experience.

Interpreting the correlation between n Change and *E* is, like Dominance, dependent upon how one construes the meaning of the Edwards variable. Previous research suggests a negative relationship with measures of personality disturbance (Smith, 1958) and a positive relationship with the *Ma* scale of the MMPI (Merrill, 1956). It will be noted from Table 1 that *Ma* is positively related to *E* although not significantly. On the basis of this sketchy evidence we may tentatively surmise that n Change carries an implication of emotional strength and a freedom from the staid and tried which may permit a readier empathy for the frequently atypical behavior of psychotherapy clients than would be possible if one were to prefer less flexibility and novelty in his experience.

The consistency variable is one about which little is known except that especially low scores may invalidate scores on other scales. The one possibility for interpreting it as the opposite of n Change is negated by the lack of correlation between the two (Edwards, 1959). Problems of interpretation also arise in the cases of Nurturance and Abasement. Since Abasement has previously been shown to correlate with indices of anxiety and maladjustment (Smith, 1958; Merrill, 1956), one would expect it to correlate negatively with empathy which it does not. However, it is not an anxiety scale and perhaps is more heavily weighted with other kinds of variants that are unrelated to empathy. Nurturance has face validity with regard to empathy but apparently that is all. The scale has not held up well in other research and perhaps is in general more reliable than valid.

The lack of a correlation between E and scores on the Davitz measure of accuracy in perceiving emotional meanings is disappointing. It could have resulted from any of several possibilities: (a) the restricted range of Davitz scores for the present sample as compared with the standardization samples, (b) the fact that the Davitz measure indicates perceptual accuracy and not the ability to communicate that accuracy, whereas E is dependent upon both of these factors, or (c) the measure is simply not a valid one with regard to "live" emotional communication of the type occurring in psychotherapy.

The significant correlation between supervisor ratings and E enhances the value of the relationships between E and the various personality variables by showing the relevance of E to an independent criterion supplementary to those indicated in the introduction.

A question arises, however, regarding whether E is actually contributing significantly to the supervisor ratings. Since age, overt anxiety, "Dominance," and Empathy all correlate with SR it would be of interest to determine their relative contributions to SR by means of a multiple regression equation. Unfortunately, the varying N's for each of the variables made these computations impossible. Retaining only those Ss for whom we had all of the relevant scores would have yielded an N unreasonably small for such purposes. Since age and "Dominance" correlate with E as well as SR, it is conceivable that these two variables account for the correlation between E and SR, thus leaving indeterminate the issue of whether therapist empathy, as measured, actually contributes to supervisor evaluations of competence.

The lack of relationship between measures of academic achievement and E is most interesting in light of the oft-repeated assertion that therapeutic skill requires qualities of emotional sensitivity which are quite different from the abilities necessary to enter successfully and compete in Ph.D. or M.D. training programs. The implication that the training of therapists may well be conducted independently of much of the traditional academic content is not surprising. We know that a basic minimum knowledge of research, personality theory, etc. was attained by all of these therapists (all had passed Ph.D. qualifying exams). We may conclude that beyond that minimum level differential attainment does not contribute to empathic ability. Whether differential attainment below that level would effect empathic skill is not presently answerable.

The lack of relationship between GRE aptitude scores and E similarly implies that for a group of professional level persons, differences in intellectual ability have no effect on ability to be empathic in therapy. Whether lower GRE scores would be associated with more or less empathy than for our Ss is indeterminate.

Some implications of the data are important for the selection and training of psychotherapists. Since personal attributes rather than academic training are related to Empathy, we may need to move in the direction of appropriately relevant standards for the selection of clinical psychologists, particularly for those who are to become practitioners. However, questions still remain regarding the influence of personality variables on factors in therapeutic ability other than Empathy, and the modifiability of those personal qualities detrimental to client change still remains an issue.

Another training issue pertains to the observation that *all* therapists in this study valued empathy as essential in therapeutic work. The fact that only those therapists who had been specifically coached in developing this ability attained it to a significant degree indicates that verbal espousal of a position does not of itself lead to its practice. Explicit learning via imitation of models with high Empathic ability, on the other hand, did lead to such an eventuality.

The fact that only one aspect of therapeutic functioning has been examined here, that therapist empathy has been found a valid predictor of eventual outcome in studies other than the present one, and that we have demonstrated correlation and not causation prevents us from stating that the presence of any of the variables found related to E causes low or high empathy and, therefore, negative or positive therapy outcome. It is, however, gratifying to find that some of our shop-worn notions regarding the therapist's personal influence upon his client's progress are closer to clear explication and that we have some additional hypotheses to work on. The simple fact of finding significant correlations between personal variables and a therapeutic behavior known to produce personality change provides a beginning toward isolating the most potent therapeutic agents while at the same time eliminating factors that interfere with the power of those agents to product positive change.

REFERENCES

BANDURA, A. Psychotherapist's anxiety level, self-insight, and psychotherapeutic competence. *Journal of Abnormal and Social Psychology*, 1956, 52, 333-337.

BANDURA, A., LIPSHER, D. H., and MILLER, PAULA E. Psychotherapists' approach-avoidance reactions to patients' expressions of hostility. *Journal of Consulting Psychology*, 1960, 24, 1-3.

BERGIN, A. E. The effects of psychotherapy: Negative results revisited. *Journal of Counseling Psychology*, 1963, 10, 3, 244-250.

BETZ, BARBARA. Experiences in research in psychotherapy with schizophrenic patients. In H. H. Strupp and L. Luborsky (Eds.), *Research in psychotherapy*. Vol. 2. Washington, D.C.: American Psychological Association, 1962. Pp. 41-60.

CUTLER, R. C. Countertransference effects in psychotherapy. *Journal of Consulting Psychology*, 1958, 22, 349-356.

DAVITZ, J. R. *The communication of emotional meaning*, New York: McGraw-Hill, 1964.

EDWARDS, A. L. *Edwards Personal Preference Schedule*. Revised. New York: Psychological Corporation, 1959.

ELLIS, A. Requisite conditions for basic personality change. *Journal of Consulting Psychology*, 1959, 23, 538-540.

FIEDLER, F. E. The concept of an ideal therapeutic relationship. *Journal of Consulting Psychology*, 1950, 14, 239-245.

FIEDLER, F. E. A comparison of therapeutic relationships in psychoanalytic, non-directive, and Adlerian therapy. *Journal of Consulting Psychology*, 1950b, 14, 436-445.

KRASNER, L. The therapist as a social reinforcement machine. In H. H. Strupp and L. Luborsky (Eds.), *Research in psychotherapy*. Vol. 2. Washington, D.C.: American Psychological Association, 1962. Pp. 61-94.

MCNAIR, D. M., CALLAHAN, D. M. and LORR, M. Therapist "type" and patient response to psychotherapy. *Journal of Consulting Psychology*, 1962, 26, 425-429.

MARLOWE, D. Some psychological correlates of field independence. *Journal of Consulting Psychology*, 1958, 22, 334.

MERRILL, R. M. and HEATHERS, LOUISE B. The relationship of the Minnesota Multiphasic Personality Inventory to the Edwards Personal Preference Schedule on a college counseling sample. *Journal of Consulting Psychology*, 1956, 20, 310-318.

MURRAY, E. J. A content-analysis method for studying psychotherapy. *Psychological Monograph*, 1956, 70. No. 13 (Whole No. 420).

ROGERS, C. R. The necessary and sufficient conditions of therapeutic personality change. *Journal of Consulting Psychology*, 1957, 21, 95-103.

ROSENTHAL, D. Changes in some moral values following psychotherapy. *Journal of Consulting Psychology*, 1955, 19, 431-436.

SMITH, G. M. Six measures of self-concept discrepancy and instability: Their interrelationships, reliability, and relationships to other personality measures. *Journal of Consulting Psychology*, 1958, 22, 101-112.

TRUAX, C. B. A scale for the measurement of accurate empathy. *Psychiatric Institute Bulletin*, University of Wisconsin, 1961a, 1, No. 12.

TRUAX, C. B. Therapeutic conditions. *Psychiatric Institute Bulletin.* University of Wisconsin, 1961b, 1, No. 10 (c).

TRUAX, C. B. Effective ingredients in psychotherapy: An approach to unraveling the patient-therapist interaction. *Journal of Consulting Psychology,* 1963, 10, 3, 256-263.

13

Basic Methodologic Issues

Implicit in Psychotherapy

Process Research*[1]

DONALD J. KIESLER

I would like to present some methodologic issues arising out of the psycho-therapy process research with which I am connected. These problems have come into focus as a concomitant of a five-year study of individual psycho-therapy with hospitalized schizophrenic patients (Rogers, 1962). The study was initiated as an attempt to verify the theoretical formulations of Carl Rogers which have been presented in several places (Rogers, 1958, 1959a, 1959b, 1961; Rogers, Walker and Rablen, 1960; Rogers, 1957), but perhaps most succinctly in his 1957 paper, "The Necessary and Sufficient Conditions of Therapeutic Personality Change" (Rogers, 1957). The results of this five-year study are to be presented in an upcoming book which will go to the publishers this summer.

My purpose is not to focus on the findings of our study, but rather to con-centrate on the methodologic problems confronting us in the process of obtaining those results. We have come to the position that these issues are so fundamental that our findings have little meaning unless these methodologic

* From *American Journal of Psychotherapy,* Vol. 20, No. 1, January, 1966, pp. 135-155. Reproduced by permission.

[1] Presented at the Third National Meeting of the Association for the Advancement of Psychotherapy, Los Angeles, Calif., May 3, 1964. I would like to thank my colleagues, Philippa L. Mathieu and Marjorie H. Klein for their contribution to the clarification and elucidation of many of the ideas presented here.

issues are clarified. It is also our contention that anyone doing process research in a study similar to ours must also deal with these same issues. If these issues are not met, the interpretation of any results obtained is at best confounded.

Let me define more specifically the research focus within which these issues arose. In his "Necessary and Sufficient Conditions" paper Rogers hypothesizes three therapeutic attitudes that the therapist must possess and communicate to his patient before constructive personality change in that patient can occur. These are the attitudes of empathic understanding, congruence or genuineness, and unconditional positive regard. The research project attempted to measure these therapist dimensions in two ways: (1) by Barrett-Lennard's Relationship Inventory (Barrett-Lennard, 1959, 1962), a questionnaire that was filled in periodically by the patients and their respective therapists; and (2) by rating scales for these variables that were devised to be applied to the tape recordings of the psychotherapy interviews.

Besides these therapist dimensions, Rogers also postulates a patient "process" dimension (Rogers, 1958, 1959a, 1961; Rogers, Walker and Rablen, 1960) which should reflect patient growth or positive change over the therapy encounter. Although this process conception is multistranded, it embraces a general continuum ranging from perceptual and conceptual rigidity to flexibility: "from fixity to changeingness, from rigid structure to flow, from stasis to flow" (Rogers, 1958, p. 143). The empiric necessity for the research project was the development of a patient "process" scale that would reliably and validly measure this theoretical continuum. The scale resulting was that of patient Experiencing (Gendlin and Tomlinson, 1961; revised by Mathieu and Klein, 1963).

The primary hypothesis to be tested by the study was that a high relationship exists between the three therapist conditions and patient process, as both are manifested in the therapy encounter. More exactly, the hypothesis was stated as follows: *The greater the degree to which the conditions of therapy exist in the relationship, the greater will be the evidences of therapeutic process or movement in the client.*

Hence, it is apparent to you that the two essential empiric tasks of the research project were (1) the *development* of rating scales measuring both the postulated therapist "conditions" and patient "process" variables, and (2) the *application* of these scales to the tape-recorded individual-therapy interviews of the study. As anyone knows who has attempted to develop scales measuring such abstract dimensions, the problems of development are horrendous, and require a high degree of research patience, creativity, and pure luck. However, for the purposes of this paper let me assume that one possesses patient or therapist scales that show high construct validity and can be applied in a highly reliable way. The major research problem then becomes: How does one validly apply these scales to the recorded psychotherapy interviews?

To spell out this problem still further: Most of the process research to date has focused on the intensive analysis of one or several interview interactions. For example, scales developed by Strupp, Bordin and his collaborators at the University of Michigan, Howe and Pope at the University of Maryland, and rogerian researchers have been applied primarily to typewritten transcripts of a *single* therapy hour, or *several* therapy hours. Some have been applied to tape-recordings but again the number of interviews considered is relatively small.

Now consider the data problem of our study. At the end of the data collection phase of the project we possessed *1,204 hours* of tape-recorded therapeutic interaction with 28 hospitalized schizophrenic patients! How does one go about applying four rating scales to such a formidable collection of recorded psychotherapy data? Clearly, it is practically impossible to rate every minute of each of the 1,204 therapy tapes. I want to focus on the basic methodologic issues that arise when one is confronted with this mass of data. Whenever possible, I will attempt to illustrate the problem with our data results that bear on the issue.

What then are the major methodologic issues one is confronted with when applying rating scales to a mass of psychotherapy data? I would like to divide the issues into four major categories: (1) Problems of sampling from the therapy interviews; (2) Problems of data form and mode of data presentation; (3) Problem of validity when different subjective viewpoints are used in applying scales or questionnaires; and finally (4) The reliability and validity issues centering around particular rating scales.

1. The Problem of Sampling from the Therapy Interviews

This problem can be stated as follows: Given the practical fact that one cannot analyze the total recorded data of the therapy interaction, how does one decide how much of the therapy continuum, and which stages of that continuum, are to be analyzed intensively? The first point I would like to make regarding this issue is that the sampling problem has to be considered within the particular theoretical framework in which one is working. That is, there is no uniform answer to this sampling question, but rather different answers depending on the questions one is asking of the data. For example, the rogerian variables, which were the focus of our interest, were theoretically formulated to be pervasively operative over the entire therapy encounter. The therapist attitudes postulated by Rogers as "necessary and sufficient" to patient constructive personality change were theoretically described as operating independently of any problem content being discussed in therapy; as being effective only in a cumulative way over the therapy encounter. Therefore, the sampling issue for our data was defined relatively simply: Since the therapeutic attitudes should be operative and manifest at every point of the therapy encounter, the major sampling concern was to sample at points of the therapy interviews continuum that would be representative of the entire therapy interaction.

This position then required only one further decision: Should one focus on a small number of interview hours for each patient, studying them in their entirety? Or would it be more profitable to take smaller samples from many interview hours for each patient? That is, should one focus on accurately representing several particular 50-minute interview interactions, or rather focus on representing accurately the entire interaction for the therapy cases? Again, the decision was made in terms of the theoretical formulation. Since Rogers' formulation emphasizes the pervasive and cumulative action of the therapist variables, it was felt to be more important to sample accurately the entire interviews continuum, rather than concentrate exhaustively on several interviews for each patient.

One could very easily make other sampling decisions, working with different variables within a different theoretical framework. For example, within an analytic freudian framework one would likely be interested in therapist variables such as Depth of Interpretation on which Bordin and his collaborators have focused or therapist Activity Level or degree of therapist Ambiguity, with which Howe and Pope have been concerned. Insofar as the patient is concerned one might be interested in variables such as patient Resistance interfering with free therapy communication such as Speisman has operationalized (Speisman, 1959), or a measure of Free-Association performance, with which Bordin has most recently been concerned (Bordin, 1963). Or one might be interested in developing measures of defense mechanisms such as reaction formation, repression, or projection described so lucidly by Anna Freud. However, given any roster of analytic therapist and patient variables such as these it seems one would *not* sample a set of data such as ours in the way that we proceeded. For the operation of the Freudian therapist variables, as defined, seems much more specifically focused than the Rogerian variables on specific problem or content areas of the patients' verbalizations. For example, the operation of therapist Depth of Interpretation or Verbal Activity in the content area of a patient's specific heterosexual problem would not be expected to be reflected in patient resistance behavior in the area of problems centering around authority. Or Depth of therapist interpretation may be related to a reduction in the operation of the patient's defense mechanism of projection in the area of authority problems, but not in the areas of peer or heterosexual relationships. Or therapist Ambiguity may be related in one way to the Free Association ability of the patient in certain problem areas, and in another way when the interaction is focused on transference or countertransference phenomena.

In other words, if researchers of the freudian analytic approach were confronted with our mass of data it seems they would be forced to different sampling decisions than the ones we utilized. It seems they would be forced at least to an editing of each psychotherapy case into different problem or content areas, as well as into different interactive conditions of the patient and therapist. It seems further, that the test of freudian hypotheses would be the limited to specific content or interactive areas in turn, with the resultant expectation of differential therapist and patient behavior in the respective areas. The sampling-location problem would be much more complex for a test of the Freudian theoretical system than it would be for the Rogerian formulation.

In any case, the point being made here is that the sampling-location decisions cannot be made uniformly for all theoretical systems, but must be made in a manner consistent with the theoretical position of immediate empiric interest.

Once we had decided for our study to sample the therapy continuum at all stages of the interaction, two further sampling issues arose: (1) What size should this brief sample from the 50-minute therapy hour be? and (2) At which point of the particular therapy hour (early, middle, or late) should the brief sample be taken? Let me now turn to these problems.

The Size of the Sample-Segment. The basic question here is: Given particular therapist or patient variables that one is attempting to measure by means of rating scales, what is the most economical *segment-size* that will still represent accurately the functioning of that variable in the total 50-minute hour? A pilot study early in the project indicated that interrater reliability was not affected by different sample sizes, ranging from 30 seconds to five minutes. As a result of this study, four-minute samples from tape-recorded therapy interviews represented the basic raw data for our therapist and patient variables. We have recently finished a second, more extensive study (Kiesler, Mathieu, and Klein, 1964) of the effect of different sample sizes on the major patient "process" variable of our study, the concept of Experiencing (Gendlin, 1962). This dimension ranges from the low end of the scale where the patient's verbalizations manifest little ownership of feelings, to the high end of the scale where the patient owns his feelings in a very intimate way, and can travel among different feeling and attitude areas with ease and with the ability to integrate these feelings with his self-concept. The question this study was asking was: What differential effect in terms of the Experiencing ratings obtained does one get if one varies segment-length?

We randomly selected seven patients each from a pool of normal, psychoneurotic, and hospitalized schizophrenic patients for whom we possessed tape-recorded interview sessions, a total of 21 patients. We selected an early (within first five interviews) and a late (within last five therapy interviews) tape for each of the 21 patients. From each of the 42 resulting tape-recorded hours of therapy we extracted overlapping segments of two, four, eight, and 16 minutes length. These four sets of 42 segments, each set of different segment-lengths, were then rated by four independent groups of raters on the Experiencing dimension.

The following results were obtained from analysis of variance of the data. 1) The interrater and rate-rerate reliability of the EXP ratings is not affected by segment-length (the intraclass reliability values range from from .83 to 91). Judges rate a 16-minute segment as reliably as a two-minute segment.

(2) There is no significant difference in the range of EXP ratings made from segments of different lengths. Ratings for stages one through five are equally likely for the different length segments. (3) The ratings made from the different lengths produce an equivalent reflection of individual differences for the three diagnostic groups, with the neurotic patients manifesting a significantly higher level of Experiencing than both the psychotic and normal patients. The last two groups of patients were indistinguishable in terms of the Experiencing dimension. (4) The segment-length ratings reflected early to late change in Experiencing for the three diagnostic groups to an equivalent degree. (5) The only difference emerging from the study was that the longer segment-lengths evoked higher absolute levels of patient Experiencing for all three groups. That is, the longer segments produced higher, deeper levels of patient Experiencing than did the shorter.

Hence, for the Experiencing scale, which was the basic patient "process" measure of our study, the findings indicate very clearly that different segment-lengths make little difference in terms of the results obtained. One gets the same results in terms of interrater reliability, range of the scale stages used, reflection of individual differences, and reflection of patient change. The only difference resulting was in terms of the absolute value of the rating obtained. Thus, since our project study was geared toward relative differentiation of individual differences and differential change among the hospitalized schizophrenic patients, the conclusion was reached that it makes no difference whether one extracts two-minute or 16-minute segments from the therapy hour. In terms of the Experiencing variable the results are identical. However, a corollary of these findings is that one cannot indiscriminately mix segment-lengths for a particular study. For if this is done, the longer segments would be biased in favor of higher or deeper levels of patient Experiencing.

Segment Location for the Individual Hour. Having discovered for our Experiencing scale that any segment-length is satisfactory as a sample of the individual recorded hour so long as it is standardized, the next question becomes: Can we take the sample randomly from any place in the 50-minute hour? Or should one sample in a standardized manner? The a priori decision made for the schizophrenic study was to take four-minute segments, randomly selected from the last half of the recorded hour. This decision was made on the judgment that one would be more likely to encounter meaningful therapy interchange in the latter half of the therapy hour. But is this decision empirically justifiable?

We recently completed a second sampling study (Kiesler, Mathieu, and Klein, 1965), using a different sample of eight subjects each from the three diagnostic groups. The purpose of this study was to determine what the trend of Experiencing is over the 50-minute interview hour. To answer the question, 24 therapy hours, chosen from both early and late interview points, were each divided into five subsequent eight-minute segments. That is, for each hour there were five segments, representing the first, second, third, fourth, and fifth eight minutes of the hour. These 120 segments were then presented in a random order to a group of five judges for Experiencing ratings.

The results of this study are presented in Figure 13.1. It is apparent that the

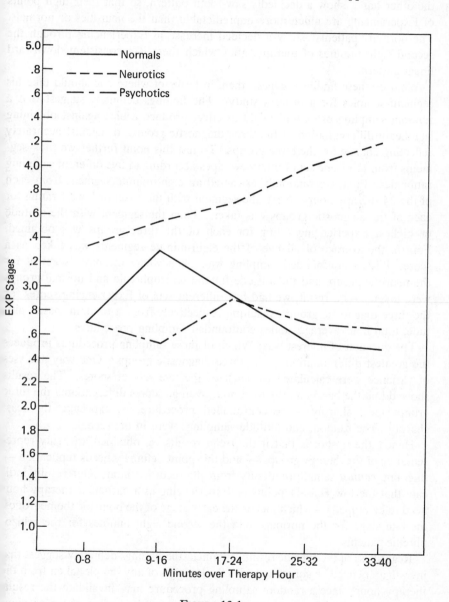

FIGURE 13.1

Trends of Peak *EXP Ratings for 9-minute Segments over the Recorded Psychotherapy Hour for Three Diagnostic Groups (n=8 in each group)*

Experiencing behavior of the three diagnostic groups over the therapy hour is significantly different. The neurotic patients show a consistently upward linear pattern of Experiencing, so that they are talking most meaningfully about themselves near the end of the therapy hour. The schizophrenic patients, on the other hand, show a decidedly saw-tooth pattern, so that their high points of Experiencing are much more unpredictable than the neurotics or normals. The normal "patients" show a decided increase in Experiencing through the second eight minutes of therapy, after which there is a consistent downward linear pattern.

What do these findings suggest, then, in terms of where one should take his segment-samples for a process study? The findings definitely suggest that a random sampling procedure might in effect produce a bias against obtaining significant differentiation of the three diagnostic groups, or against accurately reflecting change for the three groups. To test this point further we took segments from *this* same *set* of interview tapes according to five different sampling rationales. First, we randomly extracted an eight-minute segment from each of the 24 therapy hours. Next, the segment with the basal or lowest rating for each of the diagnostic groups was taken. Then the segment with the altitude or highest Experiencing rating for each of the three groups was obtained. Fourth, the average of all five of the eight-minute segments was taken as a score. Last, a confounded sampling was taken where the basal segment for the neurotic group, and the altitude for the schizophrenic and normal groups were taken. As a result, we had five different sets of Experiencing scores for the three diagnostic groups, resulting respectively from a random, basal, altitude, total hour average, and a confounded sampling procedures.

The question of interest was: Which of these sampling procedures produces the greatest differentiation of the three diagnostic groups? One way analyses of variance were calculated for each of the five sets of scores. The results showed that the basal and the total hour average scores differentiated the three groups most sharply — the confounded procedure, as expected, the least sharply. The random and altitude samplings were in between.

Hence, the upshot is that if the trend results we obtained are truly representative of the therapy groups — and this point definitely needs replication — then one *cannot* sample randomly from the recorded hour. Our results indicate that the low (basal) points of Experiencing in a particular therapy hour need to be tapped — which means the early stage of the hour for the neurotics, the late stage for the normals, and the second eight minutes for the schizophrenic patients.

Regardless of the specific results obtained, the findings definitely suggest that investigators need be concerned with the location of any sample taken from the therapy hour, since a random sampling procedure may invalidate the result obtained. Incidentaly, this second study replicated the finding of the previous one that the level of Experiencing of neurotic patients in therapy is significantly higher than that of both the schizophrenic and normal subjects. The frequenc distribution of the EXP ratings obtained by the three groups is shown in Figure 13.2.

Sample Location over the Therapy Interviews. The preceding discussion has been limited to sampling from the *individual* 50-mintue therapy hour. The problem I would now like to consider is: At what locations of the therapy interviews continuum — the entire therapy case — should one sample in order to validly represent the changes that occur over the total therapy encounter? The findings for our study of hospitalized schizophrenics suggest that an early

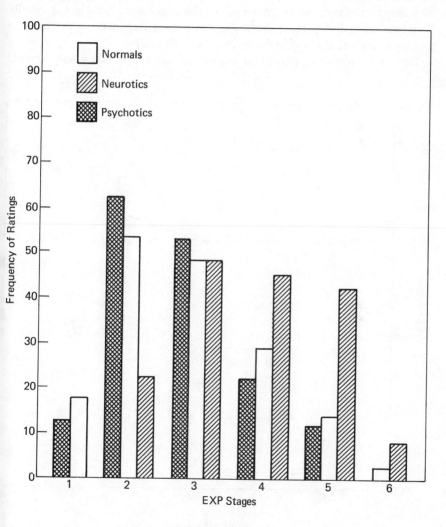

FIGURE 13.2

Frequency Distribution of EXP Ratings over the Therapy Hour for Normal, Neurotic, and Psychiatric Therapy Patients

and late therapy interview sample only will not suffice. Figures 13.3 and 13.4 show respectively the trend of the therapy patients' Experiencing over the thirds of the total therapy encounter, and over the first 30 interviews. EXP ratings for the study were made on segments from every interview through interview 50, and every fifth interview thereafter for the longer cases. Figure 13.3 shows the trend over the thirds of the total interview encounter. The slope is linear in an upward direction, showing a change over therapy to a slightly higher level of Experiencing for the patients as a whole. However, if we look at Figure 13.4, which gives the trend of Experiencing over the first 30 therapy interviews, we find a noticeably different curve. It takes a decidedly U-shaped form, indicating a sharp drop in patient Experiencing to the 15th therapy interview, and a continuous linear rise thereafter.

The upshot of this significant finding for our subjects is that if one sampled

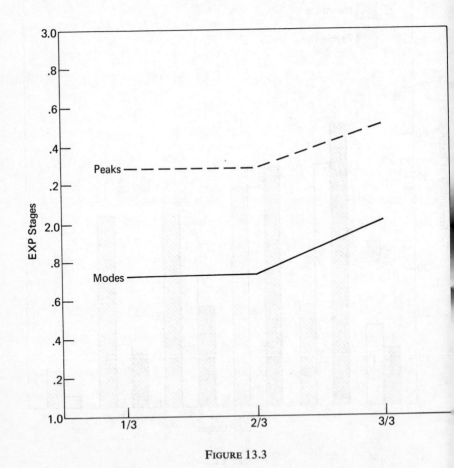

FIGURE 13.3

Trend of EXP Modal and Peak Ratings, for the Total 14 Therapy Patients over the Three "Thirds" of the Therapy Interviews (1/3, 2/3, 3/3)

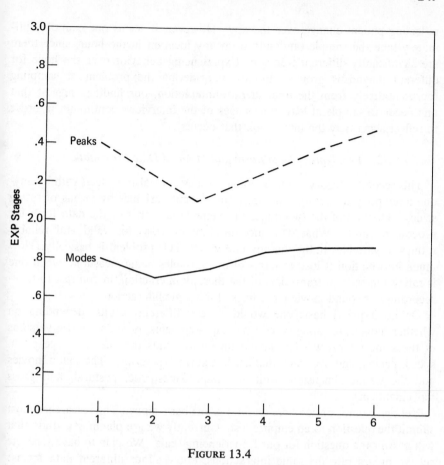

FIGURE 13.4

*Trend of EXP Modal and Peak Ratings, for the Total 14 Therapy
Patients over the First 30 Therapy Interviews (1-6)*

only early and late in the therapy interaction one would not be accurately
representing the Experiencing behavior occurring over the encounter. One
would miss the U-shaped function, with the sharp drop to the fifteenth interview, and might conclude erroneously that the function is linear. It seems
that in light of these results *at least four* stages of the therapy encounter must
be sampled in order to reflect accurately the total interaction.

   To summarize this discussion concerning the first category of methodologic
issues, that of sampling from the recorded psychotherapy interaction: First,
the sampling decisions made must be made in terms of the particular theoretical
system in which a researcher is operating. Second, regarding sampling from
a particular 50-minute recorded hour, our findings suggest two conclusions.
One may take any size sample from the hour and obtain similar results in
terms of reliability, differentiation of diagnostic groups, and equivalently

reflecting patient change over therapy. However, it seems one cannot legitimately take the sample randomly from any location in the hour, since there are significantly different trends of Experiencing behavior over the hour for different diagnostic groups. Finally, considering the problem of sampling representatively from the total therapy interaction, our findings suggest that one needs to sample at least four stages of the interviews continuum in order to reflect accurately the interaction that occurs.

2. *Problems of Data Form and Mode of Data Presentation*

This second category of methodologic issues must also be dealt with by anyone attempting to measure therapist and patient variables by means of rating scales. The first of the two major problems here is that of the data form for process research. What data medium best provides for valid and reliable ratings of variables in the therapy interview? This problem is basically: How much information is lost, in terms of the variables being measured, when one is rating typewritten transcripts of the therapy interaction, in contrast to tape-recordings or sound-movie recordings of the same interaction?

On an a priori basis one would expect different results, depending on whether judges are rating typescripts, tape-segments, or sound-movie versions of the same interview. The audial dimension adds the cues of voice pitch, speed, pacing, and overtones that are lost in the typescripts. The sound movies add the visual dimension, with additional kinesthetic, postural, and gross movement cues.

Yet one cannot decide here on an a priori basis alone. The researcher must submit the question to an empiric test. Currently we are planning a study that will answer the question for our Experiencing scale. We plan to have separate sets of judges rate the same interactions, but via four different data forms: typescripts only, tape-recordings only, silent motion-picture recordings, and sound motion-picture recordings. This study should answer the question: How valid are the different media in representing the "real" therapy interaction that occurred.

The second issue arises when one is measuring, by rating scales, both therapist and patient dimensions from the *same recorded segments*. The basic problem is that of confounding. Since the judges are listening to both the therapist and patient verbalizations in the same segment, what assurance do we have that judges rating the therapist's behavior are not in effect making their judgments from the patient's behavior instead?

That is a major problem we experienced with our study. Separate sets of judges rated independently the Empathic Understanding of the therapist and the Experiencing behavior of the patient. We found a significantly high correlation between therapist empathy and patient experiencing. But the methodologic question is: Were both sets of judges in effect rating the same thing? For example, is it possible to rate the therapist's empathic understanding from his statements alone? Or can the rating of empathy only be made in terms of the patient response to what the therapist says? This is a basic interpretive problem that must be dealt with before the findings can be interpreted unequivocally. We plan a study for the Empathy and Experiencing scales where the separate variables will be rated from the therapist's comments alone (with the patient's speech edited out), from the patient's verbalization only (with the therapist's speech edited out), and with both participants present (the unedited version). If differential values are obtained for the therapist Empathy and patient Experiencing scales under the separate conditions, the application of the scale needs to be modified accordingly.

To summarize the discussion of this second category of methodologic issues: The effects of both the data medium (typescript vs. tape-recording vs. sound movie) as well as the mode of data presentation (patient or therapist's verbalizations alone or together) on the resulting scale ratings must be assessed before one can validly interpret the findings regarding a particular rating scale.

3. Problem of Validity of Different Subjective Viewpoints

A surprising, yet very interesting finding, emerged from our therapy study which calls into question the validity of employing a single subjective viewpoint in attempting to describe accurately the process of therapy. As I mentioned previously, we measured the therapist conditions of empathic understanding, congruence, and unconditional positive regard from three viewpoints. Psychiatrically naïve judges (undergraduates of the University of Wisconsin) rated these dimensions while listening to many separate four-minute segments of the therapy hours. The patients themselves were periodically asked to describe their respective therapists by means of a questionnaire instrument devised by Barrett-Lennard (1959, 1962) to measure the same therapist variables. Finally at the same intermittent time points, the therapists were asked to describe themselves on this same questionnaire as to their own perception of their attitudinal behavior.

The interesting result is that the three separate viewpoints — judge, patient, and therapist — yielded divergent pictures of the therapist's behavior. The judges and the patients agreed consistently regarding the level of "conditions" being offered a patient by his respective therapist. Both disagreed with the therapist's viewpoint of the same behavior. That is, there was a positive correlation between the judges' ratings and the patients' perceptions (in many cases significantly positive); whereas there was a negative correlation between the therapists' perceptions and both the judges' ratings and patients' perceptions (in many cases significantly so). Thus, for our patient population, a therapist who viewed himself as offering a relatively high level of empathic understanding, congruence, and positive regard was perceived by his patient and by objective judges as exhibiting a relatively low level of these conditions. Further, the judges' and patients' conditions measures correlated positively and significantly with patient level of Experiencing in therapy; while the therapist conditions measure correlated negatively.

This finding at least points up the necessity of obtaining several viewpoints of either the therapist's or the patient's process behavior in therapy. Different viewpoints do yield different results, and the discrepancies must be dealt with. Traditionally we have accepted the proposition that the therapy relationship is dyadic. Our findings further suggest that the perceptions of therapist and patient are also dyadic. Any monadic perceptual focus, as a result, yields data inadequately describing the process of therapy.

4. Reliability and Validity Issues for Rating Scales

This final category of methodologic issues centers around rating scale issues that are both implicit and explicit in the preceding discussion. It, therefore, can be presented best as a summary of the issues a researcher must face once he develops a rating scale for measuring either therapist or patient variables in the psychotherapy interaction.

(1) First, he must develop his scale to the point that good interrater and intrarater *reliability* is obtained. (2) He must be concerned that his scale is in effect tapping an *unidimension,* rather than several dimensions. This is crucial before accurate interpretation of the scale dimension is possible. Low interrater reliability generally indicates the presence of several dimensions in a scale. The very precise work of Bordin and his collaborators and Howe and Pope has primarily focused on this dimensionality problem. Bordin's group of researchers has applied Coomb's scaling techniques while Howe and Pope have used Osgood's Semantic Differential measure as vehicles for extracting and describing the dimensions that are operative in their respective therapist scales. (3) Third, the researcher must attempt to obtain some measure of the *face validity* of his scale. For example, do other clinicians consider his scale variable as an operative or crucial dimension of the therapy encounter? Would other clinicians agree with the ranking continuum explicit in his scale? (4) He must be concerned about the problem of *construct validity.* That is, if his scale is indeed measuring the theoretical construct intended, then predictions can be made and empirically tested concerning relationships with other constructs.

For example, in the case of our Experiencing scale, a crucial question might be: How does patient Experiencing relate to measures of patient anxiety or defensiveness? Also the Experiencing scale should differentiate diagnostic groups in a manner that is theoretically consistent. Likewise, it should be able to reflect changes in the patient's behavior over the therapy encounter. (5) The researcher must make attempts to show that his scale results cannot be explained by *more parsimonious variables.* Again, in the case of our Experiencing scale, is it possible that variables such as the amount of patient silence, the number of silences, or the frequency of his interruptions of silence by themselves can explain the results we get with the Experiencing scale? These are a few of the variables with which Saslow and Matarazzo have been concerned, utilizing Chapple's Interaction Chronograph technique.

We currently have underway a study to answer the questions, using the interaction chronograph approach. (6) The researcher must define and *resolve the sampling problems* involved in applying his scale to the process data of therapy. He must first *define* these sampling problems in a manner appropriate for the test of the theoretical system in which he is interested. He must empirically attack the problems of *sample size* and *location* for the particular therapy hour, and of location for the total therapy interviews continuum. (7) He must assess the differential results obtained when using different *data media* (typescripts versus tape-recordings versus sound-movies). Likewise he must be concerned about the potential confounding arising when *therapist and patient behavior are rated* from segments where both of their verbalizations are present. (8) Finally, the researcher needs to assess *both the patient's and the therapist's viewpoint* of what is occurring in therapy, as a check on the validity of the viewpoint arrived at by judges using his scale.

Conclusion

The upshot of all this is that one is committed to a large scale program of methodologic research whenever one introduces a new scale which one feels has crucial relevance for psychotherapy process research. Yet, it is only by this painstaking confrontation of these basic methodologic issues that psychotherapy process research will move forward on a firm foundation. This is the theme of the talk today.

A Postscript

One final finding of our study which seems to me to have a very crucial bearing on the therapy outcome problem: Therapy outcome studies have been rather disappointing to date in terms of demonstrating a differential outcome effect for therapy in contrast to control patients. Eysenck has documented this view rather well, although glossing over some of the methodologic problems inherent in this demonstration.

It is my contention that outcome studies contrasting therapy patients as a group with control patients are doomed to failure. It seems this is so since the therapy-control dichotomy rests on a false assumption — that is, the assumption that all therapy contacts are homogeneous; that "therapy" as an event is the same, no matter who the therapist, no matter what the nature of the interaction.

The findings of our study challenge this assumption. If we compare our therapy patients as a group with control patients, no differences are apparent in adjustment change over therapy as is the case with such measures as the

MMPI, Wittenborn Psychiatric rating scales, TAT, diagnostic assessments of change, or per cent time out of the hospital one year after therapy termination. Likewise, we find no significant differences in patient Experiencing as measured in an independent, standardized interview session to which both the therapy and control patients were exposed. That is, an independent psychiatrist, at regular intervals, met for half-hour sessions with both the therapy and control patients for the duration of the project. These tape-recorded "sampling interview" sessions were rated on the Experiencing dimension. Here also we find no differences in Experiencing change from early to late in therapy, for the therapy patients in contrast to the control patients.

However, if we divide our therapy patients in terms of those receiving high and low therapist conditions, we find differential trends as shown in Figures 13.5 and 13.6. Figure 13.5 gives the differential Experiencing trends for the high and low conditions therapy patients, and for the control patients over the sampling Interviews. As can be seen both the high and low conditions, patients have a similar trend, with the high conditions patients only, however, ending

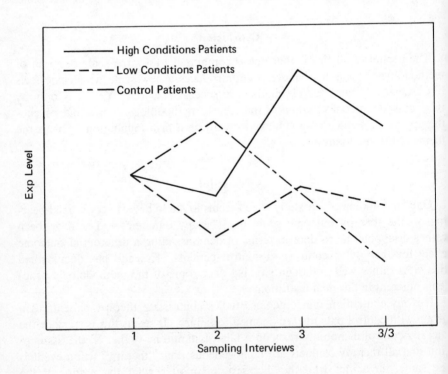

FIGURE 13.5

The Trend of Patient Experiencing over the Sampling (Combining the First Three and Thirds data) for the High Conditions and Low Conditions Therapy Patients and for the Control Patients

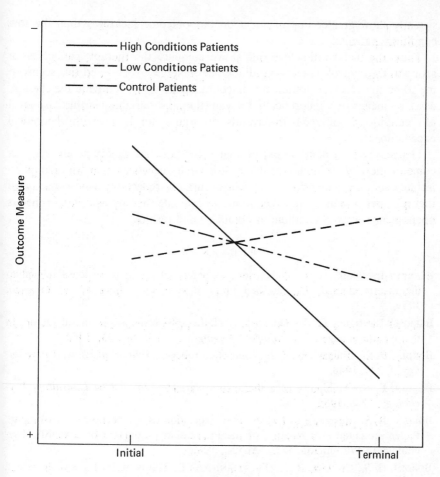

FIGURE 13.6

Test Outcome Change (Initial to Terminal) over Therapy for High Conditions and Low Conditions Therapy Patients, and for the Control Patients

the sampling interview session at a level of Experiencing higher than that obtained initially. Both the low conditions patients and the controls show an over-all decline in Experiencing.

Figure 13.6 gives the typical outcome measure finding when the high and low conditions groups are compared with the control groups. This curve could represent any of our measures of initial to terminal outcome change — let us say, for example, per cent time in the hospital for one year after termination. Again, the high conditions group shows the greatest positive change (out of the hospital a significantly greater percentage of time) than both the low conditions therapy patients and control patients. In fact, the control patients consistently show greater improvement on our outcome measures than the low conditions patients.

Thus, the picture indicates that if we compare the therapy patients as a group to the control patients, no differences emerge. Yet — and this seems to me to be the crucial question for outcome studies — if we divide the therapy cases by means of a theoretically relevant therapist variable (in this case level of "conditions" offered) the results are quite consistent with theoretical expectation.

Hence, my final point would be that before we can validly assess the outcome or therapy evaluation problem, it is vitally necessary that we attempt to isolate therapist dimensions that will accurately reflect the heterogeneity of therapist performance. If we continue to evaluate therapy as a homogeneous phenomenon we will continue to obtain invalid results.

REFERENCES

BARRETT-LENNARD, G. T. Dimensions of perceived therapist response related to therapeutic change. Unpublished Ph.D. dissertation. University of Chicago, 1959.

BARRETT-LENNARD, G. T. Dimensions of therapist response as causal factors in therapeutic change. *Psychological Monographs,* 76, No. 43, 1962.

BORDIN, E. S. Dimensions of the counseling process. *Journal of Clinical Psychology,* 4, 240, 1948.

BORDIN, E. S. Ambiguity as a therapeutic variable. *Journal of Consulting Psychology,* 19, 9, 1955.

BORDIN, E. S. Response to task of free-association as a reflection of personality. Paper presented at a meeting of the International Congress on Scientific Psychology in Washington, D.C., August, 1963.

BORDIN, E. S., CUTLER, R. L., DITTMANN, A. T., HARWAY, N. L., RAUSH, H. L., and RIGLER, D. Measurement problems in process research in psychotherapy. *Journal of Consulting Psychology,* 18, 79, 1954.

COLLIER, R. M. A basis for integration rather than fragmentation in psychotherapy. *Journal of Consulting Psychology,* 14, 199, 1950.

COLLIER, R. M. A scale for relating responses of the psychotherapist. *Journal of Consulting Psychology,* 17, 321, 1953.

DITTMANN, A. T. The interpersonal process in psychotherapy: Development of a research method. *Journal of Abnormal Social Psychology,* 47, 236, 1952.

FISHER, S. Plausability and depth of interpretation. *Journal of Consulting Psychology,* 20, 249, 1956.

GENDLIN, E. T. *Experiencing and the creation of meaning.* New York: Free Press of Glencoe, 1962.

HAIGH, G. Defensive Behavior in client-centered therapy. *Journal of Consulting Psychology,* 13, 181, 1949.

HARWAY, N. I., DITTMANN, A. T., RAUSH, H. L., BORDIN, E. S., and RIGLER, D. The measurement of depth of interpretation. *Journal of Consulting Psychology,* 19, 247, 1955.

HOFFMAN, A. E. A study of reported behavior changes in counseling. *Journal of Consulting Psychology,* 13, 190, 1949.

HOWE, E. S. An empirical scale of therapist verbal activity level in the initial interview. *Journal of Consulting Psychology,* 25, 510, 1961.

HOWE, E. S. Anxiety-arousal and specificity: Rated correlates of the depth of interpretative statements. *Journal of Consulting Psychology,* 26, 178, 1962a.

HOWE, E. S. A study of the semantic structure of ratings of interpretive responses. *Journal of Consulting Psychology,* 26, 285, 1962b.

HOWE, E. S. Therapist verbal activity level and diagnostic utility of patient responses. *Journal of Consulting Psychology,* 26, 149, 1962c.

HOWE, E. S. and POPE, B. The dimensionality of ratings of therapist verbal responses. *Journal of Consulting Psychology,* 25, 296, 1961.

KIESLER, D. J., MATHIEU, P. L., and KLEIN, M. H. Sampling from the recorded therapy interview: A comparative study of different segment lengths. *Journal of Consulting Psychology,* 28, 349-357, 1964.

KIESLER, D. J., MATHIEU, P. L., and KLEIN, M. H. Sampling from the recorded therapy interview: The problem of segment location. *Journal of Consulting Psychology,* 29, 337-344, 1965.

MATARAZZO, J. D. Stability and modifiability of personality patterns during a standardized interview. In P. A. Hoch and J. Zubin (Eds.), *Psychopathology of Communication.* New York: Grune & Stratton, 1958.

MATARAZZO, J. D., SASLOW, G. and GUZE, S. B. Stability of interaction patterns during interviews: A replication. *Journal of Consulting Psychology,* 20, 267, 1956.

MATARAZZO, J. D., SASLOW, G., and MATARAZZO, R. G. The interaction chronograph as an instrument for objective measurement of interaction patterns during interviews. *Journal of Psychology,* 41, 347, 1956.

MATARAZZO, J. D., SASLOW, G., MATARAZZO, R. G., and PHILIPPS, J. S. Differences in interview interaction pattern among five diagnostic groups. Paper read at a meeting of the American Psychological Association, New York City, September, 1957.

MATARAZZO, R. G., MATARAZZO, J. D., SASLOW, G., and PHILIPPS, J. S. Psychological test and organismic correlates of interview interaction behavior. *Journal of Abnormal Social Psychology,* 56, 329, 1958.

RAUSH, H. L., SPERBER, Z., RIGLER, D., WILLIAMS, J., HARWAY, N. I., BORDIN, E. S., DITTMANN, A. T., and HAYS, W. L. A dimensional analysis of depth interpretation. *Journal of Consulting Psychology,* 20, 43, 1956.

ROGERS, C. R. The necessary and sufficient conditions of therapeutic personality change. *Journal of Consulting Psychology,* 21, 95, 1957.

ROGERS, C. R. A process conception of psychotherapy. *American Psychologist,* 13, 142, 1958.

ROGERS, C. R. A tentative scale for the measurement of process in psychotherapy. In E. A. Rubinstein and M. B. Parloff (Eds.), *Research in psychotherapy.* Washington, D.C.: American Psychological Association, 1959a. Pp. 96-107.

ROGERS, C. R. A theory of therapy, personality, and interpersonal relationships as developed in the client-centered framework. In S. Koch (Ed.), *Psychology:*

A study of science, Vol. III. Formulations of the person and the social context. New York: McGraw-Hill, 1959b. Pp. 184-256.

ROGERS, C. R. The process equation of psychotherapy. *American Journal of Psychotherapy*, 15, 27, 1961.

ROGERS, C. R. *A study of psychotherapeutic change in schizophrenics and normals: Design and instrumentation.* Psychiatric Research Reports, American Psychiatric Association, 15, 51-60, April, 1962.

ROGERS, C. R., WALKER, A., and RABLEN, R. Development of a scale to measure process change in psychotherapy. *Journal of Clinical Psychology*, 16, 79, 1960.

SASLOW, G. Psychotherapy. *Annual Review*, 5, 311, 1954.

SASLOW, G., GOODRICH, D. W., and STEIN, M. Study of therapist behavior in diagnostic interviews by means of the interaction chronograph. *Journal of Clinical Psychology*, 12, 133, 1956.

SASLOW, G., MATARAZZO, J. D., and GUZE, S. B. The stability of interaction chronograph patterns in psychiatric interviews. *Journal of Consulting Psychology*, 19, 417, 1955.

SASLOW, G., MATARAZZO, J. D., PHILLIPS, J. S., and MATARAZZO, R. G. Test-retest stability of interaction patterns during interviews conducted one week apart. *Journal of Abnormal Social Psychology*, 54, 295, 1957.

SASLOW, G., and PETERS, A. A follow-up study of "untreated" patients with various behavior disorders. *Psychiatric Quarterly*, 30, 283, 1956.

SEEMAN, J. A study of the process of nondirective therapy, *Journal of Consulting Psychology*, 13, 157, 1949.

SHEERER, E. T. An analysis of the relationship between acceptance of and respect for self and acceptance of and respect of others in ten counseling cases. *Journal of Consulting Psychology*, 13, 169, 1949.

SNYDER, W. U. An investigation of the nature of nondirective psychotherapy. *Journal of General Psychology*, 33, 193, 1945.

SPEISMAN, J. C. Depth of interpretation and verbal resistance in psychotherapy. *Journal of Consulting Psychology*, 23, 93, 1959.

STOCK, D. An investigation into the interrelations between the self-concept and feelings directed toward other persons and groups. *Journal of Consulting Psychology*, 13, 176, 1949.

STRUPP, H. H. A multidimensional analysis of techniques in brief psychotherapy. *Psychiatry*, 20, 387, 1957a.

STRUPP, H. H. A multidimensional comparison of therapist activity in analytic and client-centered therapy. *Journal of Consulting Psychology*, 21, 301, 1957b.

STRUPP, H. H. A multidimensional system for analyzing psychotherapeutic techniques. Psychiatry, 20, 293, 1957c.

STRUPP, H. H. The performance of psychiatrists and psychologists in a therapeutic interview. *Journal of Clinical Psychology*, 14, 219, 1958a.

STRUPP, H. H. The performance of psychoanalytic and client-centered therapists in an initial interview. *Journal of Consulting Psychology*, 22, 265, 1958b.

14

Some Implications of Psychotherapy

Research for Therapeutic Practice*[1]

ALLEN E. BERGIN

A survey of psychotherapy research findings is digested into 6 broad conclusions, and implications for practice and research are drawn from them. They are: (a) Psychotherapy causes clients to become better or worse adjusted than controls, (b) Control Ss improve with time as a result of informal therapeutic encounters, (c) Therapeutic progress varies with therapist warmth, empathy, adjustment, and experience, (d) Client-centered therapy is the only interview-oriented method that has been validated by research, (e) Traditional therapies are seriously limited in effectiveness and are relevant for a small minority of disturbances, and (f) Behavior therapists have considerable promise for enhancing therapeutic effectiveness and should be utilized or experimented with more widely.

The material to follow is a digest of research findings which have implications for practice and research in psychotherapy. It has been formulated in terms of six conclusions and implications which appear justifiable and defensible. This catalogue of conclusions is based upon a comparative handful of

* From *Journal of Abnormal Psychology*, 1966, Vol. 71, pp. 235-246. Copyright 1966 by the American Psychological Association, and reproduced by permission.

[1] Based in part on a paper read at the Pre-Convention Institute of the Ontario Psychological Association, London, Ontario, February, 1964. Read at a symposium: "Implications of empirical research for innovations in therapeutic practice and research," American Psychological Association Convention, Los Angeles, September, 1964.

research reports which have been carefully selected from the present empirical chaos for their relative adequacy of conceptualization, design, and outcome. Conclusions have been drawn only in those areas where the results appear to have substance and where they have been replicated; consequently, many areas of study are excluded.

The Deterioration Effect

Conclusion 1. Psychotherapy may cause people to become better or worse adjusted than comparable people who do not receive such treatment.

Recently, a curious and provocative finding occurred in the preliminary results of the Wisconsin schizophrenia project conducted by Rogers, Gendlin, and Truax (Rogers, 1961; Truax, 1963; Truax and Carkhuff, 1964). It was that the patients in psychotherapy tended to become either better or worse in adjustment than their matched control-group counterparts.

At that time two earlier studies were analyzed (Barron and Leary, 1955; Cartwright, 1956; Cartwright and Vogel, 1960) in which similar findings had occurred; but being incidental to other results, they had not been emphasized in proportion to their true import (Bergin, 1963). Since then, four additional studies with similar findings have been discovered (Fairweather, Simon, Gebhard, Weingarten, Holland, Sanders, Stone, and Reahl, 1960; Mink, 1959; Powers and Witmer, 1951; Rogers and Dymond, 1954). In all seven studies, although there tends to be no difference in the average amount of change between experimentals and controls, there does tend to be a significant difference in *variability* of change. The criterion, or change, scores for treatment groups attain a much wider dispersion than do those of control groups, even though the mean change in both groups is quite similar. Typically, control subjects (Ss) improve somewhat, with the varying amounts of change clustering about the mean. On the other hand, experimental Ss are typically dispersed all the way from marked improvement to marked deterioration. Now frequently documented, this information is alarming to say the least. Psychotherapy can and does make people worse than their control counterparts! Because of the controversial nature of this conclusion, the following material is presented as detailed substantiating evidence in its support.

Table 14.1 is reproduced from Cartwright's (1956) reanalysis of the well-known Barron and Leary study (1955).

Cartwright comments on the data as follows:

> For many scales the variance results suggest that mean differences between the groups are absent because differences of two kinds, opposed in sign, are present. It seems that some therapy patients *deteriorated* to a greater extent than did the waiting-list controls, while some therapy patients *did improve* significantly more than the controls (pp. 403-404).

TABLE 14.1

*Variances of Discrepancy Scores on MMPI Scales for Individual
Psychotherapy and Nontreatment Groups*

Scale	Individual psychotherapy $(N = 42)$	Nontreatment group $(N = 23)$	F
	V [a]	V	
L	19.89	23.43	1.18
F	215.21	22.94	9.38**
K	55.95	31.70	1.76
Hs	127.46	64.16	1.99*
D	244.30	93.32	2.62**
Hy	113.21	87.80	1.29
Pd	155.00	89.68	1.73
Pa	111.94	68.06	1.64
Pt	208.51	73.27	2.85**
Sc	272.91	74.13	3.68**
Ma	126.79	75.34	1.68
Es	43.56	14.82	2.94**

[a] Variances computed from *SD* data reported by Barron and Leary (Table 2, p. 243).
* $p < .05$.
** $p < .01$.

It should be noted that this occurred only for individual and not for group therapy.

It is a fascinating fact that Cartwright's observation has lain unattended in the literature for years, while implicit in his statement is a clear means of resolving much of the controversy over negative results in therapy-outcome studies. It is even more fascinating that Cartwright himself participated in a study (Rogers and Dymond, 1954) in which a similar phenomenon occurred, but just as with the data in the Barron and Leary study it was never emphasized in proportion to its true import. The classic features in this study apparently overshadowed the passing references to a *client-deterioration phenomenon*. While the study is properly famous for other reasons, it provides supporting bits of evidence for the thesis that negative change in therapy is not an isolated or chance occurrence. A careful reading of the report indicates that of 25 therapy *S*s, 6 or 24 percent declined in self-ideal correlation between pretherapy and follow-up testing. A quick computation of the mean change in self-ideal correlation indicates that those who increased averaged an increment of .49 in their correlations, whereas those who declined a decrement of − .40, a difference that is striking considering the fact that the mean pretherapy correlations were not different for these two subgroups. While some chance fluctuations in scores are to be expected, these changes in both directions can hardly be attributed to the effects of imperfect test reliability. While Butler and Haigh (1954) do not examine these possibilities in the data, they do allude to them in passing: "It is of interest, though it does not bear directly upon the hypothesis, that there has also been a marked increase in the degree of variation of correlations (self-ideal) over this period" (p. 63).

It may be argued, of course, that decline in self-ideal correlation can be an indication of improved adjustment, particularly when the correlation is extremely high as in the case of some paranoid *S*s. However, the pretest correlations of all six *S*s who declined in this study were low, ranging from .28 to − .12. The question of whether self-ideal correlations actually measure adjustment at all is still a subject of some debate, so it would seem unwise to draw conclusions about psychotherapy in general from data based on this measure alone. In another section of Rogers and Dymond (1954), an analysis of behavior observations made of the clients independently of therapist progress ratings yielded results similar to those found with the self-ideal measure:

> During the whole period from pre-therapy to followup, observers saw a definite increase in the maturity of behavior of those clients whose therapy was rated as successful and a sharp decrease in the maturity of behavior of those clients rated as unsuccessful. The relationship was statistically significant (p. 228).

While there are additional fragmentary evidences of deterioration phenomena in the book, these suffice to illustrate the point.

In a controlled study of counseling with high school students, Mink (1959) observes the same phenomenon: "Counseling affected the expression of social adjustments on the California Test of Personality. The forms of expression indicate both improvement and recession" (p. 14).

The excellent multifactor design executed by Fairweather et al. (1960) yielded similar results:

> Generally, significantly different variances occurred on most instruments between treatments and diagnoses. The control group usually had the smallest variance and the three psychotherapy groups the largest (p. 24). In these three interactions, one or all of the three long-term psychotic groups in psychotherapy demonstrated changes in the maladaptive scale direction (MMPI) while the controls remain(ed) relatively the same or change(d) in the adaptive direction (p. 9).

Cartwright and Vogel (1960) discovered the same type of differential effect in a neurotic sample using different criterion measures:

> Thus, as measured by the Q score, adjustment changes, regardless of direction, were significantly greater during a therapy period than during a No-Therapy period (p. 122). The Post-therapy tests showed those in therapy with experienced therapists to have improved significantly on both tests,

whereas those in therapy with inexperienced therapists not to have improved . . . , in fact they bordered on a significant decrease in health on the TAT (p. 127).

Turning back several decades to the Cambridge-Somerville youth study (Powers and Witmer, 1951) which was initiated in 1937, the same phenomenon is found with a group of predelinquent boys:

> When the Study Services were effectual most of the boys did function better than their C-twins. This conclusion can be accepted, however, only if its opposite is also accepted: that some of the boys who were not benefited may have been handicapped in social adjustment by the organization's efforts. If this is true, we can conclude that the apparent chance distribution of terminal adjustment ratings . . . was due to the fact that the good effects of the Study were counterbalanced by the poor (p. 455).

Elsewhere the authors indicate that in a significant proportion of cases where the counselor's efforts were judged as poor, the boys "were more socially maladjusted than their control twin" (p. 509). It is unfortunate that this excellently designed and executed study is one leaned upon most heavily by Eysenck (1960, 1965) in his bold denial of the usefulness of psychotherapy, for while the study shows no difference between experimentals and controls, it demonstrates the efficacy of treatment as well as its deteriorative effect.

Finally, to cite the recent Wisconsin project on therapy of schizophrenia which has been published (Truax, 1963) thus far only in tempting bits and pieces:

> High levels of therapist-offered conditions during therapy are related to patient improvement, but . . . low levels . . . are related to patient deterioration, so that if all the therapy combined is indiscriminately compared to control conditions there is little average change. Thus, psychotherapy can be for better or for worse (p. 256).

Since the length of therapy varied in these seven studies from a few months to several years, it seems doubtful that the observed deterioration can be accounted for by the temporary regression that sometimes occurs during treatment. The views of most writers would indicate that the average deterioration due to this effect for a treatment group would be small after brief and lengthy periods of therapy but large in between; whereas the findings reported here suggest a consistent, rectangularly distributed, amount of regression, regardless of the length of time transpired prior to obtaining outcome estimates. Unfortunately, so little controlled empirical work has been done with analytic therapies, which are presumably the richest sources of such data, that it is difficult to compare the findings reported here with what might be found if research were done on them.

Fortunately, these various data indicate that psychotherapy can make people considerably better off than control *Ss*. Therefore, contrary to the notions of some critics, psychotherapy can produce improvement beyond that which may occur due to spontaneous remission alone. Consistently replicated, this is a direct and unambiguous refutation of the oft-cited Eysenckian position (Eysenck, 1960, 1965).

A general paradigm is suggested by the double-edged effect observed in the studies cited which may be schematized as shown in Figure 14.1. Such a startling phenomenon certainly deserves a name, and *The Deterioration Effect* is suggested here.

It is interesting to note that a phenomenon similar to the great variability in the quality of therapeutic effects noted here has also been observed in relation to the accuracy of diagnostic evaluations (Garfield, 1963). Apparently, even well-known diagnosticians vary greatly in the accuracy of their judgments. When all of these judgments are pooled, average predictions or discriminations often are not different from chance estimates; but some individuals appear to far exceed chance predictions while others actually do worse than chance.

Implication 1. (*a*) The practice of psychotherapy should not be given up as some have advocated. (*b*) Those engaged in this field should be more cautious and critical of their own practices, carefully eliminating any ineffective or harmful therapeutic techniques. They should find out whom they are making worse or better, and how, with all due speed. (*c*) They should find out if some therapists make people better and if some make them worse, or if individual therapists do both. After that, comes the ticklish business of making changes in technique personality, or personnel as may be necessary to eliminate negative influences and accentuate positive ones.

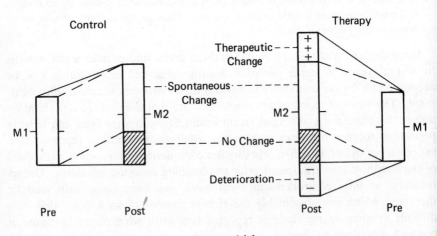

FIGURE 14.1

The Deterioration Effect. (Schematic representation of pre- and post-test distributions of criterion scores in psychotherapy-outcome studies.)

Natural Therapeutic Conditions

Conclusion 2. (*a*) It has been frequently replicated, and is now a well-established fact that control Ss who do not receive psychotherapy change positively as a group with the passage of time. This is the so-called "spontaneous remission" effect (Eysenck, 1952, 1960, 1965). (*b*) Three studies (Frank, 1961; Gurin, Veroff, & Feld, 1960; Powers & Witmer, 1951) indicate that many of these disturbed persons who receive no formal psychotherapy seek and obtain help from various professional and nonprofessional sources such as friends, clergymen, physicians, teachers, and occasionally even psychotherapists (Bergin, 1963).

All this has typically been unknown to the researchers who were depending upon these so-called controls to be a baseline for comparison with their treatment cases. It seems clear that this aid has an ameliorative effect, as the people improve, although it would be impossible to substantiate this fully without further study of the influences upon control Ss in their "natural" habitat. To the extent that this position is correct, it further undermines the Eysenck-type position, because it shows that control Ss often change due to the influence of therapy or therapy-like procedures. Thus, "spontaneous remission" is just another name for the effects of informal therapy.

Implication 2. (*a*) Researchers who utilize control groups should carefully ascertain that these groups are indeed controls, or, if necessary, should directly measure the effects of nonexperimental influences which they cannot control. (*b*) The fact that some of these previously uncontrolled influences are much like therapy, but frequently occur outside of a professional setting, implies that nonprofessional help can stimulate positive personality change. This may consist partly of individuals with "therapeutic personalities" who are sought out for counsel and catharsis by many people. It may be also that unrecognized, but powerful, therapeutic agents exist naturally in everyday life. Just as cures for various physical disorders have been discovered by studying health, so it may be possible to discover antidotes for some of the mental disorders that confront us by discovering conditions already existing in "nature" which support or promote personality integration.

Ingredients of Therapy

Conclusion 3. Therapeutic progress varies as a function of therapist characteristics such as warmth, empathy, adequacy of adjustment, and experience.

In a recent review, Gardner (1964) cited a smattering of positive results to the effect that the more a therapist has an attitude of *liking and warmth* the more likely he is to obtain positive change in his clients. While some of the studies enumerated are of questionable design or generalizability, they are relatively consistent when compared with many other areas of research.

A recent questionnaire study of patients' retrospective reports regarding their therapeutic experience (Strupp, Wallach, and Wogan, 1964), which was not reported by Gardner, further confirms this general finding. While the study is uncontrolled and appears to be contaminated by artifactually inflated correlations, it is of interest that it strongly emphasizes the importance of therapist warmth and genuineness in relation to patient-perceived outcome ($r = .53$).

Additional data on this point come from the client-centered group in a series of studies with neurotics and psychotics. It should be noted that some of the therapists studied were *not* client-centered. These studies are consistent in discovering a significant relationship between operational measures of Rogers' concept of positive regard and independent indices of therapeutic progress or outcome (Truax and Carkhuff, 1964, 1965a; Barrett-Lennard, 1962). Measures of the therapist's attitudes have included ratings by both the therapist himself and the patient. Three types of analysis have resulted in similar findings and in different studies with different samples of clients and therapists. It has thus become increasingly clear, within the limits of these studies, that a therapist's ability to be warm and positively inclined toward his patients is an effective therapeutic ingredient. The effects of intentional authoritarian demands or other forms of planned therapist aggression which are sometimes advocated have not been studied and thus cannot be compared with these findings.

Acknowledging the past confusion and contradiction involved in studies of *empathy,* it is suggested that the recent data summarized at Chicago (Barrett-Lennard, 1962), Wisconsin (Truax, 1961b; Truax & Carkhuff, 1964), and Kentucky (Dickenson & Truax, 1965; Truax & Carkhuff, 1965a; Truax, Carkhuff, & Kodman, 1965; Truax & Wargo, 1965) offer promising leads. Analyses of recorded therapist behavior and ratings by clients of their therapists during the process of treatment have yielded consistently positive relationships between empathic understanding and outcome.

The strength of these findings lies in careful design (Rogers, 1961) and in the analysis of therapist behavior *in vivo,* which is unusual in empathy research. A new empathy measure has been operationalized by Truax (1961b) and is defined by Truax and Carkhuff (1964) as accurate "sensitivity to current feelings *and* the verbal facility to communicate this understanding in a language attuned to the patient's current being" (p. 8). While the scale is still crude and might not be accepted by analysts as measuring their "kind" of empathy, its usefulness has been relatively substantial in these studies.

The third characteristic, *adequacy of adjustment,* has not been studied as thoroughly as the others, but thus far the data are relatively consistent. Those therapists who are more anxious, conflicted, defensive, or "unhealthy" are least likely to promote change in their cases.

Several studies have indicated that supervisor and client ratings of the therapists' competence are negatively related to his degree of anxiety or maladjustment (Arbuckle, 1956; Bandura, 1956; Bergin and Solomon, 1963). Other studies have yielded similar findings when the therapist's actual in-therapy behavior and the patient's response to it was evaluated and used as a criterion of competence. For example, Bandura, Lipsher, and Miller (1960) found that therapists' hostility anxiety was directly associated with avoidance responses to patients' expressions of hostility toward them. The more hostility conflict a therapist had, the more likely he was to avoid his patient's hostility and consequently the patients' self-exploration in this area diminished and his conflicts remained unresolved. A practically identical result was found by Winder, Ahmad, Bandura, and Rau (1962) with regard to dependency anxiety.

In another study (Bergin and Solomon, 1963) it was found that measures of the therapist's degree of personal disturbance correlate negatively with his level of empathy as measured by ratings of tape-recorded psychotherapy interviews. Independent measures of personality strength, on the other hand, correlated positively with degree of "live" empathy. In addition, ratings of therapist anxiety level correlated negatively with independent ratings of therapeutic competence.

Additional data come from the client-centered studies already cited with regard to warmth and empathy, in their examination of therapist congruence. Congruence (Rogers, 1957, 1959) means essentially the healthiness of the therapist in his relationship with his client — his spontaneity, nondefensiveness, openness, or genuineness. Like positive regard and empathy, this variable has also been related to therapeutic progress, and further confirms the general finding of a direct connection between level of therapist adjustment and therapeutic effectiveness.

The three elements of warmth, empathy, and congruence have been found, in the Wisconsin studies, to vary directly with outcome in both negative and positive directions. That is, when these therapist characteristics were at a low level, the patients were getting worse; when they were high, the patients improved (Truax and Carkhuff, 1964). These studies thus provide a partial answer to the question raised earlier as to how negative change occurred in the outcome studies reviewed, although they are limited in that the observed differences were not large, and there is also some question as to whether the division into high and low conditions was done before or after the fact. The other studies cited here in the same realm further clarify the point, although none of the data are precise enough to make practical selection decisions possible.

With regard to the much debated variable of therapist experience, it may be asserted that, in general, more experienced therapists are more effective and successful. This is based on four studies (Barrett-Lennard, 1962; Cartwright and Vogel, 1960; Chance, 1959; Fiedler, 1950a, 1950b, 1951), one of which suggests that highly inexperienced therapists may actually cause patient deterioration (Cartwright and Vogel, 1960).

Implication 3. (*a*) Since psychotherapists are effective partly as a function of personal adjustment, they should be selected for this quality and not solely on the basis of academic and intellectual abilities. Future practice of therapy should therefore be modified by new selection procedures which will bring healthier personalities to bear upon problems of pathology, and by closer self-scrutiny and exposure of one's work among present practitioners.

There is presently no evidence that personal therapy for a disturbed therapist can qualify him for practice and should not be depended upon to perform that function until such evidence is provided. This does not, of course, prove that the experience of being treated cannot be useful to a student therapist whose functioning is within a relatively normal range. There are no studies in which treated neurotics have improved to a level of functioning which is similar to that of control normals even though they do change in level of adjustment; therefore, treatment should not be counted upon to take care of errors in selection. The behavior ratings and personality inventories used in the studies reviewed could provide a beginning in research geared specifically toward the selection problem.

(*b*) Given the necessary personal attributes, therapists should develop their abilities in the realm of warmth and empathic communication, particularly in the case of empathy which is known to be subject to training and experience influences. Further study should be conducted so that clear, measurable standards of performance can be required of aspirants to professional status before they are permitted to practice. As an example, the Truax Empathy Scale (Truax, 1961b) could be used as a beginning to assess one's level of functioning via analysis of recorded interviews.

(*c*) Inexperienced potential therapists should be very carefully introduced to practice with clients, perhaps with much more stringent care than is now commonly exercised. Since all beginners make many mistakes, it may be useful and ethical to have them see more resilient, normal people until they reach a criterion level of interview performance, measured perhaps on dimensions such as warmth and empathy which appear to be accepted by most schools of therapy as vital though not necessarily sufficient for successful treatment.

Conclusion 4. To date, the only school of interview-oriented psychotherapy which has consistently yielded positive outcomes in research studies is the client-centered approach (Rogers and Dymond, 1954; Shlien, Mosak, and Dreikurs, 1962; Truax and Carkhuff, 1964).

The fact that other schools have not subjected their methods to systematic study of this sort is important but it should not deter one from accepting the fact that client-centered treatment has some positive value when properly conducted according to Rogers' (1957) paradigm. The implications for practice seem quite clear, particularly in view of the consistently dismal reports on percentages of improvement in psychoanalytic therapy (Eysenck, 1965; Wolpe, 1964b).

It appears from these reports that the poorest results were obtained with more classical, long-term psychoanalysis, namely a lower percentage of improved cases than the 67 per cent "spontaneous" remission rate. Briefly, analytically oriented eclectic psychotherapy was more promising in that the percentage improvement equaled the spontaneous remission figure. This type of therapy was also used in some of the studies cited in this paper on the deterioration effect; therefore, despite the generally negative evidence, some analytically oriented therapists must be having a positive effect beyond that occurring in control groups.

It should also be noted that the technique of "moderate interpretation" (Speisman, 1959), which derives from the analytic tradition, has potential therapeutic significance. Its definition is very similar to that given for "good" interpretation by various analysts (Fenichel, 1941) and it is related to productive patient self-exploration. It consists of responding to client affect just below the surface and labeling, identifying, or emphasizing it. This does not involve making connections between past and present, being diagnostic or theoretical, nor telling the patient about feelings he "really has" when he's not experiencing them. It is, rather, an instance of good empathy. If one looks carefully at the definitions and operations for identifying accurate empathy and moderate or good interpretation, it is very difficult to distinguish between them. Truax and Carkhuff (1964) refer to this notion in an interesting comment:

> "accurate empathy" has much in common with the "good psychoanalytic interpretation," in that it makes use of both verbal and nonverbal cues presented by the patient. It differs from some good psychoanalytic interpretations in its insistence that the therapist's empathic response focuses upon feelings and experience of the patient from the patient's own unique viewpoint.

The importance of these observations should not be underestimated, for if they are accurate it appears that effective variables cut across schools of treatment and thus provide the basis for applying techniques on the basis of known effects rather than on doctrines promulgated by warring factions. This also indicates that titles, degrees, or years of training should not define the psychotherapist, but rather what the individual can do. Thus one might call himself "client-centered" and espouse the teachings of that school while at the same time presenting the low level of therapist empathy found to result in client deterioration. On the other hand, a psychoanalyst might be functioning at a high level according to the client-centered empathy scale.

Conclusion 5. In spite of all so far stated about the possibilities for substantially improving consulting-room effectiveness, some stubborn facts still require confrontation. One is that even when the various sources of slippage and inadequacy are accounted for, interviews still do not generaly produce very dramatic changes in people. Another is the now well-known fact that many types of people simply are not helped at all by this procedure.

Studies of the relationship between client qualities and therapeutic outcome indicate consistently and clearly that positive outcome is limited or nil with many personality types. It is common for private practitioners and even clinics either to refuse to treat, or reluctantly to accept for treatment, cases that do not fit their conception of psychotherapy. To a great extent this is realistic because traditional methods do not work with these cases. These "rejects," as compared with "accepted" cases, tend to be less intelligent, less anxious, less educated, less verbal and insightful, more concrete and action-oriented, more severely disturbed, more impulsive in the sociopathic sense, and often find the typical consulting-room procedure rather meaningless (Barron, 1953; Cartwright, 1955; Fulkerson and Barry, 1961; Garfield and Affleck, 1961; Hollingshead and Redlich, 1958; Kirtner and Cartwright, 1958a, 1958b). This general observation has been made fairly frequently by various clinicians and is currently rather well-substantiated by the research literature.

Implication 5. The implication of these data, which only confirm an already widely believed idea, is that novel or modified techniques must be developed for dealing with a vast population whose problems are not amenable to standard methods. The importance of novel approaches is further emphasized by the fact that standard methods are not dramatically effective even in those cases where they are applicable, except in rare instances. The latter unusual cases would be a proper subject of study in themselves and may actually suggest innovations even though they arise in "traditional" therapy.

There are three primary sources of possible innovation that might alleviate this predicament. One is creative work in the clinical setting; another is naturally existing conditions in society; and another is that general area of research which is concerned with personality and behavior change such as studies of learning, attitude change, and personality development.

The Promise of Behavior Therapy

Conclusion 6. Studies of learning have thus far been very fruitful in generating principles and methods for promoting personality change. The work by Wolpe (1958), Lazarus (1963), Lang and Lazovik (1963), Lindsley (1963), and others has been both provocative and fruitful. The cases presented and research studies reported provide more positive evidence of the usefulness of these methods than is the case in any form of traditional interview or dynamic psychotherapy, including client-centered therapy.

They involve clinical adaptation of learning principles, such as counterconditioning or extinction of anxiety symptoms, positive reinforcement in shaping adaptive responses and developing appropriate discriminations, aversive conditioning of maladaptive approach responses, and modeling. It is the effects of these methods which are important here. Wolpe (1964a) cites over 200 cases of neurosis in 89 per cent of which he has obtained substantial recovery. Lazarus (1963), in England, reports 408 cases with a similar improvement rate. The striking aspect of these results is that they have been achieved with difficult symptom pictures in brief periods of time. Unfortunately, these are clinical reports by individual therapists who rate their own case outcomes. Independent criteria and control *S*s are completely lacking, and it is difficult to discern how comparable their cases are with those reported in other studies. Still, it is rare to find such high rates of claimed cure even in the clinical literature.

A number of well-designed studies appear to substantiate the clinical reports of Wolpe and Lazarus. Lang and Lazovik (1963) were able significantly to alter snake phobias with brief desensitization procedures. Effects of testing and training in relaxation were controlled, and no symptom substitution occurred during 6 months of follow-up. Lazarus (1961) demonstrated substantial and rapid change of phobic symptoms and impotence by group desensitization methods. A comparison group being treated by traditional interpretive group therapy showed considerably less improvement, only 2 of 17 cases becoming symptom free after 22 sessions. These same cases were subsequently treated by group desensitization and after a mean of 10 sessions each, two thirds were symptom free. Paul (1966) found that desensitization procedures were far more effective in eliminating speech anxieties than brief insight therapy, an attention-placebo condition, and a no-therapy control condition.

In a study of operant conditioning methods, which are different from Wolpe's techniques, King, Armitage, and Tilton (1960) found that substantial changes could be effected even in schizophrenic cases. They were able to produce clinically observable improvement in cases so treated which was greater than the changes occurring in conventional interview therapy, recreational therapy, or no therapy. Ayllon and Michael (1959) effected substantial positive changes in ward behavior of psychotics by programing the reinforcements of their hospital environment according to operant principles. Lovaas, Schaeffer, and Simmons (1966) appear to have induced important changes in the social behavior of difficult cases of childhood autism by systematic use of negative reinforcement. In a review, Lindsley (1963) argues for the general promise of operant techniques; although the evidence thus far pertains primarily to simple motor and verbal behaviors. Conceivably, this approach will prove to be more useful with the more primitive behaviors of psychotics and small children than with the more complex, symbolically involved adult neuroses.

A most interesting development in behavior therapy involves the systematic application of principles of imitative or observational learning. Bandura

(1965b) argues persuasively from the vantage point of extensive experimental work (Bandura, 1965a, 1965c) that modeling procedures provide powerful conditions for the acquisition of new responses and the modification of old ones. Though controlled clinical applications have just begun, they already lend considerable substance to Bandura's view (Berberich and Schaeffer, 1965; Frank, 1965; Hoehn-Saric, Frank, Imber, Nash, Stone, and Battle, 1965; Krumboltz and Thoreson, 1964; Krumboltz and Schroeder, 1965; Krumboltz, Varenhorst, and Thoreson, 1965; Nelson and Bijan, 1965; Thoreson and Krumboltz, 1965; Truax and Carkhuff, 1965b).

Several extensive reviews further substantiate the generality of Conclusion 6 (Bandura, 1965b; Bandura and Walters, 1963; Eysenck and Rachman, 1965; Franks, 1964; Grossberg, 1964; Krasner and Ullman, 1965; Ullman and Krasner, 1965; Wolpe, 1964b).

In spite of the fact that the evidence is favorable, these techniques have been criticized by clinicians as removing symptoms without changing basic pathology and as being limited to very simple neuroses. Neither criticism, however, fits the evidence. Wolpe (1964a) cites data on 88 cases which indicate that a high proportion of complex neuroses can be successfully treated (89 per cent) and in a much briefer time than is typical of traditional methods (Table 14.2).

TABLE 14.2

Comparison of Numbers of Sessions in Complex and Simple Neuroses

Neuroses	N	Mdn No. sessions	M No. sessions
Complex	65	29	54.8
Simple	21	11.5	14.9
Total	86	23	45.4

Note: The total is only 86 because 2 cases that turned out to be schizophrenic are excluded.

The more telling critique of this work is Breger and McGaugh's (1965) point regarding the uncontrolled case reports, which are the basis for the high cure rates, and the rater bias in estimating outcomes encountered in many of the experimental studies. Faulty as a proportion of these reports are, the overall record still represents the best there is in the field of psychotherapy.

In addition to the fact that difficult cases show improvement in a short time, these reports indicate that significant relapses are rare. This is perhaps the most persuasive evidence that behavior therapists are right when they assert that "symptoms" are not symptoms of psychoanalytic-style pathology, but that they are learned behaviors subject to modification via relearning.

Some learning theorists have criticized Wolpe in particular, claiming that his techniques do not derive directly and logically from learning principles and thus do not have the scientific base he claims (Breger and McGaugh, 1965; Mowrer, 1963). While this may be true to some extent, it is irrelevant to the question of the technique's effectiveness and ignores the possibility that these clinical phenomena may eventually become the basis for reformulating learning theories in terms of complex, socially significant human behavior. In this case, one would not expect principles of behavior therapy to conform rigorously to conceptions derived largely from animal research.

Implication 6. The implications of this work seem quite clear. Since these techniques are effective with many types of symptomatology, they should be used. With regard to some of the more complex and difficult problems, behavior therapists argue that it would be better to spend time developing more complex social learning paradigms for treatment than to expend equal energy modifying less promising traditional interview methods. It appears that special effort should be devoted to integrating these methods with others and in some cases substituting them for the other methods. It would seem important to avoid a current tendency to isolate behavior therapies from the mainstream of treatment and thus create another rigid "school" which will gradually become as impervious to new ideas as the traditional schools already are.

Conclusion

In conclusion, it is only regrettable that comment upon so many topics of research has had to be excluded. Suffice it to say that the results in many of those not mentioned are not as yet amenable to synthesis. A good example is the material on the patient-therapist relationship. Nearly all of this research actually pertains to therapist qualities and has nothing to do with an analysis of interactional factors. An unusual exception is the work of Barrett-Lennard (1962) which was cited briefly in the discussion of therapist qualities. The few other useful facts in this domain were also included in that section. Another promising line of investigation is that on patient-therapist similarity; but the meaning of the data is still quite ambiguous (Sussman, 1964).

In spite of the fact that much of what is called psychotherapy research is appalling in its inadequacy, to have found a handful of reliable conclusions is gratifying. The groundwork seems well laid by these studies for initial steps at productive innovation in therapeutic treatment.

REFERENCES

ARBUCKLE, D. S. Client perception of counselor personality, *Journal of Counseling Psychology*, 1956, 3, 93-96.

AYLLON, T., and MICHAEL, J. The psychiatric nurse as a behavioral engineer. *Journal of the Experimental Analysis of Behavior,* 1959, 2, 323-334.

BANDURA, A. Psychotherapist's anxiety level, self-insight, and psychotherapeutic competence. *Journal of Abnormal and Social Psychology,* 1956, 52, 333-337.

BANDURA, A. Behavioral modification through modeling procedures. In L. Krasner and L. Ullmann (Eds.), *Research in behavior modification.* New York: Holt, Rinehart & Winston, 1965a. Pp. 310-340.

BANDURA, A. Psychotherapy conceptualized as a social-learning process. Paper read at the Kentucky Centennial Symposium on Psychotherapy, University of Kentucky, April 1965b.

BANDURA, A. Vicarious processes: A case of no-trial learning. In L. Berkowitz (Ed.), *Advances in experimental social psychology.* Vol. 2. New York: Academic Press, 1965c. Pp. 3-48.

BANDURA, A., LIPSHER, D. H., and MILLER, P. E. Psychotherapists' approach-avoidance reactions to patients' expressions of hostility. *Journal of Consulting Psychology,* 1960, 24, 1-8.

BANDURA, A., and WALTERS, R. H. *Social learning and personality development.* New York: Holt, Rinehart & Winston, 1963.

BARRETT-LENNARD, G. T. Dimensions of therapist response as casual factors in therapeutic change. *Psychological Monographs,* 1962, 76 (43, Whole No. 562).

BARRON, F. Some test correlates of response to psychotherapy. *Journal of Consulting Psychology,* 1953, 17, 235-241.

BARRON, F., and LEARY, T. Changes in psychoneurotic patients with and without psychotherapy. *Journal of Consulting Psychology,* 1955, 19, 239-245.

BERBERICH, J., and SCHAEFFER, B. Establishment of verbal behavior through imitation. Paper read at American Psychological Association, Chicago, September 1965.

BERGIN, A. E. The effects of psychotherapy: Negative results revisited. *Journal of Counseling Psychology,* 1963, 10, 244-250.

BERGIN, A. E., and SOLOMON, S. Personality and performance correlates of empathic understanding in psychotherapy. *American Psychologist,* 1963, 18, 393. (Abstract)

BREGER, L., and McGAUGH, J. L. Critique and reformulation of "learning-theory" approaches to psychotherapy and neurosis. *Psychological Bulletin,* 1965, 63, 338-358.

BUTLER, J. M., and HAIGH, G. Changes in the relation between self-concepts and ideal concepts consequent upon client-centered counseling. In C. R. Rogers & R. F. Dymond (Eds.), *Psychotherapy and personality change.* Chicago: University of Chicago Press, 1954. Pp. 55-75.

CARTWRIGHT, D. S. Success in psychotherapy as a function of certain actuarial variables. *Journal of Consulting Psychology,* 1955, 19, 357-363.

CARTWRIGHT, D. S. Note on "changes" in psychoneurotic patients with and without psychotherapy. *Journal of Consulting Psychology,* 1956, 20, 403-404.

CARTWRIGHT, R. D., and VOGEL, J. L. A comparison of changes in psychoneurotic patients during matched periods of therapy and no-therapy. *Journal of Consulting Psychology,* 1960, 24, 121-127.

CHANCE, E. *Families in treatment.* New York: Basic Books, 1959.

DICKENSON, W. A., and TRUAX, C. B. Group counseling with college underachievers: Comparisons with a control group and relationship to empathy, warmth, and genuineness. Unpublished manuscript, University of Kentucky, 1965.

EYSENCK, H. J. The effects of psychotherapy: An evaluation. *Journal of Consulting Psychology,* 1952, 16, 319-324.

EYSENCK, H. J. The effects of psychotherapy. In H. J. Eysenck (Ed.), *Handbook of abnormal psychology.* New York: Basic Books, 1960. Pp. 697-725.

EYSENCK, H. J. The effects of psychotherapy. *International Journal of Psychiatry,* 1965, 1, 97-178.

EYSENCK, H. J., and RACHMAN, S. *The causes and cures of neurosis.* San Diego: Knapp, 1965.

FAIRWEATHER, G. W., SIMON, R., GEBHARD, M. E., WEINGARTEN, E., HOLLAND, J. L., SANDERS, R., STONE, G. B., and REAHL, J. E. Relative effectiveness of psychotherapeutic programs: A multicriteria comparison of four programs for three different patient groups. *Psychological Monographs,* 1960, 74 (5, Whole No. 492).

FENICHEL, O. *Problems of psychoanalytic techniques.* Albany: Psychoanalytic Quarterly, 1941.

FIEDLER, F. E. A comparison of therapeutic relationships in psychoanalytic, nondirective, and Adlerian therapy. *Journal of Consulting Psychology,* 1950a, 14, 436-445.

FIEDLER, F. E. The concept of the ideal therapeutic relationship. *Journal of Consulting Psychology,* 1950b, 14, 239-245.

FIEDLER, F. E. Factor analyses of psychoanalytic, nondirective, and Adlerian therapeutic relationships. *Journal of Consulting Psychology,* 1951, 15, 32-38.

FRANK, J. D. *Persuasion and healing.* Baltimore: Johns Hopkins Press, 1961.

FRANK, J. D. The role of hope in psychotherapy. Paper read at the University of Kentucky Centennial Psychotherapy Symposium, April 1965.

FRANKS, C. (Ed.) *Conditioning techniques in clinical practice and research.* New York: Springer, 1964.

FULKERSON, S. D., and BARRY, J. R. Methodology and research on the prognostic use of psychological tests. *Psychological Bulletin,* 1961, 58, 177-204.

GARDNER, G. G. The psychotherapeutic relationship. *Psychological Bulletin,* 1964, 61, 426-437.

GARFIELD, S. L. The clinical method in personality assessment. In J. Wepman and R. Heine (Eds.), *Concepts of personality.* Chicago: Aldine, 1963. Pp. 474-502.

GARFIELD, S. L., and AFFLECK, D. C. Therapists' judgments concerning patients considered for psychotherapy. *Journal of Consulting Psychology,* 1961, 25, 505-509.

GROSSBERG, J. M. Behavior therapy: A review. *Psychological Bulletin,* 1964, 62, 73-88.

GURIN, G., VEROFF, J., and FELD, S. *Americans view their mental health.* New York, Basic Books, 1960.

HOEHN-SARIC, R., FRANK, J. D., IMBER, S. D., NASH, E. H., STONE, A. R., and BATTLE, C. C. Systematic preparation of patients for psychotherapy: I. Effects on therapy behavior and outcome. *Journal of Psychiatric Research,* 1965, 2, 267-281.

HOLLINGSHEAD, A. B., and REDLICH, F. C. *Social class and mental illness.* New York: Wiley, 1958.

KING, G. F., ARMITAGE, S. G., and TILTON, J. R. A therapeutic approach to schizophrenics of extreme pathology. *Journal of Abnormal and Social Psychology,* 1960, 61, 276-286.

KIRTNER, W. L., and CARTWRIGHT, D. S. Success and failure in client-centered therapy as a function of client personality variables. *Journal of Consulting Psychology,* 1958a, 22, 259-264.

KIRTNER, W. L., & CARTWRIGHT, D. S. Success and failure in client-centered therapy as a function of initial in-therapy behavior. *Journal of Consulting Psychology,* 1958b, 22, 329-333.

KRASNER, L., and ULLMANN, L. (Eds.) *Research in behavior modification: New developments and implications.* New York: Holt, Rinehart and Winston, 1965.

KRUMBOLTZ, J. D., and SCHROEDER, W. W. The effect of reinforcement counseling and model-reinforcement counseling on information-seeking behavior of high school students. *Personnel and Guidance Journal,* 1966.

KRUMBOLTZ, J. D., and THORESON, C. E. The effect of behavioral counseling in group and individual settings on information-seeking behavior. *Journal of Counseling Psychology,* 1964, 9, 324-333.

KRUMBOLTZ, J. D., VARENHORST, B., and THORENSON, C. E. Non-verbal factors in the effectiveness of models in counseling. Paper read at American Personnel and Guidance Association, Minneapolis, April 1965.

LANG, P. J., and LAZOVIK, A. D. Experimental desensitization of a phobia. *Journal of Abnormal and Social Psychology,* 1963, 6, 519-525.

LAZARUS, A. A. Group therapy of phobic disorders by systematic desensitization. *Journal of Abnormal and Social Psychology,* 1961, 63, 504-510.

LAZARUS, A. A. An evaluation of behavior therapy. *Behavior Research and Therapy,* 1963, 1, 69-79.

LINDSLEY, O. R. Free-operant conditioning and psychotherapy. In J. H. Masserman (Ed.), *Current psychiatric therapies.* Vol. 3. New York: Grune & Stratton, 1963. Pp. 47-56.

LOVAAS, O. I., SCHAEFFER, B., and SIMMONS, J. Q. Building social behavior in autistic children by use of electric shock. In J. O. Palmer and M. J. Goldstein (Eds.), *Perspectives in psychopathology: Readings in abnormal psychology.* New York: Oxford University Press, 1966. Pp. 222-236.

MINK, O. G. A comparison of effectiveness of non-directive therapy and clinical counseling in the junior high school. *School Counselor*, 1959, 6, 12-14.

MOWRER, O. H. Freudianism, behavior therapy, and "self-disclosure." *Behavior Research and Therapy*, 1963, 1.

NELSON, K., and BIJAN, G. Teaching social behaviors to schizophrenic children through imitation. Paper read at American Psychological Association, Chicago, September 1965.

PAUL, G. L. *Effects of insight, desensitization, and attention placebo treatment of anxiety.* Stanford: Stanford University Press, 1966.

POWERS, E., and WITMER, H. *An experiment in the prevention of delinquency.* New York: Columbia University Press, 1951.

ROGERS, C. R. The necessary and sufficient conditions of therapeutic personality change. *Journal of Consulting Psychology*, 1957, 21, 95-103.

ROGERS, C. R. A theory of therapy, personality, and interpersonal relationships, as developed in the client-centered framework. In S. Koch (Ed.), *Psychology: A study of a science.* Vol. III. New York: McGraw-Hill, 1959. Pp. 184-256.

ROGERS, C. R. A theory of psychotherapy with schizophrenics and a proposal for its empirical investigation. In J. G. Dawson and N. P. Dellis (Eds.), *Psychotherapy with schizophrenics.* Baton Rouge: Louisiana State University Press, 1961. Pp. 3-19.

ROGERS, C. R., and DYMOND, R. F. *Psychotherapy and personality change.* Chicago: University of Chicago Press, 1954.

SHLIEN, J. M., MOSAK, H. H., and DREIKURS, R. Effect of time limits: A comparison of two psychotherapies. *Journal of Counseling Psychology*, 1962, 9, 31-34.

SPEISMAN, J. C. Depth of interpretation and verbal resistance in psychotherapy. *Journal of Consulting Psychology*, 1959, 23, 93-99.

STRUPP, H. H., WALLACH, M. S., and WOGAN, M. Psychotherapy experience in retrospect: Questionnaire survey of former patients and their therapists. *Psychological Monographs*, 1964, 78 (11, Whole No. 588).

SUSSMAN, A. Patient-therapist similarity as a factor in psychotherapy. Unpublished manuscript, Teachers College, Columbia University, 1964.

THORESON, C. E., and KRUMBOLTZ, J. D. Relationship of counselor reinforcement of selected responses to external behavior. *Journal of Counseling Psychology*, 1966.

TRUAX, C. B. A scale for the measurement of accurate empathy. *Psychiatric Institute Bulletin*, Wisconsin Psychiatric Institute, University of Wisconsin, 1961a, No. 10.

TRUAX, C. B. The process of group psychotherapy: Relationships between hypothesized therapeutic conditions and intrapersonal exploration. *Psychological Monographs*, 1961b, 75 (7, Whole No. 511).

TRUAX, C. B. Effective ingredients in psychotherapy. *Journal of Counseling Psychology*, 1963, 10, 256-263.

TRUAX, C. B., and CARKHUFF, R. R. For better or for worse: The process of psychotherapeutic change. In *Recent advances in behavioral change.* Montreal: McGill University Press, 1964.

Truax, C. B., and Carkhuff, R. R. Experimental manipulation of therapeutic conditions. *Journal of Consulting Psychology,* 1965a, 29, 119-124.

Truax, C. B., and Carkhuff, R. R. Personality change in hospitalized mental patients during group psychotherapy as a function of the use of alternate sessions and vicarious therapy pretraining. *Journal of Clinical Psychology,* 1965b, 21, 225-228.

Truax, C. B., and Carkhuff, R. R., and Kodman, F. Relationships between therapist-offered conditions and patient change in group psychotherapy. Unpublished manuscript, University of Kentucky, 1965.

Truax, C. B., and Wargo, D. G. Human encounters that change behavior: For better or for worse. Unpublished manuscript, University of Kentucky, 1965.

Ullmann, L., and Krasner, L. (Eds.) *Case studies in behavior modification.* New York: Holt, Rinehart & Winston, 1965.

Winder, C. L., Ahmad, F. Z., Bandura, A., and Rau, L. Dependency of patients, psychotherapists' responses, and aspects of psychotherapy. *Journal of Consulting Psychology,* 1962, 26, 129-134.

Wolpe, J. *Psychotherapy by reciprocal inhibition.* Stanford: Stanford University Press, 1958.

Wolpe, J. Behavior therapy in complex neurotic states. *British Journal of Psychiatry,* 1964a, 110, 28-34.

Wolpe, J. The comparative clinical status of conditioning therapies and psychoanalysis. In J. Wolpe, A. Salter, and L. J. Reyna (Eds.), *The conditioning therapies.* New York: Holt, Rinehart & Winston, 1964b. Pp. 5-20.

PART FOUR

New Directions in Therapy

Schoolboys quickly learn that not all good ideas fly. In this the fine art of flying paper planes and the psychotherapeutic arts are the same. An idea that thinks good, sounds good, and looks good can still flop. Therapy is a practical art; all theories about therapy must eventually meet the test of practice. A theory may persuade us that something should work, and research may prove that it has worked, but the only crucial and convincing test, finally, is the test within the therapist's own experience.

It is appropriate, then, that these chapters at the center of our book be about the practice of therapy. Whatever else a psychotherapy orientation is — a theory of personality, an ethic, a body of research, a program for social change — it must be capable of answering this simple question: How does one person help another?

The answer must begin with the realization that therapy is doing. A therapist has more in common with a mechanic or potter than with a physicist. A therapist must be person-oriented, which is why the people who write or do research about therapy are not necessarily, nor even typically, the best therapists. People and professions can be divided into those that are dominantly process-oriented, case-oriented, or person-oriented.

Identification of the process orientation is easy. Attention is directed to events, and its goal is to observe and discern conceptually those laws and principles that describe and explain process regularities. The professional model for the process orientation is the scientist.

If the case and person orientations were as easily identified and differentiated as the process orientation, many confusions about the psychotherapist's role would be dispelled. But confusions persist; partly because many psychologists, psychiatrists, counselors, pastors, and social workers have not been taught the difference between a case-oriented profession, such as medicine, and a person-oriented profession, such as psychotherapy or the ministry. It can even be argued (see Chapter 30) that the concept of a "professional" is incompatible with the fostering of person-to-person relationships. This argument says that the "scientist-professional" dispute, which is so vociferously debated in discussions about the clinical psychologist's proper role, includes the wrong disputants. The basic tension in the practice of psychotherapy is between adherents of the case and person orientations, not between the process and case orientations.

The practitioner who thinks of his job in relation to "cases" fits the model of the physician and engineer. He is an applied scientist. The person-oriented practitioner, by contrast, thinks of himself as a craftsman or artist. One tries to apply techniques to diagnosed problems to achieve predictable results. The other is himself a tool of the art he practices; the forms he helps to create are, *at best,* unpredictable. One practitioner strives for control, the other for creativity. One enjoys order and precision while the other enjoys the surprises that come when he sees that special kind of orderly disorder or disorderly order that emerges from freedom.

All chapters in Part Four align themselves, more or less, with the person orientation, a well-established client-centered alignment. From its inception the client-centered orientation has opted for an unusual blending of the process and person orientations rather than the more common psychotherapeutic case orientation. The development of client-centered therapy can be viewed as a threefold effort to find new ways of making the person orientation work, new explanations for why it works, and research demonstrations that it does work. (For a discussion of client-centered therapy's special blend of the person and process orientations see Chapter 28 on the "Literal-intuitive axis.") In Part One these client-centered developments were surveyed; Part Two presented theoretical rationales for the person orientation, with special emphasis on the theory of experiencing; Part Three contained research validations of its workability; and in this Part new forms and extensions of the orientation are described.

An important result of accepting the person orientation is that professional credentials for therapists are minimized or ignored. We can readily see that the two most prestigious advanced degrees, the M.D. and the Ph.D., require kinds of training that are irrelevant or antithetical to this orientation. Medical candidates are encouraged to be case-oriented, doctoral candidates process-oriented; in neither training program are students encouraged to identify with the person orientation. The obvious conclusion is that therapists need not and perhaps should not be professionals. What this conclusion looks like in action is shown in each of the following chapters. Nonprofessionals appear in every chapter as therapists. In some settings, as in Goodman's "Companionship as therapy," the nonprofessionals are the only therapists, while in others, such as Gendlin's "Research in psychotherapy with schizophrenic patients," they work on an equal footing with the professionals. In all settings, the research indicates that "non" is not synonymous with "un"; the nonprofessionals are neither unsuccessful nor unskilled.

One question that may be asked about these chapters is, to what extent are these "new directions" in therapy? This is not easy to answer. In one sense, none of the chapters, except Gordon's on parent effectiveness training, is wholly new. And in another sense they are all new, new to client-centered therapy. But so what? Other therapies have done psychotherapy with schizophrenics, conducted basic encounter groups, brought families into therapy, and used nonprofessionals as therapists — none of these directions originated with client-centered therapy.

But the importance of a new direction has very little to do with whether or not it is new in the sense of "first." What is important is whether something of value is added to the practice of therapy. The first art work within a new form is usually inferior to that which follows, and so it is in psychotherapy. We should not devalue the achievements of Melanie Klein or Anna Freud because they were not the first therapists to work with children. Nor is the work of Freida Fromm-Reichman or Sullivan diminished because they were not the first therapists to work with schizophrenics. Advances are made when new directions of practice are integrated with conceptualizations that guide and explain the practical explorations.

This is the sense in which we believe each chapter in Part Four brings something new to the practice of therapy, something derived from that unique blend of the process and person orientations which characterizes client-centered therapy.

15

Research in Psychotherapy

with Schizophrenic Patients

and the Nature of that "Illness"*[1]

EUGENE T. GENDLIN

This is a report on a five-year research program at the University of Wisconsin and Mendota State Hospital. The research was originated and sponsored by Carl Rogers. It attempted a number of radical things and employed research rigor and measurements that are extremely rare in the field of psychotherapy.

The Research Design

The difficulties and the many discouraging aspects of doing psychotherapy with schizophrenics as reported by others were also found by us. We did not walk in and empty out the hospital. But we did have some successes in the therapy. Similarly, we found the research difficulties almost as hard as we were told we would. The attempt at rigorous measurements of psychotherapy

* From *American Journal of Psychotherapy*, Vol. 20, No. 1, 1966, pp. 4-16. Reproduced by permission.

[1] Presented at the Second National Meeting of the Association for the Advancement of Psychotherapy, St. Louis, Mo., May 5, 1963. The project was supported by the National Institute of Mental Health, directed by Carl R. Rogers, Eugene T. Gendlin, and Charles B. Truax, at the University of Wisconsin Psychiatric Institute and Mendota State Hospital, Madison, Wis.

in a hospital was said to be impossible. We found that it was not impossible, but, at times, it was extremely close to that.

Our schedule called for testing each patient regularly, but the human condition plus the conditions of a hospital prevent anything from being quite regular. Whereas we wanted to test the patients every six months, we were fortunate to obtain at least one good instance of adequate testing early in therapy (not always in the beginning) and at least one instance late in therapy. Hence we can compare these patients early and late in therapy.

We had a no-therapy control group. That is also a very difficult matter. How can one arrange to prevent therapy for the control group without making them worse by such arrangements? If one makes the control group worse, naturally the psychotherapy group will look better. What will then seem like a good finding will mean little. Ideally, one wants a group of controls with whom nothing like therapy is done so that one can later estimate whether improvements in the psychotherapy group are really due to psychotherapy, or whether they happen just as much by spontaneous remission without therapy. But in our treatment-oriented hospital, group therapy is common and individual work not infrequent. To isolate the control group in some special way would have singled them out for worse treatment. So we merely tested them and otherwise let them get whatever the hospital gives. Most controls had group therapy, and two were in individual therapy.

Our main concern was to test Rogers' (1957) original hypotheses — that the patients will get better to the extent that the therapist is *genuine* (really himself as a person), to the extent that he is *empathic* (understands what is going on in the patient), and to the extent that he shows the patient *unconditional positive regard* (like the patient regardless of all of the patient's difficulties and bad feeling). I will rename these three conditions realness, understanding, and liking. We took on the task of measuring the extent to which the therapist is really himself, understands and likes his patient. This involves measuring in-therapy behavior itself, not only before-and-after tests outside of therapy. We are new at measuring psychotherapy itself, as it goes on during the interview hours. But, if psychotherapy research is to make real progress, one has to begin to define and measure what occurs in the psychotherapy hours. So by realness, understanding, and liking of the therapist, we meant what he does *during* the psychotherapy hours.

In addition to these three aspects of the therapist's interview behavior we are also measuring the patient's behavior. To what exent does the patient behave in ways that indicate an involvement in an experiential psychotherapy process? Beginning with Rogers' Process Scale (1959, 1960), we have refined an Experiencing Scale with indices of the extent to which the patient avoids feelings and felt meanings, and uses verbalizations that do not involve his experiencing, externalizes, and the extent to which he is really involved in a psychotherapy process, his reactions and phrasings being fresh expressions of experiencing (Gendlin and Tomlinson, 1967).

We hypothesized that therapists who measured highest on realness, under-standing, and liking would have patients who not only showed the most improvement at the end, but who during the course of therapy would show the highest and most increasing degree of this experiential therapy process.

To put it all in one sentence: Will the cases that show highest therapeutic behavior by therapists also be those that show the highest degree of patient therapeutic behavior — and will these be the patients who are most improved at the end?

Method of Scaling

We developed quite specific rating scales to apply to the tape-recorded inter-views. Except for interviews in seclusion rooms or on the ward, we tape record all the psychotherapy hours. We have walls lined with stored tape recordings. We randomly took from each of the tape recordings little four-minute bits and re-recorded them onto small separate, coded reels. We instituted some little researches to determine whether we should use four minutes, ten minutes, or two minutes. Four minutes was most reliable and valid (Hart, 1960). Despite the long psychotherapy case and the full hour's psychotherapy tape, listening to a four-minute excerpt gives a surprisingly definite impression of what sort of relationship the two people have. Of course, we use very many such excerpts.

To define the therapist and patient behavior which we measure on these tapes, we first began with simple general descriptions. For example, we had *one general* description of how a therapist is genuine. He does not use false fronts, does not present only a professional image, a mere exercise of his doc-toral role. Instead, he is the person he really is, responding as a human being to the patient. Then, below such a description we had numbers: 1, 2, 3, 4, 5, 6, 7. Number 1 was "very little," number 7 was "very much." That was our rating scale. We asked raters to rate this one general concept. That is how we began.

We keep our raters separate so that they do not talk to each other. We code all these bits of tape recording so that their only identifying aspect is a code cipher such as "segment #3245J." The rater does not know if this is an early bit or a late bit, or if this is thought to be a success case or not. If these raters, rating separately, give approximately the same ratings (applying a good deal of higher mathematics to estimate the extent to which they are rating the same way), then we know we are measuring something. If they disagree too much, then we know we are failing to measure anything.

Raters did not show sufficient agreement until we moved from this very vague rating scale, to a much more exact specification of exactly what tape-recorded observations were to be given exactly what number on the scale. Here are some examples of our *many specific* definitions of various scale points: Stage 2: The therapist sounds very uninvolved as though nothing that happens here could possibly affect him. Stage 3: There is artificiality and stiffness in the therapist's behavior, indicating that he is having trouble with the patient. Stage 4: He sounds quite personal, but this is a style that always remains the same throughout; a stereotyped repetitious professional style controls his response. Stage 7: In responding to the patient there are spontaneous expressions of the therapist's. Of course he responds to the patient's meanings, but what he says is a direct expressive outcome of his own experiencing of these meanings. Stage 8: In addition to saying whatever seems necessary according to his method of therapy, he also intends to, and does, express some of his own inner processes, steps, and feelings at the moment. And finally Stage 9: There are times when he "rolls out" with some very potent feelings of personal involvement or closeness or care. This series of examples gives some of the rating scale definitions of what we expect the raters to observe on these tape recordings.

Our research has brought science about half-way toward really defining observations well enough so that rating scales become scientific instruments rather than subjective impressions of the listener, as they were before. We have not yet reached the point where these observations are so clearly defined that if you listen to a tape recording, you can simply say "I heard that behavior" or "I didn't hear it." We may very well reach that point of precision in another decade. If we do, we will then have scientifically defined observation. Even now, the scale definitions — not subjective impressions, are being measured. We know that because the scales can be used reliably by undergraduates who know nothing of psychotherapy, clinical language, or concepts. Such raters now show more agreement in their ratings than do sophisticated clinicians (who usually project their own subjective views and attitudes into what they hear). This indicates that we are succeeding in precisely describing observable events so that they can be picked out on these tape recordings. On the other hand, we are succeeding only to the extent of reliabilities of .6 to .8 — not yet precise enough.

The prediction was that the more the therapist behaves with realness, understanding, and liking, the more the patient will get better — as I originally called it. By this we meant that on our before-and-after tests the patient would show improvement. Outcome tests, on the whole, do indicate whether the patient has gotten better or not. However, the various tests do not always agree with each other. An individual may improve on one test and not on another. Furthermore, even such tests correlate somewhat better with each other than with the judgment of the therapist, the patient, and the hospital staff. These tend to be different. A somewhat different group of patients improved according to the judgment of the ward staff than those who improved on the tests, or those of whom the therapists call improved. But, there is considerable overlap, fortunately. Hence, we are able to define fairly clearly which group of patients are successful and which are not.

Clinical Learning

It is already certain that the patients did a great deal to us. I might say that our own improvement has been remarkable. It is well known that schizophrenic patients have a way of changing their therapists. They give their therapists powerful experiences, producing growth in them. I think also that if the patients fail to change us, if we hold up our professional images to such an extent that we do not let them change us, then I doubt very much if we are giving them the kind of relationship in which they can get better. Thus, for example, genuineness has changed for us from the mere absence of a false front, to a very active, self-expressive mode of making an interaction (Gendlin, 1961b; 1962b, c; 1963, 1964a).

It used to be common that if the client was silent and had nothing to say, the client-centered therapist also sat in a receptive, respectful silence, and waited for the inner process of the client to produce something. I still advocate silence when it is the kind where a person (who has been talking) goes deeply into himself. I still feel strongly that psychotherapy needs periods of silence. These permit concretely felt depth. But, with schizophrenic people we met a different kind of silence, one in which a patient is simply cut off, in which little is happening, clearly an impasse. Here the patient does not know what to do, and I do not know what to do. In that kind of silence I have now learned always to do something. I may talk about the feelings I have. I may talk about being puzzled or wishing I heard something from the patient. I may express a very personal sense of what I wish were happening, what I wishfully imagine he might be doing; I may wonder aloud whether he might be thinking about this or that; I might tell him that I know it is hard to talk about some things. Perhaps that is some of what he is feeling.

I do not say many different things at one moment. I stand or sit for a few silent minutes. I have many feelings. I express one feeling that seems all right to express. A few silent minutes later, I may again say something of what is going on in me. I find that when I am not getting anywhere with a patient, quite a lot is going on in me (1964a). I can be very frustrated, I can be very concerned to do something with him, and I can feel very badly that I do not know what to do. I can be very curious, personally interested. I can get quite angry because so much of my own welcoming for this patient is wasted. He is not getting any of it. He has so sense of my waiting for him. All of this makes a very rich "stew" from which I can always take something that feels quite real to me and might give him a sense of what kind of a situation this is. I am perfectly willing, at first, for the patient not to know how to take that, what to do with it, not to be able to respond overtly. I know that when I express myself in this fashion, it constitutes a relationship we *both* have, even if he remains silent. If my expressions are quite personal, that kind of interaction is going on for both of us, even though he can say nothing. I have the power all by myself to make the kind of relationship I want to happen. I used to wait for it somehow or other to happen, but now I find that nobody can really stop me from making it happen.

We have quite a number of tape recordings in which a very, very moving interaction is going on, but you never hear the patient speak. Instead of T (therapist) C (client) — T C T C T C T C — the typed transcription is T — T — T — T. The entire tape is silences and therapist speaking. One can see how these patients have changed our basic notion of genuineness. The principle is the same as it was: the therapist is the real person he is, rather than a professional front or a professional model. The principle is the same, but we behave quite differently, in an active, positive, self-manifesting interaction-making.

A similar development occurred with "empathic understanding." This used to mean, and still means, responding to what is going on in the client. But we used to limit ourselves to what the client said or conveyed, what we *knew* to be going on. Now we find we can respond to "what goes on in the client" even if he does not say anything. Of course, we may not know what it is we are responding to, but that does not mean we cannot respond! "You look like you feel very sad. I wonder, are you feeling sad? You haven't said anything, so of course I don't know." Or, I can say "I know you are having a rough time" (because I do know that). That is not saying much, but yet it is responding to, referring to, what happens in him. I can always *refer to* his concrete feelings, although crudely, roundly, vaguely, stupidly, sentimentally, imaginatively, foolishly, roughly, inconsiderately, wrongly, but I can point at whatever *is* going on in him. It may be altogether different than I guess or very vague to him, but I refer to (*that* in him,) whatever he *does* feel, and I show in what spirit I view such feelings.

I have described this situation with the most difficult example, when the patient says nothing, shows no expressive behavior, not even with his face or body. But even when people are speaking quite articulately, we want to respond not to the words we hear and know, but to the felt experiencing, the felt referent, the mass of inner momentary felt meaning, which we do not fully know. This felt experiencing is not what people say but rather what they *talk from.* And only as they work with this experiencing, and as its felt meanings evolve, does change happen in any psychotherapy (1961a, 1962b, 1964b). We can respond to, and follow not only the logic of what is said or the external situations people talk about. Even when people make perfect realistic and logical sense, it is still vital to respond to their felt meanings rather than only to abstract conceptual meanings. For this reason, psychotherapy is not really so different when the patient gives us no concepts. We know less, but we can still respond to the concretely felt events going on in him.

With schizophrenics, the therapist must often not only initiate the interaction, but also keep on making it happen all the time. It does not just develop and continue of its own momentum. When it gets started, that does not mean it will be there next time. At least it may not be at all visible next time. Over and over again the therapist must *make* a moment of interaction. If he does not, nothing happens.

The Nature of Schizophrenia

What is the nature of that "illness"? First of all, "schizophrenia" is (and in our research we took it as) the catch-all category in hospitals, a label attached to anyone who is not clearly manic-depressive, alcoholic, epileptic, or something else one can define. This means it includes about half the hospital's population, and consists of just anyone. Some of these people are no different from anyone else, except that things recently happened to them which made life impossible and pushed them out of the world, so to speak. If someone can help them back into the world, they are not fundamentally different from other people.

Another group in that mixed population were perhaps pushed out of the world very early, never quite fully got into the human interpersonal world. These people may be much more difficult to help. However, I use the same words about them. I think schizophrenics suffer from being disconnected from the world. Being in a hospital, particularly a state hospital, is a late, visible, physical dramatization of their being disconnected from the world. And this is the disease we try to treat in the hospital! At first, these people were abandoned and isolated as persons and often lived in situations which seemed externally all right. Other persons could have existed interpersonally in such a situation, but this person could not. His inward isolation explains why finally he could not last (Shlien, 1961). Being isolated in a hospital in physical space is at least the second sense in which he has been abandoned. First he was abandoned many many times in interpersonal space.

The point I want to make is that human beings are not machines who have loose-wires in them or burnt-out tubes. There is not in us the kind of broken machinery that an ideal surgeon can reach and fix, or readjust, or take out the thing that is wrong, or reconnect something inside this machine. We are interactive, experiential organisms (Gendlin, 1964b; Gendlin, 1965; Bowen, 1960; Sullivan, 1953; Jackson, 1960). *When I* respond to what goes on in a person, *then* something goes on *in him*. Of course, something goes on in him also before I respond. He is in pain, anxious or dulled, he has lost his sense of himself, he does not have any feelings, everything is flat. When I respond (or let us say, when I succeed in responding, because I often try and fail for weeks and months) then something more is suddenly going on, he does feel something, there is a surprising sense of self and he feels "Gee, maybe I'm not lost." He does not say that. On the contrary, only then does he first say he feels lost. That is when he first says "There is no place for me in the world." A person can *feel* and express anything only as he *is in an ongoing process*. Without *any* place or world he feels nothing, only weird and selfless. With me there is enough of a place and world so that he feels interactively ongoing. Then he feels lost. It is not the inside that is sick. The "illness" is not internal pieces we have to eradicate. The "illness" is not "in" the human being as if he were a separated, boxed, packaged machine. We live as interactive processes.

How we live toward the world and others, how we sense ourselves in situations and referred to by others, that is us. If there is nothing there to refer to me personally, and if I have not somehow learned in other relationships to respond to myself personally, or cannot now do so, then I am not there, and everything gets very flat, very strange, and very weird. If you have ever spent five or six days by yourself without talking to anyone else, then you know something of the quality of feeling it is. But many people can live well toward nature, or with their own responses to themselves. Others find only stoppage and weirdness when intolerable events and feelings have been ground into dullness and inner isolation has long been permanent.

What kind of an illness is that? We talk of *"resolving the symptoms* and not reaching *the basic illness."* This would be the case when there are no more hallucinations but the person is still miserable, cut off, alone. It is then said that "the basic personality trouble" has not changed. Thus, "schizophrenia" is not really the "crazy" symptoms as such. Then again, other people talk of just the opposite: "I know many schizophrenics who are out there in the streets, who are working, and they are all right, but they still have the same crazy experiences," says one well-known therapist. Here the personality difficulty seems ameliorated, but *that* is not what schizophrenia is, either. Despite solutions in personality difficulty, these people still have "schizophrenic" experiences. It is the symptom-mode which is "crazy." But, we say that the symptoms also are not quite what schizophrenia is. These symptoms can go on or off within minutes. When we cure the symptom we are not content. The overt psychotic manifestations do not really define schizophrenia.

A third factor is indicated in the evidence that schizophrenia is really a relationship (Bowen, 1960; Jackson, 1960). It is a sick way of being married, or a sick family, it is an untenable way of being with another person. One is "isolated" from the world by reacting always within a given single intolerable relationship. Within this relationship one's experiential feeling processes can not be interactively ongoing — yet one is stuck within that relationship and not in the world (Gendlin, 1964b). Not the bad relationship as such, but the stoppage of experiential process in it, is the "illness."

The policy of many hospitals (in Wisconsin, for example) is to send patients back to the same relatives that signed the patient in. This policy sends him back exactly to the relationship in which he can be no more than his sickness. We are tending in two directions with that problem. One is to treat the whole family, which gives some recognition to this interactive nature of the illness. The other direction is to try and make a new life possible for the patient (protected workshops, halfway houses, new lodgings, and work). But, the possibility of a new life for the patient should be held out to him right at the beginning, when he is sitting there silent, has no hope, and nothing to say. I can say to him "I think I can help you get out of the hospital and, if you want to, you can live in the city instead of going home. I suppose you don't believe that you could get out of here, but I do. First you work upstairs, and then we will help you find a job outside, and then I'll help you find another job and a room in town, if you want one. I'll stick with you and get you out of here. I know you don't think that's possible now." If that is held out to patients when it still makes little sense, then the fundamental cut-offness can yield to a beginning interaction process into the world. We must *begin* by overcoming the break that has happened between the patient and the world, his sense that he is not in the world and can't be. Inside himself he is not feelingly alive to think about this, or feel and express himself about it, hence we must begin by restoring the possibility for such feelings and thoughts.

My conception of the illness: *It is not so much what is there, as what is not here.* The interactive experiential process is lacking, stuck, deadened in old hurt stoppages, and in disconnection from the world. It cannot be ongoing, except in and toward someone and in the world. If a toaster is unplugged, would you take it apart to find out what is wrong inside of it?

The concrete reality of humans is the experiential process, and this is no purely internal thing, but a feeling-toward others in situations. If it is not ongoing, then it cannot be made ongoing, except as we respond empathically to make interaction happen, as well as reconnect the person at least to a promised and imagined outside situation in which he might be able to live. And only if he can later actually try such situations long before he is objectively well enough to do so, can he usually become well enough to do so. Later, we really must help him with job and room, be available for calls at night and meetings in odd places. It was through what some released patients taught me in this respect that I came to promise such things to other patients at the start.

Of course, we do not yet really understand what schizophrenia is. We cannot claim to know. In addition to symptoms, personality difficulty, and experiential interactive stoppage, there may be physiologic conditions both etiologic and accumulated results of long isolation. If pharmologic help is found, it may greatly speed the recovery. But, someone must respond. Only in being responded to does the patient then seem to *have* ongoing feelings and therefore, the ability to "be aware" of them. It seems likely that the absence of this experiential interaction process is schizophrenia.

Postscript

The above talk was given in the Spring of 1963. Since then, some preliminary findings have been reported (Matarazzo, 1965; Stoler, 1963). The project has been completed, and the findings are in print (Rogers, 1967). Here is a brief summary of the findings:

The only test measure which showed statistically significant differences between the therapy group as a whole and the control group was the TAT.

The therapy group appeared significantly more improved than the controls on Barrington's TAT analysis (rated "blindly," that is, coded, so that the TAT analyst could not know early from late or success from failure cases).

Both therapy and control groups as a whole showed some degree of improvement. However, if psychotherapy is effective, the group, all of whom received it, should have shown clearly greater changes on most measures.

But, to which patients in the therapy group was effective therapy given? In past researches one had no way of knowing who of the "therapy group" received "psychotherapy" as the researcher would have defined it, and who did not. In the present research we defined "psychotherapy" in terms of both patient and therapist behavior during the interviews. The group, all of whom did receive this psychotherapy, should do clearly better than the controls (even granting that some of them might also have received it).

In the present research it was our main aim to define actual in-therapy behavior. The hundreds of randomly selected, coded segments were analyzed along three variables of therapist behavior (empathy, genuineness, and positive regard) as defined by Rogers (1957), and as operationally defined on our rating scales in terms of specific aspects of therapist behaviors. On the patient side, with developments from Rogers' *Process Scale* (1959, 1969), we measured the patient's level of "experiencing" (Gendlin and Tomlinson, 1967).

Those *patients* who showed the highest level of experiential engagement in the process of therapy also (with statistical significance) showed the greater improvement on most of our diagnostic tests, and on the MMPI, than either the low process group or the controls.

Similarly, those patients whose *therapists* were high on empathy and genuineness showed significantly greater improvement both on diagnostic measures and MMPI changes, than either controls or patients whose therapists were low on empathy and genuineness.

Finally, the patients who showed high levels of the process of therapy were also significantly those whose therapists showed the highest levels of empathy and congruence (as already implied above, since both variables correlate significantly with the positive outcome changes).

These findings raise the question: To what extent is belonging to the high group due to therapist characteristics, and to what extent might it be due to patient characteristics? In one part of our project (Gendlin, 1961b) therapists regularly visited one ward so that many patients could see the same therapist, and each therapist could see many of the patients. As a result, we could later measure the extent to which (in that part of the project) the differences between therapists affected the process level of the same patient, as well as the extent to which different patients receive different therapeutic levels from a given therapist. Both effects were found (van der Veen, 1965a, b), but the effect of the therapist is stronger.

The above findings concern the *level* (throughout therapy) at which the patient engages in an experiential therapy process. Originally, we had predicted that successful patients would *increase* this level over the course of therapy. Since then we have found, both with schizophrenic and with more usual neurotic clients (Gendlin, et al., 1962; Tomlinson and Hart, 1962) that there is only a slight increase during therapy. If the level of engagement in experiential process is sufficient, the individual succeeds in therapy even without a great rise in this level later in therapy.

The Experiencing Scale enables us to measure the extent to which effective psychotherapy is actually ongoing in a given tape-recorded psychotherapy interview (that is, whether that sort of patient behavior is *now* ongoing which is associated with *later* successful outcome changes).

There may be considerable implications, both for research design and for practical clinical policies (Gendlin, 1967) in the fact that, on both patient and therapist behavior variables, we can measure whether or not effective psychotherapy is now taking place, without having to wait some years for outcome measures to tell us so.

Considering these many findings, one should not miss the fact that the degree of success, and the length of time involved (six months to three years) in our work with these patients was broadly speaking not much better or swifter than has been reported by others. Only approximately half of our patient group were really greatly improved. On the other hand, that was the group in which both therapists and patients showed *measurably* higher levels of that sort of interview behavior we defined as psychotherapy.

REFERENCES

BOWEN, M. Family participation in schizophrenia. In R. D. Jackson (Ed.), *Schizophrenia.* New York: Basic Books, 1960.

GENDLIN, E. T. Experiencing: A variable in the process of psychotherapeutic change. *American Journal of Psychotherapy,* 15, 233, 1961a.

GENDLIN, E. T. Initiating psychotherapy with "unmotivated" patients. *Psychiatric Quarterly,* 1961b, 34, 1.

GENDLIN, E. T. Client-centered developments and work with schizophrenics. *Journal of Counseling Psychology,* 1962a, 9, 205.

GENDLIN, E. T. *Experiencing and the creation of meaning.* New York: The Free Press, 1962b.

GENDLIN, E. T. Need for a new type of concept. *Review of Existential Psychology and Psychiatry,* 1962c, 2, 37.

GENDLIN, E. T. Subverbal communication and therapist expressivity. *Journal of Existential Psychiatry,* 1963, 4, 105.

GENDLIN, E. T. Schizophrenia: Problems and methods of psychotherapy. *Review of Existential Psychology and Psychiatry,* 1964a, 4, 168.

GENDLIN, E. T. A theory of personality change. In P. Worchel and D. Byrne (Eds.), *Personality change.* New York: John Wiley, 1964b. (See Chapter 7.)

GENDLIN, E. T. Expressive meanings. In J. Edie (Ed.), *Invitation to phenomenology*. Chicago, Illinois: Quadrangle Books, 1965.

GENDLIN, E. T. The social significance of the research. In C. Rogers (Ed.), *The therapeutic relationship and its impact: A study of psychotherapy with schizophrenics*. Madison, Wisconsin: University of Wisconsin Press, 1967.

GENDLIN, E. T., KLEIN, M., and TOMLINSON, T. M. Process scale movement in neurotic cases. Mimeographed research report, Wisconsin Psychiatric Institute, University of Wisconsin, 1962.

GENDLIN, E. T. and TOMLINSON, T. M. The process conception and its measurement. In C. Rogers (Ed.), *The therapeutic relationship and its impact: A study of psychotherapy with schizophrenics*. Madison, Wisconsin: University of Wisconsin Press, 1967.

HART, J. T. Some inter-rater and intra-rater reliability properties of the process scale. Unpublished M.A. thesis, University of Wisconsin, 1960.

JACKSON, D. D. *The etiology of schizophrenia*. New York: Basic Books, 1960.

MATARAZZO, J. D. Psychotherapeutic processes. In *Annual Review of Psychology*, Vol. 16. Palo Alto, California: Annual Reviews, 1965. P. 181.

ROGERS, C. R. The necessary and sufficient conditions of therapeutic personality change. *Journal of Consulting Psychology*, 1957, 21, 95.

ROGERS, C. R. A tentative scale of the measurement of process in psychotherapy. In E. A. Rubenstein and M. B. Parloff (Eds.), *Research in psychotherapy*. Washington, D. C.: American Psychological Association, 1959.

ROGERS, C. R. Significant trends in the client-centered orientation. In D. Brower and L. E. Abt (Eds.), *Progress in clinical psychology*, Vol. IV. New York: Grune & Stratton, 1960.

ROGERS, C. R. (Ed.). *The therapeutic relationship and its impact: A study of psychotherapy with schizophrenics*. Madison, Wisconsin: University of Wisconsin Press, 1967.

SHLIEN, J. M. A client-centered approach to schizophrenia: First approximation. In A. Burton (Ed.), *Psychotherapy of the psychoses*. New York: Basic Books, 1961.

STOLER, N. Client likability: A variable in the study of psychotherapy. *Journal of Consulting Psychology*, 1963, 27, 175.

SULLIVAN, H. S. *The interpersonal theory of psychiatry*. New York: W. W. Norton, 1953.

TOMLINSON, T. M. and HART, J. T. A validation of the process scale. *Journal of Consulting Psychology*, 1962, 26, 74. (See Chapter 10.)

TRUAX, C. B. Effective ingredients in psychotherapy. *Journal of Counseling Psychology*, 1963, 10, 256.

VAN DER VEEN, F. The effects of the therapist and the patient on each other's therapeutic behavior early in therapy. *Journal of Consulting Psychology*, 1965a, 29, 19.

VAN DER VEEN, F. Therapists' judgments, interview behavior and case outcome. *Psychotherapy: Theory, Research and Practice*, 1965b, 2, 158.

16

The Process of the Basic

Encounter Group*

CARL R. ROGERS

I would like to share with you some of my thinking and puzzlement regarding a potent new cultural development — the intensive group experience.[1] It
has, in my judgment, significant implications for our society. It has come very
suddenly over our cultural horizon, since in anything like its present form it is
less than two decades old.

I should like briefly to describe the many different forms and different labels
under which the intensive group experience has become a part of our modern
life. It has involved different kinds of individuals, and it has spawned various
theories to account for its effects.

As to labels, the intensive group experience has at times been called the
T-group or *lab group,* "T" standing for training laboratory in group dynamics.
It has been termed *sensivity training* in human relationships. The experience
has sometimes been called a *basic encounter group* or a *workshop* — a workshop in human relationships, in leadership, in counseling, in education, in
research, in psychotherapy. In dealing with one particular type of person —
the drug addict — it has been called a *synanon.*

* From Challenges of Humanistic Psychology by James F. T. Bugental. Copyright ©
1967, McGraw-Hill, Inc. Used by permission of McGraw-Hill Book Company.

[1] In the preparation of this paper I am deeply indebted to two people, experienced in work
with groups, for their help: Jacques Hochmann, M.D., psychiatrist of Lyon, France, who
has been working at WBSI on a U.S.P.H.S. International Post-doctoral Fellowship, and
Ann Dreyfus, M.A., my research assistant. I am grateful for their ideas, for their patient
analysis of recorded group sessions, and for the opportunity to interact with two original
and inquiring minds.

The intensive group experience has functioned in various settings. It has operated in industries, in universities, in church groups, and in resort settings which provide a retreat from everyday life. It has functioned in various educational institutions and in penitentiaries.

An astonishing range of individuals have been involved in these intensive group experiences. There have been groups for presidents of large corporations. There have been groups for delinquent and predelinquent adolescents. There have been groups composed of college students and faculty members, of counselors and psychotherapists, of school dropouts, of married couples, of confirmed drug addicts, of criminals serving sentences, of nurses preparing for hospital service, and of educators, principals, and teachers.

The geographical spread attained by this rapidly expanding movement has reached in this country from Bethel, Maine (starting point of the National Training Laboratory movement), to Idyllwild, California. To my personal knowledge, such groups also exist in France, England, Holland, Japan, and Australia.

In their outward pattern these group experiences also show a great deal of diversity. There are T-groups and workshops which have extended over three to four weeks, meeting six to eight hours each day. There are some that have lasted only 2½ days, crowding twenty or more hours of group sessions into this time. A recent innovation is the "marathon" weekend, which begins on Friday afternoon and ends on Sunday evening, with only a few hours out for sleep and snacks.

As to the conceptual underpinnings of this whole movement, one may almost select the theoretical flavor he prefers. Lewinian and client-centered theories have been most prominent, but gestalt therapy and various brands of psychoanalysis have all played contributing parts. The experience within the group may focus on specific training in human relations skills. It may be closely similar to group therapy, with much exploration of past experience and the dynamics of personal development. It may focus on creative expression through painting or expressive movement. It may be focused primarily upon a basic encounter and relationship between individuals.

Simply to describe the diversity which exists in this field raises very properly the question of why these various developments should be considered to belong together. Are there any threads of commonality which pervade all these widely divergent activities? To me it seems that they do belong together and can all be classed as focusing on the intensive group experience. They all have certain similar external characteristics. The group in almost every case is small (from eight to eighteen members), is relatively unstructured, and chooses its own goals and personal directions. The group experience usually, though not always, includes some cognitive input, some content material which is presented to the group. In almost all instances the leader's responsibility is primarily the facilitation of the expression of both feelings and thoughts on the part of the group members. Both in the leader and in the group members there is some focus on the process and the dynamics of the immediate personal interaction. These are, I think, some of the identifying characteristics which are rather easily recognized.

There are also certain practical hypotheses which tend to be held in common by all these groups. My own summary of these would be as follows: In an intensive group, with much freedom and little structure, the individual will gradually feel safe enough to drop some of his defenses and façades; he will relate more directly on a feeling basis (come into a basic encounter) with other members of the group; he will come to understand himself and his relationship to others more accurately; he will change in his personal attitudes and behavior; and he will subsequently relate more effectively to others in his everyday life situation. There are other hypotheses related more to the group than to the individual. One is that in this situation of minimal structure, the group will move from confusions, fractionation, and discontinuity to a climate of greater trust and coherence. These are some of the characteristics and hypotheses which, in my judgment, bind together this enormous cluster of activities which I wish to talk about as constituting the intensive group experience.

As for myself, I have been gradually moving into this field for the last twenty years. In experimenting with what I call *student-centered teaching,* involving the free expression of personal feelings, I came to recognize not only the cognitive learnings but also some of the personal changes which occurred. In brief intensive training courses for counselors for the Veterans Administration in 1946, during the postwar period, I and my staff focused more directly on providing an intensive group experience because of its impact in producing significant learning. In 1950, I served as leader of an intensive, full-time, one-week workshop, a postdoctoral training seminar in psychotherapy for the American Psychological Association. The impact of those six days was so great that for more than a dozen years afterwards, I kept hearing from members of the group about the meaning it had had for them. Since that time I have been involved in more than forty ventures of what I would like to term — using the label most congenial to me — *basic encounter groups.* Most of these have involved for many of the members experiences of great intensity and considerable personal change. With two individuals, however, in these many groups, the experience contributed, I believe, to a psychotic break. A few other individuals have found the experience more unhelpful than helpful. So I have come to have a profound respect for the constructive potency of such group experiences and also a real concern over the fact that sometimes and in some ways this experience may do damage to individuals.

The Group Process

It is a matter of great interest to me to try to understand what appear to be common elements in the group process as I have come dimly to sense these. I am using this opportunity to think about this problem, not because I feel I have any final theory to give, but because I would like to formulate, as clearly as I am able, the elements which I can perceive at the present time. In doing so I am drawing upon my own experience, upon the experiences of others with whom I have worked, upon the written material in this field, upon the written reactions of many individuals who have participated in such groups, and to some extent upon the recordings of such group sessions, which we are only beginning to tap and analyze. I am sure that (though I have tried to draw on the experience of others) any formulation I make at the present time is unduly influenced by my own experience in groups and thus is lacking in the generality I wish it might have.

As I consider the terribly complex interactions which arise during twenty, forty, sixty, or more hours of intensive sessions, I believe that I see some threads which weave in and out of the pattern. Some of these trends or tendencies are likely to appear early and some later in the group sessions, but there is no clear-cut sequence in which one ends and another begins. The interaction is best thought of, I believe, as a varied tapestry, differing from group to group, yet with certain kinds of trends evident in most of these intensive encounters and with certain patterns tending to precede and others to follow. Here are some of the process patterns which I see developing, briefly described in simple terms, illustrated from tape recordings and personal reports, and presented in roughly sequential order. I am not aiming at a high-level theory of group process but rather at a naturalistic observation out of which, I hope, true theory can be built.[2]

Milling Around. As the leader or facilitator makes clear at the outset that this is a group with unusual freedom, that it is not one for which he will take directional responsibility, there tends to develop a period of initial confusion, awkward silence, polite surface interaction, "cocktail-party talk," frustration, and great lack of continuity. The individuals come face-to-face with the fact that "there is no structure here except what we provide. We do not know our purposes; we do not even know one another, and we are committed to remain together over a considerable period of time." In this situation, confusion and frustration are natural. Particularly striking to the observer is the lack of continuity between personal expressions. Individual A will present some proposal or concern, clearly looking for a response from the group. Individ-

---

[2] Jack and Lorraine Gibb have long been working on an analysis of trust development as the essential theory of group process. Others who have contributed significantly to the theory of group process are Chris Argyris, Kenneth Benne, Warren Bennis, Dorwin Cartwright, Matthew Miles, and Robert Blake. Samples of the thinking of all these and others may be found in three recent books: Bradford, Gibb, and Benne (1964); Bennis, Benne, and Chin (1961); and Bennis, Schein, Berlew, and Steele (1964). Thus, there are many promising leads for theory construction involving a considerable degree of abstraction. This chapter has a more elementary aim — a naturalistic descriptive account of the process. [See Chapter 17 of *The challenges of humanistic psychology* (J. F. T. Bugental, ed.). In that discussion, Jack and Lorraine Gibb present a synopsis of their theory to which Rogers refers above. The chapters by Haigh (22), Thomas (23), and Clark (27) also deal with aspects of the basic encounter group.]

ual B has obviously been waiting for his turn and starts off on some completely different tangent as though he had never heard A. One member makes a simple suggestion such as, "I think we should introduce ourselves," and this may lead to several hours of highly involved discussion in which the underlying issues appear to be, "Who is the leader?" "Who is responsible for us?" "Who is a member of the group?" "What is the purpose of the group?"

Resistance to Personal Expression or Exploration. During the milling period, some individuals are likely to reveal some rather personal attitudes. This tends to foster a very ambivalent reaction among other members of the group. One member, writing of his experience, says:

> There is a self which I present to the world and another one which I know more intimately. With others I try to appear able, knowing, unruffled, problem-free. To substantiate this image I will act in a way which at the time or later seems false or artificial or "not the real me." Or I will keep to myself thoughts which if expressed would reveal an imperfect me.
>
> My inner self, by contrast with the image I present to the world, is characterized by many doubts. The worth I attach to this inner self is subject to much fluctuation and is very dependent on how others are reacting to me. At times this private self can feel worthless.

It is the public self which members tend to reveal to one another, and only gradually, fearfully, and ambivalently do they take steps to reveal something of their inner world.

Early in one intensive workshop, the members were asked to write anonymously a statement of some feeling or feelings which they had which they were not willing to tell in the group. One man wrote:

> I don't relate easily to people. I have an almost impenetrable façade Nothing gets in to hurt me, but nothing gets out. I have repressed so many emotions that I am close to emotional sterility. This situation doesn't make me happy, but I don't know what to do about it.

This individual is clearly living inside a private dungeon, but he does not even dare, except in this disguised fashion, to send out a call for help.

In a recent workshop when one man started to express the concern he felt about an impasse he was experiencing with his wife, another member stopped him, saying essentially:

> Are you sure you want to go on with this, or are you being seduced by the group into going further than you want to go? How do you know the group can be trusted? How will you feel about it when you go home and tell your wife what you have revealed, or when you decide to keep it from her? It just isn't safe to go further.

It seemed quite clear that in his warning, this second member was also expressing his own fear of revealing *himself* and *his* lack of trust in the group.

Description of Past Feelings. In spite of ambivalence about the trustworthiness of the group and the risk of exposing oneself, expression of feelings does begin to assume a larger proportion of the discussion. The executive tells how frustrated he feels by certain situations in his industry, or the housewife relates problems she has experienced with her children. A tape-recorded exchange involving a Roman Catholic nun occurs early in a one-week workshop, when the discussion has turned to a rather intellectualized consideration of anger:

Bill: What happens when you get mad, Sister, or don't you?
Sister: Yes, I do — yes I do. And I find when I get mad, I, I almost get, well, the kind of person that antagonizes me is the person who seems so unfeeling toward people — now I take our dean as a person in point because she is a very aggressive woman and has certain ideas about what the various rules in a college should be; and this woman can just send me into high "G"; in an angry mood. *I mean this.* But then I find, I. . . .
Facil.:[3] But what, what do you do?
Sister: I find that when I'm in a situation like this, that I strike out in a very sharp, uh, *tone,* or else I just refuse to respond — "All right, this happens to be her way" — I don't think I've ever gone into a tantrum.
Joe: You just withdraw — no use to fight it.
Facil.: You say you use a sharp tone. To *her,* or to other people you're dealing with?
Sister: Oh, no. To *her.*

This is a typical example of a *description* of feelings which are obviously current in her in a sense but which she is placing in the past and which she describes as being outside the group in time and place. It is an example of feelings existing "there and then."

Expression of Negative Feelings. Curiously enough, the first expression of genuinely significant "here-and-now" feeling is apt to come out in negative attitudes toward other group members or toward the group leader. In one group in which members introduced themselves at some length, one woman refused, saying that she preferred to be known for what she was in the group and not in terms of her status outside. Very shortly after this, one of the men in the group attacked her vigorously and angrily for this stand, accusing her of failing to cooperate, of keeping herself aloof from the group, and so forth. It was the first *personal current feeling* which had been brought into the open in the group.

Frequently the leader is attacked for his failure to give proper guidance to the group. One vivid example of this comes from a recorded account of an early session with a group of delinquents, where one member shouts at the leader (Gordon, 1955, p. 214):

[3] The term "facilitator" will be used throughout this paper, although sometimes he is referred to as "leader" or "trainer."

You will be licked if you don't control us right at the start. You have to keep order here because you are older than us. That's what a teacher is supposed to do. If he doesn't do it we will cause a lot of trouble and won't get anything done. [Then, referring to two boys in the group who were scuffling, he continues.] Throw 'em out, throw 'em out! You've just *got* to make us behave!

An adult expresses his disgust at the people who talk too much, but points his irritation at the leader (Gordon, 1955, p. 210):

It is just that I don't understand why someone doesn't shut them up. I would have taken Gerald and shoved him out the window. I'm an authoritarian. I would have told him he was talking too much and he had to leave the room. I think the group discussion ought to be led by a person who simply will not recognize these people after they have interrupted about eight times.

Why are negatively toned expressions the first current feelings to be expressed? Some speculative answers might be the following: This is one of the best ways to test the freedom and trustworthiness of the group. "Is it really a place where I can be and express myself positively and negatively? Is this really a safe place, or will I be punished?" Another quite different reason is that deeply positive feelings are much more difficult and dangerous to express than negative ones. "If I say, 'I love you,' I am vulnerable and open to the most awful rejection. If I say, 'I hate you,' I am at best liable to attack, against which I can defend." Whatever the reasons, such negatively toned feelings tend to be the first here-and-now material to appear.

Expression and Exploration of Personally Meaningful Materials. It may seem puzzling that following such negative experiences as the initial confusion, the resistance to personal expression, the focus on outside events, and the voicing of critical or angry feelings, the event most likely to occur next is for an individual to reveal himself to the group in a significant way. The reason for this no doubt is that the individual member has come to realize that this is in part *his group*. He can help to make of it what he wishes. He has also experienced the fact that negative feelings have been expressed and have usually been accepted or assimilated without any catastrophic results. He realizes there is freedom here, albeit a risky freedom. A climate of trust (Gibb, 1964, Ch. 10) is beginning to develop. So he begins to take the chance and the gamble of letting the group know some deeper facet of himself. One man tells of the trap in which he finds himself, feeling that communication between himself and his wife is hopeless. A priest tells of the anger which he has bottled up because of unreasonable treatment by one of his superiors. What should he have done? What might he do now? A scientist at the head of a large research department finds the courage to speak of his painful isolation, to tell the group that he has never had a single friend in his life. By the time he finishes telling of his situation, he is letting loose some of the tears of sorrow for himself which I am sure he has held in for many years. A psychiatrist tells of the guilt he feels because of the suicide of one of his patients. A woman of forty tells of her absolute inability to free herself from the grip of her controlling mother. A process which one workshop member has called a "journey to the center of self," often a very painful process, has begun.

Such exploration is not always an easy process, nor is the whole group always receptive to such self-revelation. In a group of institutionalized adolescents, all of whom had been in difficulty of one sort or another, one boy revealed an important fact about himself and immediately received both acceptance and sharp nonacceptance from members of the group.

George: This is the thing. I've got too many problems at home — uhm, I think some of you know why I'm here, what I was charged with.
Mary: I don't.
Facil.: Do you want to tell us?
George: Well, uh, it's sort of embarrassing.
Carol: Come on, it won't be so bad.
George: Well, I raped my sister. That's the only problem I have at home, and I've overcome that, I think. *(Rather long pause.)*
Freda: Oooh, that's *weird!*
Mary: People have problems, Freda, I mean ya know. . . .
Freda: Yeah, I know, but *yeOUW*!!!
Facil. *(to Freda)*: You know about these problems, but they still are weird to you.
George: You see what I mean; it's embarrassing to talk about it.
Mary: Yeah, but it's O.K.
George: It *hurts* to talk about it, but I know I've got to so I won't be guilt-ridden for the rest of my life.

Clearly Freda is completely shutting him out psychologically, while Mary in particular is showing a deep acceptance.

The Expression of Immediate Interpersonal Feelings in the Group. Entering into the process sometimes earlier, sometimes later, is the explicit bringing into the open of the feelings experienced in the immediate moment by one member about another. These are sometimes positive and sometimes negative. Examples would be: "I feel threatened by your silence." "You remind me of my mother, with whom I had a tough time." "I took an instant dislike to you the first moment I saw you." "To me you're like a breath of fresh air in the group." "I like your warmth and your smile." "I dislike you more every time you speak up." Each of these attitudes can be, and usually is, explored in the increasing climate of trust.

The Development of a Healing Capacity in the Group. One of the most fascinating aspects of any intensive group experience is the manner in which a number of the group members show a natural and spontaneous capacity for dealing in a helpful, facilitative, and therapeutic fashion with the pain and suffering of others. As one rather extreme example of this, I think of a man in charge of maintenance in a large plant who was one of the low-status members of an industrial executive group. As he informed us, he had not been "contaminated by education." In the initial phases the group tended to look down on him. As members delved more deeply into themselves and began to express their own attitudes more fully, this man came forth as, without doubt, the most sensitive member of the group. He knew intuitively how to be understanding and acceptant. He was alert to things which had not yet been expressed but which were just below the surface. When the rest of us were paying atttention to a member who was speaking, he would frequently spot another individual who was suffering silently and in need of help. He had a deeply perceptive and facilitating attitude. This kind of ability shows up so commonly in groups that it has led me to feel that the ability to be healing or therapeutic is far more common in human life than we might suppose. Often it needs only the permission granted by a freely flowing group experience to become evident.

In a characteristic instance, the leader and several group members were trying to be of help to Joe, who was telling of the almost complete lack of communication between himself and his wife. In varied ways members endeavored to give help. John kept putting before Joe the feelings Joe's wife was almost certainly experiencing. The facilitator kept challenging Joe's façade of "carefulness." Marie tried to help him discover what he was feeling at the moment. Fred showed him the choice he had of alternative behaviors. All this was clearly done in a spirit of caring, as is even more evident in the recording itself. No miracles were achieved, but toward the end Joe did come to the realization that the only thing that might help would be to express his real feelings to his wife.

Self-acceptance and the Beginning of Change. Many people feel that self-acceptance must stand in the way of change. Actually, in these group experiences, as in psychotherapy, it is the *beginning* of change. Some examples of the kind of attitudes expressed would be these: "I *am* a dominating person who likes to control others. I do want to mold these individuals into the proper shape." Another person says, "I really have a hurt and overburdened little boy inside of me who feels very sorry for himself. I *am* that little boy, in addition to being a competent and responsible manager."

I think of one governmental executive in a group in which I participated, a man with high responsibility and excellent technical training as an engineer. At the first meeting of the group he impressed me, and I think others, as being cold, aloof, somewhat bitter, resentful, and cynical. When he spoke of how he ran his office it appeared that he administered it "by the book," without any warmth or human feeling entering in. In one of the early sessions, when he spoke of his wife, a group member asked him, "Do you love your wife?" He paused for a long time, and the questioner said, "OK, that's answer enough." The executive said, "No. Wait a minute. The reason I didn't respond was that I was wondering if I ever loved anyone. I don't think I *ever* really *loved* any-one." It seemed quite dramatically clear to those of us in the group that he had come to accept himself as an unloving person.

A few days later he listened with great intensity as one member of the group expressed profound personal feelings of isolation, loneliness, and pain, reveal-ing the extent to which he had been living behind a mask, a façade. The next morning the engineer said, "Last night I thought and thought about what Bill told us. I even wept quite a bit by myself. I can't remember how long it has been since I have cried, and I really *felt* something. I think perhaps what I felt was love."

It is not surprising that before the week was over, he had thought through new ways of handling his growing son, on whom he had been placing extremely rigorous demands. He had also begun genuinely to appreciate the love which his wife had extended to him and which he now felt he could in some measure reciprocate.

In another group one man kept a diary of his reactions. Here is his account of an experience in which he came really to accept his almost abject desire for love, a self-acceptance which marked the beginning of a very significant experi-ence of change. He says (Hall, 1965):

> During the break between the third and fourth sessions, I felt very droopy and tired. I had it in mind to take a nap, but instead I was almost compul-sively going around to people starting a conversation. I had a begging kind of a feeling, like a very cowed little puppy hoping that he'll be patted but half afraid he'll be kicked. Finally, back in my room I lay down and began to know that I was sad. Several times I found myself wishing my roommate would come in and talk to me. Or, whenever someone walked by the door, I would come to attention inside, the way a dog pricks up his ears; and I would feel an immediate wish for that person to come in and talk to me. I realized my raw wish to receive kindness.

Another recorded excerpt, from an adolescent group, shows a combination of self-acceptance and self-exploration. Art had been talking about his "shell," and here he is beginning to work with the problem of accepting himself, and also the façade he ordinarily exhibits:

Art: I'm so darn used to living with the shell; it doesn't even bother me. I don't even know the real me. I think I've uh, well, I've pushed the shell more away here. When I'm out of my shell — only twice — once just a few minutes ago — I'm really me, I guess. But then I just sort of pull in the [latch] cord after me when I'm in my shell, and that's almost all the time. And I leave the [false] front standing outside when I'm back in the shell.

Facil.: And nobody's back in there with you?

Art *(crying)*: Nobody else is in there with me, just me. I just pull everything

> into the shell and roll the shell up and shove it in my pocket. I take the
> shell, and the real me, and put it in my pocket where it's safe. I guess
> that's really the way I do it — I go into my shell and turn off the real
> world. And here: that's what I want to do here in this group, ya know,
> come out of my shell and actually throw it away.
> Lois: You're making progress already. At least you can talk about it.
> Facil.: Yeah. The thing that's going to be hardest is to stay out of the shell.
> Art *(still crying)*: Well, yeah, if I can keep talking about it, I can come out
> and stay out, but I'm gonna have to, ya know, protect me. It hurts; it's
> actually hurting to talk about it.

Still another person reporting shortly after his workshop experience said,
"I came away from the workshop feeling much more deeply that 'It is all right
to be me with all my strengths and weaknesses.' My wife has told me that
I appear to be more authentic, more real, more genuine."

This feeling of greater realness and authenticity is a very common experience. It would appear that the individual is learning to accept and to *be* himself, and this is laying the foundation for change. He is closer to his own
feelings, and hence they are no longer so rigidly organized and are more open
to change.

The Cracking of Façades. As the sessions continue, so many things tend to
occur together that it is difficult to know which to describe first. It should
again be stressed that these different threads and stages interweave and overlap. One of these threads is the increasing impatience with defenses. As time
goes on, the group finds it unbearable that any member should live behind a
mask or a front. The polite words, the intellectual understanding of one another
and of relationships, the smooth coin of tact and cover-up — amply satisfactory for interactions outside — are just not good enough. The expression of
self by some members of the group has made it very clear that a deeper and
more basic encounter is *possible,* and the group appears to strive, intuitively
and unconsciously, toward this goal. Gently at times, almost savagely at others,
the group *demands* that the individual be himself, that his current feelings not
be hidden, that he remove the mask of ordinary social intercourse. In one
group there was a highly intelligent and quite academic man who had been
rather perceptive in his understanding of others but who had not revealed
himself at all. The attitude of the group was finally expressed sharply by one
member who he said, "Come out from behind that lectern, Doc. Stop giving
us speeches. Take off your dark glasses. We want to know *you.*"

In Synanon, the fascinating group so successfully involved in making per-
sons out of drug addicts, this ripping away of façades is often very drastic.
An excerpt from one of the "synanons," or group sesessions, makes this clear
(Casriel, 1963, p. 81):

> Joe *(speaking to Gina)*: I wonder when you're going to stop sounding so good
> in synanons. Every synanon that I'm in with you, someone asks you a

question, and you've got a beautiful book written. All made out about what went down and how you were wrong and how you realized you were wrong and all that kind of bullshit. When are you going to stop doing that? How do you feel about Art?

Gina: I have nothing against Art.

Will: You're a nut. Art hasn't got any damn sense. He's been in there, yelling at you and Moe, and you've got everything so cool.

Gina: No, I feel he's very insecure in a lot of ways but that has nothing to do with me. . . .

Joe: You act like you're so goddamn understanding.

Gina: I was *told* to act as if I understand.

Joe: Well, you're in a synanon now. You're not supposed to be acting like you're such a goddamn healthy person. Are you so well?

Gina: No.

Joe: Well why the hell don't you quit acting as if you were.

If I am indicating that the group at times is quite violent in tearing down a façade or a defense, this would be accurate. On the other hand, it can also be sensitive and gentle. The man who was accused of hiding behind a lectern was deeply hurt by this attack, and over the lunch hour looked very troubled, as though he might break into tears at any moment. When the group reconvened, the members sensed this and treated him very gently, enabling him to tell us his own tragic personal story, which accounted for his aloofness and his intellectual and academic approach to life.

The Individual Receives Feedback. In the process of this freely expressive interaction, the individual rapidly acquires a great deal of data as to how he appears to others. The "hail-fellow-well-met" discovers that others resent his exaggerated friendliness. The executive who weighs his words carefully and and speaks with heavy precision may find that others regard him as stuffy. A woman who shows a somewhat excessive desire to be of help to others is told in no uncertain terms that some group members do not want her for a mother. All this can be decidedly upsetting, but as long as these various bits of information are fed back in the context of caring which is developing in the group, they seem highly constructive.

Feedback can at times be very warm and positive, as the following recorded excerpt indicates:

Leo (*very softly and gently*): I've been struck with this ever since she talked about her waking in the night, that she has a very delicate sensitivity. (*Turning to Mary and speaking almost caressingly.*) And somehow I perceive — even looking at you or in your eyes — a very — almost like a gentle touch and from this gentle touch you can tell many — things — you sense in — this manner.

Fred: Leo, when you said that, that she has this kind of delicate sensitivity, I just felt, *Lord yes*! Look at her eyes.

Leo: M-hm.

A much more extended instance of negative and positive feedback, triggering a significant new experience of self-understanding and encounter with the group, is taken from the diary of the young man mentioned before. He had been telling the group that he had no feeling for them, and felt they had no feeling for him (Hall, 1965):

> Then, a girl lost patience with me and said she didn't feel she could give any more. She said I looked like a bottomless well, and she wondered how many times I had to be told that I *was* cared for. By this time I was feeling panicky, and I was saying to myself, "My God, can it be true that I can't be satisfied and that I'm somehow compelled to pester people for attention until I drive them away!"
>
> At this point while I was really worried, a nun in the group spoke up. She said that I had not alienated her with some negative things I had said to her. She said she liked me, and she couldn't understand why I couldn't see that. She said she felt concerned for me and wanted to help me. With that, something began to really dawn on me, and I voiced it somewhat like the following. "You mean you are all sitting there, feeling for me what I say I want you to feel, and that somewhere down inside me I'm stopping it from touching me?" I relaxed appreciably and began really to wonder why I had shut their caring out so much. I couldn't find the answer, and one woman said: "It looks like you are trying to stay continuously as deep in your feelings as you were this afternoon. It would make sense to me for you to draw back and assimilate it. Maybe if you don't push so hard, you can rest awhile and then move back into your feelings more naturally."
>
> Her making the last suggestions really took effect. I saw the sense in it, and almost immediately I settled back very relaxed with something of a feeling of a bright, warm day dawning inside me. In addition to taking the pressure off of myself, however, I was for the first time really warmed by the friendly feelings which I felt they had for me. It is difficult to say why I felt liked only just then, but, as opposed to the earlier sessions, I really *believed* they cared for me. I never have fully understood why I stood their affection off for so long, but at that point I almost abruptly began to trust that they did care. The measure of the effectiveness of this change lies in what I said next. I said, "Well, that really takes care of me. I'm really ready to listen to someone else now." I *meant* that, too.

Confrontation. There are times when the term "feedback" is far too mild to describe the interactions which take place, when it is better said that one individual *confronts* another, directly "leveling" with him. Such confrontations can be positive, but frequently they are decidedly negative, as the following example will make abundantly clear. In one of the last sessions of a group, Alice had made some quite vulgar and contemptuous remarks to John, who was entering religious work. The next morning, Norma, who had been a very quiet person in the group, took the floor:

Norma *(loud sigh)*: Well, I don't have *any* respect for you, Alice. *None!*
(Pause.) There's about a hundred things going through my mind I want
to say to you, and by God I hope I get through 'em all! First of all, if
you wanted us to respect you, then why couldn't you respect *John's* feelings last night? Why have you been on him today? Hmm? Last night
— couldn't you — couldn't you accept — *couldn't you* comprehend in
any way at all that — that *he felt* his unworthiness in the service of
God? Couldn't you accept this, or did you have to dig into it today to
find something *else there*? And his respect for womanhood — he *loves*
women — yes, he does, because he's a real person, but you — you're
not a real woman — to me — and thank God, you're not my mother!!!!!
I want to come over and beat the hell out of you!!!! I want to slap you
across the mouth so hard and — oh, and you're so, you're many years
above me — and I respect age, and I respect people who are older than
me, *but I don't respect you, Alice. At all!* And I was so *hurt* and *confused* because you were making someone else feel *hurt* and *confused.* . . .

It may relieve the reader to know that these two women came to accept each
other, not completely, but much more understandingly, before the end of the
session. But this *was* a confrontation!

The Helping Relationship Outside the Group Sessions. No account of the
group process would, in my experience, be adequate if it did not make mention of the many ways in which group members are of assistance to one
another. Not infrequently, one member of a group will spend hours listening
and talking to another member who is undergoing a painful new perception
of himself. Sometimes it is merely the offering of help which is therapeutic.
I think of one man who was going through a very depressed period after having told us of the many tragedies in his life. He seemed quite clearly, from his
remarks, to be contemplating suicide. I jotted down my room number (we
were staying at a hotel) and told him to put it in his pocket and to call me any-
time of day or night if he felt that it would help. He never called, but six
months after the workshop was over he wrote to me telling me how much that
act had meant to him and that he still had the slip of paper to remind him of it.

Let me give an example of the healing effect of the attitudes of group members both outside and inside the group meetings. This is taken from a letter
written by a workshop member to the group one month after the group sessions. He speaks of the difficulties and depressing circumstances he had
encountered during that month and adds.

I have come to the conclusion that my experiences with you have profoundly affected me. I am truly grateful. This is different than personal
therapy. None of you *had* to care about me. None of you had to seek me
out and let me know of things you thought would help me. None of you
had to let me know I was of help to you. Yet you did, and as a result it has
far more meaning than anything I have so far experienced. When I feel the

need to hold back and not live spontaneously, for whatever reasons, I remember that twelve persons, just like those before me now, said to let go and be congruent, to be myself, and, of all unbelievable things, they even loved me more for it. This has given me the *courage* to come out of myself many times since then. Often it seems my very doing of this helps the others to experience similar freedom.

The Basic Encounter. Running through some of the trends I have just been describing is the fact that individuals come into much closer and more direct contact with one another than is customary in ordinary life. This appears to be one of the most central, intense, and change-producing aspects of such a group experience. To illustrate what I mean, I would like to draw an example from a recent workshop group. A man tells, through his tears, of the very tragic loss of his child, a grief which he is experiencing *fully,* for the first time, not holding back his feelings in any way. Another says to him, also with tears in his eyes, "I've never felt so close to another human being. I've never before felt a real physical hurt in me from the pain of another. I feel *completely* with you." This is a basic encounter.

Such I-Thou relationships (to use Buber's term) occur with some frequency in these group sessions and nearly always bring a moistness to the eyes of the participants.

One member, trying to sort out his experiences immediately after a workshop, speaks of the "commitment to relationship" which often developed on the part of two individuals, not necessarily individuals who had liked each other initially. He goes on to say:

> The incredible fact experienced over and over by members of the group was that when a negative feeling was fully expressed to another, the relationship grew and the negative feeling was replaced by a deep acceptance for the other. . . . Thus real change seemed to occur when feelings were experienced and expressed in the context of the relationship. "I can't *stand* the way you talk!" turned into a real understanding and affection for you the *way* you talk.

This statement seems to capture some of the more complex meanings of the term "basic encounter."

The Expression of Positive Feelings and Closeness. As indicated in the last section, an inevitable part of the group process seems to be that when feelings are expressed and can be accepted in a relationship, a great deal of closeness and positive feelings result. Thus as the sessions proceed, there is an increasing feeling of warmth and group spirit and trust built, not out of positive attitudes only, but out of a realness which includes both positive and negative feeling. One member tried to capture this in writing very shortly after the workshop by saying that if he were trying to sum it up, ". . . it would have to do with what I call confirmation — a kind of confirmation of myself, of the uniqueness and universal qualities of men, a confirmation that when we can be human together something positive can emerge."

A particularly poignant expression of these positive attitudes was shown in the group where Norma confronted Alice with her bitterly angry feelings. Joan, the facilitator, was deeply upset and began to weep. The positive and healing attitudes of the group, for their own *leader,* are in unusual example of the closeness and personal quality of the relationships.

Joan *(crying):* I somehow feel that it's so *damned* easy for me to — to put myself *inside* of another person and I just guess I can feel that — for John and Alice and for you, Norma.

Alice: And it's *you* that's hurt.

Joan: Maybe I am taking some of that hurt. I guess I am. *(crying.)*

Alice: That's a wonderful gift. I wish I had it.

Joan: You have a lot of it.

Peter: In a way you bear the — I guess in a special way, because you're the — facilitator, ah, you've probably borne, ah, an extra heavy burden for all of us — and the burden that you, perhaps, you bear the heaviest is — we ask you — we ask one another; we grope to try to accept one another as we are, and — for each of us in various ways I guess we reach things and we say, *please* accept me. . . .

Some may be very critical of a "leader" so involved and so sensitive that she weeps at the tensions in the group which she has taken into herself. For me, it is simply another evidence that when people are real with each other, they have an astonishing ability to heal a person with a real and understanding love, whether that person is "participant" or "leader."

Behavior Changes in the Group. It would seem from observation that many changes in behavior occur in the group itself. Gestures change. The tone of voice changes, becoming sometimes stronger, sometimes softer, usually more spontaneous, less artificial, more feelingful. Individuals show an astonishing amount of thoughtfulness and helpfulness toward one another.

Our major concern, however, is with the behavior changes which occur following the group experience. It is this which constitutes the most significant question and on which we need much more study and research. One person gives a catalog of the changes which he sees in himself which may seem too "pat" but which is echoed in many other statements:

I am more open, spontaneous. I express myself more freely. I am more sympathetic, empathic, and tolerant. I am more confident. I am more religious in my own way. My relations with my family, friends, and co-workers are more honest, and I express my likes and dislikes and true feelings more openly. I admit ignorance more readily. I am more cheerful. I want to help others more.

Another says:

Since the workshop there has been a new relationship with my parents. It has been trying and hard. However, I have found a greater freedom in talking with them, especially my father. Steps have been made toward being closer to my mother than I have ever been in the last five years.

Another says:

It helped clarify my feelings about my work, gave me more enthusiasm for it, and made me more honest and cheerful with my coworkers and also more open when I was hostile. It made my relationship with my wife more open, deeper. We felt freer to talk about anything, and we felt confident that anything we talked about we could work through.

Sometimes the changes which are described are very subtle. "The primary change is the more positive view of my ability to allow myself to *hear,* and to become involved with someone else's 'silent scream.'"

At the risk of making the outcomes sound too good, I will add one more statement written shortly after a workshop by a mother. She says:

The immediate impact on my children was of interest to both me and my husband. I feel that having been so accepted and loved by a group of strangers was so supportive that when I returned home my love for the people closest to me was much more spontaneous. Also, the practice I had in accepting and loving others during the workshop was evident in my relationships with my close friends.

Disadvantages and Risks

Thus far one might think that every aspect of the group process was positive. As far as the evidence at hand indicates, it appears that it nearly always is a positive process for a majority of the participants. There are, nevertheless, failures which result. Let me try to describe briefly some of the negative aspects of the group process as they sometimes occur.

The most obvious deficiency of the intensive group experience is that frequently the behavior changes, if any, which occur, are not lasting. This is often recognized by the participants. One says, "I wish I had the ability to hold permanently the 'openness' I left the conference with." Another says, "I experienced a lot of acceptance, warmth, and love at the workshop. I find it hard to carry the ability to share this in the same way with people outside the workshop. I find it easier to slip back into my old unemotional role than to do the work necessary to open relationships."

Sometimes group members experience this phenomenon of "relapse" quite philosophically:

The group experience is not a way of life but a reference point. My images of our group, even though I am unsure of some of their meanings, give me a comforting and useful perspective on my normal routine. They are like a mountain which I have climbed and enjoyed and to which I hope occasionally to return.

Some Data on Outcomes. What is the extent of this "slippage"? In the past year, I have administered follow-up questionnaires to 481 individuals who have been in groups I have organized or conducted. The information has been obtained from two to twelve months following the group experience, but the greatest number were followed up after a three- to six-month period.[4] Of these individuals, two (i.e., less than one-half of 1 per cent) felt it had changed their behavior in ways they did not like. Fourteen per cent felt the experience had made no perceptible change in their behavior. Another fourteen per cent felt that it had changed their behavior but that this change had disappeared or left only a small residual positive effect. Fifty-seven per cent felt it had made a continuing positive difference in their behavior, a few feeling that it had made some negative changes along with the positive.

A second potential risk involved in the intensive group experience and one which is often mentioned in public discussion is the risk that the individual may become deeply involved in revealing himself and then be left with problems which are not worked through. There have been a number of reports of people who have felt, following an intensive group experience, that they must go to a therapist to work through the feelings which were opened up in the intensive experience of the workshop and which were left unresolved. It is obvious that, without knowing more about each individual situation, it is difficult to say whether this was a negative outcome or a partially or entirely positive one. There are also very occasional accounts, and I can testify to two in my own experience, where an individual has had a psychotic episode during or immediately following an intensive group experience. On the other side of the picture is the fact that individuals have also lived through what were clearly psychotic episodes, and lived through them very constructively, in the context of a basic encounter group. My own tentative clinical judgment would be that the more positively the group process has been proceeding, the less likely it is that any individual would be psychologically damaged through membership in the group. It is obvious, however, that this is a serious issue and that much more needs to be known.

Some of the tension which exists in workshop members as a result of this potential for damage was very well described by one member when he said, "I feel the workshop had some very precious moments for me when I felt very close indeed to particular persons. It had some frightening moments when its potency was very evident and I realized a particular person might be deeply hurt or greatly helped but I could not predict which."

Out of the 481 participants followed up by questionnaires, two felt that the overall impact of their intensive group experience was "mostly damaging."

[4] The 481 respondents constituted 82 per cent of those to whom the questionnaire had been sent.

Six more said that it had been "more unhelpful than helpful." Twenty-one, or 4 per cent, stated that it had been "mostly frustrating, annoying, or confusing." Three and one-half per cent said that it had been neutral in its impact. Nineteen per cent checked that it had been "more helpful than unhelpful," indicating some degree of ambivalence. But 30 per cent saw it as "constructive in its results," and 45 per cent checked it as a "deeply meaningful, positive experience."[5] Thus for three-fourths of the group, it was *very* helpful. These figures should help to set the problem in perspective. It is obviously a very serious matter if an intensive group experience is psychologically damaging to *anyone*. It seems clear, however, that such damage occurs only rarely, if we are to judge by the reaction of the participants.

Other Hazards of the Group Experience. There is another risk or deficiency in the basic encounter group. Until very recent years it has been unusual for a workshop to include both husband and wife. This can be a real problem if significant change has taken place in one spouse during or as a result of the workshop experience. One individual felt this risk clearly after attending a workshop. He said, "I think there is a great danger to a marriage when one spouse attends a group. It is too hard for the other spouse to compete with the group individually and collectively." One of the frequent aftereffects of the intensive group experience is that it brings out into the open for discussion marital tensions which have been kept under cover.

Another risk which has sometimes been a cause of real concern in mixed intensive workshops is that very positive, warm, and loving feelings can develop between members of the encounter group, as has been evident from some of the preceding examples. Inevitably some of these feelings have a sexual component, and this can be a matter of great concern to the participants and a profound threat to their spouses if these feelings are not worked through satisfactorily in the workshop. Also the close and loving feelings which develop may become a source of threat and marital difficulty when a wife, for example, has not been present, but projects many fears about the loss of her spouse — whether well founded or not — onto the workshop experience.

A man who had been in a mixed group of men and women executives wrote to me a year later and mentioned the strain in his marriage which resulted from his association with Marge, a member of his basic encounter group:

> There was a problem about Marge. There had occurred a very warm feeling on my part for Marge, and great compassion, for I felt she was *very* lonely. I believe the warmth was sincerely reciprocal. At any rate she wrote me a long affectionate letter, which I let my wife read. I was *proud* that

[5] These figures add up to more than 100 per cent since quite a number of the respondents checked more than one answer.

Marge could feel that way about *me*. [Because he had felt very worthless.] But my wife was alarmed, because she read a love affair into the words — at least a *potential* threat. I stopped writing to Marge, because I felt rather clandestine after that.

My wife has since participated in an "encounter group" herself, and she now understands. I have resumed writing to Marge.

Obviously, not all such episodes would have such a harmonious ending.

It is of interest in this connection that there has been increasing experimentation in recent years with "couples workshops" and with workshops for industrial executives and their spouses.

Still another negative potential growing out of these groups have become evident in recent years. Some individuals who have participated in previous encounter groups may exert a stultifying influence on new workshops which they attend. They sometimes exhibit what I think of as the "old pro" phenomenon. They feel they have learned the "rules of the game," and they subtly or openly try to impose these rules on newcomers. Thus, instead of promoting true expressiveness and spontaneity, they endeavor to substitute new rules for old — to make members feel guilty if they are not expressing feelings, are reluctant to voice criticism or hostility, are talking about situations outside the group relationship, or are fearful of revealing themselves. These old pros seem to be attempting to substitute a new tyranny in interpersonal relationships in the place of older, conventional restrictions. To me this is a perversion of the true group process. We need to ask ourselves how this travesty on spontaneity comes about.

Implications

I have tried to describe both the positive and the negative aspects of this burgeoning new cultural development. I would like now to touch on its implications for our society.

In the first place, it is a highly potent experience and hence clearly deserving of scientific study. As a phenomenon it has been both praised and criticized, but few people who have participated would doubt that *something* significant happens in these groups. People do not react in a neutral fashion toward the intensive group experience. They regard it as either strikingly worthwhile or deeply questionable. All would agree, however, that it is *potent*. This fact makes it of particular interest to the behavioral sciences since science is usually advanced by studying potent and dynamic phenomena. This is one of the reasons why I personally am devoting more and more of my time to this whole enterprise. I feel that we can learn much about the ways in which constructive personality change comes about as we study this group process more deeply.

In a different dimension, the intensive group experience appears to be one cultural attempt to meet the isolation of contemporary life. The person who has experienced an I-Thou relationship, who has entered into the basic encounter, is no longer an isolated individual. One workshop member stated this in a deeply expressive way:

> Workshops seem to be at least a partial answer to the loneliness of modern man and his search for new meanings for his life. In short, workshops seem very quickly to allow the individual to become that person he wants to be. The first few steps are taken there, in uncertainty, in fear, and in anxiety. We may or may not continue the journey. It is a gutsy way to live. You trade many, many loose ends for one big knot in the middle of your stomach. It sure as hell isn't easy, but it is a *life* at least — not a hollow imitation of life. It has fear as well as hope, sorrow as well as joy, but I daily offer it to more people in the hope that they will join me. . . . Out from a no-man's land of *fog* into the more violent atmosphere of extremes of thunder, hail, rain, and sunshine. It is worth the trip.

Another implication which is partially expressed in the foregoing statement is that it is an avenue to fulfillment. In a day when more income, a larger car, and a better washing machine seem scarcely to be satisfying the deepest needs of man, individuals are turning to the psychological world, groping for a greater degree of authenticity and fulfillment. One workshop member expressed this extremely vividly:

> [It] has revealed a completely new dimension of life and has opened an infinite number of possibilities for me in my relationship to myself and to everyone dear to me. I feel truly alive and so grateful and joyful and hopeful and healthy and giddy and sparkly. I feel as though my eyes and ears and heart and guts have been opened to see and hear and love and feel more deeply, more widely, more intensely — this glorious, mixed-up, fabulous existence of ours. My whole body and each of its systems seems freer and healthier. I want to feel hot and cold, tired and rested, soft and hard, energetic and lazy. With persons everywhere, but especially my family, I have found a new freedom to explore and communicate. I know the change in me automatically brings a change in them. A whole new exciting relationship has started for me with my husband and with each of my children — a freedom to speak and to hear them speak.

Though one may wish to discount the enthusiasm of this statement, it describes an enrichment of life for which many are seeking.

Rehumanizing Human Relationships. This whole development seems to have special significance in a culture which appears to be bent upon dehumanizing the individual and dehumanizing our human relationships. Here is an important force in the opposite direction, working toward making relationships more meaningful and more personal, in the family, in education, in government, in administrative agencies, in industry.

An intensive group experience has an even more general philosophical implication. It is one expression of the existential point of view which is making itself so pervasively evident in art and literature and modern life. The implicit goal of the group process seems to be to live life fully in the here and now of the relationship. The parallel with an existential point of view is clear cut. I believe this has been amply evident in the illustrative material.

There is one final issue which is raised by this whole phenomenon: What is our view of the optimal person? What is the goal of personality development? Different ages and different cultures have given different answers to this question. It seems evident from our review of the group process that in a climate of freedom, group members move toward becoming more spontaneous, flexible, closely related to their feelings, open to their experience, and closer and more expressively intimate in their interpersonal relationships. If we value this type of person and this type of behavior, then clearly the group process is a valuable process. If, on the other hand, we place a value on the individual who is effective in suppressing his feelings, who operates from a firm set of principles, who does not trust his own reactions and experience but relies on authority, and who remains aloof in his interpersonal relationships, then we would regard the group process, as I have tried to describe it, as a dangerous force. Clearly there is room for a difference of opinion on this value question, and not everyone in our culture would give the same answer.

Conclusion

I have tried to give a naturalistic, observational picture of one of the most significant modern social inventions, the so-called intensive group experience, or basic encounter group. I have tried to indicate some of the common elements of the process which occur in the climate of freedom that is present in such a group. I have pointed out some of the risks and shortcomings of the group experience. I have tried to indicate some of the reasons why it deserves serious consideration, not only from a personal point of view, but also from a scientific and philosophical point of view. I also hope I have made it clear that this is an area in which an enormous amount of deeply perceptive study and research is needed.

REFERENCES

BENNIS, W. G., BENNE, K. D., and CHIN, R. (Eds.). *The planning of change.* New York: Holt, Rinehart and Winston, 1961.

BENNIS, W. G., SCHEIN, E. H., BERLEW, D. E., and STEELE, F. I. (Eds.). *Interpersonal dynamics.* Homewood, Ill.: Dorsey, 1964.

BRADFORD, L., GIBB, J. R., and BENNE, K. D. (Eds). *T-group theory and laboratory method.* New York: Wiley, 1964.

CASRIEL, D. *So fair a house.* Englewood Cliffs, N.J.: Prentice-Hall, 1963.

GIBB, J. R. Climate for trust formation. In L. Bradford, J. R. Gibb, and K. D. Benne (Eds.), *T-group theory and laboratory method.* New York: Wiley, 1964.

GORDON, T. *Group-centered leadership.* Boston: Houghton Mifflin, 1955.

HALL, G. F. A participant's experience in a basic encounter group. (Mimeographed) Western Behavioral Sciences Institute, 1965.

17

The Self-Directed Group:

A New Direction

In Personal Growth Learning*

LAWRENCE N. SOLOMON   BETTY BERZON

A major shift has occurred in the conceptualization of psychotherapy over the past few years, due largely to the influence of Rogers' client-centered approach. Treatment, as traditionally conceived, was seen as "doing something to" another person, manipulating him in some way, "adjusting" his behavior so that he functions in more socially acceptable ways. Recently, increased emphasis has been put upon the creation of a therapeutic climate within which the individual can seek out the solutions to his own problems and can become more fully aware of himself and his relatedness to others.

Rogers indicates this change in his own thinking when he states, "One brief way of describing the change which has taken place in me is to say that in my early professional years I was asking the question, How can I treat, or cure, or change this person? Now I would phrase the question in this way: How can I provide a relationship which this person may use for his own personal growth?" (1961, p. 32)

The increasing emphasis upon the therapeutic nature of certain interpersonal relationships has created opportunities for a variety of innovations in this field. First of all, such emphasis implies that formal, professional train-

* This paper is a revision of "The Self-Directed Therapeutic Group: Three Studies," *Journal of Counseling Psychology,* 13, 1966, 491-497. Revision used by arrangement with the American Psychological Association.

ing may not be, indeed in many cases *is* not, requisite to a helping relationship. It follows that *anyone,* if he possesses the necessary sensitivity and personal characteristics, may create that kind of interpersonal relationship which can be used for personal growth by one or both of the partners. Never before has the use of the self as a therapeutic tool been so clearly or definitively stated as in the recent writings of the client-centered theorists.

A logical extension of this approach is the one taken by the present authors in their research on the use of small groups for personal growth learning. The basic rationale for the use of self-directed groups may be developed as follows. From theory comes the statement that, to be helpful in a therapeutic relationship, *what you know* is not as important as *how you are* as a person (Rogers, 1957). Therefore, the professional diploma may only indicate mastery of prescribed cognitive materials in graduate school; it may say little about the personal characteristics of the individual who holds the degree. One implication of this statement is that intervention in the life of a troubled person by someone trained in a helping profession may not actually be as helpful as intervention by an empathic, accepting, congruent, untrained individual.

The Final Report of the Joint Commission on Mental Illness and Health (1961) came close to a full recognition of the therapeutic potential that exists as an essentially unused resource in the population. In recommending the use of nonmedical workers in the field of mental health, the Joint Commission allied itself with the expanding utilization of indigenous nonprofessionals in this area (Reiff and Riessman, 1964; Pearl and Riessman, 1965). The present authors feel strongly that the careful implementation of self-directed groups can be another important step in dealing with problems presented by the professional manpower shortage.

From research come findings which indicate: (a) Subjective reports of critical incidents from members of therapeutically-oriented small groups indicate that about as many helpful growth experiences involve interaction between peers as involve interaction between group member and group leader. Contrary to much professional opinion, people in groups *can* help one another, without professional guidance or intervention, and certain kinds of group interaction may be identified that predictably lead to therapeutic experiences (Berzon, Pious, and Farson, 1963).

(b) In a recent study of psychiatric in-patients, it was found that conventional leader-led group therapy sessions were significantly more depressed and tended to be more tense than unled sessions. There was a tendency for unled sessions to be warmer and more supportive (Harrow, Astrachan, Becker, Miller, and Schwartz, 1967). The present authors have observed that members of self-directed groups become very protective of one another and tend not to enter into tabooed areas unless group consensus legitimates it. Leader-led groups usually follow the direction set or implied by the professional leader, and he may lead the group into areas with which it is not ready to deal. The leader's single judgment, although it may be "professional," can, in many cases, be less accurate than the consensually validated judgment of the group members.

(c) From the research in group dynamics, particularly the classic studies of White and Lippitt (1953) and Coch and French (1948), come clear implications that self-initiated change from democratic and egalitarian participation in a group problem-solving task leads to personal growth, increased autonomy, leadership ability, and self-esteem. Just as in a personal growth group, the applied behavioral scientist working with task groups in organizational settings seeks to promote increased interpersonal responsibility, a mature commitment, involvement, and trust among the group members. Surely these aims are not of any different order than those sought by the sensitivity trainer or group "facilitator" in a basic encounter group.

From these and other theoretical and research foundations the present authors derive their rationale for the self-directed group as a new direction in personal growth learning. As the term implies, the self-directed group is one that has no professionally-trained leader to guide its interaction. The potential of this approach for extending a personal growth experience to many who would never encounter a professional mental health worker is obviously enormous. Is this approach effective? Can it be implemented and experimentally assessed without posing unwarranted risks for the clients served? Would careful experimental evaluation of such an approach support the contentions of client-centered theorists? The studies detailed below represent one approach to finding answers to these questions.

Study I: Exploration

Initially, the task of researching self-directed groups was considered with great caution (Berzon and Solomon, 1964). Two groups of adult men and women, who had come voluntarily for group therapeutic experience in a research institute setting, met weekly for eighteen weeks. They were observed through a one-way vision window by an "on call" therapist, who could be summoned into the group upon unanimous agreement of its members that it was necessary to do so.

During the eighteen weeks, the therapist was summoned only three times in each group. The subjects saw the experience through, none appeared to have been injured by it, and some reported they had found it helpful. There was none of the physical acting-out that, strangely enough, seemed to be the focus of concern for many professionals who criticized the endeavor. The worst that was envisaged, when the study began, was not that too much would happen, but that too little would happen. And this proved right; too little did happen. Nevertheless, it was concluded that self-directed therapeutic groups are generaly feasible, as judged against the specific criteria of absenteeism and attrition, their ability to function without a leader, and subjective evaluation of the experience by the group members.

In the attempt to discover why so little that was therapeutic happened in the pilot study, it became apparent that an important precondition to therapeutic effectiveness was previous experience in some type of therapeutic activity (individual therapy, sensitivity training, etc.). Those group members who were experienced in this activity were more prone to take responsibility for what happened in the group, either to themselves or to their fellow members. Inexperienced members were reluctant to assume this responsibility. From Study I emerged a major variable for further study: previous experience. Additionally, Study I suffered methodologically from the lack of a "control" group with which to compare the findings from the self-directed group. It was decided to design a more elaborate study in which self-directed groups would be compared with professionally-directed groups, and in which the influence of group members' previous therapeutic experience could be evaluated. The two major variables, direction and experience, defined the parameters of Study II.

Study II: Evaluation

Twelve eight-person groups met weekly for eighteen weeks. Six of the groups were professionally-directed by a designated leader, a qualified professional with significant experience working with groups and whose regular staff assignment included such work. The other six groups were self-directed, without a professionally-trained, designated leader, and with no one "on call" as was the case in Study I. Three of the six professionally-directed groups were composed of individuals who had had some kind of previous individual or group therapeutic experience; three were composed of subjects who had not had prior individual or group therapeutic experience. The self-directed groups were similarly composed.

The subjects were adult men and women who came voluntarily, on a non-paying basis, to serve as participants in a research project. The groups were compared on five dimensions: (1) personality changes were evaluated with pre- and post-MMPI scores; (2) S's perceptions of therapeutic conditions present in the group were measured by a modified form of the Relationship Inventory (Barrett-Lennard, 1959) questionnaire; (3) therapeutic process was rated by trained judges on two scales developed to measure the degree of "facilitative behavior" and the level of "intrapersonal exploration" discernible in four-minute recorded excerpts from the groups' second, tenth and sixteenth sessions; (4) S's subjective reports of "therapeutic events" were quantitatively and qualitatively analyzed; and (5) attendance and attrition rates were computed.

Contrary to what might have been expected, there were no clear-cut differences among the four treatment conditions on any of the five dimensions, with one exception: experienced Ss were more facilitating and achieved deeper levels of intrapersonal exploration than did the inexperienced.

The presence or absence of professional leadership did not significantly affect the group's ability to establish facilitative conditions, nor the ability of most of its members to engage in the therapeutic work in a meaningful way. The results of Study I appeared to demonstrate the potential usefulness of the self-directed therapeutic group as an important mental health resource (Berzon, 1964). However, there were some indications that those groups which accomplished the least therapeutically were the self-directed, inexperienced groups. While prior experience seemed to compensate for the absence of a professionally-trained leader, naïve subjects, left entirely on their own, generally did less well than did their professionally-directed counterparts.

The results of Studies I and II were consistent in affirming the feasibility of self-directed therapeutic groups. They were also consistent in underscoring the need for development of stimulus materials that could be presented to nonexperienced self-directed groups to enhance their effectiveness. Accordingly, in Study III attention was turned specifically to the task of developing "program" materials to guide and enhance the therapeutic interaction of non-experienced subjects.

Study III: Programming [1]

First Year — 1965

In the first year of this study, an eighteen-session program of stimulus materials was developed and tested with a vocational rehabilitation client population.[2]

Eight small groups met twice weekly for nine weeks. Four of the groups were professionally-directed (PD) and did not use the stimulus materials. The other four groups did not have professional leadership; instead, they used the materials. These were the self-directed groups (SD).

A basic assumption was made about the vocational rehabilitation client population: they were, typically, persons with low self-esteem and an unfavorable self-concept. Therefore, the program was designed to increase the probability that the participant would come away from the group with a sense of personal contribution to cohesive group interaction. He would have the opportunity, through identification with peer group interaction, to test his own leadership capability and to perceive himself as a responsible participant. These experiences, it was assumed, would specifically influence his sense of self-esteem and his self-concept in a positive direction.

Structurally, the program consisted of eighteen booklets, one for each of eighteen sessions. Each group member had a booklet and the contents were read aloud, a paragraph at a time, the group members taking turns reading

---

[1] This investigation was supported, in part, by a research grant No. RD-1748 from the Vocational Rehabilitation Administration, Department of Health, Education, and Welfare, Washington, D.C.
[2] This program was written by Betty Berzon, Lawrence N. Solomon, and Melinda Sprague.

around the circle. The program was written in this way to (a) encourage total participation and (b) promote a continuing focus on the here-and-now aspect of the group's interaction.

Each session had a cognitive component, or "message," and an interactive component, or "exercise." The exercise followed the reading of the message and required the group to engage in a task specifically designed to provide direct experiencing of the phenomena discussed in the message section. There were also review sections in several sessions.

Quantitative assessment was made using a battery of seven research instruments. They included pre- and post-tests to measure personality and self-concept change and counselor-rated progress toward vocational rehabilitation, early and late subject-ratings of the therapeutic conditions perceived to be present in the group, session-by-session subject ratings of their own degree of self-disclosure, session-by-session ratings of the "therapeutic climate" in the group made by observers monitoring the live interaction through a one-way vision window, and a session-by-session subject-reported checklist of therapeutic events.

Pre-post measures. Administered to both experimental and control subjects, these were given the week preceding the group experience and the week following. They consisted of the following:

(1) *The Constructive Personality Change Index* (CPC), a selection of 162 items from the MMPI, all of which are phrased in the present or future tense, designed to assess personality changes in the direction of positive mental health (Truax, 1962e).

(2) *Self-Concept Rating Scale,* composed of ten seven-point semantic differential rating scales on which the subject rates the concept, "The Way I See Myself." The scales are defined by polar-opposite adjectives, such as strong-weak, active-passive, and useful-useless (modified from Aiken, 1965).

(3) *Vocational Rehabilitation Progress Scale* (VRP) rating was made for each subject by his counselor at the Division of Vocational Rehabilitation. This instrument consisted of a set of four seven-point scales on which each subject's counselor rated progress toward vocational rehabilitation in terms of (a) suitability of present employment objective, (b) effective utilization of DVR resources, (c) removal or reduction of barriers to employment, and (d) overall movement toward vocational rehabilitation.

(4) *The Relationship Inventory,* a multiple-choice questionnaire that yields a score measuring the degree to which certain conditions hypothesized as being necessary to therapeutic change are perceived to be present in a given relationship (Barrett-Lennard, 1962). This instrument was administered to the experimental groups after either the second or third session and again after the eighteenth (last) session.

Session-by-session measurements. Several session-by-session measurements were made of the experimental groups as described below:

(1) *Therapeutic Group Event* (TGE) questionnaire, consisting of a checklist of twelve categories of events (5 cognitive, 5 affective, 2 behavioral) that had been reported by previous groups as the most significant and helpful occurrences to them personally (Berzon *et al.,* 1963, Berzon *et al.,* 1964). The group members were instructed at the end of each session to check those categories of events which they experienced, and additionally, to indicate the degree of intensity with which the event occurred by checking one of three adverbs: slightly, quite a bit, extremely.

(2) *Self-Disclosure Index,* composed of a set of five seven-point semantic differential rating scales on which each subject separately rated two concepts after each group session: "The way I felt inside" and "How I must have seemed to others." The scales are defined by polar-opposite adjectives, such as friendly-unfriendly, tense-relaxed, and angry-pleased (Goodman, 1962). The degree of discrepancy between the ratings of "The way I felt inside" and "How I must have seemed to others" was taken as an index of self-disclosure. If S rated his subjective feelings and objective behavior similarly on the semantic differential scales, then the discrepancy was small and perceived self-disclosure was high; conversely, a large discrepancy between ratings of subjective feelings and objective behavior indicated a low degree of perceived self-disclosure.

(3) *Evaluation of Therapeutic Climate Scales* (ETC) consisted of two rating scales designed to measure (a) to what extent and at what depth members of a therapeutic group are engaged in self-exploration (Truax, 1962a; van der Veen and Tomlinson, 1962; Gendlin and Geist, 1962), and (b) the extent to which members of a therapeutic group respond to one another with behavior that encourages and enables the exploration of feelings, beliefs, and personally relevant material (Truax, 1961, 1962b, 1962c, 1962d). These ratings were made independently every fifteen minutes during the group's interaction by two trained observers who monitored the group through one-way vision windows.

(4) An *Attendance and Attrition Record* was completed each session by the observers. On it were recorded the names of the group members present that session and those absent, as well as those who were dropouts.

(5) *Vocational Rehabilitation Progress Scale* was also used as a follow-up measure. Each counselor completed a VRP on those clients in the study whose cases were still open one year after the termination of the group sessions.

Experimental Groups

Thirty-four subjects were assigned to the professionally-directed (PD) condition. Four groups of approximately eight persons each were conducted. Twenty-nine subjects were assigned to the self-directed (SD) condition, in four groups of approximately seven each. Twenty subjects were included in the control condition, with data collection on ten subjects taking place concurrently with that of the PD groups, and data collection on ten additional subjects taking place concurrently with that of the SD groups. All four PD groups were conducted during the same nine-week period, as were the SD groups.

Results[3]

Pre-Post Measures

Constructive Personality Change Index (CPC). The differences between pre- and post-scores on the CPC reveal little difference among the PD, SD, and Control conditions. The mean change for the PD condition was 2.38; for the SD condition, .01; and for the Control condition, .24. These differences are not statistically significant.

Self-Concept Rating Scale. The distribution of change scores on this instrument, for the three conditions, is presented in Figure 17.1.

[3] Data analysis was performed by Clifford Weedman of the WBSI staff.

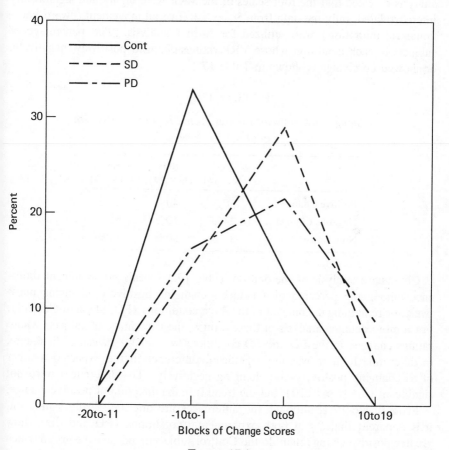

FIGURE 17.1

*Distribution of Subject's Pre- to Post-Change Scores
on Self-Concept Scale, 1965*

It is evident from an analysis of these results that subjects in the PD and SD groups tended to change their self-concept ratings in the direction of more positive evaluation, as compared to control subjects who tended to show the opposite tendency. Fifty-nine per cent of the PD *S's* and 70 per cent of the SD *Ss* changed their ratings in a positive direction, whereas 71 per cent of the Control *Ss* changed their ratings in a negative direction. Statistical analysis of the change in self-concept score for the three conditions reveals a significant difference between the experimental conditions (PD and SD) and the control condition (p. < .05). No significant difference was found between the PD and SD conditions.

Vocational Rehabilitation Progress Scale (VRP). Changes in counselor ratings on the VRP were analyzed according to the *direction* of change, either positively, negatively, or no change from pre- to post-measurement. Since analysis revealed that the four scales of the VRP were highly and significantly intercorrelated, only the data from Scale #4 (overall movement toward vocational rehabilitation) were utilized for further analysis. The percentage of subjects in each condition whose VRP ratings changed positively, negatively, or showed no change is shown in Table 17.1.

TABLE 17.1

Changes in Counselor Ratings, from Pre- to Post-Measure on the VRP Scale

	PD (N = 34)	SD (N = 29)	Control (N = 20)
Positive Change	38%	40%	25%
Negative Change	24%	10%	55%
No Change	38%	50%	20%

Chi-square analysis of the data in Table 17.1 reveals no significant difference among the percentage of subjects changing positively, changing negatively, or remaining unchanged in the three conditions (PD, SD, and Control). For a more detailed analysis of these ratings, the percentage of subjects whose ratings changed in the PD and SD conditions was analyzed, using chi-square, to determine if there was any significant difference in the expected number of *Ss* changing positively and changing negatively. The differences were not significant (.05 < p < .10), but the trend is in the direction of positive change.

From Table 17.1, although the differences are not statistically significant, it is apparent that *S's* in both experimental conditions (PD and SD) show greater positive change than do the Control subjects; and that the group which shows the greatest negative change is the Control group.

At the time of the one year follow-up, only fifteen members of the PD group, eleven members of the SD group, and fourteen members of the Control group were still active clients of the DVR, hence, available for rating. Their counselors rated them on the VRP scale, and the *direction* of change from the post-rating made one year previously was noted. Table 17.2 presents the percentage of *Ss* in each condition whose ratings changed positively, negatively, or not at all.

TABLE 17.2

Changes in Counselor Ratings, from Post-Measurement to One Year Follow-Up, on the VRP Scale

	PD (N = 15)	SD (N = 11)	Control (N = 14)
Positive change	36%	27%	7%
Negative change	14%	45%	43%
No change	50%	27%	50%

Due to attrition, the sample size was too small at the time of the one year follow-up to allow for statistical analysis of the data. However, it is interesting to note that the trend toward positive change for the two experimental groups is still apparent, as compared to the Control group. As far as negative change is concerned, it appears that the SD group is now on a par with the Controls, while the PD group still enjoys the advantage it had a year earlier.

Early-Late Measure

Relationship Inventory (RI). Each *S's* rating of the degree to which certain conditions, hypothesized by Rogers (1957) as necessary to therapeutic change, were present in his group during Session 2 or 3 was compared to that *S's* same rating for Session 18. The direction of change in the rating was then assessed and change scores computed for each of the four dimensions measured by the instrument. The four dimensions are: Congruence, Empathic Understanding, Unconditionality of Regard, and Level of Regard.

Statistical analysis of the data reveals that, as perceived by the *Ss* in the SD condition, there was a significant *decrease* in Congruence, Unconditionality of Regard, and Level of Regard from early to late in the group sessions ($p < .05$). However, no significant change was found from early to late for Empathic Understanding in the SD condition. For the PD group, there was no significant change on the RI, from early to late, for any of the four dimensions assessed.

Session-by-Session Measures

Evaluation of Therapeutic Climate Scales (ETC). The observers' ratings on the two ETC subscales (self-exploration and facilitative behavior) were combined and a mean scale rating calculated for each session for both the PD and SD conditions. The mean scale ratings are presented in Figure 17.2.

Analysis of the data in Figure 17.2 indicates that there is a significant increase in therapeutic climate, from Sessions 1-9 to Sessions 10-18, of the PD group, as judged by trained observers ($p < .50$). However, no significant difference was found for the SD conditions between Sessions 1-9 and Sessions 10-18.

Observation of Figure 17.2 reveals that the mean ETC ratings for the PD condition are consistently higher than those ratings for the SD conditions across all eighteen sessions. This difference between PD and SD conditions is statistically significant ($p < .05$).

Self-Disclosure Index. A median discrepancy score was computed for each PD and SD subject's ratings of the statements, "The way I felt inside" and "How I must have seemed to others," over the two blocks of sessions, 1-6 and 13-18. The difference between the discrepancy scores for these two blocks of sessions, for both PD and SD subjects, was statistically significant, indicat-

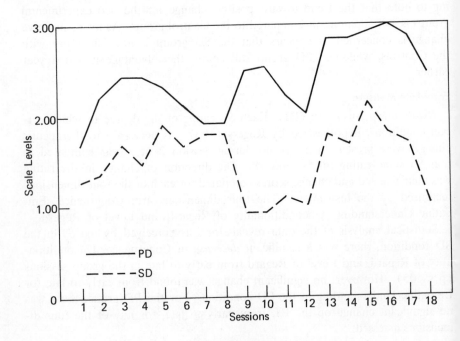

FIGURE 17.2

Mean "Evaluation of Therapeutic Climate" Ratings, 1965
(Scale levels ranged from 1 to 5)

ing a marked increase in perceived self-disclosure in both conditions (p < .05). A further analysis revealed no significant difference between PD and SD conditions on this instrument.

Attendance and Attrition. Attendance and attrition results are presented in Figures 17.3 and 17.4.

Chi-square analysis of the data in Figures 17.3 and 17.4, analyzed in blocks of six sessions each (1-6, 7-12, and 13-18), reveals no significant differences in either absences or dropouts between the PD and SD conditions.

Therapeutic Group Events Scale (TGE). The percentage of total *Ss* who checked the adverb "extremely" on each item in the TGE was computed for both PD and SD conditions for each of the eighteen sessions. Statistical analysis of these data reveals no significant differences between the two

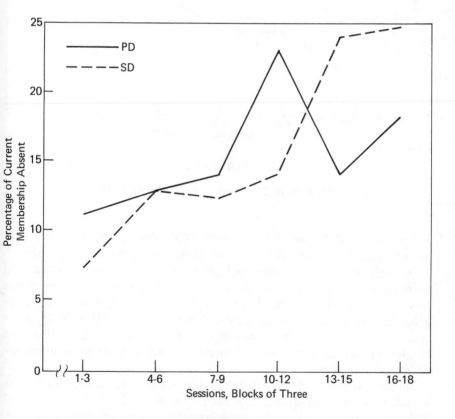

FIGURE 17.3

Absences over 18 Sessions, 1965

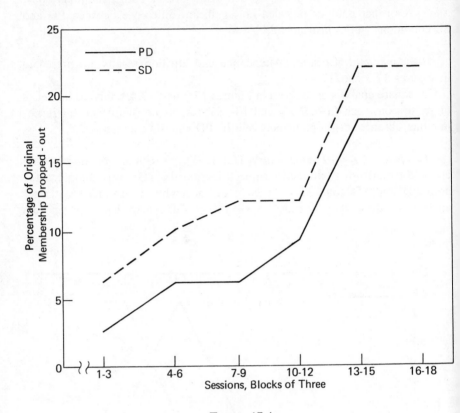

FIGURE 17.4

Cumulative Drop-outs over 18 Sessions, 1965

groups on any of the twelve items on the TGE, although the PD group consistently showed a higher percentage of *Ss* responding to each TGE item.

In order to assess the differential effectiveness of the various structuring exercises in the program, an analysis was made of the TGE categories checked each session by the SD group only. Table 17.3 indicates the categories that were checked by more than 70 per cent of the SD *Ss* in any given session. The 70 per cent figure was chosen because it appeared liberal enough to allow for a number of sessions to qualify for inclusion but stringent enough to be discriminating.

Summing across sessions in Table 17.3, it appears that Categories 1, 5, 6, 8, and 10 were checked by a high percentage of the *Ss,* while Categories 7 and 9 were not checked at all. Summing across categories, Sessions 2, 3, 4, 14, and 15 appeared to evoke the greatest number of therapeutic events; whereas Sessions 16, 17, and 18 seemed to evoke the least.

TABLE 17.3

*TGE Items Checked by at Least 70% of the SD Subjects,
for Each Session*

		Cognitive						Affective				Behavioral	
	Categories	Recognizing similarity to others	Achieving heightened awareness of intrapersonal self	Achieving heightened awareness of intrapersonal self	Seeing self as seen by others	Acquiring information about persons, issues, or group process	Feeling responded to positively by another or others in the group	Feeling responded to negatively by another or others in the group	Feeling positive emotions toward another or others in the group	Feeling negative emotions toward another or others in the group	Feeling increased warmth, trust, or cohesiveness in the group	Expressing self concurrently, articulately, or assertively in the group	Reaching out to help another
Exercise	Session No.	1	2	3	4	5	6	7	8	9	10	11	12
Introductions	1	X					X		X				
Focus on feelings	2	X				X	X		X		X	X	X
Feed-back charts	3	X	X	X	X	X	X		X		X		X
Feed-back charts	4	X	X	X		X	X		X		X		
Metaphors	5	X		X	X		X						
Problem members	6	X				X	X		X		X		
Angry feelings	7	X					X						
Unfortunate circumstance	8	X				X	X		X		X		
Plan the picnic	9	X					X		X				
Picnic	10						X		X		X		
Group as metaphor	11	X					X						
Draw-the-group	12	X				X	X		X		X		
Group members' positive contributions	13	X			X		X		X				
Re-do-feed-back charts	14	X	X	X	X	X	X		X				
Focus on change	15	X	X	X	X	X	X				X		
Significant other reports	16	X											
Significant other reports	17	X											
Free discussion	18	X											

An Additional Instrument: Post-Sessions Reaction Questionnaire

A Post-Sessions Reaction Questionnaire was administered after Session 18 to those in the SD condition only. On this instrument the *Ss* rated the degree of benefit they derived from the group experience, on a five-point scale, ranging from (1) "very helpful" through (2) "quite helpful," (3) "neither helpful nor harmful," (4) "slightly harmful," to (5) "very harmful." The percentage of *Ss* that reported the group experience to be helpful was 79.2; 12.5 per cent rated it harmful; and 8.3 per cent rated it neither helpful nor harmful.

From an impressionistic point of view, the following weaknesses and strengths were notable in the program.

Weaknesses

Obviously, there was an attempt to cover too much. The participants' time was overstructured. Too little time was allowed to let the idiosyncratic material come out — the raw material — without which we often have only the illusion that something meaningful is happening.

Too little time was allotted to develop themes and to work through conflicts that emerged among group members.

In general the program was too cognitive and not experiential enough.

Strengths

On the positive side, there was definitely more dealing with personally relevant material in these groups than there was in the self-directed groups of naïve persons that the writers had studied earlier.

There was also more confrontation in these self-directed groups than in those studied in the past. They not only confronted each other, but they confronted the experiment as well. They often discussed the value of what they were doing, talked about alternative choices open to them, and expressed the resentment and frustration they felt toward the experimenters when particular sessions did not work at all. In other words, they dealt directly with their own fate. This was not as true of self-directed groups studied in the past, and it is taken as a gain in what the program was able to bring about.

Second Year [4] — 1966

In the second year of Study III major changes were made in research design and in program format and content.

Since it was felt that the professionally-directed and structured self-directed groups in the first year were sufficiently comparable, the professionally-directed condition was eliminated.

A shift was made from semi-weekly meetings to daily intensive sessions. Groups met for two sessions a day, five consecutive days in one week, and four consecutive days in the following week. The intensity of such scheduling appears to contribute greatly to the increased effectiveness of the program, as compared to sessions previously conducted on a semi-weekly basis.

Another major change involved the presentation of the program on audio-

---

[4] This program was written by Betty Berzon, Lawrence N. Solomon, Melinda Sprague, and Clifford Weedman for use in vocational rehabilitation settings.

tape, rather than in booklet form. Group members were told, during a brief orientation period at the beginning, that they would find a new tape on the machine each session and they need only turn on the recorder to begin the session. Instructions for each session's exercise usually took about ten minutes, though the tape continued to run silently for the entire two hours. Also, the members were given a Participant's Notebook that included forms needed for certain exercises as well as some of the material presented on the tapes, for the participants' later reference.

In addition to changes in format, the content of the program was completely revised, based on learnings from the first year. The new program is described below in some detail.

Revised Program

General Goal of the Program

The general goal of the program is to enhance the individual's ability to make fuller use of his social and vocational potential through better understanding and broadened experiencing of himself in relation to other people.

Specific Goals of the Program

To accomplish the general goal, a set of specific goals was designed to focus on the impact of feelings and behavior on interpersonal relationships.

The specific goals are for the participant to *experience more fully in awareness:*

(1) His own feelings (OF)
(2) How his own feelings affect his own behavior (OF ⟶ OB)
(3) How his own behavior affects another's feelings (OB ⟶ AF)
(4) How another's feelings affect his behavior (AF ⟶ AB)
(5) How another's behavior affects his own feelings (AB ⟶ OF)

A simple graphic model is used for this set of relationships.

Criterion Behaviors

For the specific goals to be met, two things must happen to the individual in the group. He must (1) symbolize what he is experiencing and talk about it and (2) listen with relatively accurate understanding when others talk.

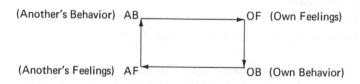

FIGURE 17.5

From the specific goals, a set of criterion behaviors were developed along two dimensions: talking and listening. These are the behaviors to be evoked in the group and they are presented below as they relate to the specific goals.

Goal: To experience more fully in awareness one's own feelings.
Intermediate behavior:
 Talking about public aspects of self.
 Talking about private aspects of self.
 Talking about private aspects of self with description of feelings.
Criterion behavior:
 Talking with direct expression of here-and-now feelings.

Goal: To experience more fully in awareness how one's own feelings affect one's own behavior.
Criterion behavior:
 Talking with recognition of feelings and of their meaning for own behavior in relation to others.

Goal: To experience more fully in awareness how one's own behavior affects another's feelings.
Intermediate behavior:
 Listening with accurate understanding of the content of what others are saying.
 Listening with accurate understanding of the feelings others are describing.
Criterion behavior:
 Listening with accurate understanding of others' here-and-now feelings and how they have been affected by one's own behavior.

Goal: To experience more fully in awareness how another's feelings affect his behavior.
Criterion behavior:
 Listening with an accurate understanding of others' feelings and how they affect their behavior.

Goal: To experience more fully in awareness how another's behavior affects one's own feelings.
Criterior behavior:
 Talking with direct expression of own here-and-now feelings and recognizing the effect of others' behavior on these feelings.

Note that on both behavioral dimensions, talking and listening, there is a general sequential movement from (1) public to private, (2) there-and-then to here-and-now, and (3) simple to complex.

Exercises

To evoke the intermediate and criterion behaviors, a series of exercises were presented via the tape recording. (Because the tape continues to run for the entire two hours, it is possible in some exercises to intervene with additional instructions during the session.)

A brief session-by-session outline of exercises appears below. It is obviously not a complete description of program content, but is presented to give an idea of the nature of the structuring used.

Session IA — Orientation. The main purpose of this session is to establish group norms along the lines of trust building and facilitative behavior. This is done by presentation of (1) a set of "Group Ground Rules" and (2) a list of ten characteristics employers look for in a "good employee," the latter heavily weighted with interpersonal factors. The exercise is to rank order the "ten characteristics" in terms of their relative importance. This is a group task, and the rank ordering must be a consensual one.

Session IB — Listening Lab: Triads. In this session, "rules for good listening" are presented and a checklist using these rules is provided in the Participant's Notebook. The exercise is to devide into triads, or three-person groups, in which one person takes the role of the "talker," one the "listener," and one the "observer," who uses the checklist to rate the "listener" on his listening behavior. The "talker's" task is to talk for ten minutes about why he came to the Department of Rehabilitation. The roles are then rotated so each person has a chance to take each role. During the last fifteen minutes of this session, the group consensually rank orders its membership on "good listening" and the results are recorded on a "Feedback Chart" on the wall of the group room.

Session 2A — Paraphrasing. This exercise is built on the previous session's material. Each person tells the group what his "talker" told him about why he came to the agency. This task serves the dual purpose of underlining the importance of listening to understand others and of making information about each participant available to the entire group.

In this "go around" exercise, as in others to follow, the instruction is for each group member to take a given number of minutes. As he talks, he holds a simple kitchen timer set for the designated time, usually ten minutes. When the timer goes off, he finishes and hands it to the next person, in a sense giving up the floor to him and passing on the responsibility of participation. This provides an effective way of encouraging active participation and distributing it equally.

Session 2B — Self-Appraisal. In a "go around" each group member selects one of the "ten characteristics of a good employee" that he thinks he needs to work on to make himself more sought after as an employee.

The last fifteen minutes is spent on the Feedback Chart. This time the group consensually rates each other in terms of "Participation."

Session 3A — Unfortunate Circumstances. In a "go around" group members are asked to tell the most unfortunate circumstance in their life and to discuss their feelings about it.

Session 3B — Listening Lab: Cue Cards. One group member is designated a "talker" and one a "listener." They sit in the center of the room facing a row of "talker's helpers" on one side, and "listener's helpers" on the other. The "talker" continues discussion about the feelings he had during the unfortunate circumstance described in the previous session. The "listener" practices the "rules of good listening" to facilitate the "talker's" job. The "helpers," with the aid of large cue cards, encourage "talker" and "listener" to fulfill their roles, using the various principles of self-disclosure and understanding that have been presented earlier in the program.

Feedback Chart for this day is again for "good listening."

Session 4A — Descriptions: Other. In a "go around" each group member describes every other group member metaphorically, thus initiating here-and-now interpersonal feedback in an indirect way.

Session 4B — Descriptions: Self. In another "go around" each individual describes himself metaphorically, providing an opportunity for group members to make themselves better known to the group. Feedback Chart is for "participation."

Session 5A — Feeling Pooling. In this session, individuals anonymously write out a strong feeling they have about another group member. These are placed in a pile, drawn out one at a time, and read aloud by others who comment on why they think someone would feel that way about the person named. Group members are encouraged to elaborate, using their own feelings toward the person.

Session 5B — Motion Giving. In an effort to build a bridge from the individual's group experience to his life outside, the group gives each member a specific task to do over the intervening weekend. The task is related to a problem the member has discussed or manifested in the group, a task he is having difficulty working through. He is asked at least to "go through the motions" of doing something about the problem. Additionally, each group member selects a partner, and then, over the weekend, writes a story about what he hopes his partner will do in carrying out his "motion."

Feedback Chart this session is for "willingness to try to improve self."

Session 6A — Motion Reporting. Participants describe what happened when they tried to go through their "motion," telling particularly what their feelings were. Each "partner" then reads his prediction and discusses his feelings about what the person did in relation to what he thought he would do.

Session 6B — Free Session. In this session, it is suggested that the participants use their time to deal with, or go more deeply into anything that has occurred in the group so far.

Feedback Chart is again for "willingness to improve self."

Session 7A — Secret Pooling.[5] Group members are asked to write anonymously a personal secret. The papers are scrambled, and each person then reads the secret he selected and tells how he thinks it would feel to have a secret like that.

Session 7B — Free Session. Feedback Chart is for "willingness to be known by others."

Session 8A — Confrontation.[6] Group members stand in a circle. One at a time, each goes around the circle stopping before each person. The instruction is, "look directly at the person, touch him, and tell him how you feel about him."

Session 8B — Free Session. Feedback Chart is for "emotional honesty."

Session 9A — Self-Reappraisal. Participants are asked to look again at the list of "ten characteristics of a good employee" and to select the one they now think they need to work on the most or to talk about any other way in which they think they need to make an effort to change.

Session 9B — Going Home. The instruction is to "pretend you are on the way home after the group has ended" (this is the last session). Think about the things you did not do or say in the group when you had the chance. Then, tell the group what those things are.

To assist in understanding the relationship of the exercises to the criterion behaviors and the specific goals, the outline is presented below in Table 17.4.

In the second year, the battery of instruments used to assess the program's effectiveness was modified on the basis of the first year's experience, changes in research design, and altered program format. Seven measurements were taken over three different time periods. The one pre-post measure employed from the previous year's battery was the Self-Concept Rating Scale. This

---

[5] The authors are grateful to Gerald Goodman for this exercise.
[6] The authors are grateful to William Schutz for this exercise.

TABLE 17.4

Program Design Outline, 1966

Session No.	Exercises	Intermediate and Criterion Behaviors	Specific Goals
1A	Orientation		
1B	Listening Lab: Triads	Talking about public aspects of self; listening to understand content.	
2A	Paraphrasing	Talking about public aspects of self; listening for accurate understanding of content.	
2B	Self-Appraisal	Talking about private aspects of self.	
3A	Unfortunate Circumstance	Talking about private aspects of self-description of feelings; listening for feelings.	
3B	Listening Lab: Cue Cards	Listening for accurate understanding of feelings described.	
4A	Descriptions: Other	Talking with indirect expression of own feelings about another.	
4B	Descriptions: Self	Talking about self with indirect expression of own feelings.	
5A	Feeling Pooling	Talking with direct expression of here-and-now feelings.	Experience more fully in awareness own feelings.
5B	Motion Giving	Understanding how another's feelings affect his behavior.	
6A	Motion Reporting	Talking with recognition of how own feelings affect own behavior; listening with accurate understanding of other's feelings and how they affect his behavior; listening with accurate understanding of other's here-and-now feelings and how they have been affected by one's behavior.	Experience more fully in awareness how own feelings affect own behavior; experience more fully in awareness how other's feelings affect their behavior.

6B	Free		
7A	Secret Pooling	Understanding how others' feelings affect their behavior relative to more deeply personal material.	Experience more fully in awareness how others' feelings affect their behavior.
7B	Free		
8A	Confrontation	Talking with direct expression of own here-and-now feelings, recognizing effect of other's behavior on these feelings.	Experience more fully in awareness how other's behavior affects one's own feelings.
8B	Free		
9A	Self-Reappraisal		
9B	Going Home		

instrument was also used for a six-month follow-up measure. Additionally, two new pre-post measures were added: the *Who Knows You Inventory* and an *Employability Interview*. Session-by-session measures were taken, using, from the previous year, a Self-Disclosure Index, the Evaluation of Therapeutic Climate Scales (ETC), attendance and attrition records. The early-late use of the Relationship Inventory and the session-by-session use of the Therapeutic Group Event (TGE) questionnaire, which were part of the 1965 design, were changed in the 1966 design to the daily administration of a *Group Experience Rating* form. These new instruments incorporated into the evaluation procedures in 1966 are detailed below.

The *Who Knows You Inventory* assesses the amount and content of the *S's* self-disclosure to selected "target persons" on a four-point scale. The content of potentially disclosable items dealt with personal finances, worries and concerns, beliefs and attitudes. The target persons used in the questionnaire were: *S's* best friend of the same sex, *S's* best friend of the opposite sex (or spouse), and *S's* counselor at the Department of Rehabilitation. The form of this instrument used in the present study was a modification of the test developed by Jourard and Dutton and revised by Greening (1965).

The *Employability Interviews* were tape-recorded ten-minute personal interviews conducted by the research team in which *S's* motivation for work and self-understanding were explored. Each *S* was asked the following questions: what job that you could get would you like to have?; what three things would you do in order to get this job?; what do you see yourself doing five years from now?; what is the best thing you can tell about yourself as an employee?; and what is the worst thing you can tell about yourself as an employee? The first three questions were designed to assess motivation to work; the last two, self-understanding. The interview was conducted a third time six months after the post-measure as a follow-up assessment.

The *Group Experience Rating* form requested the *Ss* to indicate "How I Felt About the Group Today." A two-part instrument was designed to assess:

(1) The degree to which certain conditions, hypothesized by Rogers (1957) as necessary to therapeutic change, were present in the group, by using a modification of the Relationship Inventory (previously described) in a semantic differential format;

(2) Degree of similarity between self and others in the group along dimensions of genuineness, risk-taking, sensitivity to others, and personal openness, by requiring *S* to assign a number between 1 (low) and 5 (high) to himself and each of the other group members indicating the extent to which he perceived those characteristics to be present during the day.

Experimental Groups

Experimental subjects (N = 24) were again recruited from the client population of the San Diego Office of the California Department of Rehabilitation, Division of Vocation Rehabilitation. The control subjects (N = 23) were recruited from the Sheltered Workshops of San Diego, employing the same criteria as were used for the selection of experimental *Ss*. The experimental *Ss* were divided into three groups. Data collection on the control *Ss* was conducted concurrently with data collection on the experimental subjects.

Results[7]

Pre-Post Measures

Self-Concept Rating Scale. Pre- and post-measurements were analyzed by the F-test. As in the previous year's study, the experimental group showed a significant change in self-concept toward more positive evaluation (p < .05) while the control group showed no such change. However, this finding did not hold up on a six-month follow-up measure.

Who Knows You Inventory. In order to compare pre- and post-measurements on this instrument, two separate analyses were performed on the data

(1) The responses on the inventory were dichotomized into two categories, those indicating a willingness to disclose self to others (scale positions "1," "2," and "3"), and those indicating a complete lack of willingness to disclose self (scale position "4"). The number of times experimental and control *Ss* chose the "4" response ("I would not tell the person even if that person asked me to reveal the information") was tabulated and analyzed for significance of difference between pre- and post-measure, summing over all target persons. Results of this analysis indicated that there was a significant increase in self-disclosure (as shown by a decrease in nondisclosure) for the experimental *Ss* with no change for the controls.

---

[7] Data analysis was performed by Mr. David P. Davis of the WBSI staff.

(2) To reveal changes in self-disclosure vis-à-vis specified target persons, the data were analyzed separately for each target person. Mean pre- and post-ratings assigned to each target individual by the experimental and control *Ss* were compared and a mean change score computed for each target person. Scale values were transformed so that a higher value indicated a greater degree of disclosure. These data are presented in Table 17.5.

TABLE 17.5

Mean Change Scores for Target Persons on the
"Who Knows You" Inventory

	Best Friend Same Sex	Best Friend Opposite Sex (or Spouse)	Counselor
Experimental *Ss*	1.1	1.9	2.1
Control *Ss*	−0.5	−0.1	−2.9

F-test analysis of these data indicate that none of the differences reach statistical significance. However, the trends are interesting. The experimental *Ss* consistently show a change in the direction of *increased* disclosure to each target person, as compared to the control *Ss*. Also, the greatest change in disclosure occurred with reference to the counselor; but the direction of change is exactly opposite for experimental and control *Ss* — experimental *Ss* increase and control *Ss* decrease in willingness to disclose self to their counselor.

Employability Interviews. The pre-, post-, and follow-up interviews for five experimental and five control *Ss* were randomly selected for assessment by a panel of four expert judges. Blind ratings of the tape-recorded interviews were made by the judges regarding (a) motivation to work (on a seven-point scale) and (b) self-understanding (on a five-point scale).

The ratings were analyzed statistically and indicated a significant increase in *motivation to work* for the experimental group, as compared to the control group. Mean pre-, post-, and follow-up measures for the control group all fell in the center interval on the seven-point scale, indicating a neutral position between being motivated to work and showing resistance to work. In contrast, the mean prerating for the experimental subjects fell in the "slightly resistant" interval, while both the mean post- and follow-up measures fell in the "slightly motivated" interval.

Analysis of the ratings on *self-understanding* showed no significant changes over time for either the experimental or control groups. All three mean ratings for the experimental group fell in the "moderate amount" interval; the mean pre-measure for the controls fell in the "modern amount" interval, but their mean post- and follow-up measures moved down the scale to the "slight amount" interval. Figure 17.6 illustrates these findings.

Session-by-Session Measures

Self-Disclosure Index. A mean discrepancy score was computed for each experimental *S's* rating of the statement, "The way I felt inside" versus the rating on the same set of scales of the statement, "How I must have seemed to others." These discrepancy scores were computed for eight consecutive sampling periods. The scores were analyzed by the F-test, and differences among sampling periods were found to be significant ($p < .05$). A mean deviation score was computed for the combined deviation scores of all three

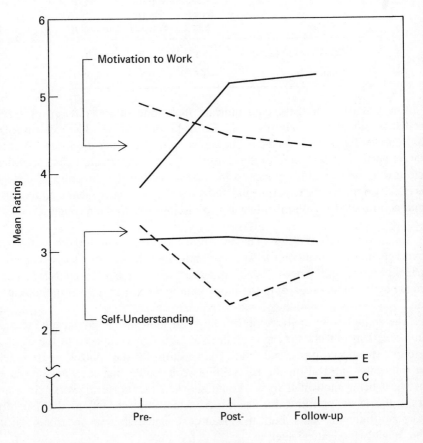

FIGURE 17.6

Mean Employability Ratings for Experimental (E) and Control (C) Subjects, 1966. (Maximum rating possible for the Self-Understanding Scale is 5.00, and for the Motivation to Work Scale is 7.00.)

experimental groups and plotted for each daily sampling period. A trend analysis was performed on the mean self-disclosure ratings over sampling periods and a significant increase in self-disclosure was found.

Attendance and Attrition. Attendance was recorded as percentage of the current membership absent each day. A cumulative percentage of dropouts from the original membership was also computed for each day. Attendance and attrition data are presented below in Figures 17.7 and 17.8 respectively.

For comparison, the same data from the 1965 study are included in these figures. A chi-square analysis of the attendance data in Figure 17.7 indicated that there were significantly fewer absences among the 1966 group than among the 1965 SD groups. Figure 17.8 reveals that there were consistently fewer dropouts over sessions among the 1966 groups than for the 1965 SD groups.

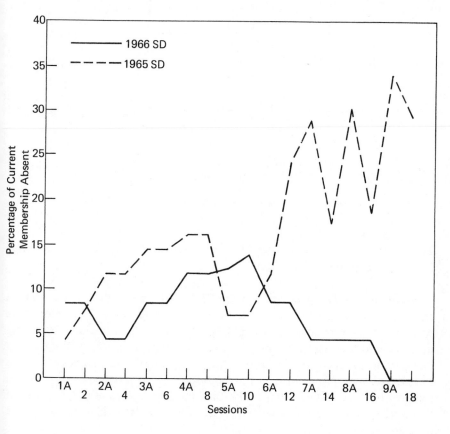

FIGURE 17.7

Absences over Sessions, 1965 and 1966

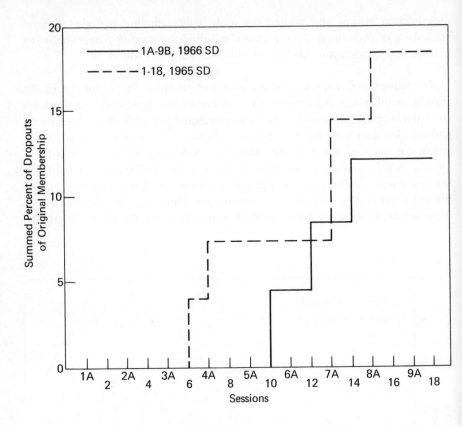

FIGURE 17.8

Cumulative Drop-Outs over Sessions, 1965 and 1966

The total percentage of dropouts for the 1965 SD groups was 18 per cent; for the 1966 groups, 12 per cent.

Evaluation of Therapeutic Climate (ETC). The mean therapeutic climate rating was computed for each of both sessions on each day. Data for these process ratings were collected via audio-tape recordings of sessions. Sampling units were four-minute excerpts of verbal interaction from early, middle, and late portions of each session. From the three groups, 162 samples were collected, and were re-recorded in random sequence on six tapes, twenty-seven samples per tape. Blind ratings were then made independently by a panel of four raters, with two raters per tape. Each rater judged three tapes, with a different partner each time.

Figure 17.9 indicates that, for the 1966 groups, Sessions 2B, 4A, 4B, 5B, and 9A tended to produce the highest ratings of therapeutic climate, while

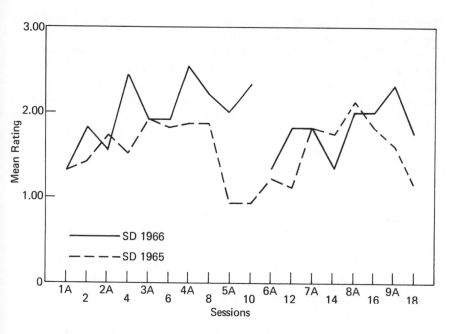

FIGURE 17.9

*Mean "Evaluation of Therapeutic Climate" Ratings, 1965 and 1966.
(1965 groups had one session daily, and the 1966 groups had two
sessions daily. The maximum possible rating is 5.00.)*

Sessions 1A, 2A, 6A, 7B, and 9B tended to produce the lowest ratings. Statistical analysis of the 1966 data indicates: (a) there is a significant difference in ratings over days and (b) the trend of the mean ratings reveals an increase in therapeutic climate over Sessions 1A through 5B and another increase over Sessions 6A through 9B. For ease of interpretation, the data points for Sessions 5B and 6A in Figure 9 are not connected; the interval between those Sessions is the weekend break.

Daily Measure

Group Experience Rating. The responses to the semantic differential form of the Relationship Inventory were analyzed by the F-test. No significant change was found in the *S's* perception of the presence of Rogers' therapeutic conditions over days.

The peer-ratings of genuineness, risk-taking, sensitivity to others, and openness were analyzed by F-test and revealed: (a) no significant change over days in perceived genuineness among group members, (b) a significant increase in sensitivity to others, (c) a significant increase in risk-taking over Days 1 through 7, followed by a decrease over Days 8 and 9, and (d) a significant increase in perceived openness over Days 1 through 6, followed by a significant decline over Days 7 through 9.

In addition to the analysis of the peer-ratings, the *S's* self-rating was analyzed in the following way. On each of the four dimensions assessed, the deviation between *S's* own self-rating and his median peer rating was computed. The sign-test was employed; no significant difference was found from the early part of the program (Days 1 and 2) to the later part of the program (Days 8 and 9) in the deviation between the way *S* saw himself and the way he was seen by the others in the group.

Discussion

What do these findings mean, overall? Four years of experimentation with self-directed groups has led to two conclusions: that such groups are effective in promoting increased interpersonal responsibility, and that stimulus materials can be developed for significant enhancement of this effectiveness. Specifically, results indicate that self-directed groups, using program materials, promote positive changes in the subjects' ability to be more open, congruent, self-accepting, and self-motivating.

A closer look at each dependent variable reveals:

(1) A change in the self-concept, in the direction of more positive evaluation, for the 1965 PD and SD *Ss* and for the 1966 experimental groups. However, analysis of the follow-up data on the 1966 experimental *Ss* reveals a marked *drop* in positive self-evaluation, indicating that the changes induced by the small group experience were not sustained over the six months following the termination of the groups. Such findings might imply the desirability of a continuing small group experience to sustain the gains shown at the time of the post-testing.

(2) A significant increase in "self-disclosure" from early sessions to late sessions, for both 1965 and 1966 experimental *Ss*. Improved self-concept and increased self-disclosure were achieved in the 1965 SD condition to the same extent as was possible under the guidance of a professionally-trained group leader. This finding was consistent for the 1966 groups.

Additionally, the 1966 data from the "Who Knows You Inventory" tended to corroborate the self-disclosure findings.

From Figure 17.9 it is apparent that the 1966 program material was more effective in generating a therapeutic climate (as rated by trained observers), since the data points for the 1966 results tend to be generally higher than those for the 1965 results. Two further aspects of Figure 17.9 deserve discussion: (1) the marked drop in the 1965 curve on Sessions 9 and 10 is accounted for by the nature of the task that was posed for the group by the 1965 program material; (2) the 1966 curve appears to be best interpreted as two separate curves, created by the weekend intermission. That is why the data points for Sessions 5B and 6A are not connected.

In reference to the TGE findings in 1965, close examination of Table 17.5 reveals that certain of the sessions in that year's program evoked a higher percentage of therapeutic events than did others in the judgment of the group members themselves. These sessions were, for the most part, those which involved the systematic use of "feedback" information and direct confrontation between group members. As judged by trained raters, those sessions in the 1965 program which produced the highest ratings of "therapeutic climate" (see Figure 17.9) were also those involving the systematic use of feedback. The ETC ratings for 1966 (also shown in Figure 17.9) continue this trend and, in addition, reveal that systematic *self*-confrontation also generates high "therapeutic climate" ratings.

The 1965 SD groups seem to do about as well as the 1965 PD groups in terms of counselor-rated movement toward rehabilitation, but differences between experimental and control groups are not statistically significant. However, the trends are in an encouraging direction. In the 1966 study the VRP scale was replaced by the Employability Interview, which more clearly reveals increased motivation to work among the experimental *Ss*.

Close inspection of Figure 17.6 shows an initial difference between the experimental and control groups in motivation to work. The control group shows a slightly higher motivation to work than the experimental group on the pre-measure. This may be accounted for if, as some readers may prefer, the control group for the 1966 study is considered as another "treatment" group rather than a "control" group in the traditional sense. The *Ss* who comprised the controls for the 1966 study were vocationally handicapped individuals, as were the experimental *Ss*. However, they were all employed at the time of testing as workers at the Sheltered Workshop. Although no formal group treatment program was available to them (as it was to the experimental group) the Sheltered Workshop experience may be thought of as another form of therapeutic intervention. Without becoming unduly speculative about changes over time for the control subjects' motivation to work, it does seem warranted to infer that an explanation of the initial difference between experimental and control groups in motivation to work may be found in the differential occupational status of the two groups at the beginning of the study.

There were significantly fewer absences and consistently fewer dropouts over sessions in the 1966 groups than in the 1965 SD groups. It seems apparent that both these changes may be accounted for by the change in format and the more intensive nature of the 1966 group experience.

The *Ss* perception of therapeutic conditions in his group was measured in two ways, by using the Relationship Inventory as an early-late measure in 1965, and by using items from the Relationship Inventory in a semantic differential format as a daily measure in 1966. In general, there appears to be a lack of correlation between results on these instruments and group outcome, as we found previously by van der Veen (1965).

Two questions were asked of the data from the second part of the Group

Experience Rating form: (1) do group members perceive each other as increasing in genuineness, risk-taking, sensitivity to others, and openness over sessions? Although perceived genuineness does not show a significant change, sensitivity to others does modify in the expected direction. Risk-taking and openness also change in the direction expected, although these variables appear to be susceptible to the "end effect" and (2) do the group members come to see themselves as the other group members see them on the four dimensions assessed, over the course of the group experience? Contrary to expectations, results indicate that they do not.

Third Year — 1967

In the third year, additional changes were made in program format and content, though they generally reflected the orientation adopted in the second year with regard to a more experiential program, an intensified session schedule, and presentation via audio-tape recordings.

The revised Program[8] is called PEER for "Planned Experiences for Effective Relating." The goals were redefined and the format modified as follows:

Purpose and Design

The general purpose of PEER is to help people learn to relate more fully and effectively to the world around them. To accomplish this, PEER provides a series of structured opportunities for each participant to: (1) express more easily his genuine feelings and receive the genuine feelings of others, (2) inquire more actively into his own experience, and (3) try new behaviors in the group, thereby enabling the individual to increase his awareness of the choices available to him, understand better how he functions in groups, and gain more control over what happens between him and other people.[9]

To make the best use of the resources participants bring with them, PEER emphasizes: (1) *personal strengths,* rather than weaknesses, and potentialities rather than deficiencies; (2) *learning through experience,* the immediate, shared experience of the group, to which all members make meaningful contribution; and (3) *self-direction,* in that the group can conduct its own sessions using the PEER guidelines, thereby making it unnecessary to have a professional leader.

In other words, PEER's orientation is positive, experiential, and self-directing.

Format

PEER consists of ten sessions. Each session is approximately two hours long and begins with an exercise, instructions for which are presented on an audio-

[8] This program was written by Betty Berzon and Jerome Reisel.
[9] The PEER goals are based on those defined by Warren G. Bennis in "Goals and Meta-Goals of Laboratory Training," *NTL Human Relations Training News,* Vol. 6, No. 3, 1962.

tape recording. After the instructions are given, the tape continues to run silently for the remainder of each session, enabling intervention with additional instructions during certain exercises.

The ten PEER exercises can be accommodated to a variety of schedules, from a three-and-a-half day workshop with three sessions a day, to ten weeks with one session a week.

Content

Outline of Session Goals

Sequence	*Session No.*	*Session Goals*
I. Group Building	1	Effect personal involvement in the group
	2	Establish group norms
	3	Orient to facilitative feedback
	4	Review of concepts presented
II. Data Flow and Feeling Intensification	5	Generate interpersonal trust
	6	Identify coping abilities
	7	Deepen interpersonal participation in the group
	8	Focus on growth motivation
	9	Re-inforce growth motivation
III. Separation	10	Recognize behavior change and bind off separation process

The PEER Package

The PEER materials are presented as a package, which includes five tape recordings, an Operations Manual, and forms for evaluation by participants of the effectiveness of PEER.

The Operations Manual contains suggestions for composing groups, structuring expectations of potential group members, initial orienting of groups, administering of evaluation forms, and so on.

The Operations Manual is for use by the group leader, the sponsoring organization, or whoever is taking responsibility for setting up the group. All that is needed in addition to the PEER Package is a tape recorder and a meeting place.

Evaluation of PEER

At the time this chapter was written, the program described above was in the process of being evaluated.

The Future

It is anticipated that in future development of this approach the emphasis will be on customized programs for use in such settings as family groups, corrections and rehabilitation, community relations, and the professional training of teachers, counselors, ministers, et al. There is no doubt in our minds that the use of self-directed groups does have a future.

REFERENCES

AIKEN, E. G. Alternate forms of a semantic differential for measurement of changes in self-description. *Psychological Reports,* 1965, 16, 177-178.

BARRETT-LENNARD, G. T. Dimensions of therapist response as causal factors in therapeutic change. *Psychological Monographs,* 1962, 76 (43, Whole No. 562).

BERZON, BETTY. The self-directed therapeutic group: An evaluative study. Western Behavioral Sciences Institute, La Jolla, California, 1964. Also, paper read at American Psychological Association, Los Angeles, California, 1964.

BERZON, BETTY, PIOUS, CONSTANCE, and FARSON, R. E. The therapeutic event in group psychotherapy: A study of subjective reports by group members. *Journal of Individual Psychology,* Fall 1963.

BERZON, BETTY and SOLOMON, L. N. The self-directed therapeutic group: An exploratory study. *International Journal of Group Psychotherapy,* 1964, 14, 366-369.

BERZON, BETTY, PIOUS, CONSTANCE, DREYFUSS, ANN and FARSON, R. D. Personal experience in therapeutic groups. Mimeographed paper. Western Behavioral Sciences Institute, La Jolla, California, 1964.

COCH, L. and FRENCH, J. R. P., JR. Overcoming resistance to change. *Human Relations,* 1948, 1, 512-532.

GENDLIN, E. T. and GEIST, MARILYN. Experiencing scale. Wisconsin Psychiatric Institute, University of Wisconsin, 1962.

GOODMAN, G. E. Emotional self-disclosure in psychotherapy. Unpublished Ph.D. dissertation, University of Chicago, 1962.

GREENING, THOMAS C. The transparent self: UCLA extension course. Psychological Service Associates, Los Angeles, California. Mimeographed paper, 1965.

HARROW, M. ASTRACHAN, B., BECKER, R., MILLER, J. and SCHWARTZ, A. Influence of the psychotherapist on the emotional climate in group therapy. *Human Relations*, 1967, 20, 49-64.

JOINT COMMISSION ON MENTAL ILLNESS AND HEALTH. *Action for mental health: Final, report of the Joint Commission on Mental Illness and Health.* New York: Basic Books, 1961.

PEARL, A. and RIESSMAN, F. *New careers for the poor.* New York: Free Press, 1965.

REIFF, R. and RIESSMAN, F. The indigenous nonprofessional: A strategy of change in community action and community mental health programs. *Community Mental Health Journal*, Monograph Series, No. 1, 1965.

ROGERS, C. R. The necessary and sufficient conditions for therapeutic personality change. *Journal of Consulting Psychology*, 1957, 21, 95-103.

ROGERS, C. R. *On becoming a person.* Boston: Houghton Mifflin Company, 1961.

TRUAX, C. B. A scale for the measurement of accurate empathy. Wisconsin Psychiatric Institute, University of Wisconsin, 1961.

TRUAX, C. B. The measurement of depth of intrapersonal exploration. Wisconsin Psychiatric Institute, University of Wisconsin, 1962a.

TRUAX, C. B. A tentative scale for the measurement of therapist genuineness of self-congruence. Wisconsin, 1962b.

TRUAX, C. B. A tentative scale for the measurement of unconditional positive regard. Wisconsin Psychiatric Institute, University of Wisconsin, 1962c.

TRUAX, C. B. A tentative approach to the conceptualization and measurement of intensity and intimacy of interpersonal contact as a variable in psychotherapy. Wisconsin Psychiatric Institute, University of Wisconsin, 1962d.

TRUAX, C. B. Constructive personality change. Mimeographed paper. University of Wisconsin, 1962e.

VAN DER VEEN, F. Dimensions of client and therapist behavior in relation to outcome. Proceedings of the 73rd Annual Convention of the American Psychological Association, 1965, 279-280.

VAN DER VEEN, F. and TOMLINSON, T. M. Problem expression scale. Wisconsin Psychiatric Institute, University of Wisconsin, 1962.

WHITE, R. and LIPPITT, R. Leader behavior and member reaction in three "social climates," in D. Cartwright and A. Zander (Eds.), *Group dynamics: Research and theory.* Evanston, Ill.: Row, Peterson and Company, 1953. Pp. 585-611.

18

Companionship as Therapy:

The Use of Nonprofessional Talent*

GERALD GOODMAN

Our work at Berkeley is based on the assumption that untutored therapeutic talent can be discovered and put to use. We built and are studying an experimental program that uses one-to-one relationships differing from the traditional therapy enterprise in several important ways. The "therapists" were male college students, and their "clients" were fifth- and sixth-grade boys referred by parents as having emotional problems. They met two or three times a week, according to convenience and inclination, and meetings lasted from one to five hours. The relationships were limited to the span of a school year. Their "office" was the community. The "method" was companionship.

Most of the questions put to the project are still unanswered because our research is in progress — so our findings are limited. We will tell of several innovations for selecting students, forming dyads, and studying companionship process. We will also describe our methods for orienting and supervising students and some general companionship patterns. However, the center of our project may be most visible through the following abbreviated description of one companionship described by a student.

* The Interpersonal Relations Project was initiated and coordinated by Stiles Hall-University YMCA under a grant from the National Institute of Mental Health Applied Research Branch (#00992) in collaboration with the Berkeley Public Schools and the Institute of Human Development (University of California, Berkeley). This chapter was written with the help of my associate director, Earl C. Brennen, and our staff: Warren Robinson, Barbara Short, Evelyn Sheffer Talbert, and Bonny Kay Parke. I am grateful to Drs. Henry Maas, Brewster Smith, and Mr. William Davis for their guidance.

Walt and Tim

First visit: I picked up Tim at school as we had previously arranged and drove to the park. We hiked in the hills for an hour or so and then sat down to talk. He was eager to talk about his activities at school, particularly sports. I talked a little about photography but spent most of the time listening to him.

Sixth visit: I met Tim after school and we drove up to the park. We walked around the hills, throwing rocks, looking at things, and shouting. Since we met, Tim seemed to be acting as if he felt inferior to me or at least felt he had to agree to my suggestions. I told him that if we were to be friends, we had to be able to look at each other more as equals — this struck a responsive chord. Later he told me about his brother who had died last year.

Eighth visit: . . . He showed me an album of pictures of his dead brother and told me how sad he was about it, which moved me — it made me feel sad too — and I told him how I felt; we were very close for a few moments. We then went out and I showed him how to ride his bike. He did very well and seemed happy. I think this has been our best session so far.

Twelfth visit: . . . We decided to make some repairs on Tim's bike. He mentioned not getting along well with his mother. I asked him why, and he spent some time telling me of his difficulties with her. Then we talked more about his family (his father left home) and he told me many of his feelings about it. I said that I was very interested but was afraid to show it because he might think I was prying. He said 'No' — and that he felt much better after talking to me like this. The rest of the meeting was quiet; we worked on his bike and then watched TV.

Fourteenth visit: Tim said he had some difficulty in describing me [during an interview with a project staff member] so I told him about my family problems and how I felt lonesome and inferior as a boy. He said that his description of me was indeed right and that he felt that way too. We talked more and more easily about feelings this time then ever before, but I'm worried about how to handle the situation because Tim seems to have mixed feelings about talking. Sometimes he really likes it — other times he is very nervous. Tim wanted to work on an old train set. We worked without success for an hour or so on the train. While we worked, Tim got talking about how he visited the doctor the other day and how modest he is — though he knows it's silly. I unwittingly felt I had to tell him how I used to be modest also. This seemed to disappoint him as I think he just wanted to tell me something about himself. We then went and played baseball for a couple or more hours. Relaxed and enjoyed it but not talking much.

Sixteenth visit: He told me of his disgust at having his head examined by a doctor, about the headaches he's been having for several years. We printed some photos that we had taken. Tim was happy about how the pictures came out. He told me later that he thought it was great that a kid like him and me were friends.

Seventeenth visit: After the movie, he told me he was having a tough time sleeping and said he had a lot of problems. I asked him 'what?' but he said he didn't want to talk about it. We started painting a picture together and really enjoyed it. He painted a picture of me with a question mark on it and said I was 'un-understandable.' That was, I assume, a broad hint that I should talk more about myself — something I have rarely done.

Eighteenth visit: As we were carving soap he told me he had a lot of problems but didn't want to discuss them with me then. I told him that I wanted to hear about them whenever he wanted to talk about them.

Nineteenth visit: ... We went for a coke with his mother, brother, sister, and several of her friends. Tim seemed very anxious to show me off as his friend.

Twentieth visit: We went to the ice skating rink. I'd never skated before and Tim seemed anxious to teach me something new and exciting as I taught him how to ride a bike. I learned fairly quickly, and we enjoyed ourselves. Tim seemed to enjoy my obvious nervousness and the opportunity it gave him to encourage and teach me ...

Twenty-fourth visit: We took pictures of Tim's dog. Tim was rather nervous and hard to talk to. He said he felt things too deeply and alluded to his brother's death. But when I asked him what he meant, he quickly shifted the subject. Tim said he was doing better in school and his (tension) headaches were gone.

Twenty-seventh visit: We got talking about beggars — whom he said shouldn't beg. I got excited and launched into a speech on the "other America" and basic economics — but ended talking about my own mother who lives rather poorly and can't get work. Tim took the talk about my mother with great sympathy, making me glad I had told him. We went down and shot pool for a couple of hours afterwards.

Thirtieth visit: ... One time as I was kidding him about the mess he had made of the kite strings, he said between bursts of laughter 'you little bastard.' I laughed and said, 'I'm not a little bastard, I'm a big bastard.' We laughed some more. Funny, I never expected to find joy at someone calling me a bastard, but I felt wonderful. This was something Tim could not have done before and it made me feel that he liked me. I tried to tell him later that I liked the fact that we were so open with each other as I had very few people I could be open and free with and say what I wanted. Tim said little but I felt he understood and agreed it was good.

Thirty-first visit: ... While we were flying the kite, we talked about his turtle, his father — whom he dislikes — and sex. He wanted me to describe how it feels to have intercourse. I tried to tell him but admitted that it was almost impossible to give an adequate description ... we agreed that it was important for us to be able to talk over ideas, questions, and problems with each other.

Thirty-seventh visit: Tim seemed very selfish to me and I got angry with him. Before we left he asked what made me mad and I told him. He said he was sorry. I felt embarrassed and said to forget it.

Forty-second visit: During the two hours in the darkroom we managed to print only three pictures. I get rather perfectionistic about photography technique and though I tried to let Tim do what he wanted, I was heavy-handed with him and he was both bored and angry. I was angry both at him and at myself for making the visit bad and realized both then and after that I was making the same mistake as before: not letting things flow comfortably but trying to structure them rigidly. We exchanged a few hot words.

Forty-third visit: ... Tim's mother and I got into a discussion on the recent events on campus. Tim was angry because he had been ignored and told me so. I apologized.

Forty-fourth visit: We rode our bikes around the park. Tim told me about his family and his mixed feelings towards both his mother and his father. I told him my feelings toward him and tried to explain a few things that I thought fouled up our last couple of meetings. I also told him how joining the project and my relationship with him had changed my career plans. I now want to do something where I can work directly with people.

Forty-fifth visit: While we were playing chess, I put, unthinkingly, my feet up on the coffee table. He told me I was very rude and treated things in his house with no respect. I was mad and told him he had hurt my feelings. I said that he might find some way to criticize me without making me feel that bad. He apologized and we agreed to forget it, but it left a breach between us for the rest of the meeting. We played chess for a while longer and, although interested, we didn't have a very good time.

Forty-seventh visit: I feel that we are not so close now as we have been before. I don't know why and it bothers me. I haven't brought it up yet with Tim, but I plan to very soon.

Fifty-third visit: I wanted to walk around in the hills and talk, but he didn't. We agreed after some argument to go down and shoot some pool. We didn't have a very good time shooting pool. Tim got depressed because he did not do very well. As we were driving home, he asked me how I was going to write up this visit. I told him I would put it down as "so-so." He felt that it was a bad visit and said he wished we had followed my suggestion to walk and talk.

Fifty-fourth visit: Tim talked about my teaching him how to ride a bike about five or six months ago and said he felt I was successful where others had failed because we were friends . . . since I liked him, I was patient. This really made me feel good and I told him. We had a bare knuckles sparring match for a few minutes (no hiting above the neck or below the belt). We occasionally do this and I, for lack of space, rarely report it to the project, but I have noticed a definite change in these sparring matches since we started having them. At first they bothered me a little as Tim seemed really aggressive while at the same time scared like he didn't trust me. Sort of hard to describe but definitely there. Now the sparring matches are a lot of fun for both of us. I feel that he trusts me much more completely than he used to. This is a subtle change but it's only one example of many things which have made us more comfortable with each other. There is another change — until a few weeks ago, Tim never asked me how I described our relationship to the project. Now we regularly talk about it. I told him I would describe this visit as very good. Though we had not discussed anything personal, I felt very comfortable and good with him. He said 'Yes, there is something between us, a feeling of warmth.' I told him that it was great simply to be able to be with him and say whatever came into my mind without wondering 'will he like that or not' which I worried about during our earlier meetings. Tim said he would call me tomorrow. This is another change. Until about a month ago, Tim would never call me and this hurt me a little. I felt sometimes he didn't care. On the way down to the Photo Club Tim talked about the short time we have left together on the project — it is very much on his mind recently — and said he hated to lose me as I was the only person he could talk 'personally' to. Tim seems jealous of time in the face of the end of the project. He really wants to talk a lot, and is unhappy when we don't. He has always felt that our talks were 'the best part' of our relationship, but before they just happened — now he is actively pushing them. He seems to want my understanding more than ever before.

Sixtieth visit: As we carved our soap figures Tim talked about his family. I just listened. He was much more open than he had been in the past about his brother. He said that he didn't like his brother and only realized his affection for him when the brother died. We were quiet for a while. Then Tim said 'how great' this session was. Then he said 'I love you, Walt, I really like you, I really like you a lot.' I said that I thought he was right the first time in saying 'love' although it was a little embarrassing for me as well as for him to use the term — I said that I felt that way about him too. He nodded and said 'yes, love' . . . We both felt completely at ease, talking as we felt like it and working on our carvings. I felt that Tim was happy to be able to express his feelings openly towards me, and it made me feel good for him to be able to do so.

Sixty-sixth (last) visit: After buying chemicals we drove back to Tim's house while he talked a mile a minute about his experiments. He also talked about the friendship he has with his school teacher. He is very proud and happy about this friendship. When we got up to his house we talked more about his experiments. I told him I thought I had changed a lot during the eight months we had been together. I was more interested in people and had changed my career plans. He said that he had changed a lot too, that at the beginning he had not liked people very much and had few friends at school, but that just last week he formed a club of boys and was president. Tim wanted to mix some chemicals but I told him I didn't want to, so we went outside instead. His mother was there. Tim told us that he thought I was terrible the first time we met but got to like me more as time went on until he liked me so much he couldn't say it well. I thought this was really important because Tim talked so openly about himself and me in front of his mother. This is the first time he has done this.

In this companionship we can note the clear and apparently systematic growth of acceptance, emotional disclosure, and empathic understanding — elements that seem to make a therapeutic environment. The relationship began through the manufacture of a research project — a companionship with contract — but it grew into a genuine friendship characterized by mutual respect, honesty, and understanding.

Walt's peers and our staff described him as open, warm, and understanding during a selection group session. We hired him for these qualities. When he joined the project, Walt was a twenty-year-old political science major who wanted to teach in college. He was active in student affairs and was arrested for participating in the Free Speech Movement sit-in on the Berkeley Campus.

Working on the project changed his career plans, and he is now a graduate student in psychology. Walt's description of his relationship with Tim was drawn from a visit report form, which is filled out by all counselors after each visit.

Tim was ten; his mother applied to the project because ". . . it seems that his last hope for a close relationship with men in his own family is gone." She said he had to struggle to assert himself with three strong-minded females. Tim was further described as being extremely modest, feeling unsure of himself with people, and not liking himself. The number and intensity of his personal problems appeared higher than the average applicant to the project. His teacher described him as somewhat isolated and attention-seeking, but his classmates saw few problems and considered him quite likable. He rejected professional psychotherapy. Most of Tim's problems were still with him as the program ended even though both his mother and teacher saw the beginnings of improvement, especially in his self-esteem and relations with other children. One year later, the changes were more noticeable. Tim liked himself and had more self-confidence with friends.

If we could have tape-recorded the complete dialogue of Walt's and Tim's companionship, a number of segments would probably be indistinguishable from various forms of professional therapy. Much of it might sound like client-centered therapy because our orientation and supervision of counselors was influenced by client-centered theory. We wanted our counselors to avoid making interpretations, giving advice, using tactical questions, adopting an authoritarian stance, or trying other treatment strategies commonly seen as belonging to the "expert" therapist. The limited training our counselors received focused on the functions of empathic understanding, the spontaneous sharing of feelings, and the acceptance of behaviors boys sometimes use to take care of themselves. That is, we asked our counselors to incur the emotional risks of self-disclosure, vigorous listening, and respecting the other's defenses. We do not know how often these conditions were met in the fifty companionships established each year. Adequate study would have required tape recordings or other forms of intervention difficult to implement or capable of cancelling the dyads' sense of freedom. Some clues as to the influence of our orientation on companionship interaction are currently being drawn from counselors' visit reports.

Some Assumptions and Questions

It was our assumption that client-centered conditions were within the experience of our counselors, and we hoped they would try them out in a more sustained manner with their boys. Half of the counselors attended weekly small group sessions aimed at the implementation of these conditions. The staff was immediately available to those who were having difficulty. The assumption that our counselors were familiar with the conditions we hoped to establish in the companionships rested on their successful behavior during the selection session (an experimental group assessment of interpersonal traits to be described later). We also assumed that listening to feelings without predilection and reflecting them with genuine self-disclosure is something most people have done on occasion. In fact, our entire project is built on the idea that some people are "naturals" at creating a therapeutic climate in a fairly wide range of situations. These people can provide an important pool of therapeutic talent, talent that can be used "as is" or slightly trained for both traditional and novel therapy enterprises.

Most current programs using nonprofessionals in some direct therapeutic capacity have been primarily concerned with administrative feasibility and have not studied the critical psychological questions: are those useful criteria for describing untutored therapeutic talent? If so, can reliable selection procedures be built? What brings people to such work? What special methods are needed to begin studying process and outcome? The future use of nonprofessionals will be shaped by these questions, and they are targets of our research. We have no solid answers yet. However, data have been collected, new methods have been developed and tried, and analysis is underway. I can offer our current reactions to the above questions, along with descriptions of our methods and a few tentative findings.

Are There Useful Criteria for Untutored Therapeutic Talent?

At times I feel there will never be any generally accepted criteria for therapeutic talent. Each system of therapy holds its own view of effective therapist behavior and its own training methods. Clinical training programs in and out of the universities have offered little empirical or theoretical work on therapeutic talent, which appears to be thought of as a minor variable or an impossible concept. Schools usually select their students with criteria based on academic achievement and letters of recommendation limited to the amplification of academic achievements. Evidence of therapeutic talent is generally missing, and committees, at best, attempt to extrapolate intuitively a few clues about personality into judgments of future success in the therapy role. The major concern is predicting compatibility with a given training program. Of course, a few selected students are eventually screened out because they disappoint their clinical supervisors, evidence pathology, fail academically, or leave by choice — but these factors can be unrelated to therapeutic talent.

In general, therapists are brought into professional training on evidence that often has little to do with the critical skills they must actually use in the field. This situation is accompanied by a shortage of research on the prediction of therapeutic effectiveness, which left us without a successful model for selecting nonprofessional therapists. A model could be built by creating a picture of personal requisites that seem most likely to generate conditions outlined by various therapy theories. For our purposes the therapy theory would have to be convertible to a program using nonexperts.

This last consideration limited our choice because most therapy theories imply, specify, or simply generate a therapy environment established by an expert. The therapist may formulate his patient, offer advice, take on a neutral stance, or even prescribe desensitization schedules. The medical styles of "patient management" and professional distance have surely influenced the mainstream of psychotherapy practice. Being an expert, omitting personal reactions, and specifying antecedent causes of current distress are necessary conditions or by-products of most therapy theory. The traditional therapist usually attempts to use the "power of knowledge" in understanding his patient better than his patient understands himself. In short, his therapeutic techniques seldom depart from the historical conception of a professional healer. These theories cannot provide a working model for nonprofessional therapists who do not have the expertise to formulate or prescribe.

In contrast, client-centered theory seems to provide an appropriate model for selecting nonprofessional criteria. Each of the necessary and sufficient conditions of therapeutic personality change formulated by Rogers (1957) can be seen in everyday behavior, even though their simultaneous and sustained appearance is less evident outside the therapist's office. Some people are regarded by those close to them as "good listeners," good at knowing what the other person's feelings mean to him. Others are better at being spontaneous, open, "straight," self-disclosing. Some people who do not need many specific conditions to feel positive regard for humans are often described as having "an accepting nature." A few unusual people possess these traits in strong combinations and are clearly seen by many to be straight, accepting, good listeners. They should be able occasionally to approximate the conditions of client-centered therapy without trying, and, with orientation or slight training, they might create this type of therapeutic environment quite frequently.

This reasoning led us to adapt a set of criteria for therapeutic talent based on client-centered theory. We wanted to find people with these traits and needed a quick reliable selection procedure. Some previous work showed promising results at assessing client-centered conditions from tape recordings of interviews (e.g., Carkhuff and Truax, 1965) and questionnaires (e.g., Barrett-Lennard, 1962), but they were too elaborate for our large-scale selection program. We decided to build a new assessment procedure. Early attempts using multiple interviews with several rating instruments generated unsatisfactory results. Eventually, it seemed that a small group assessment method would do the job.

The project's attempt to operationalize and quantify such vague variables as openness, understanding, and acceptance can be most kindly described as a crude but promising first step. We simply manufactured a structured small group situation in which students were asked to rate one another after trying to listen and disclose to a stranger. The sessions were often stunning, stressful, and revealing for staff and students. However, much work is needed to clarify the relation between this selection procedure and client-centered conditions.

For example, the constancy of interpersonal style over time and situation is still a question for study. Variance among assessment groups and between group and dyadic behavior will reduce predictability. Still, some early informal observations and a few findings suggest that this new technique can be superior to interviews or paper-pencil self-descriptions at quantifying interpersonal traits such as openness, understanding, and acceptance. We refer to the procedure as GAIT (Group Assessment of Interpersonal Traits).

GAIT. Seven or eight applicants gather into structured groups where they perform several interpersonal tasks and prepare systematic descriptions of one another. As they enter the room, each applicant receives a written set of instructions and a sociometric rating scale, along with a rationale for the entire procedure. A warm-up period invites students to ask the group a personal question "as if" it were an individual. Anyone who wishes can answer the question briefly, and the questions and answers continue around the group until all have asked and answered once. Now the applicants are asked to think of two immediate interpersonal concerns they could share with the group and to state them briefly in writing during a coffee break. The majority of these statements tell of discomfort with alienation, guilt, dependency, self-worth, and honesty; they usually involve girl friends, parents, pals, and siblings. These self-descriptive statements are used as catalysts to start dialogues between pairs of applicants, where one person elaborates or explores his own statement as his partner attempts to understand feelings. Here is an outline of the procedure:

(1) The applicants sit in a circle and wear letter tags. "Mr. A" begins by reading one of his statements to the group. We call him the "Discloser."

(2) Any applicant can spontaneously respond to the Discloser and engage him in a five-minute dialogue. We call him the "Understander." The remainder of the group is asked to remain silent.

(3) In the rare instance (about one in fifty) where no response is offered to the Discloser's first statement within a minute, the Discloser is asked to read his second statement.

(4) Understanders are asked to avoid giving advice, making judgments, asking questions, or offering interpretations (a difficult request for many applicants). We suggest they reflect feelings, disclose their own relevant thoughts or immediate reactions, or simply "listen very hard" while saying nothing.

(5) When the five-minute dialogue has terminated, the Understander tries a brief (thirty second) recap of the interaction.

(6) The recap is followed by the Discloser's re-reading of his initial statement. This contrast between initial statement and recap gives the group a sharper view of the Understander's grasp of the situation and

his success at facilitating the expansion of the "presenting problem."

(7) The recap ends the first dyadic interaction. A second dyad is formed as "Mr. B" becomes the Discloser and anyone who has not been an Understander responds to him. The group continues to form dyads in this manner until everyone in the circle has performed both tasks.

(8) When finished, the group has observed each of its members in two dyads. All have attempted to be genuine and understanding in a mild stress situation. At this point they are asked to rate one another (but not themselves) on sociometric scales describing interpersonal traits: Understanding, Openness, Acceptance, Rigidity, etc. Attending staff members use the same scale to rate applicants.

(9) Finally, when the scales are completed, the group is open for free discussion, with the staff answering questions. The entire procedure takes about an hour and a half.

We realized this task would ask a great deal of applicants, and we told them so. Some would be dissatisfied with their performance; we also told them that. But a sustained relationship with a troubled boy might ask more of them and cause frequent feelings of self-dissatisfaction. For us, the central product of GAIT is the direct assessment of each applicant's solution for solving two difficult interpersonal problems before he assumes the trials of an actual project companionship. These interpersonal problems are: (a) how best to take the risk of disclosing an important part of one's self in conditions far from ideal (being assessed by a manufactured group of strangers) and (b) how to enter another person's frame of reference and understand his feelings with few questions, no judgments, interpretations, or advice-giving (all in five minutes!). A perfect solution was quite improbable.

Applicants feeling much anxiety about performing the tasks were left with avenues of escape. They could simply leave the group during the coffee break or after reading instructions; they could remain and avoid disclosing themselves by reading a less personal or abstract statement to the group. Avoidance of the listening task was infrequently accomplished by interjecting small lectures on unrelated matters or turning away from the Discloser's statement with unrealistic "quickie" solutions, etc. Those few appearing to need escape were usually rejected through the poor ratings given by other applicants and staff.

The sociometric instrument contained seven statements descriptive of interpersonal style. It also contained space for rank ordering the applicants on judged potential as successful project counselors. The statements below were linked with six-step scales ranging from "very much like him" to "very much not like him." Terms in parentheses are variable names; asterisks denote selection criteria variables thought to reflect attributes suggested by client-centered theory.

SOCIOMETRIC ITEMS	VARIABLE NAME
(1) I feel he understands what others really mean.	*(Understanding)
(2) He seems sad, blue, discontented.	(Depressed)
(3) He appears honest, frank, emotionally open.	*(Open)
(4) I see him as a mild, reserved, quiet person.	(Quiet)
(5) He seems warm, patient, and accepting.	*(Accepting-Warm)
(6) He appears set in his ways.	(Rigid)
(7) I see him as a relaxed, easy-going person.	(Relaxed)
(8) A composite of Items #1, 3, and 5.	*(Therapeutic Talent)

Eventually, we decided to dichotomize the scale ratings of the above items into "yes-no" attributions, and individual scores became the percentage of "yes" responses for each trait. The correlation of applicant and staff ratings on the Therapeutic Talent variable produced an estimated reliability of .56 (Spearman-Brown formula). It should be noted that the reliability of these "therapeutic" traits is not far below one of the most "visible" interpersonal dimensions: Quiet versus Outgoing (.69). The ratings of applicants and staff seemed close enough to combine so that an individual's score on each trait was usually generated by nine observers: six applicants and three staff members.

The following criteria were used for hiring applicants: (1) a minimum score of 60 per cent Therapeutic Talent (the composite index containing the Understanding, Open, and Accepting-Warm variables). That is, 60 per cent of the raters must produce scores on this index that fall on the "yes" side of the scale. (2) A minimum score of 50 per cent on each of the three separate criterion traits. An applicant with a score of less than 50 per cent on any one of these traits was not hired. (3) At least 30 per cent of the group must rank the applicant in the upper half on judged potential as a project counselor. (4) Finally, any of the attending staff (two experienced clinicians and a graduate student) could veto those candidates who caused them any doubt or appeared emotionally unstable. (These rather complex criteria were based on empirical and intuitive considerations during the pilot phase of GAIT.) Incidentally, Walt (who described his companionship earlier in this chapter) was ranked in the top 25 per cent of all applicants.

The GAIT criteria asks much of students. Of 179 applicants who applied for the final two program years, fifty-six failed to meet the criteria (a 31 per cent rejection rate). However, it would be erroneous to infer that 69 per cent of the male students at Berkeley would meet the criteria. Certain forms of screening are operative before the student attends GAIT. It seems that considerable self-selection is involved in applying to the project in the first place. We suspect the applicant group views the prospect of this interpersonally demanding job with more comfort than the average student. In addition, our applicants seem to have considerable prior experience working with children e.g., as camp counselors. A surprising number eventually join the Peace

Corps, Vista, and the like. Just how atypical our applicants are cannot be known at this time. Considering both motivation and talent to meet GAIT criteria, we guess they are quite special — but still available in enough quantity to form an important pool of mental health manpower. More self-selection occurs in the period between initial application and GAIT assessment. About 25 per cent of those who prepared applications decided to withdraw; some are discouraged after a preliminary talk with a staff member in which project demands are clarified.

Even though we consider GAIT a useful first step in the selection of therapeutic talent, further revision and study is needed to provide elegant assessment.[1] Some of the problems we anticipated during the planning stage have been solved, some have remained, and a few appeared to be pseudo-problems. For example, we wondered if the Understanding and Disclosure scores might be primarily determined by an applicant's partner. An extremely cooperative, self-disclosing, articulate Discloser may provide the stimuli for a higher Understanding score; conversely, a receptive, warm, empathic Understander might generate behavior in his partner that would be rated a high score on Openness. It seemed that this type of dyadic specificity and unequal stimuli could severely bias the assessment of any individual (correcting the unequal stimuli problem through the use of an actor or movies, or by modifying GAIT so that each applicant has several partners for each task would create a new set of problems to solve). As we left our paper-planning and applied GAIT to a live situation, it became apparent that our target traits were observable beyond the influence of partner's style. Good listeners could display their ability to see and hear the reserve of a recalcitrant Discloser. Those willing to be self-disclosed, paired with a poor Understander, could be open by disclosing their immediate experience of not being known, etc. Some Disclosers switched from their initial statement to revealing immediate anxiety at being personal with the group, and they generally received high scores on Openness. In addition, the severely limited Understanders and Disclosers were rare and stood out; they obviously reduced the opportunity of their partners, and the group rating somehow seemed to compensate for the problem. Nevertheless, it does seem likely that a few applicants were rejected solely because of their unlucky pairing with poor Understanders and Disclosers.

GAIT looked good to us. It appeared to be getting at important aspects of interpersonal competence. A systematic test of these impressions was difficult because there are no clear external criteria for the Openness, Understanding, and Acceptance-Warmth variables. Asking GAIT scores to predict the eventual success of a counselor — as measured by boy outcome data — seems too severe a test at this time. Such a design must rely on two large intervening assumptions irrelevant to GAIT validity. First, we must assume that our

---

[1] A book on companionship-therapy (in progress) will report our current research on GAIT's reliability and success in predicting field performance.

assessment of change in troubled boys is valid, and second, that Openness, Understanding, and Acceptance-Warmth indeed create a therapeutic climate in our project. A weakness in either assumption would erroneously appear as a weakness in GAIT's predictive ability. We will study GAIT's prediction of outcome, but our preliminary work has employed questionnaires as external criteria.

The questionnaires given to applicants after successfully completing GAIT were directed at students' attitudes toward human nature (Wrightsman, 1964), their patterns of self-disclosure (Jourard, 1964), and their degree of social insight (Chapin, 1942). We did not administer these questionnaires to rejected applicants; asking them to submit to additional assessment after being rejected seemed like a rude imposition. Our failure to collect these data prevented us from comparing the lowest GAIT criteria scores with the bulk of our external measures. Thus, the analyses were weakened — being limited to applicants scoring "medium" and "high" on Open, Understanding, and Accepting-Warm.

A sample of findings seems necessary to round out this picture of GAIT. Students receiving high scores on Accepting-Warm were compared with those receiving medium scores. The two groups were compared on the questionnaires mentioned above, and on two forms administered earlier to all applicants: the ACL (Adjective Check List, Gough and Heilbrun, 1965) and an application form requesting information on family background, etc.

Those high on GAIT Accepting-Warm had more "person-oriented"[2] vocational goals ($p = .05$).[3] Their self-descriptions on the ACL were less Dominant (.01), more Deferent (.05), less Achieving (.05), and somewhat less Defensive (.10). They described human nature as less Favorable (.01), less Independent (.05), and more Complex (.05) on the Philosophies of Human Nature Questionnaire. Accepting-Warm students were clearly more "Quiet" on our composite Quiet-Outgoing measure (.01). During the GAIT session they were frequently chosen as Best Potential Counselor (.05) and described as more Understanding (.05) and less Rigid (.05). Half of the counselors attended weekly sensitivity training sessions throughout the year and were described by the group after each session. The high Accepting-Warm counselors were seen as less assertive (.05) during the sessions.

This sample of findings on one GAIT variable makes some sense even though the absence of rejectees' scores hinders the comparisons. It seems reasonable that accepting and warm people should choose person-oriented vocations, be less defensive and dominant, etc. Their tendency to describe human nature as complex and less favorable could also seem reasonable with some juggling of assumptions. Findings on other GAIT variables also suggest that some enduring interpersonal styles are being measured. For example

[2] From an empirically developed occupation rating scale (Rosenberg, 1957).
[3] Mann-Whitney "U"-Test (Siegal, 1956).

those seen as Mild in the group assessment were a little less active in high school and college and described themselves as less exhibiting and so forth. The top Understanders did somewhat better on the Social Insight Test and described people as, for example, more complex. Those described as Depressed had unfavorable self-descriptions and often chose vocations oriented away from people, etc. GAIT-Rigid students said that they disclosed a bit less to friends and described others as less changing and more simple, etc. In sum, this method for assessing interpersonal style shows much promise, and, with more research, may become a reliable measure of therapeutic talent.

Organizing Counselor and Boy Pairs

The GAIT was also used to help us divide our counselors into "Quiet" (approximating introvert) and "Outgoing (extrovert) groups. An individual's score on GAIT-Mild was combined with his ACL-Exhibit score and his direct self-description of "quiet" or "outgoing" (application questionnaire) into a single composite score. Incidentally, these three variables involving the views of self and others intercorrelated at .37 (N = 179). All counselors were rank ordered on the composite score and divided at the midpoint to form contrasting groups. These two groups were divided again by assigning half to group training and half to a "self-directed" status. The manipulations gave us four subgroups of counselors: quiet-trained, quiet-self-directed, outgoing-trained, and outgoing-self-directed. Research into the effects of training and the counselors' effectiveness in the field is enhanced by these refinements. To ensure that the four groups of counselors would be paired with four balanced groups of boys, a complex process of matching and pairing was instituted prior to the actual first meeting of counselor and boy.

Briefly, all the boys who applied in any one program year (about 120 each year) were first sorted into pairs matched on five variables: quiet-outgoingness, degree of pathology, race, father-in-home, and socioeconomic background.[4] One boy from each matched pair was then randomly chosen as a participant and the other was assigned to the nonparticipating control group. The participant boys were next divided into four groups, each containing a nearly equal number of Negroes, quiet boys, fatherless boys, and so on. The four equal groups of boys were evenly paired with the four groups of counselors to form an exceptionally symmetrical arrangement of counselor-boy pairs. We could now study the differential success, for example, of quiet counselors and outgoing counselors, knowing that training and certain boy characteristics were controlled. We could also compare outcome scores of quiet and outgoing boys, knowing that counselor type and training were controlled.

---

[4] Some other gross characteristics were already "matched" through restricting the program to fifth- and sixth-grade boys attending Berkeley public schools who were referred as emotionally troubled by their parents.

Counselor Orientation

All the counselors attended an orientation meeting, which comprised the bulk of "training" for many counselors. Our instructions were few and simple enough to fit on one sheet of paper. We wanted to be very open with the students, sharing our concerns, assumptions, research design, and administrative structure whenever possible or relevant. The following quotes from an information sheet should characterize the orientation.

> Counselors and boys will be paired on the basis of specific research criteria. When you have completed three teaching machine[5] sessions, we will send you general information about the boy assigned to you including his age, interests, and hobbies. It will be your task to call the parents immediately and arrange a meeting with them and their boy. They will be expecting your call. We want to know when this meeting occurs and if it has proven satisfactory for everyone. Parents will call our office if they do not feel you and the boy will get along well.
>
> You should call our office the afternoon following the initial meeting. If you and the parents and the boy feel good about starting, we will consider the relationship in progress. Arrangements for future meetings are now the responsibility of you, the boy, and his parents. . . . In sum, your obligations are: (1) call parents upon receiving our letter, (2) visit the boy's home, (3) call us the next afternoon, (4) if things go well, see your mailbox and make further arrangements to see the boy.
>
> We have prepared a brief, convenient form (Visit Report) for you to use as an aid in describing each contact. If these forms are not properly filled out by counselors, our ability to make some sense out of the relationship will be severely hampered because your observations are a crucial aspect of the program. The form asks what you did, how long it took, and what and whom you talked about. The entire task should take ten to fifteen minutes and should be done within a few hours after you leave the boy.
>
> We will soon provide you with a list of activities in which counselors and boys participated last year. Some of these may help you in finding activities of mutual interest to you and your boy. . . . Boys should not be taken into your homes, dorms, or fraternity houses without their parents' consent.
>
> Since it is our intention to establish one-to-one relationships, it would be best to avoid including a third person unless there are special circumstances. Should a third person join you during an activity, please note it on your visit report. We would like you and your boy to have much opportunity for two-person conversations that will allow the boy greater opportunity to experience trust and a feeling of closeness. Frequent spectator activities such as movies or inclusion of other people may reduce your chance of establishing a meaningful relationship.
>
> Do not promise more than you can deliver. Try not to promise the boy

---

[5] A programmed instruction course on interpersonal relations that must be taken simultaneously by two persons. It involves role playing and other forms of structured interaction designed to enhance empathy, openness, etc. (Berlin and Wyckoff, 1964.)

some activity unless you are fairly certain that it will occur. You can create an atmosphere conducive to trust by not disappointing the boy — keep your goals modest — try hard to anticipate correctly. If a visit has to be brief, let the boy know at the start. If there is some possibility that you will be late or cannot make it next time, let the boy know. In short, try to share all the things you know that touch on the relationship between you and your boy. This sharing may be difficult for you at first, but it will make you a more comfortable person to be with.

Don't use "strategy." Don't try to "treat" the boy or offer explanations for his emotional aches and growing pains. Remember that you are not a professional. Just be as honest with yourself and the boy as possible. Counselors who are genuine with their boys usually create the best relationships. We selected you carefully from a large number of applicants and feel your best resource is your personality. Take it easy with personal advice. Let the boy know that you are getting paid (at the same time, you can let him know that you are interested in working with kids). It is absolutely necessary during the early visits that you let the boy know that the relationship will end in June. If you neglect this point the boy may not be prepared for the separation and he may feel badly let down.

Please see the boy two or three times every week — no less, no more. Try not to visit less than one hour nor more than four hours. Also try not to see the boy less than four hours every week or more than eight hours every week. In sum:

	MINIMUM	MAXIMUM
Visits per week	2	3
Hours per visit	1	4
Hours per week	4	8

We feel this procedure will give the boy a sense of continuity, allow for a degree of consistency between relationships, and help us keep within our budget. You may break these limits on occasion if you feel it necessary, but let us know the reason.

Please remember that we want these relationships to be comfortable and want you to call us any time if you run into any difficulty, feel troubled, or are just curious. We may not have the answer, but we will work with you toward a solution. The chances are that you will find it easy to get along with your boy. Most ten- and eleven-year-olds enjoy the exclusive attention of adults — they usually relax when adults relax.

(A copy of this information sheet will be sent to parents.)

Consultation and Supervision

Counselors were looked after and watched over through several administrative structures. They described each contact on a visit report form. This brief form had check lists of activities, topics discussed, and feelings observed where counselors could describe their boys and themselves. Visit reports were closely read by staff members who were looking for signs of difficulty that might require staff intervention. Counselors experiencing problems and wanting help had easy access to the staff for consultation, during and after office hours. Another form of supervision came from parents. Early during the companionships parents were asked to write accounts of what they saw and felt about the project. They were also invited to call us with any concern about the companionships. A final form of consultation, for half the counselors, occurred in the sensitivity training groups where peers and their leaders often helped counselors work through problems with themselves or their boys.

Here are a few examples of counselor problems that were brought to us — along with staff reactions.

Often, counselors were expecting "deep" problem-oriented discussions rather early in the relationship. They seemed to doubt whether any benefit could come from simply being a friend to their boy. We responded to their concern with our belief that the companionship itself might be helpful through offering the boy an opportunity to try out new ways of being with people. For example, one of the boys was described by his parents as being fearful and too dependent upon others. While the pair did not discuss this problem directly, the counselor did things with the boy that involved independent behavior, such as riding bikes and meeting at new places away from home. The parents later reported their surprise that Johnny suddenly learned to ride a bike and was now taking the bus by himself for the first time.

Early in the program some counselors felt like "glorified baby-sitters" because they saw their boys as lacking problems. Occasionally, counselors would ask for details about the "presenting problems," but they were refused. These occasions were among the few instances where secrets were kept from counselors. We told them that the project advertised for troubled boys who were selected through the descriptions of parents, teachers, and peers, but these descriptions were never revealed. Some boys could be having problems that only appeared outside the companionships. It was our intention for counselors and boys to learn about each other from each other only, not through the eyes of outside observers. Our purpose would be defeated if counselors saw their boys as a bundle of symptoms in need of treatment. In short, counselors were told of our anti-diagnostic approach. As the companionships strengthened they found challenge and self-worth in trying to be genuine and understanding and accepting of the way their boys needed them. Looking for problems to correct seemed a minor concern for counselors after the first few months.

A few counselors were disenchanted because their boys were "uncooperative," "indifferent," or "ungrateful." They seemed to be saying "My boy should reach out to me more often; what's wrong with him?" But with more experience or with consultation, some counselors changed their tune to something like "I'm afraid my boy doesn't like me very much, and I want him to what's wrong with me?" When these problems came to us, our consultation usually took the form of listening, with few questions and scarce advice. In many ways, we approached our counselors as we wished them to approach their boys. Our favorite question, or piece of advice, was "Would you be able to tell your boy what you just told me?" It is in accord with our assumption that self-disclosure and emotional risk-taking usually facilitate relationships.

Some Companionship Patterns

The visit report form counselors used to describe each meeting contained various checklists and space for an open-ended description. (The description of Walt and Tim, at the start of this chapter, was drawn from visit reports.) Thus, much of our view of the companionships is through the counselors' eyes. As the companionships ended, both boys and counselors retrospectively described the entire relationship, but this material has not been analyzed. The findings in this section are from our first look at the visit reports. They are a distillation of about 4400 visits from eighty-eight dyads and only provide gross parameters of the companionships.

Here are a few relevant background statistics. The average dyad met about fifty times over the school year. Their usual meeting lasted a little less than three hours. The mean expense for snacks, hobby material, admissions, etc., was 62¢ a visit. Counselors were paid about $1.50 an hour. In general, each dyad cost the project less than $250, excluding research and administration.

The first checklist on the visit report form contained sixteen classes of activities, e.g., quiet games, sitting down to talk, and so on, and a blank space for unlisted activities.

Fourteen per cent of the average dyad's total activities consisted of participation in active sports. A similar proportion involved visits to the boys' homes. Nine per cent of the activities included a third person (usually a friend or the boys' parents). Quiet games, taking walks, and sitting down to talk each comprised about 8 per cent. The following activities are listed in rank order: working on a hobby (7 per cent); eating lunch or dinner together (6 per cent) visiting a public place (6 per cent); watching TV or listening to records (5 pel cent); taking a bike or car ride (5 per cent); visiting counselors' homes (4 per cent); spectator sports (3 per cent); seeing a movie (2 per cent); collab orating on boys' homework (less than 2 per cent); visiting friends' home (1 per cent).

The visit reports also contained a twenty-four-item checklist and blank spac for describing topics of discussion. Instructions asked for topics that wer themes of definite conversations and brief incidental subjects only when th counselor felt they were significant.

Most frequently, the dyads talked about their immediate activities or thos of past meetings (15 per cent of all reported topics). Plans for future visit and discussion of the boys' school activities were next in frequency (eac about 9 per cent). The boys' skills and talents occupied much conversatio

(8 per cent). Next in frequency came the boys' friends (6 per cent), boys' behavior or personality, boys' families, counselors' activities (each about 5 per cent). Each of the following topics, presented in rank order, were central to less than 5 per cent of the conversations: boys' mothers; boys' feelings about their counselors; counselors' feelings about their boys; the project; counselors' skills; boys' trips; boys' fathers; counselors' personality and behavior; boys' teachers; counselors' travels; counselors' friends; boys' duties at home; counselors' families in general; and counselors' mothers, fathers, and professors.

The final section of the reports contained a set of bipolar adjective items for the counselors to use in describing themselves and their boys, e.g., Bored-Interested, Sad-Happy, Relaxed-Tense, etc. The opposing words were separated by six-step scales: extremely, quite, slightly — slightly, quite, extremely. In order to study changes in the process of the companionships over time, the ratings for each dyad were divided into three equal periods (about seventeen visits in each period for the average dyad). We found that counselors tended to describe themselves as significantly less bossy during the third period of the companionship as compared to the second period. They also described their boys and themselves as becoming more relaxed and comfortable over these periods. A significant increase in ratings of emotional openness and warmth occurred between each of the three periods for both boys and counselors.

The data collected on feelings, topics discussed, and activities may eventually help us learn what aspects of companionship process can predict change in boys and counselors. We are beginning to relate these process variables to assessed changes in boys and counselors, "dyad types," background information, and other things known about the dyads. It also may be possible to outline some developmental stages of companionship. Early findings have increased our confidence in the validity of our four dyad classifications. For example, the dyads assessed and designated as "double-outgoings" (a boy with aggressive-active problems paired with an extroverted counselor) report the highest percentage of "robust" activities involving active sports and spectator sports, while "double-quiets" (a withdrawn boy paired with an introverted counselor) are highest on visits to the boy's home and going for a ride. Another tentative finding, based on parent observation, shows that boys in "double-outgoing" dyads become less aggressive and better adjusted at home than boys in other types of dyads.

In sum, our early findings on companionship process suggest that counselors become less controlling as tension is reduced over the last two-thirds of the companionships, while openness and warmth show a steady and significant increase from beginning to end. These types of analyses may give clues as to effective matching of boy-counselor pairs, the usefulness of counselor training, and which aspects of companionship process generate significant change. However, a great deal will depend upon our success at solving the disheartening methodological problems in assessing the project's effect on the rapidly changing lives of ten-year-old boys.

Closing the Companionships

Termination of the companionships was coincident with the end of the school year, but was not rigidly fixed. Most of the last "official" visits occurred within a three-week span. Participants were told that the project would pay for extending the companionships in cases where separation appeared unduly hard on the boy. This option was used only once. Most of the counselors planned future contact with their boys. Sixty per cent of the boys specifically asked for letters or phone calls from counselors remaining in Berkeley. Our incomplete followup data suggests that roughly one-third of the counselors will see their boys after the last official visit and that over one-third will phone or write.

Counselors were urged to discuss openly the end of the project at the beginning of the relationship. This point was emphasized during the orientation, the workshop, and the sensitivity training sessions. A note to both counselors and boys reminding them to prepare for termination was sent one month before the project's close. We asked parents to give us their impressions. Our first concern about the boys being let down hard by the separation was lessened by experience. We will know more about the qualities of disappointment and the effect on boys from our followup study.

A Design for Studying Change in Boys and Counselors

We are currently in the midst of studying the program's effects on boys. The design will include observations from parents, teachers, classmates, counselors, and the participant boys from two duplicate program years (N = 86). A group of rejected applicants (N = 73) and randomly selected boys (N = 200) will serve as controls. Three timepoints will be used: (1) pre-program — before the companionships began; (2) Post-program — as the companionships terminated; and (3) Followup — about one year after termination. The collection of post-data has recently been completed and some early findings suggest no dramatic difference in Pre-Post gains between the total participant and matched control groups. Incidentally, the boy described earlier in this chapter ("Tim") gained more than his matched control on most indices of change, especially those based on parent and teacher observations. But the differences were small. One of our staff comparing the two boys wrote "Tim wins — but not by a hell of a lot." Maybe Tim's case will be characteristic of our general findings. However, an adequate analysis of the program's effect on boys will require one year followup observations to see if there are delayed gains and a breakdown of the total sample into various subgroups, e.g., Negro versus Caucasian boys, Quiets versus Outgoings, fatherless boys versus boys from intact homes, boys initially described as mildly, moderately, and markedly troubled, etc.

When data collection is complete we will have parents' descriptions of their boys over three timepoints on the Adjective Check List (Gough & Heilbrun, 1965) and a thirty-five-item Problem Check List for Elementary School Boys (Goodman, 1964). Parents' estimates of change in self-esteem, attitudes toward school, and getting along with others, etc., are collected at Post and at Followup through the Retrospective Change Questionnaire (Goodman, 1965). Changes in the school situation will be studied through sociometric ratings made by classmates and teachers on the Peer Nominations Inventory (Wiggins & Winder, 1961). This empirically derived instrument has factorial scales labelled Isolation, Hostility, Likeability, and Attention-Seeking, to which we have added an Atypicality scale. Entire classrooms are rated to conceal the identity of the boys being studied.

Eventually we hope to locate subgroups defined by dyadic, counselor, or boy characteristics that clearly benefit from the program. The discovery of such subgroups could lead to more therapeutic pairing and location of the companionship process patterns related to significant change.

One of the few things we are certain about at this point is the positive attitude of parents toward the program. One item on the Parents Retrospective Questionnaire asked: "Do you think it was a wise decision to let your boy join the project — or to put it another way, if you could go back in time and had a chance to do it all over again, would you let your boy join? Yes____ or No____ (Please discuss)." About 95 per cent clearly answered "yes." The few negative or ambivalent responses were elaborated by complaints about the counselors' introversion, unconcern, the program's ineffectiveness or its demands upon parents, e.g., ". . . although both Tommy and I liked Jerry, I would have liked to see Tommy with someone more stimulating — but not to the point of being competitive," . . . "We wanted to help by picking up and dropping off the counselor which really took too much time," . . . "Though I hoped he would get more out of it than he did, I feel he didn't lose anything by it."

Most parent comments had a testimonial flavor and many could be fairly described as enthusiastic, e.g., "We have noticed tremendous improvement in Cliff. We don't have competence to state that none of the changes would have occurred had Cliff not participated, but, our guess is that the project deserves a great deal or all of the credit," . . . "an extremely helpful program for Warren . . . he has developed more self-confidence and widened interests." Sometimes parents mentioned change in specific problems:

> Billy now vents feelings he used to keep to himself. He expresses disappointments where he used to be long suffering. Moreover, he able to get angry at his mother and resistant to his father's avoidance tactics, even to the point of demanding answers or disagreeing vehemently.

Ernie has always felt less apt at sports than other boys, which colored his attitude. Now, he has developed his basketball interest to the point where he will not let the better coordinated boys dissuade him from playing. And just the fact that he could talk about his college friend and all the things they did gave him greater prestige within his own mind. He now travels freely on the bus with his confidence — and mine, and is even beginning to question the more absolute answers of adults.

The satisfaction of parents can only serve as a tentative clue to the program's effectiveness. More useful answers will have to come from the comparative changes between participants and controls over the three timepoints using the systematic observations of teachers, classmates, and parents.

With a less elaborate design, we are studying the project's effect on counselors. They are being compared with a group of nonparticipating students paid to be assessed at the project's start and end.

Research from other programs using students in helping relationships with institutionalized adults suggests an increased interest in pursuing mental health careers (Scheibe, 1965; Umbarger, Dalsimer, Morrison & Breggin, 1962). We also want to know if working closely with a troubled child alters students' attitudes toward human nature or changes their self-concepts or their tendency to disclose to others or their performance on a social insight test, etc. A satisfactory study of counselors cannot be made by considering them as one group confronted with a rather uniform experience. Some went to weekly sensitivity training groups while half did not. Some were with more seriously troubled boys. Half the counselors were "Quiet" and half "Outgoing," and so on. Looking for differential changes between various subgroups of counselors and their nonparticipating controls appears to be the best approach. We may also have to do some followup study on counselors because it seems that some change career goals during the year after participation. A surprising number of counselors go on to other social service programs such as Vista, the Peace Corps, and mental hospital work.

At this point we have a few findings on the total counselor sample from a single program year. These counselors report very significant gains in the quality (and often quantity) of their interpersonal relations when compared with nonparticipating controls ($p = .01$). This is our strongest early finding. As might be expected, in contrast to controls, they describe dramatically heightened interest in the behavior of children, emotionally troubled people in general, and in their own relationships with friends (all at the .01 level). A question asking about change of interest in political activity was inserted to catch possible acquiescence set in the counselors' self-descriptions. It produced almost identical scores for the two groups, which makes the differences observed on other items more persuasive. On Pre-Post testing, using Jourard's Self-Disclosure Questionnaire (1964), counselors show more increase than controls in disclosing aspects of their personality and feelings about schoolwork (both at .05). They also report telling their pals much more about themselves (.01).

There are a few more miscellaneous findings. Counselors see psychotherapy as more helpful than do controls. This may be a reflection of their faith in the psychologically helping relationship. Most of the group-trained counselors were positively impressed with the groups. Many gave convincing details on how the training created important changes in their lives. The two-person teaching machine (Berlin and Wyckoff, 1964, p. 23) received negative comments from about half the counselors. However, they claimed it taught them something despite its redundancy and condescending flavor. Outgoing counselors reported they disclose a bit more than quiet counselors. Untrained counselors showed more discrepancy between what they "would tell" their boys and what they "did tell" their boys during the project. Perhaps group training helped counselors discuss things they wanted to disclose with their boys. These odds and ends suggest that we may eventually find working with troubled boys changes students in important ways.

Here are some other questions about counselors and boys that we hope to answer. Does the group assessment method produce patterns of scores that predict effective counselors? More specifically, will ratings of counselors' self-disclosure, warmth, ability to understand, depression, rigidity, and surgency predict measures of change in boys from observations of parents, peers, and teachers? (Some incomplete data suggest that boys with counselors who score high on GAIT Disclosure gain more than their controls on parents' ratings of adjustment.) Are quiet or outgoing counselors more effective with quiet or outgoing boys? Are variables such as age, vocational goal, quality of school work, and attitude toward human nature related to effectiveness? Is the counselor's measured effectiveness predicted by his previous experience in working with children? His training in the project? His having received psychotherapy? His expressed motive for joining the project? His perception of the boy during visits? The types of things he tells his boy? And so on. Finally, can patterns or clusters of these variables help us locate students who can help troubled boys the most? We will ask this set of questions separately of counselors with several different types of boys. As you can see, we are trying to find out what kinds of students work best with what kinds of boys under what kinds of conditions. A few small but solid answers should make us happy. We also want to know how many boys get worse and if enough get better to make the entire enterprise worthwhile. If the research eventually shows that the program flops, we will advertise our errors in a book so others won't repeat them. If it succeeds, we will prepare a "cook book" for distribution to the many communities throughout the country who may want to start their own programs.

REFERENCES

BARRETT-LENNARD, G. T. Dimensions of therapist response as causal factors in therapeutic change. *Psychological Monographs,* 1962, 76, Whole No. 562.

BERLIN, JEROME I. and WYCKOFF, BENJAMIN L. Human relations training through dyadic programmed instruction. American Personnel and Guidance Association Convention, 1964. (Mimeo., Human Development Institute, 1299 W. Peachtree Street, N.E., Atlanta, Ga.)

CARKHUFF, ROBERT R. and TRUAX, CHARLES B. Training in counseling and psychotherapy: An evaluation of an integrated didactic and experimental approach. *Journal of Consulting Psychology,* 1965, 29, 333-336.

CHAPIN, F. STUART. Preliminary standardization of a social insight scale. *American Sociological Review,* 1942, 7, 211-225.

GOODMAN, GERALD M. Problem check list for elementary school boys, 1964. Retrospective change questionnaire, 1965. (Interpersonal Relations Project, Psychology Department, UCLA, Franz Hall)

GOUGH, HARRISON G. and HEILBRUN, Alfred B., Jr. *The adjective check list manual.* Palo Alto, California: Consulting Psychologist Press, 1965.

JOURARD, SIDNEY M. *The transparent self.* New York: Van Nostrand, 1964.

ROGERS, CARL R. The necessary and sufficient conditions of therapeutic personality change. *Journal of Consulting Psychology,* 1957, 21, 95-103.

ROSENBERG, MORRIS. *Occupations and values.* Glencoe, Illinois: The Free Press, 1957.

SCHEIBE, KARL E. College students spend eight weeks in mental hospital: A case report. *Psychotherapy: Theory, Research, and Practice,* 1965, 117-120.

SIEGAL, SIDNEY. *Nonparametric statistics for the behavioral sciences.* New York: McGraw-Hill, 1956 (Chapter 6).

UMBARGER, C. C., DALSIMER, J. S., MORRISON, A. P., and BREGGIN, P. R. *College students in a mental hospital: An account of organized social contacts between college volunteers and mental patients in a community hospital.* New York: Grune and Stratton, 1962.

WIGGINS, JERRY S. and WINDER, C. L. The peer nominations inventory: An empirically derived sociometric measure of adjustment in preadolescent boys. *Psychological Reports,* 1961, 9, Mon. Supp. 5-V9, 643-677.

WRIGHTSMAN, LAWRENCE S. *Measurement of philosophies of human nature scale.* July, 1966. Mimeo.

19

Filial Therapy*[1]

BERNARD G. GUERNEY, JR.   LOUISE F. GUERNEY

MICHAEL P. ANDRONICO

The traditional practice in treating emotionally disturbed young children has been to separate distinctly the child's own therapy sessions from the counseling or psychotherapy offered to the parent. The treatment procedures, regardless of any verbal reassurances to the contrary, have tended to suggest to the parent that his potential as an ally for ameliorating the child's problems was not taken seriously; and that the role he played in the development and continuation of the problem was the important factor.

Filial therapy is a new method for treating emotionally disturbed children up to ten years of age. In contrast to the orientation just depicted, it uses parents as allies — in fact, the agents — for effecting therapeutic change in the child; delegating to the parents functions that have traditionally belonged to therapists. Because of this reversal of the traditional picture, it seems to many an abrupt and startling change. Viewed as a total system, the change is admittedly a radical one, but in addition to having partial historical precedents all the way back to Freud himself, it can be viewed as one of the logical extensions of several historical trends in relation to the theory and practice of psychotherapy (Fidler, Guerney, et al., 1964). In order to place the filial technique in this perspective, we will now briefly describe these trends.

As do professional therapists, the medium that the parents use in filial therapy to effect change is play sessions with the child. The idea that play

* From the *Yale Scientific Magazine*, March, 1966, Vol. 40, No. 6, p. 60, and reprinted by permission.

[1] This research in filial therapy has been partially supported by Public Health Service Grant MH 11975-01 from the National Institute of Mental Health.

affords a salutary outlet for troubling emotions has been traced at least as far back as Aristotle (Mitchell and Mason, 1948). In the early 1920's, the systematic utilization of play to facilitate the treatment of emotionally disturbed children was developed independently by Sigmund Freud's daughter, Anna Freud (1946), and Melanie Klein (1950), who was also a Freudian psychoanalyst. The former initially used it largely as a means of facilitating a positive and influential emotional relationship between the therapist and the child. Melanie Klein viewed the specific content of the child's play — for example, the way in which a child made use of toys, the stories a child acted out in playing with dolls — as comparable in many ways to the free associations or dreams of adult psychoanalytic patients, and she directly interpreted the child's actions to him in terms of their hitherto unconscious meanings.

Today, professionals engaged in what has come to be called "play therapy" agree with their predecessors that the fantasies of children do reflect those emotional concerns that have had and are having the greatest impact on the formulation of the child's personality. They also agree that in his play with others — particularly under the special atmosphere that can be created in play therapy — the interpersonal patterns the child displays reflect important dimensions of his own emotional needs and his perceptions and expectations of other people. They agree that under the permissive conditions of play therapy the child often returns to events, wishes, or types of interpersonal interaction that have become laden with anxiety or with undischarged emotions of the past, and that the child can use play to release these tensions and emotions in a more satisfying way. In this way he can learn gradually to express and master his emotional responses to experiences that previously frightened him and needed to be repressed — kept outside of his present experience and perceptions.

Child-Therapist Relationships

But many such professionals, possibly the majority, no longer feel that the major benefit to be derived from play therapy is to be achieved by imparting an intellectual understanding to the child as to the "true" meaning of his behavior in the play sessions. There is less reliance too, in modern thinking, on explaining to the child how events of the child's past are linked to those of the present. There is, instead, an emphasis on the importance of the *relationship* between the therapist and the child as the critical factor in psychotherapy. This conceptual change is traceable to the theories of Rank (1945) that were applied to play therapy by Taft (1933) and Allen (1942).

The development of client-centered therapy by Carl Rogers (1951) supplied more specific methods by which the therapist could foster the type of relationship believed to be especially therapeutic, and at the same time provided a consistent theoretical framework for understanding its importance in the therapeutic process. Work in play therapy consonant with or derived from Rogers' views has been carried out and enriched by such people as Axline (1947), Dorfman (1951), and Moustakas (1953). Central to the client-centered method was the idea that what the therapist needed to impart to the child (or adult) "client" was the feeling that he was completely respected, understood, and deeply and warmly accepted as a worthwhile person by the therapist, that no view or feeling expressed by the child would change this permissive understanding and accepting attitude. This attitude, conveyed to the child, was the essential element that would enable him to choose those paths of self-expression and interpersonal behavior within the therapeutic situation that would enable him to overcome his emotional difficulties and most fully develop his potentialities.

According to this more recent (but by no means universal) view, the therapist's function thus becomes not one requiring knowledge and facility with respect to Freudian psychodynamics, nor, in fact, complicated psychodynamics of any sort. Rather, his function under this orientation is to be able empathically to understand and accept the ideas, wishes, and feelings of the child at any given moment, and to convey this understanding and acceptance to the child. Moreover, Carl Rogers and his followers have carefully described the nature of the therapist's task and his verbal responses. Thus, this type of therapy can be more readily taught than many other types of therapy.

Now we go back to Freud and his immediate followers to trace the second historical change that has occurred in orientation toward psychotherapy. The dimension we are concerned with here is the locus of the problem of an emotionally troubled child. One's conception of this locus determines the target and nature of the treatment effort. Following the medical and scientific models prevalent in his time, Freud's emphasis was on the stresses and conflicts that existed within the individual, rather than between individuals. It was the individual's own psyche and the patterns of interaction among the differing aspects of the psyche — id, superego, and ego — that absorbed most of the energies of the Freudians in theory construction and treatment. The patient was, in effect, studied in a state of isolation. Contact with associates of the patient and with family members of patients was kept to a minimum for fear that such contacts would be harmful to the treatment process.

In more recent years, especially since the second World War, the conceptual focus of psychotherapy with adults has expanded, so that much more attention has been paid to *interpersonal interaction:* relationships among people. Such broadening of theoretical horizons has been reflected in the development of new modes of psychotherapeutic treatment: individual therapies stressing "ego psychology" and interpersonal relations, group psychotherapy, conjoint therapy sessions with husbands and wives, and family group therapy.

The third trend to which we wish to call attention is the increasing realization that the traditional therapeutic techniques based on a one-to-one contact between a professional therapist and patient via hourly sessions spread over many months or years, cannot hope to resolve the mental health problem the country faces. The supply of such people, using such techniques, could not conceivably keep up with the need for mental health services. It is increasingly realized that new techniques are needed that afford the professional therapist greater leverage in the use of his time, and indeed, the physical facilities at his disposal.

These trends are what have encouraged the conception of filial therapy. The first suggested that the highly intellectual, expensive, and prolonged training in psychodynamics theory was not essential in learning to play a therapeutic role. The second suggested that with emotionally disturbed people, and particularly with children and their parents, one should attempt to modify directly the *relationship* between people and not only its psychic representation as it exists separately in the minds of each. The third trend provided the sense of urgency and necessity that energizes experimentation, and influ-

FIGURE 19.1

This photograph illustrates how parents observe the therapist conducting a play session as part of their training. At Rutgers, The State University, parents wear headphones to listen, and observe through glass that appears to be a mirror when seen from the playroom. The therapist is Dr. Bernard Guerney, Jr.

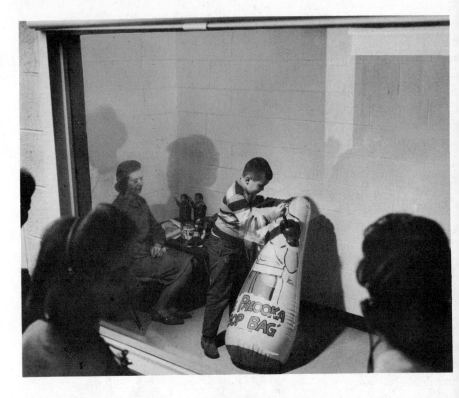

FIGURE 19.2

*Both boys and girls are used in (separate) demonstrations, because they
tend to play differently, and thus call forth a wider range of therapist
responses than would the use of one sex alone. Once the children
realize they are free to structure the play in their own way, they frequently ignore the fighter pictured on the "bop bag" and, as one would
wish, assign other identifications to it. Here, the child is attacking it
with a rubber knife. The therapist is Dr. Louise Guerney.*

enced the formulation of a technique that involves very high leverage in terms
of the professional time and facilities.

The Rationale for Using Parents

In addition to the potentially high leverage it provides in the use of professional time and resources, the rationale for the use of parents as therapeutic
agents was based on a variety of considerations (Guerney, 1964). As a minimum, it was felt that the extra and undivided attention the child would be
receiving would alone have some degree of positive effect in enhancing the
child's sense of belonging and worthiness, and make him feel somewhat less

negative and more "giving" toward the parents. But much more important, it was reasoned that if the parent could be taught to execute the essentials of the role usually taken by therapists, the parent would conceivably be more effective than a professional. This was taken to be so because (a) the parent has more emotional significance to the child, (b) anxieties learned in the presence of, or by the influence of, parental attitude could most effectively be unlearned, or extinguished, under similar conditions, and (c) interpersonal mis-expectations should be efficiently corrected if appropriate delineations were made clear to the child by the parent himself as to what is, and what is not, appropriate behavior according to time, place, and circumstances.

It was further assumed that an approach that made it very clear to the parent that his good intentions toward the child could be harnessed to directly benefit the child would provide a strong motivation for the parent to undertake a therapy program and to continue treatment for the necessary time. It was felt that the parents would learn to play the role required of them sufficiently well, because they would be asked to play it for only short periods of time under special conditions, and while receiving feedback and encouragement from the therapist and other parents making the same attempt. The very difficulties that the parent encountered in trying to adopt such a role might prove illuminating to him with respect to his general pattern of relationships with the child. The fact that the parent would, through his learning of a new role for the sessions, deliberately break certain previous patterns of interaction for at least a limited amount of time, might also be expected to enhance his ability to explore and adopt new patterns outside of the sessions. With these considerations in mind, the following technique was developed.

The Filial Method

The age of ten is ordinarily the upper limit for the maximum effectiveness of a play format for psychotherapy. When a child below ten is deemed, after diagnostic testing and interviewing, to have an emotional problem (as opposed to, say, an intellectual or neurological one), the general nature of this problem is explained to the parent. Such problems arise in large measure, and with differing specific patterns in each case, from a lack of self-confidence on the part of the child, from a lack of sufficient feeling on the part of this child that he is accepted as a worthwhile individual by the parents, from the child's fear of, and consequent need to hide, certain kinds of significant feelings from other people and from himself, and from a lack of communication and understanding between parents and child that would enable the child to express his needs in such a way as to allow these difficulties to be overcome. This is explained to the parent in a manner that fits the individual case. It is then explained that we can teach the parent a specific way of interacting with his child, at special times, and in a special place set aside for this purpose. This special interaction we expect will enable the child to express his feelings and needs more freely and adequately, and build his sense of worthiness and confidence. It should also help the parent to understand better the previously hidden or distorted inner needs and feelings of the child, and thus enable him to respond more appropriately to the child.

If, after full discussion, the parent accepts the recommendation for this type of help, the mother and/or father are placed in a group of six to eight other parents also beginning filial therapy. A group may be comprised of mothers, of fathers, of spouses, or of mothers and fathers of different families. The parents then attend a group meeting with the therapist every week thereafter until the parent terminates therapy, which is usually between six and eighteen months thereafter.

The first two or three group sessions are devoted to explaining further to the parent the nature and purpose of the role he will be asked to assume in the weekly sessions he will be having with his child. The parent's role is modeled as closely as possible after that taken by a client-centered play therapist. The basic things that the parent must learn are: (a) to be empathic with the child during the sessions — to make every effort to understand how the child is viewing himself and his world at the moment and what his feelings of the moment are; (b) to be fully understanding and accepting of the child — i.e., his feelings and thoughts, whatever their nature; (c) to leave the directions that the play sessions take (within certain clearly defined limits to be discussed later) completely to the child; and (d) most of all, to *convey* this understanding and acceptance to the child. It is explained to the present how the creation of these conditions will tend to allow the child to express more freely his previously repressed feelings and needs. It is explained to the parent that the repressed needs and denied feelings that contribute to the child's difficulties continue to press on him for expression and realization, but because he has learned through earlier experiences to fear them, the child denies them. This leads him to distort personal and interpersonal realities and/or to satisfy his needs in devious and ultimately unsatisfactory ways. As his anxiety about losing status in the eyes of his parent and in his own eyes diminishes and he reveals his true feelings, he can come to grips with these feelings more and more effectively — mastering them rather than denying them or being overwhelmed by them. As this anxiety goes down and the child experiences his true range of feelings while remaining fully accepted by the parent, his sense of worth and confidence and his desire to give to others increases, while his frustrations and concomitant hostilities decrease.

But were there not legitimate reasons for his not expressing some such feelings openly in the past, and even now? The answer to this question is contained in a consideration of time, place, and mode of expression. The emotionally disturbed child for whom both the traditional and the filial mode of therapy is appropriate is in trouble largely because: (a) he has *over*learned certain inhibitions — now overextending restrictions originally placed on overt

FIGURE 19.3

Although convenient, elaborate observational facilities are not essential. Prior to the installation of new equipment, the one-way screen used for teaching the parents at the Hunterdon Medical Center was a portable blackboard with a white cloth replacing the slate. Differential lighting then makes the observers less visible, and thus less distracting. Dr. Michael Andronico is giving the demonstration.

behavior to the experiencing of the related *emotions* as well; and/or (b) he has *under*learned the need to restrict the expression of certain feelings, and instead acts on them directly and overtly without restraints appropriate to the time and place. The latter circumstance brings us to consideration of limitations, mentioned parenthetically above, that are imposed on the child during the session.

Limitations to the Child

These limitations are very modest by ordinary standards, and most of them become relevant only after the child has come to realize the freedom of the sessions, and expresses feelings such as anger very strongly and directly. The child is not permitted to extend the time of the session; he is not allowed to break a certain (expensive) toy of those that are provided him to play with in the sessions; and he is not allowed to physically hurt his parent. There are a number of reasons for imposing these "limits" aside from the obvious practical ones. Prominent among them are the following two. First, the essential ingredient of the sessions is the empathic understanding felt and conveyed by the parent. Professionals do not expect themselves to be able to fully maintain this attitude while being physically abused, nor do we expect it of parents. Second, parents as parents — especially parents of the children with under-learned behavioral restraint — benefit from knowing and practicing the art of setting firm limitations on their children's *behavior* while nevertheless accepting the child's feelings as real, and while continuing to convey a sense of valuing the child as a person. When parents successfully practice that art, children derive a sense of security and safety — knowing that they cannot go too far — as well as learning what is socially appropriate.

All of the above matters are not taught in lecture fashion. The parents are encouraged to express their own feelings and ideas, and often arrive at certain of these principles themselves, through group discussion.

Next, the therapist, using children not under treatment, conducts two or three play sessions himself as demonstrations for the parents. The parents observe these sessions through a oneway screen and later discuss what they have seen from the point of view of technique and from the point of view of what meanings the behaviors of the therapist and the child held for the child. Then each of the parents brings in his own child and conducts sessions under observation by the therapist and the rest of the group, followed by discussion as just described. When the parents and therapist feel they are ready — usually two to three months after the meetings began, after two practice sessions under observation, and after having observed some 15 or 20 sessions — the parents begin to conduct their sessions at home. Every so often, sessions are again conducted at the Clinic under the observation of the group. The parents use the most appropriate room they have — a basement, garage, kitchen, or bedroom, perhaps — and a prescribed set of toys designed to permit expression of certain basic psychological needs, interpersonal fantasy, or role-playing. The toys include, for example, a "Joe Palooka" punching bag, a baby bottle, a family of dolls, a family of puppets, a toy gun, clay, crayons, and paper. This particular set of toys is available to the child only during his sessions. Other young children in the family are also given sessions. Originally, the session is once a week, and a half hour in duration. Later, if practical and appropriate, the sessions may be extended to 45 minutes and up to several times a week. This time is devoted exclusively to the child — to the extent of not answering the phone, etc.

In the continuing weekly meetings with the therapist, a description of the home session by each parent serves as a starting point for discussion. Problems of technique and interpretation of the meaning of sessions, and the parents' emotional reactions to the sessions, are given high priority. However, the parents are free to go into other matters of emotional significance to them or their child. The work of the therapist, then, is a combination of a didactic role with respect to the home sessions and a more traditionally therapeutic one in dealing with emotional concerns of the parent, as in other forms of group therapy (Andronico, Fidler, et al., 1965).

The fact that the parents are all striving to play a similar role in their home sessions provides an extra dividend with respect to their group sessions in that it gives the members of the group a standard situation — a common framework — in which to view their children's problems and reactions and their own problems and reactions. This facilitates mutual comparison and understanding among them. The home sessions and the group sessions seem to make both separate and mutually facilitating contributions toward helping the parent and child establish a better relationship and adjustment.

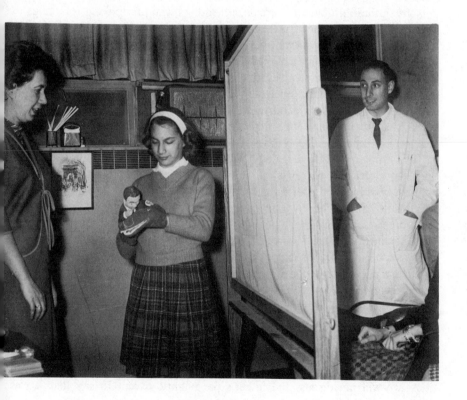

FIGURE 19.4

A mother plays the required role with her own child while Dr. Michael Andronico and the rest of the group observe. Afterward, the group and therapist will discuss with the mother the way in which she did and did not fulfill the requirements of the role.

A Case Illustration

The particular case to be presented was chosen for several reasons. The obvious ones are that it proceeded according to our expectations, was successful, and rather dramatic in content; which, of course, is not always the case. But, in addition, it is particularly interesting because the mother, who was the parent selected to be trained to work with the child, was regarded — to quote from summaries of the diagnostic and interpretive interviews before therapy began — as "a challenge to the limits and capacity of filial therapy to motivate parents. . . ." This guarded assessment of the mother's capacity for conforming to the required role was based partly on her personality, and also on her strongly expressed feeling that "the idea of interacting with the child in a play situation is emotionally repulsive." Further, Mrs. S's (the name and initial are fictitious) attitude toward psychology and psychiatry was quite negative. Because of a previous brush with someone in an allied field, she regarded persons in these professional areas as meddlers who are looking for things to criticize, under the guise of presenting an individual with insight about himself.

Her boy, Fred, was a seven-year-old referred to the Rutgers Psychological Clinic by the county mental health clinic. It was reported that he was a nervous child, had frequent headaches, ate poorly, was enuretic, had nightmares, masturbated excessively, bit his nails, and manifested tic-like throat clearings. Socially, he was quiet, easily offended, with no friends. He feared physical aggression, and took flight from play with peers when games of this sort were introduced.

Tests of personality revealed that he perceived his home life as highly uncomfortable. He perceived his mother as directing and assertive, always guiding, warning, and protecting, in a most unwelcome way. Father was seen as a hostile figure. There was some indication that the mother was regarded as the more threatening figure "behind the scene," but Fred refused to acknowledge hostility in himself or his mother. The examiner's summary pictured Fred as a bright, anxious child, developing compulsive behavior and manifesting many nervous symptoms. Fear of physical aggression and some hypochondriacal behavior were also present.

Mrs. S. was a very bright, well-read woman in her late thirties. She was rigid and controlling in all phases of her life. She injected herself into all phases of Fred's existence, demanding appreciation for all that she did. She constantly instructed and moralized. She was in awe of authority figures she respected, very scornful toward those she did not. Because of space limitations, we will not discuss the father's personality, except to say that it was relatively bland.

Group Membership

Mrs. S. initially reacted against the idea of being a member of a group. She found the other members' comments rather worthless, and felt that only the psychologist's statements had any real meaning. She particularly disliked one group member and attacked her from time to time in terms of how people like her made the group idea a poor one. Mrs. S's criticisms were handled as reflective of her personality rather than a realistic appraisal of the group approach. Ultimately, Mrs. S. confessed to the group that she did, after all, see value in a group approach, because she felt that she had gained as a person in learning to be more accepting of antagonistic views, in contrast to her previous need to attack them. She regarded the behavior of the therapist, which served as a model in this respect, as inducing this change in herself. Toward the end, more than once, she led the group in relating how the group discussions had benefited them.

With respect to the play session technique, Mrs. S. asked meaningful questions from the beginning. She doubted the wisdom of simply reflecting the child's own feelings, and felt that directing and interpreting his behavior would be more productive. However, she was willing to give the approach a try, and learned to play the role required in the play periods very well. Her biggest problem was in refraining from asking leading questions, which she did control for the most part. While she did not achieve the ultimate in empathic attitude, she became fairly warm and relaxed, and even had a genuinely good time during the play periods — joining in play, as requested by her boy, in a good-natured manner with no airs of adult superiority. Fred accepted the sessions with enthusiasm, and kept up a high level of interest in them until close to the end, when he could take them or leave them. (When problems diminish, motivation to work on them generally lessens as well.) Some of his play periods read like textbook sessions. He expressed, and apparently worked through, Oedipal feelings, castration fears, ambivalence toward his parents and himself, conflict over aggressive feelings, and self-destructive impulses; and, in the end, genuine positive feelings toward himself and his family emerged.

Fred entered into the play situations eagerly, and centered most of his activity for the initial sessions around the Joe Palooka "bop bag" (which bounces back and allows the subject to feel he is really fighting). He commented that he did not want to try to make anything with the Tinkertoy for fear that it would turn out badly. Until Session 4, his mother's special role did not fall under scrutiny. At Session 4, he seemed to be annoyed by the style of her comments and made various critical remarks about them. This abated after a few weeks, when he apparently realized she was not going to change her behavior, and because she handled these remarks by reflecting and accepting his annoyance. Thus, he learned that his mother could tolerate his criticisms — and aggression — and in turn respond uncritically, and even sympathetically.

By Session 6, Fred was able to assemble Tinkertoy objects without fear of making mistakes, and used them quite creatively. However, in quantity and dynamic quality of play, Joe Palooka continued to remain the focus. In the course of the sessions, this punching bag was at times labeled with his father's nickname and soundly beaten. As Father, Palooka had his penis cut off with a rubber knife (no penis actually appears on the figure). As Mother, it was beaten, stabbed, shot, hugged, and told Fred loved it. As Sister, it was killed, "with blood gushing from its head."

Early in the sessions, Fred had accidentaly hit Mother with the punching bag. He then received a warning that hitting mother in any form would not be permitted, and would cause the session to end. A few weeks later he did it again; the session was ended. The next week, Fred asked Mother to be sure to tell him when he had one minute left. Mother did, and Fred immediately walloped her with the punching bag. She pointed out that he seemed to have been wanting to do that all of the session (as indicated by various remarks), but that he had waited until the end. He explained that this way he lost only one minute and was still able to hit her. This system he devised continued from this until Session 45. After that, on the rare occasions when Joe Palooka or some other object hit her, it seemed to be truly an accident.

In puppet play, his family was wiped out by crocodiles, storms, huge monsters, Nazis, etc. Father was always first to go — with the son looking after mother, usually until the last minute, when everyone was killed.

Change in Tone

Around Session 40, a different tone began to emerge in Fred's play. He included Mother in more activities, wanted her to join him in beating up Palooka, help him by giving him clay bombs to throw, play cards with him, and the like. More often Joe Palooka was Mother, whom he hugged, kissed, and said to, "I adore you." However, there was an increase also in the hostility directed toward her. As Palooka, Mother's nipples were bitten off after he sucked them. He named her the daughter of Frankenstein, made Palooka into his daughter, and bombed her with clay bombs. He drew war pictures with swastikas, which he knew from experience outside the session she did not like, sat on her lap like a baby, and then stuck his tongue out at her. She came into focus as the main figure of interest, and great conflict about her was revealed. He loved her, wanted her, needed her, etc., but could not do so unconditionally. Strong negative feelings were present as well, and feelings of anxiety about his aggressive feelings toward her.

In addition to providing catharsis for the child, this play made it possible for the mother to see that he reacted to her with a variety of feelings, depending on his anxiety level, most pressing emotional needs, etc. It was easier to see why in real life she did not see consistent devotion, obedience, etc., but these positive feelings were actually present. She was able to adjust her expectation of his emotional commitment to her to more realistic levels, saving herself from disappointment when he was not all "love." This, combined with newfound ability to resist being manipulated by him in the hope of "buying his appreciation" made their relationship much more satisfying to both.

By the time 55 home play sessions were held, all symptoms were completely removed or greatly diminished. After 11 more sessions, Mrs. S. decided that though he was still somewhat introverted she could accept this degree of introversion, and therapy was terminated.

Toward the end, the sessions were calmer and less emotional in content. More of them were devoted to simple play-poker, target games, etc. However, Palooka was still important. Fred usually played the role of world champ and beat him up soundly. (At this point, he started wrestling with Father in real life.) Finally, after it was announced to Fred that sessions would end after two more, he had a very symbolic session where he staged "pretend temper tantrums" and then assumed his normal voice and laughed. Mrs. S. remarked that "Big Fred is laughing at Baby Fred," and he agreed. He seemed to be exorcising the babyish element in himself in this way, bidding it goodbye good-humoredly, because he was ready to do so.

Status of Research

Evaluated from the point of view of preliminary clinical experience — with about a dozen groups completed or under way — most of the assumptions underlying the technique seem to hold up, and the technique seems an effective one; for us, more effective than more traditional approaches. We are fully cognizant, however, of the role experimenter enthusiasm and bias inevitably play in making such judgments. At the same time, the problems presented in attempting to subject the effectiveness of psychotherapy to rigorous experimental test are extraordinary. They range from the philosophical and ethical through complex problems of measurement to the practical matter of the enormous expense involved in seeing sufficient numbers of subjects in a reasonable span of time. For such reasons, the practice of psychotherapy in general rests on clinical experience and evidence, and not quantitative experimental evidence. An enormous amount of work remains to be done before this situation can be effectively reversed. Much of our present effort is viewed as being along lines of trying to develop more efficient therapy by clinical methods and evaluation. If more efficient methods can be developed in this way, experimental methods of evaluation will then become more feasible.

At this time, we are trying to evaluate qualitatively and clinically the effects of different types of parent groups and the types of parents and children most amenable to the technique, and we are trying variations in the technique with the idea of improving it further. On the quantitative side, we are trying out certain measuring instruments and attempting to adapt or develop others appropriate to young children. In the area of process (as opposed to "outcome") research, an experimental research project is currently being carried out by the senior author and Mrs. Lillian Stover, part of which objectively and quantitatively tests the assumption that parents can learn and apply the prescribed role. Preliminary results comparing trained parents and children with a similar group of untrained parents and children indicate that they can. Moreover, the children begin to respond to that role in ways predicted by client-centered theory as early as the second training session.

We regard the essence of the filial technique to be that of systematically tapping a relatively neglected but potentially powerful resource: the energy of parents in working for the betterment of their children. We have hope that this principle can be applied also to other age groups of emotionally disturbed children and also to different types of problems. We are hopeful, for example, that underprivileged children's educational motivation and scholastic skills might be increased by applying the same sort of positive orientation to the use of parents, with appropriate modifications of the method of working with the parents and skills the parents are taught. In the future, we hope to be able to conduct research along these lines as well.

REFERENCES

ALLEN, F. H. *Psychotherapy with children*. New York: W. W. Norton, 1942.

ANDRONICO, M. P., FIDLER, J., GUERNEY, B. JR., and GUERNEY, LOUISE F. The combination of didactic and dynamic elements in filial therapy. Paper presented at the 1965 American Group Psychotherapy Association Convention.

AXLINE, VIRGINIA M. *Play therapy*. Boston, Mass.: Houghton Mifflin, 1947.

DORFMAN, ELAINE. Play therapy. Chapter in C. R. Rogers (Ed.), *Client-centered therapy*. Boston: Houghton Mifflin, 1951.

FIDLER, J. W., GUERNEY, B., JR., ANDRONICO, M. P., and GUERNEY, LOUISE. Filial psychotherapy as a logical extension of current trends. Paper presented at the Sixth International Congress of Psychotherapy, London, 1964.

FREUD, ANNA. *The psychoanalytic treatment of children*. London: Imago, 1946.

GUERNEY, B., JR. Filial therapy: Description and rationale. *Journal of Consulting Psychology,* 1964, 28, 304-310.

KLEIN, MELANIE. *The psychoanalysis of children*. London: Hogarth, 1950.

MITCHELL, E. D., and MASON, B. S. *The theory of play*. New York: A. S. Barnes, 1948. P. 77.

MOUSTAKAS, C. E. *Children in play therapy*. New York: McGraw Hill, 1953.

RANK, D. *Will therapy* and *Truth and reality*. New York: Knopf, 1945.

ROGERS, C. R. *Client-centered therapy*. Boston: Houghton Mifflin, 1951.

TAFT, JESSIE. *The dynamics of therapy in a controlled relationship*. New York: Macmillan, 1933.

20

Client-Centered Family Therapy:

Some Clinical and

Research Perspectives

NATHANIEL J. RASKIN   FERDINAND VAN DER VEEN[1]

Along with therapists of many orientations, those of the client-centered persuasion have become increasingly interested in therapy with family groups. The aims of the present paper are to survey new directions in client-centered theory and practice that are consistent with its application to the family, to formulate some of the distinctive aspects of family therapy carried out within this approach, including recorded case examples, and to present a program of research that shows promise for investigating this complex area.

Developments within the Client-Centered Orientation

Throughout the development of client-centered therapy there has been an intensive focus on the moment-to-moment experience of the client (Raskin, 1948; Hart, 1961). For a number of years, Carl Rogers (1951) and many of his students concentrated their efforts on purifying the attitude of appreciating what the client felt, what the client thought, and what the client saw, uncontaminated by thoughts *about* him.

A corollary of this individual phenomenological concentration was that the person who came for therapy was seen as the exclusive channel of change.

[1] Work on this chapter by the second author was supported in part by USPHS Grant No. MH 13633, "Family Concepts, Psychotherapy, and Child Adjustment."

The therapist as a person and relatives of the client were not seen as significant participants in the therapeutic process, although relatives could become clients themselves, and thereby become the objects of the acceptance and respect to which client-oriented therapists were deeply dedicated.

The responsibility of the individual client was prized, and the respect for him as an agent of change was no less if he happened to be a child. No other therapeutic orientation had taken the position so clearly that a child could be helped in therapy without the participation of his parents (Axline, 1947).

This belief was maintained at the same time that a substantial interest was exhibited in group processes, such as in group therapy (Hobbs, 1951), teaching (Rogers, 1951), industrial organizations and group leadership (Gordon, 1956). In all these situations — child and group therapy, teaching, group leadership — the conceptualization of the therapist or group leader has been fundamentally the same: he is seen as a person who deeply respects the strength of individuals, irrespective of age or group status, to assume the initiative for their own growth.

What brought about the change that has led, among other things, to "client-centered family therapy?" Several reasons can be identified; some have occurred within the client-centered approach, some outside it. In the late 1940's, the concept of the therapist as a personal participant in the therapeutic process began to germinate (Raskin, 1952a), and in the 1950's the factor of therapist "congruence" or genuineness joined "empathy" and "unconditional positive regard" as the triumvirate of Rogers' "necessary and sufficient conditions" of therapy (Rogers, 1957). The last two factors represented the further development of Rogers' original focus on the client; "congruence" gave formal recognition to the importance of the therapist as a person in the process and was defined in terms of his genuineness, his openness to his own feelings, and the ease with which he could express these feelings.

With congruence in the list of therapeutic conditions, the "client in relationship" automatically became important in client-centered therapy. The therapist's field of operations now included his own feelings, his personal reactions to the client as well as the client's reaction to him. There was now an element of *encounter* in the therapeutic process, which led many client-centered therapists to add or substitute the label of "experiential" or "existential" to their identification tags. Empirical support for the mutual influence of client and therapist on each other has come from several recent research studies (van der Veen, 1965; Moos and Clemes, 1967).

With greater freedom for therapeutic action, *therapist involvement* has become a more salient aspect of the client-therapist relationship. The therapist has become more *expressive*, particularly with clients who are withdrawn or not able to relate (Gendlin, 1967). He has increased his involvement through *multiple therapy* — two or more therapists present at the same time — a mode of participation that gives the therapist a widely increased range of expressive freedom and opportunity for growth without lessening his responsibility (Whitaker and Malone, 1953; Mullen and Sanguiliano, 1964).[2] Of particular relevance here the therapist also increased his involvement by being open to the client's *community,* especially the client's *family relationships.* The client-centered therapist in family therapy has manifested greater personal expressiveness and has learned to deal directly with the client's significant family relationships. A parallel development has occurred with groups, where the "basic encounter group" for nonclinic populations has witnessed the increasingly free and personal involvement of the therapist and the direct focus of the group members on their relationships with one another (Rogers, 1967b).

Turning now to formulations about the person of the client, the core construct of client-centered personality theory has been the self concept of the individual (Raimy, 1948; Lecky, 1945; Snygg and Combs, 1949; Rogers, 1959). In the development of the self, particular attention has been paid to the origin of self-regarding attitudes in the child, a process in which the parents exert great influence (Raskin, 1952b). The core of psychological maladjustment is viewed as the *absence* of the consistent experience of making a positive difference to others in early childhood (Standal, 1954).

In view of the critical importance of the individual's family experience for his personal growth and psychological health, an additional construct has been formulated. It is the person's concept of his family or, more simply, his *family concept* (van der Veen et al., 1964). The family concept consists essentially of the feelings, attitudes, and expectations each of us has regarding his or her family life. The family concept encompasses a relatively stable and potent set of psychological attributes. It is assumed to have several characteristics: it influences behavior; it can be referred to and talked about by the individual; and it can change as a result of new experience and understanding. These characteristics are evident in family therapy, where the family changes as a result of talking about, sharing, and changing various aspects of the family concepts of the members. Some promising research findings regarding family concepts will be presented in a later section of this chapter.

Developments External to Client-Centered Therapy

Outside the client-centered approach, work with the family unit has received impetus from several orientations. Early conceptual work in sociology by Burgess (1926) provided a new outlook, reflected in the title of his article, "The family as a unity of interacting personalities." He writes,

> The study of the patterns of personal relationships in family life led directly to the conception of the family as a unity of interacting persons. By a unity

Though these authors are not identified with the client-centered approach, they are mentioned here because their work is so relevant to multiple therapy and has much in common with client-centered developments.

of interacting personalities is meant a living, changing, growing thing. . . . The family is even more than an interaction of personalities. In this interaction the family develops a conception of itself . . . . A family that had no conception of its role in the community, and of the responsibilities of its individual members would not be an institution, not even a family (p. 5).

Ackerman developed the clinical application of this theme in an early paper on "The unity of the family" (1938). Irene Josselyn, a child analyst actively invested in social work, stated succinctly that "The family is as much a part of the individual as the individual is part of the family" (1953, p. 342). Notable contributions from psychology include the ground-breaking practical formulation for family therapy by John Bell (1961), and the beginning of a theoretical and scientific foundation for the study of the family unit by Handel (1965).

It is apparent that interest in the study of the family unit and the treatment of family disturbance has received impetus from a wide range of disciplines and a growing body of clinical practice.

A Contrast to Other Approaches

While those with client-centered orientations were thereby further stimulated to get into the "family act," they have done it in a distinctive way, a way that now includes the concepts of therapist participation, expressivity, and involvement, but also retains the fundamental client-centered principle that the therapist facilitates a process in which clients are their own architects. In contrast, the bulk of the literature on family therapy seems overwhelmingly "therapist-centered." We read about *the therapist deciding* which members of the family are to be seen and in what order, *the therapist finding out* how the neurotic patterns of wife, husband, and children feed into each other, *the therapist confronting* the family members with his insights and discoveries. The reader's attention is called to some quotations from Ackerman and Franklin, MacGregor and Satir to show how strongly the therapist dominates the family scene. While there are some elements of management in Bell's (1961) approach, they are not nearly as strong as those reflected in the following quotations.

Evaluative comments by Ackerman and Franklin (1965) on a filmed interview include such remarks as:

Therapist continues to test danger of daughter's closeness with father.
The therapist's use of the term "gripe" is not a slip on his part. His reinforcement of daughter's complaint against father is purposeful.
Therapist challenges mother's denial of being intrusive, like grandmother.
Therapist challenges father as to his submerged violence.
Therapist stirs patient's hope of a man of her own.
Therapist neutralizes patient's fear and resistance.
Therapist wants a commitment: is sex allowed, yes or no?

MacGregor et al. (1964):

> In this project, intake was not a screening step, but a planning step that performed a therapeutic as well as a diagnostic function. These conferences provided clues to the strengths and weaknesses of the family, and helped the team to determine a treatment plan suited to that particular family.
>
> In the briefing session, the team set initial objectives, sometimes diagraming them so that each therapist might have a clearer idea of the tactics of each team member.

The client was obviously not an active or equal participant in the planning process.

Satir (1964):

> I almost always start family therapy with what I call a "family life chronology" or history taking process.
>
> The therapist helps the patient to see how past models influence his expectations and behavior . . . . The therapist delineates roles and functions . . . . The therapist completes gaps in communication and interprets messages.

A Client-Centered Approach to Family Participation

The antithesis of therapist management is respect for the self-determination of family members. In contrast to the handling of Satir and others, the composition of family groups may be determined by the family members themselves. Suggestions about participation may be made by the therapist, based on his perception of the attitudes of the individual members, but he is governed by the family's reactions to these suggestions and to the experience of the members themselves. The client-centered therapist does not begin with a preconceived idea of who should be seen in which order, nor does he see himself as the skilled diagnostician who will call the shots on participation as he goes along. The following is an example of how family composition evolved in one situation. (Pseudonyms are used throughout.)

Mrs. Maxwell called and expressed the concern of herself and her husband about their 11-year-old son's negative attitude toward school. The therapist invited both parents to come in for a first interview, responding to the concern and motivation for seeking help that was present in both parents.

The tape-recorded interview began this way:

Therapist: You told me a little bit about the situation over the phone, but why don't we start all over.
Mother: (to father) Why don't you start?
Father: Let's see, where should we start. Then you can check our story. We have two children; one is thirteen, one is eleven. We have difficulty with Tommy. We just think we need help. We need your help because we'd like to know, "where do we do something wrong?" It's obvious that it's on us.

Mr. Maxwell went on to explain that, as part of his work, he and his family lived part of the time in Europe, and that Tommy had done very well academically in a particular European city a few years earlier, but had felt crushed and had "gone down" since returning to the United States. Mr. Maxwell also noted that the family was bilingual.

To resume the verbatim account:

Father: Now it may be that we pushed him too hard; we didn't mean to, but I'm sure this is part of it, the intellectual pushing.

Therapist: You mean all the way through.

Father: It may be all the way through. You know, you believe one thing, but then you still would like to push a child. It may be this is part of it; it may be the language is part of it. It may be that part of it is that Tommy rejects part of the cultural duality — the European-American duality. Part of it is the sister, Linda, is very sure of herself, and is an artist in some ways. Competition with the older sister surely plays a role. And so Tommy hates to go to *school*. And right now Tommy's grades are terrible, which doesn't matter. This is one thing we have learned to live with lately.

Mother: Well, terrible — you would have to say — he has just gotten a report card. He has one A, two or three B's and the rest are C's. Now that is not a terrible report card. But we feel, and of course this may be a wrong projection from the parent's point of view, that he is capable of doing more. He has done better. He doesn't hand in his work; what he does hand in is alright, he often gets A's on these. . . .

Father: He still wets . . . very irregularly, but above all when it comes to school, wouldn't you say, in his school time.

Therapist: When he's feeling school pressures, do you mean?

Mother: I'm not sure that that's true, because he also wets the bed during the summer. . . .

Father: That's right.

Therapist: M-hm, m-hm.

Mother: . . . so that it can't be completely . . . that's right.

Father: He has times in which he is extremely regressive, in which he wants to play the little tiny child. He has times — this is the interesting thing, this is partly what fooled us — in which you can discuss with him very intelligently. He has quite a lot of profound common sense . . . I can discuss with him . . . this may be part of our difficulties.

Mother: He's much interested, for example, in questions having to do with his father's work, and very intelligently.

Father: And other matters too. And then suddenly, he's a tiny child, on the level of four or six, emotionally.

Mother: He'll suck his thumb. He'll watch television and almost always, he'll be sucking his thumb.

Therapist: What do you think of that?

Mother: Well, until recently, I didn't think too much of it because his sister did the same thing, and she stopped. So I assumed. . . .

Therapist: I wasn't thinking specifically of sucking his thumb, but as part of . . . you know you were saying that he had all these adult interests and then suddenly he's a little child. I wonder if this means anything in particular to you.

Father: To me it means he needs it. He needs it. He needs a great deal of love. I hold him; he comes to my lap . . . He needs physical love.

Mother: Well, it just seems to balance somehow. His discussion that he has is beyond his years, so here comes the balance to it.

Therapist: You think of this childishness as being a reaction to his overextending himself intellectually? He can't be quite that grown up so he compensates by being a little child?

Mother: That's been an opinion, right or wrong.

Therapist: But you (to father) would put it more as simply his needing love — to be loved like a little child is loved. . . .

After this both parents brought out additional opinions about both children, about themselves as children, about their present family and some of the stresses that might exist in it, especially those they themselves might be originating. In addition to bringing out problems, they expressed considerable satisfaction with the family, agreeing that it represented a definite improvement over those in which they had grown up. Toward the end of the hour, the therapist brought up the question of how to meet the next time, as follows:

Therapist: I've been wondering about how to go on from here. I found myself wondering about the possibility of the whole family meeting and talking together, and then I thought, "Well, you don't really see the *family* as having problems as much as you do. . . ."

Father: Yes, I do.

Therapist: Well, which would be more the case, that you see the family as having problems or that you see Tommy as having some problems.

Father: Let me interject something. Linda is very much . . . Linda is bossy to him.

Mother: But that's normal.

Father: That's normal, sure (laughing) that's the older sister complex. But she sure is part of the picture, wouldn't you say?

Therapist: She probably is.

Mother: Well, I think of it as the family, as a family unit, very strongly.

Therapist: I have the idea that the children could join you in talking about things, going by their age and the way you describe them.

Mother: Yes, I feel certain of that, if you'd like that. I think that the children would both be capable of joining us.

Father: They sure would be.

Therapist: Well, if you're willing to do that, perhaps we could meet that way next time and explain to them that this started because you were concerned about Tommy's attitude toward going to school and also that you felt he should be doing better in school than he is, so you came in to talk about that, and as we talked about it we got the idea that it might be worthwhile to have the whole family talking about how they feel about things in the family.

Mother: Certainly, I think that would be interesting. I hope the children speak freely, I think they would.

Father: I hope they would. Oh, they will. Don't worry, they will.

Mother: We'll certainly try to encourage them to.

Father: At our table there's one big discussion. Oh, they'll talk, don't worry; it'll be fun.

Therapist: Well, I won't be crushed if they don't talk, but I would guess they probably would and the important thing is, "Would it help?"

Father: Yes, that's the question, "Do you think it would help us?"

Mother: Well, at least you could see where to go from there, if it doesn't help.

Therapist: Yes, I still would like to look on this as . . . I feel like always throwing the ball back to you. I really don't know whether this is the best way to go ahead, I don't think anybody knows. I guess you know enough about the field to know that we don't have specific treatments for specific problems. I think the most realistic way to look at this is that we are all in this together and that maybe because I see a lot of families and a lot of people with problems I can add something to your family's consideration of your problems. But I also see you as two intelligent, sensitive people who are right in the middle of this and the way you are going to wind up living is going to come mostly out of the way you are and what makes sense to you, not the advice you get from an outsider.

Father: Yes, yes, yes.

Since this approach depends upon what makes sense and feels right to different families, the client-centered therapist finds that he ends up working with families in many different patterns: in one situation all three family members are seen together; in another, the parents are seen together at one time and one child individually at another time; in another, one parent is seen by one therapist and the other by a second therapist, with the child wanting nothing to do with it; in still another, it is the father who wants nothing to do with it, and the therapist sees the son and the wife individually.

The principle here is for the therapist to be open to a full family encounter and to be able to suggest this *when it is consistent with the attitudes expressed by the family members with whom he is in contact.* A corollary principle is to modify the family group in accordance with the reactions of the participants as they experience it. In the example quoted above, the daughter decided, after coming once, to discontinue, leaving a group of mother, father, and son.

An Example of Interaction in Client-Centered Family Therapy

We turn to a consideration of the group process and the nature of the therapist participation in the family meetings. Again, the therapist with a client-centered orientation finds himself antagonistic to an approach based on therapist-discovery-and-disclosure-of-neurotic-patterns; the antithesis of this is an empathic attitude that leaves the initiative with the family members. This locus does *not* shift when the therapist expresses personal feelings or reactions consistent with a basically empathic attitude.

The following is taken from the third interview with the Maxwell family described above. The 13-year-old daughter, Linda, decided not to return after the second session, so that the participants in this third meeting included Mr. and Mrs. Maxwell, 11-year-old Tommy, and the therapist. The discussion has been about Tommy's frequent feeling of boredom, especially over the weekend, and the problems this has created for the family.

Therapist: Is it tied up with a kind of expectation, "You (parents) should be, or other people should be, doing something for me?"

Tommy: No.

Mother: Or *with* me, certainly.

Tommy: Yes.

Father: Very much so, *very* much so.

Therapist: I guess I'm interested in whether you have that kind of feeling, and if you don't, what is the feeling you have a lot of the time.

Tommy: I just think that with two people there's always something you can do, but alone there's not so many things you can do.

Therapist: M-hm. And you feel that you are put in the position of being alone too much.

Tommy: Quite often.

Therapist: Do you get the feeling that everybody else in the family is busy with their own stuff?

Tommy: Most of the time, yes.

Father: That's the strange contrast . . . Linda's always doing something. And I think part of the big trouble started when Linda began to do things on her own. About two years ago she really began to have a desire to lock herself off. She always played with him.

Therapist: So I can see where this would have made a big difference to Tommy.

Father: Yes.

Therapist: Another feeling I get — I wonder if Tommy has this — "I *should* be doing this or that, but I don't really *feel* like it."

Tommy: Well, there's only a couple of things you can do, and often most things you don't really want to. Cooking is one thing I always like to do. But . . .

Father: For the last two months, anyway.

Therapist: You mean, you don't know how long that's going to last.

Father: Yes, it's just two months; Tommy would have protested against cooking in December. It's just that school — it gave him a first independent creativity. That's how we interpreted it — for the first time Tommy could do something on his own. And we were very happy about it. I must say, I made my mistakes, too. Sometimes we do get a little nervous, real nervous, and say "Tommy, can't you do something?" You see, when Tommy stands around all Sunday (father and mother laugh), when he stands around doing nothing, sometimes you say, "Can't you *do* something, for heaven's sake?"

Therapist: "You mean, you can get irritated, and express anger, and you're sorry you've done this?"

Father: Yes, very much so, because I know from my own life that you cannot force somebody to do something. I know very well that it's silly to say, "Tommy, get a hobby, or do something with your Saturday, or your Sunday, or whatever it is."

An Example of Outcome

After two sessions together with the father, mother, and son, which were regarded as very helpful by the parents, Tommy decided that he would like to see the therapist alone several times. His parents agreed that this would be desirable and three individual meetings were held, which Tommy described as much more relaxed, which he used conversationally with little personal exploration, and in which he reported that his school work had improved greatly, to the point where he was practically "straight A." In the third individual meeting, he brought up the possibility of his parents coming to see me alone; this seemed to be in accordance with his wishes and theirs. He himself retained a positive attitude toward therapy; a time was arranged when, he said, he would come if it turned out to be not convenient for his parents.

As it turned out, it was his parents who came for the next interview, which began in this way:

Mother: It's been a long time since we've been here.

Father: It has.

Therapist: In a way it feels long to me; in another way it feels like you were just here.

Father: Yes, and we've learned a lot, I think, since then (he and mother laugh together in a friendly manner).

Therapist: M-hm.

Father: I really want to say this.

Therapist: You mean, it got you started in thinking about Tommy and the family and so on.

Father: Yes, in two ways. First of all, in that Tommy has improved a lot, but we think the crucial thing is that we look at things differently. You know, it got us started examining the whole thing.

Therapist: M-hm. . . .

Father: It seems to me that the major insight you gave us, and it came rather soon . . . we had the feeling that Tommy was a child who had somehow been deprived of love. But it's the other way around, I think: I think Tommy got too much. In some ways, we overprotected him.

Mother: I was going to say that perhaps it's more a question of protection than love. I think you owe your child and want to give your child all the love you can. But that doesn't necessarily involve the protection that we had given him, just short of sheltering him and doing everything for him, not allowing him to make up his own mind. . . .

Father: And thereby preventing him from growing up, I suppose. And of course, there might be a dynamic between us at stake here.

Therapist: I'm not sure what you mean by that, only in a general way.

Father: Well, I don't know what happens when parents spoil their child. We've been trying to say what is going on here (laughs together with wife). Is it that we . . . ? Why do you spoil your child? Is it that you like somebody smaller than you? You love to have something to pet and protect.

Mother: Well, in a sense perhaps you can manipulate him in a way that you can't your own partner. I don't know, is that part of it too? Here you have a personality with which you can deal and make decisions for. . . .

Therapist: M-hm, m-hm.

Mother: . . . in a way that you certainly can't. . . .

Father: One thing that has happened since . . . and, of course, it happened in some ways ever since we decided to come to see you. I am treating Tommy differently . . . I am treating him much more brutally. I want to leave him alone; I feel he needs to be left alone.

Therapist: M-hm. You're giving him more room to grow on his own terms.

Father: Yes, yes. . . .

Mother: . . . I think we've spoiled him; I think that's become pretty clear.

Father: Emotionally.

Mother: I think that's clear.

Father: We talked about that, he comes to your lap and you give him kisses and all. He always came and. . . .

Therapist: You made a lot of him?

Father: We did.

Mother: And he has stopped that; that's been interesting. He doesn't. . . .

Therapist: This is one way he's changed?

Mother: I think so. He doesn't come to my lap. In fact, when he goes to school in the morning he doesn't even give me a kiss any more, which I think is fine.

Therapist: Don't miss it? (smiling)

Mother: Not really (laughs and father joins in). Sometimes I do. But I think it's right.

Therapist: You're willing to give that up. . . .

Mother: Oh, yes.

Therapist: . . . in the larger scheme of things.

Father: M-hm. Yes, Tommy has changed quite a bit. We all have changed, I suppose, the whole . . . and strangely enough, the girl changed. She used to be extremely jealous of Tommy.

Therapist: She used to be very sensitive to the idea that he might be getting something which she was not, this kind of thing?

Father: M-hm. I think so. And that has changed. . . .

Mother: . . . she is, of course, a very sensitive child; she knows our moods without saying a word. Now Tommy is not like that.

Father: Yes, and strangely enough, even though she rebelled like fury when we came here, remember this, she is the one who changed maybe most of all.

Therapist: Hmm!

Father: She treats him much more naturally and if he has a tantrum or something, uh (to mother) what does she say?
Mother: "Don't behave like a baby." It's sort of matter-of-fact.
Therapist: M-hm.
Father: Which, in turn, helped him, of course.
Therapist: This was instead of her getting very annoyed. M-hm. . . . .

The Significant Elements

This experience with the Maxwells exemplifies a process that included these elements:

(1) The therapist was open to the participation of all the family members, and made this explicit.

(2) All members of the family were given the freedom to choose the extent and the pattern of their participation in therapy. The response of the Maxwells was a very idiosyncratic one, one the therapist could not have been able to predict in advance.

(3) The way in which each family member *did* participate seemed the most productive and comfortable for him.

(4) The therapist interacted freely with the family members without trying to manage or dominate or be the expert. He felt free to express his own feelings, maintained a continuous awareness of the clients' feelings, tried to respond to these empathically, and left the locus of responsibility for interpretation and for action with the family members. The "insight" Mr. Maxwell felt he had obtained from the therapist was based on one of many feelings verbalized by the therapist; the latter did not have the attitude of "selling" any of these.

(5) The meaning they derived from the experience, and the initiative for action and for terminating the meetings were elements left up to the Maxwells, for which they did assume responsibility.

Another Example of Family Participation and its Outcome

The following is an example from another family situation in which the same principles were operating. This one differs in that the parents chose to meet together, but separately from their 11-year-old daughter, who was regarded as their "problem child." Also, the parents had been meeting with the therapist over a period of several months. The excerpt contains some examples of the therapist's expression of personal reactions, consistent with a client-centered empathic attitude.

Father: But with Susan it seems, right now, that the worst thing we can really do is be this sensitive and this concerned. You know, here we're spending really a lot of our time and money and interest to try to get . . . and all that's coming out of the thing is that in most areas we really should try not to be this concerned and this worried. I mean, if yesterday's an example, maybe. . . .

Mother: Well, I wouldn't exactly say that yesterday ended up as a roaring success. She prepared herself to venture out from one o'clock to five o'clock in the afternoon and finally made it out the door. And all the other children were occupied, so she had nobody. . . .

Therapist: Well, apparently you (father) saw what happened yesterday as *some* accomplishment and *your* feeling about it (mother), you know, your whole tone of voice and everything conveys the feeling that it was nothing at all, that she was just kind of forced into it.

Mother: I think the fact that she got out the door was something; you know I really never expected her to get out of the house.

Therapist: M-hm.

Mother: And I think it was successful in that we didn't do any winding of the key . . . The parents' responsibility for directing their children and getting them interested and getting them started — where does that stop and where does the responsibility of the children begin — that's what isn't clear in our our minds. You don't just give up your kids . . . sure, you take them here and you take them there but then they've got to take the bit and go and you've got to let *go* and I *like* the idea of letting *go,* because I (laughs) am sick of carrying the bit (laughs) . . . There's a mobile library in Covington where we spend the summer. Well, she's been old enough for two years to get on her bike and go to the damned library and get her own books. She'll never go unless I drive her over. . . . Part of it, I think, is her difficulty in facing the librarian and going through the mechanics of it. Part of it is I think she's lazy.

Therapist: Too damned lazy. (laughs)

Mother: (laughs) No get up and go.

Therapist: I like your damned language tonight. (laughs)

Father: Yeah, she's coming on strong.

Mother: (laughs) I'm getting free, I guess.

Therapist: Maybe it's a reaction to too much, too much *worry.* . . .

Mother: . . . *feeling* and *responsibility.* You know, I'm not completely free; I like the idea of freeing myself and the more I think that Byron's and my problems are solved . . . and that's why I think, sometimes I feel as if these elongated discussions about Susan are really hedging, away from some of the basic things that really might free us really . . . sometimes I feel we're really getting. . . .

Therapist: . . . that you're not coming to grips with the real problems. . . .

Mother: . . . with what the problems really are and Susan is part of a larger problem and yes, we're arriving at certain conclusions which are good and reasonable and well to act upon, you know. But maybe this is a way of getting to them. I don't know what some of them are, really.

Therapist: You've both kind of hinted that there was more to be done about your own relationship.

Father: Oh, yeah! Oh certainly! But I'm convinced of only one thing. I think it's all really the same thing . . . My feeling is that it doesn't really matter which door you enter. It all leads to the same kind of things. It keeps coming back to authoritativeness on my part, dogmatic kind of ways, my pragmatic ways . . . I think the whole thing is to live with *each other,* to live with the *children,* to live with the *world,* and I think it's all . . . you've got to live with yourself and you've got to try to find yourself. I don't mean it that pat, I think it's quite complex.

Therapist: But the idea is something like learning to accept yourself and learning to accept the other people in the family the way they are?

Father: The other way. The other people first. I'm beginning to see a little bit of myself through Fran and through Susan. But again, I see the other side of the problem — the more emotional I get, the more relaxed, the more involved with Susan and the less I feel sure of what I'm doing, the more shaken up I get.

Therapist: So it's two forces working against each other.

Father: Yeah, but I seem to prefer this way. You know, it seems to be at least, I can see once in a while with Fran . . . I come up the stairs and I see she's upset tonight worrying about the fact that one of the girls may need an operation. I've learned at least to say, "Listen, so it's enough to be upset. So she'll be upset and I'll try not to let it upset me." You know, instead of trying to convince her that everything's going to be great and there's nothing to worry about. . . .

In this family situation, the parents were able to look more deeply at themselves than were the Maxwells; their daughter Susan had chosen to meet with the therapist individually over a period of months, had focused on her social rather than on her family relationships, and had stopped therapy having gotten something very meaningful for herself out of the meetings, without being able to or interested in exploring her family situation any more. The oldest of her three siblings was six, and their lack of involvement in therapy was no doubt a function of their age. So we see this family responding to therapy less as a unit, but also more deeply than the Maxwells and more actively involving the therapist, and this seems to have been in accordance with each person's emotional capacities and needs.

Some Research Formulations for the Study of Family Treatment and Change

There is little question that family therapy and family change need objective study. The theoretical place of the concept a person has of his or her family was mentioned earlier in the chapter. Here some of the research findings on the role of the family concept in family adjustment and change will be presented.

An instrument has been constructed called the Family Concept Q Sort which is composed of eighty family items that are relevant to psychological functioning and to actual clinical interaction. The items are placed on a series of piles ranging from *least like* to *most like* my family (or my ideal family). Among the items are ones such as "We are an affectionate family," "We have very good times together," "We just cannot tell each other our real feelings," and "We get along very well in the community." The items concern the entire family unit, not individual relationships within the family. Thus the test provides a description of the most salient aspects of a person's family experience, regardless of the specific relationships involved. It also enables an exact comparison between the views of different family members, and with other persons, such as a therapist or a friend. Also possible are comparisons across generations, between child, parent, and grandparent.

Several measures relevant to clinical treatment and family functioning have been derived from the Family Concept Q Sort. The *Family Adjustment Score* is the degree of agreement between a person's family concept and a professional concept of the ideal family, based on a sample of twenty-seven professional clinicians. The *Family Satisfaction Score* gives an estimate of the similarity between a person's family concept as it now is and his concept of the family as he would ideally like it to be. The *Real Family Congruence Score* provides an index of agreement between the real family concepts of the family members. The *Ideal Family Congruence Score* measures the correspondence between the ideal family concepts of the family members.

Reliability and validity of the Q Sort appear adequate (van der Veen, 1966). Each of the measures has been found to be significantly lower for parents who have a child with problems in social and emotional school adjustment, than for the parents of high adjustment children (van der Veen, 1965b). They are also positively related to a widely validated test of marital adjustment (van der Veen et al., 1964). The father's family satisfaction, the child's family adjustment and family satisfaction, and parent-child family congruence have been found to be clearly positively associated with the degree of socialization of adolescent children, as measured by the California Personality Inventory (Sailor, 1967). Generally, the CPI variables show a much stronger relationship to the father's family measures than the mother's. Another study has found that the family adjustment and the family satisfaction of the adolescent are higher when those of the father are higher, but this is not true in relationship to the mother. They are also higher for the adolescent when there is greater family congruence between himself and mother or father and between the two parents themselves (van der Veen, 1967a).

Hurley and Silvert (1966) have reported a positive relationship between the Q Sort Family Adjustment Score and mate-image congruity, the similarity between spouses' descriptions of *each other* on the Edwards Personal Preference Schedule. This relationship was substantially greater than the one with similarity of the spouses' *self*-description on the EPPS. Hurley and Palonen (1967) report a significant negative association between family adjustment, obtained on a multiple-choice version of the Q Sort items, and the number of children of student parents. Less adjustment was associated with greater child density (measured as number of children per years of marriage).

In a study on families with more than one adolescent child, it was found that the family concepts of a disturbed child showed lower family satisfaction and family adjustment than a nondisturbed sibling, while the sibling did not differ from normal controls. There were some distinctive differences in content emphasis in the three groups, with patients stressing emotional involvement and dependence, siblings focusing on task achievement, and normal controls emphasizing positive interpersonal relationships (Novak and van der Veen, 1968, in press). A related study on the adolescent's perception of his parents' attitudes toward him, corroborated the perception of higher client-centered parental attitudes of positive regard, genuineness, and empathic understanding by normal siblings and controls than by disturbed children (Novak and van der Veen, 1969). The findings also suggested a modification of client-centered theory for the role of unconditionality of regard in parent-child relationships. It appears that low unconditional regard is not of itself detrimental, given sufficient genuineness, positive regard, and empathy. What does appear to be essential for the child's emotional health is the degree to which he can *make sense* out of, comprehend and integrate, the conditional acceptance that is shown him by each of his parents, commonly a difficult task in disturbed families.

There is evidence, therefore, that the concepts family members have of the family are associated with the adequacy of functioning of the child and the marital adjustment of the parents, that the adolescent's family concept and personality are influenced by the family concepts of the parents, apparently more so by the father's than the mother's, and that the perception of client-centered attitudes within the family is strongly related to family satisfaction and adjustment.

Several preliminary studies shed some light on changes in family concepts associated with therapy. Ayers (1965) has investigated changes over time in a treatment group, a waiting list group, and a nonclinic group, using several instruments including the Family Concept Q Sort. Family satisfaction and real family congruence showed no group differences over a four-month period. However, there was a significant increase toward greater ideal family congruence in the parents of the treatment group. There was also significantly more change in the real family concepts of the treatment group than the other groups. Family adjustment was not computed.

Presently under way is an extensive study of changes in family concepts and in child adjustment as a result of psychotherapy (van der Veen, 1967b). The study is part of a program of research, under the direction of the second author, that originated at the Dane County Mental Health Center, Madison, Wisconsin. Several of the preceding findings have been obtained from the program. Family change is measured in a group of treatment cases seen at a family clinic, for whom a child is the identified patient. Several control groups are used, including a waiting-list group, a nonclinic low adjustment group, and nonclinic high adjustment group. The purpose of the study is to show how changes over time in family concepts are related to clinic treatment, child adjustment, and marital adjustment. The study also has developed family concept measures for clinical assessment and prevention applications, including a rapidly administered multiple choice revision of the test and an automated computer analysis of all family concepts for an entire family.

In a preliminary content analysis of family concept changes (Hamilton et al., 1966), parents in the treatment group were found to show positive changes, with little consistent change evident for nonclinic parents over equivalent time points. There is some regression by the treatment families from the post-treatment to the follow-up point six months later. Gains concerning more shared activities, greater emotional expression, and better relationships in the family maintain themselves, but emotional tension tends to increase again after the termination of therapy. Mothers, more than fathers, see less upset and better understanding within the family after treatment, while fathers see less to be ashamed of and more of interest in the family. Changes in ideal family concepts show that, unlike the other groups, clinic parents are more willing to see their ideal family as having shortcomings after therapy. At the follow-up point the clinic group shows change in the direction of seeing the ideal family as having more emotional comfort and greater strength than at the post-treatment point. Thus, there are distinct changes over therapy and over a post-therapy period in both real and ideal family concepts. More conclusive data on larger samples and additional variables will become available as the program progresses.

The research reviewed here presents an objective and clinically relevant approach to the study of the family, in terms of a person's family experience as viewed from his own frame of reference. Still eluding us, but strongly beckoning for study now, is a formulation of family therapy that will permit the testing of specific hypotheses about its effects and its effectiveness. If there is some consistency with other findings (Rogers, 1967a; van der Veen, 1967c), the dimensions of effective therapist behavior delineated in client-centered research are likely to bear fruit for the study of family therapy as well. These dimensions most centrally concern the attitudes of the therapist and his reliance on the inherent capacity of family members to shape their own growth, both as individuals and as a group.

REFERENCES

ACKERMAN, N. W. The unity of the family. *Archives of Pediatrics,* 1938, 55, 51-61.

ACKERMAN, N. W. *The psychodynamics of family life.* New York: Basic Books, 1958.

ACKERMAN, N. W. and FRANKLIN, P. F. Family dynamics and the reversibility of delusional formation: A case study in family therapy. In I. Boszormenyi and J. D. Framo (Eds.), *Intensive family therapy,* New York: Hoeber, 1965, Ch. 6.

AYERS, E. G. A study of conflict between parents in clinic and non-clinic families. Unpublished doctoral dissertation, University of Kansas, 1965.

AXLINE, VIRGINIA M. *Play therapy.* Boston: Houghton Mifflin, 1947.

BELL, J. E. *Family group therapy.* Public Health Monograph No. 64. United States Government Printing Office, 1961.

BURGESS, E. W. The family as a unity of interacting personalities. *Families,* 1926, 7, 3-9.

GENDLIN, E. T. Therapeutic procedures in dealing with schizophrenics, In C. R. Rogers, (Ed.), *The therapeutic relationship and its impact.* Madison, Wisconsin: University of Wisconsin Press, 1967. Ch. 16.

GORDON, T. *Group-centered leadership.* Boston: Houghton Mifflin, 1956.

HAMILTON, R. B., HUNTER, J. B., and RENTMEESTER, J. A. Changes in family perceptions due to psychotherapy. Unpublished M.A. thesis, University of Wisconsin, 1966.

HANDEL, G. Psychological study of whole families. *Psychological Bulletin,* 1965, 63, 19-41.

HART, J. T. The evolution of client-centered psychotherapy. Wisconsin Psychiatric Institute Discussion Papers, 1961, 26 pp.

HOBBS, N. Group-centered psychotherapy. In C. R. Rogers, (Ed.), *Client-centered therapy.* Boston: Houghton Mifflin, 1951. Ch. 7.

HURLEY, J. R., and PALONEN, DONNA J. Marital satisfaction and child density among university student parents. *Marriage and Family Living,* 1967, 29, 483-484.

HURLEY, J. R., and SILVERT, DIANE M. Mate-image congruity and marital adjustment. *Annual Convention Proceedings.* Washington, D.C.: American Psychological Association, 1966, 219-220.

JOSSELYN, IRENE. The family as a psychological unit. *Social Casework,* 1953, 34, 336-343.

LECKY, P. *Self-consistency, a theory of personality.* New York: Island Press, 1945.

MACGREGOR, R. *et al. Multiple impact therapy with families.* New York: McGraw-Hill, 1964.

MOOS, R. H., and CLEMES, S. R. Multivariate study of the patient-therapist system. *Journal of Consulting Psychology,* 1967, 31, 119-130.

MULLEN, H. and SANGUILIANO, IRIS. *The therapist's contribution to the treatment process.* Springfield, Illinois: Charles C. Thomas, 1964.

NOVAK, A., and VAN DER VEEN, F. Differences in the family perceptions of disturbed adolescents, their normal siblings and normal controls. *76th Annual Convention Proceedings.* Washington, D.C.: American Psychological Association, 1968, 481-482.

NOVAK, A., and VAN DER VEEN, F. Perceived parental relationships as a factor in the emotional adjustment of adolescents. *77th Annual Convention Proceedings.* Washington, D.C.: American Psychological Association, 1969, 563-564.

Novak, A., and van der Veen, F. Family concepts and emotional disturbance in the families of disturbed adolescents with normal siblings. *Family Process,* in press.

Raimy, V. C. Self-reference in counseling interviews. *Journal Consulting Psychology,* 1948, 12, 153-163.

Raskin, N. J. The development of non-directive therapy. *Journal Consulting Psychology,* 1948 12, 92-110.

Raskin, N. J. Client-centered counseling and psychotherapy. In L. E. Abt and D. Brower (Ed.), *Progress in clinical psychology.* New York: Grune and Stratton, 1952.

Raskin, N. J. An objective study of the locus-of-evaluation factor in psychotherapy. In W. Wolff and J. A. Precker (Eds.), *Success in psychotherapy.* New York: Grune and Stratton, 1952b. Ch. 6.

Rogers, C. R. *Client-centered therapy.* Boston: Houghton Mifflin, 1951.

Rogers, C. R. The necessary and sufficient conditions of therapeutic personality change. *Journal of Consulting Psychology,* 21, 1957, 95-103.

Rogers, C. R. A theory of therapy, personality, and interpersonal relationships as developed in the client-centered framework. In S. Koch (Ed.), *Psychology: A study of a science,* Vol. III, *Formulations of the person and the social context.* New York: McGraw-Hill, 1959, 184-256.

Rogers, C. R. (Ed.). The therapeutic relationship and its impact: A study of psychotherapy with schizophrenics. Madison, Wisc.: University of Wisconsin Press, 1967a.

Rogers, C. R. The process of the basic encounter group. In J. F. T. Bugental (Ed.), *Challenges of humanistic psychology.* New York: McGraw-Hill, 1967b. (See Ch. 16.)

Sailor, W. S. Family perception and its relation to personality and adjustment factors in the child. Unpublished M.A. thesis, University of Kansas, 1967.

Satir, Virginia. *Conjoint family therapy.* Palo Alto: Science and Behavior Books, 1964.

Snygg, D. and Combs, A. W. *Individual behavior.* New York: Harper and Bros., 1949.

Standal, S. W. The need for positive regard: A contribution to client-centered theory. Unpublished doctoral dissertation, University of Chicago, 1954.

van der Veen, F., Huebner, B., Jorgens, Barbara, and Neja, P., Jr. Relationships between the parent's concept of the family and family adjustment. *American Journal of Orthopsychiatry,* 1964. 34, 45-55.

van der Veen, F. Effects of the therapist and the patient on each other's therapeutic behavior. *Journal of Consulting Psychology.* 1965a, 29, 19-26.

van der Veen, F. The parent's concept of the family unit and child adjustment. *Journal of Counseling Psychology,* 1965b, 12, 196-200.

van der Veen, F. The family concept Q sort: A brief review of findings and studies in progress. University of Kansas, 1966 (mimeo).

VAN DER VEEN, F. Adjustment factors in the family concepts of adolescents and their parents. University of Kansas, 1967a (mimeo).

VAN DER VEEN, F. Family concepts, child adjustment and psychotherapy: A research proposal. Institute for Juvenile Research, 1967b.

VAN DER VEEN, F. Basic elements in the process of psychotherapy: A research study. *Journal of Consulting Psychology.* 1967c, 31, 295-303.

VAN DER VEEN F., and NOVAK, A. Perceived parental attitudes and family concepts of disturbed adolescents, normal siblings and normal controls. Institute for Juvenile Research, mimeo, 1969.

WHITAKER, C., and MALONE, T. *The roots of psychotherapy.* New York: Blakiston, 1953.

21

A Theory of Healthy Relationships

and a Program of

Parent Effectiveness Training

THOMAS GORDON

Because our society can never solve its mental health problems by waiting to treat people after they have already developed psychological disorders, we must find new *preventive approaches* to this serious problem. On both theoretical and logical grounds, it would seem that the most fruitful place to start prevention would be with children. Society urgently needs to come up with innovative ways of preventing emotional problems in children.

The most direct and ultimately the most effective way to prevent children's emotional problems is to modify that human relationship that exerts the most influence on children's psychological health — the *parent-child relationship*. Modification is required because obviously something is radically wrong with the parent-child relationship in our society. Despite the fact that most parents sincerely want to raise emotionally healthy children, we have ample evidence that far too few parents seem able to do it.

Part of the problem, of course, is that parents are not trained for the job of parenthood. Few parents in our society even accept the fact that they do not enter into parenthood inherently equipped to do an effective job. It is therefore not a commonly held belief in our society that being an effective parent requires special training, just as surely as does being effective in any endeavor. It is a rare parent who actively seeks parent training, despite the fact that most parents today do realize that the way a child is treated, trained, and

407

talked to by his parents is probably the single most important determiner of his future emotional health, his happiness, his ability to cope with the problems he will face, and his effectiveness in relating to others in his world. Preparation for parenthood in our society does not go much beyond buying the new bassinet, repainting a borrowed crib, or purchasing a paperback by Dr. Spock.

Furthermore, it is hard to believe that in our psychologically sophisticated society even those few parents who do feel a need for training would have real difficulty finding a training program. There simply are not very many parent training programs readily available. Girls in high school can learn cooking and sewing, but not how to be an effective parent. Even the small percentage of students who take a course in child psychology in college discover that it is generally a course about how the child's mind and body develops, not about parenthood. How to discipline a child is seldom covered, nor is much of anything else a parent actually needs to know. There are parent education courses in the adult education programs of many of our school districts, yet only a handful of parents avail themselves of this opportunity.

However, there appears to be an even more important reason why parents seem to be doing such an ineffective job of rearing their children. Much of what is written about child-rearing is both confusing and misleading to parents. This is particularly true in the area of discipline, control, and authority. Parents today are warned against being strict and using authority, yet urged to be firm and set definite limits. Child-rearing experts convincingly assure parents that children actually want parental authority and limits to their freedom, then turn around and warn parents that children will rebel against and resist parental authority. Authors of books for parents write about the virtues of democracy in the home but within the covers of the same book tell parents not to let the children defy parental authority. Parents are told not to be strict and not to be lenient, not to be permissive and not to be authoritarian. Parents are blamed for giving children too much freedom, yet are simultaneously told that children need to become independent. Parents hear that they should discipline their children, yet are told that parental discipline can block the development of self-discipline. Is it any wonder parents are confused or skeptical about finding practical answers to their questions about child-rearing?

Those of us on the firing line — the professionals who see the countless numbers of emotionally troubled children, work with them in the classroom, try to give them counsel and guidance, seek ways to rehabilitate those who are failing to cope with their lives or who have broken the laws of our communities — all of us share a deep conviction that we can not possibly provide help for all these children, or that we will never make serious inroads on the larger problems of community mental health until some kind of significant change is brought about in the way children are being reared by their parents. Professional efforts that are focused primarily on treating children *after* they develop emotional problems will continue to be a losing battle.

What is urgently needed then is a new approach for parents to help them out of their dilemma about discipline and authority, and a practical method of providing training for them in this new child-rearing approach. In this chapter, I will describe a project in which I have made an effort, first, to construct a new *theory of parent effectiveness,* and then, to develop a specific program based upon that theory — *a program of parent effectiveness training.*

While the theory was developed specifically with the parent-child relationship in mind, it is actually a general theory of all healthy human relationships. I am now quite certain that the characteristics of a healthy or "therapeutic" relationship between parent and child are identical to those of healthy relationships between husband and wife, boss and subordinate, teacher and student, group and group, and nation and nation.

This general theory takes into account three aspects of human relationships usually neglected in other theories: (1) the existence of a *power differential* between persons, (2) *the inevitability of conflicts* in all relationships; and (3) the methods utilized in human relationships for *conflict-resolution.* In my opinion, power, conflict, and conflict-resolution have not been adequately dealt with by previous theories of human relationships, a serious omission in view of the extreme importance of these factors relative to the health of personal relationships.

Similarly, the specific program I have developed to modify parent-child relationships, unlike most "parent education" programs which are child-oriented, focuses principally on modifying the behavior of the one with the power — the parent. From years of experience as a professional "helping agent" working with relationships in which power differentials exist, such as the boss-subordinate relationship in organizations, the teacher-student relationship in families, I have developed a conviction that *significant* change in such relationships is brought about only when the focus of change is directed toward the person with the most power. It is the person in the power position who must be trained, so that he can *initiate* the process of making the relationship a more healthy one. Consequently, our program to modify the parent-child relationship focuses primarily on modifying the *parent,* hence is called "Parent Effectiveness Training."

Features of "Parent Effectiveness Training"

Parent Effectiveness Training is a laboratory or workshop course designed to facilitate a change in parents' *attitudes* as well as to teach them specific *skills* and *methods* for implementing those attitudes. There are no educational prerequisites and no grades or examinations. The full course consists of twenty-four hours of classroom instruction, which include lectures, demonstrations, listening to tape-recordings, classroom participation experiences, role-playing, buzz sessions, and general group discussion. Each parent is also given a workbook containing supplementary reading, self-instructional skill-practice materials, self-administering diagnostic inventories, and at-home activities requiring application of the methods taught in the classroom. Parents pay a fee for the course.

Classes generally meet one night a week for eight successive weeks, each session lasting three hours. Classes are limited to no more than twenty-five parents. On the average, 75 per cent of the class is couples and 25 per cent a single parent. The dropout rate is less than one-half of 1 per cent.

Classes are started in a community in several different ways:

(1) Any parent may organize a small group of fifteen neighbors or friends and arrange for an instructor to come to that home and conduct one three-hour demonstration class. Enrollment for the full course may be made after the demonstration class. When twenty to twenty-five enrollments have been accumulated, a full twenty-four-hour P.E.T. class is scheduled in that community.

(2) Churches, nursery schools, PTA units, or other organizations may organize a group of no less than fifteen parents and arrange to have an instructor give the full course.

(3) In communities where P.E.T. has become rather well-established classes are regularly scheduled throughout the year. Announcements of such classes are placed in the local newspaper or in the P.E.T. newsletter sent to all alumni. Parents simply phone the local P.E.T. instructor and ask to be registered for the next scheduled class.

(4) Organizations may sponsor a public lecture given by one of the P.E.T. instructors, after which the organization may decide to sponsor a regular P.E.T. class.

Instructors for the course have been recruited from two main sources:

(1) Parents who, after taking the course, express a desire to teach others. Most of these have been mothers who have demonstrated a high degree of aptitude for applying the new methods in their families and who have had some experience either in teaching or organizational leadership. They enter a training program that consists of outside reading, discussion of course content, training in role-playing, training in group leadership skills, practice teaching and co-teaching with an experienced P.E.T. instructor.

(2) Professionals who express a desire to become an instructor or to launch the program in their particular community. Our present group of instructors includes at least one clinical psychologist, psychiatric social worker, minister, marriage counselor, nursery school teacher, school counselor, school principal, rehabilitation counselor, and school psychologist. Before teaching, they took the course themselves, after which they usually co-taught one or two classes with an experienced instructor before taking a class alone.

In the seven-year period since I taught the first class in the community of Pasadena, the program has been introduced into one hundred and twenty-five different communities throughout California. Two hundred and fifty instructors have been trained and over 10,000 parents have taken the course. The growth of the program, measured by the number of parents trained, has averaged around 125 per cent each year.

Many school districts have contracted to have the course given to their administrators, counselors, and teaching staff, for they have seen that the theory and the methods taught in the course are equally applicable to the teacher-student relationship and to the counselor-student relationship. The program was recently included in a research project, funded by the Office of Education, in which two schools were set up as demonstration schools to show both the process and outcomes of a new theory of education called Self-Enhancing Education.[1] P.E.T. classes were offered the parents of the students in these two experimental schools so the parents might learn more "self-enhancing methods" of communicating with their children and solving conflicts in the home. In this way, the parents would reinforce what the teachers were trying to do in the classroom.

It is apparent both from the past rate of growth and from predictions of future growth that P.E.T. is meeting a felt need in communities not only on the part of parents but also other adults who are working with children.

"Parent Effectiveness Training" can be viewed as one kind of new model for a low-cost preventive approach to the problems of juvenile delinquency and mental health in our society:

(1) It can be made available to any number of communities.
(2) It can utilize nonprofessionals as instructors and thus does not rely on the availability of highly trained members of the helping professions.
(3) It can be made available at a relatively low cost for parents and other adults.
(4) It is an educational approach rather than a "therapeutic" or treatment approach in helping to modify adult-child relationships.
(5) It attracts parents *before* serious problems with their children have developed. Hence it is truly a preventive approach.
(6) It utilizes both classroom instruction and at-home materials for self-instruction.
(7) It is a group rather than an individual approach, hence uses the potency of the group in facilitating attitudinal and behavior change.
(8) It has appeal to many fathers as well as to mothers.
(9) The focus is on training the parent rather than on "treating the child." The program is parent-centered, not child-centered.

[1] For information about this project, the reader may write Mrs. Norma Randolph, Cupertino Unified School District, Cupertino, California.

(10) It is methods-oriented rather than solution-oriented — parents are taught methods that are applicable to all problems and all ages of children.

(11) The ideas and methods taught are presented and programmed with a deliberate effort to make them easily understood by parents irrespective of their level of formal education.

The Theory of Healthy Relationships

The theory will be presented as a set of principles or a list of requirements for only *one* person in a relationship. Actually, however, the requirements are the same for both persons in that relationship, but inasmuch as the primary responsibility for *initiating* change in a relationship must be assumed by the one with power, the focus will be on the requirements for that person.

I. Feeling Accepting of the Other

I must feel quite accepting of the other. The more of his behavior I can accept, the better for his growth and health, because acceptance is a powerful therapeutic force.

At those times when I am genuinely feeling acceptance toward another, I am in possession of a tool that can produce startling therapeutic changes. I can be influential in his learning to accept and like himself and to acquire a sense of his own worth, I can greatly facilitate his development and utilization of the potential with which he was genetically endowed, I can accelerate his movement away from dependence and toward independence and self-direction, I can help him learn to solve for himself the problems that life inevitably brings him rather than depend upon others to solve them for him, and I can give him the strength to deal constructively with the inevitable disappointments and pain of life. To accept another is truly an act of love, and to feel accepted is to feel loved. We have only begun in our science of psychology to realize the tremendous power of being loved — it can promote the growth of both the mind and body, and it is probably the most effective therapeutic force we know for *repairing* both psychological and physiological damage to the organism.

Exactly *how much* of the other's behavior I must accept has not been established by research. Certainly, however, I need not and cannot accept all of his behavior — I can never be "unconditionally accepting" of another. This can be represented by the following diagrams:

Letting the area within the rectangle represent all the behaviors of the other person, it is thus clear that some of his behaviors I can readily accept and some I cannot. This is inevitable in all human relationships.

Just where the line of demarcation will be in a parent-child relationship is a function of (1) the parent, (2) the child, and (3) the situation. Some *parents* are simply more accepting than others — not just of a child's behavior,

| All the Behaviors of the Other | Acceptable Behavior |
| | Nonacceptable Behavior |

but usually of the behavior of other people in general. Some *children* are simply easier to accept than others because of their own characteristics. Similarly, in some *situations,* a parent can be more accepting of the child's behavior than he can in another situation involving the same behavior. For example, when grandparents or friends are visiting, previously acceptable behavior to the parent can become unacceptable because of the parent's need to look like a good parent to his (her) parents.

Thus, the line of demarcation between acceptable and nonacceptable behavior constantly moves up or down, depending upon the parent, the child and the situation:

Thus, a parent-child relationship is a constantly changing dynamic system with respect to whether the parent can feel accepting of some particular behavior of the child or how much of the child's behavior he can accept. This single diagram has some significant effects upon the parents in our training program:

(1) It relieves a lot of their guilt about not always feeling accepting — it sanctions their having some nonaccepting feelings.
(2) It relieves a lot of their guilt about feeling more accepting of one child than another because of the characteristics of the child.

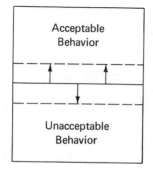

FIGURE 21.1

(3) It helps them understand and accept that differences in the degree of acceptance of a child can exist between husband and wife.

(4) It helps them accept the knowledge that their degree of acceptance can be solely a function of themselves as persons or of how they feel at a particular moment.

(5) It refutes the notion that parents have to be "consistent" — it sanctions their feeling different degrees of acceptance at different times.

(6) It helps parents be more sensitively aware of what they are feeling toward a child at a particular time, be it acceptance or nonacceptance.

II. Demonstrating Acceptance of the Other

Because it is one thing to feel accepting of the other person and another thing for him to perceive that acceptance, I must demonstrate or communicate my acceptance clearly and effectively.

We tend to think of acceptance as a passive thing — a state of mind, an attitude, a feeling. But to be an effective therapeutic force in influencing another, acceptance must be actively communicated or demonstrated. Thus, I must continue to try to find more effective ways of *implementing my attitude of acceptance.* Generally, this will be done through talk, although we also communicate nonverbally.

Talk can be therapeutic and foster constructive change, but talk can also be nontherapeutic and destructive. I must somehow learn to refrain from evaluating, judging, warning, threatening, preaching, arguing, interpreting, diagnosing, reassuring — all the frequently-used kinds of messages that carry a high risk of communicating to the child that I do not accept him as he is and want very much for him to be different.

The client-centered therapist's empathic nonevaluative "Active Listening" has been for me one of the most consistently effective ways of communicating my acceptance of another. Both research and clinical experience have demonstrated the powerful "therapeutic" effect of this way of responding to others. Nevertheless, this type of listening is not easy to learn. It also carries its own risk — I might be changed by what I hear. So I have to develop a degree of courage and personal security to employ this method of communication, in view of the fact that what I hear from my child may change my own attitudes and beliefs.

However, Active Listening, is not the only kind of "therapeutic talk." Other kinds of communication can demonstrate acceptance — expressing feelings of caring for the other, sharing my own experiences with him at appropriate times, touching him, being *with* the relationship when I'm *in* it, and other expressions of "giving of myself." These take courage, too, for they expose me to possible rejection, criticism, or rebuke.

Parents in P.E.T. are trained in how to communicate acceptance by several basic teaching methods. First, through a classroom exercise they are shown how they typically respond to their children's communications or their behavior. By presenting parents with three situations involving a child expressing a strong opinion, a personal problem, and a strong negative emotion, we elicit the parent's own responses, which invariably include all the following:

(1)	Ordering, Commanding	"You must . . ."
(2)	Admonishing	"You ought to . . ."
(3)	Warning, Threatening	"You had better . . ."
(4)	Advising, Suggesting	"You might . . ."
(5)	Instructing, Teaching	"You need to know . . ."
(6)	Criticising, Disagreeing	"You are wrong . . ."
(7)	Praising, Agreeing	"You are right . . ."
(8)	Name-calling, Ridiculing	"You're acting like a baby . . ."
(9)	Interpreting, Analyzing	"You're doing this because . . ."
(10)	Reassuring, Sympathizing	"You'll be okay . . ."
(11)	Probing, Questioning	"Who? When? How? Why?"

The parents are then shown how these typical ways of responding often communicate nonacceptance, how they can communicate a desire to change the child, how they often show disrespect for his needs, and how they can block further communication. Most parents have never thought of "categories of talk," and so this exercise is a very meaningful one to them. Parents often report that after this exercise, they are more sensitively aware of their own pattern of talk. They also report how amazed they are at the frequency of their nontherapeutic talk.

Parents are then introduced to ways of responding to children that communicate genuine acceptance, the most effective being the client-centered counselor's "reflection of feeling" called in P.E.T. simply "Active Listening."

Despite the widespread familiarity with Carl Rogers' writings and with Haim Ginott's books for parents, both of which clearly identify the technique of "reflection of feelings," almost all the parents who enroll in P.E.T. find Active Listening a totally new way of responding to the verbal messages of children. Even though some have understood the concept of acceptance, few have ever thought of the necessity of communicating this attitude by means of a particular verbal response to their children's talk. Therefore, it comes as a revelation to our parents that they can learn a specific skill with which they can implement their felt acceptance.

They are even more convinced of the effectiveness of Active Listening when they are shown how it functions as a "Feedback mechanism" for checking on the accuracy of their understanding.

Many parents acquire a surprising level of skill in Active Listening by the end of the twenty-four-hour course. Some have immediate success experiences at home. Others report that it is effective with one child but not another. Still others have rather disappointing experiences at first. This latter group is invariably made up of those parents whose level of acceptance is still low or whose children have already stopped communicating with their parents. Some parents initially have some reluctance about using Active Listening, yet they do become conscious of when they use the "roadblocks to communication" and report a marked decrease in such communication with their children.

Many parents report improvement in the communication between husband and wife as a result of training in Active Listening. Husbands also report applying it successfully in their relations with subordinates. Clearly, Active Listening is one of the most useful tools parents acquire in the course.

III. Trying to Become Accepting of More of the Other's Behavior

I must have a genuine desire to try to extend my area of acceptance — to try to bring about a condition in which less and less of the other's behavior is unacceptable to me. Or conversely, I must try to increase my "therapeutic potential" by becoming more accepting or by feeling acceptance more often.

Parents in P.E.T. are shown three basic ways of doing this: (1) modifying themselves, (2) modifying the environment, and (3) modifying the child's behavior. Discussions center around how parents can modify their own attitudes through enlarging their understanding of children in general or their own children in particular. Books about children are recommended, and parents are encouraged to recall their own behavior as a child. Discussions about values, morals, and standards are encouraged. The relationship between acceptance of self and acceptance of others is pointed out. Parents are shown how important it is for them to acquire self-acceptance from their own achievement and self-fulfillment rather than from their children's achievements.

P.E.T. seems to influence parents to become more accepting of their children by means of the following:

(1) Less accepting parents learn from more accepting parents as different "common" problems are discussed in class.

(2) Parents acquire insights into themselves by applying what is taught in the course to their relationships with their *own parents*.

(3) Parents acquire a better understanding of their own biases, prejudices, or unrealistic standards.

(4) Parents begin to realize how much of their nonacceptance is a result of their own needs to be seen as a good parent by friends and relatives.

(5) Parents begin to understand how much of their nonacceptance is a result of their lack of acceptance of themselves as persons or the lack of fulfillment in their own lives.

(6) Some parents begin to realize that their unaccepting feelings toward their children are a function of their relying too much on them to bring feelings of gratification, because they are not obtaining sufficient gratification from their relationships with their spouses.

P.E.T. also shows parents how often they can "modify the environment" to prevent the occurrence of behaviors by the child that would be unacceptable to the parent. Examples of the many ideas given to parents are:

(1) Substitute an acceptable object for one the parent finds unacceptable for the child to play with.
(2) Inform the child ahead of time of changes that are going to take place (e.g., a new baby-sitter, a trip, a new house, a new food, etc.).
(3) Child-proof the home.
(4) Set aside a corner of the house or the garage for "messing" or painting.
(5) Take along things for a child to play with when visiting friends or taking a trip.

P.E.T. also teaches parents ways of *influencing the child to modify his own behavior* — behavior the parent finds unacceptable.

(1) Ask him to alter his behavior and give him a reason for your request.
(2) Inform the child of the consequences of what he is doing.
(3) Model or demonstrate the new behavior for the child.
(4) Confront the child with the parent's own feelings — directly, honestly, and unambiguously.

This last idea deserves further comment because among the parents who take the course we have found an almost universal reluctance to be honest and open in sharing their feelings with their children. This leads to our fourth and fifth principles.

IV. Becoming Aware of Nonaccepting Feelings

I must learn to be aware of and admit to myself the existence of my non-accepting feelings toward the other's behavior whenever I have them.

If the child persists in behaving in a way that bothers me or interferes with meeting some needs of my own, I must not pretend to be accepting when actually I am not. I must not be guilty of "false permissiveness." Children are amazingly sensitive in picking up nonverbal clues — they are like sensitive radar when it comes to perceiving incongruent (false) messages. Consequently, we try to show parents how they must continuously find ways of getting more in touch with their feelings and accept them for what they are. Discussions center on the influences in society that keep people from being in touch with feelings, both negative and positive. Parents are introduced to Rogers' concept of "congruence" and Jourard's concept of the "transparent self." In addition, through role-playing in the classroom and at-home self-instructional exercises, parents are made more sensitive to times when they are not in touch with what they are feeling in various encounters with children.

Many parents are greatly relieved to get "sanction" for having negative feelings toward their children. Undoubtedly, much of the literature that gets into the hands of parents either fails to deal with the inevitability of parents having negative feelings or actually admonishes them against having such feelings. The "sweetness and light" philosophy of parental behavior is all too prevalent in books and popular magazines.

V. Communicating Unaccepting Feelings

I must also learn to act congruently or honestly. I must have the courage to be "transparently real" — to be what I am feeling. My communications must match my inner state.

But why should I communicate to my child how I feel? What is the purpose of this? When I become aware of nonaccepting feelings toward the child, I first may try to change these to accepting feelings, recognizing that nonaccepting feelings are nontherapeutic to the child and uncomfortable to me. Or I might try to modify myself in some way — for example, I might remember that I behaved similarly when I was a child, the memory of which makes me now feel accepting of my own child's behavior. Or I might try modifying the environment or the child in some way so his unacceptable behavior ceases. However, if neither of these works, and I still feel unaccepting, then I must be willing *to confront him* — to communicate to him openly and directly how I feel about his behavior. Now, knowing how his behavior makes me feel, he *might* choose to change his unacceptable behavior. If he does, so much to the good, for now I can feel accepting of him again.

Parents in our P.E.T. courses almost universally reveal a fear or a reluctance about openly expressing strong negative (and often strong positive) feelings to their children. It shocks them when our instructors urge them to match their feelings with appropriate words and feeling-tone: "I am very angry at you, Bobby, for hurting your baby brother," or "I felt very mad when I had to empty the garbage that you forgot to take out this morning." So many of our parents "undershoot" or "soften the blow" as they role play various parent-child encounters in the classroom. They fear hurting the child's feelings, or are concerned about frightening the child or damaging his ego, or have a vague apprehension that the child will lose "respect" for a parent who gets angry (reveals his humanness).

VI. Communicating My Unaccepting Feelings Nonevaluatively

Realizing that communicating my true feelings may be upsetting to another, depending upon how I do it, I must learn certain ways of communicating my feelings that are less threatening.

Communication that implies evaluation, blame, or judgment is usually threatening ("You are acting very childish," or "You are being a bad girl"). However, it is far less threatening when I can communicate only *my* feelings and communicate them in a way that implies that I *own* them — they belong to *me,* as opposed to the child being responsible for them. Less likely to produce defensiveness are "I"-messages such as "I am embarrassed when you act like that" or "I am too tired now to want to play with you." I must learn, therefore, to avoid "You"-messages and communicate only what is inside *me.*

Even if I send an "I"-message, however, the child seldom *wants* to hear that I am feeling embarrassed, tired, angry, hurt, or the like. No one really likes to learn that his behavior is making another person uncomfortable. Yet a person is much less threatened and more likely to modify his behavior when the message he hears is how the *other* feels than when the message implies evaluation or judgment of him.

Rogers has made this point convincingly in his paper, "A tentative theory of interpersonal relationships."[2] In P.E.T. we greatly simplify this concept by our device of differentiating between "I"-messages and "You"-messages.

This simple scheme seems to have great meaning for our parents after role playing and at-home exercises. Some parents report immediate successes from this technique at home, bringing back to the class dramatic instances of children responding for the first time to their parent's feelings or expressed needs. Parents accustomed to having to "nag" report that their children are responding immediately to "I"-messages. In short, most of our parents are delighted to discover a way of getting their children to listen to them for a change and to show consideration for their parents' needs.

VII. Refusing to Use Power in Conflict-Resolution

I must commit myself to refuse to use my power to resolve conflicts between myself and the other. Power, punishment, threats of punishment, unilaterally established limits, discipline through fear — none of these belongs in a healthy or therapeutic relationship between people or between groups.

If my efforts to become accepting of a child's particular behavior fail (if I am still feeling unaccepting), or if I have not been able to modify his unacceptable-to-me behavior by telling him how I feel, then our relationship for the moment has a *conflict* — a "conflict of needs" situation exists. What does a parent do when such a conflict occurs? Probably, *the most critical requirement* for a healthy relationship is that the person with the power must commit himself to avoiding the use of that power to impose a solution that would meet *his* need but not that of the other person. As an effective parent I must be unwilling to *win* at the expense of the child having to *lose.*

We have adequate research to convince us of the harmful and destructive effects of parental authority and power on both the child and the relationship itself. Yet psychologists have made almost no headway in influencing parents to discard this method of conflict-resolution. Today's children, like yesterday's children, invariably respond to this method by fight, flight, or submis-

[2] Rogers, C. R., "A tentative theory of interpersonal relationships" (unpublished manuscript).

sion. It is *the* method of choice to guarantee hostility, resentment, and rebellion; lying, covering up, and tattling; dependence and submissiveness; withdrawing and shyness. Furthermore, parents who rely on this method in the children's early years discover to their dismay that as their children move into adolescence the parents inevitably begin to lose their power and are eventually left with no effective means of influencing the adolescent's behavior. Nevertheless, this method of conflict-resolution has been and continues to be the most frequently used method in the families of our society. While the authoritarian method of conflict-resolution is rapidly losing ground in labor-management relationships, in boss-subordinate relationships, in relationships between husbands and wives, and even in relationships between nations, the parent-child relationship is one of the last strongholds for the advocacy of power to settle conflicts. The teacher-student relationship is one other that has steadfastly resisted change.

The idea of not using power in the parent-child relationship comes as a real shock to parents in our P.E.T. classes. It provokes initial resistance because it threatens one of the oldest and most sacred beliefs in our society, namely, that parents *must* exercise their authority over their children. We find, too, that our principle of refusing to use parental power is almost invariably a brand-new idea for these parents. Almost without exception, it is the *first* time our parents have ever encountered this idea. Even so-called "permissive" parents believe in using power when the chips are down.

At first, this surprised me until I began systematically to examine the writings of educators, pediatricians, psychiatrists, and psychologists in the area of child-rearing and parent-child relationships. It became increasingly apparent that *almost none of this vast literature even deals with conflict and conflict resolution.* Books and articles either avoid this fundamental aspect of the parent-child relationship or treat it with vague abstractions or outright inconsistencies. Even research studies of the parent-child relationship have failed to deal with this basic issue. In the hundreds of studies reviewed in Hoffman and Hoffman's recent *Review of child development research* (1964), there is hardly a reference to conflict, methods of conflict-resolution, authority, or the use of power in the parent-child relationship.

Understandably then the thousands of parents who have enrolled in our P.E.T. classes find our principle a startlingly novel one. On the other hand, when we ask them in class how *they as children* coped with and responded to their own parents' use of power to resolve conflicts in the home, our parents invariably produce a list that includes everyone of the negative effects known to professionals who work with children:

(1) Resistance, defiance, rebellion
(2) Hostility, resentment, anger
(3) Aggression, hyperactivity
(4) Retaliation, cutting-down-to-size

    (5) Lying, covering up, hiding feelings
    (6) Blaming others, tattling, cheating
    (7) Domination of others, bossiness
    (8) Competitiveness, needing to look good, hating to lose
    (9) Organizing, forming alliances, ganging up
  (10) Withdrawal, escapism, retreat, autism, regression
  (11) Submissiveness, fear, obedience
  (12) Seduction, apple-polishing, courting favor, seeking approval
  (13) Conformity, reluctance to try something new, requiring assurance of success, lack of creativity
  (14) Blaming self, guilt, feeling "bad" or no good

This classroom exercise is an eye-opener, even to those who most vigorously defend the parents' "right" or "obligation" to exercise authority.

Perhaps the most effective device for bringing about an openness to this new idea, however, is the following simple conceptual scheme to help parents understand how conflicts are typically handled between parents and children:

Method I: When a conflict-of-needs exists, it is the parent who eventually decides how the conflict is to be resolved. The parent decides the solution. His solution must prevail. If the child does not readily accept the solution, as is often the case, the parent tries different methods of persuasion, usually ending up using his power or threatening to use his power. In this method, *the parent wins and the child loses.* Consequently, the child is resentful or angry.

Method II: When a conflict-of-needs exists, it is the child who is permitted to get his way. It is the child who decides the solution. For various reasons, the parent "gives in" or "gives up," permitting the child to have his needs met, often at the expense of the parent's needs. In this method, *the child wins and the parent loses.* Consequently, the parent is resentful or angry. In a sense, the child is allowed to use *his* power over the parent.

Parents readily see the disadvantages of both methods when viewed in the frame of reference of someone winning and someone losing. In fact, one of the most valuable insights I have acquired from our parents is the fact that most authoritarian parents at a deep level are quite dissatisfied with their method of conflict-resolution, because they hate to see the child lose or they hate to deal with his subsequent hostility or resentment. However, they have not been able to give up Method I because they could not stand the only alternative they knew, namely, to have the child win while they lose (Method II). Similarly, Method II parents are generally dissatisfied with the results of letting the child win, yet for them it would be worse to switch to Method I. Most of our parents, therefore, are actually locked into a method they basically sense is unsatisfactory and ineffective because they see no other way to go.

VIII. Refusing to Give in to the Other's Use of Power

I must be unwilling to let the other impose his solution on me such that his needs are met and mine are not.

It is just as unhealthy for a parent-child relationship if the child consistently wins and the parent loses. I must not allow myself as a parent to deny my own needs begrudgingly and resentfully. Situations resulting in my feeling "OK, you win" only lead to my feeling deprived, used, disregarded, imposed upon, defeated. In the long run, I will grow to resent or even hate the child, just as certainly as he will have such feelings toward me if usually *I win* and *he loses.*

Again, we have sufficient evidence of the harmful effects upon a child of letting him have his way in the family, or permitting him to rule his parents. The overly indulged and spoiled child who has been given license to do very much what he wants when he wants it generally turns out to be unmanageable, inconsiderate, selfish, unlikeable, and emotionally unstable. He often feels insecure about being loved, principally because he so frequently is not lovable and, therefore, cannot easily be loved. Also, such a child gets a rude awakening when he goes out into the world and discovers that others are not as willing as his parents to let him have his way.

I have come to feel that this is the major dilemma of today's parents. Most of them think only in terms of these two "win-lose" methods of conflict-resolution. This "either-or" way of thinking about the parent-child relationship is almost universal in our society, among parents and professionals alike. Either the parent wins and the child loses, or the child wins and the parent loses. Both are "win-lose" methods of conflict-resolution. Parents and children see their relationship with each other grow into a power struggle, much like unfriendly nations. Thus today's parents and their adolescent children end up in a contest — or, if you will, *at war* — both thinking in terms of someone winning and someone losing.

Many parents in P.E.T. are those whose most frequent pattern of conflict-resolution has been to permit the child to have his way most of the time. Such parents are usually very intelligent and often well educated. They have been strongly influenced by nursery schools. Some have resolved to be lenient and permissive with their children in reaction to their own strongly Method I parents. Others are people who dread conflict of any kind and consequently, take a peace-at-any-price approach in child-rearing. Some have been influenced strongly by the permissive approach they perceive in Dr. Spock's books.

Rarely do the Method II parents need any convincing that their approach to conflict-resolution is unsatisfactory. Parenthood already feels like a burden to most of them and they complain about not having much control over their children. They describe their children as uncooperative and inconsiderate of the needs of others in the family. Often they look forward to the time when their children will be old enough to leave home so they can then be free to do what they want to do. Then, of course, there are those Method II parents who seem to have lost all love and affection for their children, simply because they have been so mistreated by these children.

P.E.T. has a strong impact on Method II parents. Generally they are quite relieved to learn that it is not necessary to meet all the needs of children. They naturally respond positively to the idea that *their* needs are as important as the child's. Some acquire the courage to confront their children, often for the first time. P.E.T. helps these parents understand why they have developed resentments or why they feel so angry toward their children. Such parents are only too glad to learn that there is an alternative to Method II, yet not one that would require them to be authoritarian (Method I).

IX. Resolving Conflicts By a "No-lose" Method

I must commit myself to use a "no-lose" method to resolve all the inevitable conflicts that occur in my relationships with the other.

There is an alternative to the two "win-lose" methods of conflict resolution. It is a method that involves a problem-solving approach to conflict in which parent and child join together in a mutual search for a solution that will be *acceptable to both.*

While this method is seldom used in families, it is not exactly rare in other segments of society. Conflicts are resolved every day in our society by contractual agreements, negotiation, joint decision-making, consensus, group-centered decision making, out-of-court settlements, and so on. Where power tends to be equal between persons or groups, the no-lose method is more apt to be used — as a matter of fact, it usually must be used. However, in relationships in which one person has substantially more power than another, the no-lose method is rarely used consistently. This has been true in boss-subordinate relationships, teacher-student relationships, and relationships between large nations and small nations, as well as in parent-child relationships. Apparently human beings as yet have learned only that a democratic or no-lose method of conflict-resolution is what you are forced to use when you *do not have power* over another. The idea that it can be used even when you *do have power* over another is not commonly accepted.

Nevertheless, I have become convinced that if a relationship between persons, groups, or nations is to be a healthy one — or a mutually "therapeutic" one — there *must* be a commitment that conflicts in that relationship will *always* be resolved by means of a nonpower or no-lose method.

Method III is taught parents in P.E.T. by means of: (1) playing tape recordings of actual Method III problem-solving situations that have been recorded in the homes of parents who have learned to use this method; (2) involving parents in role-playing conflict situations in the classroom; (3) encouraging parents to bring to the Classroom tape-recordings of their own attempts to use Method III; and (4) self-instructional materials used by the parents at home.

Parents' ability to acquire the skills necessary to utilize this method of conflict-resolution varies a great deal. Some parents eagerly grab the new method and immediately run to put it into effect successfully in their home, even before the course is completed and often with startling results. Others find it much more difficult, either because of their own authoritarian or permissive tendencies or because of initial resistance or distrust on the part of their children. Interestingly, few of our parents actually reject the validity or soundness of the idea of Method III. With rare exception our parents perceive Method III as an obviously sensible alternative to Method I or Method II. Many express feelings of deep gratitude to have been given their first ray of hope — to have been shown for the first time a positive way out of the dilemma about authority and discipline. A frequent response of parents is to ask why had not anyone told them about this method before?

To the parents in our classes, it is very seldom the acceptance of the *theory* of Method III that is difficult but rather the job of pulling it off effectively in their day-to-day interaction. One of the reasons for this, of course, is that Method III requires that the parents use both Active Listening and effective sending. Two-way effective communication is the prerequisite for Method III conflict-resolution. They must bring to Method III problem-solving all the other skills they have been taught in P.E.T.

A Summary of the Theory

What we are attempting to teach parents is obviously a philosophy of child-rearing that embodies a new theory of healthy interpersonal relationships. This theory itself is quite simple. I have translated the theory into everyday language in the form of a credo:

A Credo for my Relationship with my Child

You and I are in a relationship with each other. Yet each of us is a separate person having his own needs. I will try to be as accepting as I can of your behavior as you try to meet your own needs. I will even try to learn how to increase my capacity to be accepting of your behavior. But I can be genuinely accepting of you only as long as your behavior to meet your needs does not conflict with my meeting my own needs. Therefore, whenever I am feeling nonaccepting of you because my own needs are not being met, I will tell you as openly and honestly as I can, leaving it up to you whether you will change your behavior. I also will encourage you to do the same with me and will try to listen to your feelings and perhaps change my behavior. However, when we discover that a conflict-of-needs continues to exist in our relationship, let us both commit ourselves to try to resolve that conflict without the use of either my power or yours. I will respect your needs, but I also must respect my own. Consequently, let us strive always to search mutually for solutions to our inevitable conflicts that will be acceptable to both of us. In this way, your needs will be met but so will mine. As a result, you can continue to grow and achieve satisfaction and so can I. And, finally, our relationship can continue to be a healthy one because it will be mutually satisfying.

It has occurred to me that this theory is a description of a truly *democratic relationship* between persons or groups or nations. This is the way people would interact in a true democracy. This would be the basic philosophy underlying a democratic way of life or a way of living democratically with others. Could it be that a relationship that is *democratic* in a real sense would also be therapeutic, and conversely, that a relationship to be therapeutic *must* be democratic? If I can learn to live with others democratically, then it would follow that I would automatically be providing an environment or climate in which they have the greatest chance to grow, to develop, to actualize themselves — as would I. In democracy, have we found what is maximally therapeutic for people? And in therapeutic relationships have we found an operational definition of democracy?

A democratic way of life, then, would become more than "a system of government" or one of the several "political philosophies." Rather, it would be a set of conditions for *all* human relationships, if people are to fulfill their maximum potential, become what they are capable of being, and continue to relate to one another in mutual respect, friendship, love, and *peace*.

REFERENCES

HOFFMAN, MARTIN L. and HOFFMAN, L. W. Review of child development research. New York: Russell Sage Foundation, 1964.

ROGERS, CARL R. A tentative theory of interpersonal relationships. Unpublished manuscript.

PART FIVE

Values at Work

Among the schools of thought that make up the psychotherapeutic institution, none have been more concerned with the issue of human values than client-centered therapy. From the outset, Rogers and his collaborators have emphasized the dignity and worth of the individual, and fundamental to that position is the premise that, given an appropriate atmosphere and relationship, each person has within himself a self-actualizing drive to grow and develop to his full potential.

This value orientation stretches far beyond the boundaries of psychotherapy. This section, for example, contains papers that deal with value issues relevant to the total society as well as to the practice of client-centered therapy. In this context it is appropriate that the first paper be by Carl Rogers and that it concern itself with a modern (i.e., new) approach to value development. It is significant that in Rogers' view the source of this development is the human organism itself, rather than the traditional "out there" agents of society. As such, Rogers rejects the compulsive rules-for-rules-sake stance of the greater society, and stands instead with those who have chosen to behave in response to their inner (organismic) experience of the world.

Reliance on one's own internal valuing sense often carries with it the possibility of conflict with conventional norms. Indeed, the motivating force of dissidence in this country is a product of the gap between human experience and conceived values. The conceived values are being challenged, because for many it is clear that these values do not gibe with their internal sense of what is "right." And so students protest against irrelevant education, blacks protest against the killing insensitivity of whites, hippies protest against the ethic of money, and on and on it goes. Some of the protest may be gratuitous and some of it may seem to be a product of the egregious impertinence of youth, but in the final analysis it is a charge born from the society's failure to develop a system of values that fosters the growth of every individual's self-fulfillment. The answer, Rogers suggests, is not in a reinstatement of a universal set of values given by rulers, priests, philosophers, or psychologists, but rather in "the possibility of universal human value directions *emerging* from the experiencing of the human organism." The trick is to place the individual in touch with his own organismic valuing process, and then to provide the cultural atmosphere in which that internal awareness can grow in directions that "would make for the survival and enhancement of the human race."

In the second chapter in this section, "Professional psychology and the control of human behaviour," G. T. Barrett-Lennard focuses the discussion on the "ethical and psychological issues connected with the involvement of professional psychologists in the control and modification of human behaviour." Barrett-Lennard discusses the value differences that underlie the Behaviorist and Rogerian positions, and describes how the two approaches differ in terms of their conception of human personality, therapeutic goals, method, and values. He makes no direct attempt to evaluate the potential social impact of the two approaches, but points out that they have quite different implications for the future of society, conceiving as they do of utterly disparate "states of being of which man is capable."

Focusing more sharply on psychotherapy, the values theme is continued by Tomlinson's discussion of the relationship of values and strategy in client-centered therapy. Tomlinson argues that the polemic about efficacy among the various therapies is a product of their differing value systems rather than issues of effect and outcome. Each method has an effect and produces an outcome that may or may not be reflected in a given criterion of results. Choice of treatment method is more appropriately based on the valued goals of the practitioner, together with evidence that the therapeutic strategy is consistent with achieving those goals. Tomlinson then describes the particular value orientation of client-centered therapy and how and why the client-centered method, in pure form, is a valid and internally consistent method for the achievement of certain valued outcomes.

In the next chapter, "The interpersonal relationship in the facilitation of learning," the discussion broadens a bit as Rogers addresses himself to the dilemma of teaching versus facilitation of learning in the school system. Teaching in the sense of "making people know," "showing, guiding, and directing," etc., is rejected by Rogers on the grounds that such methods stultify and rob the student of the opportunity to develop an *internal* thirst for knowledge. An educational facilitator, on the other hand, by establishing the same climate for learning as is found in the therapeutic relationship, provides a context for the development of personal responsibility for the educational process and allows the student to develop his own unique potential, unrestricted by the encouragement of "facts." Rogers does not argue for "permissive education" in the sense that an uninvolved teacher allows his students unrestricted activity within the classroom. Instead Rogers argues that the teachers should display the same characteristics to their students that have been found to facilitate learning and the development of human relationships in other settings. Thus, Rogers pleads for teachers to prize and accept their students, to be transparently real (congruent) persons in the classroom, and to interact through the medium of empathic understanding rather than authority. The aim is to create a classroom situation in which it is safe for the students to be what they are and thereby to become what they can be. This is best accomplished by a teacher who, through his own behavior as an educational facilitator, rather than an imparter of knowledge, allows the student to generate his own interest in obtaining the knowledge available to him.

This section ends with a paper that has created a swirl of controversy, Rogers' "Current assumptions in graduate education: A passionate statement." In it Rogers lays out and challenges the common assumptions that govern graduate training in most major colleges, and which in his view, consummate the slow intellectual death of American education by rigidifying and/or ejecting students who show the greatest promise for independent and creative thought and action.

Summing together, this section presents a view of the working values that permeate the thought, theory, and practice of those who describe themselves as client-centered therapists. The system of values, however, extends far beyond the boundaries of psychotherapy into all walks of professional educational endeavor. It is a controversial view: few colleges accept Rogers' view of the problems of higher education; few teachers conduct their classes in the style described and endorsed by Rogers; and few people trust themselves (or others) sufficiently to accept the guidelines for behavior that spring from their own experiencing process. But the words have been said, the challenge has been issued. The ferment and unrest of the past decade testify to the need and bear witness to the change.

22

Toward a Modern Approach

to Values: The Valuing Process

in the Mature Person*

CARL R. ROGERS

A description is given of the change in the value orientation of the individual from infancy to average adulthood, and from this adult status to a greater degree of psychological maturity attained through psychotherapy or fortunate life circumstances. On the basis of these observations, the theory is advanced that there is an organismic basis for the valuing process within the human individual; that this valuing process is effective to the degree that the individual is open to his experiencing; that in persons relatively open to their experiencing there is an important commonality or universality of value directions; that these directions make for the constructive enhancement of the individual and his community, and for the survival and evolution of his species.

There is a great deal of concern today with the problem of values. Youth, in almost every country, is deeply uncertain of its value orientation; the

* From Carl R. Rogers, "Toward a Modern Approach to Values: The Valuing Process in the Mature Person," *The Journal of Abnormal and Social Psychology*, Vol. 68, No. 2, pp. 160-167. Copyright 1964 by the American Psychological Association. Reproduced by permission.

values associated with various religions have lost much of their influence; sophisticated individuals in every culture seem unsure and troubled as to the goals they hold in esteem. The reasons are not far to seek. The world culture, in all its aspects, seems increasingly scientific and relativistic, and the rigid, absolute views on values which come to us from the past appear anachronistic. Even more important, perhaps, is the fact that the modern individual is assailed from every angle by divergent and contradictory value claims. It is no longer possible, as it was in the not too distant historical past, to settle comfortably into the value system of one's forebears or one's community and live out one's life without ever examining the nature and the assumptions of that system.

In this situation it is not surprising that value orientations from the past appear to be in a state of disintegration or collapse. Men question whether there are, or can be, any universal values. It is often felt that we may have lost, in our modern world, all possibility of any general or cross-cultural basis for values. One natural result of this uncertainty and confusion is that there is an increasing concern about, interest in, and a searching for, a sound or meaningful value approach which can hold its own in today's world.

I share this general concern. As with other issues the general problem faced by the culture is painfully and specifically evident in the cultural microcosm which is called the therapeutic relationship, which is my sphere of experience.

As a consequence of this experience I should like to attempt a modest theoretical approach to this whole problem. I have observed changes in the approach to values as the individual grows from infancy to adulthood. I observe further changes when, if he is fortunate, he continues to grow toward true psychological maturity. Many of these observations grow out of my experience as therapist, where I have had the mind stretching opportunity of seeing the ways in which individuals move toward a richer life. From these observations I believe I see some directional threads emerging which might offer a new concept of the valuing process, more tenable in the modern world. I have made a beginning by presenting some of these ideas partially in previous writings (Rogers, 1951, 1959); I would like now to voice them more clearly and more fully.

Some Definitions

Charles Morris (1956, pp. 9-12) has made some useful distinctions in regard to values. There are "operative values," which are the behaviors of organisms in which they show preference for one object or objective rather than another. The lowly earthworm, selecting the smooth arm of a Y maze rather than the arm which is paved with sandpaper, is giving an indication of an operative value.

There are also "conceived values," the preference of an individual for a symbolized object. "Honesty is the best policy" is such a conceived value.

There is also the term "objective value," to refer to what is objectively preferable, whether or not it is sensed or conceived of as desirable. I will be concerned primarily with operative or conceptualized values.

Infant's Way of Valuing

Let me first speak about the infant. The living human being has, at the outset, a clear approach to values. We can infer from studying his behavior that he prefers those experiences which maintain, enhance, or actualize his organism, and rejects those which do not serve this end. Watch him for a bit:

> Hunger is negatively valued. His expression of this often comes through loud and clear.
> Food is positively valued. But when he is satisfied, food is negatively valued, and the same milk he responded to so eagerly is now spit out, or the breast which seemed so satisfying is now rejected as he turns his head away from the nipple with an amusing facial expression of disgust and revulsion.
> He values security, and the holding and caressing which seem to communicate security.
> He values new experience for its own sake, and we observe this in his obvious pleasure in discovering his toes, in his searching movements, in his endless curiosity.
> He shows a clear negative valuing of pain, bitter tastes, sudden loud sounds.

All of this is commonplace, but let us look at these facts in terms of what they tell us about the infant's approach to values. It is first of all a flexible, changing, valuing *process,* not a fixed system. He likes food and dislikes the same food. He values security and rest, and rejects it for new experience. What is going on seems best described as an organismic valuing process, in which each element, each moment of what he is experiencing is somehow weighed, and selected or rejected, depending on whether, at that moment, it tends to actualize the organism or not. This complicated weighing of experience is clearly an organismic, not a conscious or symbolic function. These are operative, not conceived values. But this process can nonetheless deal with complex value problems. I would remind you of the experiment in which young infants had spread in front of them a score or more of dishes of natural (that is, unflavored) foods. Over a period of time they clearly tended to value the foods which enhanced their own survival, growth, and development. If for a time a child gorged himself on starches, this would soon be balanced by a protein "binge." If at times he chose a diet deficient in some vitamin, he would later seek out foods rich in this very vitamin. The physiological wisdom of his body guided his behavioral movements, resulting in what we might think of as objectively sound value choices.

Another aspect of the infant's approach to values is that the source or locus of the evaluating process is clearly within himself. Unlike many of us, he *knows* what he likes and dislikes, and the origin of these value choices lies strictly within himself. He is the center of the valuing process, the evidence for his choices being supplied by his own senses. He is not at this point influenced by what his parents think he should prefer, or by what the church says, or by the opinion of the latest "expert" in the field, or by the persuasive talents of an advertising firm. It is from within his own experiencing that his organism is saying in nonverbal terms, "This is good for me." "That is bad for me." "I like this." "I strongly dislike that." He would laugh at our concern over values, if he could understand it.

Change in the Valuing Process

What happens to this efficient, soundly based valuing process? By what sequence of events do we exchange it for the more rigid, uncertain, inefficient approach to values which characterizes most of us as adults? Let me try to state briefly one of the major ways in which I think this happens.

The infant needs love, wants it, tends to behave in ways which will bring a repetition of this wanted experience. But this brings complications. He pulls baby sister's hair, and finds it satisfying to hear her wails and protests. He then hears that he is "a naughty, bad boy," and this may be reinforced by a slap on the hand. He is cut off from affection. As this experience is repeated, and many, many others like it, he gradually learns that what "feels good" is often "bad" in the eyes of significant others. Then the next step occurs, in which he comes to take the same attitude toward himself which these others have taken. Now, as he pulls his sister's hair, he solemnly intones, "Bad, bad boy." He is introjecting the value judgment of another, taking it in as his own. To that degree he loses touch with his own organismic valuing process. He has deserted the wisdom of his organism, giving up the locus of evaluation, and is trying to behave in terms of values set by another, in order to hold love.

Or take another example at an older level. A boy senses, though perhaps not consciously, that he is more loved and prized by his parents when he thinks of being a doctor than when he thinks of being an artist. Gradually he introjects the values attached to being a doctor. He comes to want, above all, to be a doctor. Then in college he is baffled by the fact that he repeatedly fails in chemistry, which is absolutely necessary to becoming a physician, in spite of the fact that the guidance counselor assures him he has the ability to pass the course. Only in counseling interviews does he begin to realize how completely he has lost touch with his organismic reactions, how out of touch he is with his own valuing process.

Perhaps these illustrations will indicate that in an attempt to gain or hold love, approval, esteem, the individual relinquishes the locus of evaluation which was his in infancy, and places it in others. He learns to have a basic distrust for his own experiencing as a guide to his behavior. He learns from others a large number of conceived values, and adopts them as his own, even though they may be widely discrepant from what he is experiencing.

Some Introjected Patterns

It is in this fashion, I believe, that most of us accumulate the introjected value patterns by which we live. In the fantastically complex culture of today, the patterns we introject as desirable or undesirable come from a variety of sources and are often highly contradictory. Let me list a few of the introjections which are commonly held.

Sexual desires and behaviors are mostly bad. The sources of this construct are many — parents, church, teachers.

Disobedience is bad. Here parents and teachers combine with the military to emphasize this concept. To obey is good. To obey without question is even better.

Making money is the highest good. The sources of this conceived value are too numerous to mention.

Learning an accumulation of scholarly facts is highly desirable. Education is the source.

Communism is utterly bad. Here the government is a major source.

To love thy neighbor is the highest good. This concept comes from the church, perhaps from the parents.

Cooperation and teamwork are preferable to acting alone. Here companions are an important source.

Cheating is clever and desirable. The peer group again is the origin.

Coca-Colas, chewing gum, electric refrigerators, and automobiles are all utterly desirable. From Jamaica to Japan, from Copenhagen to Kowloon, the "Coca-Cola culture" has come to be regarded as the acme of desirability.

This is a small and diversified sample of the myriads of conceived values which individuals often introject, and hold as their own, without ever having considered their inner organismic reactions to these patterns and objects.

Common Characteristics of Adult Valuing

I believe it will be clear from the foregoing that the usual adult — I feel I am speaking for most of us — has an approach to values which has these characteristics:

The majority of his values are introjected from other individuals or groups significant to him, but are regarded by him as his own.

The source or locus of evaluation on most matters lies outside of himself.

The criterion by which his values are set is the degree to which they will cause him to be loved, accepted, or esteemed.

These conceived preferences are either not related at all, or not clearly related, to his own process of experiencing.

Often there is a wide and unrecognized discrepancy between the evidence supplied by his own experience, and these conceived values.

Because these conceptions are not open to testing in experience, he must hold them in a rigid and unchanging fashion. The alternative would be a collapse of his values. Hence his values are "right."

Because they are untestable, there is no ready way of solving contradictions. If he has taken in from the community the conception that money is the *summum bonum* and from the church the conception that love of one's neighbor is the highest value, he has no way of discovering which has more value for *him*. Hence a common aspect of modern life is living with absolutely contradictory values. We calmly discuss the possibility of dropping a hydrogen bomb on Russia, but find tears in our eyes when we see headlines about the suffering of one small child.

Because he has relinquished the locus of evaluation to others, and has lost touch with his own valuing process, he feels profoundly insecure and easily threatened in his values. If some of these conceptions were destroyed, what would take their place? This threatening possibility makes him hold his value conceptions more rigidly or more confusedly, or both.

Fundamental Discrepancy

I believe that this picture of the individual, with values mostly introjected, held as fixed concepts, rarely examined or tested, is the picture of most of us. By taking over the conceptions of others as our own, we lose contact with the potential wisdom of our own functioning, and lose confidence in ourselves. Since these value constructs are often sharply at variance with what is going on in our own experiencing, we have in a very basic way divorced ourselves from ourselves, and this accounts for which of modern strain and insecurity. This fundamental discrepancy between the individual's concept and what he is actually experiencing, between the intellectual structure of his values and the valuing process going on unrecognized within — this is a part of the fundamental estrangement of modern man from himself.

Restoring Contact with Experience

Some individuals are fortunate in going beyond the picture I have just given, developing further in the direction of psychological maturity. We see this happen in psychotherapy where we endeavor to provide a climate favorable to the growth of the person. We also see it happen in life, whenever life provides a therapeutic climate for the individual. Let me concentrate on this further maturing of a value approach as I have seen it in therapy.

As the client senses and realizes that he is prized as a person[1] he can slowly begin to value the different aspects of himself. Most importantly, he can begin,

---

The therapeutic relationship is not devoid of values. When it is most effective it is, I believe, marked by one primary value, namely, that this person (the client) has *worth*.

with much difficulty at first, to sense and to feel what is going on within him, what he is feeling, what he is experiencing, how he is reacting. He uses his experiencing as a direct referent to which he can turn in forming accurate conceptualizations and as a guide to his behavior. Gendlin (1961, 1962) has elaborated the way in which this occurs. As his experiencing becomes more and more open to him, as he is able to live more freely in the process of his feelings, then significant changes begin to occur in his approach to values. It begins to assume many of the characteristics it had in infancy.

Introjected Values in Relation to Experiencing

Perhaps I can indicate this by reviewing a few of the brief examples of introjected values which I have given, and suggesting what happens to them as the individual comes closer to what is going on within him.

> The individual in therapy looks back and realizes, "But I *enjoyed* pulling my sister's hair — and that doesn't make me a bad person."
> The student failing chemistry realizes, as he gets close to his own experiencing, "I don't like chemistry; I don't value being a doctor, even though my parents do; and I am not a failure for having these feelings."
> The adult recognizes that sexual desires and behavior may be richly satisfying and permanently enriching in their consequences, or shallow and temporary and less than satisfying. He goes by his own experiencing, which does not always coincide with social norms.
> He recognizes freely that this communist book or person expresses attitudes and goals which he shares as well as ideas and values which he does not share.
> He realizes that at times he experiences cooperation as meaningful and valuable to him, and that at other times he wishes to be alone and act alone.

Valuing in the Mature Person

The valuing process which seems to develop in this more mature person is in some ways very much like that in the infant, and in some ways quite different. It is fluid, flexible, based on this particular moment, and the degree to which this moment is experienced as enhancing and actualizing. Values are not held rigidly, but are continually changing. The painting which last year seemed meaningful now appears uninteresting, the way of working with individuals which was formerly experienced as good now seems inadequate, the belief which then seemed true is now experienced as only partly true, or perhaps false.

Another characteristic of the way this person values experience is that it is highly differentiated, or as the semanticists would say, extensional. The examples in the preceding section indicate that what were previously rather solid monolithic introjected values now become differentiated, tied to a particular time and experience.

Another characteristic of the mature individual's approach is that the locus of evaluation is again established firmly within the person. It is his own experience which provides the value information or feedback. This does not mean that he is not open to all the evidence he can obtain from other sources. But it means that this is taken for what it is — outside evidence — and is not as significant as his own reactions. Thus he may be told by a friend that a new book is very disappointing. He reads two unfavorable reviews of the book. Thus his tentative hypothesis is that he will not value the book. Yet if he reads the book his valuing will be based upon the reactions it stirs in *him,* not on what he has been told by others.

There is also involved in this valuing process a letting oneself down into the immediacy of what one is experiencing, endeavoring to sense and to clarify all its complex meanings. I think of a client who, toward the close of therapy, when puzzled about an issue, would put his head in his hands and say, "Now what *is* it that I'm feeling? I want to get next to it. I want to learn what it is." Then he would wait, quietly and patiently, trying to listen to himself, until he could discern the exact flavor of the feelings he was experiencing. He, like others, was trying to get close to himself.

In getting close to what is going on within himself, the process is much more complex than it is in the infant. In the mature person it has much more scope and sweep. For there is involved in the present moment of experiencing the memory traces of all the relevant learnings from the past. This moment has not only its immediate sensory impact, but it has meaning growing out of similar experiences in the past (Gendlin, 1962). It has both the new and the old in it. So when I experience a painting or a person, my experiencing contains within it the learnings I have accumulated from past meetings with paintings or persons, as well as the new impact of this particular encounter. Likewise the moment of experiencing contains, for the mature adult, hypotheses about consequences. "It is not pleasant to express forthrightly my negative feelings to this person, but past experience indicates that in a continuing relationship it will be helpful in the long run." Past and future are both in this moment and enter into the valuing.

I find that in the person I am speaking of (and here again we see a similarity to the infant), the criterion of the valuing process is the degree to which the object of the experience actualizes the individual himself. Does it make him a richer, more complete, more fully developed person? This may sound as though it were a selfish or unsocial criterion, but it does not prove to be so, since deep and helpful relationships with others are experienced as actualizing.

Like the infant, too, the psychologically mature adult trusts and uses the wisdom of his organism, with the difference that he is able to do so knowingly. He realizes that if he can trust all of himself, his feelings and his intuitions may be wiser than his mind, that as a total person he can be more sensitive and accurate than his thoughts alone. Hence he is not afraid to say, "I feel that this experience [or this thing, or this direction] is good. Later I will probably know *why* I feel it is good." He trusts the totality of himself, having moved toward becoming what Lancelot Whyte (1950) regards as "the unitary man."

It should be evidence from what I have been saying that this valuing process in the mature individual is not an easy or simple thing. The process is complex, the choices often very perplexing and difficult, and there is no guarantee that the choice which is made will in fact prove to be self-actualizing. But because whatever evidence exists is available to the individual, and because he is open to his experiencing, errors are correctable. If this chosen course of action is not self-enhancing this will be sensed and he can make an adjustment or revision. He thrives on a maximum feedback interchange, and thus, like the gyroscopic compass on a ship, can continually correct his course toward his true goal of self-fulfillment.

Some Propositions Regarding the Valuing Process

Let me sharpen the meaning of what I have been saying by stating two propositions which contain the essential elements of this viewpoint. While it may not be possible to devise empirical tests of each proposition in its entirety, yet each is to some degree capable of being tested through the methods of psychological science. I would also state that though the following propositions are stated firmly in order to give them clarity, I am actually advancing them as decidedly tentative hypotheses.

Hypothesis I. There is an organismic base for an organized valuing process within the human individual.

It is hypothesized that this base is something the human being shares with the rest of the animate world. It is part of the functioning life process of any healthy organism. It is the capacity for receiving feedback information which enables the organism continually to adjust its behavior and reactions so as to achieve the maximum possible self-enhancement.

Hypothesis II. This valuing process in the human being is effective in achieving self-enhancement to the degree that the individual is open to the experiencing which is going on within himself.

I have tried to give two examples of individuals who are close to their own experiencing: the tiny infant who has not yet learned to deny in his awareness the processes going on within; and the psychologically mature person who has relearned the advantages of this open state.

There is a corollary to this second proposition which might be put in the following terms. One way of assisting the individual to move toward openness to experience is through a relationship in which he is prized as a separate person, in which the experiencing going on within him is empathically understood and valued, and in which he is given the freedom to experience his own feelings and those of others without being threatened in doing so.

This corollary obviously grows out of therapeutic experience. It is a brief statement of the essential qualities in the therapeutic relationship. There are already some empirical studies, of which the one by Barrett-Lennard (1962) is a good example, which give support to such a statement.

Propositions Regarding the Outcomes of the Valuing Process

I come now to the nub of any theory of values or valuing. What are its consequences? I should like to move into this new ground by stating bluntly two propositions as to the qualities of behavior which emerge from this valuing process. I shall then give some of the evidence from my experience as a therapist in support of these propositions.

Hypothesis III. In persons who are moving toward greater openness to their experiencing, there is an organismic commonality of value directions.

Hypothesis IV. These common value directions are of such kinds as to enhance the development of the individual himself, of others in his community, and to make for the survival and evolution of his species.

It has been a striking fact of my experience that in therapy, where individuals are valued, where there is greater freedom to feel and to be, certain value directions seem to emerge. These are not chaotic directions but instead exhibit a surprising commonality. This commonality is not dependent on the personality of the therapist, for I have seen these trends emerge in the clients of therapists sharply different in personality. This commonality does not seem to be due to the influences of any one culture, for I have found evidence of these directions in cultures as divergent as those of the United States, Holland, France, and Japan. I like to think that this commonality of value directions is due to the fact that we all belong to the same species — that just as a human infant tends, individually, to select a diet similar to that selected by other human infants, so a client in therapy tends, individually, to choose value directions similar to those chosen by other clients. As a species there may be certain elements of experience which tend to make for inner development and which would be chosen by all individuals if they were genuinely free to choose.

Let me indicate a few of these value directions as I see them in my clients as they move in the direction of personal growth and maturity.

> They tend to move away from façades. Pretense, defensiveness, putting up a front, tend to be negatively valued.
> They tend to move away from "oughts." The compelling feeling of "I ought to do or be thus and so" is negatively valued. The client moves away from being what he "ought to be," no matter who has set that imperative.
> They tend to move away from meeting the expectations of others. Pleasing others, as a goal in itself, is negatively valued.
> Being real is positively valued. The client tends to move toward being

himself, being his real feelings, being what he is. This seems to be a very deep preference.

Self-direction is positively valued. The client discovers an increasing pride and confidence in making his own choices, guiding his own life.

One's self, one's own feelings come to be positively valued. From a point where he looks upon himself with contempt and despair, the client comes to value himself and his reactions as being of worth.

Being a process is positively valued. From desiring some fixed goal, clients come to prefer the excitement of being a process of potentialities being born.

Sensitivity to others and acceptance of others is positively valued. The client comes to appreciate others for what they are, just as he has come to appreciate himself for what he is.

Deep relationships are positively valued. To achieve a close, intimate, real, fully communicative relationship with another person seems to meet a deep need in every individual, and is very highly valued.

Perhaps more than all else, the client comes to value an openness to all of his inner and outer experience. To be open to and sensitive to his own *inner* reactions and feelings, the reactions and feelings of others, and the realities of the objective world — this is a direction which he clearly prefers. This openness becomes the client's most valued resource.

These then are some of the preferred directions which I have observed in individuals moving toward personal maturity. Though I am sure that the list I have given is inadequate and perhaps to some degree inaccurate, it holds for me exciting possibilities. Let me try to explain why.

I find it significant that when individuals are prized as persons, the values they select do not run the full gamut of possibilities. I do not find, in such a climate of freedom, that one person comes to value fraud and murder and thievery, while another values a life of self-sacrifice, and another values only money. Instead there seems to be a deep and underlying thread of commonality. I believe that when the human being is inwardly free to choose whatever he deeply values, he tends to value those objects, experiences, and goals which make for his own survival, growth, and development, and for the survival and development of others. I hypothesize that it is *characteristic* of the human organism to prefer such actualizing and socialized goals when he is exposed to a growth promoting climate.

A corollary of what I have been saying is that in *any* culture, given a climate of respect and freedom in which he is valued as a person, the mature individual would tend to choose and prefer these same value directions. This is a significant hypothesis which could be tested. It means that though the individual of whom I am speaking would not have a consistent or even a stable system of conceived values, the valuing process within him would lead to emerging value directions which would be constant across cultures and across time.

Another implication I see is that individuals who exhibit the fluid valuing process I have tried to describe, whose value directions are generally those I have listed, would be highly effective in the ongoing process of human evolution. If the human species is to survive at all on this globe, the human being must become more readily adaptive to new problems and situations, must be able to select that which is valuable for development and survival out of new and complex situations, must be accurate in his appreciation of reality if he is to make such selections. The psychologically mature person as I have described him has, I believe, the qualities which would cause him to value those experiences which would make for the survival and enhancement of the human race. He would be a worthy participant and guide in the process of human evolution.

Finally, it appears that we have returned to the issue of universality of values, but by a different route. Instead of universal values "out there," or a universal value system imposed by some group — philosophers, rulers, priests, or psychologists — we have the possibility of universal human value directions *emerging* from the experiencing of the human organism. Evidence from therapy indicates that both personal and social values emerge as natural, and experienced, when the individual is close to his own organismic valuing process. The suggestion is that though modern man no longer trusts religion or science or philosophy nor any system of beliefs to *give* him values, he may find an organismic valuing base within himself which, if he can learn again to be in touch with it, will prove to be an organized, adaptive, and social approach to the perplexing value issues which face all of us.

REFERENCES

BARRETT-LENNARD, G. T. Dimensions of therapist response as causal factors in therapeutic change. *Psychological Monograph*, 1962, 76 (43, Whole No. 562).

GENDLIN, E. T. Experiencing: A variable in the process of therapeutic change. *American Journal of Psychotherapy*, 1961, 15, 233-245.

GENDLIN, E. T. *Experiencing and the creation of meaning.* Glencoe, Ill.: Free Press, 1962.

MORRIS, C. W. *Varieties of human value.* Chicago: University of Chicago Press, 1956.

ROGERS, C. R. *Client-centered therapy.* Boston: Houghton Mifflin, 1951.

ROGERS, C. R. A theory of therapy, personality and interpersonal relationships. In S. Koch (Ed.), *Psychology: A study of a science.* Vol. III. *Formulations of the person and the social context.* New York: McGraw-Hill, 1959. Pp. 185-256.

WHYTE, L. I. *The next development in man.* New York: Mentor Books, 1950.

23

Professional Psychology and

the Control of

Human Behaviour*[1]

G. T. BARRETT-LENNARD

This paper is a discussion of ethical and psychological issues connected with the involvement of professional psychologists in the control or modification of human behaviour — especially in therapeutic practice. The grounds on which the psychologist assumes responsibility for influencing behaviour and personality, and establishes the objectives of his influencing function, are explored briefly. Two basic kinds of orientation to therapeutic control of behaviour are examined and contrasted: approaches based on learning theory and the Rogerian position. The comparison reveals that these orientations involve sharply differing views of what impels man's actions, of the way his personality is organized and how constructive change in behaviour occurs, and that they are directed to the attainment of different kinds of desired or valued goals. These opposing conceptions of man's nature and the different human consequences of professional practice from one or other standpoint confront us with critical problems both of scientific discrimination and of value choice.

* From the *Australian Journal of Psychology*, Vol. 17, No. 1, 1965, pp. 24-34. Reproduced by permission.

[1] Developed from a paper given in a symposium on "Psychology and the control of human behaviour" held at the Annual Conference of the Australian Branch of the British Psychological Society in Perth, August, 1962.

Understanding and controlling human behaviour has apparently always been one of man's basic concerns. Behavioural sciences and related fields of professional practice are a formidable new expression of this old interest. Looking ahead on the basis of present accomplishments and the accelerating pace of development in the behavioural sciences, some awesome possibilities are posed regarding the power that this increasing knowledge could give to those who apply it. Already the situation raises ethical issues and problems of social responsibility that are becoming matters of grave concern to many psychologists (e.g. Hobbs, 1959; Krasner, 1962; Lowe, 1959; Patterson, 1958; Rogers and Skinner, 1956; Smith, 1961; Watson, 1958).

These authors are mainly concerned with considerations that confront the psychologist as he becomes directly involved in modifying human behaviour. The more ambiguous, difficult, but perhaps equally important problem of the ethical issues facing the scientific psychologist, as scientist, has not yet become a matter of serious explicit concern. The purist may argue that his aim is solely to extend knowledge, because to do so is both valuable and satisfying in its own right; applications arising from this knowledge are the business and responsibility of a different class of people, namely, psychological practitioners or technologists. In practice, however, this argument is usually inapplicable or difficult to defend, for a number of reasons: (a) The behavioural scientist, either through intrinsic interest or expedient opportunity, frequently selects research problems because of their practical implications. (b) If he makes discoveries that seem afterwards to have potentially significant applications, even though this was not his prior aim, he may understandably be concerned to advocate or develop these applications. A notable case in point consists of the programmed learning methods stemming from Skinner's originally "basic" research on operant conditioning. (c) Frequently, he has direct interest and responsibility both in research and applied work. In these circumstances, his research is most likely to grow out of observations and concerns at a practical level, and to contribute to evaluation and perhaps revision of this practice.

Thus, it is difficult to see any clear demarcation between the domain of the scientist and that of the practitioner in psychology. In either function, our work has significant immediate or potential effects on other people which call for ethical concern and professional judgment. This discussion will focus on the resources we need and concepts and procedures we employ at the level of practice, but has bearing also on the consequences and responsibilities of our role as scientific investigators.

In professional psychology we are directly confronted with the problem and the challenge of controlling or influencing human behaviour for practical ends. Clearly, the knowledge that behaviour *can* be controlled in particular ways provides no answer to the question of whether it *should* be. From this distinction arise the specific issues the writer wishes to examine.

These issues are considered here with particular reference to psychological counselling and therapy, but are viewed as relevant in principle to professional psychology generally. Our professional aim in this helping context is to promote effects that are "good" for the people we work with, that enable them to function in more rewarding and constructive ways. How do we decide what is good or constructive for other people, that is, how do we choose the desired outcomes of our influencing or controlling function? What does or can justify us in making this kind of decision? What sorts of objectives do we establish, and what forms of control do we use in pursuing them?

One issue related to the choice of objectives has already been implied. This is the question of whether scientific procedure can establish criteria of healthy or adequate personality functioning without resorting, at any point, to what we or other persons selectively value through our experience and observation of human living. Perhaps it is labouring the obvious to assert that science has no such power, that it consists of methods to discover what is, not what should be. Scientific knowledge of the way behavioural patterns or personality qualities are interrelated and determined can be used either constructively or destructively within the context of any given value system. Increase in such knowledge enlarges its potential hazards to man as much as its possible benefits.

It might be argued that we can reduce our responsibility for value choices by relying on our clients (in therapy, industry, government, etc.) to establish their own objectives. Particularly if a person seeks our assistance on his own initiative he helps at least to determine the objectives of our efforts together. However, if we were to apply our efforts solely toward achieving the expressed aims of those who call on our services we would still be making a significant, implied choice; a decision to adopt externally given objectives as our own aims in the situation. Thus we would not be freeing ourselves of responsibility, but variably defining this responsibility to accord with the purposes and standards of other individuals or authorities. Clearly, this alternative would not be consistent with any meaningful system of professional ethics or valued objectives.

In practice, at least in a therapeutic context, we do make what amounts to a prior choice (as far as any particular client is concerned) of kinds of goals or objectives. Typically, there is a consistency to our theoretical and procedural orientation in therapy, which necessarily implies objectives of one kind rather than another. In effect, we offer "help" in terms of certain values, although these may not be explicit or may seem to be externally given rather than something we personally share responsibility for.

To the first question raised the answer is given, therefore, that we choose or accept the objectives of our professional controlling function on the basis of some implicit or explicit valuing process. What, then, does or can qualify us to make such choices — in particular to decide what is more or less constructive or desirable among different modes of psychological functioning? The only general answer evident to the writer is that the combination of our special training and qualities as persons may justify such judgments.

The principal emphasis of our basic academic preparation in psychology is typically that of developing knowledge and critical appreciation of psychology, as a scientific discipline. So far as judgment and valuing are concerned, the focus is on becoming more resourceful in critically assessing theory, research methods and findings in psychology. Granted the importance of these goals in their own right, what are their limitations in the present context? In the writer's view, their pursuit does not contribute to self-understanding that makes an effective difference in our own living. It does not significantly enrich our understanding of and response to other persons in real life situations. It is not geared to the aim of helping us to become more functionally aware of the consequences to the individual and those he influences of different modes of personal organization and functioning.

However, our development in such ways as these is considered vitally relevant to our qualification for psychological intervention in the lives of other persons. It follows from this argument that, at least in the context of avowedly professional preparation in psychology, it is necessary to provide conditions that do foster self-discovery and assist the student in his own becoming as a person. The extent to which he will justify the trust of professionally influencing the behaviour and personalities of other individuals depends on his own maturity and wisdom in a total personal-professional sense. The relevance of this maturity transcends the precise way in which it is conceived. Regardless of detailed definition, its facilitation implies a training situation in which the individual's specialized resources become a vital, authentic, continually developing aspect and expression of himself rather than a relatively static, ready-made professional repertoire and role.

In answer to the second issue raised, therefore, it is argued that dependable judgment of what are more or less adequate and rewarding ways of functioning arises from experiential learning where the individual's thinking has its basic roots and meaning in direct experience. This implies that the student needs to be involved as a person in the learning process, in ways that foster increasing awareness and integration of the primary data of his own experience and a growing sensitivity to the inwardly experienced worlds of other persons. From the interaction of this process and his exposure to the operational criteria and judgments of other professionals he can evolve bearings for his own professional activity that are both deeply and significantly rooted and open to continued development.

The third question and primary focus of this discussion concerns the particular aims and methods of "control" that we, as psychologists, employ or advocate. It is clear that we vary widely among ourselves in this respect. Although many viewpoints could be distinguished, there appear to be two basic divergencies whose roots go far back in history and whose consequences may largely define the nature of the contribution that psychology makes to the human condition, at least in our time.

Allport (1955) has pointed out that one of these streams may be identified historically with John Locke (Fraser, 1894) and developments that followed his work. Locke's proposal that man's mind is initially a *tabula rasa,* which passively acquires its contents and structure through sensory stimulation and associative processes, is represented in modern psychology by conceptions based on formal learning theories; for in such theories the person is regarded as essentially a *re*active agent whose behavioural patterns are built up by their association with drive-reduction. These drives are generally conceived of as stemming either directly or indirectly from biological tissue needs.

The opposing stream may be traced, for example, to Leibnitz's conception of man's mind as active and purposive in its inherent nature, prone to organizing sensory experience, and disposed to rational, reflective thought which acts upon and goes beyond the products of sense-experience (Leibnitz, 1949; Loemker, 1956). For Leibnitz, the emphasis is on man seeking and using experience (in terms of inherent dispositions and capacities) rather than being a result of it, although both kinds of process occur. For Locke, the emphasis is sharply reversed. The counterpart of the Leibnitzian view is found, to some extent, in modern cognitive theories involving principles of perceptual organization, of expectancy, cognitive maps and allied concepts. But it is developed on a different level, and most fully in the writer's view, in dynamic organismic personality theories that postulate self-actualization or an equivalent construct as a basic, unifying motivational principle. (See, e.g. Angyal, 1941; Allport, 1955; Goldstein, 1940; Maslow, 1962; Rogers, 1959b, 1963b.)

If our professional work is rooted theoretically in a learning-theory conception, such as that employed by Dollard and Miller or Skinner or Eysenck, we establish targets of a specific nature and apply conditions designed literally to undo existing patterns of response and to substitute selected alternative patterns. From a Skinnerian standpoint, for example, we would set in motion a carefully planned operant learning schedule by consistently rewarding the target behaviours and avoiding any reinforcement of the behaviours to be eliminated.

Skinner has said that the first task of the therapist (following diagnosis) is to establish or consolidate his power or control in relation to the patient. He may do this by various means including the reinforcement of direct approval. Once this control is achieved, the therapist is in a position effectively to suggest modes of behaviour designed to alter or eliminate certain kinds of reinforcements or to introduce other kinds. Merely by virtue of his role as a "nonpunishing" audience, the therapist can exercise decisive influence in making possible the progressive extinction of maladaptive behaviour based originally on negative (punitive) reinforcement (Skinner, 1953, pp. 269-271).

Skinner evidently regards the patterning of all human behaviour to be due literally to reinforcement by external reward and punishment. The new picture given by behavioural science is, in his view, sharply different from our previous conceptions. "Man's vaunted creative powers, his original accomplishments in arts, science, and morals, his capacity to choose and our right to hold him responsible for the consequences of his choice — none of these is conspicuous in this new self-portrait. Man, we once believed, was free to express himself in art, music, literature, to enquire into nature, to seek salvation in his own way. He could initiate action and make spontaneous and capricious changes of course. . . . But science insists that action is initiated by forces *impinging on the individual* . . ." (present author's italics) (Skinner, 1955-56).

Dollard and Miller do speak of a person attaining "the free use of his mind." What they mean, however, is conveyed by their statement that "when thought is free, conscious anticipation of punishment and reward replaces repression, and maximum freedom to act adaptively is gained" (Dollard and Miller, 1950, p. 249). This is a "freedom" that Skinner would probably accept too. Like Skinner, they also assert that in the presence of the therapist's permissive, calm, nonjudgmental response the patient talks about frightening topics. As he is not punished by the therapist his fears and associated neurotic habits are gradually extinguished.

The deconditioning of fear, repression and associated neurotic habits, and an accompanying increase in adaptive behaviour, are central objectives of therapeutic control in the conception of Dollard and Miller. As for the nature of this control, although the authors speak repeatedly of the therapist as permissive and nonjudgmental they also emphasize that "the rule of free association [their central therapeutic technique] is not a mere invitation to speak freely. It is an absolute obligation which is the foundation of the therapeutic situation. . . . This rule defines the 'patient's work' which is to drive ruthlessly through the pronouncement of sentences which may evoke sickening anxiety. The rule is a force which is applied against the force of neurotic fear" (Dollard and Miller, 1950, p. 241). However, the pressure or stress on the patient must be carefully controlled by the therapist, according to his judgment of the patient's limits of tolerance. This process is referred to as "dosing anxiety."

Other techniques employed by the therapist include selective use of sympathy or approval for positive reinforcement, timely "labelling" of previously unverbalized features of the patient's experience, and the process of teaching the patient to discriminate between responses judged by the therapist to be appropriate and inappropriate in his contemporary relationships and life-situation. Thus, for Dollard and Miller, the therapist's function is to guide the patient step-by-step through learning experiences that undo his symptoms and patterns of neurotic response and replace them with modes of response judged "realistic" and adaptive.

Eysenck and associated behaviour therapists go significantly further than Dollard and Miller in reducing the processes of behaviour control to strictly behaviouristic conditioning models and procedures. In a typical statement Eysenck asserts that "Learning theory . . . regards neurotic symptoms as simple learned habits; there is no neurosis underlying the symptom, but merely the symptom itself. *Get rid of the symptom and you have eliminated the*

neurosis" (Eysenck, 1959, p. 65). All the symptoms or (more strictly) maladaptive habits are regarded as falling into one of two major categories:
surplus conditioned reactions and deficient conditioned reactions. Deficient
reactions are response patterns necessary for adaptive behaviour, that have
not been acquired by the individual due to defective conditioning powers or
inadequate environmental conditions. In this case, the method of behaviour
control is some form of positive conditioning designed specially to bring the
missing reaction into play.

More commonly, in "neurotic" people, maladaptive habits are surplus
conditioned reactions. After identifying what form these habits take in a
given case, treatment aimed at displacing or de-conditioning them is instituted.
The specific methods of behaviour control advocated include aversion therapy
(pairing some form of punishment with the symptom); conditioned inhibition
(building up inhibition by massive voluntary practice of the symptom); and
reciprocal inhibition (involving elaboration of a conditioned response incompatible with the symptom to be abolished) (Eysenck, 1960).

The orientation standing in contrast to the learning-theory approaches to
behaviour control is represented notably among contemporary psychologists
in the work of Carl R. Rogers. From a Rogerian viewpoint, a major outcome
of successful therapeutic control is that the client gains a genuine and vital
sense of inner freedom, autonomy, self-responsibility and of worth as a
unique person. He becomes open to his own experience and his self-concept
changes to become congruent with the full range of his inner experience and
his outward actions and encounters. His behaviour becomes more varied,
adaptive, and resourceful, and he lives more fully in his relationships with
others (Rogers, 1963a). He moves from a relatively fixed, closed, self-
perpetuating condition *not* to another kind of invariant but adequate organization but rather to an open, integratively changing, emergent state of being
(Rogers, 1959a).

In view of our fundamental assumption of psychological determinism we
might ask, with Skinner, whether this potent sense of inner freedom and self-
direction, of freedom to be and to choose, is merely an illusion. If, in accordance with the behaviourist learning theory orientation, we view man as an
essentially reactive agent, as a being conditioned by external forces originating
independently of him, then a concept of inner freedom or true choice does
become meaningless. But if we take the contrary view that man is *inherently*
active, purposeful, striving and searching, that he is motivated essentially to
develop his potentialities and exercise his capacities, then concepts of inner
freedom and choice can be deeply meaningful. If this second description is
accurate, and providing the tendencies indicated are not blocked or distorted,
one would expect man to *feel* free and responsible. He would *be* free in the
sense that the essential initiative for what he does and strives to become arises
from an inherent tendency to maintain, express and actualize his experiencing
being.

Evidently, therapeutic control of behaviour must be a different sort of process from this second standpoint than it is within the learning-theory orientation. It is conceived, essentially, to be a matter of providing a relationship which has certain qualities that are actually communicated to and experienced by the client. The crucial factors are, first, the therapist's empathic understanding of his client. This implies, optimally, that the therapist is sensing the feelings and personal meanings that the client is experiencing, at each moment, perceiving them as they seem to the client but without confusing them with feelings and meanings originating in himself. The second factor is the therapist's attitude of unconditional or unqualified positive regard for the client. Optimally this attitude consists of deep unwavering, nonjudgmental acceptance and caring for the client. The third factor is the therapist's genuineness or congruence in relation to his client, such that he is fully open to conscious discrimination of what he is experiencing in this relationship, and that his outward response is consistent with this awareness (Rogers, 1957b).

The therapist takes the initiative in providing these relationship qualities. Ideally however, in the moment of the relationship, he is not consciously calculating his response to try to maximize them. Rather, he is living them as a natural expression of himself in the situation. Together they are conceived as providing the conditions or nutrients for adequate, integrated psychological regeneration and growth.

The whole theoretical and procedural structure of the Rogerian orientation has evolved within the context of helping psychologically troubled individuals. As such, its development has been dominated by humanitarian values, and its concept of the whole or fully-functioning person is undoubtedly influenced strongly by the ideals of a democratic culture. Rogers has not merely acknowledged the problem of values but searched repeatedly to clarify and explicate the philosophical underpinnings of his system and of psychological science generally (Rogers, 1955, 1957a, 1961, 1964).

The learning-theory position has its origin in the search for basic scientific laws and principles in the domain of behaviour. Its major concepts have evolved largely through controlled studies of infra-human learning. Generally, advocates of this approach have not applied their efforts to help the individual toward some explicitly conceived optimum state of being, but rather to overcome particular functional deficiencies. Although they (rightly, in the writer's view) reject the traditional medical concept of mental illness or disease, it is not difficult to interpret their procedures as seeking to eliminate infected components of behaviour and promote the growth of healthy behaviour patterns in the regions involved. In most cases, they seem not to have seriously examined the value-systems implicit in what they advocate and practise in the realm of therapeutic control of behaviour.

In summary, the two types of orientation outlined differ in the following crucial respects:

(1) They rest on sharply different conceptions of human personality. (a)

The learning-theory approaches involve a mechanistic associationist view of personality, in which component aspects can be understood and modified in their own right, without reference to the whole. The Rogerian approach implies that the person is an organized, dynamic whole, in which component features can only be adequately comprehended and influenced in accordance with their function and relationships in the complete system. (b) In the former position, human motivation takes the form of multiple physiological and derived "secondary" drives, which spur the person to tension-reducing behaviour. In the latter approach, specific motivations all stem from a basic and pervasive growth and actualizing tendency, and the person normally reaches out for the fullest development and expression of himself that he can attain under the conditions and possibilities that he experiences. (c) In the one case, behaviour change is conceived as resulting from the cumulative effects of specific instances of reinforcement or its opposite. In the other, significant change involves shifts in the balance, organization and functional unity of a complex whole, mediated by the actualizing tendency of this whole. (d) The behaviourist learning theories have no serious use for a construct such as self or ego. The self — as know to the individual — is a pivotal construct in Rogers' conception.

(2) For the learning-theory therapist, control of behaviour is oriented directly toward specific maladaptive habits or to implicit, internal response patterns considered to mediate the maladaptive behaviour. For the Rogerian therapist, control is oriented toward internal factors restricting the individual's access to his own experience, particularly his awareness of himself. The former is concerned with environmental adjustment and the latter emphasizes the attainment of personal integration or congruence.

(3) Methods of control are based, for the learning-therapist, on non-punishing responses to fear and expectation of punishment, or on specific reward or punishment schedules; and, for the Rogerian, on a *relationship* in which the therapist responds as a congruent person, with sensitive empathy and unqualified caring that, in learning-theory terms, rewards the clients as much for one behaviour as for any other.

(4) In the sphere of values, the learning-theory approaches appear to rest their case implicitly on the assumption that man can and should be shaped to live comfortably and productively in his society. From the Rogerian standpoint, man's greatest need is to be at one with himself, true to his own nature which has an inherent tendency to be constructive, forward-moving, socialized and responsible. Exponents of the former view generally show little explicit concern with values; adherents of the second position have presented a conception of inner, psychological freedom which they hold as a paramount human value.

In their view of man's nature, and the aims and methods of modifying his behaviour, the two types of system presented stand too far apart for present reconciliation. In the light of present research evidence, both approaches achieve results in their own terms. In the author's view, both have the potentiality for exercising powerful and extensive influence on human conduct and personality. As professional psychologists our responsibility and opportunities demand that we examine and consider the basis on which we make our own stand, whether in accord with one of these orientations or some other alternative. An inescapable determinant of our choice is the relative value we place on the different states of being of which man is capable.

REFERENCES

ALLPORT, G. W. *Becoming: Basic considerations for a psychology of personality.* New Haven: Yale University Press, 1955.

ANGYAL, A. *Foundations for a science of personality.* New York: Commonwealth Foundation, 1941.

DOLLARD, J. and MILLER, N. E. *Personality and psychotherapy.* New York: McGraw-Hill, 1950.

EYSENCK, H. J. Learning theory and behaviour therapy. *Journal of Mental Science,* 1959, 105, 61-75.

EYSENCK, H. J. Personality and behaviour therapy. *Proceedings of the Royal Society of Medicine.* 1960, 53, 504-508.

FRASER, A. C. (Ed.) *Locke's essay concerning human understanding.* Oxford: Clarendon Press, 1894. Vol. 1.

GOLDSTEIN, K. *Human nature in the light of psychopathology.* Cambridge: Harvard University Press, 1940.

HOBBS, N. Science and ethical behaviour. *American Psychologist,* 1959, 14, 217-225.

KRASNER, L. Behaviour control and social responsibility. *American Psychologist,* 1962, 17, 199-204.

LEIBNITZ, G. W. (Trans. A. G. Langley). *New Essays concerning human understanding.* Illinois: Open Court, 1949. (3rd ed.)

LOEMKER, L. E. (Ed. and trans.) *G. W. Leibnitz: Philosophical papers and letters.* Chicago: University of Chicago Press, 1956.

LOWE, C. M. Value orientations — an ethical dilemma. *American Psychologist,* 1959, 14, 687-693.

MASLOW, A. H. *Toward a psychology of being.* Princeton: Van Nostrand, 1962.

PATTERSON, C. H. The place of values in counselling and psychotherapy. *Journal of Counseling Psychology,* 1958, 5, 216-223.

ROGERS, C. R. Persons or science? A philosophical question. *American Psychologist,* 1955, 10, 267-278.

ROGERS, C. R. A therapist's view of the good life. *The Humanist,* 1957a, 17, 291-300.

ROGERS, C. R. The necessary and sufficient conditions of therapeutic personality change. *Journal of Consulting Psychology,* 1957b, 21, 95-103.

ROGERS, C. R. A tentative scale for the measurement of process in psychotherapy. In E. A. Rubenstein and M. B. Parloff (Eds.), *Research in Psychotherapy*. Washington: A.P.A., 1959a.

ROGERS, C. R. A theory of therapy, personality, and interpersonal relationships, as developed in the client-centered framework. In S. Koch (Ed.), *Psychology: A study of a science*. Vol. III, *Formulations of the person and the social context*. New York: McGraw-Hill, 1959b.

ROGERS, C. R. *On becoming a person*. Boston: Houghton Mifflin, 1961. Chs. 20-21.

ROGERS, C. R. Learning to be free. In S. M. Farber and R. H. Wilson (Eds.), *Conflict and creativity: Control of the mind, Part 2*. New York: McGraw-Hill, 1963a.

ROGERS, C. R. The actualising tendency in relation to "motives" and to consciousness. In M. R. Jones (Ed.). *Nebraska symposium on motivation*. Lincoln: University of Nebraska Press, 1963b.

ROGERS, C. R. Toward a science of the person. In T. W. Mann (Ed.), *Behaviourism and phenomenology: Contrasting bases for modern psychology*. Chicago: University of Chicago Press, 1964.

ROGERS, C. R. and SKINNER, B. F. Some issues concerning the control of human behaviour. *Science*, 1956, 124, 1057-1066.

SKINNER, B. F. Freedom and the control of men. *American Scholar*, 1955-56, 25, 47-65. (Also in B. F. Skinner, *Cumulative Record*. New York: Appleton-Century-Crofts, 1959. Pp. 3-18.)

SKINNER, B. F. *Science and human behaviour*. New York: Macmillan, 1953.

SMITH, M. B. Mental health reconsidered: A special case of the problem of values in psychology. *American psychologist*, 1961, 16, 299-306.

WATSON, G. Moral issues in psychotherapy. *American Psychologist*, 1958, 10, 574-576.

24

Values and Strategy in

Client-Centered Therapy:

A Means to an End

T. M. TOMLINSON   RICHARD E. WHITNEY

Introduction

The principle, and in the context of this book, perhaps reactionary, point which this chapter makes is that client-centered therapy in its "pure" state is a self-contained, internally consistent therapeutic system, the goals of which, while value determined, are logically related to the method. Toward this end other therapy systems will be briefly discussed to make the point that their goals are also based on the explicit and implicit values contained within the theory, and therefore that evaluations of effect must take into account the values as well as (or perhaps instead of) the conventional criteria of "cure." It is important to examine the relationship of method to goals in evaluating the adequacy of given therapeutic systems simply because the criteria of outcome (goal attainment) may be logically unrelated to the method used to attain the goals and thus fail to reflect the changes which actually do take place. For if the values (goals) are of one kind and the method is inconsistent with the attainment of those goals, then the evaluation of efficacy must inevitably reflect the "noise" resulting from the poor fit between method and goals. In this case the criteria of outcome ought to be oriented to the method rather than to the goals on the assumption that the therapy's method or strategy has an effect, but that effect is not fully measurable in terms of value determined, and, from the viewpoint of method, largely irrelevant, goal criteria.

In this context client-centered therapy is examined for the fit between its method and its goals. Certain types of therapist communication which are rejected by client-centered therapists are discussed and their inconsistency with client-centered goals demonstrated. Alternative and accepted communication forms are similarly shown to be logically related to the goals endorsed by the theory and value system. The aim is not to make critical comparisons between client-centered therapy and other systems of treatment, but only to make the case that client-centered therapy is a "fully functioning" system whose method and goals, given an appropriate evaluation procedure, are sufficient in themselves to justify the continued exercise of the practice.

Values as Outcomes

Debates about the effects and effectiveness of various therapeutic approaches have over the years consumed considerable time and energy. The issues that make up the most recent polemic, between what London (1964) has called the "action" (behaviorist) and "insight" (talking therapy) approaches to psychotherapy, are typical. Arguments have been offered, countered, and reoffered regarding the actionists' claim to greater therapeutic efficacy and scientific respectability (for example, Breger and McGaugh, 1965; Rachman and Eysenck, 1966; Breger and McGaugh, 1966). These arguments, like many of those in the past, do not consider what probably is the most important, however unscientific, distinction between the two groups, namely, the explicit and implicit values each holds. The justification for this statement rests in the fact that, while the difference in both therapeutic strategy and research support are ambiguous, there is relatively little ambiguity about the differences in the value systems upon which each of the major approaches is grounded. Furthermore, as will be shown, there is little doubt that the values which inhere in a given therapeutic approach in large measure determine the goals approved of and sought. Wiener and Ehrlich (1960) suggest, in fact, that neither therapists nor clients make a functional distinction between values and goals. That is, when a therapist speaks of therapeutic goals, he is at the same time speaking of the values he holds, and these values determine the direction and results he seeks during the course of psychotherapy. Approved outcomes are so deeply rooted in the therapist's value system (whether personally or theoretically determined) that no criterion of improvement which fails to consider his philosophy of living will be satisfactory.

Therapists typically believe they know what kind of client behavior is desirable, and though they may not actively strive to develop such behavior, they still evaluate their own efficacy in terms of the degree to which they can observe the presence of that behavior in the client's emergent self. Further, for a client to be marked an unqualified success he must fulfill the important criteria the therapist holds, and these criteria are invariably ideal in nature. The client who does not achieve the ideal will be marked down accordingly.

Thus the measure of outcome must be in terms of what the therapist and his theory designate as the ideal man, and these considerations are rooted in values, not in objective considerations of adjustment.

That values do play a large part in both the conduct and evaluation of psychotherapy has received ample testimony. Marmor (1961), speaking from a psychoanalytic stance, points out that the analyst, whether he intends it or not, plays the part of teacher, model, and/or ideal person to his patients. The analyst must recognize that he influences his patients along these lines and that this influence is a central fact in psychoanalysis.

Krasner (1962) has written extensively on the presence of behavior control in insight therapies despite the therapist's disavowal of controlling intent. Krasner feels that the insistent denial of control stems from an insight therapist's unwillingness to confront the moral, ethical, and legal problems that would result from the assumption of responsibility for the patient's behavior and the changes which result from the psychotherapy experience. But he neglects to consider the possibility that many insight therapists occupy a philosophical position which extols the development of individual responsibility and deplores external control. Thus, rather than avoiding issues, these therapists are simply maintaining a particular value stance which is in opposition to Krasner's theme. Their therapeutic goal is to create a situation in which therapist influence is minimized and the opportunity for the client to come to grips with his own philosophy of life is maximized.

Lowe (1959) takes a meta-theory stance in his discussion of the ethical dilemma stemming from conflicts over four possible sets of therapeutic values. His essential point is that values stem from scientific, cultural, human, and theistic concerns, any one of which may be defended and seized upon as justification for a given therapeutic approach. Within this framework the Freudian is bound to operate in terms of a value system dictated by his belief in the scientific method. In the interest of truth, he is ethically bound to impose his value system on the patient, that is, to abrogate the patient's use of illusion and self-deception. At this point, science replaces therapy as the primary therapeutic goal. Cure or relief is less important than truth, a position which is apparent even in psychoanalytic writings. ". . . psychoanalytic treatment has lengthened and this we can only justify if we regard it as educational (in the broad sense) and preventive rather than *merely* therapeutic" (Menninger, 1958, p. 6) (italics ours). Despite his scientificism Freud was prey to more mundane values such as his belief in the nature of man (bad) and his belief in the relationship between instincts and civilization (inherently conflictual). Thus Freud, like those who came after him, had a value system he imposed on his observations and which quite distinctly colored his therapeutic aims and behavior.

However, the central point is not that psychoanalytic (or client-centered or behaviorist) theory carries with it a built-in value system; discussions of values in psychotherapy have burgeoned in the past fifteen years, and it is hardly a point of contention to suggest that values play a part in the therapy process. The critical issue now is the way the values contained within a given theory contribute to the derivation of therapeutic method, and hence influence the client's therapeutic experience.

As a case in point, let us compare two prominent "insight" methods, psychoanalysis and client-centered therapy. The methods of the two have been detailed elsewhere (Menninger, 1958; Rogers, 1951, 1962) and may be briefly characterized here as follows:

(1) Psychoanalysis — in the presence of a passive (verbally inactive) therapist the patient reclines on a couch and emits verbal behavior which, it is hoped, is uncensored by conscious or ego processes. The nature of the patient's utterances tend to dwell initially on past events and later, with the help of interpretations, on the relationship of these events to present behavior. The passivity of the therapist has the overt intent of encouraging the patient to act out with the therapist his neurotically determined interpersonal distortions, that is, the creation of a transference neurosis. The therapist, by interpreting the "real" meaning of the acting-out to the patient, provides the patient with the "insight" necessary to understand and gain control over his behavior. Presumably, when the patient comes to understand the meaning of his own behavior or shows insight, he is finished with analysis and may be called a successful analysand.

(2) Client-centered therapy — as described by Rogers (1951, 1962) and Gendlin (1964), the client assumes a face-to-face sitting position across from the therapist, whose primary aim is to help the client gain full awareness of hitherto unsymbolized or poorly symbolized aspects of his internal experiencing process. The central aim is to provide for increased congruence between the client's cognitive processes and his internal valuing process. The therapist attempts to engage the client in a genuine relationship by presenting himself transparently to the client — the therapist attempts to be no other person than what he really is, namely (and ideally) an honest and personally congruent human being. In providing this genuine person, the therapist also attempts to provide a "psychologically safe" atmosphere wherein the client may uncover his own distortions of experience at his own rate. Therapy ends successfully when the client states that he feels at one with himself and his life.

Superficially, both approaches aim to instigate insight, psychoanalysis by making the patient aware of the nature of his neurotic interaction which stems from early experience, and client-centered therapy by providing a climate wherein the client becomes aware of and moves into congruence with his internal experiencing process. Presumably each method leads the client to a greater awareness of his internal processes as they effect his day-to-day functioning.

There are, however, some very fundamental and important differences between the two. These differences stem from the quite different types of relationships established in the two situations and the basic attitudes each holds toward the nature of man. The psychoanalytic relationship provides for regression of the patient to an even more infantile level than he was at when he presented himself for analysis (Menninger, 1958, p. 48). The client-centered relationship aims to instigate growth and maturity from the inception of therapy. Instead of encouraging the patient to become more infantile, client-centered therapy encourages him to engage in an encounter with another human being who displays himself as a *human being*. Through the device of interpretations, psychoanalysis helps to provide the meaning by which the patient understands his experience. Client-centered therapy develops a situation wherein the client generates his own understanding of the meaning of his experience. The therapist at no time furnishes an interpretation of the *meaning* of the client's experience or experiencing process. Psychoanalysis is interested in developing the patient's awareness of the influence of past experience on the assumption that awareness of that influence places the patient in a better position to control his current behavior. Client-centered therapy, on the other hand, is interested in the development of the client's internal experiencing process on the assumption that the feeling process is a vital and sufficient, but rejected, guide for the conduct of life. Finally, psychoanalysis views man as restricted and determined by past experience, whereas client-centered therapy takes the point of view that man is a developing organism who strives toward personal actualization.

Obviously, the values inherent in the two systems are different. Psychoanalysis seems aimed at the instigation of greater personal control while client-centered therapy is aimed at the production of greater freedom of expression. Freud was pessimistic about the nature of man; Rogers is sanguine. Client-centered therapy sees a human relationship devoid of façade and pretense as absolutely necessary to constructive therapeutic experience, while psychoanalysis provides a peculiar amalgam of doctor-patient, mentor-student relationship, which is purposely constructed to elicit a particular response from the patient. The upshot is that the values implicit in the therapeutic method of both approaches contribute in large measure not only to the development of different goals, but also to very different strategies for attaining these outcomes. These differences stem from the nature of the relationship within the two approaches, from the nature of the goals which are overtly or covertly established by the therapist as desirable, and from the style of communication each elects to achieve those goals.

Comparing psychoanalysis and client-centered therapy to the various learning theory approaches provides an even more stark contrast in goals and values. The general behaviorist philosophy places no particular emphasis on either the development of personal control or personal freedom. Rather, the intended main thrust is a straightforward intent to remove the "foreign body" (symptom, anxiety) from the client. Treatment is a product of an expeditious application of learning principles uncomplicated by analytic talk. General (nonsymptomatic) enhancement of the organism presumably occurs as a by-product of the loss of the symptom or the reduction of anxiety. Theoretically, little attention is paid to the development of the cognitive processes necessary to entertain the possibility of self-generated growth and change. The method pointedly avoids interaction which would lead the client to explore hitherto unconceptualized areas of his life, on the grounds that symptom removal is the first and only important order of business and the internal rumination necessary for insight is only useless by-play on the road to cure (although Breger and McGaugh [1965] suggest that that position may be more theoretical than factual).

But values do play a part in Behaviorist theory; they provide a rationale for avoiding the therapist-client interplay necessary to produce the outcome of insight and personal knowledge. The expressed value is symptom removal and behavior change. But the outcomes of the method are neither good nor bad, rather they are one of a set of alternatives each of which yields its own product.

The Relationship of Strategy to Outcome

By now it should be clear that values play a role in determining the goals of the various therapies. This fact complicates the evaluation picture since it precludes the use of a single, all-purpose evaluation dimension for comparing the several therapeutic approaches. Evaluation should take into account each value-determined goal and should therefore go beyond a general definition of outcome. Outcome measures such as "personality change" (unspecified), "adjustment," and "symptom removal" should be replaced, or at least supplemented, by method-specific measures which reflect and do justice to the goals unique to the method. Client-centered therapy is one therapeutic approach which has developed measures to tap the outcomes unique to the method, thereby illustrating the use of theory and method-revelant measures. (See Part Three for specific examples.)

In like manner the methods of each therapy should be examined for their logical relation to the intended outcome. One of the crucial variables in determining the adequacy of a given therapeutic method (or theory) is its internal consistency. That is to say, given a goal, the operations necessary to achieve the goal ought to relate logically to one another and in turn should relate logically to the goal itself. It is beyond the scope and intent of this chapter to analyze all the therapeutic systems in this manner, but an attempt will be made to explicate the relationship between the client-centered method and certain valued goals.

Strategy

The basic theory of client-centered therapy states that if the therapist offers certain conditions (empathic understanding, unconditional positive regard, personal congruence), then certain client responses will result (less dependence, reduced perceptual distortions, greater reliance on his own valuing process, and less reliance on "introjected values"). The evident goal of client-centered therapy is to allow the client to become aware of and accept the validity of his own experiencing process (organismic valuing process) as a guide for his own behavior. In doing so, the client becomes increasingly disengaged from reliance on the "shoulds" and "oughts" of societal rules, and more reliant on his sense of having experience and more willing to use his own interpretation of that experience as a behavioral guide. Experience and cognition are congruent; they match and the individual is no longer compelled to fight with himself about his behavior and feelings.

The client's task is to work through the discrepancies between what he feels and what he does, with the ultimate ideal goal being the development of a personal set of values and a behavioral style which is both satisfying and growth producing.[1] The therapeutic strategy employed to achieve the goal of personal independence and the development of an internal valuing process takes a certain form. Such a personal system must be self-created if it is to be both meaningful to the client and internalized. A "system" of conduct which is presented to the client (as for example the rules of conduct taught by one's parents) may or may not be believed, and may or may not have personal significance. In either event, rules, whether personal or societal in origin, must be understood as to their meaning and personal relevance to be effective.

Overt suggestions for behavior change or direct applications of "action" methods are invariably based on inexact and, at times, wholly distorted perceptions of both therapist and client. The objective of client-centered therapy is to get people to assume responsibility for their own lives and their own behavior. Therapeutic behavior which works against that goal is in the end destructive, however well intentioned the therapist may be in "helping" the client. In this light let us examine some common types of "therapeutic" communciation, and by analyzing the implicit meaning of these communications perhaps gain a better understanding of the relationship of client-centered method to valued outcomes. Four types of common communications will be considered: "helping" questions; "helping" advice; "helping" support; and "helping" interpretations.

Helping Questions

Questions by their nature are designed to elicit information and by definition they demand a response from the object of the interrogation. Questions are invariably a product of the interrogator's own conception of information that

---

[1] The value assumption that this growth will benefit both the person and his fellow citizens is obvious but defensible (Hobbs, 1962), and it does not preclude client actions which may move against the "rules' but which are nevertheless a product of the client's growth process.

would be useful to him or of areas of exploration that should be examined by the client, e.g., "tell me about your relationship with your parents," "when did you first do 'X'," "did you get along with your brothers and sisters," "do you like your boss," etc.

The response to such questions serves to remove the client's attention from his internal sense of having experience, from his internal referents, and shifts it to that of answering or responding to external stimuli. The process is generally a cognitive one and except in rare instances the question serves to alert or engage defensive processes. Thus the client may justify his perception of the world because he feels the person interrogating him is after information which would incriminate him, or he may distort the response, feeling that damaging information, which he is fearful to reveal, may be pulled from him. In these cases the interrogator (therapist) is viewed as dangerous to the continued maintenance of the self-concept.

A second, and in the long run more damaging, consequence of questions is the production or reinforcement of dependency in the client. Questions lift the responsibility for self-exploration from the client. The therapist-interrogator now becomes the source and guide for self-examination. The client is prevented from learning to refer spontaneously to his own experiencing process as a guideline for interaction. Thus, however helpfully intended, questions disrupt (1) the focus of attention upon internal events, (2) the development of personal responsibility for the unfolding of experience, and (3) the development of reliance on the experiencing process as a guide for behavior.

Helping Advice

The immediate flaw in advice-giving is in the building of a dependency relationship in which the client remains susceptible to external influence. Thus, assuming the client takes the advice offered, he is behaving in terms of the therapist's interpretation of what is "correct" behavior, and he remains naïve about the course of action that is most suitable for his particular case. The advice-giving therapist implicitly assumes that his conception of the proper course of action is appropriate for the client. The fact that he may not know the client's conception of the world and that that conception may invalidate the direction for action indicated by the advice is often overlooked. Frequently the outcome is similar to that described by Eric Berne (1964) in his "game" of "Why don't you, yes but . . .". Here the advice-giver supplies an apparently useful suggestion and is responded to with "I would do that, but . . .", which response is a rebuttal of the advice together with a justification for maintaining the current stand. Thus advice-giving simply reminds the client either of something he has previously thought of but which failed to achieve the desired end, or it elicits from him a justification for continuing on his present course of action. In either event, he is again taken away from an internal focus and engaged in the business of defending himself against the advice.

Advice-giving is seldom useful in the production of responsibility and personal growth. If suggestions for change (advice) are given and followed, the likely outcomes assume two forms: if the change is effective, the therapist is reinforcing dependency in the client (the client learns that following the therapist's suggestion leads to improvement and, as a result, he fails to learn to follow his own lead); if the change attempt fails to work, the client comes to mistrust and doubt the therapist's understanding of him, with consequent damage to the relationship.

In all advice-giving situations the client does not see the instigation for action as self-determined, whether the advice succeeds or fails. He is not allowed to enjoy the experience of personal responsibility for his behavior as such. He is diverted from learning that he is capable of autonomy and effective decision-making, and instead learns to depend on or blame the therapist for his outcomes. Advice-giving removes the opportunity for the client to learn to evaluate his own experience and arrive at alternatives for behavior which best suit him at a given moment within the context of his total experience.

Helping Support

Support is probably the best intentioned of the nongrowth responses. The giving of support usually follows some utterance of pain by the client to which the therapist attempts to indicate his understanding or sympathy by statements such as these: "It's all right, I've felt the same way in the past," or "gee, you shouldn't feel that way, I think you're nice," or "don't feel badly, that happens to a lot of people." The aim of all these statements is to relieve pain by reducing the seriousness or uniqueness of the complaint. However, the motive of the pain-reliever is not so altruistic as it would seem, and in the long run he may do more damage than help with his support.

The unstated meaning conveyed in a message of support is that the communicator is made so anxious by the client's painful sounds that he cannot tolerate its expression, and must somehow reduce it, that is, the therapist is made so uncomfortable by the perception of pain in his client that he is moved to relieve it by supporting a view *contrary* to the client's. Thus the motive for support is not so much to do the other good as it is to reduce one's own anxiety generated by the other's pain.

An additional assumption is that the person is either too weak to bear the pain without help or that he is weak for having the pain. Support frequently carries and communicates the implicit message that the other's experience is of lesser or little importance since "I've had one like it, or worse." When the response to painful feelings is "you shouldn't feel that way . . . ," the message again is that your feelings are either wrong or unimportant.

Whatever the outcome of the support statement, the important result, and the debilitating one, is that the client is never allowed to express, fully explore, and own the pain. The support statement takes the client away from a thorough self-examination (which fulfills the supporter's intention) and he is never able truly to come to grips with his pain.

Therefore, giving support is really a response to avoid the anxiety generated by another's feelings of pain and serves ultimately to defeat the goal of personal growth. The pained person is never allowed to experience deeply and understand his feelings since to do so he must continue in the face of someone who is afraid of his feelings and who implicitly says "I'd rather you didn't feel that way," i.e., "don't talk about it and I won't be disturbed."

Helping Interpretations

The ostensible purpose of interpretations is the production of insight. The therapeutic aim is to tie together aspects of experience in a hitherto unthought of manner and thereby achieve "understanding." Having tied up the experiential package, the client would ideally say and feel "aha, so that's it" — yet this seldom happens. What's more, even when it does occur, it is of doubtful therapeutic benefit since there is no evidence that insight leads to change. Rather, according to Hobbs (1962), insight is merely a by-product of an underlying dimension of growth and by itself is of little worth. If insight is of little therapeutic use, then other considerations become important in considering the use of interpretations as a therapeutic tool. For even in response to "correct" interpretations the client attends to the therapist's input, away from his internal experience. If the interpretation is "premature" or "incorrect" (only the client can ever confirm these things), then he typically engages in a rebuttal, justification, or at best a "so-what" response. In both instances the therapist has interfered with the client's internal focus.

Interpretations are not a direct product of the client's experiencing process, they are the product of the therapist's conceptualization of "how-it-ought-to-be" according to his best information or belief system. It is merely another external communication. Indeed, the interpretation may be accepted as truth as a product of the therapist's credibility as an information source, but in this case the end product is little better than that stemming from advice. The client is evidencing only susceptibility to external influence. He remains dependent upon an external source to supply meaning to his experience. He is shunted away from an internal focus in the direction of attending to the "correctness" of the therapist's interpretation. The net effect is the client's continued failure to utilize his own experiencing process to provide meaning to perceptual data.

In sum, if the aim of the relationship is to provide true growth, i.e., to equip the person to be his own man, to evaluate his experience in terms of the meaning it has for him and not for "someone out there," then advice, questions, support, and interpretations will generally work to prevent this development. Communications of the type just described are logically inconsistent with the achievement of goals valued by client-centered therapy, and for this reason are seldom used.

There is however a style of communication and a context for its delivery consistent with the stated goals. Rogers (1957) and more recently, Gendlin (Chapter 7) have advanced a conception of the type of relationship within which personal knowledge and individual growth are maximized. The nature of this relationship provides a working definition of the type of relationship which should lead to the development of personal autonomy, self-responsibility, and increased awareness of one's own experiencing process as a valid guide for living.

As the "necessary and sufficient" conditions for the production of personal growth, Rogers (1957) suggests that the following characteristics should be present in the therapist's behavior:

(1) Positive regard. The therapist must value or "prize" the client. He must have a fundamental respect for the client as a person. This concept assumes a basic commitment to the worth of the individual and the principle that each man has the right to self-worth and self-determination. Positive regard may or may not include personal liking for the individual, although it seems likely that if one values a person, he is apt to "like" him also.

(2) Congruence. In the relationship to his client the therapist presents himself exactly as he is; there is no façade or pretense at being something other than a human being. He is open to his own feelings and willing to acknowledge them to himself and, if necessary, to the client. He can allow himself to be aware of his own fears or his own perplexities without having to erect defenses against these feelings.

(3) Empathy. This condition involves the therapist's ability to understand the meaning of his client's words. As the client describes his experiences (both internal and external), the therapist is empathic to the degree that he perceives and understands the client's descriptions "as if" they were his own. The condition of empathic understanding is fulfilled when the therapist moves in the same world of meaning as the client. At that point he truly understands the client.

(4) Unconditionality. This condition is closely related to positive regard, in that it calls for the therapist to avoid placing "conditions of worth" on the client. By this is meant that regardless of how the client presents himself, whether he says good or bad things about himself, the therapist will not make evaluations of "good" and "bad." He accepts whatever the client says without passing judgment.

(5) Finally, given the presence in optimum degree of the four therapist conditions, the client must perceive their presence at least to a minimal degree. He must be able to experience being understood, positively regarded, and so on, before growth can take place.

Operating within this framework, the therapist's communication is governed in the following ways. In being empathic the therapist is being asked to understand and communicate his understanding of the client's experiencing process. He is not being asked to work up a formulation which permits an interpretation which ties together related aspects of the client's experience, or to think of questions he might ask to elicit important data, or to express sympathy. He is being asked only to understand what the client is saying and feeling and to communicate that understanding to the client. This communication takes place in the form of expressions which attempt to capture the meaning, both surface and implicit, of the client's utterances. To the degree the therapist is able to express himself in a way which fits the client's own experience (and that experience may not yet be verbalized, because it is preconceptual) he advances or helps the client to advance his (the client's) understanding of his own ongoing experience. The empathic therapist always maintains the focus of the communication on the client's expressed or implicit experiential referent, thereby maintaining a continuous focus on the issue occupying the client's attention.

In being unconditional the therapist accepts the client exactly as he is, i.e., he accepts the client's pain as well as his pleasure, the client's "bad" as well as his "good" self, in short, the whole person who is the client. Under these circumstances, if the client expresses hatred of himself, the therapist doesn't attempt to reduce that feeling with support. Rather he accepts it, treating the expression as another dimension of the client's experience which is worthy of understanding as it exists in the person. Nor does the therapist give advice in these circumstances, because in granting "unconditional positive regard" he is confirming the client's personhood and acknowledging the client's ultimate capability of taking responsibility for himself.

Thus the relationship format of client-centered therapy is so constructed as to provide a style of therapist communication which is consistent with the method's stated goals. Empathic understanding enables the client to unfold his experience at his own rate, and in a manner which allows him to place his own interpretations of meaning on self-generated data and to draw his own conclusions about the action implications of his self-understanding. In this fashion he is being taught to be independent and to rely on his own experiential sense as a guide for behavior. In learning to rely on his experiencing process the client has embarked on the first step to self-actualization; in trusting his organismic sense he has captured the sense of self-propelled change which should provide for future positive growth and self-enhancement.

Two questions remain: (1) how in this relationship does self-exploration produce personal knowledge, and (2) what kind of knowledge does it produce? At the core of the client-centered position is the concept of experience. Central therapeutic questions concern the manner in which the client construes his experience, how the therapist can come to know and understand the client's experience of the world, and how the client can come to know and more realistically evaluate the meaning of his own experience and experiencing process. Gendlin (Chapter 7) has developed a theory of personality change which employs the client's experiencing process, that is, his sense of having experience, as the primary mode of personal growth. By differentiating between "experience" (concrete psychological events) and "experiencing" (a felt process), Gendlin describes how the experiencing process" (concrete, bodily feelings) may be used to discover the "basic matter of psychological and personality phenomena."

Gendlin points out that anyone at any time can refer directly to his inward sense of experiencing, and, by so doing, one's sense of having experience provides a "direct referent" to internal feelings. The feeling or direct referent to which the person refers contains meaning. Frequently the meaning is not well symbolized and thus is not susceptible to detailed articulation. However, the *feeling* is in awareness and may, therefore, be referred to, however unclearly. The unverbalized — implicit — meanings can be better or more completely symbolized if they are directly referred to and talked about. The process of focusing on a preconceptual meaning provides the client with the chance to complete or carry forward the preconceptual, implicit meaning of a bodily feeling.

Gendlin also notes that this process of self-exploration is best completed in a relationship of the kind previously described. When a person can feel safe enough to focus on an anxiety-producing bodily feeling, he is in a position for thorough exploration of the heretofore vague, implicit meanings that accompany the anxiety experience.

As the client begins to refer directly to his bodily feelings, the anxiety which ordinarily accompanies the experience and which typically prevents focused self-examination begins to dissipate. The dissipation of the anxiety is the client's cue that he is correctly symbolizing the felt meaning.

The paradox of anxiety reduction accompanying focused attention on a feared experience or experiencing process is rather easily resolved. The client is made anxious by his ignorance of the meaning of his feelings. He can't understand why he feels the way he does, and it is frightening to him. His inability to gain mastery over his feelings, to understand their full meaning, leads him to feel helpless with himself. Coming to know the complete meaning of one's feelings reduces fear because the person is fulfilling his "need" to know about himself. He is now in control of his feelings; he knows exactly what they mean. He can continually refer to his experiencing for confirmation that the current symbolization of the bodily feelings is correct. It "feels right" to have described his experiencing process in a certain way. An erroneous description of the internal process "feels wrong"; the client knows he is incorrect, and anxiety rises.

Thus step by step the client unfolds his felt meaning. He may grapple with a felt referent by attempting to symbolize it in a number of ways. He may dramatically hit upon the "right" description as, for example, when he announces, "Yes, that's it. That's the way I've always felt, but I didn't know what it meant."

During these periods of unfolding, as the client more and more accurately symbolizes the direct referent, there will be times when he sees a more general application of the discovered meaning. He may say something to the effect that he now sees that he treats everyone in terms of the uncovered construct, or that he has repeated the same behavior over and over again, without previously recognizing the fact.

As the more general nature of the direct referent, i.e., the experiencing process to which the client is referring, becomes known, it begins to feel different. The heretofore implicit meanings are now changed. The direct referent is seen in a new context and now, as a product of referent movement, the client shifts his focus to the referent's new meaning.

The process of directly referring to an imprecise, preconceptual felt meaning and of unfolding and symbolizing aspects of the referent leads to referent movement. As the referent moves, the client starts again on the "new" referent and repeats the process. The continuous exploration of changing but more completely symbolized referents exerts continuous pull on the client's attention. It is something he must attend to, something he must finish. He may be sidetracked, but he is compelled to return to the felt referent. The compelling nature of referent exploration is called the self-propelled feeling process, and it is this self-propelled quality that permits the client to proceed on his own. As one becomes able and accustomed to focus on and symbolize vague internal feelings he also is enabled to continue the process alone. A therapist who can facilitate the unfolding, who can help the client to verbalize the implicit meanings, is critically important. But for initiating what has been called the "actualizing process," the client must develop the ability to refer to *and* understand his feeling process without a therapist's help. In this light, therapy is an experience which initiates the growth process. But for continued growth to occur, the client must learn to use his inner, organismic experience as a guide. Only then can he know what he wants and needs, and fully engage in the behavior which leads to his own fulfillment.

To sum up, the therapy which grows out of client-centered theory moves beyond conventional treatment interests in the direction of not only helping the disturbed person but also of providing him with an experience which will contribute to his long-range growth and self-realization. The goal is not merely to return the person to some previous level of psychological functioning, but to contribute to an enhanced richness of living which surpasses that which was known before.

The process by which this goal is attained focuses sharply on the relationship between the client and his therapist, and on the development of a heightened awareness of inner experience to provide meaning to one's personal experience. As the person comes to know how he feels and is able to symbolize that experiencing process accurately, he effectively comes to rely upon himself to provide meaning to his experience and set himself meaningful goals of life. His susceptibility to external influence drops proportionally as he learns to trust himself to provide meaning to what he sees. He is freed to give himself direction and to develop his own style of life, one which is uniquely suitable to him. If necessary, he is able to move to unconventional, hopefully creative goals, since he is not constrained by growth-retarding self and societally imposed rules. But he is responsible to his fellow men and gives cause for their disapproval only when his own sense of personal integrity permits him no recourse. Having done so, he willingly acknowledges his action and responsibility for the direction he takes having learned that it is he and only he who chose to act.

REFERENCES

BERNE, E. *Games people play: The psychology of human relationships.* New York: Grove Press, 1964.

BREGER, L., and MCGAUGH, J. L. Critique and reformulation of "learning theory" approaches to psychotherapy and neurosis. *Psychological Bulletin,* 1965, 63, 338-357.

BREGER, L., and MCGAUGH, J. L. Learning theory and behavioral therapy: A reply to Rachman and Eysenck. *Psychological Bulletin,* 1966, 65, 170-173.

GENDLIN, E. T. A theory of personality change. In P. Worchel and D. Byrne (Eds.), *Personality change.* New York: John Wiley, 1964. (See Chapter 7.)

HOBBS, N. Sources of gain in psychotherapy. *American Psychologist,* 1962, 17, 741-747.

KRASNER, L. Behavior control and social responsibility. *American Psychologist,* 1962, 17, 199-204.

LONDON, P. *The modes and morals of psychotherapy.* New York: Holt, Rinehart and Winston, 1964.

LOWE, C. M. Value orientations: An ethical dilemma. *American Psychologist,* 1959, 14, 687-693.

MARMOR, J. Paper presented to the Academy of Psychoanalysis, Chicago, May 1961.

MENNINGER, K. *Theory of psychoanalytic technique.* New York: Basic Books, 1958.

RACHMAN, S. and EYSENCK, H. J. Reply to a "critique and reformulation" of behavior therapy. *Psychological Bulletin,* 1966, 65, 165-169.

ROGERS, C. R. *Client-centered therapy.* Boston: Houghton Mifflin, 1951.

ROGERS, C. R. The necessary and sufficient conditions of therapeutic personality change. *Journal of Consulting Psychology,* 1957, 21, 95-103.

ROGERS, C. R. *On becoming a person.* Boston: Houghton Mifflin, 1962.

WEINER, D. and EHRLICH, DANUTA. Values and goals. *American Journal of Psychotherapy,* 1960, 73, 615-617.

25

The Interpersonal Relationship

in the Facilitation of Learning

CARL R. ROGERS

. . . It is in fact nothing short of a miracle that the modern methods of instruction have not yet entirely strangled the holy curiosity of inquiry; for this delicate little plant, aside from stimulation, stands mainly in need of freedom; without this it goes to wrack and ruin without fail.

ALBERT EINSTEIN

I wish to begin this paper with a statement which may seem surprising to some and perhaps offensive to others. It is simply this: Teaching, in my estimation, is a vastly overrated function.

Having made such a statement, I scurry to the dictionary to see if I really mean what I say. Teaching means "to instruct." Personally I am not much interested in instructing another. "To impart knowledge or skill." My reaction is, why not be more efficient, using a book or programmed learning? "To make to know." Here my hackles rise. I have no wish to *make* anyone know something. "To show, guide, direct." As I see it, too many people have been shown, guided, directed. So I come to the conclusion that I *do* mean what I said. Teaching is, for me, a relatively unimportant and vastly overvalued activity.

* Reprinted with permission of the Association for Supervision and Curriculum Development and Carl R. Rogers. Copyright © 1967 by the Association for Supervision and Curriculum Development.

But there is more in my attitude than this. I have a negative reaction to teaching. Why? I think it is because it raises all the wrong questions. As soon as we focus on teaching, the question arises, what shall we teach? What, from our superior vantage point, does the other person need to know? This raises the ridiculous question of coverage. What shall the course cover? (Here I am acutely aware of the fact that "to cover" means both "to take in" and "to conceal from view," and I believe that most courses admirably achieve both these aims.) This notion of coverage is based on the assumption that what is taught is what is learned; what is presented is what is assimilated. I know of no assumption so obviously untrue. One does not need research to provide evidence that this is false. One needs only to talk with a few students.

But I ask myself, "Am I so prejudiced against teaching that I find no situation in which it is worthwhile?" I immediately think of my experience in Australia only a few months ago. I became much interested in the Australian aborigine. Here is a group which for more than 20,000 years has managed to live and exist in a desolate environment in which a modern man would perish within a few days. The secret of his survival has been teaching. He has passed on to the young every shred of knowledge about how to find water, about how to track game, about how to kill the kangaroo, about how to find his way through the trackless desert. Such knowledge is conveyed to the young as being *the* way to behave, and any innovation is frowned upon. It is clear that teaching has provided him the way to survive in a hostile and relatively unchanging environment.

Now I am closer to the nub of the question which excites me. Teaching and the imparting of knowledge make sense in an unchanging environment. This is why it has been an unquestioned function for centuries. But if there is one truth about modern man, it is that he lives in an environment which is *continually changing*. The one thing I can be sure of is that the physics which is taught to the present day student will be outdated in a decade. The teaching in psychology will certainly be out of date in 20 years. The so-called "facts of history" depend very largely upon the current mood and temper of the culture. Chemistry, biology, genetics, sociology, are in such flux that a firm statement made today will almost certainly be modified by the time the student gets around to using the knowledge.

We are, in my view, faced with an entirely new situation in education where the goal of education, if we are to survive, is the *facilitation of change and learning*. The only man who is educated is the man who has learned how to learn; the man who has learned how to adapt and change; the man who has realized that no knowledge is secure, that only the process of *seeking* knowledge gives a basis for security. Changingness, a reliance on *process* rather than upon static knowledge, is the only thing that makes any sense as a goal for education in the modern world.

So now with some relief I turn to an activity, a purpose, which really warms me — the *facilitation of learning*. When I have been able to transform a group — and here I mean all the members of a group, myself included — into a community of *learners,* then the excitement has been almost beyond belief. To free curiosity; to permit individuals to go charging off in new directions dictated by their own interests; to unleash curiosity; to open everything to questioning and exploration; to recognize that everything is in process of change — here is an experience I can never forget. I cannot always achieve it in groups with which I am associated but when it is partially or largely achieved then it becomes a never-to-be-forgotten group experience. Out of such a context arise true students, real learners, creative scientists and scholars and practitioners, the kind of individuals who can live in a delicate but ever-changing balance between what is presently known and the flowing, moving, altering, problems and facts of the future.

Here then is a goal to which I can give myself wholeheartedly. I see the facilitation of learning as the aim of education, the way in which we might develop the learning man, the way in which we can learn to live as individuals in process. I see the facilitation of learning as the function which may hold constructive, tentative, changing, process answers to some of the deepest perplexities which beset man today.

But do we know how to achieve this new goal in education, or is it a will-of-the-wisp which sometimes occurs, sometimes fails to occur, and thus offers little real hope? My answer is that we possess a very considerable knowledge of the conditions which encourage self-initiated, significant, experiential, "gut-level" learning by the whole person. We do not frequently see these conditions put into effect because they mean a real revolution in our approach to education and revolutions are not for the timid. But we do find examples of this revolution in action.

We know — and I will briefly describe some of the evidence — that the initiation of such learning rests not upon the teaching skills of the leader, not upon his scholarly knowledge of the field, not upon his curricular planning, not upon his use of audio-visual aids, not upon the programmed learning he utilizes, not upon his lectures and presentations, not upon an abundance of books, though each of these might at one time or another be utilized as an important resource. No, the facilitation of significeant learning rests upon certain attitudinal qualities which exist in the personal *relationship* between the facilitator and the learner.

We came upon such findings first in the field of psychotherapy, but increasingly there is evidence which shows that these findings apply in the classroom as well. We find it easier to think that the intensive relationship between therapist and client might possess these qualities, but we are also finding that they exist in the countless interpersonal interactions (as many as 1,000 per day, as Jackson [1966] has shown) between the teacher and his pupils.

What are these qualities, these attitudes, which facilitate learning? Let me describe them very briefly, drawing illustrations from the teaching field.

Realness in the Facilitator of Learning

Perhaps the most basic of these essential attitudes is realness or genuineness. When the facilitator is a real person, being what he is, entering into a relationship with the learner without presenting a front or a façade, he is much more likely to be effective. This means that the feelings which he is experiencing are available to him, available to his awareness, that he is able to live these feelings, be them, and able to communicate them if appropriate. It means that he comes into a direct personal encounter with the learner, meeting him on a person-to-person basis. It means that he is *being* himself, not denying himself.

Seen from this point of view it is suggested that the teacher can be a real person in his relationship with his students. He can be enthusiastic, he can be bored, he can be interested in students, he can be angry, he can be sensitive and sympathetic. Because he accepts these feelings as his own he has no need to impose them on his students. He can like or dislike a student product without implying that it is objectively good or bad or that the student is good or bad. He is simply expressing a feeling for the product, a feeling which exists within himself. Thus, he is a person to his students, not a faceless embodiment of a curricular requirement nor a sterile tube through which knowledge is passed from one generation to the next.

It is obvious that this attitudinal set, found to be effective in psychotherapy, is sharply in contrast with the tendency of most teachers to show themselves to their pupils simply as roles. It is quite customary for teachers rather consciously to put on the mask, the role, the façade, of being a teacher, and to wear this façade all day removing it only when they have left the school at night.

But not all teachers are like this. Take Sylvia Ashton-Warner, who took resistant, supposedly slow-learning primary school Maori children in New Zealand, and let them develop their own reading vocabulary. Each child could request one word — whatever word he wished — each day, and she would print it on a card and give it to him. "Kiss," "ghost," "bomb," "tiger," "fight," "love," "daddy" — these are samples. Soon they were building sentences, which they could also keep. "He'll get a licking." "Pussy's frightened." The children simply never forgot these self-initiated learnings. Yet it is not my purpose to tell you of her methods. I want instead to give you a glimpse of her attitude, of the passionate realness which must have been as evident to her tiny pupils as to her readers. An editor asked her some questions and she responded: " 'A few cool facts' you asked me for. . . . I don't know that there's a cool fact in me, or anything else cool for that matter, on his particular subject. I've got only hot long facts on the matter of Creative Teaching, scorching both the page and me" (Ashton-Warner, 163, p. 26).

Here is no sterile façade. Here is a vital *person,* with convictions, with feelings. It is her transparent realness which was, I am sure, one of the elements that made her an exciting facilitator of learning. She does not fit into some neat educational formula. She *is,* and students grow by being in contact with someone who really *is.*

Take another very different person, Barbara Shiel, also doing exciting work facilitating learning in sixth graders.[1] She gave them a great deal of responsible freedom, and I will mention some of the reactions of her students later. But here is an example of the way she shared herself with her pupils — not just sharing feelings of sweetness and light, but anger and frustration. She had made art materials freely available, and students often used these in creative ways, but the room frequently looked like a picture of chaos. Here is her report of her feelings and what she did with them.

> I find it (still) maddening to live with the mess — with a capital M! No one seems to care except me. Finally, one day I told the children . . . that I am a neat, orderly person by nature and that the mess was driving me to distraction. Did they have a solution? It was suggested they could have volunteers to clean up. . . . I said it didn't seem fair to me to have the same people clean up all the time for others — but it *would* solve it for me. "Well, some people *like* to clean," they replied. So that's the way it is (Shiel, 1966).

I hope this example puts some lively meaning into the phrases I used earlier, that the facilitator "is able to live these feelings, be them, and able to communicate them if appropriate." I have chosen an example of negative feelings, because I think it is more difficult for most of us to visualize what this would mean. In this instance, Miss Shiel is taking the risk of being transparent in her angry frustrations about the mess. And what happens? The same thing which, in my experience, nearly always happens. These young people accept and respect her feelings, take them into account, and work out a novel solution which none of us, I believe, would have suggested in advance. Miss Shiel wisely comments, "I used to get upset and feel guilty when I became angry — I finally realized the children could accept *my* feelings, too. And it is important for them to know when they've 'pushed me.' I have limits, too" (Shiel, 1966).

Just to show that positive feelings, when they are real, are equally effective, let me quote briefly a college student's reaction, in a different course. ". . . Your sense of humor in the class was cheering; we all felt relaxed because you showed us your human self, not a mechanical teacher image. I feel as if I have more understanding and faith in my teachers now. . . . I feel closer to the students too." Another says, ". . . You conducted the class on a personal level and therefore in my mind I was able to formulate a picture of you as a person and not as merely a walking textbook." Or another student in the same course,

[1] For a more extended account of Miss Shiel's initial attempts, see Rogers, 1966a. Her later experience is described in Shiel, 1966.

. . . It wasn't as if there was a teacher in the class, but rather someone whom we could trust and identify as a "sharer." You were so perceptive and sensitive to our thoughts, and this made it all the more "authentic" for me. It was an "authentic" *experience,* not just a class (Bull, 1966).

I trust I am making it clear that to be real is not always easy, nor is it achieved all at once, but it is basic to the person who wants to become that revolutionary individual, a facilitator of learning.

Prizing, Acceptance, Trust

There is another attitude which stands out in those who are successful in facilitating learning. I have observed this attitude. I have experienced it. Yet, it is hard to know what term to put to it so I shall use several. I think of it as prizing the learner, prizing his feelings, his opinions, his person. It is a caring for the learner, but a nonpossessive caring. It is an acceptance of this individual as a separate person, having worth in his own right. It is a basic trust — a belief that this other person is somehow fundamentally trustworthy.

Whether we call it prizing, acceptance, trust, or by some other term, it shows up in a variety of observable ways. The facilitator who has a considerable degree of this attitude can be fully acceptant of the fear and hesitation of the student as he approaches a new problem as well as acceptant of the pupil's satisfaction in achievement. Such a teacher can accept the student's occasional apathy, his erratic desires to explore byroads of knowledge, as well as his disciplined efforts to achieve major goals. He can accept personal feelings which both disturb and promote learning — rivalry with a sibling, hatred of authority, concern about personal adequacy. What we are describing is a prizing of the learner as an imperfect human being with many feelings, many potentialities. The facilitator's prizing or acceptance of the learner is an operational expression of his essential confidence and trust in the capacity of the human organism.

I would like to give some examples of this attitude from the classroom situation. Here any teacher statements would be properly suspect, since many of us would like to feel we hold such attitudes, and might have a biased perception of our qualities. But let me indicate how this attitude of prizing, of accepting, of trusting, appears to the student who is fortunate enough to experience it.

Here is a statement from a college student in a class with Morey Appell.

Your way of being with us is a revelation to me. In your class I feel important, mature, and capable of doing things on my own. I want to think for myself and this need cannot be accomplished through textbooks and lectures alone, but through living. I think you see me as a person with real feelings and needs, an individual. What I say and do are significant expressions from me, and you recognize this (Appell, 1959).

One of Miss Shiel's sixth graders expresses much more briefly her misspelled appreciation of this attitude, "You are a wonderful teacher period!!!"

College students in a class with Dr. Patricia Bull describe not only these prizing, trusting attitudes, but the effect these have had on their other interactions.

> . . . I feel that I can say things to you that I can't say to other professors. . . . Never before have I been so aware of the other students or their personalities. I have never had so much interaction in a college classroom with my classmates. The climate of the classroom has had a very profound effect on me . . . the free atmosphere for discussion affected me . . . the general atmosphere of a particular session affected me. There have been many times when I have carried the discussion out of the class with me and thought about it for a long time.

> . . . I still feel close to you, as though there were some tacit understanding between us, almost a conspiracy. This adds to the in-class participation on my part because I feel that at least one person in the group will react, even when I am not sure of the others. It does not matter really whether your reaction is positive or negative, it just *is*. Thank you.

> . . . I appreciate the respect and concern you have for others, including myself. . . . As a result of my experience in class, plus the influence of my readings, I sincerely believe that the student-centered teaching method does provide an ideal framework for learning; not just for the accumulation of facts but more important, for learning about ourselves in relation to others. . . . When I think back to my shallow awareness in September compared to the depth of my insights now, I know that this course has offered me a learning experience of great value which I couldn't have acquired in any other way.

> . . . Very few teachers would attempt this method because they would feel that they would lose the students' respect. On the contrary. You gained our respect, through your ability to speak to us on our level, instead of ten miles above us. With the complete lack of communication we see in this school, it was a wonderful experience to see people listening to each other and really communicating on an adult, intelligent level. More classes should afford us this experience (Bull, 1966).

As you might expect, college students are often suspicious that these seeming attitudes are phony. One of Dr. Bull's students writes:

> . . . Rather than observe my classmates for the first few weeks, I concentrated my observations on you, Dr. Bull. I tried to figure out your motivations and purposes. I was convinced that you were a hypocrite. . . . I did change my opinion, however. You are not a hypocrite, by any means. . . . I do wish the course could continue. "Let each become all he is capable of being." . . . Perhaps my most disturbing question, which relates to this course is: When will we stop hiding things from ourselves and our contemporaries? (Bull, 1966).

I am sure these examples are more than enough to show that the facilitator who cares, who prizes, who trusts the learner, creates a climate for learning so different from the ordinary classroom that any resemblance is, as they say, "purely coincidental."

Empathic Understanding

A further element which establishes a climate for self-initiated, experiential learning is empathic understanding. When the teacher has the ability to understand the student's reactions from the inside, has a sensitive awareness of the way the process of education and learning seems *to the student,* then again the likelihood of significant learning is increased.

This kind of understanding is sharply different from the usual evaluative understanding, which follows the pattern of, "I understand what is wrong with you." When there is a sensitive empathy, however, the reaction in the learner follows something of this pattern, "At last someone understands how it feels and seems to be *me* without wanting to analyze me or judge me. Now I can blossom and grow and learn."

This attitude of standing in the other's shoes, of viewing the world through the student's eyes, is almost unheard of in the classroom. One could listen to thousands of ordinary classroom interactions without coming across one instance of clearly communicated, sensitively accurate, empathic understanding. But it has a tremendously releasing effect when it occurs.

Let me take an illustration from Virginia Axline, dealing with a second grade boy. Jay, age 7, has been aggressive, a trouble maker, slow of speech and learning. Because of his "cussing" he was taken to the principal, who paddled him, unknown to Miss Axline. During a free work period, he fashioned a man of clay, very carefully, down to a hat and a handkerchief in his pocket. "Who is that?" asked Miss Axline. "Dunno," replied Jay. "Maybe it is the principal. He has a handkerchief in his pocket like that." Jay glared at the clay figure. "Yes," he said. Then he began to tear the head off and looked up and smiled. Miss Axline said, "You sometimes feel like twisting his head off, don't you? You get so mad at him." Jay tore off one arm, another, then beat the figure to a pulp with his fist. Another boy, with the perception of the young, explained, "Jay is mad at Mr. X because he licked him this noon." "Then you must feel lots better now," Miss Axline commented. Jay grinned and began to rebuild Mr. X (Adapted from Axline, 1944.).

The other examples I have cited also indicate how deeply appreciative students feel when they are simply *understood* — not evaluated, not judged, simply understood from their *own* point of view, not the teacher's. If any teacher set herself the task of endeavoring to make one nonevaluative, acceptant, empathic response per day to a pupil's demonstrated or verbalized feeling, I believe he would discover the potency of this currently almost non-existent kind of understanding.

Let me wind up this portion of my remarks by saying that when a facilitator creates, even to a modest degree, a classroom climate characterized by such realness, prizing, and empathy, he discovers that he has inaugurated an educational revolution. Learning of a different quality, proceeding at a different pace, with a greater degree of pervasiveness, occurs. Feelings — positive and negative, confused — become a part of the classroom experience. Learning becomes life, and a very vital life at that. The student is on his way, sometimes excitedly, sometimes reluctantly, to becoming a learning, changing being.

The Evidence

Already I can hear the mutterings of some of my so-called "hardheaded" colleagues. "A very pretty picture — very touching. But these are all self reports." (As if there were any other type of expression! But that's another issue.) They ask, "Where is the evidence? How do you know?" I would like to turn to this evidence. It is not overwhelming, but it is consistent. It is not perfect, but it is suggestive.

First of all, in the field of psychotherapy, Barrett-Lennard (1962) developed an instrument whereby he could measure these attitudinal qualities: genuineness or congruence, prizing or positive regard, empathy or understanding. This instrument was given to both client and therapist, so that we have the perception of the relationship both by the therapist and by the client whom he is trying to help. To state some of the findings very briefly it may be said that those clients who eventually showed more therapeutic change as measured by various instruments, perceived *more* of these qualities in their relationship with the therapist than did those who eventually showed less change. It is also significant that this difference in perceived relationships was evident as early as the fifth interview, and predicted later change or lack of change in therapy. Furthermore, it was found that the *client's* perception of the relationship, his experience of it, was a better predictor of ultimate outcome than was the perception of the relationship by the therapist. Barrett-Lennard's original study has been amplified and generally confirmed by other studies.

So we may say, cautiously, and with qualifications which would be too cumbersome for the present paper, that if, in therapy, the client perceives his therapist as real and genuine, as one who likes, prizes, and empathically understands him, self-learning and therapeutic change are facilitated.

Now another thread of evidence, this time related more closely to education. Emmerling (1961) found that when high school teachers were asked to identify the problems they regarded as most urgent, they could be divided into two groups. Those who regarded their most serious problems, for example, a "Helping children think for themselves and be independent"; "Getting student to participate"; "Learning new ways of helping students develop their maximum potential"; "Helping students express individual needs and interests" fell into what he called the "open" or "positively oriented" group. When

Barrett-Lennard's Relationship Inventory was administered to the students of these teachers, it was found that they were perceived as significantly more real, more acceptant, more empathic than the other group of teachers whom I shall now describe.

The second category of teachers were those who tended to see their most urgent problems in negative terms, and in terms of student deficiencies and inabilities. For them the urgent problems were such as these: "Trying to teach children who don't even have the ability to follow directions"; "Teaching children who lack a desire to learn"; "Students who are not able to do the work required for their grade"; "Getting the children to listen." It probably will be no surprise that when the students of these teachers filled out the Relationship Inventory they saw their teachers as exhibiting relatively little of genuineness, of acceptance and trust, or of empathic understanding.

Hence we may say that the teacher whose orientation is toward releasing the student's potential exhibits a high degree of these attitudinal qualities which facilitate learning. The teacher whose orientation is toward the shortcomings of his students exhibits much less of these qualities.

A small pilot study by Bills (1961, 1966) extends the significance of these findings. A group of eight teachers was selected, four of them rated as adequate and effective by their superiors, and also showing this more positive orientation to their problems. The other four were rated as inadequate teachers and also had a more negative orientation to their problems, as described above. The students of these teachers were then asked to fill out the Barrett-Lennard Relationship Inventory, giving their perception of their teacher's relationship to them. This made the students very happy. Those who saw their relationship with the teacher as good were happy to describe this relationship. Those who had an unfavorable relationship were pleased to have, for the first time, an opportunity to specify the ways in which the relationship was unsatisfactory.

The more effective teachers were rated higher in every attitude measured by the Inventory: they were seen as more real, as having a higher level of regard for their students, were less conditional or judgmental in their attitudes, showed more empathic understanding. Without going into the details of the study it may be illuminating to mention that the total scores summing these attitudes vary sharply. For example, the relationships of a group of clients with their therapists, as perceived by the clients, received an average score of 108. The four most adequate high school teachers as seen by their students, received a score of 60. The four less adequate teachers received a score of 34. The lowest rated teacher received an average score of 2 from her students on the Relationship Inventory.

This small study certainly suggests that the teacher regarded as effective displays in her attitudes those qualities I have described as facilitative of learning, while the inadequate teacher shows little of these qualities.

Approaching the problem from a different angle, Schmuck (1963) has shown that in classrooms where pupils perceive their teachers as understanding them, there is likely to be a more diffuse liking structure among the pupils. This means that where the teacher is empathic, there are not a few students strongly liked and a few strongly disliked, but liking and affection are more evenly diffused throughout the group. In a later study he has shown that among students who are highly involved in their classroom peer group, "significant relationships exist between actual liking status on the one hand and utilization of abilities, attitude toward self, and attitude toward school on the other hand" (1966, p. 357-358). This seems to lend confirmation to the other evidence by indicating that in an understanding classroom climate every student tends to feel liked by all the others, to have a more positive attitude toward himself and toward school. If he is highly involved with his peer group (and this appears probable in such a classroom climate), he also tends to utilize his abilities more fully in his school achievement.

But you may still ask, does the student actually *learn* more where these attitudes are present? Here an interesting study of third graders by Aspy (1965) helps to round out the suggestive evidence. He worked in six third-grade classes. The teachers tape-recorded two full weeks of their interaction with their students in the periods devoted to the teaching of reading. These recordings were done two months apart so as to obtain an adequate sampling of the teacher's interactions with her pupils. Four-minute segments of these recordings were randomly selected for rating. Three raters, working independently and "blind," rated each segment for the degree of congruence or genuineness shown by the teacher, the degree of her prizing or unconditional positive regard, and the degree of her empathic understanding.

The Reading Achievement Tests (Stanford Achievement) were used as the criterion. Again, omitting some of the details of a carefully and rigorously controlled study, it may be said that the children in the three classes with the highest degree of the attitudes described above showed a significantly greater gain in reading achievement than those students in the three classes with a lesser degree of these qualities.

So we may say, with a certain degree of assurance, that the attitudes I have endeavored to describe are not only effective in facilitating a deeper learning and understanding of self in a relationship such as psychotherapy, but that these attitudes characterize teachers who are regarded as effective teachers, and that the students of these teachers learn more, even of a conventional curriculum, than do students of teachers who are lacking in these attitudes.

I am pleased that such evidence is accumulating. It may help to justify the revolution in education for which I am obviously hoping. But the most striking learnings of students exposed to such a climate are by no means restricted to greater achievement in the three R's. The significant learnings are the more personal ones — independence, self-initiated and responsible learning; release of creativity, a tendency to become more of a person. I can only illustrate this by picking, almost at random, statements from students whose teachers have endeavored to create a climate of trust, of prizing, of realness, of understanding, and above all, of freedom.

Again I must quote from Sylvia Ashton-Warner one of the central effects of such a climate.

> . . . The drive is no longer the teacher's, but the children's own. . . . The teacher is at last with the stream and not against it, the stream of children's inexorable creativeness (Ashton-Warner, p. 93).

If you need verification of this, listen to a few of Dr. Bull's sophomore students. The first two are mid-semester comments.

> . . . This course is proving to be a vital and profound experience for me. . . . This unique learning situation is giving me a whole new conception of just what learning is. . . . I am experiencing a real growth in this atmosphere of constructive freedom. . . . The whole experience is very challenging. . . .

> . . . I feel that the course has been of great value to me. . . . I'm glad to have had this experience because it has made me think. . . . I've never been so personally involved with a course before, especially *outside* the classroom. It's been frustrating, rewarding, enjoyable and tiring!

The other comments are from the end of the course.

> . . . This course is not ending with the close of the semester for me, but continuing. . . . I don't know of any greater benefit which can be gained from a course than this desire for further knowledge. . . .

> . . . I feel as though this type of class situation has stimulated me more in making me realize where my responsibilities lie, especially as far as doing required work on my own. I no longer feel as though a test date is the criterion for reading a book. I feel as though my future work will be done for what *I* will get out of it, not just for a test mark.

> . . . I have enjoyed the experience of being in this course. I guess that any dissatisfaction I feel at this point is a disappointment in myself, for not having taken full advantage of the opportunities the course offered.

> . . . I think that now I am acutely aware of the breakdown in communications that does exist in our society from seeing what happened in our class. . . . I've grown immensely. I know that I am a different person than I was when I came into that class. . . . It has done a great deal in helping me understand myself better. . . . Thank you for contributing to my growth.

> . . . My idea of education has been to gain information from the teacher by attending lectures. The emphasis and focus were on the teacher. . . . One of the biggest changes that I experienced in this class was my outlook on education. Learning is something more than a grade on a report card. No one can measure what you have learned because it's a personal thing. I was very con-

fused between learning and memorization. I could memorize very well, but I doubt if I ever learned as much as I could have. I believe my attitude toward learning has changed from a grade-centered outlook to a more personal one.

. . . I have learned a lot more about myself and adolescents in general. . . . I also gained more confidence in myself and my study habits by realizing that I could learn by myself without a teacher leading me by the hand. I have also learned a lot by listening to my classmates and evaluating their opinions and thoughts. . . . This course has proved to be a most meaningful and worthwhile experience . . . (Bull, 1966).

If you wish to know what this type of course seems like to a sixth grader, let me give you a sampling of the reactions of Miss Shiel's youngsters, misspellings and all.

. . . I feel that I am learning self abilty. I am learning not only school work but I am learning that you can learn on your own as well as someone can teach you.

. . . I have a little trouble in Socail Studies finding things to do. I have a hard time working the exact amount of time. Sometimes I talk to much.

. . . My parents don't understand the program. My mother say's it will give me a responsibility and it will let me go at my own speed.

. . . I like this plan because thire is a lot of freedom. I also learn more this way than the other way you don't have to wate for others you can go at your on speed rate it also takes a lot of responsibility (Shiel, 1966).

Or let me take two more, from Dr. Appell's graduate class.

. . . I have been thinking about what happened through this experience. The only conclusion I come to is that if I try to measure what is going on, or what I was at the beginning, I have got to know what I was when I started — and I don't. . . . So many things I did and feel are just lost . . . scrambled up inside. . . . They don't seem to come out in a nice little pattern or organization I can say or write. . . . There are so many things left unsaid. I know I have only scratched the surface, I guess. I can feel so many things almost ready to come out . . . maybe that's enough. *It seems all kinds of things have so much more meaning now than ever before.* . . . This experience has had meaning, has done things to me and I am not sure how much or how far just yet. I think I am going to be a better me in the fall. *That's one thing I think I am sure of* (Appell, 1963).

. . . You follow no plan, yet I'm learning. Since the term began I seem to feel more alive, more real to myself. I enjoy being alone as well as with other people. My relationships with children and other adults are becoming more emotional and involved. Eating an orange last week, I peeled the skin off each separate orange section and liked it better with the transparent shell off.

It was jucier and fresher tasting that way. I began to think, that's how I feel sometimes, without a transparent wall around me, really communicating my feelings. I feel that I'm growing, how much, I don't know. I'm thinking, considering, pondering and learning (Appell, 1959).

I can't read these student statements — 6th grade, college, graduate level — without my eyes growing moist. Here are teachers, risking themselves, *being* themselves, *trusting* their students, adventuring into the existential unknown, taking the subjective leap. And what happens? Exciting, incredible *human* events. You can sense persons being created, learnings being initiated, future citizens rising to meet the challenge of unknown worlds. If only one teacher out of one hundred dared to risk, dared to be, dared to trust, dared to understand, we would have an infusion of a living spirit into education which would, in my estimation, be priceless.

I have heard scientists at leading schools of science, and scholars in leading universities, arguing that it is absurd to try to encourage all students to be creative — we need hosts of mediocre technicians and workers and if a few creative scientists and artists and leaders emerge, that will be enough. That may be enough for them. It may be enough to suit you. I want to go on record as saying it is *not* enough to suit me. When I realize the incredible potential in the ordinary student, I want to try to release it. We are working hard to release the incredible energy in the atom and the nucleus of the atom. If we do not devote equal energy — yes, and equal money — to the release of the potential of the individual person, then the enormous discrepancy between our level of physical energy resources and human energy resources will doom us to a deserved and universal destruction.

I'm sorry I can't be coolly scientific about this. The issue is too urgent. I can only be passionate in my statement that people count, that interpersonal relationships *are* important, that we know something about releasing human potential, that we could learn much more, and that unless we give strong positive attention to the human interpersonal side of our educational dilemma, our civilization is on its way down the drain. Better courses, better curricula, better coverage, better teaching machines, will never resolve our dilemma in a basic way. Only persons, acting like persons in their relationships with their students can even begin to make a dent on this most urgent problem of modern education.

I cannot, of course, stop here in a professional lecture. An academic lecture should be calm, factual, scholarly, critical, preferably devoid of any personal beliefs, completely devoid of passion. (This is one of the reasons I left university life, but that is a completely different story.) I cannot fully fulfill these requirements for a professional lecture, but let me at least try to state, somewhat more calmly and soberly, what I have said with such feeling and passion.

I have said that it is most unfortunate that educators and the public think about, and focus on, *teaching*. It leads them into a host of questions which are either irrelevant or absurd so far as real education is concerned.

I have said that if we focused on the facilitation of *learning* — how, why, and when the student learns, and how learning seems and feels from the inside, we might be on a much more profitable track.

I have said that we have some knowledge, and could gain more, about the conditions which facilitate learning, and that one of the most important of these conditions is the attitudinal quality of the interpersonal relationship between facilitator and learner. (There are other conditions, too, which I have tried to spell out elsewhere [Rogers, 1966b].)

Those attitudes which appear effective in promoting learning can be described. First of all is a transparent realness in the facilitator, a willingness to be a person, to be and to live the feelings and thoughts of the moment. When this realness includes a prizing, a caring, a trust and respect for the learner, the climate for learning is enhanced. When it includes a sensitive and accurate empathic listening, then indeed a freeing climate, stimulative of self-initiated learning and growth, exists.

I have tried to make plain that individuals who hold such attitudes, and are bold enough to act on them, do not simply modify classroom methods — they revolutionize them. They perform almost none of the functions of teachers. It is no longer accurate to call them teachers. They are catalyzers, facilitators, giving freedom and life and the opportunity to learn, to students.

I have brought in the cumulating research evidence which suggests that individuals who hold such attitudes are regarded as effective in the classroom; that the problems which concern them have to do with the release of potential, not the deficiencies of their students; that they seem to create classroom situations in which there are not admired children and disliked children, but in which affection and liking are a part of the life of every child; that in classrooms approaching such a psychological climate, children learn more of the conventional subjects.

But I have intentionally gone beyond the empirical findings to try to take you into the inner life of the student — elementary, college, and graduate — who is fortunate enough to live and learn in such an interpersonal relationship with a facilitator, in order to let you see what learning feels like when it is free, self-initiated and spontaneous. I have tried to indicate how it even changes the student-student relationship — making it more aware, more caring, more sensitive, as well as increasing the self-related learning of significant material.

Throughout my paper I have tried to indicate that if we are to have citizens who can live constructively in this kaleidoscopically changing world, we can *only* have them if we are willing for them to become self-starting, self-initiating learners. Finally, it has been my purpose to show that this kind of learner develops best, so far as we now know, in a growth-promoting, facilitative, relationship with a *person*.

REFERENCES

APPELL, M. L. Selected student reactions to student-centered courses. Mimeographed manuscript, 1959.

APPELL, M. L. Self-understanding for the guidance counselor. *Personnel and Guidance Journal,* October, 1963, 143-148.

ASHTON-WARNER, S. *Teacher.* New York: Simon and Schuster, 1963.

ASPY, D. N. A study of three facilitative conditions and their relationship to the achievement of third grade students. Unpublished Ed.D. dissertation, University of Kentucky, 1965.

AXLINE, VIRGINIA M. Morale on the school front. *Journal of Educational Research,* 1944, 521-533.

BARRETT-LENNARD, G. T. Dimensions of therapist response as casual factors in therapeutic change. *Psychological Monographs,* 76, 1962. (Whole No. 562.)

BILLS, R. E. Personal correspondence. 1961, 1966.

BULL, PATRICIA. Student reactions, Fall 1965. State University College, Cortland, New York. Mimeographed manuscripts, 1966.

EMMERLING, F. C. A study of the relationships between personality characteristics of classroom teachers and pupil perceptions. Unpublished Ph.D. dissertation, Auburn University, Auburn, Alabama, 1961.

JACKSON, P. W. The student's world. University of Chicago. Mimeographed, 1966.

ROGERS, C. R. To facilitate learning. In Malcolm Provus (Ed.), NEA Handbook for Teachers, *Innovations for time to teach.* Washington, D.C.: Department of Classroom Teachers, NEA, 1966a.

ROGERS, C. R. The facilitation of significant learning. In L. Siegel (Ed.), *Contemporary theories of instruction.* San Francisco, California: Chandler Publishing Co., 1966b.

SCHMUCK, R. Some aspects of classroom social climate. *Psychology in the Schools* 3, 1966, 59-65.

SCHMUCK, R. Some relationships of peer liking patterns in the classroom to pupil attitudes and achievement. *The School Review* 71, 1963, 337-359.

SHIEL, BARBARA J. Evaluation: A self-directed curriculum, 1965. Mimeographed, 1966.

26

Current Assumptions in

Graduate Education:

A Passionate Statement*

CARL R. ROGERS

Over the past decade I have become more and more keenly disturbed by the damage which is done to students during their graduate training in the various professional fields. In 1963 I attempted to document my concern in a paper, "Graduate Education in Psychology: A Passionate Statement." It was submitted to the leading professional journal in psychology, but was rejected because it was too controversial and might have a divisive effect upon the science and profession of psychology! I let it be known that the document existed, and since then thousands of copies have been distributed upon request to individuals in a variety of fields. I suspect it has become one of the most widely read unpublished papers of the past decade. This is its second appearance in print.[1]

The letters I have received in response make it clear that the fallacious assumptions I see in graduate education in psychology exist also in other fields. This is especially borne out in the article by Arrowsmith (1966), "The Shame of the Graduate Schools." His ringing protest is

* "Current Assumptions in Graduate Education: A Passionate Statement" is from *Freedom to Learn*, Chapter 8, by Carl R. Rogers, Columbus, Ohio: Charles E. Merrill, 1969. Reproduced by permission.

[1] This article first appeared in *Freedom to Learn* by Carl R. Rogers (Charles E. Merrill, 1969).

against education in the humanities, *and he rather blithely assumes that all is well in graduate education in the sciences.*

Hence, though the content of this chapter deals with the graduate education of psychologists, since that is the field I know intimately, it is my firm belief that the statements in it apply equally to most secondary schools, to most undergraduate education, and indeed to almost every phase of our vast educational enterprise.

So I simply suggest that educators at every level ask themselves, "Do the assumptions listed here apply to any degree to the educational program in which I am involved?" If the answer is "No," they are indeed fortunate.

I wish in this chapter to express a strong and growing personal concern about the educational policies which are operative in most departments of psychology in their graduate training programs. Very briefly, the theme of my statement is that we are doing an unintelligent, ineffectual, and wasteful job of preparing psychologists, to the detriment of our discipline and society.

My concern has its basis in the knowledge that the future of civilization may depend on finding the solutions to psychological problems. It is a truism that man has made great progress in solving many of the material problems of his existence, but that he may well be defeated, and perhaps annihilated, by his failure to solve the *psychological* problems which face him — interpersonal, interracial, and international frictions, delinquency, the disturbances labelled "mental illness," the growing loss of a sense of purpose, and the inability to learn at a rate which will keep up with our expanding knowledge. Thus, the logic of our culture *demands* that the behavioral sciences play an increasingly important part in the foreseeable future of our society as it confronts these problems.

Obviously this situation constitutes a challenge to psychology and the other behavioral sciences. We should be selecting and training individuals for creative effectiveness in seeking out and discovering the significant new knowledge which is needed. Furthermore, since psychology, more than the other sciences, has access to the cumulating research knowledge regarding learning, creativity, and the development of autonomous persons, it would seem that our programs for the preparation of psychologists should be superior to programs in other fields.

Is this the case? I fear not. As Sigmund Koch has recently said of psychologists, "We are not known for our readiness to be in the wavefront of history." Granting that American psychologists have not been noted as pioneers, it seems to me unnecessary that in our graduate programs we should so frequently display timid or reactionary patterns which put us in the backwaters rather than the wavefront of history.

In recent years I have had opportunity to observe a number of psychology departments. I have gathered material from graduate students in widely divergent places. For me these observations and this material raise profound and disturbing questions about the general pattern of scientific and professional education in our discipline. When we examine what we *do,* rather than what we *profess* in this area, the picture which emerges is, in my estimation, a sorry one.

I am well aware that members of other sciences and professions often feel similarly critical of graduate education in their own areas. I am limiting my remarks to the field of psychology for two reasons. It is the only field in which I can speak from firsthand knowledge. It is also the science which should be leading the way in preparation of new members of its science and profession.

Implicit Assumptions

I believe that we may best consider our programs of graduate education by examining the implicit assumptions on which they appear to be based. I will present these assumptions as I see them, and some of the evidence which challenges them. I trust the reader will think of these statements in relation to some departmental situation he knows and see to what extent they apply.

Implicit Assumption 1: *The student cannot be trusted to pursue his own scientific and professional learning.*

This is an extremely pervasive assumption in the great majority of departments. One might suppose that the graduate student who has chosen to become a psychologist could be trusted to pursue that purpose, and that the function of the faculty would be to give help in fulfilling his aim of learning the material of his science and profession. Instead, it is almost uniformly true that the faculty attitude is one of mistrustful guidance. Work must be assigned; the completion of this work must be supervised; students must be continually guided and then evaluated. It is very rare indeed that the graduate student finds his program to be an experience in which he is *set free* to pursue the learnings which are of importance to himself.

Many years ago I endeavored to state the divergent views on this point:

> Many believe that the goals of graduate education can best be reached by requiring students to work through a carefully guided program in which the content to be required, the credits to be gained, and the courses to be taken, are quite carefully and clearly defined. They believe that a carefully planned curriculum which sets forth the knowledge and skills to be acquired is perhaps our best method of achieving such a goal.

> Others believe that quite a different method is called for in achieving these goals. To them it seems that the best education, and particularly the best

graduate education, is that which frees the student to pursue the knowledge, skills, attitudes and experiences which seem to him related to his own goals of ultimate professional and scientific competence. To this second group this seems to be more in accord with what we know of the laws of learning and the principles of individual development and growth.

A graduate student discusses the same issue with more feeling. She says:

> The general attitude in higher education today is one of student *vs.* faculty rather than student *with* faculty. I wonder if this "opposing attitude" in education doesn't go back to the system of learning in the primary and elementary system. Here the student is asked to memorize rules rather than to understand intrinsically the basic concepts and reasons for these rules. One is "taken to" learning by the hand, rather than "guided toward" knowledge by desire. Professors have learned this way, and the majority of them carry this "opposition learning" to the student. It is what they have experienced, and thus, it is what they transfer to the next fellow.

Later in her statement she gives an appealing view of the alternative possibility:

> In my mind, the two most basic, and at the same time, most general, qualities that should exist in learning, are freedom and responsibility. Freedom of time and freedom of thought, allowing students to relax and become "swept up" by a stimulating environment; to become involved, to be able to give to as well as take from. Responsibility should be felt and accepted by the student — a responsibility to himself, and to his field; to learn, to be involved, to question what he does and thinks and what others do and think.

Her statement is strongly echoed by a distinguished group of nine psychologists who spent four weeks in formulating the principles by which graduate education in psychology might lead to more initiative for research, and more significant research. They say:

> The attitudes, the independence of thought, and the willingness to persist in one's own interest and beliefs that characterize good research work are often the very traits that lead an individual to resist actively pressures toward conformity to a given pattern of study, toward mastery of given areas of knowledge, or toward acceptance of given ways of thinking. Consequently, the imposition of standardized patterns may often operate to exclude individuals with traits desirable for research (*American Psychologist* 1959, p. 173).

Thus, there seems reason to believe that trusting the student would be a much sounder assumption than the present attitude of mistrust which has a definitely damaging effect upon self-confidence. MacKinnon, in studying creativity in architects, gives a list of the factors in the early life of these men which are highly associated with their present creativeness (as judged by their fellows). The first such background factor is: "An extraordinary respect for the child and confidence in his ability to do what was appropriate" (1963, p. 20).

We might try extending such respect and confidence to our graduate students.

Implicit Assumption 2: Ability to pass examinations is the best criterion for student selection and for judging professional promise.

The best candidate to be selected for training as a psychologist is one who has passed examinations in the past. The most promising graduate student is the one who best passes the examination in this department.

This assumption, again implicit in the great majority of departments, leads to a heavy stress on the academic record and the grade point average in the process of selecting graduate students. It also leads to the use of measures such as the Graduate Record Examination and the Miller Analogies Test, in the hope that they will predict "academic success," that is, the ability to pass courses similar to undergraduate courses. It also, of course, leads to the use of examinations as the primary criterion for assessing the promise of those students who have been selected for graduate work.

While it is clear that examination-passing ability is a useful skill, and has a place in professional training, it almost certainly emphasizes rote learning and mental agility rather than originality of thought and scientific curiosity, traits which in the long run are more valuable. Guilford has pointed out that education . . .

> . . . has emphasized abilities in the areas of convergent thinking and evaluation, often at the expense of development in the area of divergent thinking. We have attempted to teach students how to arrive at "correct" answers that our civilization has taught us are correct. This is convergent thinking. . . . Outside the arts we have generally discouraged the development of divergent thinking abilities, unintentionally but effectively (1957, p. 19).

Likewise, in terms of the research by Getzels and Jackson, it would appear that our present methods of selection and assessment tend to place value on what they term the high-I.Q. individual rather than the creative individual. It is useful to think of our usual assessment procedures in the light of their comments about these two types of student:

> It seems to us that the essence of the performance of our creative adolescents lay in their ability to produce new forms, to risk conjoining elements that are customarily thought of as independent and dissimilar, to "go off in new directions." The creative adolescent seemed to possess the ability to free himself from the usual, to "diverge" from the customary. He seemed to enjoy the risk and uncertainty of the unknown. In contrast, the high-I. Q. adolescent seemed to possess to a high degree the ability and the need to focus on the usual, to be "channeled and controlled" in the direction of the

right answer — the customary. He appeared to shy away from the risk and uncertainty of the unknown and to seek out the safety and security of the known (1963, p. 172).

The effect of this second assumption is that students who are selected and valued as psychologists-to-be tend to excel in examination passing, rather than in those qualities which would give them promise as independent discoverers of new knowledge.

Implicit Assumption 3: *Evaluation is education, education is evaluation.*

It is incredible the way this preposterous assumption has become completely imbedded in graduate education in the United States. Examinations have become the beginning and the end of education. They are a way of life for the graduate student, and a more stultifying way of life could hardly be imagined. In one university the graduate student in psychology is faced with these major evaluation hurdles:

(1) Examination in first foreign language
(2) Examination in second foreign language
(3) First six hour qualifying examination
(4) Second six hour qualifying examination (both of these in the first graduate year)
(5) Three hour examination in methodology and statistics
(6) Four hour examination in a chosen major field of psychology
(7) Two hour examination in a minor field
(8) Oral examination on Master's thesis
(9) Committee evaluation of Ph.D. proposal
(10) Committee evaluation of Ph.D. thesis
(11) Oral examination on Ph.D. thesis

Since 10 to 50 per cent of those taking any of these examinations are failed on the first attempt, the actual number of examinations taken is considerably greater than indicated above. Understandably, the anxiety on the second attempt is considerably (sometimes unbearably) greater. Furthermore, these examinations are so spaced out that during the four to seven years of his graduate work the student's main concern is with the next sword of Damocles which hangs over his career. As if the above list were not enough, it should be made clear that these major examinations are *in addition to* any quizzes, mid-semester and final examinations given in his courses.

Obviously the student cannot possibly have the sense of fully independent freedom which is clearly at the base of creative professional work. Small wonder that a graduate student leaving this program wrote:

> I don't mind a certain amount of academic hazing of graduate students by the faculty. I know that they feel that they must "get tough." But at this

university the point is never reached at which the student feels, "The department is now behind me in my endeavor to get a degree."[2]

The way in which examinations stultify real learning is indicated by a student from another university who writes:

> A lot of people are never sure when they write an exam what grade range they are in. The grade on the exam depends upon whether you have hit the point or points that the professor is looking for. In class you have to tune your mind into the wave length of the instructor. You would like to understand what he is getting at but this is barred by trying to determine what he wants fed back on an exam (Clark, 1962, p. 42).

Another graduate student in still another university expresses something of the bitterness which this approach engenders:

> One leaves the course knowing gobs of jargon, and most of "the" answers. He has filled all the pages of his notebook with the professor's speeches, and on the final exam, he has hopefully given back to the professor most of the important facts and basic ideas. The professor looks for and expects a blind acceptance; he wants back what he gave you, not giving you the opportunity for digestion and reaction. There is little chance for synthesis. The student is requested to conform to the instructor's view, and no reward is given for creative thought and individual reaction to the material. The subject is presented as black and white, and one-dimensional. As I write this I feel frustrated. It is a feeling of bitterness, a rebellion, feeling all steamed up inside, but without a hole in the kettle spout to let out some steam; it is a burning steam.

Frequently, for the major examinations, the student is given almost no clues as to what the examination will cover. It will simply be an examination in "general psychology" or "social psychology," or some other field. But since the student knows that the examination questions will be formulated by Professors X and Y, he does not waste his time concentrating on what for him is important in general or social psychology. He focuses instead on learning the interests and prejudices of the two professors. One student, commenting on this aspect, says:

> One spends so much time trying to "second guess" what exam questions will be that he has no time to learn what he wants to learn.

Lest one feel that these are merely the rantings of callow graduate students, let me add one more quotation from a scientist looking back on some of his experience:

---

[2] It is important to note that all of the graduate students quoted in this paper are doing highly creditable graduate work. One holds a National Science Foundation Fellowship; others hold other national fellowships based on merit. One is known to have a straight A graduate record. None of the quotations are "gripes" from marginal or failing students. For reasons of diplomacy, the authors of the quotations prefer not to be identified.

This coercion had such a deterring effect (upon me) that, after I had passed the final examination, I found the consideration of any problem distasteful for me for an entire year.

This is a statement by Albert Einstein. It portrays very well the impact of an evaluative system upon a sensitive, inquiring, and creative mind. A less restrained statement is said to have been made by another mature scientist, a noted astronomer. He states that real advances in knowledge come from people who are doing what they like to do. We all know the effect on children of compulsory spinach and compulsory rhubarb. It is the same with compulsory learning. They say "It's spinach and to hell with it." Though I cannot prove the authenticity of this statement it certainly expresses the same point of view as is held by most scientists.

It is difficult to exaggerate the damage done to promising graduate students by this completely fallacious assumption that they learn by being threatened, time after time, with catastrophic failure. While I am sure most faculty members would deny that they hold to this assumption, their behavior shows all too clearly that this is the operational principle by which they work.

Implicit Assumption 4: *Presentation equals learning: What is presented in the lecture is what the student learns.*

It scarcely seems possible that intelligent men could hold to this assumption. Yet one has only to observe a hard-working, seriousminded committee of faculty members arguing over the topics to be included in a graduate survey course in psychology to realize that in their view of the course, what is "covered" (a marvelous term!) is what is learned.

Here is the reaction of a graduate student in the midst of taking such a carefully planned course:

> Worst of all, I think, is the fact that not many of the students feel that they are learning anything at all. They feel that it is just a continuation of the idiocy of undergraduate school in which huge amounts of material are thrown at you and you are expected to regurgitate most of it on a test, and then supposedly you have learned something. You may indeed have gained some separated facts about psychology, but none of them can be integrated in any coherent way.

The assumption that learning is equivalent to hearing a lecture is closely tied in with the preceding assumption that education is evaluation. They are both closely related to the next assumption.

Implicit Assumption 5: *Knowledge is the accumulation of brick upon brick of content and information.*

One might think that psychology, of all the scientific disciplines, would be the least likely to hold this implicit assumption. It is psychologists who have shown that learning takes place primarily and significantly when it is directly related to the meaningful purposes and motives of the individual. Yet most graduate departments proceed upon the conviction that there are a series of fundamental building blocks in the science of psychology which must be mastered sequentially by the student, whether or not they fit in with his current interests.

Some of the best minds in psychology know differently. The Conference on Education for Research in Psychology, mentioned previously, makes these important observations:

> A knowledge of facts of psychology is important for research. How much of this is to be imparted during graduate study, however, is not easy to determine. Much of the factual knowledge of the mature scientist has been accumulated during the course of his career and probably cannot be duplicated by explicit instruction. Morever, substantive courses inevitably compete for the student's time with practical experience in the methods and art of research. For all these reasons, we urge caution against the overloading of an individual's graduate program with substantive courses, either as the result of department requirements or as the result of choice by the student (*American Psychologist,* 1959, p. 172).

> In general, we question the assumption that the more formal preparation the individual has for research, the more productive and creative he will be in research. Specifically, we doubt that the more complete the individual's mastery of statistical and other tools, the more effective he will be in research; we doubt that the greater his scholarly knowledge of the literature, the more likely he will be to contribute to that knowledge; we doubt that the value of theory in research increases continuously as it becomes more formalized and detailed (*American Psychologist,* 1959, p. 170).

I believe it is pertinent to note that Harvard and a number of other leading medical schools have done away with the pre-med undergraduate major, a requirement based on the "brick-by-brick" philosophy. Harvard found that by the third year of medical school those without the pre-med major were doing slightly better in their grades than those with such a major, besides having greater breadth and greater promise.

Implicit Assumption 6: *The truths of psychology are known.*

In some departments with which I am acquainted this assumption of an orthodoxy of knowledge is quite evident. In other departments there is much more acceptance of divergence. To the extent that there is only one acceptable view, this seems most unfortunate in a developing science. One graduate student describes his experience:

> There is an orthodoxy here. [He then describes the ritual and dogma of his particular department in terms which might be identifying.] . . . Here, it seems, one speaks only in imitation of one's elders. The result is a "new

scholasticism"; stultifying repetition of the thoughts and prejudices of the faculty.

One related procedure, which struck me most forcefully in my first class session, is what I call "study-citing behavior," name-dropping about any member whatsoever of certain approved classes of research. It is behavior well calculated to gain the favor of the faculty; it serves the further end of eliminating any necessity for the citer having to think and is also effective in cutting off an opponent in argument. While appeal to research findings can have value if it does not itself become an authoritarianism, it is indicative of the closed-mindedness of the department that only certain brands of research have approved citing status. . . . One learns here rather quickly what is expected of him.

There is no point in belaboring this issue. Often faculty members talk critically about dogmatism, yet display an extreme degree of it in their behavior. Sometimes the orthodoxy is in regard to method, and it is the "truth methods" of scientific psychology that are regarded as immutable. In any event, where attitudes such as those described above exist in a department, the atmosphere is opposed to any true scientific endeavor. Only a pseudoscience can result.

Implicit Assumption 7: *Method is science.*

Here is an assumption which I find particularly widespread in American psychology. A rigorous procedure is often considered (if one may judge by faculty behavior) as far more important than the ideas it is intended to investigate. A meticulous statistics and a sophisticated research design seem to carry more weight than significant observations of significant problems.

Here again, when prominent scientists in the field of psychology think together about graduate training, they resolutely reject such an assumption:

Education for research must do more than develop competence in designing, executing, and interpreting experimental or other studies. Development of such competence is important, but much more important is the development of the individual's creativeness — his ability to discover new relations, to reformulate or systematize known facts, to devise new techniques and approaches to problems (*American Psychologist*, 1959, p. 170).

Implicit Assumption 8: *Creative scientists develop from passive learners.*

A number of the preceding assumptions make it evident that many departments believe, operationally, that the student who absorbs and then gives back on examinations is the one on whom they are placing their bets for the future. Yet I know of no studies in the field which would support this assumption. Anne Roe, from her extensive work in studying leading scientists comes to the conclusion that some of the factors in our educational procedures which adversely affect students in their development as scientists are the following:

(1) Insufficient valuation of problem solving attitudes in the school.

(2) The general tendency of teachers to sweeping devaluation of "wild" or "silly" ideas.

(3) Restriction upon curiosity (1963).

Similarly a broadly based study of several hundred colleges by Thistlethwaite (1963) shows that vigorous class discussions and flexibility of a curriculum are significantly associated with the number of Ph.D.'s in the social sciences produced by these colleges, relative to enrollment. Interestingly enough these same elements are somewhat negatively associated with the production of Ph.D.'s in the natural sciences. Here is an issue worth further study.

MacKinnon, from his extensive work in the investigation of creativity, points up a fact which is too litttle considered. He says:

> . . . *ledge,* the second element in the word *knowledge,* means sport. Knowledge is the result of playing with what we know, that is, with our facts. A knowledgeable person in science is not, as we are often wont to think, merely one who has an accumulation of facts, but rather one who has the capacity to have sport with what he knows, giving creative rein to his fancy in changing his world of phenomenal appearances into a world of scientific constructs (1963, p. 23).

I think I know what would happen, in most departments, to the graduate student who gave "creative rein to his fancy!"

Yet when students are *taught* to defer judgments about ideas, and are encouraged in a permissive atmosphere simply to *produce* ideas no matter how unreasonable they may seem, they are found to produce a greater quantity and a higher quality of problem-solving ideas than a control group, as research by Parnes and Meadow (1963) has shown.

In my judgment, in our insecurity as a profession, we attach enormous importance to turning out "hardheaded" scientists, and strongly punish any of the sensitive, speculative, sportive openness which is the essence of the real scientist. What departments of psychology of your acquaintance would value these qualities in their graduate students?

> Students who are "unusually appreciative of the intuitive and non-rational elements of their nature; distinguished by their profound commitment to the search for esthetic and philosophic meaning in all experience" (Taylor and Barron, 1963, p. 386).

> Students who exhibit "an openness to their own feelings and emotions, esthetic interests, and a sensitive awarenesss of self and others" (MacKinnon, 1963, p. 36).

Yet these statements are taken from summaries of the objective characteristics of outstanding young scientists and outstandingly creative professional men. They are, however, the type of personal qualities which many psychologists fear in themselves and in their students.

Implicit Assumption 9: *"Weeding out" a majority of the students is a satisfactory method of producing scientists and clinicians.*

To me it seems a scandalous waste of manpower that of the carefully selected graduate students whom we take into our programs, only a small proportion ever obtain their degrees. It is indicative of the irresponsible attitude of our discipline that most departments have no idea of what percentage of their students obtain a Ph.D. It appears that in fortunate departments perhaps one out of two students is successful. In some departments only one out of five, or even one out of seven of those who start actually obtain the degree. Usually this is regarded as evidence that the department maintains "high standards." I know of no other field of work in which such an attitude would be taken. Medicine has long ago recognized that when they select a talented group as medical students, the profession has an obligation to conserve this potentiality. Failure is seen as being as much a reflection upon the medical school as upon the student. Industry, too, realizes that it must conserve talented manpower. But in psychology it is not so.

The shameful attrition rate referred to above occurs in part because students fail some of the numerous evaluative hurdles previously mentioned and are eliminated from the program or discouraged from continuing. But it also occurs in considerable part because students with an original turn of mind become disenchanted with the sterility of a program based on the assumptions outlined in these pages and leave for other fields. As I have watched this process it is my conviction that among the students who leave our psychology departments one would find both the least promising and the most promising of our potential future psychologists. Any system of continuous evaluation weeds out some of the less competent or less intelligent. Yet, it also tends very definitely to eliminate the most unique and creative of our students who simply refuse to, as they say, "put up with all that Mickey Mouse."

All in all, it seems clear that most departments are quite satisfied with a weeding out process which wastes the vast majority (from 50 to 85 per cent) of the graduate students who have been so carefully selected. The thought that the profession has a responsibility to "grow psychologists" out of the talented individuals they select, seems scarcely to have entered our thinking. In my opinion, every student who leaves a department should be considered as a possible failure on the part of the department, either in selection, in teaching, in faculty-student relationship, or in the provision of a stimulating professional and scientific climate. His leaving should be carefully considered from each of these angles, in order that deficiencies may be corrected. Industry endeavors to learn from its "exit interviews." Psychology might do likewise.

Implicit Assumption 10: *Students are best regarded as manipulable objects, not as persons.*

Certainly in a number of departments the relationship between students and faculty is remote and impersonal. This seems to grow out of two causes. In the first place the current ultra-behavioristic philosophy which underlies today's psychology tends to see all individuals simply as machines, managed by reward and punishment. Hence students are dealt with on this same basis. Since students do not like to be treated as objects, the net effect is low morale. Students even tend to treat each other in the same fashion. In some departments where there is a very heavy stress on evaluation, student A will not give help to student B because any improvement in B's showing will automatically put A lower "on the curve." This seems to be a vicious sort of attitude for a professional person who will later be expected to be a part of a scientific or professional team.

There is another factor in this remoteness of faculty-student relationship. It is that it is almost impossible to be close to a student if one's primary relationship to him is that of a judge and evaluator. This is hinted at by a graduate student who describes the faculty-student relationship at his university:

> I see . . . instructors hiding behind a mask of impersonal, "scientific" objectivity in order to avoid the risk involved in *personal* interpersonal relationships, and perhaps out of distaste for the evaluative task they have imposed upon themselves.

In some instances faculty members put the student in a real "double bind" situation by giving him a contradictory message. It is as if the faculty member said: "I welcome you to a warm and close interpersonal relationship — and when you come close I will clobber you with my evaluation." The analogy to the parents of schizophrenics is painfully clear.

Again, solid evidence exists to contradict this tenth assumption. Thistlethwaite, in a study referred to previously, found that faculty "informality and warmth of student-faculty contacts" in the institution is significantly related to the rate of production of Ph.D.'s in the natural sciences, and also in the arts, humanities and social sciences (1963). Psychology may be hurting its own future by its insistence that the individual is nothing more than a machine.

Why These Assumptions?

Why is it that departments cling to these behaviors and their underlying assumptions, when even a casual study would expose their fallacies? Why is it that advancement and prestige in departments of psychology depends on adherence to these shaky assumptions? Why is it, for example, that a faculty member who fails half his students on an examination is likely to be regarded as a better (because more "tough-minded") instructor than his colleague who fails none? Why is it that the man who treats his students as persons, as human beings, as junior colleagues, is apt to be looked on with some suspicion by his fellows? How is it that the behaviors described have been so rewarding that they have become embedded in American psychology, in spite of their fallacious base?

I can only speculate. No doubt one reason is that students, consciously or unconsciously, after sixteen years of academic spoonfeeding, tend to demand more of the same. Another reason may be that original, curious, autonomous students, pursuing their own goals, are nearly always disturbing to have around. They challenge pet beliefs and fixed ways of doing things, and hence, as faculty members we may tend to avoid producing them. Still another reason is that as Research has become an end rather than a means, various results follow. Teaching is devalued, purity of research design becomes all important, and students are a means of getting research done. There is little concern with the true nurture of young scientists. Most important of all, perhaps, is that the philosophical views of psychologists regarding education and the nature of man seem not to have caught up with the advances in their own field. These are only possibilities. The question needs a great deal more investigation. There must be a rational explanation for the stubborn way in which psychology departments cling to these outmoded ideas.

The Other Side of the Coin

I am well aware that not all of the teaching which goes on in graduate programs operates on the assumptions I have listed. One graduate student, after making a number of complaints, writes:

> More rarely, I will leave a class feeling inspired, excited, and stimulated. Here is the rare professor who encourages freedom of thought. He does not yield to the pressures of having to see his students pass the "finish line," but realizes that there is no finish line. A questioning, thought-provoking atmosphere exists. The student has the opportunity to react openly and honestly, and to lend his own creative thoughts to the subject. The professor does not want his students to take what he says for granted, but rather he encourages them to think about what he says; to think, to react, to question; to accept, to reject, to incorporate.

It is the good fortune of psychology to have a number of such teachers, operating on a very different set of hypotheses, whose open-minded venturesome honesty leads to scientific curiosity and excitement in their students.

Although the operational procedures in most of our graduate programs tend to be in line with the assumptions I have listed, it would not be too difficult to implement a vastly improved program, based upon sharply different principles. Many of the elements of such a program have already been set forth in the report on "Education for research in psychology" to which

I have made several references. I endeavor to spell out such a program in Chapter 9 of *Freedom to learn* (Rogers, 1969).

A Final Challenge

If the day comes when psychology wishes to make a thoughtful appraisal of its methods of professional preparation, it will, I believe, throw out most of its current assumptions and procedures. I have tried to indicate, however, that lying all about, in the research literature of psychology itself, are the facts and findings upon which we could build a graduate program of which we could be proud — a program productive of freely independent, openly curious psychologists, unafraid in their search for genuinely new and deeply significant approximations to the truth.

REFERENCES

AMERICAN PSYCHOLOGIST. Education for research in psychology. (Report of a seminar group sponsored by the Educational and Training Board of the American Psychological Association), 1959, 14, 167-179.

ARROWSMITH, W. The shame of the graduate schools. *Harpers Magazine*, March, 1966, 232 (1390), 51-59.

CLARK, J. V. Education for the use of behavioral science. Los Angeles: Institute of Industrial Relations, UCLA, 1962.

GETZELS, J. W., and JACKSON, P. W. The highly intelligent and the creative adolescent. In C. Taylor and F. Barron (Eds.), *Scientific creativity: Its recognition and development*. New York: John Wiley and Sons, 1963.

GUILFORD, J. P. A revised structure of intellect. *Reports from the Psychological Lab.*, #19, Los Angeles: University of Southern California, 1957.

MacKINNON, D. W. The nature of creativity. In *Creativity and college teaching*. Proceedings of a conference held at the University of Kentucky. Bulletin of the Bureau of School Service, 1963, 35, #4, College of Education, University of Kentucky, Lexington, Kentucky.

PARNES, S. J. and MEADOW, A. Development of individual creative talent. In C. Taylor and F. Barron (Eds.), *Scientific creativity: Its recognition and development*. New York: John Wiley and Sons, 1963.

ROE, ANNE. Personal problems and science. In C. Taylor and F. Barron (Eds.), *Scientific creativity: Its recognition and development*. New York: John Wiley and Sons, 1963.

ROGERS, CARL R. *Freedom to learn*. Columbus, Ohio: Charles E. Merrill, 1969.

TAYLOR, C. and BARRON, F. (Eds.), *Scientific creativity: Its recognition and development*. New York: John Wiley and Sons, 1963.

THISTLETHWAITE, D. The college environment as a determinant of research potentiality. In C. Taylor and F. Barron (Eds.), *Scientific creativity: Its recognition and development*. New York: John Wiley and Sons, 1963.

PART SIX

Directions of Change

How should a book end? Certainly a psychotherapy book must end with some new beginnings. Research, theory, and practice — each needs to be extended and improved. Research on therapy must continue the sensitive examination of helpful interactions while making outcome investigations more comprehensive. Theory must more cogently intertwine with both research and practice. And therapists must continue to teeter, as they practice their art, on that wobbly balance between professionalism and innovation.

This final section discusses those directions within client-centered therapy so new they are just beginning — and in some instances they have not yet begun. Such an endeavor has its risks. Fortune-tellers are notoriously sanguine. They look at the world through pink-colored crystal balls. But if one listens to forecasts with the right amount of skepticism, insights can be heard. At the very least, fortunes tell us about the needs of the present. How, or whether, those needs will be met is always elusive. Our four fortune-tellers — Rogers, Shlien, Gendlin, and Hart — attempt to predict both.

There are several forecasts on which they agree. One: therapy will continue to develop new forms outside the usual one-to-one office meetings characterizing traditional psychotherapy. Two: nonprofessional therapists of all types will be trained and widely used. Three: theoretical and empirical emphasis on the development of potentialities rather than on the correction of pathologies will continue. And four: eclectic empiricism and general theories of personality change will replace schools of psychotherapy. Probably most therapists, at least most humanistic therapists, would agree with these propositions. Naturally then, more far-out forecasts are the more interesting, and our fortune-tellers provide these too.

We begin with the "A conversation with Carl Rogers." Throughout his career Rogers has never found it difficult to conjure provocative forecasts

499

and work to make his forecasts a reality. Nor does he now: "I have a feeling that what we used to think of as the function of the true university is increasingly going to leave universities and be carried on by peripheral institutions. Universities are so big, with so much production machinery, and develop such a bureaucracy, that probably the exciting new things will develop either in ad hoc organizations that form a particular task force, or institutes that serve a particular specialized function." In this conversation Rogers comments about client-centered therapy's past and its future; he talks about people and ideas and institutions; he speculates about new developments in the philosophy of science. He is both incisively critical and gently hopeful: "I think the intensive group experience is a really significant modern invention that deserves to be classified along with radar or penicillin in importance. . . . It is interesting that I don't know of a single university that gives it any real backing except through schools of business administration. It has no standing in any of the professions. It has nothing except its own vitality and public support. Perhaps some day the universities and professions will catch up with it."

The next chapter, "The literal-intuitive axis and other thoughts," by John Shlien, continues the emphasis on innovation begun in Rogers' chapter. Dr. Shlien, who is now at Harvard, succeeded Dr. Rogers as Director of the University of Chicago's Counseling Center. He brought to that job a catholicity of interests and a graceful humor that helped to preserve and increase the Center's stature as a training ground for counselors and psychotherapists. The same qualities are evident in his chapter, which explores the continuing significance of that unusual blend of the literal and intuitive to be found in client-centered therapy. In doing this he is able to show how prized but uncommon personal qualities, such as courage, which are usually overlooked within the technicalities or reductionalisms of other orientations, can be understood and encouraged. "Client-centered therapy has moved closer to becoming an 'action' therapy in this sense: the objective is to develop a *capacity* rather than to attack a particular problem or symptom. We work toward the exercise of a *capacity to see,* not toward a particular vision itself." (This stress on the development of capacities is also found in Hart's Chapter 30, in which he describes one branch of applied psychology as "psychotechnics — or, psychology as the science of will.")

Gendlin's chapter can be read as a complement to his earlier chapter on the theory of personality change (Chapter 7). Experiential theory is here considered in relation to the practical consequences that will follow as the experiential method is "applied to society as a whole and to our methods of thinking in science." The experiential method is "responsivity to specific felt meaning" which "at each step engenders, carries forward, and changes the individual's ongoing experiential process."

Applying this formulation of the experiential method, Gendlin shows how the old rules that characterized nondirective therapy can be given new and broader meanings. For example, "don't interpret," means don't shift the client's attention away from his preconceptual felt meanings and into generalizations. "But once we have formulated this experiential principle underlying the rule, 'don't interpret,' we can interpret. We can use every and any promising diagnostic notion that strikes us as therapists. It won't be generalized but will point specifically to a short step that can be taken from where the client is." With this experiential method Gendlin can generate a comprehensive set of ideas and techniques that go beyond any single orientation to the practice of therapy. He predicts that *"there will be a universal 'experiential' method of psychotherapy using all useful procedures in reference to the individual's own process."* And he goes on to make seven other predictions about what this experiential method will mean when applied to society and how it can be applied.

In the last chapter of the book Hart presents a program for a new applied psychology that is "Beyond psychotherapy." His program has two parts. The first part, psychotechnics, extends the Rogerian-Rankian emphasis on will psychotherapy to the whole endeavor of developing man's capacity to do and to be. In this extension he tries to retain the concern with persons that characterizes the best in psychotherapy while broadening its scope: the goals of psychotechnics "are not prediction, explanation, and control; they are self-awareness, self-understanding, and self-control. Psychotechnics does not fit into professional models inherited from the engineer, physician, scientist, educator, or even the psychotherapist. The psychotechnist comes closest to the teacher of the arts, the teacher of drawing, painting, sculpture, music — but in psychotechnics the materials and forms are in the student."

The second part of this new applied psychology Hart calls "experimental mysticism — or, psychology as the science of soul." Here he attempts to lay the foundations for what is essentially an applied psychotheology. Although psychotherapists have given some attention to religion, and theologians and clergymen have been influenced by Freud, and Jung, and Rogers, Hart argues that experimental mysticism is a necessary part of applied psychology that has never been seriously worked upon.

With these new and controversial beginnings we bring this study of new directions in client-centered therapy to a close.

27

Looking Back and Ahead:

A Conversation with Carl Rogers*

CARL R. ROGERS   JOSEPH HART

Reminiscences

Hart: Let's begin by getting some of your reminiscences about people who influenced your early life and career. Do some people stand out in your memory?

Rogers: Well, yes. I think of a high school principal, Miss Graham, who was also a teacher of English. She helped me realize that it was all right to be original and unique, like writing themes on crazy topics. She has had quite some significance for me. Then in college perhaps two people — one was a teacher of agriculture that I remember for quite other things than agriculture. He's the one who used to say . . .

Hart: Yes, I remember that saying, "Don't be a damned ammunition wagon, be a rifle."

Rogers: That's right. And the other was a crusty old gent named George Sellery, who later became Dean of the College of Letters and Science. He was a professor of history when I worked with him. He was a scholar himself, and he appreciated my scholarship. Then there were other teachers in the department of history too, but I think of him particularly because I worked very closely with him and I was flattered that he would let me do my bachelor's thesis

* Editor's note: This conversation was tape-recorded in Dr. Rogers' home, August 5, 1966.

with him. That was an unusual thing. In those days you did a bachelor's thesis as well as a master's; I worked out some ideas on the source of authority in Luther's thinking — the source of truth or what I would call today the "locus of evaluation" in the life of Martin Luther. That was a good experience for me. Then in graduate school, Goodwin Watson was my sponsor. He was a very good teacher, but I particularly appreciated the fact that he was quite wiling to let me go my own way in my graduate work and research. Then still another person in graduate school was Leta Hollingworth, who at that time was known in psychology for her work on gifted children. I had my first courses in clinical psychology with her — I've always been pleased with that because she was very much interested in children and very much interested in people. Clinical psychology with her was a far cry from the kind of cold approach I feel is typical today. Then at the Institute for Child Guidance where I interned, I gained a great deal from E. K. Wickman, who had a real feeling for research and true open-mindedness. *Teacher's behavior and children's attitudes,* I think was the title of the book he wrote. That book has always intrigued me because he started out to study one problem, and then found that his data really showed up something entirely different and so he turned the purpose of the thing around, which I think very few people are open-minded enough to do. I was stimulated by David Levy, who brought the Rorschach to this country. But one thing about my teachers is that there has never been any one outstanding person in my learning and I think this is fortunate. I regret sometimes that for some of my students I have been the outstanding figure in their intellectual life. I have come to feel this is unfortunate. I think I was very fortunate that no one dominated my intellectual development, so as I went on there was no one I had to rebel against or leave behind.

Hart: I guess for intellectual paternity it's best to have multiple fathers.
Rogers: Yes, the large family milieu.
Hart: When you started talking about your bachelor's thesis, I wondered if writing has always been interesting and easy for you.
Rogers: I think I've always liked to write. I don't know whether I would say that it has been easy, although obviously I write more easily than many people. Yes, I guess that goes back as far as I can remember. I skipped first grade and entered second grade — that was my first year of school — because I could already read. I remember — this is one of those real childhood memories — I remember that a story I wrote, which was a very childish but imaginative story, was posted by the teacher on the bulletin board. So it must be that even from those early days I liked to write.

Hart: You said that you liked to write but it hasn't been easy. Do you mean there's a struggle?

Rogers: What do I mean by that? I do enjoy writing. Let me put it this way — some people talk very easily — Abe Maslow or Abe Kaplan are both good examples of that. Either one of them can give a lecture at the drop of a hat, they don't have to have advance notice, they are very facile with words. I wouldn't say that my writing is like that. I guess that's why I say it isn't easy. I work at it but I do enjoy trying to put things in a way I think will communicate. I guess this is a characteristic that goes back a long way too. I don't really know its roots. Perhaps you could argue that I was sufficiently an oddball and loner during my childhood and youth that there were few people that I communicated with, but I could communicate through writing. Then I had lots of training in writing. When I was at the theological seminary we used to have to write sermons; that was a good exercise for we continually had to meet deadlines. In my first clinical job at Rochester we had to write reports for court hearings and for social agencies and nearly always there was a deadline on that. You had to do the best you could and get it done — and get it done clearly so it would get across.

Hart: Some of your critics probably feel that you're still writing sermons.

Rogers: I think they do. I guess I feel that writing without commitment is not much good. Writing to try to persuade people to your point of view is not much good either, probably sometimes I fall into that. But I guess that whatever real sermon elements they find in my writing I would be opposed to also.

Hart: But the commitment in the writing is important.

Rogers: That's right. Taking a stand for certain values I wouldn't apologize for — it's the attempt to say that other people should hold the same values that I would criticize. I think that every person who writes or every person who does scientific work has a real commitment to certain values. It is the fashionable thing in the behavioral sciences today to conceal those values — that I don't accept at all.

Hart: Is it concealment, or is there one value system that dominates? Whenever a value system is shared people don't bother to talk about it. Not until it becomes a point of dissension do people begin to talk and write about the values behind their work. I think some of your work has tried to introduce just those points of dissension.

Rogers: I think that insofar as there is a shared value system among workers in the behavioral sciences most of their value assumptions are very definitely questionable.

Hart: I suppose that value neutrality is one of the assumptions that you would want to question.

Rogers: Yes, a pseudo-neutrality is wrong. And the belief that the behavioral sciences can be completely objective in the sense that the scientist as a person plays no role in his research and that his subjects are simply manipulable objects — I think those are assumptions that are very common, and I think each one is questionable.

Hart: The clinical psychologist often adopts the model or paradigm popular in other areas of applied psychology; it is a paradigm that emphasizes external control and external manipulation. Expressed as a paradigm, I think it goes something like this (you can read this in most introductory psychology textbooks): "psychology is the science of behavior which attempts to predict, understand, and control behavior." Psychotherapists have not always accepted the emphasis on external control embodied in the paradigm — although present-day behavior therapists tend to align themselves with that emphasis. Psychotherapists keep saying self-control is the important kind of control. *Self-direction* is what they value and try to promote.

Rogers: I would agree, and I think it is the *experience* of the psychotherapist that leads him to that point of view. As you know I'm devoting all the time I can now to a consideration of the philosophy of the behavioral sciences, precisely because I believe that this paradigm you mentioned and the way it is implemented is really a Newtonian model of science. Psychology is following a very outdated model of science. It isn't that I see clearly what the model *should* be; I don't think anyone has come up yet with the picture of what the science of man might be, but I feel that a Newtonian model of manipulable objects following clear-cut laws is a model that leaves out a great deal of the subject that behavioral science is supposed to be studying. I look forward to some brilliant man or group to provide us with a more adequate model of the science of man. I have a feeling it will have a phenomenological flavor. It will have some background, I think, in existential philosophy. It will not throw overboard the positivism and operationalism that has become part of our thinking, but I hope that it will find new and better ways of encompassing more of the richness of man's subjective mind. I've tried to spell out some of that thinking in a recent paper (Rogers, 1965).

Hart: I'd like to come back to that topic later, perhaps when we discuss the third stream movement within psychology. But let's become chronological again. The promotion of significant learning and understanding has long been an important concern for you. Did your early teachers establish some direction for you? Did they exemplify in their own teaching some of the later emphases you've made?

Rogers: Only two I would say. One I neglected to mention in the first list. That was William H. Kilpatrick. He really tried to encourage students to think for themselves; that was the essence of his approach. The same would be true with Goodwin Watson. On the other hand, it has intrigued me that several of the other teachers who have been significant in my experience have tended to be people quite different from the kind of person I would want to be as a teacher, and different from the ways that I would encourage someone else to be as a teacher.

Hart: There's a puzzle there.

Rogers: Yes, that is a puzzle. McGiffert at Union Seminary was, I think, one of the most profound scholars I have ever known. One reason he appealed was that he himself was very scholarly in his presentation — he always lectured, I don't remember any discussion in his classes. But he did manage to convey the feeling that it was *his* viewpoint about a certain man or a certain philosophy that he was presenting — *you* were entirely free to develop your own. I don't quite know how he communicated that, because he certainly didn't do it verbally. So it shows that the fundamental attitudes of the teacher probably come through no matter what kind of approach he uses. A lecture can be something very guiding, where you had better think the same as the teacher does, or it can be something that exists in the context of saying "this is what I'm presenting, but you can hold whatever view you wish."

Hart: The attitudes of the students are crucial, too. Some teachers with some students promote a kind of entanglement where the students get what they want, which is careful guidance, guidance that eventually becomes intellectual dependency. From what you say, when you were a student you were already fairly independent. It didn't make too much difference what the style of the teacher was because you had your own style. But a different kind of student, with a dominating teacher, becomes dominated.

Rogers: Yes, I think that's true — it is one of the advantages of being a rebel. I suppose I have been a rebel. I don't know if I can date it, but certainly from the age of twelve or thirteen on I can remember specific incidents of rebellion against the thinking of my parents. I never rebelled in behavior very much, not until much later. But in a sense I did feel that nobody was going to dominate me. So I'm sure that with every teacher I used all the freedom they were willing to give. I think you're right, if the teacher senses that a student will use freedom then it's easier to grant it.

Scientific Styles

Hart: That must be a paradoxical side of your own relationships with people who come to you; you must see both kinds of teacher-student styles emerging. It is surprising, I suppose, to find yourself with disciples.

Rogers: The students who are my *disciples,* in the real sense of that word, are the ones that I have less respect for. And you're right that no matter how much freedom of thinking and action you try to give people, some do have a strong need for dependence and will be dependent no matter what you may try to do to free them.

Hart: We've talked about how that dependency works on the student. I wonder how it works on the person, the leader, the one surrounded by disciples. What about very creative people, scientists and artists and others, who in some way lose their creativity? We can draw graphs showing when creative achievements occur and these graphs seem to show creative people "peaking out" very early. One idea I have about this peaking-out phenomenon is that a stultifying and retrograding influence develops with fame. The influence acts both ways, on both the leader and his followers. It might be invigorating if every person who becomes famous would after ten years of plaudits change his name and start anew. Instead of submitting papers as Carl Rogers or as B. F. Skinner or as Harry Harlow or as Erich Fromm, the famous person would take a pseudonym.

Rogers: In a sense I have tried to follow a somewhat different pathway that accomplishes the same thing. It isn't accidental that I left Chicago and the Counselling Center at a point when it would have been the easiest time in my life to say, "Here I've got it made. I am surrounded by a very congenial group of people, who all think well of me, who are doing lots of significant work and this is the place to stay." Well, it seemed to me precisely the time to move. When I came to Chicago, I needed a kind of isolation, and freedom to develop my own way of doing things, and I needed to surround myself with students who could help me move in the directions I wanted to go. Those needs had been satisfied. When I went to Wisconsin I hoped I would not need this tight group of students but could make my way in the general academic world, both in psychology and psychiatry. To a limited extent I was able to do this in Psychiatry, but in Psychology I realized I was never able to make a dent. Then as we started our research at Wisconsin, there was again the building up of a group of students and researchers somewhat similar to the Chicago group.

Hart: I've noticed that your intellectual hopping and your moving around has had some curious effects. One effect is that the people who come from one place know a certain Carl Rogers and a certain brand of Rogerian therapy, which is sometimes a great deal different from the brand that existed in another place. You didn't change your name but you did change your ideas and what you were doing — perhaps you changed your style as well, I don't know about that. If we look at different times and places in your career — Rochester, Ohio, Chicago, Wisconsin, WBSI — you're different. I think that if a panel of ex-students were assembled from each of those periods and asked to identify the real Carl Rogers, they couldn't possibly do it because they would all be pointing at a somewhat different person.

Rogers: Yes, there is some truth in that, particularly the last statement, because I think that each one of those groups did see a different me and do see a different me. The differences between the students themselves and their own points of view I think could be exaggerated, because it has been my experience that the best ones go on developing their own thinking. Often it is quite heartening to find that as they've moved on they've discovered some of the things I've discovered too as I've moved on in other places in another situation. That's kind of confirming to feel that they've discovered some of the same elements on their own.

One reason I have enjoyed working with groups of business executives is that it is practically like changing my name. Many of them have never heard of me, so I enter a group of businessmen and really start from scratch, start fresh. The same is true in being a consultant at Cal Tech — there are really only one or two people in the groups I work with who know me in the sense of knowing my professional background and reputation. To the others I am just a strange guy who seems to operate in ways they don't understand; that forces me again to test out the basic hypotheses with which I work.

Hart: What is the activity at Cal Tech?

Rogers: Well, that's been quite a story — being called in as a person to consult on the human and educational problems at Cal Tech. Not having any idea of how to go about that I gradually worked out a pattern. A number of us who were there thinking together about the problems decided that it would be best if I worked with a faculty group. I insisted that the faculty groups should have no formal status, no standing, no authority. It was simply a group to get together and think. We even decided that I would invite the members of the group so they could easily turn down the invitation if they wished. If it had come from the president or some other administrative authority there might have been pressure to accept. For two years this group has met and talked about educational and human issues and have become more personally involved with one another. They're strictly hard scientists and many of them would show the *strongest* feelings in *denying* that feelings are of any importance, consequently we've had interesting struggles. But I feel when I've been at my best in that group I have served a catalytic purpose, entering in as a person only on issues where I feel I have some real commitment. Of course, it has been exciting to work with very high level scientists from various fields. I think all would agree that our discussions together have had a real impact on the educational policies of Cal Tech. We've never taken any direct action ourselves as a group. Whatever influence we have had has been by osmosis. Yet a great many things have happened where it seems quite clear that some changes, such as the dropping of freshman grades, would not have happened had they not been first thoroughly thought through and discussed in our group. At the very outset I expected a certain phenomenon to happen; I thought we would come to be looked on as sort of a secret group, a secret power group of some kind, and I was puzzled to know how we should avoid that. Actually, it took quite a long while for that to develop; it wasn't until we had been meeting nearly two years that it became a problem. So then the group decided rather reluctantly to disband and we started two new groups seeded with members of the original Honker Group.

Hart: What is the name of the group? The Honker Group?

Rogers: Yes, I wanted to give it an ambiguous name because any name that attempted to describe its function would have sounded very presumptuous. We met the first time at the Honker Restaurant so we decided that was a fine name for it. The two new groups that have formed, one adopted a name I am not so pleased with; they call themselves Rogers' Rangers. The other one I really do like, that is FOG, an acronym for the Far-Out-Group.

Hart: Have you noticed contrasts while working with scientists from very different fields?

Rogers: Yes. In many ways I think that physical scientists are less defensive and more exciting to work with than psychologists. I think I would have had a much tougher time doing the same job with some psychology departments. Physical scientists are more secure in their scientific approach, so they are willing to be imaginative and free-wheeling and speak off the cuff, and they are not stuffy by and large. On the other hand, although I've never had an exactly comparable experience, I have found psychologists and psychiatrists to have the greatest difficulty in expressing their feelings.

They have the greatest fear of departing from orthodoxy of any group I know. It's typical, for example, that in a recent conference on philosophy of science[1] at which many people spoke up in the discussions, which were recorded, the only two people who refused to let their remarks be quoted were chairmen of psychology departments.

Hart: It's ironic that social scientists whose business it is to understand and promote social change are perhaps the most resistant to it.

Rogers: Well, you see, I think that many of them would not agree with you that it is their purpose to understand and promote social change.

Hart: That's right.

Rogers: They feel their purpose is to hold grimly to this little developing science and make sure it never becomes unscientific. That is the opposite of the theoretical physicists at Cal Tech. They would just as soon go off on a free-wheeling fantasy about some speculative hunch they have. One good example in the group at Cal Tech has been Dick Feynman. I mention him because he is very well known since he received the Nobel Prize. You would have to look all over the world, I think, to find a psychologist like Dick Feynman. He is just a small boy who has never grown up, in the sense of being absolutely curious about everything. He is highly opinionated, and yet if you say "but here is the evidence that you're wrong," then he will accept that. He is very emotional, very impulsive, but primarily he is deeply curious. He is curious about *everything*. A question came up as to whether research could be done in psychotherapy — it was something that was mentioned in one of our group discussions. He said in the meeting that "those *witch doctors* don't even know what research is." Before the next meeting of the group he had read and carefully studied *Psychotherapy and personality change* (Rogers and Dymond, 1954) and had acquired both a real respect for it and an appreciation for the difficulties. He said, "My God, it's hard to do research in this field." And he also had plenty of pertinent criticisms to make about it, which showed he had thought deeply about the whole thing. I finally said to him, "Dick, where did you ever find time to read this?" "Oh," he said, "I finished it one morning about 3:00 o'clock." He had stolen time to delve into a question he had suddenly become curious about.

Hart: It's helpful for me to recognize two types of scientists. One is trained to follow certain rules. His products are publications that show he has followed those rules. The other kind I admire much

[1] Conference on "Man and the Science of Man," sponsored by WBSI, with the collaboration of UCSD and The Salk Institute of Biol. Studies, March 1966.

more because he has trained himself to seek new insights. He sometimes uses a scientific rule although his special capability is to suspend the rules and use fantasy. An adventurous searching characterizes his work.

Rogers: Yes, and I think that adventurousness is *not* something that characterizes most psychological research today. There are beginning to be some exceptions and mostly those fall entirely outside the mainstream of psychology. Some of the research on dreams is adventurous, but it isn't the kind of psychology that would be approved in most psychology departments.

Hart: I think it will be a while before psychology recognizes, to the extent that it no longer needs to be debated, that there are three events that must be studied in a complete psychology: behavioral events; physiological events; and experiential events. The bringing together of three event levels is true in some research on dreaming.

Rogers: Yes, I think when a scientist can move easily back and forth in those three, depending upon what his particular problem demands, he will be much more mature as a scientist.

Professional Involvements

Hart: I want to ask you about the changes you have noticed in psychology. At one time you were very much involved in professional affairs and then, I discern from reading your autobiography, that there was a pulling away from further involvement. Either you pulled away from the involvement or it pulled away from you, or both, I don't know. Could you characterize some of your professional involvements?

Rogers: In my younger days I wanted to influence professional directions and felt that could come about through professional organizations. It is interesting that I didn't even join the APA until 1939. I think I had been out of graduate school twelve or thirteen years at that time. During all that period I felt psychology was not doing anything that I was much interested in. I joined the psychiatric social workers and moved up to national office in their professional society, the American Association of Social Workers. Then when the American Association for Applied Psychology developed, that *did* seem to be going in directions that interested me, and I moved into that and again was very active in professional affairs; this time in psychology.

Hart: When was that?

Rogers: About 1939 or 1940. I worked hard on professional issues at that time. I'm not quite sure of my own motivations. Part of it was straight ambition for leadership, but I think a more important part of it was that here, at last, was an organization that wasn't as stuffy as the APA. I finally became President of the AAAP in 1944-45. About that time Robert Yerkes particularly, and some other people in the APA, realized the harm that might come from having these two separate and competing organizations. Unless they were brought together soon, they probably never *would* be brought together. While I was skeptical at first, I could see the wisdom of union if we could revise the APA and make it into a democratic organization, which it most certainly was not at that time. So I worked hard as a member of a group which brought about a constitutional convention of the two organizations and reunited the two. Partly as a result of that, I found myself elected the second president of the newly reunited APA, in 1946-47. Then following that I tapered off. I think there is no doubt that I have been the one who has withdrawn. I have turned down all kinds of opportunities to serve on professional committees and things of that sort. I felt I had sort of done my stint on organizational matters and that I had more pressing business and that organizational work was better suited to the people who were coming up through the profession. Later, I did accept the presidency of the Clinical Division for one year, but for the most part, I have gone out of professional affairs and now feel quite remote from them. Both because I really don't care for more committee and organizational work and, also, there is a deeper cause. I feel somewhat alienated from the directions psychology is taking. I'd like to have influence on those directions but feel that probably my chance of influence is much greater through writing than it is through getting active in organizational work again.

Hart: One direction within the organization is toward a new split between experimental psychology and clinical and applied psychology, a direction that would reinstate the old division.

Rogers: Yes, fences are being built up again. For a while the barrier between experimental and clinical psychology was quite low but now it has become very high again.

Hart: We now have the Psychonomic Society, which in some ways competes with the APA; but today, the majority-minority relationship between clinical and experimental psychology has been reversed.

Rogers: Yes, when I first entered psychology the few clinicians were a struggling minority with no voice at all, and now that has quite reversed.

Hart: The pressures against progress are stronger I think within clinical psychology than the pressures outside.

Rogers: I agree.

Hart: I think, for example, that certification and the use of boards to put the stamp of approval on various clinical practices and clinical myths are stultifying. Once something becomes certified, it becomes very hard to change. Indeed, people are certified in skills that may not exist.

Rogers: I feel that in a sense there always will be this tension within a profession between the conserving and protecting forces — particularly the concerns of the profession about protecting society from malpractice — and the innovating forces. I quite agree with what you said about certifying boards but I myself had a part in some of this in the formation, for example, of the American Board of Examiners in Professional Psychology. I acted with many qualms at the time, feeling that it could easily lead to stultification, and I think it has. But also at that time there was a need for some protection of society. Society needed to know who really was qualified. Now I think the influence and authority of the Board could be greatly reduced. The pressures *outside* clinical psychology are for a great expansion of that field into new areas. It is absurd that all the new developments — basic encounter groups or T-groups, self-directed groups, family therapy — almost all those go on outside formal clinical psychology. Students don't get trained in such areas, they are not told of these developments, yet the demands are enormous. Many clinical psychologists are involved, but it is not experience that would help you pass your board examinations, nor is it anything that would help you get a degree.

Hart: I think that part of the new wave of influence by behavior therapists comes from their rushing in with great promises. They promise an armamentarium of very visible techniques. The therapist can say, "I can do this and no untrained person can do it as well because it takes technical knowledge." There is a proliferation of technical jargon; it identifies the therapist as a professional, a possessor of techniques not available to the man in the street.

Rogers: Also it's much more acceptable to the orthodox department of psychology.

Hart: That's right, it carries the accepted image of man and the specialist. These images are, I think, counter to some of the emphases within your thinking and within humanistic psychology. As I read some of your ideas and interpret some recent experiments concerning the use of nonprofessional therapists,[2] it seems that psychotherapeutic expertise is taught long before people get to graduate school. It's an expertise in living and in being. If people haven't learned at least a little of that by the time they get to professional schools, they can't be rescued as therapists.

Rogers: It's even one degree worse than you say. Both in psychiatry and

[2] See Part Four of this book for relevant articles.

clinical psychology much of the training students receive tends to inhibit or destroy the very qualities that might have permitted them to be good therapists. One research study Ernest Poser in Canada did a number of years ago has finally come out (1966). He had a group of psychiatrists and psychologists treating groups of schizophrenics. He felt it would make sense for the control groups to have an equal number of hours of contact with someone who was not professional, who was completely untrained. So he just got some undergraduate girls, some senior girls from a nearby college, to spend an equivalent number of hours with the control groups of schizophrenics. He was really frightened by the outcome, which was that the control groups showed a greater degree of change than the groups in therapy. I suppose it says something about psychology that most psychologists would be afraid to take a square look at a study like that, and its significance and meaning. We could learn very deeply from it, but it's too threatening.

Hart: This relates to the protection issue. Recently I've had a little contact with some of the people from whom psychology wanted to protect the public. People like scientologists and various religious cultists who do psychotherapy, although now they don't call it psychotherapy. These people sometimes seem to be extraordinarily effective. And I believe it isn't merely a religious placebo effect. They are effective because, in some cases, they've been working with people a long time; they were interested in working with people when they began. Now it's really unfashionable for a psychology student to write on his application to graduate school that he's going into psychology because he wants to help people. But these nonprofessional therapists are doing what they're doing because of that motivation and they sometimes do it very well. They have developed ideas and techniques that would benefit psychology. Usually the ideas are imbedded in an offbeat religious terminology that is hard to chop through. But if you ignore the terminology and look at their empirical knowledge, it's impressive.

The Geography of a Career

Hart: I'd like to ask you now to look more directly at some of the periods in your career before we move on to discuss some of your current ideas. For example, what about Rochester?

Rogers: I think that in Rochester I was very fortunate in the degree of isolation. I wasn't connected with a university, no one was looking over my shoulder from any particular treatment orientation, it was simply that these were a group of social agencies who wanted help with children. They didn't give a damn how you proceeded but hoped you could be of some assistance. This made for a very free atmosphere. I really don't remember ever thinking during that period, "well, is this something a psychologist should be doing, or do psychologists approve of what we're up to?" We worked with whatever skills and knowledge we had.

One of the real impacts on me at that time was the thinking of Otto Rank, which came mainly indirectly. We had social workers in Rochester from the Philadelphia School of Social Work, which was Rankian in orientation. We did bring Otto Rank for a two-day seminar, which was fruitful and interesting but it was just for two days. All in all, the emphasis on responding to the feelings of the client spring, I think, from that stream of thought. I'm not particularly indebted to any one person but to a whole series of influences that came from the Rankian group. I would include in that Jesse Taft's book on *The dynamics of therapy* (1933), which I think is still a small masterpiece of writing and thinking.

I have never regretted all the practical pressures of that period. You can't do treatment with everyone, you can't do therapy with everyone; what is the best plan you can work out for this individual? I've always felt pleased that while I was there, we had a highly cooperative arrangement with many other agencies. We would get together and really built a coordinated plan for the child that then would be put into effect because it was agreed to by all concerned. The school would do what it could do, the placement agency or the probation agency, or whatever, would also take steps to do what they could do — it was a working system that really operated. I feel that in so many places, psychologists in psychological clinics make studies of individuals, especially children and make their reports and those reports are filed away and nothing ever happens. This was a way of planning which had its own built-in implementation and that was good.

Hart: While there you wrote *The clinical treatment of the problem child?*

Rogers: I more or less stole the time for that, with a couple of short leaves of absence and a lot of work on the side and during vacations.

Hart: Was it that book that made it possible for you to go to Ohio State? You recommend that a person go into a university as a full professor. I very much agree with that advice but haven't been able to put it into practice.

Rogers: I always say that with tongue in cheek, but it was an incredible situation where a lot of circumstances fitted together. Clinical psychologists were very few in number; by writing the book, I suppose I demonstrated that here was a person with practical experience in the field who also could do a reasonably scholarly job of bringing together much of the evidence. Ohio State at that time was looking around for a replacement for Henry Goddard, who was one of the first people in the clinical field, and they invited me to come there. And I came in the best mood that one can come for getting a job. I really didn't think I wanted the position. I had just finished setting up a new and independent clinic in Rochester, the Rochester Guidance Center, separate from any other social agency, and felt I was obligated to stay there. So they offered me an associate professorship and could see that it was very much touch and go as to whether I would even be interested in their offer. Then they upped it to a full professorship. I must confess I sometimes think I've been a very naïve person professionally. The really enormous difference between the first offer and the second I didn't realize until years afterward. But at any rate I finally decided to go, partly at Helen's insistence. She said, "Now look. You've always liked teaching, you've always thought you wanted to get into a university sometime; here's a good opportunity and you shouldn't be too bound by the Rochester situation." She had quite an influence on that decision and I guess the outcome of that has helped me to make other decisions, leaving places when everyone else would say that in the obvious light of common sense I should *not* leave. And it's always worked out well.

Hart: That's right. You really haven't followed the program a leader is supposed to follow. That's why when people ask about where the center of client-centered therapy is, it's impossible to answer them.

Rogers: It's sometimes embarrassing to me. People write wanting to know what are the centers of client-centered therapy, and I can't give them a list. Well, I have always felt that — not *always,* I'm not sure that *always* is the word, but for the most part, and certainly after the first years in Chicago — I have avoided starting a *movement.* I've been aware of the fact that I could easily promote this school of thought into a quite specific and organized movement. I have leaned over so far backward away from that view that I sometimes think that I have leaned too far. But at any rate I abhor the notion of a school of thought because I think it tends to become rigidified. One consequence of this unwillingness to form a movement or a school of psychotherapeutic thought, one unforeseen consequence, is that I have had an impact on many different fields. I think if I had gotten caught up in organizing a movement in psychotherapy that probably the influence would not have been nearly so diffuse. As I said to someone the other day, I think that realistically, I don't have very much standing at the present time in psychology itself, and I couldn't care less. But in education and industry and group dynamics and social work and the philosophy of science and pastoral psychology and theology and other fields, my ideas have penetrated and influenced in ways I never would have dreamt. It certainly wasn't planned that way. I believe it has come about partly because there is no organized movement or school so it is simply a diffusion of both writings and people who have found some of the ideas congenial and have put them to work in their own fields.

Hart: If you had started an institute or a school, you would inevitably have become involved in filling in the gaps in your ideas, putting in periods and punctuation marks. Instead, there have been drastic changes. There is a core of values which have been maintained, I believe, but as for basic ideas about therapy and about human relationships, they've changed.

Rogers: Yes, I would agree that it is possible to focus on either end of the spectrum, and you could make a case for the view that the client-centered orientation has not basically changed at all, and you can make a very good case that it has changed drastically.

Hart: Why don't you explore both cases; I think that would be interesting.

Rogers: Well, I think the relatively unchanging aspect of it has to do with the core idea that the individual does have, within himself, a capacity — which can be released under suitable conditions — for understanding himself, for living his life, for dealing with the problems of his life, or moving toward a greater degree of self-actualization. That idea has probably become clearer and perhaps been better phrased, and yet in a fairly profound sense, it has been there from the beginning. You can date this core idea. The book on *The clinical treatment of the problem child,* written about 1937 and published in 1939, never questions the manipulative aspects of treatment that are on practically every page of the book. Between 1937 and 1941, I became infected with Rankian ideas and began to realize the possibilities of the individual being self-directing. This certainly fitted in with earlier ideas I had absorbed from Kilpatrick and John Dewey. I was clearly fascinated by Rankian ideas but didn't quite adopt his emphases for myself until I felt Rochester. But the core idea did develop. I came to believe in the individual's capacity. I value the dignity and rights of the individual sufficiently that I do not want to impose my way upon him. Those two aspects of the core idea haven't changed since that time.

Hart: Were they first formally expressed in the book *Counseling and psychotherapy?*

Rogers: Yes, that book was written about 1941 or 1942. There was a quite sharp philosophical difference between *Clinical treatment of the problem child* and *Counseling and psychotherapy.* I guess I must have written the first book at about the time I was leaving that point of view behind. Because otherwise it would seem like a very sharp flipflop; and I know that's not the case.

Hart: I think that's the reason authors sometimes bemoan the slowness of the writing process, because they're already developing new directions of thought. It requires discipline to stay with the old ideas long enough to express them in writing.

Rogers: There's another thing too, and that's the willingness to express the imperfect. I think many people feel, "When I get this thoroughly worked out, then I'll be willing to write it." That point never comes; by the time you feel you're approaching it, you're already leaving it behind. And whether it's for better or for worse, sometimes definitely for worse, I have been willing to put down the way I see things *now,* realizing that in all likelihood I could do it better a few years later. Or what is more accurate is that in all likelihood I will see things from a different *perspective* later. This going along with my feeling that the greatest contribution a professor can make to students is to let them know his tentative thinking; the thinking which seems imperfect and only partly worked out is often far more stimulating than the complete exposition with a lot of support. I think this is one of the reasons why I've valued contact with students and graduate students especially, much more than contacts with colleagues. I've learned much more from students. For me it's a rare thing, quite a rare thing, to learn something really significant from a colleague, but I've learned all kinds of things from graduate students. In fact I think most of my more significant ideas have come from younger people who did very little with the ideas themselves. Frequently they were people whose thinking was not very clear cut, often they were screwballs. At Rochester, for example, there were three people in social agencies who had a lot of contact with Rank's thinking. I learned very deeply from their ideas and their work. None of them ever made anything of the ideas, or particularly went on from there. It's not that they didn't use those values, they did. They just never pushed beyond.

Hart: What about the second case? What about some of the significant changes?

Rogers: When did those come about? Let me think out loud a bit. It seems to me offhand that those have come about through being exposed to different circumstances and through stimulation from graduate students. Working with hospitalized schizophrenics brought me face-to-face for the first time with people who didn't want help, who came from a lower social and educational strata, were inarticulate, and so on. So that brought about quite a few changes in mode of working, and there certainly were innovations in therapy by people like Gendlin and you and others. I feel I sort of followed along. Then here at WBSI I've had a chance to fulfill the third part of my tentative long-range professional plans. I've been working a lot

with so-called normal individuals, people from the community, educators, business executives — working with groups. That has also
very much changed my mode of expression and action in interpersonal relationships.

Hart: What do you mean by that?

Rogers: I find that I've changed in the willingness to express myself and my
feelings openly, as data for the other person to use, but not as a
guide or an imposition. If I am angry, I will express that anger as
something within myself, not as a judgment on the other person.
I am much more free-wheeling in stating personal feeling reactions
to what the other person has said or done. I have been amazed
when listening to recordings of group sessions in which I have been
perceived as the facilitator. Not only by the sort of expressions
I just described and by the confrontation of others with my feeling
reactions, but also by the extent to which I become a participant,
expressing problems and concerns of my own. Only when I sense
that someone in the group is hunting, or groping to find himself, do
I find myself expressing primarily the empathic feelings I experience,
as sensitively and accurately as I can. In these moments, it is very
similar to my individual therapy, where my primary concern is
creating the atmosphere where the person can explore himself.
But at other times, I am very much a multifaceted person in the
interaction.

I think I have at least touched upon a number of the changes
I see in my manner of working.

Hart: I'll react to some of the things you have been saying by giving you
my categorization scheme for the changes in client-centered therapy.
The scheme may force the changes too neatly into periods, but see
how it strikes you. I see the book on *Counseling and psychotherapy*
as an expression mainly of the value stance. Then I see the book on
Client-centered therapy as expressing the first-stage theoretical ideas,
with an emphasis upon the reflection-of-feeling technique to implement the ideas. Also in that book, there is an emphasis on the self-
concept as a way of conceptualizing and measuring the changes that
occur during therapy. Then out of your many later papers I'd select
"A process conception of psychotherapy" (Rogers, 1958) and
"The necessary and sufficient conditions of therapeutic personality
change" (Rogers, 1957) to exemplify your recent thinking. The
process paper expresses a changing emphasis. Instead of a focus on
self-concepts or the contents of experience, your focus there is on
modes of experiencing. In the paper about necessary and sufficient
conditions, I see an emphasis upon therapist characteristics, traits,
interaction capabilities, rather than specific techniques. The reflection-of-feeling technique loses its dominance in the orientation.

Although reflecting feelings is sometimes compatible with the task of creating the necessary and sufficient conditions, it is only one technique among many. In that paper are conceptual precursors of changes that actually came about when working with schizophrenics.

Rogers: I can give my own picture of some of those same events. It has some different shadings. I see the book on *Counseling and psychotherapy* as being partly focused on the value stance and heavily focused on techniques. A couple of whole chapters and the inclusion of the recorded case were all intended to present *technique*; if you will recall the footnotes in the recorded case, every response is taken as significant in itself and I try to analyze how the responses could have been a little better this way or that. So I see it as a very technique-oriented book, but based on a value stance. The therapy at that point as indicated in the recorded cases includes quite a lot of reflection of feeling but other procedures too.

Hart: Yes, I certainly agree with that.

Rogers: Then, by the time I wrote *Client-centered therapy,* I was impressed with the fact that this should be a *pure* approach so that research at that time showed that almost all the counselor's responses now were empathic ones and nothing else was permitted to come in. And you're quite right that in *Client-centered therapy* there also was the beginning of a real theoretical formulation that was almost completely lacking in *Counseling and psychotherapy.* That theory formulation finally reached its climax in the chapter in Koch (Rogers, 1959) written about 1953-4, which was of considerable value to me. However, like everything that has *closure,* that chapter could very well be serving a deleterious purpose. Then the paper on "Necessary and sufficient conditions," I agree with you, was a real turning point toward a more general formulation of the relationship. The "Process" paper I also feel was a new step forward into formulating a theory of process that later has, I think, shown itself to have wide application in many fields. Both of those are rather good examples of the value of presenting something before you are entirely sure of it. I remember how very tentative I felt when I gave the "Necessary and sufficient conditions" paper to a University of Michigan audience because I wasn't at all sure of it myself, and I was trying it out on them. Yet that paper has probably sparked as much research as anything I've ever written. And the "Process" paper has had much the same result. I was desperate on that. I was forced to meet a deadline, having received the APA Scientific Contribution Award in 1956. One of the requirements was that the recipient was obligated to give an important paper the next year. I thought at the beginning of the year that I could work through to a good new statement on the process of therapy but realized when I finally *had* to write the paper in time for the conference, that it was far from complete or clear in my own thinking. Yet I've never regretted having put it forth. Another in that same category, another paper that was quite a turning point though not really too good as a paper, was my address as President of the APA (Rogers, 1947). Again, I was trying to think through something for myself, about the self and the organization of personality. For the first time I really tried to formulate the place the self had in its various aspects. Anyone could tear that paper apart from many points of view. It received very little attention at the time. But it was good to put it forth; it did help to crystallize some ideas about the self at that point. It is interesting to me that in recent years it has been widely reprinted. As I say, at the time I think the paper was quite a disappointment to the members of APA and didn't receive much recognition.

Hart: You mentioned the Koch volume. I think the pressure to make a complete statement often becomes pressure for a comprehensive statement. The Koch volumes perfectly represent the pressure that is always present to build a very big theory; the theorist is urged to make a statement about nearly everything psychological.

Rogers: Yes, I've felt those pressures from time to time. I think that for the most part I've resisted them. How should I put it? Unless they seemed, unless it seemed natural to me to do it. What I mean is this. In the book on *Client-centered therapy,* or in the book *On becoming a person,* I launch out into education, family relationships, and various other fields. But that isn't out of any sense of pressure to give a complete and comprehensive picture. It's just that I've gotten excited about the implications in this field or that. The Koch paper is an exception because in that I felt both external and internal pressure to try for a comprehensive effort, toward something complete and rounded. I don't apologize for it particularly, it has sparked a lot of research, but I'm less proud of it than of a number of other things I've done.

Values

Hart: One of the other contributors in the Koch volume also resisted the pressures to say something about everything psychological, and he did it in a way that I thought was very original and very personal, and yet he's a person who very often seems to represent a value stance counter to yours. I'm thinking, of course, of Skinner (1959). I've enjoyed the sharpness of your dialogues (1956, 1964), because the encounters represent a basic confrontation between two nearly polar positions within psychology.

Rogers: Yes, I have enjoyed our confrontations too. I think one reason we've been able to hold sharp discussions, and differ about philosophical assumptions about as completely as anybody could, is the fact that both of us are trying to be honest about our assumptions, our points of view, and the implications they would have. When you have that kind of situation, you don't feel the other person is trying to use some false shield to hide behind. I think the only thing I've ever regretted about any of our meetings is that Skinner has never been willing to release the full transcript, nor even the full tape recordings, of our nine hours of encounter in Duluth in 1962. I know intellectually that at some point there will be some overarching resolution of our seemingly incompatible points of view. But I think that resolution becomes more likely the more clearly and completely the two different approaches can be spelled out.

Hart: How would you spell out some of the differences?

Rogers: It fascinates me the way Skinner not only makes objects out of other people, but an object out of himself. This is one of the things I respect in him; he's fully consistent. I think it was at the Duluth meeting that he told how he tries to set up rewards for himself for working and to condition himself into certain working habits as though he were an experimental subject. It seems to me he overlooks the fact that this is self-control, but he does try to be thoroughgoing in his approach. The question of whether a word like "choice" has any meaning is something we differ very sharply on. He feels it does not have. I feel it has a great deal of meaning. What you might call the human or subjective dimension of living is something that he clearly values — when you hear him play the piano or engage in lively conversation you know that the subjective meaning of experience has value to him — but he tries very rigorously to shut it out of his thinking in psychology. I feel there may be definite limits as to the extent to which the experiential can be made a part of the science of psychology, but I feel it's tragic to close our eyes to it because we're shutting out one of the largest bodies of data in our field. My perception of one of the points on which we differ most sharply is that Skinner has a point of view of what constitutes science, and so that dictates what it is he will do in trying to understand, predict, or control human behavior. My own point of view, in contrast, is that here is the human being with all his manifestations and *that* is our field of interest. I ask, how can we understand these manifestations more deeply, in ways that have the various types of validity that science can have, not a final but at least a tentative kind of validity? I feel that *any* approach that helps us to *understand* more deeply is a legitimate part of psychological science. This means that you must admit a tentative, beginning, intuitive part of science, before you get to the confirmation stage. I hate to see so much of the material ruled out before we start.

Hart: I think that the choice issue and the subjective experience issue are at the nub of your disagreements. But I want to focus on the choice issue because I think that's the one that really polarizes the discussion between you and Skinner or, indeed, the discussion between you and the majority of psychologists today. I think it's the choice issue that sometimes earns you the label "mystic" for some of your views.

Rogers: Right. I don't know how much further I can push it now. I think that is at the heart of it. Perhaps I should try soon to formulate some of my own thoughts, and some of the material that's becoming available, more extensively. I would say, from my biased perception, that the trend of the times is on my side. I think Skinner's very narrow definition of what psychology means is steadily losing ground.

Hart: One thing that's happening today is that a few psychologists are beginning to take the metaphors of psychology very seriously. In the past, psychologists used metaphors but didn't follow them far. Our favorite metaphor has been, "man the machine." The kind of machine has changed — from hydraulic clocks to switchboards to computers. But to work with a machine, we have to understand the machine's full capabilities. It isn't enough to study a biological machine only insofar as it resembles a simpler machine. If that were true, we'd be reduced to a search for the simplest machine analogy, which I think is in essence the S-R formulation. But if you take seriously the notion of man as a machine, then you must realize that he is a very special kind of machine. One of his machine capabilities is the capability of understanding his own mechanical workings; with that understanding comes a capability for directing those mechanical workings. The machine metaphor can be used as an expansive metaphor as well as a reductive metaphor.

Rogers: This leads to another more general difference I have with Skinner. I feel his view of human beings could just never comprehend or take in the kind of thing that can happen in one week in a basic encounter group, for example. You'd really have to disregard practically every significant event. You could catch a minute fraction of it, pointing out that such and such events are conditioned behaviors, but the major aspect of what occurs is lost in his thinking. The whole impulse toward expansion of consciousness, actualization, personal change, needs a very large and complex notion of man to fit the facts.

Hart: Yes, we'll need a new image of man. I think our images lead our scientific concepts. Once a new image gains acceptance, then concepts compatible with that image begin to be researched.

Rogers: I would agree.

Hart: One person who represents the antithesis of the Skinnerian position at least as much as you do is Abraham Maslow. He is identified with humanistic psychology or the third stream of psychology with which you are also identified. But I've had the impression, I don't know where I got it, that your acceptance of that identification wavers. Sometimes you wholeheartedly identify yourself with that direction but at other times you don't. What is your reaction to that characterization, and what do you see as the potentialities and limitations of humanistic psychology?

Rogers: I think I would definitely identify myself with the current interest in humanistic psychology. It's the organization of the movement that I often feel somewhat skeptical about. In other words, I feel that the humanistic trend is setting in, in psychology, and I'm gambling on it as being the wave of the future; but some of the spokesmen for it, and the organization of it, seem to me often to be disappointingly conventional and to fall into old patterns.

Hart: What specifically?

Rogers: Well, for example, the American Association for Humanistic Psychology brought together about twenty-five people at very considerable expense last year for a conference to think about the future of humanistic psychology. It was a splendid selection of people and a very exciting prospect, but in spite of protest from a couple of us, what did they do? They got together for two and one-half days and six or eight members delivered speeches to the other members. That just shows a lack of imagination and understanding that I find very disappointing in a new trend. I think Maslow is probably the most visible and the most verbal and most out-in-front of the humanistic psychology trend. He embodies within himself some of the things that both stimulate me and concern me. A lot of his ideas are very exciting, and he's continually formulating new ideas. But I think he has very little concern with tieing humanistic psychology to science. Yet if we simply *talk* a good game of humanistic psychology, I fear that's not going to mean very much nor is it going to have any very profound effect. Science is the language of our times. It has enormous advantages as well as bringing enormous social threats. I feel that if we're going to develop a humanistic psychology that amounts to anything, we've somehow got to come to terms with the question of how we can regard people as human beings and at the same time include them within some model of science that fits them. The last time I talked to the Association for Humanistic Psychology I talked like a hard-boiled psychologist because I feel it's a question of whether or not we're facing up to the challenge of this movement. On the other hand, if I were talking to an ordinary psychology department, I would defend the movement.

Hart: Your description of the current state of the movement prompted me to liken humanistic psychology to parapsychology. Parapsychology has been on the fringe of psychology for many, many years and it seems it may continue there unless something striking happens. What will have to happen is a demonstration or a series of demonstrations going beyond case studies and going beyond statistically significant results. Instead, parapsychologists must demonstrate *powerful* results. Even though the claims made by parapsychologists call for a revision of assumptions, assumptions are never truly challenged until a powerful experiment, a powerful demonstration, is made. Statistical results are all very well, but people don't begin to challenge their assumptions on the basis of statistical findings. They have to be shown. Until someone can say, "Come to this room at this date and I will demonstrate to anyone's satisfaction this parapsychological phenomenon," until then, there isn't going to be a fundamental challenge. And the same thing is required in humanistic psychology. Perhaps some of your work on basic encounter groups tries to go in this direction.

Rogers: I would quite agree with all that you're saying, and for me the greatest probability at present of demonstrating a really potent psychological effect lies within the basic encounter group. I do feel that I could say to skeptics, if you will come with me and form a group and cut yourself off from other obligations for six or seven days so that we can meet eight to ten hours a day, you will experience something, the potency of which can't be denied. It is my feeling that science is advanced by investigating *potent* phenomena. There is the potent possibility of constructive change and growth in a basic encounter group — and there is also some possibility of damage.

Hart: Potent phenomena are probably always potent in several directions.

Rogers: That's right. I think it would be an excellent starting point for significant humanistic research and demonstration.

Hart: It's important to distinguish between the potency of a phenomenon and its tractability. Traditional experimental psychology has more often moved toward tractable phenomona. It's absolutely fatal for a new movement to adopt the methodological presuppositions that deal with more tractable phenomena. That's the mistake of parapsychology. It could very easily occur in humanistic psychology.

Rogers: That's why I've stated that I would like to draw some experimental psychologists into a basic encounter group with the notion that

	they would experience something in themselves. This wouldn't prove anything in the scientific sense, but I don't think they could ever quite get over the fact that they had experienced a potent phenomenon that falls quite outside the tractable domain of experimental psychology. And in the long run, it would have an effect.
Hart:	I think it would. That kind of demonstration is very much in line with the new philosophy of science Polanyi, Kaplan, Gene Gendlin, and others are presenting.
Rogers:	An idea that has been very appealing to me is that science starts from the dim recognition of a pattern of related events in nature. Then the means taken to try to *verify* that pattern is science as we know it, but the much more important thing is the perception of the pattern. This is something that tends to happen at the gut level; it demonstrates that the scientist, like every other human being, is really wiser than his mind alone. This is why in any kind of significant science there is a total or gut level experience that is the most valuable guide to the direction that science will take. So, selfishly, that's why I'd like to get some physicists and experimental psychologists and sociologists, preferably people who have a very hardheaded scientific view, into groups of this sort, so they can begin to feel something that would, I think, help them see patterns they've never seen before.
Hart:	It's interesting to me that there is a confluence of interests, ideas, and strivings from several directions that ordinarily don't mix. One direction is philosophy of science, another is religion, particularly mystical religion. Gene Gendlin, in a recent paper (1966), argues that a new sort of logic has to be recognized, existential or experiential logic, that must be given equal consideration along with scientific logic. Scientific logic, he argues, moves from assertion to evidence or proof to conclusion to next assertion, and so on. Experiential logic proceeds from experience to formulation to next experience to reformulation to next experience.
Rogers:	Yes, I think George Leonard, one of the editors of *Look* magazine (1966), has stated this whole idea very well. We're starting out toward the next frontier, the exploration of our inner selves and our interpersonal relationships. I believe there are many indications that this is the case. It is particularly true, perhaps, on the West Coast, but the trend will gradually extend to other parts of the country.
Hart:	I like that simile enough to make it an analogy, because when we talk about frontiers and explorations, we have to recognize dangers. And there will be just as many dangers and just as many misadventures as on other frontiers; just as many mishaps as successes.

Rogers: Having been a great reader of frontier stories in my boyhood, I feel the analogy is very close. There'll be a lot of people who get drowned without help around, people who get lost in the woods, maybe some people who strike it rich, some people who settle down as solid settlers in the new territory — there will be all kinds.

Recent History

Hart: I want to retrace a few of our steps and obtain some comments from you about your activities in Wisconsin and Chicago before we move toward the end and focus on what you are doing and what you plan to do.

Rogers: OK. I'll back up one step further and include Ohio State. I'll try to characterize briefly each of those periods. At Ohio State I was certainly developing new ideas, but one of the most important things is that I came into a department at a time when it was, I believe, past its peak but still attracting excellent graduate students. They had already been well trained in a rigorous type of approach, were bored stiff because they found nothing very significant in it, and were just ready to pounce on this new field. It seemed to them exciting and worthwhile. It was a very fortunate combination of circumstances; there were people like Nick Hobbs, Victor Raimy, Bill Snyder, Tom Gordon, Don Grummon, and many others. They were well trained young scientists before they became infected with this other kind of approach — which made a good combination.

The Chicago period was notable primarily because there, due to the protection given by Ralph Tyler, Dean of Social Sciences, and Bob Strozier, Dean of Students, I was really given the freedom to develop an enterprise in any way that I wanted to. They were often skeptical about what I was doing but never seriously interfered with my freedom to develop the Counseling Center in any way that I felt was sound.

Hart: Did you develop it from nothing or did you change an already existing organization?

Rogers: From nothing. That was another very nice part of it. It was difficult at the time; it was during the war when all the people I most wanted to obtain were in the service. But we started with a young, fresh group and developed it exactly as we wanted it. I resisted all pressures to unite with other guidance activities on the campus. I said to hell with that.

Hart: Is that when you fought some battles with psychiatry?

Rogers: Well, psychiatry wanted us abolished entirely. They didn't care to have us amalgamate. They just wanted to get rid of us. Both at Rochester and Chicago, there were great battles with psychiatrists. At Ohio State that was not true; psychiatry was not strong. They were either cooperative or ignorant of what was going on. In Wisconsin, there was a great deal of cooperation from psychiatry. But in Rochester and Chicago, there were plenty of strenuous battles.

In Chicago we started from scratch, developed a group, developed new ways of working together as well as new ways of working with clients, and all of us were committed to a research point of view. Some people were not very keen about being researchers, but they certainly were willing to cooperate to the extent of helping to collect the data. This made possible many research studies.

Then in Wisconsin — I look back on that as the most unsatisfactory professional period of my life from many points of view. I misjudged what I could do in Psychology. I knew when I went there that the department did not see eye-to-eye with me, but this didn't concern me, because at Chicago I had been able to develop a group working with me, and if it didn't always fit into other things that were going on in Psychology, that made no difference. That could have happened at Wisconsin, too, if it hadn't been for the fact that the really terrible examination system was governed by the department. *Everyone* had to pass *all* the requirements so that there was no allowance for different fields of interest. It meant that students who would have gotten very much involved in their work with me got involved to the extent that they could, but their major goal had to be the passing of exams in other fields they were not particularly interested in. I regard it as a great triumph, not for me since it happened years after I left, but for that department, that just a few months ago they finally did away with the proseminar, the worst feature of the department program, as it was administered. Now the students are permitted to set up their doctoral program in accordance with their interests, under the supervision of a committee.

Hart: That's a great departure from the traditional Midwestern program.

Rogers: But I really was defeated by that, defeated in what I wanted to do in Psychology, by that examination system. Students who wanted to work with me were severely handicapped by the system. This meant that, where at Chicago I had been turning out Ph.D.s at a rapid rate, at Wisconsin they were practically nonexistent. It never troubled me that other members of the department viewed things very differently. I'm pretty good at living and letting live, but when they wouldn't let my *students* live that became a dissatisfying experience.

Hart:　　That's when you began to formulate some of the ideas in your "Passionate statement on graduate education." [3]

Rogers:　Yes, I felt deeply emotional about it. One time I felt so upset about a particular matriculation exam on which they had failed the majority of the graduate students taking the exam, I knew I couldn't control my voice if I tried to talk to them in the department meeting so I recorded a little speech to them and played it at the department meeting. I think they were rather shocked and thought it was another manifestation of my strange behavior.

Then in Psychiatry at Wisconsin, I made some mistakes too, and so did they. Although, by and large my continuing relationship with the members of the Department of Psychiatry was considerably better than my relationship with members of the Department of Psychology, I knew that I represented quite a threat to the Department of Psychiatry. I had a reputation, came in at the top level, and was identified with a particular point of view that few of them liked. Perhaps there would have been no way of remedying that situation at all, but I tried to handle it by sort of soft-pedalling myself in the department, making it clear that I was not a threat. I think I probably overdid it and this only made people more suspicious about what I was up to. I did this somewhat in dealing with the psychiatric residents. I didn't want to try simply to sell them one point of view and have someone else try to sell them another point of view. So I think I held back in some respects. I think I realized I'd been holding back when I finally made the decision to leave Wisconsin. The best teaching that I did with the residents was after I decided I was leaving. I really gave them a good experience in the last semester I was there.

Hart:　　That might be a good recommendation for a reversal of tenure procedures. New professors should be told that, regardless of what they do, they must leave at the end of five years. Then instead of being freed in their last year they will have five years of good teaching.

Rogers:　There must be something to that, because the University of Wisconsin had what they called The Last Lecture Series, in which I participated. I always laughed at it because they seemed to think that only if a man thought he was giving his last lecture would he really say what he thought. It amused me but I realize there is some truth to it.

Hart:　　Did you have many reactions to your statement on graduate education?

[3] See Chapter 26.

Rogers: I should say I have! It runs the risk of being the most widely read unpublished article in existence.[4] We've sent out something like 2,500 copies from WBSI, and that's only the smallest fraction of what has been distributed. Partially because single copies are passed from person to person but even more because many people have duplicated the paper and distributed it on their own, so I really have no idea how many copies have been distributed. Partly because of the unorthodox method of distribution, I think it has been read by almost everyone who gets a copy of it.

Hart: I'm sure of that; it's been like a banned book.

Rogers: That's right. I read somewhere the other day that the average number of readers for an article in a psychological journal is 200. When the *American Psychologist* turned down the article, it was like being banned in Boston.

Hart: When you made the decision to leave Wisconsin, had you definitely decided to come to WBSI?

Rogers: Well, it was a two-part decision. I resigned from the Department of Psychology in the Spring of 1963 when I was at The Center for Advanced Study in the Behavioral Sciences. I made a couple of attempts to get the department to take some actions that would have made it possible for me to stay, but they were quite unwilling to budge at all in their whole examination system. So I resigned from the Department of Psychology. I made arrangements with President Harrington to give noncredit, interdepartmental seminars. I thought that between those interdepartmental seminars and the work in the Department of Psychiatry that I would stay at Wisconsin. Then during the summer of 1963 WBSI made me an offer that I promptly turned down, saying that I belonged in a university. Then I began to think about how much profit it had been to me in the last ten years to be in a university and the more I thought about that, the more I felt the advantage to me had been very slight. So I finally made my decision in the early autumn of 1963 and left in December of 1963. I've never regretted it.

Current Activities

Hart: It would be interesting, to learn about what you're doing, and what you're planning.

Rogers: I don't quite know all the reasons, but I've had many more significant dealings with faculty members since I've been outside the university than I had when I was in. Now various faculties want

---

[4] We hope that the readership will continue to expand even though the paper has now moved from the vigor of ditto blue to the respectability of print black.

me to come and meet with them. Cal Tech is one of the outstanding examples, but there have been a number of others, too. When I've met with faculties, it has been on serious issues, educational policy, or what constitutes learning, all kinds of significant issues that almost never get discussed within the university. I've had much more direct contact with many learners than I had for the last half-dozen years I was in a university. For the most part, these have been brief, intensive group experiences. Yet they've had a pretty profound impact. For example, I went to the University of Colorado for a four-day workshop, under many difficult restrictions, with graduate students in clinical psychology. I heard just the other day that the reverberations of that still continue. I'm sure I could have been at Colorado for a year and taught a standard number of courses and not have had anything like that influence on students. So I haven't been disappointed in my contact with learners — students and others. Then at WBSI it's been a fulfillment of a third aspect of a pattern that I hoped to achieve long ago in Chicago. In Chicago, I was working with troubled or maladjusted people but at least these people functioned in the community. I felt that to round out my own learning I would like to work with hospitalized psychotics and also to work with normal people. I tried to combine that in the research at Wisconsin. The arrangements didn't work out with normals, but at least I had a chance to work with hospitalized schizophrenics. That was a valuable experience even though a toughly discouraging one. All of us felt that discouragement. Now, coming out here, I've had full opportunity to work with normal individuals. Within the past year I've had the opportunity, for example, to work with two groups of presidents of corporations, which has given me quite a new facet of experience. I'm not accustomed to working with people to whom the use of power comes naturally and who are accustomed to this power. They're a very intriguing group. Partly because of my research interests, I've always avoided private practice. I wanted to work with people with whom one didn't have to consider questions of power and politics and influence and that kind of thing. Also, ordinary people who simply came for help were more willing to enter into research programs. So this is a really new experience. During workshops in Australia and in France, I have recognized some of the sharp cultural differences and the wide variety of attitudes toward the client-centered point of view. I have feeling that what we used to think of as the function of the true university is increasingly going to leave universities and be carried on by peripheral institutions. Universities are so big, with so much production machinery, and develop such a bureaucracy, that probably the exciting new things will develop either in ad hoc organizations that form a particular task force, or institutes that serve a particular specialized function. I'm inclined to question whether cutting edge ideas very frequently come from universities. I may be a little too pessimistic about universities. Perhaps a more modest statement would be that a great many of the cutting edge ideas will come from organizations that are outside of and peripheral to the universities.

Hart: That's an argument that a number of people are making, including Paul Goodman and Timothy Leary. Perhaps students can rescue the universities; students are increasingly unwilling to be processed.

Rogers: I regard student unrest on some of the campuses as one of the healthiest things that has happened in years. I'm sure there will be some damaging effects and some foolish extremes, but by and large I regard it as a very healthy influence on university life.

Hart: I'd like to pause a minute and see whether there are any other directions we might consider. We talked about the way intuitions lead concepts. I wonder whether there are directions that you are intuiting to which you could give some preliminary exposure.

Rogers: I think I've mentioned most of them, but I'll sort of review them again. I have the intuitive feeling that we're on the edge of developing a new model of science in the behavioral science field. I think I could even sketch a few of the qualities that it might have, but I have no idea what the model will eventually be. I feel intuitively that we're on the verge of a revolution in education that will be opposed by most of the people now in education. It may be a difficult or even a psychologically bloody struggle, I don't know, but I think everything in life is pointing to the fact that education as we have known it has got to be plowed under or turned upside down because it's just not suitable for modern life. There I feel I have one very practical approach I want to try. It's a proposal for the concentrated use of the basic encounter group at all levels of a given school system. The only requirement for choosing a system would be that one or two of the people at the top would be open to change and willing to get involved in it. The plan is to hold basic encounter groups first with administrative personnel, perhaps including the board of trustees. They would then really have experienced such a thing, experienced some changes in themselves, become more open and less authoritarian, and come to relate more to people as people. Then that same approach would be used with groups of teachers who were willing to volunteer — all this would be voluntary — then with class units including the teacher, supervising teacher, and assistant teachers, and the janitor if he has anything to do with the class, exposing them to an intensive group experience where real feelings and attitudes would come out. Then begin to do some cross-cutting in groups, so that there might be a couple of parents, and a member of the board of trustees, an a school principal, and a couple of teachers, and some students, and a couple of school drop-outs, all in one group, where they would come to understand and communicate with each other as persons instead of as roles. And then the final proposal is to take people from the school system who have been turned on by some of these experiences and train them to be facilitators of such groups, so that a continuing self-directed change process would be developed.[5] Obviously no outside group could realy get into all the aspects of a school system, but we would develop a continuing change process within the system. Then as a parallel part of this, to add what I think is much needed in this field, one group would be studied very vigorously, taking before and after measures and process measures to get a real notion about what detailed changes occur. One feature of the research plan is to use pocket transmitters so that interpersonal behavior could be sampled before their group experience and at varying periods after their group experience.

This development of the basic encounter group, which has now taken all kinds of forms of expression through art, through body movement, through verbal expression, is a part of a very significant modern trend in which people are endeavoring to fight alienation, overcome alienation, endeavoring to explore more of themselves, endeavoring to *become* more of themselves, endeavoring to find more meaning in relationships with others, endeavoring to use themselves differently. I think the intensive group experience is a really significant modern invention that deserves to be classified along with radar or penicillin in importance. It may lead into other things; I don't know what it will flow into. It has its faults and dangers but it's part of a social trend. It is interesting that I don't know of a single university that gives it any real backing except through schools of business administration. It has no standing in any of the professions. It has nothing except its own vitality and public support. Perhaps some day the universities and professions will catch up with it.

This project has been funded and is now underway in Los Angeles.

REFERENCES

GENDLIN, E. T. Existentialism and experimental psychotherapy. In C. Moustakas (Ed.), *Existential child therapy*. New York: Basic Books, 1966. (See Chapter 5.)

LEONARD, G. B. Where the California game is taking us. *Look,* 1966, 30, June 28 108-116.

POSER, E. G. The effect of therapist training on group therapeutic outcome *Journal of Consulting Psychology,* 1966, 30, 23-89.

ROGERS, C. R. Some observations on the organization of personality. *American Psychologist,* 1947, 2, 358-568.

ROGERS, C. R. Some issues concerning the control of human behavior. (Sympo sium with B. F. Skinner) *Science,* 1956, 124, 1057-1066.

ROGERS, C. R. A theory of therapy, personality, and interpersonal relationships as developed in the client-centered framework. In S. Koch (Ed.), *Psychology A study of a science.* Vol. 3. New York: McGraw-Hill, 1959. Pp. 184-256

ROGERS, C. R. Toward a science of the person. In T. W. Wann (Ed.), *Behaviorism and phenomenology: Contrasting bases for modern psychology.* Chicago: Uni versity of Chicago Press, 1964. Pp. 109-140.

ROGERS, C. R. Some thoughts regarding the current philosophy of the behaviora sciences. *Journal of Humanistic Psychology,* 1965, 5, 182-194.

ROGERS, C. R. and DYNARD, R. F. (Eds.), *Psychotherapy and personality change* Chicago: University of Chicago Press, 1954.

ROGERS, C. R. and SKINNER, B. F. *Dialogue.* Two-hour edited tape recording o dialogue at Duluth, June, 1962. Distributed by AAP Tape Library, 6420 Cit Line Ave., Philadelphia, Pa.

SKINNER, B. F. A case history in scientific method. In S. Koch (Ed.), *Psychology A study of a science.* Vol. 2. New York: McGraw-Hill, 1959. Pp. 359-379.

TAFT, J. *The dynamics of therapy.* New York: Macmillan, 1933.

28

The Literal-Intuitive Axis

and Other Thoughts*

JOHN M. SHLIEN

It is hard to peer into the future of clients who will be living as people in
a period of genuine social revolution. Some old problems may disappear,
new problems may emerge, with the possibility of different kinds of solutions
than those to which we are now accustomed. The environment will become
more complex. Like it or not, the great society lies ahead of us, and if it is
not great, it will at least be big. As Nicholas Hobbs has pointed out, in this
coming society the future of individual psychotherapy is itself somewhat in
doubt, perhaps bound to give way to various community mental health efforts
based on new models of helping. This poses a problem since, to my mind,
client-centered therapy has always had a particularly phenomenological base
and will require some theoretical modification or extension to adapt to group
contexts. The sources of this theoretical development are not yet clear, but
from what we hear of Carl Rogers' current interests in intensive group therapy,
he might be one source.

There is another gap. Though client-centered therapy developed out of
work with children in the Rochester Clinic it soon became and has largely
remained in theory and practice a matter of adult repair. Presently, as surely
as one works with groups and larger communities, one is led to thoughts of
preventive work in those problems of living which endanger mental health.
As soon as one thinks of prevention, one is led to thoughts of working with

* Paper given at the Symposium, "The Future of Client-Centered Therapy," at the
American Psychological Association Meeting in Los Angeles, September, 1964, with
Carl R. Rogers, John M. Butler, and Eugene T. Gendlin.

535

younger and younger people, eventually children. This is the other gap. We need still more in the way of a theory of child development and of creative education. Again, the sources of these future developments are not clearly visible. One wonders why they have been absent and neglected. Economics? Age-graded interests of adult therapists? Apparent need?

Now as for the idea of change and the directions of change. True prophets are most often those who work toward the fulfillment of their predictions. I would rather try to forecast what might be the "natural history" of the future, though admittedly this will reflect my personal interests.

I think there will be no single line of development, but that change is assured in several directions. Change as a motif is built into the system by the founder, with his notable distaste for dogma, and by the inventive mavericks attracted to the system. Indeed, during my own early years at the Counseling Center, when Carl Rogers was its leader, I often got the impression that there was a directive: to become neo-Rogerian as quickly as possible. Even so, in the past, client-centered therapists, according to studies by Strupp (1960) and others, have been more homogeneous in their practice than have other schools. This is understandable; intelligent reflections will vary a good deal less than equally intelligent interpretations. But client-centered therapy has had somewhat the quality of a protest movement, with some forced cohesive effects. Now the missionary zeal is tempered, our protests have been drawn into the main stream (on the surface at least), and the organization is big and steady enough to contain what in the past might have been spin-offs. A more heterogeneous set of behaviors is predictable, remaining, I hope, more or less client-centered. With regard to changing of techniques, there is another factor. Techniques become tiresome. Reflection was, and is, a good tool. It takes a surprising amount of skill to apply it deftly and without woodenness, since it is actually quite foreign to our conventional repertoire (such as advice, persuasion, etc.). For those attitudes which Rogers set forth and to which we subscribed reflection serves to implement as no other technique would. Yet, after twenty years, it is incomplete, a bit restrictive and tiresome. A technique may be excellent, but if it becomes tedious and confining, the therapist's own need for novelty and originality or for personal expression will force modifications. I do not mean that "understanding is not enough" or that reflection will be dropped; it will be laced with new variations and probably be the better for it.

The Future in General

Even though client-centered therapy is entrenched in the universities and more barricaded by research than is any other, it seems to me that we must share to some extent the future of psychotherapy in general. The future in general has been commented on by a number of observers, who have noted a measure of turmoil, confusion, and even "chaos." None sees disaster ahead but to me the situation looks serious. Granted the demand is there; therapy is favorably represented on TV, and studies of the metropolis show a large proportion of the population in need of treatment. (In this connection, let me parenthetically remark that I believe psychotherapy is an urban substitute for a deep and satisfying contact with nature. Indeed, if it were required to prescribe one and only one method of bringing a mental health measure to the public on a massive scale, I would say, give each person a tree of his own to grow and contemplate). The demand is there, and the profession is growing lustily as a profession. However, that profession may be afflicted by problems attending popularization, and by a "market mentality" which might be our undoing if we cannot deliver to the mass culture. Already, those long clinic waiting lists have in them some who have been patients once or twice elsewhere.

Meanwhile, from the inside, Schofield suggests that anxiety and psychotherapy may have been overrated and oversold; Szasz challenges the "myth of mental illness"; Leary takes some jabs at the "psychotherapy game"; and Mowrer tells us that the neurotic endeavor is a shirking of guilty responsibility which most therapy only perpetuates. These are all intelligent men whose messages deserve some attention. From the outside, we have the much publicized critiques such as Eysenck's (1952), still not thoroughly refuted and perhaps not to be.[1] Brill has recently surveyed outcome studies and concluded that currently the results total only ten studies to nine on balance favorable in their effects. Recent research evidence (Rogers, 1967) shows what we have always known — that in the ubiquitous one-third rated "not improved," some are not only not improved but according to outcome measures, rated lower than their initial status. Something is wrong, though given the general ineffectiveness of all sorts of work in all other fields, we might be foolish to expect otherwise. Indeed, proficiency is bound to be imperfect. It is always a combination of incomplete theory and imperfect practice. The product is like the multiplication of fractions.

A private survey of my own suggests that in the opinion of therapists in practice, about 20 per cent of their colleagues are judged to be of so little competence that one would not consider referral to them.[2] If this is so, the 70 per cent improvement rate generally reported and generously accepted by critics is remarkable! It means that some therapists are quite efficient. Others are not. We are hard put to identify any of these therapists at any point in their career. Further, effectiveness surely fluctuates, and all attempts at evaluation are complicated by problems of inadequate sampling, patient differences, criteria, and so on. Yet this is a problem that we cannot continue

Editor's Note: Chapter 13 by Donald J. Kiesler is a reply to Eysenck's critique.

[2] This was carried out by asking some variant of the question "to whom would you send a close friend or a member of your family." It has since come to my attention that Dr. Paul Meehl, using much the same technique, supposes that only one-third or one-fourth of the "professional helpers" are regarded as competent by their colleagues.

to avoid. It points to the question of competence — the personal competence of the therapist. There is probably no such thing as a "good therapist," whose efforts never fail or whose results are never disappointing, but rather therapists who are more or less good with some people, at some times, and not with others. I think we see one reaction to this problem in the development of new systems. That there were five, then thirty-six, now 100 systems of therapy does not testify simply to the excitement and inventiveness and freedom in the field. It also reflects the failure of *any* system to produce sufficient results *as a system*. A hundred more will not save us while the fault lies not so much in our system as in ourselves.

If this is so, client-centered therapy (once scorned as a homeopathic method of study counsel), with its demonstrably increased range and potency of application, shares this problem. What can we do about it? I predict that in the next ten years the therapist's behavior and personality will be subjected to such scrutiny as has been applied only to patients and clients in the past. Focus on the selection and training of therapists has and will come from many quarters: from group therapy, where he is on public display; from visits by actors and journalists trained to represent patients (two instances have already been reported); from the results of various outcome studies. All this may carry discomfort, potential mismanagement, unjustified sampling, and other abuse. But the therapist, in spite of a good deal of recording and some films, continues to work largely in private with only one true potential collaborator, the client. From this latter source, I believe, will come the next major client-centered effort to find a way to develop and maintain advanced competence in keeping with its general principles. In the past, an apprentice therapist was often judged promising if his behavior matched the teacher model, and supplementarily, if the client responses indicated confirmation of the therapist's understanding. The latter aspect has to be developed and amplified. Our ultimate criterion has to be the client's own perspective. Whatever faults this basis has, it is no more flawed than any other source, and in the end every other criterion *has* to connect with this one. The next step is to take the client in as an active research collaborator. The myth of the naïve subject is fading in the rest of social science. It is absurd now in therapy to assume that the client does not know what is being measured, or what process is being experienced. What I envision is, first, a move toward sophisticated self-study by the therapist and the client, with both trained in introspective and observational methods; second, a new form of collaboration in which the process of interaction is closely examined by these two participants, perhaps with the aid of a third party. When the client and therapist together analyze their own actions and interactions, we will see some new subtleties only dimly perceived or not even suspected before. Of course, this procedure will depart from the ordinary uninvestigated therapy, but so does any other research strategy. For us, the future will either hold a sophisticated rigorous self-study involving candid and intelligent therapists aided and appraised by clients, or therapy will turn more and more to *external* criteria and end as a conditioning operation, since external criteria logically lead to "behavior modification."

There will be, then, a serious concentration upon the problem of competence. It will involve intensive study of the therapist, self-study with the collaboration of the client, we hope. With it, much new can be learned. Without it, individual therapy may wither away even as a laboratory, since studies of patient or client outcome cannot support it indefinitely. By no means is this to say that individual therapy is not or cannot be good, when it is often very good indeed, and a source of satisfaction to both clients and practitioners. It may remain as a research laboratory, a training procedure, and a luxury trade item in private practice. However, it cannot continue to meet either its scientific or social obligations without some new developments.

The Literal-Intuitive Axis

Client-centered therapy is much more than a method of therapeutic endeavor. It is also an intellectual-theoretical position — a way of looking at and understanding behavior. The characteristics of this range along an axis which features a highly literal approach at one end, and at the other, a deeply intuitive one.

The intuitive side has attracted many, with its emphasis on feelings, inner experience, the philosophy of phenomenology and its consequent ultimate individualism, man's nature and his relation to nature. When intuitive knowledge is invoked, it is a type of knowing called "feeling" and it draws on what was always there; the unitary and universal in knowledge, as the slave boy intuitively knew the geometry of the triangle when Socrates led him to it, and as the flower in the crannied wall represents the transcendent whole when understood in depth. There is an organic tone to it. It smacks of soil, sea weed, tree roots; when Rogers dips his toe into the blue Caribbean, he gets an infusion of that oceanic feeling and writes about the personal side of science. It also characterizes something of the mystical or at least mystifying (and this may mean nothing more than that of which we are ignorant or pretend to be) relationship between client and therapist, and is in fact the naturalistic touchstone of client-centered theory.

The other emphasis is the strikingly different literal quality of thought. For me, this is the greater part of the genius of this approach, and would remain as an influence if the conduct of therapy were to cease. This is not merely the instrumentation of theory with technique such as reflection to implement the other's internal frame of reference, or the penchant for verbatim recording of interviews for review. Both are valuable in themselves and as illustrations, but the literal is more than any illustration. It is a quality of description and explanation that aims to simplify operations and translate them into the currency of science. It avoids ceremonial complexities. It shuns the arcane and esoteric, but it is by no means simpleminded. It rejects the deliberate mystique of some therapies and looks for rational alternatives. Ignorance is admitted for what it is. Knowledge is advanced in the form of tentative hypotheses couched in ordinary language rather than a contrived vocabulary. I have always admired Freud's statement, "Much is won if we succeed in transforming hysterical misery into common unhappiness." This Freudian wish is in fact the kind of effort which has characterized client-centered therapy, while psychoanalytic thought, by contrast, seems to have moved in the opposite direction toward a metaphorical system.

(a) To illustrate, consider a key concept such as transference. Rogers never accepted it as a necessary condition. He spoke of "transference attitudes," which need not be cultivated, could be avoided. Butler analyzed transference in terms of learning, anticipatory response, and extinguishing. Shlien called transference "a fiction, developed and maintained to protect the therapist from the consequences of his own behavior" — which behavior could consist of no more or less than just listening and understanding and sharing the secrets of the client's experience. He accounted for positive and negative transference on the basis of the client's feeling understood or misunderstood — supported by Van Kaam's phenomenological study of "how it feels to be understood." This major hallmark, transference, has already lost much of its force. The therapist no longer holds the bland and neutral role of a screen upon which all patients' attitudes are simply projections. This now sounds silly. It always was. The predicted future examination of therapist's behavior will reveal much of his contribution to reactions which have heretofore been attributed to "transference." It is interesting to note that Franz Alexander's final statement from his research experience ran along these very lines. The most important conclusion that has emerged from this research is the fact that the traditional descriptions of the therapeutic process do not adequately reflect the immensely complex interaction between therapist and patients. The patients' reactions cannot be fully described as transference reactions.

(b) I expect that there will be new literal attacks upon other intrenched esoterica, including the stronghold of the "unconscious." This is a concept so fundamental to most psychotherapy, and as Sartre points out, so attractive as a cover-up for our conventional duplicity and stupidity, that we will have to provide a set of alternative explanations, or come to terms, or go out of theoretical business. The alternative concept of "levels of awareness" as a continuum rather than a trichotomy was a start. Snygg and Combs (1949) additionally pointed to figure-ground phenomena and also to "tunnel vision" (narrowed and rigidified perception) under conditions of threat, which is essentially the concept of span of attention as it is affected by emotion. It is thus closely connected to the concept of energy level, a level which fluctuates and thus differs from the Freudian hydraulic system. In conjunction with the interaction of span of attention and energic fluctuation, there are also the variable forces of sensations competing for enough of that attention to become perceptions. To such combinations of concepts as attention, energic fluctuation, and levels of awareness, add variability of self-concept as a filter through which perceptions are screened, and the combined literal explanation of inconsistencies or temporary ignorance takes on considerable power. Finally, consider that the sensory system is composed of multiple input channels (ears, eyes, nose, etc.), all capable of compound reception, while the expressive system is usually limited to a single output (vocal, usually) at one time. This very inbalance of rapidly accumulative multiple input and slower single output makes suppression, at least, unavoidable. All these considerations, along with clues from new "visual search" studies of scanning and selection, and other strategies from information storage and retrieval theory, should help in the future to provide literal understandings of at least some phenomena previously relegated to the hidden operations of "the unconscious." It may be that besides the emotional clearance of free and honest expression in the psychological economy, the literalist inquiry into the multiplicity of thought will require the invention of new apparatus to train and extend expressive modalities — a response piano, as it were, so that the limits of consciousness are released through a keyboard of complex chords instead of a single melodic line.

(c) This more literal stance will probably show itself also in a new understanding of sex and the role of sexual behavior. Client-centered therapy, as many have noted, has been relatively backward in this area. It is as if we invested in self-theory while psychoanalytic libido-theory was sweeping the field. Now there is a "sexual revolution." It seems real. Whether it turns out to be harmful or helpful, or leads to a counterrevolution, we cannot yet see, but certainly the restrictive pressures are off. Much of what used to be hidden is now open and perhaps less powerful. Now social-self theory rears *its* head with more validity. For instance, a client who had been almost unselectively promiscuous says, "I've come to realize that there is a man on the other end of that penis." This makes life understandable and to be understood in terms of real human interaction and humanity, rather than squeamish interpretations of sexual symbols in dreams. Another sexually active girl, for whom interpretations of sexual repression would be nonsense, says, "When I really like a man, I let him see me take down my hair." Lack of sexual experience is not a concern; lack of genuine intimacy is. Another example comes from a brilliant and attractive college student who takes the view that in each new relation she is ready for sex as soon as it feels comfortable, with the idea that if sex is not used as a lure, "then we can see if we can be friends, if he cares for me as a person, without all that phony and awkward courtship." Perhaps astonishing, perhaps over-balanced according to our traditional views, and whether this turns out to be a matter of vulnerability and exploitation or a noble experiment in the betterment of human relations we wait to see. But, plainly, self-theory takes on more validity as the force and interest of "naughty" sexuality wanes. New, more literal understandings may become possible.

Here is a better example. It has to do with an alternative understanding of an "Oedipal situation." Oedipal theory has always seemed slightly hysterical to me, and I'm appalled at the force therapists have applied to this pressure point without looking beyond the original theory. A 21-year-old male entered therapy under heavy stress. According to his Rorschach, appraised by an expert and famous clinician, this young man was a suicidal risk, near a psychotic break, ready for hospitalization, and above all, bore a deep Oedipal attachment to his mother. He certainly was very nervous, very confused. As therapy progressed, he reported and discussed a recurring dream. In his waking life, he was courting an attractive girl with whom he wanted to have intercourse, but of whom he was afraid because of his own inexperience and lack of confidence. In his dreams, he saw himself beginning to make love to the girl, and as he began to lie upon her, her face turned into his mother's face. He was shocked and puzzled. One might think, from the previous diagnosis and the power of Oedipal theory, that there was no more to be said. But, given the opportunity, the young man continued to consider the dream and his feelings about it. Why should he want his mother? "Really an old bag, after all" — when the girl he was courting was so beautiful. Then he hit upon it — "Why not! Why shouldn't I want my sex where I get my security? That's it!" There is the crux of the problem for any frightened person — to find both pleasurable adventure and sufficient security together, for severe anxiety is a detriment, sexually and otherwise. With that realization, this young man solved his own problem and, to my mind, made one new contribution toward a theory of sex. What characterized the supposedly Oedipal complex was the essential quality of the experience of security, not the being of mother, who was a metaphorical representation of that security.

(d) As a final comment on this position I submit that psychotherapy can be expressed as the composition of two primary elements — honesty and courage. Such simple terms will never win the Talcott Parsons Award; indeed, these are such simple terms for problems which have such complicated consequences that when they are unresolved, we can only rename the elements just because we lost the battle. Honesty and courage mean the ability to know the facts of experience without flinching, or at least without turning away and denying these facts to oneself, whether or not one chooses to declare them to others. The person who possesses these qualities does not need psychotherapy. He may want friendship, love, help, support, and other environmental benefits, but he does not need psychotherapy. He has a cleanliness of neurological operation, a psychological economy unburdened by deficit financing of layers of defense, and that is the value of the literal elements.

How have the therapies dealt with this basic problem? Psychoanalysis, by the rule of free association (a contradition in terms if taken literally) meaning no thought held back, and through the royal road of symbolic analysis, sought to penetrate all secrets, distortions, and self-deceits. Forced-choice honesty, that is. Client-centered therapy sought through acceptance, understanding, and safety, to promote "openness to experience." Honesty by safe conduct, that is. Whether safety in a privileged environment can produce courage outside it is a question. True, clients grow by facing their pain and surviving. They also develop a psychological integrity which they prize and know they would lose if they allowed fear to drive them back into self-deception. But client-centered therapy accidentally approaches the development of courage in another way. It has been classified as an "insight" therapy. Originally, insight was a partial objective, but it now receives less and less attention. Client-centered therapy has moved closer to becoming an "action" therapy in this sense: the objective is to develop a *capacity* rather than to attack a particular problem or symptom. We work toward the exercise of a *capacity to see,* not toward particular vision itself. Thus it is not an insight therapy in the sense of tracing causes or understanding particular content. Content has long been considered subordinate to feeling. Experiencing is increasingly emphasized but, again, more as a capacity. This capacity, regardless of content, is what may lead to courage. It is as if we encourage weight lifting, not to move a particular set of heavy objects into a new arrangement (though that is one of the effects), but to strengthen muscles. That strength can be the basis for courage.

All this leads to an increasing awareness of the component of "will" therapy. That is not to say that Rank begat Rogers, but that they have much in common. I believe that the simple virtues of honesty, courage, and personal responsibility (though without the punitive cost demanded by some who preach responsibility) may become more and more the context in which growth and successful outcome will be analyzed. Even guilt will lose much of its force as a basis for interpreting neurosis. Most therapeutic theory in the past has been based upon guilt; either this was an error adopted from religious precepts or people have changed. Guilt does not seem very important. People do not seem to suffer much from it. Social concern, yes, and social shame. Perhaps they are not very guilty. They suffer more from being scared and lonely. If it were only guilt, there is plenty of machinery to take care of that; various forms of confession, repentence, expiation, and salvation. But overcoming fear and loneliness — that takes some doing. For the scared and lonely, it is often easier to confess and analyze at length than to face life and make friends.

REFERENCES

EYSENCK, H. J. The effects of psychotherapy: An evaluation. *Journal of Consulting Psychology,* 1952, 16, 319-324.

ROGERS, C. R. (Ed.), *The therapeutic relationship and its impact.* Madison, Wisconsin: University of Wisconsin Press, 1967.

SYNGG, D. and COMBS, A. W. *Individual behavior.* New York: Harper, 1949.

STRUPP, H. M. *Psychotherapists in action.* New York: Grune and Stratton, 1960.

29

A Short Summary and Some

Long Predictions

EUGENE T. GENDLIN

Client-centered therapy has helped give birth to experiential psychotherapy. This is my summary. I will expand it a little and then turn to the forecast. The experiential method will be applied to society as a whole and to our methods of thinking in science. That is the forecast. I will expand it, too.

Summary

A little more than a decade ago client-centered therapy was embattled in emphasizing that helpful change happens only through the client's own steps of concrete feeling. It was client-centered therapy which emphasized that an individual isn't changed by concepts, by being told what's wrong, by being argued with, or by agreeing with a correct explanation. The word "client" was intended to define psychotherapy along the lines of a legal rather than a medical model. The doctor can treat the patient even without the patient's knowing what the steps of treatment are, and certainly without the patient's being in charge of the treatment. The lawyer, on the contrary, must operate entirely as an adjunct to a process of which the client always remains in charge. It would be absurd for the lawyer to sue, or not to sue, in the client's name but on the lawyer's responsibility. The same idea was then doubly encoded into the name of the orientation by terming it "client-centered," which emphasizes what the very word "client" already emphasizes.

And yet, all this was very confusing at the time. It seemed to be based on a preference for democracy, as if the therapist were saying, "As an expert I know a lot, of course, but I will deny that I know anything since it is more in

544

accord with my values that you make up your own mind and arrive at conclusions by yourself." This seemed silly to many people, and although it was certainly never phrased that way, client-centered therapy struck many people as an inappropriate application of democratic ideals.

In my early writings I tried to articulate the underlying principles that were really at stake. It was not because we preferred the client's own process that we insisted on responding only to him and not with our own ideas and diagnoses. Rather, in order for something more than our own ideas to happen, the work *had* to be with the client's own process, his own felt meanings and steps of resolution. But wasn't this always known by all therapists of any view? Yes, in general it was known, but specifically, from moment to moment in the therapy interview, it was *not* known how to respond to an individual so that this process would occur in him. Thus psychoanalysis held that interpretation was the key element, and the patient was often sent home to do the experiential work alone as "homework." Similarly, the usefulness of transference was explained in general as the need for the patient to relive (not merely rethink) his problems, but the time in therapy was spent "interpreting the transference," to show him that he was repeating old patterns. It was a mystery how the patient ever came to change. "Working through" was called the most essential part of treatment, but no exact instructions for therapists were available for anything but interpretation. In general, of course, everyone agreed to the need for an emotional process if any real change was to happen. But in specific terms, there was systematic knowledge only of how the patient *was*. There were very sophisticated ways of talking about all different sorts of maladjustment — and even a few ways of talking about adjustment. But there were no ways of talking about the steps therapists and patients should take during interviews to help the patient move toward greater health.

The Basic Principle

Client-centered therapy emphasized "reflection of feeling," which was mostly taken to mean repeating what the client says. Client-centered therapy was thus itself half in the old mold. Somehow, mysteriously, by saying what the client said, something new will occur, the client will soon say something new, and then we can respond to that. But, by featuring responsivity at every small, specific, momentary step, the client-centered method did in practice what could only later be formulated in theory. The therapist carried foward not only what the client verbally stated, but also the client's experiential process. One can *feel* a change or an impact when another person responds exactly to one's felt meaning. And "respond" can mean understand, but it can also mean "point to" or even "want to know about," as long as it is exactly this felt meaning you now have, in saying this which you just said. In another chapter,[1] I deal with the theoretical explanation of why such responding

---

[1] See Chapter 7.

"carries forward" the individual's experiential process so that he changes. Here I want only to show that *this responsivity to specific felt meaning at each step engenders, carries forward, and changes the individual's on-going experiential process.* This is the underlying principle that is implicit at the bottom of client-centered therapy and its early quaint rules for therapist responding. Note that this principle is interactive, it is what *T* does which has experiential effects in *C*. It isn't a matter of the things *T* says — often he says nothing new. It is a matter of *T* being another person, of another person responding exactly to what *C* feels — that is what changes *C*.

The interactive character of this responding is all the clearer when what *T* says verbally is already known to *C*, and what *C* says — at least initially — is also already known to *C*. To what is change due? Only to the fact that saying something to *T* is different than just saying it to oneself, and hearing oneself responded to by *T* is a new and different experience than just knowing about something in oneself.

But the "feeling" to which *T* responds was thought to be an emotion, like anger, or gladness, or fear. While such terms are often used, mostly "the feeling" isn't really an emotion. Rather, it is like "feeling worried that such-and-such would happen, and wishing it wouldn't because. . . ." In other words, feelings are always already processes of interaction, of living-in situations, of struggling but not quite succeeding in living situations well or fully.

Thus client-centered therapy has had to be reformulated. Feelings are really "felt meanings," implicitly complex experiencings of situations, of processes that are stopped, or constricted. Responsivity by a therapist, point by point, moment by moment, to the individuals' concrete, bodily felt meaning "carries forward" the process, i.e., allows present experiencing to move beyond hang-ups.

In retrospect we can now look at the old client-centered rules and understand their underlying reason, which was to engender and maximize this experiential process, staying with it, focusing on it, grappling with it, "carrying it forward." Every meaning, every hunch, and every diagnostic possibility can be referred back to it. "Is that what you feel? Was that your point in saying what you said?" A response that is not directed at the client's experience is merely getting off the track, a digression, an interesting generalization perhaps, or a good categorization, but not helpful in the real work of therapy.

Experiential felt meanings are "preconceptual," not exactly this or that concept but an organic texture of bodily felt living. Therefore, verbalized ideas are "exactly it" only if there is a concretely felt effect of saying them. Only if what we say and think makes an experiential shift, is anything changed.

As we look at the old client-centered rules and see what the reason for them was, we can now see many other ways to serve this same reason. In general, we have reversed most of the rules we used to obey — and still we serve the same basic principle in doing so. We can do that because we can now formulate the principle. Not to distract or digress from the experiential process of the client's concretely felt meanings, but to point to them, help him wrestle with them, carry them forward by our personal and exact response to them or inquiry concerning them — that is the principle.

Old Rules — New Meanings

We used to have the rule: *"Don't interpret."* (Most of our rules said "don't." In obeying these don'ts we implicitly acted in ways which only now can we formulate and define.) Why not interpret? Because it will get the client off his experiential track (we can now say). Interpretations will get him off, shift his attention away from his concrete mass of confused and preconceptual felt meaning and into generalizations, intellectualizations, and concepts that are interesting in themselves but apply to him only indirectly. Rather than getting into touch with himself, interpretations send the client off to know himself through knowing a general idea that fits him. An interpretation tells him what category he is in, and thus he deals with general categories rather than with himself.

But once we have formulated this experiential principle underlying the rule, "don't interpret," we can interpret. We can use every and any promising diagnostic notion that strikes us as therapists. It won't be generalized but will point specifically to a short step that can be taken from where the client is. Diagnostic interpretive ideas *might* help the client discover an avenue of experiential "give," of movement in his directly felt referent, an "opening up," or "unfolding." I emphasize "might" because it may not. To use interpretive ideas in responding experientially means precisely that we use them in reference to the concrete felt meaning the client now has or *can* now have. We know that a response was useless, if what we said produces no felt shift, no "aha," no experiential corroboration in him, no series of steps that he now goes through. It is important, in that case, to bring the client quickly back onto his experiential flow where he was a moment before. If the client says "yes, that *must* be true, ah, I guess," I might say something like "that seems true to you, but it doesn't really get at this. You were just saying. . . ." And I thereby bring us back to where I distracted him. In this way, moments later, I may say something based on totally different theories, or memories of other patients, or psychopathological categories. It would be foolish for me to try to decide then which was right, this response or the one before. Interpretations used experientially, used in reference to experiencing, aren't used as factual statements, and it doesn't work to ask which is right or if they are both wrong. Rather, they either open up experiential corrobration so that the client goes through a whole series of steps ("and another thing is, and yes, that also fits with . . . and furthermore. . . .") or we gained nothing with it, however much the client may agree that it *must* be so.

Also, if I have a certain diagnostic notion I have in some way gotten my impressions from the client's behavior. Usually I try to remember specifically and then to re-translate my diagnostic notion into what it was in what he said or did which gave me that impression. Or, if I have forgotten, I wait till I sense it again. I find a very short step from what he is now saying that he might take in the direction of my notion. If I am right, a sequence of experiential steps will begin there, and if I am wrong, I will have gotten him off the track only very minimally. It is like tapping along the wall looking for a hollow sound. The rightness of where you tap is shown by where loose bricks can be pulled out, where a hidden stairway reveals itself, where one can *go* down that stairway . . . many steps. By the time we are down the stairs, it is a silly question whether indeed that first hollow sound was or wasn't a hollow. However right we may be in general, we can't go down a stairway that we only insist *must* be behind some brick that doesn't give.

All our old client-centered rules become more exact "do" rules. By applying the principle of responding to specific felt meanings, "don'ts" become "do's."

Take *"don't answer the client's questions."* Why did we hold that rule? Because if we answer we don't find out why he asks, and we don't continue on his track, we don't explore that whole mass of felt concern that is only hinted at obliquely in his question. But, nowadays, I first honestly answer just about any question — and then very soon thereafter I say, "why do you ask?" Answering often gives me a chance to show what I think about the client, which usually is very close to his own experience but still in my words, with my way of seeing things.

We used to tell therapists *"don't express your own opinion."* Now if I am asked for it, I almost always do express my opinion, rather briefly, but showing exactly the steps of thought I go through. Then I say, "but it isn't likely that that would fit you, because you're a different person, and besides, you probably thought of that already anyway and it doesn't work." And I return him to his own track. (Of course he might have all sorts of feelings about the fact that I have the opinion I have, but these too we can explore, if he expresses or lets me sense these reactions in him. That too will again be his process, and we will try to respond to each other honestly in reference to his process and his concretely felt steps.)

In effect, we previously urged therapists *"if you're puzzled about something, don't mention it."* We wanted to pursue what the client was puzzled about, not the therapist's questions, associations, and ideas about it. And we still avoid distracting questions. But, now we think that expressing our puzzlement about his felt expressions will lead to clarification. The client will have the added solidity of having laid out the steps clearly, he may even discover something new, and he experiences the fact that his therapist really follows every step or else says that he doesn't. It makes what is at first an often complex, compressed maze of autistic meaning into a clearly interpersonal chain of meanings that are given interactive solidity, point by point.

We used to say *"if you didn't respond rightly to something a minute ago, the moment has passed. Don't bring it up now. You have to wait till the client brings it up again."* All our effort was to maximize and not derail the client's process. But now I can say, "just a minute, I am still mulling over what you said a while ago, and I. . . ." I can even say, "this reminds me, all week I've been thinking about what you said last week, and I said XYZ. That wasn't right, really you must have meant. . . ." The client should know that I think all week about what he said, if I do. The principle is to respond to his experiential process. Our rules achieved that indirectly, by *not* doing all the other things, as in this example, by not deciding when and what will be talked about.

We used to teach:

"If you have strong liking and appreciation for the client, don't mention it."

"If there is something you think he ought to talk about, forget it."

"If he is silent, you must remain silent also, indefinitely."

A look at how we learned to work with silent schizophrenics shows how far we have come.[2] There, too, we had to grasp the underlying principle. Then we learned how to use ourselves to serve that principle, to respond to a silent patient's experiential process.

You will notice that I have been saying what the therapist ought to do, all in one principle: maximizing the client's experiential process, using our own to do so. But this can be said specifically in terms of the three "conditions" which phrased it in more old-fashioned language. *Empathy* seemed to be restating the client's verbal content, although really it always meant pointing sensitively to his felt meaning to help him focus on it and carry it further. *Congruence* seemed to mean saying what we as therapists thought. Really it meant responding from out of our own ongoing experiential process, showing the steps of thought and feeling we go through, responding not stiltedly or artificially, but out of our felt being. As verbal content, congruence seems contradictory to empathy (in empathy we tell only exactly about the client, while in congruence we tell about ourselves). As experiential processes, empathy and congruence are exactly the same thing, the direct expression of what we are now going through with the client, in response to him. Finally, *unconditional positive regard* as content contradicts the other two. "If you don't like him now, then you aren't unconditional, and if you say so, you're not empathic, but if you keep still about it, you're incongruent." But unconditional regard really meant appreciating the client as a person regardless of not liking what he is up against in himself (responding to him in his always positive struggle against whatever he is trapped in). It includes our expressions of dismay and even anger, but always in the context of both of us knowing we are seeking to meet each other warmly and honestly as people, exactly at the point at which we each are and feel.

Thus the therapist's erstwhile rather formal role has now become the thera-

<hr>

[2] See Chapter 15.

pist himself, his use of his own actual ongoing experiential process. This is the real meaning of the therapist conditions, rather than their contradictory literal meanings.

The basic principle we see more clearly today is: the client-centered response, which I now call *the experiential response,* is the honest untrammeled pointing at the client's *felt meaning.* That was the summary.

And now the forecast, expressed in eight predictions.

Forecast

Prediction One: There will be a universal "experiential" method of psychotherapy using all useful procedures in reference to the individual's own process.

As recently as 1910, medicine had a number of different orientations. There was no single approach until enough was known to make up a recognized body of knowledge that everyone practiced and into which new discoveries could be integrated. Psychotherapy in the next decade will also move beyond the stage of different sects or orientations. With a whole series of researches, we are showing that successful change in psychotherapy occurs when the patient engages in an experiential process. Successful clients work in a way that can be recognized in the research studies of their verbalizations. We are now at the stage where we can tell from a few samples of tape-recorded interview behavior whether the ongoing therapy is of the sort that eventuates in success or not. This is undoubtedly true of all orientations, regardless of what concepts or therapist styles are used.

Although research has not yet covered all orientations, the transition from specific rules (our client-centered "don'ts") to experiential "do" rules is just as possible in every other orientation and is now occurring in many of them. In all orientations the experiential method is implied — but not yet recognized — as making the difference between success and failure. For example, consider the Jungian "directed daydream" during which the analyst interprets the archetypal structures that arise. Jung was concerned with dreams as symbols of "transformation," since they function to produce an experiential shift the patient can feel, which then makes his further imagery different and makes him different. But too often the analyst and patient remain fascinated with the imagery as such, with their archetypal universal meaning, and there is no emphasis on the necessary zigzag between feeling and imagery to see if and when a felt difference has occurred. That fascination sometimes produces intriguing books about psychotic imagery without improvement of the patients and without attention paid to the way one can use imagery to produce the necessary experiential shifts. Similarly, Albert Ellis has renamed his "Rational Therapy"; he now calls it "Rational-Emotive Therapy" because, again, not all the rational arguments and attacks on "irrationality" count; what counts is whether and when they produce an "emotional" shift. What is essential is the emotional. Or, consider again psychoanalytic interpretation. Everything depends upon whether therapist and patient spend the hour arguing (or, for that matter agreeing) on their interpretative generalizing and analyzing, which can be endless, or whether they swiftly rummage through the variety of possible interpretations to arrive soon at one that produces what Fenichel calls a "dynamic shift." Psychoanalysis can become experiential, and is becoming so, moving constantly back and forth between its rich interpretive repertoire and the patient's direct experiential process, in shifts that alone can guide the analyst. Role-playing, changed environments, body relaxation, and body armor interpretation, all have the same potentiality to provide means for obtaining an experiential shift. They can be guided step by step in a direction the patient feels as freeing, or they can be used rather blindly, guided by a therapist's guesses, values, and diagnoses. Whether one begins inside (as we do) with words and then refers to bodily feeling by focusing one's attention on it, or begins outside, by role playing, bodily gestures, or deconditioning, in each approach one seeks to create a shift that will be felt and will lead to a person who is different in feeling and action.

But this seems to say only that the experiential method provides the essential focus, guide, and moment-by-moment aim. The procedures of the orientations all seem different from one another. What will become of the different procedures? I believe we will learn to use them all when they can be helpful. Already, most therapists no longer use solely the procedure they were taught — client-centered therapists do not merely reflect feelings, many analysts discard the couch. In the past, a new and total method of therapy originated every time someone found one useful thing to do. It was customary then to insist that the new method could handle everything, or to argue against it that it could do nothing at all. I am impressed with the power of Lindsley's Skinnerian method "pinpointing the behavior" to be changed, and then counting it when it occurs and changing what usually happens as a consequence. But although I am very far from perfect or perfectly satisfied with myself, I find few nontrivial behaviors to count and change. Different methods work for different things and at different junctures. (I would not say for different people, because we don't know that as yet.) Clearly, a cat phobia or any other isolable behavior that the patient feels is undesirable is more amenable to deconditioning than a general malaise with life in which no one or several specific behaviors stand out.

All these "methods" are really tools, procedures, useful things one can try. The basic method which cuts across them all is that any procedure, word, or deed must be used in a continual zigzag that moves toward the experiential sense of the individual, and back out of that with a new start, if there has been a change, or toward a new attempt at something else if what was tried hasn't worked, hasn't experientially shifted anything. Thus I think in the future we will all learn all the useful tools we can, and we will subordinate no human beings to these tools but will attempt to perform the reverse.

Prediction Two: Psychotherapy, or rather what we have learned from it, will be applied to the society as a whole, in social programs.

The whole trend of current thinking has shifted to the view that human beings are interactional creatures and that the nature of psychological ills is inherently interactive. It isn't that something is wrong with an individual's psychic machinery, there are no loose screws inside. We don't know how and need not know how, to replace worn-out units inside him. He isn't a machine, a self-contained box, but rather an ongoing interaction process.

Thus our definitions of psychopathology have shifted from the Freudian typology of individuals to new concepts about an individual's interactions. The new concepts aren't well worked out yet. Psychotherapy has been understood to be an interaction of patient and therapist as two genuine people who must respond to each other from out of, and to, each other's experiential processes. But, further, much of psychopathology has been recognized as a matter of family relationships (Mowrer, Bowen, Bateson, Jackson, Haley), so the patient can be thought of as "the individual in whom the family's illness manifests itself" (Bowen, 1960). Further, it has been recognized that social class (the Negro, lower class, etc.) has its peculiar sorts of psychopathology, that the community is the locus of psychopathology. This has led to an entirely new view of psychopathology, expressed for instance in the often cited fact that "these days we get very few classical hysterias. . . ." If psychopathology were a form of illness of the human psyche, why isn't hysteria around anymore? Has the mosquito that breeds the hysteria germ been wiped out?

Today we recognize that psychological ills are a function of culture, environment, community practices, and typical situations. As society changes, so do the ills of its members. A few wealthy persons might be able to afford individual psychotherapy, but today's social planners are rightly impatient with this mode of treatment because it is incapable of reaching the mass of people who need it. Instead, social programs are coming more and more to the fore. I include here poverty programs, Vista, the Job Corps, community development, community mental health programs, rural planning, and so on.

The troubled person is all one; he doesn't have one set of psychological and another set of situational problems, especially if he is poor. The mass of our patients in state hospitals are not there because of psychological problems as such, but because they can't be sent home. The masses of troubled people need help with their total situation, not just with some separate psychological part. At any rate, we can't supply them with enough "doctors" to deal with just that part. Furthermore, while they remain in an institution they cannot get fully well, and when they go home to the original sickmaking situation which hasn't changed, they get sick again, and return. A few years ago, if we arrived at this realization, we would say "to get this one patient well you'd have to change the whole system . . ." and we meant, sadly, that of course you couldn't. But now, we are setting about to do just that.

The current flood of social programs and community programs, however, will fail unless they include the sort of therapeutic conditions and individual process we have been discovering in successful cases of therapy. Social programs must build into themselves some intimate, close sensitive human interaction. They must give each individual an individual. Of course, these can't be professionals, nor even subprofessionals. There will never be enough of them. Instead, we must devise ways in which ordinary people can provide the therapeutic processes for one another.

Prediction Three: Hospital patterns of providing therapeutic interactions will be devised.

In our research on psychotherapy with schizophrenics in Wisconsin we soon saw that an individual physician or psychologist, going out to the hospital twice a week, could carry very few patients. Even these few, being schizophrenic, lower class, threatened, and unused to therapy and emotional talk, refused to see therapists. We found a way to scare them less, and we could work with very many more by providing therapists "available" on the ward. (Gendlin, 1961). These therapists were willing to speak to any patient who came, sometimes sitting quietly next to a silent patient, sometimes over many months exchanging only glances and understood signs of greeting with patients, or allowing fearful patients to approach a relationship and back off again, without thereby wasting months of therapist time. This "ward availability" pattern is also used by student volunteers (a group known as VISA) at the University of Chicago when they visit Chicago State Hospital. Among the gigantic regular hospital staff, with all their variety of different professionals, none are there just to be available for patients to talk to. It would not cost much to provide some, especially if these need not be college trained people. I am therefore sure that more and more we will leave behind the whole pattern of the office situation where two or three times weekly we are shut in with one individual for fifty minutes. We will find patterns in which a few available persons can offer intimate, sensitive, understanding relationships in many contexts.

I spoke of the structure of hospitals, but "availables" can be in schools, community organizations, in any social program whatever.

Prediction Four — Everyone will routinely learn in school the skills of experiential focusing, listening, and relating.

We are close to the time when every school system will teach skills of personal problem solving and helpful interacting to everyone, much as today we teach every child calisthenics and personal hygiene. Of course, some will go on to become very able at this (like athletes), but even those not especially talented will be taught a minimal amount.

Our researches recently have shown that successful clients engage in a type of interview behavior that shows experiential focusing right from the start (a finding which Kirtner was the first to discover in 1957).[3] Eventual

[3] See Chapter 8 by Kirtner and Cartwright and the related Chapter 10 by Tomlinson and Hart.

failure clients, though they may stay in psychotherapy for years, can be picked out from the start as those who do not focus on their felt meanings. They don't seem to know how. We have not been teaching people to do this, because we thought only therapy could show them how . . . but it turns out, instead, that therapy doesn't even begin if they don't know how. Thus we must teach this skill. Since it is a matter of focusing attention on preconceptual felt meanings, it doesn't require complex concepts and can probably be taught quite early in school.

Eventually we will teach everyone the experiential zigzag of focusing on felt meaning and verbalizing from that. We will teach everyone how to listen to another person and attend to, ask about, attempt to help them articulate their felt meaning. We will teach certain very specific skills of interaction; for example, the sort of honest self-expression that creates a close relationship because it doesn't blame the other person, one in which an individual begins honest expressions by starting with his own shortcomings and upsetting weaknesses first. Finally, to complete this envisioned teaching program, we will teach everyone how to recognize when he is in over his depth with someone, when he is being weirdly twisted around and is unable to feel whole, sound, and in touch with himself in the relationship, i.e., how to recognize the time to bring a third person into the relationship for help. Thus professionals will be needed more than ever when this society-wide teaching comes about, since more people will need more of such "supervision" or "consultation," which will then be known by some routine term.

In this way we will give psychotherapy back to people, for it cannot indefinitely remain the property of a professional group but must be translated into society-wide applicability.

The training developed so far is not yet being given routinely to everyone. We are at the half-way point, namely, the training of nonprofessionals who function in professional roles.

For example, in trying to bring together the community population and the isolated hospital patients, I devised a plan (now being put into action by the State of Illinois) for the training of "interveners." The name comes not from the word "intervention," but from the need to fill the gap which "intervenes" between hospital and community. These will be nonprofessionals, and if the desire of the Office of Manpower and Training is followed, they will be selected from the population presently called "unemployables." They will be trained to work with patients in the hospital and will spend two days a week there. But they will also be trained as community workers and will spend three days a week in a given neighborhood, its schools, churches, jails, social agencies, community organizations, and local hospital wards. They will help reconnect the patient to the community, and they will be able to discuss this with patients in advance and try them out in the community before they are quite recovered — so that they can become recovered. Interveners will be able to take patients back to the hospital where they need not become lost indefinitely — for the interveners can realistically promise to bring the patients out again. Like many other currently ongoing modes of training nonprofessionals, this project will create a new and useful, quasi-professional, job-defined role. I also consider training hospital volunteer women a vital step along this same road. I have been training such women not to pass out doughnuts and coffee or to play cards but instead to interact helpfully and sensitively with patients.

Prediction Five: There will be two new social institutions: (a) an individual relationship for everyone; (b) a group for everyone.

Hospital patients are only one subgroup of the population that needs close relationships. This is true of every other segment of our population as well. It is true of the women who now come as volunteers, but it is also true of the women who stay home with their children all day, every day. It is true of the students who are forever discussing the anomie of the large university and of the high school students who take so enthusiastically to any personally relevant activity whether group or individualized. It is the case with old people, and the same need is found in churches and factories. There is no reason to think of the hospitalized patients as the only group in need of intimate relationships. The picture makes much more sense if it is enlarged. Finally, the need for preventive measures to avoid the creation of psychotics and neurotics leads to the same conclusion, namely, the teaching for, and the providing of, routinely available close relationships so that everyone can learn to experience and express himself openly and know how to receive others who do so.

Therefore we have at last taken the plunge: in one study we are instructing pairs of ordinary individuals. They draw numbers to determine who is *T* and who is *C*. The instructions[4] then ask the one person to choose a personal

---

[4] The exact instructions were: We want 1 to choose some personal problem that is bothering you now, but which you also feel you could explore profitably with your partner during this afternoon's session. We don't expect you to reveal everything about yourself, but it would be better for you to choose a real problem that's important to you and not say everything about it, than to choose an unimportant problem that you feel very comfortable saying everything about.

We want 2 to respond as you wish to your partner, keeping in mind that the purpose of your discussion is to try to help him with the problem he chooses to explore with you.

Keep on what's crucial to you ("patient"); if you (to "patient") feel you're off on a tangent that isn't interesting to you, or if your partner is asking you questions and you would rather talk at that moment about another part of the problem, say that. Talk about what's important to you, what you feel at any moment is getting to the heart of your problem. If you find that the problem you have chosen to talk about is part of a bigger problem, then follow that where it takes you. The role we are setting up for you is not one in which you are both to hold in your real feelings until later; say what you are feeling now. If you are feeling something and wonder whether it will fit in with your role here to say it, go ahead and say it. This means anything about yourself, your partner, or your role here. You might want to say to your partner, "I don't like the way you are directing the questions" or "What is all this nonsense anyway?" We're not prescribing here the direction your discussion should take — you'll probably want to say different things — but we are encouraging you to say whatever feels important for you to say at any moment.

problem of real importance in his life. We say: we would rather you chose a really important problem even though you might not feel free to tell everything about it, than one you could say everything about but which isn't so important. In the next twenty minutes we will ask that you try to understand the problem better and to help yourself with it. We will ask the other person to help you in doing so. If you don't find what he does helpful, and you wish he would respond differently, please tell him.

After twenty minutes we then give the Focusing Manual (and plan to give further quite specific instructions) to such experimental-subject therapists and patients. Then we ask them to continue another twenty minutes. We are not ready to report findings from this research as yet, but we can already see a promising and safe method in this use of ordinary persons as therapists in combination with research to measure behaviors of both patients and as therapists.

I consider the necessary skills quite numerous and specific and am in the process of devising specific words for specific procedures of focusing, listening, and interacting. I don't think that psychotherapy is merely a general and constant attitude nor does it depend upon the sort of person you happen to be. A full-blown experiential vocabulary for instructions of this sort is now being devised and will undoubtedly develop further as many ordinary people engage in psychotherapy with each other.

The day is fast waning when one must plead "sick" to get a sensitive and impartial listener and willing interactor. Consider how foolish it has really been, that we have given this only to people who were under sufficient pressure to plead "sick" and incapable of helping themselves (which in our society is supposed to be a very bad thing). In fact, there is plenty of evidence that everyone needs someone, that humans are interaction processes in their very nature.

But we know, for example, from the Manhattan study, that up to 80 per cent of the people show measurable psychological disturbances of the sort requiring psychotherapy. Does this mean everyone is sick? Or does it mean that this is the human condition, and that our society lacks institutions that offer the sort of interhuman process needed by people? I believe it shows the latter. In the future the individual engaging in the sort of experiential process defined here won't be called a "patient," nor a "client," but a person. There will be social patterns such that everyone will routinely have some other individual with whom he is the therapist and one with whom he is the patient. For example, Goodman's[5] pattern of older high school students working with younger boys can easily be made routine in all school systems. It can become a "social institution," that is, a regular social pattern, offered routinely. Many other patterns are conceivable. To get and keep such a relationship, one would only have to want it.

[5] Refer to Chapter 18.

Prediction Six: A second new social institution: (b) everyone will belong to a group.

For a long time we haven't had anything on the group level that corresponds even to "friendship." To be in a group, one has to plead sick (therapy) or one has to have (or pretend to have) an interest in photography, adult education, or politics. Often groups want to continue to meet, though their reason for being is over (after the election, for example) and no socially understood pattern exists for continuing a group simply because there is a human need to belong to a group. But such a pattern is coming. We already have psychotherapy groups, T groups, development groups, sensitivity groups, church groups, political groups, encounter groups, marathon groups, management skills groups, brainstorming groups, all quite similar. Soon it will become understood that everyone needs to be in a group.

While these groups have different names, and in some cases deal with very different contents (e.g., religious doubts in a church group, politics in a Students for a Democratic Society group), a certain vital group process occurs in all of them: the newcomer finds himself listened to, responded to; he discovers that he makes sense, can articulate feelings and reach out to others, be accepted, understood, appreciated, responded to closely. He discovers that there is room for him as a person and not just as a maker of canned, appropriate statements or as a player of prescribed roles. His previously almost dumb and silent self becomes intensely alive, being in this group is intense and it is growth-producing. He "breaks through," finds himself as not just a player of roles, but also as speaking from himself as an experiencing, feeling, human being. He finds he can work with both roles and felt aliveness. His life outside the group naturally profits enormously from this breakthrough, as he lives other situations less constrictedly and role-definedly, and more in terms of an interplay between his real feelings and the prescribed words and roles. But typically, this is only the first stage of what often then becomes a less desirable group for him.

For a time after his breakthrough, he helps others to "break through," but does not really need to do this anymore for himself. During this period he attends partly because it is rewarding to aid others in the breaking-through process, but partly because even after breaking through one needs a group. However, the constantly new members keep such a mixed group at the breakthrough stage, and the veteran members all reluctantly drop out after getting tired of trying to pretend that they are always breaking through all over again. (This can be observed also in political and other sorts of groups, since the basic experiential process is always the same.)

In the future we will provide people with a quiet closed group in which they can move in depth, tell how things are, share life, so to speak, perhaps say little at times, perhaps do major therapeutic work when needed, but always with the sense of belonging, the anchoring which such a group provides. Then, in addition, those who want to can serve a vital function in the other type of group that is open to newcomers, where a few veterans who know how to relate intimately can swiftly bring a whole group of new people to the break-through point.

Such groups — and such individual relationships — will focus on the experiential process. In most settings an individual must be just a certain way to be appropriate, he must talk about a certain topic, or he must behave in a certain way, share attitudes, speak about himself in a certain way only. Friendship, marriage, work, church — these settings define certain narrow bands of behavior as appropriate, and nothing else will do. In the groups I think are coming, anything someone does will be appropriate if it "means something to him," i.e., has an experiential reference for him.

But, of course, this also means that discussions in such groups will go beyond abstractions. One will more often ask "why do you hold that view?" than, "Is this view tenable? What general assumptions is it based on?" The *experiential* reasons and bases of the concern may turn out to be very different, not relevant except personally, and very far from what one might have expected on abstract grounds alone. Anyone with any views might be welcomed into such a group, and people would thereby learn what sort of personal processes go into other people's having the views they do (which, currently, we can't imagine).

Prediction Seven: Modes of human thinking and discussion will become much more widely creative and very much more specific compared to current abstractionism in thought and science.

Before the nineteenth century people held that the order of nature had an underlying rational mathematical system, and that man, too, was subject to it (Vico, Spinoza). The nineteenth century discovered a whole raft of different irrational aspects in man, and rationalism was pushed back to a few last-ditch areas. Some held that by comparing different societies, both ancient and primitive, one would arrive at a lowest common denominator of human nature that would be lawful (Comte). Some held that only the laws of economics and economic change were amenable to rational scientific analysis and could then indirectly explain everything else (Marx). Some held that the laws of psychology would provide a rational scheme, which would then explain everything else (Freud). But in the twentieth century none of these attempts at a reductive science of man have been shown to work.

All rational schemes are too thin and abstract, too simple and artificial, to represent human processes. We are more complicated than our schemes. We make schemes — and a lot else besides! Schemes are tools, like words, therapeutic procedures, social roles. The tool doesn't become the thing; one must still look at the thing one works on to guide the tool.

The experiential method is based in philosophy (Gendlin, 1965a, 1962). Philosophy examines the basic types of concepts that are current, the ways of slicing up what we perceive and observe. Current philosophy, coming from the history of thought I just described, centers on the fact that schemes, models, systems, are not enough. The human activities of living, acting, and speaking in human situations are the bigger context within which any scheme, system, model, or concept must be evaluated.

But how can we evaluate the explicit, the precise, the logically formed against the "bigger context" that is implicit, preconceptual, lived and acted, but not logically formed in just one way?

In psychotherapy we do this by checking every step of verbalization (the client's and the therapist's) against the client's felt sense, his experiential, bodily felt meaning. Thus we move back and forth between explicit, precise verbalizations and preconceptual, imprecise, yet governing experiencing. In society we will seek to establish this same zigzag method between the explicit social role expectations and the individual's experiential living feel of his self. Current thinking is more and more turning to this recognition that the formed, the precise, the defined, must be held against what is experiential and implicit because while less precise it is lived, actual, existential activity.

From Linguistic Analysis in Oxford to Mysticism in San Francisco, the underlying theme is to refuse to deduce from the model, from the formed, but instead to use the formed in the context of the wider process of living that always transcends this or that form.

But of course, without precision and form we can say nothing and do little. Without form the felt and lived would be nonsensical. Experiencing is by no means lacking in form. On the contrary, it is more formed, more organized than any one scheme. Implicitly it contains history and evolution, many organic and conceptual distinctions and perceptions. Physical, animal, cultural, and individual organizations are always implicit in any living and acting. Anything actual is much *more* organized than any one system or model can tell. Therefore, when one holds precise verbalizations against the bigger context of acting and experiencing, one holds them not against something unorganized, but something organized in so many interrelated ways as to defy being represented.

The experiential method moves beyond representation. No set of words, concepts, or models can be equal to what is being experienced, lived, or done in a situation. Instead, sets of words must be seen within living and acting.

In going back and forth between felt experiencing and precise words or roles we don't discard words or social roles. We only make it possible to use these creatively, to be always more concerned with our *use* of them than with the words themselves. We are more concerned with what we are doing with them, what someone is trying to do with them, than with what can be deduced.

We will take our next set of words and our next action, not directly from what follows from some words or socially predefined roles, but from our own implicitly meaningful experiencing, which we always have as we say or do anything.

This method is another way of talking about creativity, which has long been said to depend upon an individual who does not deduce from the given way things are set up. Only by using himself, his own live felt sense of being in a particular situation, can he sense what's wrong and devise new ways, from which new possibilities will follow that weren't visible in the way things were first given.

This means that what we use is not only what the words (the role, the command) say, but what was supposed to be done with them, what was being got at in using them in the context in which they were used. It means that words aren't being viewed for what they represent (what they are a picture of), but as tools in a wider process of acting and living in situations. But this wider process is had by an individual only in a bodily, active, live felt sense. To use symbols not only in themselves, but also in whatever role they have in the wider context of living is to use them nonrepresentationally. It adds to their precise meaning the possibilities of creative change, of new definitions, and moves.

The new definitions and new moves we want aren't just any new ones. We don't want them just because they are new. (An endless number of possible new nonsense could be devised.) What we want are new definitions and new moves that will follow from, and deal with, the situations we are in, and — since situations are defined by what we seek to do in them — from our whole experiential sense of living and acting.

In this wider "nonrepresentational" method of using words and roles we ask not what a given set of words and roles is, but what one does with it.

Actually, what one does or tries to do, what an individual is getting at or pointing out, is always very, very much more specific than any of the verbalizations and schemes we have. Any human phenomenon worth studying is much more specific than the old line theories can as yet specifically locate, let alone represent. Thus, the method moves beyond theory and procedures as such, and concentrates on how they are used. In so concentrating we encourage ourselves (and others) to discriminate and work on the specific facet of observation we wish to work on — and on creating the new terms, procedures, and definitions necessary to enable others to locate the same facet.

In science this philosophy puts the emphasis on the *creation* of variables. Not that we would forego our good scientific methods of verification. We will continue to use the scientific ways of publicly checking anything we think is true. But we need to point out that our scientific method is highly developed only in the matter of *checking* conclusions and hypotheses. Where does one get hypotheses? If you think some thing A and some other thing B are connected, we have excellent methods of finding out if you're right or not. We have excellent methods of checking this in a way that doesn't depend on your own impressions. We have methods for making it possible for others to check this, to "replicate" publicly what you found. But, perhaps A and B are not the most interesting or important things to study. Perhaps R and S are also connected, and if we knew this we would be able to see and do many useful things. But no one has isolated R and S, no one has fashioned concepts for them, no one notices them as such, no one has discriminated something like R and S. We have no scientific method for first coming up with interesting items like that, interesting "variables" for scientific research. Today this is still unscientific. Every scientist is expected somehow to come up with variables, perhaps in his sleep, in the shower, or as a result of whatever naturalistic observations he conducts.

Prediction Eight: There will come about a science of man which includes the man who is the scientist and which defines specific and significant aspects of interactive living.

I have already said that, in my opinion, the chief needed advance in the science of man is the discrimination and definition of much more specific variables than the general and ambiguous ones we use today.

Furthermore, as with all symbols, scientific terms must be seen in terms of what they do, not merely what they say. Scientific terms must come to be "operational," that is, they must be tied to specific procedures, and we must study the results of these procedures. But if we place this model of operational science into the context of life, we can see that current science is a mere stick figure of what we need. We want to specify the very specific meaningful "operations" we engage in with other people, and we want to specify the results that are obtained. Client-centered research is some of the first meaningful research of this sort: it defines certain ways of approaching and acting toward someone, and it defines the sort of process that then occurs in him. Of course, we seek very much greater specificity — we seek a whole vocabulary of specific terms with which to study how we are and what we do with each other.

I am predicting a science not of individual differences, but of different specific manners of approaching and relating with each other. To dramatize this, let me cite here our discovery that, for psychotherapy purposes, schizophrenic people differ from neurotics but are very much the same as normal people! That is, normal people require some of the same specific approach behaviors by anyone who wants to relate intimately with them. In our Wisconsin Research (Rogers, 1967) we learned to work with others who did not seek to relate closely with us and who had no real idea, in advance, of what such relating would be. They seemed not to know that one could articulate and communicate one's feelings about living in the typical way we are familiar with from psychotherapy. In a very different context, we see now that the same methods are needed with the parents of children in play therapy whenever the parents do not seek psychotherapy for themselves. In short, identified here is a category of therapist behavior, and a category of client behavior, both cutting right across the usual categories of individual psychopathology. Of course, much more specific subcategories are coming.

The totally nonexpressive silent "schizophrenic" patient who sits immobile for hours and hours, and is found always in the same chair in the hospital day room — he belongs in a different category for therapist behavior than the

562 *Directions of Change*

"schizophrenic" who, while always silent, is enormously expressive, reactive, and sensitive, and presents a different expressive behavior every moment. The therapist must use his experiencing differently with each. Again this distinction cuts across the usual psychopathology, and again different ways of approaching a person must be specified for each.

This is the age in which we are becoming scientifically aware of ourselves. Just as three hundred years ago we began to develop a vocabulary of nature, we will now develop a vocabulary of man's experience. As we develop this science of experience facilitation, we will thereby make the teaching of it in school much more possible and effective.

REFERENCES

Bowen, M. Family participation in schizophrenia. In R. D. Jackson (Ed.), *The etiology of schizophrenia.* New York: Basic Books, 1960.

Gendlin, E. T. Initiating psychotherapy with "unmotivated" patients. *Psychiatric Quarterly,* 1961, 1, 34.

Gendlin, E. T. *Experiencing and the creation of meaning.* New York: Free Press, 1962.

Gendlin, E. T. Expressive meanings. In J. M. Edic (Ed.), *Invitation to phenomenology.* Chicago: Quadrangle Books, 1965a.

Gendlin, E. T. What are the grounds of explication? *The Monist,* 1965b, 49, No. 1.

Gendlin, E. T. Psychotherapy and community psychology. *Psychotherapy,* Vol. 5, No. 2, June, 1968, pp. 67-72.

Gendlin, E. T. and Beebe, J. Experiential groups. In G. M. Gazda (Ed.), *Basic innovations to group psychotherapy.* Springfield, Illinois: Charles C. Thomas, 1968.

Gendlin, E. T., Diesenhaus, H., Oberlander, M. and Pearson, L. Psychologists and government programs. In B. Lubin and E. E. Levitt (Eds.), *The clinical psychologist.* Chicago: Aldine, 1967.

Gendlin, E. T., Kelly, J. J., Raulinaitis, V. B., Spaner, F. E. Voltunteers as a major asset in the treatment program. *Mental Hygiene,* Vol. 50, No. 3, July, 1966, pp. 421-427.

Rogers, C. R. (Ed.), *The therapeutic relationship and its impact.* Madison, Wisconsin: University of Wisconsin Press, 1967.

30

Beyond Psychotherapy - The Applied Psychology of the Future[1]

JOSEPH HART

Beyond psychotherapy? Why beyond? To what beyond? How beyond? These are the questions discussed in this chapter. That the answers offered are speculative is indicated by the subtitle. This is a "programmatic essay" rather than a research summary or a theoretical integration; it is, if you like, a preface to a book not yet written.

Some people never read prefaces. But prefaces are better, in many books, than their contents. In them authors usually speak directly, personally, candidly. They tell what they sought to accomplish and why, how they began, and what remains to be done. Prefaces present programs. Now and then I've thought of a book that would be all prefaces. It would certainly please people like me who weary of the emphasis on facts in today's social and behavioral sciences. Facts spill over us like beans burst from an overfull bag. They are indigestible. As a steady diet they dull the mind. Not that I am opposed to facts (or beans), but tasty facts are what we need, facts worth remembering, facts that nourish. Most of what is served us does nothing more than produce a feeling of fullness and, later, flatulence.

I cannot see far enough to speculate for a whole book's worth of prefaces but will try to fill this chapter. The contents must be considered prefatory because nothing is discussed in detail; instead, a program for thought and action is presented. The program attempts to reformulate and redirect the task of applied psychology.

[1] I thank Dr. Alan Gross, Dr. Perry London, Dr. Steve Shapiro, and Miss Betty Egle for their careful readings of the manuscript.

563

Why Beyond? Where Beyond?

Many of the preceding chapters have already gone in directions that depart from traditional psychotherapy. The client-therapist encounter is taken out of the office into the home and community. The therapist does not wear the suit and tie of the psychologist, social worker, or psychiatrist but the jeans and sneakers of the college student. The therapist may be a housewife, a parent, a neighbor, a friend. Technique and theory are replaced by honesty, caring, warmth, and the sharing of experience. All these departures are desirable and significant; they have gone and are continuing to go in needed directions.

The conclusion to be drawn from these new directions is clear — *in helping relationships there are no professionals;* there are only people. Some people are better at helping than others. Some get paid for helping. There seems to be no necessary relationship between being paid and possessing skill as a helper.

People are frequently made less effective in giving or receiving help because of an unthinking adherence to the false belief that professionals exist. This can prevent people from being real, not only in therapy but also in other close relationships. Most children experience sometime in their lives the shock of discovery that comes when they see their mother, their father, or their teacher as a person, as a distinct individual. Often this realization comes when the child sees the familiar person in an unfamiliar setting: father at work, mother in the hospital, teacher at a party. They don't look right. They're different, and other people are different toward them. Daddy is not daddy, but Jim; mommy is Mrs. Somebody; and Miss Teacher is Evelyn. Unfortunately, this salutary shock is not reciprocal. At the next meeting, mom is still likely to act like a mom and dad like a dad and, most definitely, teacher like a teacher. People too often live their roles, not their lives. To help people live by their experience rather than by rote rules and roles, a therapist must be someone who does more than "act like a therapist." If he does not, he will merely teach others to "act like patients."

To its credit, the new psychotherapy has recognized that helping relationships are no more and no less than encounters between people. Yet the potential profundity of these encounters has not been fully realized. Psychotherapy, even after changing its locus, its participants, and its methods, continues to do repair work. Psychotherapy's usual task is to bring people from below the social norm to the norm. There is no need to quibble about the desirability of moving some people toward the norm. Many popular criticisms of "adjustment" are misdirected. An autistic child who is helped to communicate, adjusts, and that is good; a sexually frigid woman who becomes capable of sexual satisfaction, adjusts, and for the better; a hospitalized schizophrenic who is helped to live and work outside the hospital, adjusts, and his world becomes wider. Psychotherapy can and does help people adjust in ways that lessen their misery and increase their competence.

But what then? Our ability to repair people should become at least as good as our ability to repair automobiles. We should have as many expert helpers in our society as expert mechanics. But once tuned up and ready to go, where do we travel? Psychotherapists do not tell us. Asking a therapist how to live is like asking a mechanic where to drive; neither believes he should be asked and neither has useful answers.

It is a central task of applied psychology to develop a meaningful ethic. Historically science has been permitted to ask "what" and "how" while religion and philosophy have retained the "where's" and "why's," an arrangement which is becoming outmoded. Religion must become more scientific and science, more religious.

Critics of contemporary psychotherapy such as London (1964), Mowrer (1964), and Szasz (1961) have demolished the notion that psychotherapy is value-free. Their criticisms can be extended to the whole of applied social science (Gouldner, 1962). Within client-centered therapy, too, there has been a move away from insisting on a neutral value stance for the therapist toward an explicit recognition of the value commitments therapists must make. The distance from nondirective therapy to experiential therapy can be measured as much by new explications in values as by new developments in technique, theory, and research (Rogers, 1957, 1964).

Science, the religion of modern man, does not yet include ethics and religious experience; it does not help man to be religious. Science discredits the old answers to questions about the meaning of life but does not provide its own answers. This leaves modern man adrift in an ocean, floating amid the flotsam and jetsam of old moral systems which take him nowhere. He cannot cling to the old religions because he does not believe in them, but as they sink, he sinks, for there is nothing else.

An adequate applied psychology must speak to the very practical problems of ethics and religious experience. Doing so leads to more than psychotherapeutic repair work; it leads to a psychology that can guide growth as well as correct stunting. There are two parts to this new applied psychology; they might be called *psychotechnics,* or *psychology as the science of will,* and *experimental mysticism,* or *psychology as the science of soul.* Psychotechnics refers to the psychology of performance, experimental mysticism to the psychology of awareness. Psychotechnics tries to further individual fulfillment in all kinds of psychological functioning: sensory-perceptual, motor, emotional, cognitive, and social. In experimental mysticism a transformation of awareness is sought — what religionists call the realization of soul.

One immediate reservation about these directions I describe as "beyond psychotherapy" is whether they can and should be conceived as extensions of client-centered psychotherapy. Many client-centered therapists will disagree with the desirability of what I wish to encourage. They will feel that neither psychotechnics nor experimental mysticism, especially the latter, are reasonable extensions of client-centered thinking and practice.

Of course I disagree. It seems to me there are two sources in client-centered psychotherapy that lead directly to experimental mysticism as a necessary development within practical psychology. One source is in the theory of experiencing. This theory, discussed throughout this book, posits the locus of man's existence within the *flow* of his own meaningful experience. The man who cannot live in this flow lives at a lower level of consciousness, deprived of his potentiality, of his legitimate birthright. Clearly, this secular theoretical position is compatible, if not identical, with the religious attitudes of mysticism. The way to realization is within.

And what of the man who has found the way within? This is the second connection between client-centered therapy and experimental mysticism. The client-centered ideal of the person who is able to claim his birthright and live within the fulfilling being of his own experience reveals a man who discovers universals. When Rogers writes about "the possibility of universal human value directions *emerging* from the experiencing of the human organism" (1964, p. 167), he expresses in modern language the age-old mystic claim that values are *discovered* within man, not imposed from without. But this happens only if a person can open himself to the direct experience of those values. To do this he must have the courage to discover himself. He must learn to be free:

> This process of the good life is not, I am convinced, a life for the faint-hearted. It involves the stretching and growing of becoming more and more of one's potentialities. It involves the courage to be. It means launching oneself fully into the stream of life. Yet the deeply exciting thing about human beings is that when the individual is inwardly free, he chooses as the good life this process of becoming (Rogers, 1957, p. 300).

Psychology is necessarily closer to philosophy than are the other sciences. Because of this there have been many attempts in psychology's brief history to define its methods and subject matter in scientific ways that would exclude the meandering circles of philosophy. Now that psychology is beyond its era of "isms" perhaps it is possible to see once more some value in philosophical meanderings.

Philosophy seems to repeat itself, to develop in a cyclical pattern, not because philosophers have one mental leg shorter than the other, but because the same questions recur in every age — the fundamental human questions of evil, God, truth, knowledge, justice, and beauty. If we as psychologists begin to speak to these same questions (and I believe we must), then we will need to acknowledge the psychological directions taken by the great religious teachers of the world. They can tell us where to begin our search for answers, for values, for freedom.

Before we can turn, however, to a psychological examination of religion, philosophy, or mysticism for our answers, we must examine the state of modern applied psychology. Can it be of any use to us in our attempts at a greater understanding of life and our search for a fuller way of living?

The Naked King

Contemporary psychology is like the emperor with invisible clothes. It possesses most of the accoutrements of the other sciences: laboratories, computers, electronic equipment, statistics, mathematics, journals, national and international, associations, conventions, and textbooks. Psychology also has achieved the exalted status of hidden hyphenation: psychopharmacology, psychobiology, psychophysiology, neuropsychology, and so on. The divisions of the kingdom of psychology range from old fiefdoms like experimental psychology and clinical psychology to the new border areas like consumer psychology.

Still, the king is naked. The clothing of a science is made from applied knowledge, and psychology does not yet have a true fabric of applied knowledge. The reasons for this are located in three misconceptions about the nature of applied psychology, misconceptions which are widely and uncritically believed. This uncritical acceptance retards development of a genuine applied psychology. The misconceptions are: (1) applied science is fundamentally quantitative; (2) external control is the appropriate aim of applied psychology; and (3) religious experience is beyond the purview of scientific psychology. Let us now consider why these are misconceptions and how they arose.

Misconception One — Applied Science is Fundamentally Quantitative

The contrary is true — applied science is fundamentally *qualitative*. Only after both technology and scientific theory progress to very sophisticated levels does applied science emerge at all, and even further sophistication is required before applied science becomes quantitative. Technology consists essentially of qualitative observations, rules, empirical generalizations, and compendia of techniques.

Technology *precedes* theory. People knew how to build bridges and arches and cathedrals long before they could apply the formal language of mechanics to explain and predict which structures would stand and which would topple. Not until very recently in the history of physical technology were engineers able to calculate structural stresses by applying the mathematics of vector algebra.

Engineer and historian James Kip Finch says of the relationship between quantitative science and engineering:

> For centuries natural science and engineering had gone their own ways.
> It was a *developed* science and a *developed* practical art that, at long last,

uncovered a mutually stimulating liaison. Every practical art is based to some degree on a practical science stemming from rules derived from experience. . . . Some practical knowledge of mathematics and at least some simple quali-tative mechanics had, thus, long found use in engineering practice. . . . At the same time engineering remained primarily a construction art, limited to simple and plentiful materials — wood, stone, and brick — to manual labor and to long-known structural forms. Here, experience was the most impor-tant teacher. In short, the need for science in engineering unfolded slowly. It was not until the 18th century in France that attempts were made to bridge the gap between practical needs and new scientific insights. Thus, contrary to popular belief, the major role of science in engineering has been, as in medicine, the reinforcement and stimulation of the growth of a practical science within the technique of the profession itself. The major inventions in engineering and industry . . . were won through experience, patient trial-and-error rather than effects to find applications for a priori knowledge of natural science. Roads, canals, and railroads, arch and truss bridges, the steam engine and early machines, many chemical, industrial, and metallurgi-cal products and processes, and, in our own day, the internal-combustion en-gine and the airplane — these not only predated but prompted scientific study and analysis (1960, xxiv-xxv).

The same basic reliance upon empiricism and practical technology is found, both historically and contemporaneously, in medicine. Everyone knows that the surgeons of the Renaissance were barbers, but few realize that the work of today's surgeons more closely resembles the practical art of barbering than the abstract and quantitative work of the scientist.

If the two exemplars of applied science, the engineer and the physician, are, in origin and practice, technologists and artisans, then why have psycholo-gists downgraded technology? Why have we ignored the fact that technology precedes science? Why have psychologists not recognized that applied sci-ence is essentially qualitative? Or, asked differently, why is physics and not obstetrics the model for applied psychology? The answers to these questions are not difficult to find. Scientific psychology was founded by physicists and physiologists who wanted to emulate physics. Whether we pick Helmholtz or Fechner or Wundt or Titchener or Pavlov or Thorndike or Watson or Hull as *the* founder of scientific psychology, makes no difference: they all sought to make psychology a science, *like physics*. Unfortunately, their notions of both physics and applied science were excessively narrow.

Titchener was one of the most influential proselytizers for this physicalistic view of psychology; he was so effective that the behaviorists retained physical-ism while rejecting Titchener's structuralism, ". . . there can be no essential difference between the raw materials of physics and the raw materials of psychology . . . in general, the method of psychology is much the same as the method of physics" (Titchener, 1910, excerpted in Herrnstein and Boring, 1966, pp. 599, 604). A few years later Titchener's student, E. G. Boring, stated the physicalistic bias more blatantly, "Historically science is physical science. Psychology, if it is to be a science, must be like physics" (1963, p. 6).

If psychology as a pure science was to be like physics then, of course, applied psychology would need to be like engineering. But in their desire to be "scientific" psychology's founding fathers wanted no associations with the practical arts or with technology. So they sought the impossible, an applied psychology derived from pure science and dissociated from practical knowledge. Today we must recognize that for psychology, even more than for physics and physiology, there is a necessary core of applied science that is essentially qualitative.

Misconception Two — External Control is the Appropriate Goal of Applied Psychology

When psychology finally did begin to develop a kind of technological knowledge, it was not coincidence that the development was stimulated by a thinker who rejected physics as a desirable model for experimental and applied psychology. B. F. Skinner, in his writings and research, emerges as a technologist (see especially "A case history in scientific method" [Skinner, 1959] and *Walden Two* [Skinner, 1948]) who rejects mathematical models and quantitative functions as the desiderata or criteria of science. Instead, he emphasizes control, the moment-to-moment control of the individual organism:

> When you have the responsibility of making absolutely sure that a given organism will engage in a given sort of behavior at a given time, you quickly grow impatient with theories of learning. Principles, hypotheses, theorems, satisfactory proof at the .05 level of significance that behavior at a choice point shows the effect of secondary reinforcement — nothing could be more irrelevant. No one goes to the circus to see the average dog jump through a hoop significantly oftener than untrained dogs raised under the same circumstances, or to see an elephant demonstrating a principle of behavior (1959, p. 370).

In short, like all technologists, Skinner does what he must — he gets down to cases.

Good, so far. Skinner did not accept the idea that science is fundamentally quantitative. He grasped the need for a gradual acquisition of technology and he realized that model building is insignificant in the early growth of technology. But he did not extend this effort at promoting technology to the promotion of internal, self-directed control. Skinner promotes behavioral engineering, external control. He gave up one misconception only to perpetuate and enlarge another. Before extending this criticism of what Skinner did not do, consider one manifestation of his influence, behavior therapy.

The major contribution of behavior therapy to applied psychology will eventually be quite different from what its founders intended. Breger and McGaugh (1965) ably attack the pretensions of behavior therapy as a theory-based practice of therapy. The learning theories that behavior therapists espouse — whether Hullian, Skinnerian, or Pavlovian — are altogether too sparse to guide the practice of therapy with cognizing, purposeful human beings. Obviously, the practice of behavior therapy is connected only remotely with the theories said to guide the therapist. In some instances, the learning theories behavior therapists claim to apply have no terms for phenomena the therapists work with, phenomena such as images, plans, and feelings. (As an aside, it seems to me, too, that attempting to establish a technology of therapy while ignoring the personal characteristics of the therapists who apply the technology is merely another foolish attempt to emulate engineering. When someone gets around to studying those behavior therapists who are successful and those who are not, it will be found, I am sure, that many of the personal traits necessary for psychotherapist are also important for a behavior therapist.)

What is left? Just this; the value of behavior therapy is its intense practicality. Behavior therapists are attempting to develop those necessary step-by-step routines that must be the basis of every technology. When behavior therapists stop calling themselves behavior therapists and recognize that they work with much more than behavior, their techniques will be seen as very close to those of many traditional forms of psychotherapy. They will also find many affinities with Hindu psychology, as developed so elaborately in the various types of yoga.

In my view, evidence that human beings can be both purposive and conscious provides a basis for a much more significant kind of applied psychology than that envisioned by Skinner. This new applied psychology would teach people to become self-directing and self-controlling. It would be a psychology of fulfillment and transformation as developed in psychotechnics and experimental mysticism.

It is not that I reject the Skinnerian approach, but that it is conceptually incomplete. Moreover, unless people are taught to realize their capacities, they remain little more than machines, responsive objects for Skinnerian manipulations. For technology to bring forth those potentials of man beyond his machine and animal nature, a different orientation is needed. Skinner's technology is inadequate because he does not recognize emergent functions — those subjective and behavioral consequences that follow from self-development. I suppose, in one sense, Skinner's applied psychology could be called a naturalistic psychology, whereas the applied psychology I am calling for is transnaturalistic.

Skinner, like all naturalists, starts with certain behavioral givens. Then, through the precise application of reinforcement, the givens are combined and recombined, sequenced and coordinated, until a complex performance is achieved — pigeons are taught to play ping pong. Nothing else is possible unless one assumes that emergent processes can surface with training. The naturalistic applied psychologist looks only for new combinations of the givens of behavior. The transnaturalist looks for new levels of psychological functioning. The two start from contrasting assumptions about the goal of applied psychology, even though their methods often can be very similar. This difference in assumptions relates directly to the emphasis on external versus internal control. Someone who believes man can evolve from within will not try to impose outer fixed forms. Instead, he will try to discover in what ways conscious animals can become men. A full exploration of how man can discover himself requires that the psychologist relinquish both his arrogant and his timorous attitudes about religion.

Misconception Three — Religious Experience is Outside the Purview of Scientific Psychology

Anyone who adheres to Misconception One or Misconception Two also, by default, will accept the proposition that religious experience is outside the purview of scientific psychology. But it would be of no interest to discuss the position of Skinner and other behaviorists on religion because they are so attached to the assumptions of naturalism that they do not consider trans-naturalistic alternatives. Their position is no position; religious experience, along with other subjective experiences, does not exist.

Although this nonposition is certainly widespread among those who style themselves "behavioral scientists," it is perhaps less influential in the larger arena of social science than the psychoanalytic position. No doubt the psychoanalytic view is well known to most readers. Stated most simply, it is the view that religious experience is symptomatic of psychopathology. To be religious is to be sick-minded. In this view, the psychology of religion becomes a branch of abnormal psychology. Religious experiences are not informative for the person who has them; they do not impart knowledge. Rather, religion is a purveyor of illusions which must eventually fade as the hegemony of scientific analysis becomes established. It would be nonsensical, therefore, for applied psychology to concern itself with the encouragement of religious sensitivity and insight. Insofar as religious experience relates to applied psychology at all, the proper task of the applied psychologist is to rid men of the need for religious dependence.

Freud's ideas about the meaning of religion and religious experience must be considered seriously not only because of their widespread influence, but also because Freud was not misled by either of the misconceptions that influenced other applied psychologists. He recognized that the investigation of mental contents and processes must be essentially qualitative. He also recognized that the practical psychologist's basic task is the promotion of internal, not external, understanding and control. Freud did not try to make psychology an imitation of either medicine or engineering. Significantly, too, as a scientist, Freud was able to come closer than any other psychologist to the speculative, imaginative side of physics that social scientists usually ignore. Critics like Bailey (1964) who castigate Freud for excessive speculation and deficient experimentation perhaps are right about the latter but are wholly wrong about the former. The entire value of Freud's work resides in his power as a speculative thinker. He followed his imagination with boldness, scope, and subtlety, dragging the corpus of science along behind him. Critics who reject the speculative side of Freud's work with the jibe "unscientific" are themselves scientific ignoramuses, unable to discriminate between processes of scientific discovery and methods of verification.

It is regrettable that Freud did not go far enough, that he set boundaries to his speculations for *these boundaries retarded the extension of psychotherapy into pragmatic mysticism.* Freud's cautious followers mistook the boundaries for content and thereafter did not tread outside the posted domains of Freud's thought.[2]

The divisive difference between Freud and Jung was Jung's proclivity to speculate beyond the Freudian boundaries concerning religion. As Jones (1955) says,

> They brought back opposite conclusions from their studies: Freud was more confirmed than ever in his views about the importance of incestuous impulses and the Oedipus complex, where Jung tended more and more to regard these as not having the literal meaning they appeared to, but as symbolizing more esoteric tendencies in the mind (pp. 97-98).

Rieff (1966) states the difference more starkly:

> The normality of disillusion and a controlling sense of resignation, which was the most for which Freud had hoped, appeared to Jung the beginning rather than the end of therapy. He proposed to continue beyond the point where Freud felt any honest analyst must leave off. Therefore, June went about his self-appointed task of finding a new "meaning" for it all, and was paradoxical enough to be at once analytic and religious. Jung pushed the therapeutic question beyond the limit set by Freud (p. 43).

I think Freud was as limited by his commitment to the assumptions of rationalism and naturalism as the medical critics of his era were by the assumptions of materialism. In contrast to Jung, Freud never experienced personally the peak or mystical regions of subjectivity. He could only read about such experiences, and vicarious mysticism is no more convincing than vicarious dreaming. In the same way that his critics derided the idea that it might be necessary to prepare oneself before the psychic realities contained in dreams could be comprehended, so Freud refused to consider the possibility

---

[2] This criticism applies to Freudians, neo-Freudians, neo-neo-Freudians, and ego analysts. It does not apply to Norman Brown (1966), who might be called a para-Freudian. However, I do not believe that his thinking has at all influenced the *practice* of therapy, even though it has been a seminal influence among literary humanists. Yet he does point the way; "Here is the point where we have to jump, beyond psychoanalysis: They know not of Regeneration, but only of Generation. Therapy must be rebirth; but psychoanalysis does not believe that man can be born again; and so it does not believe that man is ever born at all; for the real birth is the second birth" (1966, p. 54).

that some preparatory discipline might be required to experience and comprehend the mystical:

> There is no appeal beyond reason. And if the truth of religious doctrines is dependent on an inner experience which bears witness to that truth, what is one to make of the many people who do not have that rare experience? One may expect all men to use the gift of reason that they possess, but one cannot set up an obligation that shall apply to the all on a basis that only exists for quite a few. Of what significance is it for other people that you have won from a state of ecstasy, which has deeply moved you, an imperturable conviction of the real truth of the doctrines of religion? (1957, p. 48).

As we shall see in the section on Experimental Mysticism, Freud underestimated the number of people who have mystical experiences; his "quite a few" should be read colloquially. Of course mystical experiences must be interpreted correctly; if not, they can lead to dogmatism, just as credulous dream interpretations promote word magic. Yet the fact that mystical experiences may be falsely understood and misused does not discredit their psychological reality or importance.

Apart from his own ignorance of the subjective reality of mystical experience, there was another reason for Freud's position. Even writers sympathetic to him, such as Jones and Rieff, have remarked that Freud, in his writings on religion, departed from his characteristic equanimity and became polemical. Here is an example:

> If after this survey we turn again to religious doctrines, we may reiterate that they are all illusions, they do not admit of proof, and no one can be compelled to consider them as true or to believe in them. Some of them are so improbable, so very incompatible with everything we have laboriously discovered about the reality of the world, that we may compare them — taking adequately into account the psychological differences — to delusions. Of the reality value of most of them we cannot judge; just as they cannot be proved, neither can they be refuted. We still know too little to approach them critically. The riddles of the universe only reveal themselves slowly to our inquiry, to many questions science can as yet give no answer; but scientific work is our only way to the knowledge of external reality. Again, it is merely illusion to expect anything from intuition or trance; they can give us nothing but particulars, which are difficult to interpret about our own mental life . . . (1957, pp. 54 and 55).

This polemic sounds familiar; we have heard the same criticisms before, directed *at* Freud. A polemic cacophony sounds whenever one set of metaphysical and metaphysic assumptions grates against a contrary set. As Rieff (1961) so cogently argues in *Freud: The mind of the moralist,* Freud was above all an exponent of a new morality. The new Freudian morality attempted to replace the ideal of the *religious man,* committed to intuitively known truths, with the ideal of the *psychological man,* committed to the difficult effort to be realistic and analytic. The religious man strives for transforming insight and fulfillment of his inner potential. The Freudian psychological man strives, through self-analysis, to maintain a reasonable balance between inner tension and outer release.

There is little doubt that Freud's psychological man has become the moral ideal of our age. Like most ideals, it is seen most frequently in distortions rather than realizations; the Freudian moral ideal is no easier to live than its religious counterparts. Despite these distortions, the ideal's pervasive influence is undeniable. When a moral ideal becomes sufficiently known within a culture for people to be self-conscious that they are not meeting it, then we can be sure it has become a subconscious moral precept. Psychological naïveté is as blameworthy in our culture as was sin in the Middle Ages.

Though the Freudian assumptions about religious experience and moral ideals are tacitly accepted by most social scientists, reasonable counterassumptions are available. Psychologists and other social scientists seem confused about religion. For them religion is illusion. Or, it is synonymous with religious institutions, an area of specialized study for sociologists. Or, they assume religion to be a primitive relic from prescientific cultures, something to be left to anthropologists and archeologists. Or, they assume religion is about God and creeds and therefore can be relegated to philosophers, theologians, literati, and others who have nothing more serious to think about. These views are mistaken. Religion is fundamentally about man and man's possibilities.

More explicitly, religion is about the "psychology of man's possible evolution" (Ouspensky, 1966). Sorokin states these counterassumptions clearly;

> For the partisans of the supraconscious, the total man appears not as a diadic creature, consisting of body and mind, but as a triadic being made up of body, and mind, and nous, or of body, and mind, and pneuma (or spirit or self), of the unconscious, conscious, and the supraconscious forms of beings. Accordingly, the summit of spirituality is achieved by those who succeed in identifying themselves — in their living, feeling, thinking, and acting — with the supraconscious by making their body and their unconscious and conscious mind a mere instrumentality of the immortal self (1954, p. v).

This is transnaturalism. If transnaturalism is correct or, correct or not, if it provides a tenable alternative to the prevailing assumptions of naturalism and rationalism, then social scientists must consider new approaches to religious experience.

Resume

The three misconceptions discussed here are not the only influences which opposed the development of applied psychology. But these three, taken together, sum up the biases of the modern social scientist. He prefers the quantitative and experimental to the qualitative and empirical. He emphasizes outer control by experts rather than inner control by individuals. And he adheres to the assumptions of naturalism rather than leaving room for the possibilities of transnaturalism.

Today these biases are being challenged, from within psychology by humanistic psychologists, and from outside psychology by nonprofessionals. If the histories of engineering and medicine are taken as guides, it seems likely that the significant developments in practical psychology will be accomplished mostly by nonpsychologists. Only outsiders will be free to reject the misconceptions that have curtailed applied psychology's development. I am not at all sure what the disciplinary affiliations of the new applied psychology will or should be, but I feel confident about the two kinds of practical knowledge to be developed: psychotechnics and mysticism.

Psychotechnics — Psychology as the Science of Will

The word "psychotechnics" was first used by William Stern with much the same meaning I intend here: "Today a distinction between 'applied' and 'practical' psychology is commonly made. The former is the *science* of psychological facts that are pertinent in making practical applications; the latter is the *art* and *technique* of the application itself" (1938, p. 40). Psychotechnics is the art and technique of applying psychological knowledge for human betterment.

Now consider the key work in the definition — "will." By will I mean ability or skill. Will should not be thought of as a generalized faculty or mysterious power possessed by some men and lacking in others. Will is what a person can be. Psychotechnics, the practical science of skill development, is both an art and a technology.

The word "will" connotes an image of man as an independent actor. This emphasizes that psychotechnics, unlike many other branches of applied psychology, assumes that man can act for himself. Psychotechnics is concerned with developing the range and height of man's ability to act and be. Its concern is with each person's abilities and potentialities. Psychotechnics is not psychology applied to the person but psychology used for and by the person. Its goals are not prediction, explanation, and control; they are self-awareness, self-understanding, and self-control. Psychotechnics does not fit into professional models inherited from the engineer, physician, scientist, educator, or even the psychotherapist. The psychotechnist comes closest to the teacher of the arts, the teacher of drawing, painting, sculpting, music — but in psychotechnics the materials and forms are in the student.

Both Stern's word and his program for a practical psychology were eventually supplanted by other movements in the field. Stern himself supplied some of this undermining influence. As he became more involved in the measurement of psychological abilities (he was the originator of the phrase and concept "intelligence quotient") he came to use the word "psychotechnics" to refer more to the measurement of abilities and less to their development.

The supplanting of psychotechnics by psychometrics was extremely unfortunate. Today in psychology we have many elaborate systems of measurement but only a fragmentary technology. The conceptual biases of psychometrics hindered the emergence of a practical psychology. A dictum such as "Whatever exists can be measured," although harmless and trivial in itself, fostered attitudes incompatible with the effort to put theories and principles into practice. Many psychologists came to believe that a higher level of measurement is more scientifically significant than a lower level, and even more subscribed to the belief that measuring a skill is more important than teaching it. Of course, these beliefs are merely variants of the misconceptions discussed earlier. If engineering had developed in the way psychology tried to develop, engineerometricians would still be waiting for logs to fall across streams so they could measure and compile norms for bridge spans.

Psychotechnics is a very broad practical psychology. It includes all types of psychological activities and processes for which beneficial skills can be developed: sensory-perceptual, cognitive, emotional, social, and so on. I apply the word "will" in much the same way Wallace (1967) uses "personality." Personality is what a person can do — this is Wallace's "abilities conception of personality." Will is used in much the same sense, but it includes more. Personality generally refers to those complex, high-level abilities that are socially significant. Will includes these, but also includes simpler sensory-perceptual, cognitive, and motor skills. And, what is more important, will psychology or psychotechnics emphasizes the teaching of skills, not merely their description and measurement. This is also the way psychotechnics differs from psychometrics and the general study of individual differences. One branch of psychometrics, the one concerned with the nature and measurement of intelligence, provides an instructive example of the gap between traditional psychology and psychotechnics. Only recently have a few psychologists been venturesome enough to work on the practical task of teaching "retardates" the skills of "normals" (Hunt, 1961). This is real progress. We can hope we will also be able to learn how to teach skills that take people beyond the mundanity of being normal. If we do not, psychology's reflection of man will continue to be through a mirror darkly.

I do not intend to shatter psychology's mirror for man, just polish it. We have passed beyond the era of dogmatic definitional pronouncements such as, "Psychology is the science of mind," or "Psychology is the science of behavior." Psychology is both, and more. I am not espousing another restrictive definition of what psychology should properly include and exclude, such as "Psychology is the science of will," or "Psychology is the science of soul." But to be complete, psychology must include these concerns. To omit either psychotechnics or experimental mysticism is to diminish man.

Some Examples of Psychotechnics

One possibility for the desirable development of psychotechnics is mental fluency. Fluency in manipulating mental contents is usually considered a necessary adjunct to complex cognitive performances. Nonetheless, we know almost nothing about how to teach people these subjective manipulations. Sunday supplements and popular hypnotists offer quick courses in "dynamic concentration training," but their claims exceed their knowledge.

However, if the deployment and control of inner attention has never been extensively studied by modern psychologists, it is at the core of traditional Hindu psychology. Hindu meditation manuals such as Patanjali's *Raja Yoga* (Wood, 1948) provide detailed analyses of practical techniques for achieving cognitive control. Results from recent psychophysiological experiments on hypnotic susceptibility suggest that these techniques are not mere Sanskrit esoterica. People who are susceptible to hypnotic instructions are people who can manipulate their mental contents in ways inaccessible to the unhypnotizable. The brain wave rhythm produced by these subjects is very similar to the rhythm produced by experienced yogis, swamis, and Zen practitioners when they meditate (London, Hart, Liebowitz, 1968).

To understand what this finding means, some background information is needed. Hypnosis research is now at a stage of development similar to research on intelligence in Terman's time. We have reliable measures of hypnotic susceptibility (Hilgard, 1965) but no adequate theories of hypnosis and no ways to change a person's responsiveness markedly to hypnotic instructions. We know that hypnosis is not "something special." That is, people who respond to suggestions "under hypnosis" will often respond, if sufficiently exhorted, when they are not hypnotized. Hypnosis is not caused by the hypnotist's manipulations; rather, the hypnosis setting provides an occasion for the exercise of mental skills — skills such as the production of hallucinations, remote memories, and sensory anesthesias the person might not have tried before. Some pople are skilled at responding to hypnotic instructions; some are not. These differences in skill might be viewed as differences in mental fluency. Some people can add or subtract from the contents of their minds with relative ease while others achieve only partial results or none at all.

If hypnosis is a skill, we can understand why the many attempts to find distinctive physiological indicators of the hypnotic "state" have failed. There is no state. If people skilled at manipulating their mental contents in ways called "hypnotic" are physiologically different from unskilled, they will be both "in" and "out" of hypnosis. The only difference is that "in" hypnosis, they will be more predisposed and guided in the use of their mental skills than otherwise.

There is a brain wave correlate for differences in hypnotic susceptibility (London et al., 1969). When this finding is coupled with another recent line of research showing that subjects can learn to control their own brain waves, then the way to teach people to achieve hypnotic fluency becomes clear: teach them to produce those brain wave patterns that are conducive to the self-control of mental contents. I believe, this kind of research provides an exciting and useful paradigm for many practical ventures into psychotechnics. It also shows that East and West have met and will perhaps be married in the laboratory.[3]

Other examples of psychotechnics are emerging from the many contemporary efforts to promote a more human togetherness. People can learn to feel happier within themselves and with others, and they are beginning to realize that it is not immoral or unnatural to seek new ways of being together. This new awareness is encouraging the "great group binge" of marathons, encounter groups, sensitivity training, and synanons (Hoover, 1967). The title of William Schutz's book, *Joy: Expanding human awareness* (1967), conveys the direction this movement in practical psychology is taking. The development of new institutes, such as Esalen, Shalal, and Kairos, also reflects the public's desire to learn the ways to joy.

Perhaps some readers familiar with these trends in humanistic psychology will agree with what I said about the value and need for psychotechnics but feel that it is already in the making. And in many ways it is. A special in *Psychology Today* (1967) featured the lively practice of practical psychology. A four-page foldout was included, the "Garden of Human Potential," to show the people and places "where the action is." There is no doubt that many people are seeking to develop and practice the arts and techniques of a psychology devoted to the betterment of man.

The Limits of Humanistic Psychotechnics

There are several drawbacks inherent in these otherwise encouraging developments. First is the minor drawback that most of the new programs have not found a home within professional psychology. Students in psychology, both undergraduates and graduates, will find few opportunities in their curricula to learn about marathons, encounter groups, or other developments in practical psychology. But, as I indicated earlier, this drawback may actually be an advantage for the growth of psychotechnics, if not for the students. After all, it is evident that universities are institutions for the preservation, not the creation, of cultural forms. The growth of institutes, "free universities," extension programs, and other new institutions may be one of the most significant contributions of the new psychology.

The second drawback is more important. The new programs in humanistic psychology exist like bright fragments of a broken bottle. They are so jaggedly and sharply different that we do not recognize their common identity.

[3] The research on brain wave autocontrol is discussed, in relation to meditation, in the section on experimental mysticism.

Until they can be conceptually joined, each program, alone, will hold only a drop or two of knowledge. By presenting an overall rationale and program for practical psychology, I want to provide a way for the pieces to be joined. But I do not want to urge anything as patchy as the glueing together of old fragments. It would be much better to build something like the Watts Radia Towers, structures that could rise in the midst of life by holding together the most exotic and commonplace objects from the world of psychology.

The third and most important drawback is that most programs in humanistic psychology are based upon a very limited view of man's potential. This may seem surprising; it is the same objection third-stream psychologists direct to psychoanalysis and behaviorism. Still it is true, and the deleterious influence of this limitation is all the worse because it is sometimes misconstrued as a strength. The examples given of psychotechnics show the limits of technology applied to man. In every instance the aim was to increase man's pleasure and ease his pain; nothing is wrong with that, but all attempts to increase man's control over himself and the world are inevitably inadequate.

Man seeks freedom. Knowledge and power decrease man's vulnerability, but they do not yield freedom. This is the paradox of mysticism: to achieve freedom man must become as a little child. All of man's carefully learned ways of asserting and protecting himself in the world will not provide the peace and joy of freedom. To achieve he must give up his assertive ego consciousness. But to do this one becomes *like* a child; one does not become a child; one does not regress. Instead there is a progression to a new state of awareness in which the ego is suspended but not forgotten, the ego skills and knowledge remain, the ego goals expire. This is transcendence, a level of consciousness different from both the child's immature consciousness and the normal adult's consciousness. The recognition of the reality and desirability of this state distinguishes transnaturalistic from naturalistic psychology. This is what humanistic psychology lacks and what experimental mysticism is all about.

Experimental Mysticism — Psychology as the Science of Soul

By "soul" I do not mean an insubstantial entity or essence that persists after death — such a definition can have little meaning for the scientist or practicing therapist. I am talking about a level of awareness, existence, or being, a psychological phenomenon. Psychology as the science of soul attempts to understand the characteristics, contents, and processes that describe this level of awareness. Pragmatic mysticism, or the practical psychology of the soul, attempts to develop and systematize techniques that will permit man to achieve this level of awareness. This formulation of the meaning of soul not only brings it within the province of scientific psychology but also is in accord with basic religious meanings of the term (see Spinks, 1963).

Although there is no special difficulty in applying the methods of science to the study of soul, there is some in applying accepted metaphysical and epistemological assumptions. Experimental mysticism[4] may lead to quite different conceptions of what man is and what man can know. So far in this chapter nothing has been said that drastically departs from modern psychology's currents of thought. If experimental mysticism simply carried psychotechnics one step further into the study of new levels of awareness, it might provoke skepticism but would not encounter active opposition. It is possible to look at experimental mysticism this way. But it is also possible to view mysticism, or its results, as a direct challenge to contemporary assumptions about what *is* and what is *possible*.

Consequently, it seems worthwhile to sketch the contrasting philosophical assumptions of behaviorism and psychoanalysis, humanism, and mysticism. In this sketch, behaviorism and psychoanalysis can be drawn together since these approaches agree that man is a reactor; at best, he is an adaptable, flexible reactor. The humanistic psychologist drops the prefix and proceeds from the assumption that man is an actor; at best, he is a creative and self-evolving actor. Psychotechnics fully accords with the humanistic conception of man.

Now consider the mystic's assumptions; he differs radically. Although most mystics would not deny the limited validity of ideas of man as a reactor or actor, they would claim that the fully achieved man goes beyond both reaction and action to merge with the world. In the mystic's view, man is potentially an agent, receiver, or transmitter of higher awareness. Depending upon the context in which the mystical vision is described, this state of transcendence speaks of man as a vehicle of God, an expression of cosmic consciousness, or a merging point in the absolute. None of these phrases have much meaning for the modern psychologist; they are easily dismissed as poetic metaphors. It is imperative however, to realize that these counterassumptions about man's nature are no more speculative than are our familiar assumptions.

The difference between these assumptive foundations can be seen through a comparison of their conceptions of the nature of mind. For the behaviorist and psychoanalyst, mind is conceived as a repository of genetic and learned habit-memories: mind is habit. For the humanistic psychologist, mind is a simulator, a formulator, a model builder. This formulation is also true for experimental psychologists (Miller et al., 1960) who espouse mentalistic

---

[4] The phrase "experimental mysticism" is used to describe the ideals of Dr. Andrew MacPhail, a character in Huxley's novel, *Island* (1962). The island, Pala, was a utopian society that combined the resources of Eastern mysticism and the Western science. "His ideal was pure experimental science at one end of the spectrum and pure experimental mysticism at the other. Direct experience on every level and then clear, rational statements about those experiences" (p. 113). "Experimental mysticism" also appears as a chapter heading in Ouspensky's book *A new model of the universe* (1961). Ouspensky's chapter is especially interesting today because, writing in 1912, he explored many of the possibilities and limits of psychedelic mysticism.

behaviorism: mind is idea. But in both these conceptualizations the mind is *made* either from without or from within and is considered man's highest attainment. In mysticism, mind must stop, since only then can man receive, without distortion, full consciousness. The Western psychologist praises the full and active mind. The Eastern mystic seeks emptiness that he may become full. The Western asumption is that knowledge come only through observation and reasoning therefrom; the mystic's assumption is that knowledge can come directly to the mind, that intuition and revelation are informative. These epistemological differences are real and fundamental. We as Western scientists, must stay open to the possibility that our familiar ways of knowing may not be the only ways.

The present age emerged when reliance upon faith and dogma gave way to reliance upon reason and experimentation. A new age may be coming in which faith in science will be replaced just as faith in the church was replaced. Reliance upon outside, rational, and experimental proofs may yield to inner, intuitional, and experiential proofs.[5] Our introduction to experimental mysticism can best begin by considering the ideas and life of the first psychologist who tried to link scientific ways of knowing with mystical ways of knowing.

Fechner — Mystic Without a Method

Fechner is usually praised for his psychophysical methods and derided for his goal, which was to verify scientifically his mystical vision of man and the world. Biographies of Fechner tell us that he passed through a personal crisis in his life from 1840 to 1843. His difficulties began with an extremely painful eye ailment, sometimes considered psychosomatic. This forced him to give up his post as a physicist and live as a recluse in his own home. His condition worsened and he eventually was unable to read, write, or talk. He ate very little. He wore bandages over his eyes and stayed, alone, in his black-draped bedroom. His main activity during this time was fighting to control his thoughts in an effort to avert madness. This is how he described his mental anguish:

> I was unable to control my thoughts, which revolved constantly about the same point, returned to it again and again, bored and burrowed as it were in my brain, which was deteriorating to such a degree that I had a definite feeling that I should be lost irrepairably if I did not resist with all my strength. This labor, which for nearly a year occupied the greater part of each day, was after all a kind of diversion, but it was the most painful kind that can be thought of. However, it was not altogether fruitless, and I believe that I owe the restoration of my mental powers to the steadfast persistence with which I carried it off. My inner man was as it were divided into two parts; my ego and the thoughts. Both fought with one another: the thoughts sought to over-

---

[5] On this point see Gendlin's discussion of "experiential logic" in Chapters 5 and 7.

power my ego and go their way independently to the destruction of my health: my ego on the other hand exerted the whole power of its will to master the thoughts, so that when a thought would establish itself and spin itself out my ego would strive to dispell it and introduce a remoter thought in its place. *Thus my mental occupation consisted, not in thinking, but in constantly checking and expelling thoughts* (Fechner, 1946, pp. 39-40, italics mine).

After three years of this torment, Fechner recovered. He attributes his recovery to his wife's faithful devotion and the development of his religious sensitivity, "At times I actually thought of my present secluded situation as a kind of chrysalis from which I might emerge rejuvenated and with new strength, even in this life" (1946, p. 41). His new religious convictions emboldened him to try, this time more successfully, to eat more and then to expose himself once again to the light. As Fechner came into the world again, he found it transformed — faces and forms had a new beauty, a new radiance. When he ventured into his garden among the flowers, the colors and forms were so incredibly vibrant and vivid that he felt — indeed, he says he perceived — the plants as consciously alive.

Fechner's recovery was complete. He never again experienced serious ill health, and he was soon able to resume his scientific, social, and literary activities with exuberance. In 1848, not long after his recovery, he wrote the book *Nana or the soul life of plants*. It contained a clear expression of some of his metaphysical speculations, not designed to be accepted readily by his positivistic contemporaries. A later book, *Zend-avesta or about heavenly things and the hereafter from the standpoint of natural science,* published in 1851, gave fuller expression to his visions. In the same book he formulated the basic ideas which were later expressed in the *Elements of psychophysics.* (See Fechner, 1946, for a complete listing of his writings.)

In retrospect, we can see what Fechner did not, that because of his illness he became an involuntary anchorite. He changed his surroundings, his activities, his body chemistry, and his mind. And, like others who have done the same, he achived the mystical vision. Fechner's description of his attempts to control his thoughts is a clear account of one technique of meditation. It could have come directly from the quill of a medieval monk. Unfortunately, he did not fully realize the psychological meaning of what he had done; his training as a physicist and his bias toward the quantitative led him to overlook the practical techniques he had stumbled upon.

William James — Knowledge without Experience

In temperament, training, and careers, Fechner and James were opposites, but they were alike in the serious consideration they gave to the psychological significance of mystical experience. Each contributed to the psychology of mysticism, and each fell short of providing a conceptual and practical basis for experimental mysticism; Fechner, because he was misled into psycho-physics, and James, because he had, too, few direct experiences of mystical subjectivity.

In *The varieties of religious experience* James described, with charactertstic insight and balance, the essential features of mystical consciousness:

> Whether my treatment of mystical states will shed more light or darkness, I do not know, for my own constitution shuts me out from their enjoyment almost entirely, and I can speak of them only at second hand. But though forced to look upon the subject so externally, I will be as subjective and receptive as I can; and I think I shall at least succeed in convincing you of the reality of the states in question, and of the paramount importance of their function (1958, p. 292).

This is intellectual honesty at its highest, and he did succeed. His insights are likely to have more influence on the psychology of today than any of his contemporaries. James concluded his analysis of a great variety of historical instances of mystical experience by specifying four characteristics of this level of consciousness: "ineffability," a "noetic quality," "transciency," and "pas-sivity." These conclusions have been substantiated by modern empirical stud-ies, such as Maslow's (1962) investigations of "peak experiences" and Laski's (1961) studies of "ecstatic experiences." Maslow writes,

> Peak experiences, as I have defined them for this analysis, are secularized religious or mystical or transcendent experiences, or, more precisely, peak experiences are the raw materials out of which not only religions can be built but also philosophies of any kind. . . . Not only are these experiences not dependent on churches or specific religions, as James and Dewey saw, they do not necessarily imply any supernatural concepts. They are well within the realm of nature, and can be investigated and discussed in natural-istic ways (1964, p. xii).

Aside from these investigations in the intellectual tradition of William James, there are many others relevant to the subject. Since I do not intend this to be a literature review, just two predecessors of the investigations of Maslow and Laski will be mentioned: Bucke's work on *Cosmic conscious-ness* (1923) and Hall's little-known book *Observed illuminates* (1926). Both these books, like the later ones by Maslow and Laski, present objective ac-counts of mystical experiences as reported by ordinary people. William James drew mainly from the writings of monks and nuns whose entire lives were consecrated to the achievement of mystical union with God. His con-clusions could be dismissed as applicable only to saints. The findings of the others cannot be so easily set aside. But there is still something missing in these investigations.

In most examinations of mysticism there is no systematic attempt to produce new levels of awareness. The investigations are empirical rather than ex-perimental. They describe the precursors, sensations, feelings, thoughts, and consequences of the mystical experience but do not try to induce the experience. That is the task of experimental mysticism.

In this undertaking Western psychology will find much of value in the traditional psychologies of the East. Western psychology has been essentially experimental and analytic, while Eastern psychology has been practical and speculative. It is the blend we want.

The Meeting of the Twain

The relevant literature of the Eastern religions on levels of awareness is much too abundant and complex to be reviewed here. Indeed, writings from East and West about methods of achieving mystical states of awareness and the meanings of those states may constitute the single largest literature in the whole of psychology.[6] Or is it in psychology? It is revealing that the "psychology of religion" is included as a chapter in Farberow's book *Taboo topics* (1963). I will try to select a few examples showing what modern psychology can add and receive through contact with the traditional religious psychologies of the East.

Drugs and Mysticism. Mystical techniques can be divided into physical techniques (diet, posture, exercises, breathing routines, flagellation, drugs, and so on), psychological techniques, (the use of mantras and tantras, training in meditation, concentration, and contemplation), and techniques or programs that make use of both, such as Raja Yoga. Among these various techniques, none is more controversial than the use of drugs to induce ecstatic mystical experiences.

Disregarding all the shoulds and should nots surrounding the use of psychedelic drugs, what is the evidence that drugs can be used to induce mystical states of consciousness? Perhaps the clearest answer to date is provided by Pahnke's (1963) experiment on the use of psilocybin to induce mystical consciousness.

Pahnke performed a straightforward, double-blind drug experiment. He used Harvard Divinity School students as subjects; half received a thirty-milligram dosage of psilocybin, half received nicotinic acid (this placebo induces flushing and feelings of warmth). After ingesting the drugs the subjects attended a two-and-a-half hour religious service at the University chapel. The data obtained included reports written by the subjects immediately after the service and information from postdrug and follow-up questionnaires.

The results were organized in terms of a nine-category typology of mystical experience derived from the categories of James (1958) and Stace

---

[6] For starters, consult the excellent though far from comprehensive reviews by Stace (1960), Happold (1963, 1966), Underhill (1961), Maupin (1962), Deikman (1966a, b), and, of course, James' *Varieties* (1958), a bona fide classic frequently quoted but seldom read.

(1960). They were: (1) unity; (2) transcendence of time and space; (3) deeply felt positive mood; (4) sense of sacredness (5) objectivity and reality (direct insight); (6) paradoxicality; (7) alleged ineffability; (8) transiency; and (9) persisting positive changes in attitudes and/or behavior. Pahnke concluded from his content analyses of the written reports and from the questionnaire data that ". . . under the conditions of our experiment, those subjects who received psilocybin experienced phenomena which were apparently indistinguishable from, if not identical with, certain categories defined by our typology of mysticism" (Summary, pp. xi-xii).

The significance of Pahnke's experiment resides as much in the fact that it is an experiment as in his results. Clearly, experimentation and mysticism are not antithetical. Nor are practicality and mysticism at odds. This is shown by the results for Category 9, "persisting positive changes in attitudes and/or behavior." Drugs can be used to induce meaningful religious experiences. Primitive man knew it, the alchemists of the Middle Ages knew it, and modern man is learning it anew. Modern man is also rediscovering other ancient techniques. Meditation, another example of a revived coalescence of experimentation, pragmatism, and mysticism, is one of them.

Experimental Meditation. Not very long ago, maybe as few as ten years ago, meditation was a curiosity. The image of someone meditating was likely to be that of a yogi standing on his head, or of a monk in his dark cell, or perhaps of a gullible middle-aged matron trying to sit in the half-lotus position to please her swami. But no longer. Today meditation is widely practiced by college students, businessmen, housewives, physicians — by people throughout our society.

This one-time curiosity has also been brought to the laboratory, with interesting results. Perhaps the first experimental investigation of meditation was performed by Edward Maupin (1965) who now teaches meditation and other techniques for self-awareness at Esalen. In his experiment, Maupin instructed twenty-eight male college student volunteers in a zazen concentration exercise. They practiced the exercise daily in 45-minute sessions over a two- to three-week period. After each session the students reported their experiences, and their response to the exercise was rated as high, moderate, or low. These responses were then related to premeditation test measures of digit span attention, concentration on a continuous additions task, scanning control, tolerance for unrealistic experience as assessed from Rorschach responses, amount of autokinetic movement reported, and capacity for adaptive regression as measured by the Rorschach and by visual imagery during a free association test.

Both tolerance for unrealistic experience and capacity for adaptive regression, as measured from the Rorschach, were shown to be significantly correlated with the subjects' responses to the meditation exercise. Those students who were most tolerant of unrealistic experiences and most able to regress adaptively were also most responsive to the practice of meditation. Maupin concluded from the experiment and from his review of the literature (1962) that satori can be understood as a psychologically adaptive regression, and that meditation training can be conceptualized as a sequence of states of regression, each stage developing from the tolerances and skills built up in the preceding states. Significantly, several of Maupin's subjects within the short training period reached surprisingly deep and meaningful regions of subjectivity, including hallucinoid feelings and intense emotions.

Convergent evidence for Maupin's findings comes from research by the psychiatrist Arthur Deikman (1966a, 1966b, 1963). He, too, used a traditional training technique (contemplative meditation, concentration on an object without analyzing or thinking *about* the object) and subjects with no previous meditation training. Deikman found that with as few as twelve meditation sessions over a three-week training period several of his subjects experienced unusual mental states. These included time-shortening, personal attachment to the object of meditation (a blue vase), transfiguration of the object, and feelings of intense pleasure and beauty. Deikman also found marked individual differences among his subjects in the difficulties they experienced with the method and in the intensity of their experiences during meditation. Based upon the subjects' reports in postmeditation interviews, Deikman concluded that contemplative meditation induces a "de-automatization" of perceptual and cognitive experience, which permits the adult to free himself from mental stereotyping and experience a fresh and beautiful mode of being in the world. This interpretation accords with Maupin's emphasis on the capacity for adaptive regression.

Both these experimental approaches to the study of meditation need to be extended, since their findings are based upon limited testing with small numbers of subjects for short time periods; and they drew upon only two techniques of meditation from among hundreds known. Nonetheless, the results are intriguing and should encourage other scientists to do experiments on what is perhaps the most ancient and elaborate set of techniques for practical psychology, the techniques of meditation.

We can also expect Maupin and Deikman's psychological investigations to be linked to the physiological studies that have been conducted on meditation. These investigations show an intriguing convergence between the ancient and the modern, between meditation and cybernetics.

Autoregulation of Brain Processes. That yogis can control bodily processes ordinarily considered involuntary has been mentioned already and is confirmed in many experiments (Behanan, 1937; Brosse, 1946). But the results of these experiments have exerted little influence in either theoretical or applied psychology, partly because yoga training has seemed too rigorous for most people and partly, as discussed earlier, because few psychologists have been interested in practical training procedures. The only Western scientist to make use of yoga techniques extensively and explicitly is Schultz

(1959). Significantly, his autogenic therapy was developed in a European clinic, apart from the mainstream of American experimental psychology. The yoga techniques he investigated were mainly those of hatha yoga, involving disciplining the breath, postures, and other bodily functions.

More recently, scientists have demonstrated that mental meditation exercises by themselves can produce definite and consistent physiological changes, including: (a) marked increase in galvanic skin resistance; (b) slowing of respiratory rate to as few as two to three breaths per minute; (c) decreases in metabolic rate, in some instances as much as 20-30 per cent below the basal levels; and (d) changes in the EEG, increased alpha activity even with the eyes open and in deep meditation, sustained theta activity (Anand et al., 1961; Bagchi and Wenger, 1957; Kasamatsu et al., 1957, 1966; Kugler, 1964). These investigations have shown that the physiological changes induced by meditation are basically similar regardless of the type of meditation practiced; both Zen masters and Yogis show similar patterns of change.[7]

These findings are impressive, since there are no other psychological states, aside from sleep and extreme stress, which show such regular and pronounced physiological correlates. *Meditation appears to be the only training technique known to psychology for which there are clearly demonstrable physiological indicators of the training's success or failure.* But, impressive as these physiological indicators are, we might be inclined to dismiss the training techniques as having no practical importance, as nothing more than interesting curiosities. After all, we do not expect the ordinary man in the street to renounce his home, job, and family to become a Zen monk or a yogi. However, two recent developments make these findings highly relevant.

First, forms of meditation training are being introduced to the West that do not require the practitioner to renounce society and devote his life to meditation. An article in *Look* (Hedgepeth, 1968) described the widespread popularity of Maharishi Mahesh Yogi's system of transcendental meditation, especially among college students. In the Los Angeles area alone, more than 5,000 students have completed the training program (two lectures, an interview, an hour of personal instruction in the techniques of transcendental meditation, followed by three group question-and-answer sessions to check

---

[7] Alpha activity (8-13 cps) is prominent in the occipital region of the scalp. For most people the alpha wave is the most abundant single EEG rhythm, but it is very unusual for it to be sustained when the eyes are open. Theta rhythms (4-7 cps) are rarely observed in the waking record of an adult (see Hart, 1967). Probably the most interesting and distinctive changes occurring during meditation are brain wave changes, which have been studied most thoroughly by Kasamatsu and his collaborators. He found a high correlation between measured EEG patterns and the number of years of Zen practice and rankings of meditators by a Zen master. The regular and progressive changes in EEG activity Kasamatsu observed were: (a) increased alpha activity; (b) increased alpha amplitude; (c) slowing of the alpha frequency; and (d) sustained theta activity (this last pattern was observed only in subjects with twenty years or more of Zen experience). Kasamatsu also reports that the usual habituation of the alpha blocking response to click stimulation does not occur with experienced meditators.

on the correctness of the meditation practice). After the training, the students are on their own, to practice meditation twice a day, for fifteen to thirty minutes, in the morning before breakfast and in the evening before dinner.

The fact that this technique is widely practiced and is compatible with the demands of everyday life certainly indicates that pragmatic mysticism is already becoming a social force in our society.[8] Both the social effects and the techniques should soon receive the careful scrutiny of psychologists.

The other development that must influence our assessment of the relevance of meditation training comes from the psychophysiology laboratory. Psychophysiologists have demonstrated that people can learn to control their own brain waves. Autoregulation of brain waves is based upon a familiar cybernetic principle: instantaneous feedback about changes in a system must be available before the system can be self-regulating. This is true whether the system is a thermostat, an eye, a muscle, or the brain. Although the principle is simple, only recently did scientists apply it to brain wave autocontrol. In 1962, Kamiya reported that subjects in a feedback loop could be trained to discriminate alpha from nonalpha states in their own brains, and as subjects then learned to discriminate the wave states, it was also found that they could begin to produce alpha rhythms voluntarily. Mulholland (1962) and Dewan (1964) demonstrated the same effects for the control of short alpha bursts; their subjects were able to send Morse code with their brain rhythms.

The significance of autoregulation training for meditation research is twofold. First, the EEG changes associated with meditation can be mimicked in the laboratory, and second, by combining meditation trraining with autoregulation training, both may be made more effective.

This is a hopeful prospect, because *if man can learn to control his own consciousness, through a combination of age-old techniques and modern technology, we will enter a new cultural age.* But this new age of psychological technology forbodes even greater dangers than those wrought by industrial technology. To consider both prospects and dangers we must expand this discussion and move from a consideration of techniques to a discussion of the general isues involved in applying them.

Morality and Mysticism

Of the great psychologists of the past hundred years, only three were professionaly interested in mysticism: Fechner, James, and Jung. Only Fechner

[8] Transcendental meditation is not the only meditation technique growing in popularity; it is merely the best known. Antecedents of transcendental meditation worth mentioning are Subud (Barter, 1967), which is a growing practice based upon movement meditation, and modern Zen Buddhism which continues to draw Westerners to meditation. The best book about modern Zen Buddhism that I know is *The three pillars of Zen*, edited by Kapleau (1965); it includes accounts of satori experiences and transcriptions of interviews of a Zen master with his students. For a detailed psychological analysis of satori consciousness consult Benoit (1955).

dwelt long in the mystical regions of mind, and his route to mysticism was not of his choosing. Because James and Jung read widely in the literature and wrote insightfully about their reading, it is sometimes believed that they were practiced in the traditional techniques of mysticism. They were not. This cannot be attributed to a lack of opportunities, since both traveled widely and could have found a teacher had they felt impelled to do so.

Their reluctance to gain practical training is all the more puzzling because both men were obviously aware that the Eastern techniques yield results. In a letter to a friend, W. Lutoslawski, James remarked that he had not tried "Yoga discipline" but had read several books about it. He goes on to comment about his friend's reported results from the "discipline":

> Your whole narrative suggests in me the wonder whether the Yoga discipline may not be, after all, in all its phases simply a methodical way of waking up deeper levels of willpower than are habitually used, and thereby increasing the individual's vital tone and energy. It have no doubt whatever that most people live, whether physically, intellectually or morally, in a very restricted circle of their potential being. They make use of a very small portion of their possible consciousness, and of their soul's resources in general, much like a man who, out of his whole bodily organism, should get into a habit of using and moving only his little finger. . . . May the Yoga practices not be, after all, methods of getting at our deeper functional levels? And thus only be substitutes for entirely different crises they may occur in other individuals, religious crises, indignation crises, love crises, etc. (Murphy and Ballou, 1963, pp. 275-276).

Why, if James felt this way about yoga, did he not set about immediately to learn its secrets? He does not tell us. Jung gives his reasons, and I believe James' were probably similar:

> Western man has no need of more superiority over nature, whether outside or inside. He has both in almost devilish perfection. What he lacks is conscious recognition of his inferiority to the nature around and within him. He must learn that he may not do exactly as he wills. . . . Since Western man can turn everything into a technique, it is true in principle that everything that looks like a method is either dangerous or condemned to futility. Insofar as yoga is a form of hygiene, it is as useful to him as any other system. In the deepest sense, however, yoga does not mean this but, if I understand it correctly, a great deal more, namely the final release and detachment of consciousness from all bondage to object and subject . . . my criticism is directed solely against the application of yoga to the peoples of the West. . . . Western civilization is scarcely a thousand years old and must first of all free itself from its barbarous one-sidedness. This means, above all, deeper insight into the nature of man. But no insight is gained by repressing and controlling the unconscious, and least of all by imitating methods which have grown up under totally different psychological conditions. In the course of the centuries the West will produce its own yoga, and it will be on the basis laid down by Christianity (1958, pp. 535-537).

Both James and Jung distrusted the influence of Eastern mysticism. This distrust was expressed, personally, by avoiding direct immersion in its techniques and, by Jung, in his writings about the baneful effects the spread of Eastern practices could have on Western man. We should try to be informed by the reservations and fears that James and Jung intuited. Our need to recognize the truth and falsity in their ideas is all the more critical in this period in which East and West are rapidly interpenetrating.

The dangers for the Westerner exposed to the spiritual psychologies of the East are real. He may succumb to the temptations of passivity and withdrawal or, perhaps worse, he may become exploitatively spirirtual. Jung recognized both these dangers.

The first danger is based largely upon our failure to comprehend the complete teachings of the Eastern religious psychologies. Jung simply was wrong when he wrote:

> . . . if anyone should succeed in giving up Europe from every point of view, and could actually *be* nothing but a yogi and sit in the lotus position with all the practical and ethical consequences that this entails, evaporating on a gazelle-skin under a dusty banyan tree and ending his days in nameless nonbeing, then I should have to admit that such a person understood yoga in the Indian manner (1958, p. 568).

Jung has expressed here a stereotype about one path of yoga but has ignored the full teaching and many paths.

In their undistorted forms, almost all Eastern teachings present two religious ideals or ways: the way of the renunciate and the way of the householder. Each is important and each can lead to self-fulfillment, but the renunciate's way is for the few, while the householder's way is for the many. When Westerners such as Jung reject the way of the renunciate as a viable teaching for our civilization, they are correct. That way cannot serve as the single moral ideal for any civilization, Eastern or Western. But to reject the whole of Eastern teachings is to reject too much. The way of the householder and the methods to further it are needed and applicable in both Orient and Occident. The moral ideal of the householder is that of a man who is in the world but not of the world. This is the ideal of the free man, the man who transcends through action.

Only by striving to realize this ideal can we cope with the second danger that arises when East meets West — the danger of exploitative technology applied to man's inner world.[9] I have already alluded to this in discussing psychotechnics. Jung's warnings about this danger are more to the point

---

[9] The West has already experienced the stagnation of a one-sided moral ideal, in the monasticism of the Middle Ages. And, too, our culture has known, during the years of the Inquisition, the evils of exploitative spirituality. Aldous Huxley's novel *The devils of Loudun* (1952) evokes the horrors and corruptions that arise when self-righteous men are given the power to bend and break others to fit a religious ideal.

than are his fears about yogis under banyan trees. Western man does strive more to become a superman who controls and exerts power than he does to find harmony within himself and the world. We are now on the verge of applying technological goals to man's psyche. These new techniques extend all the way from the use of drugs to improve learning and memory to technological mysticism — they include new ways of controlling ourselves and others.

We can see the great dangers of exploitative technology all around us; the most technologically sophisticated society, the United States, is the most blighted. Western technology has disturbed the earth's natural balances and checks; the harmony of the earth is faulted. The same disruptions can be wrought in our inner ecology, with even more disastrous consequences.

But what does all this talk of yoga and inner ecology and psychotechnics have to do with morality? Everything. I believe, with Jung, that the West will and must develop its own yoga (pragmatic mysticism). *The psychotherapist or counselor should be at the forefront of this cultural development. By going beyond psychotherapy the therapist becomes a psychopomp, a "soulguide."* Jung is right that a psychopomp must come to know the truth of Christianity before he can guide others, but that truth is the truth of mystical experience which is at the core of all religions. As Clark (1968) says:

> By far the most interesting, instructive, and yet puzzling phenomenon of religious experience is the mystical one. I would agree with William James that "personal religious experience has its root and center in mystical states of consciousness." This characteristic seems to me to separate religious consciousness from other forms of consciousness. All other aspects of the religious life have their counterparts in man's secular life. A mystical state alone is *sui generis* and is so different from any other psychological state that subjectively it is seldom mistaken for anything other than religion. A mystical state produces a particular kind of perception involving what is probably the most intense positive psychological experience known to man (p. 43).

I have already discussed the pervasiveness of the Freudian moral ideal. Other authors have discussed its shortcomings, but no one has offered a viable alternative. The only psychologist to try is Hobart Mowrer (1964). In numerous essays and books he has counseled a return to the values of "responsibility," "community," "confession," "love," and "honesty." He has called for renewed appreciation of traditional Protestant values. As salutary as Mowrer's message is, as a means of pointing up the shortcomings of the Freudian ethic, it will not suffice. Reheated Protestantism has all the deficiencies of hash: it will not be savoured by a sophisticated culture that has tasted the spicy new morality of popularized psychoanalysis and the skepticism of science. Apart from this, Mowrer's message is also wrong.

The basic idea within Mowrer's religious psychology is that of sin: sin is real, to sin is to do wrong, and to be healthy, a man must recognize, confess, and repent his sins. This is a familiar message to anyone in our society, familiar but inadequate as a basis for moral behavior. The Protestant conception of sin is fundamentally wrong because it is a distortion of the real meaning of sin. To sin, in the early Greek phrase used in the gospels, means *to miss the mark* (Nicoll, 1950, 1954). This is not at all the same in meaning as to do wrong or to violate a law. To miss the mark is to be less than a man can be, to live on a lower level of consciousness. To live morally a man must come to live at a new level of consciousness; anyone who does not do this sins, however correct he is in outward behavior. This is the basic message of Christ, Buddha, Lao Tse, Socrates, and all honored teachers who counsel "Know thyself."

A new morality, a new age of religion can be founded only by renewed contact with the source of morality and religion which is the mystical experience. Morality follows this experience. In an age of science the way to mysticism will come from science. But the traditional stance of the scientist is outward. He seeks to control from the outside, through facts and generalizations. In contrast, the disposition of the mystic is inward; he seeks to understand and interiorize. Each seeks a way in the world; the scientist through prediction and control of the world, the mystic through comprehension and harmony with the world. As we move toward a science and technology of man, these two traditions must merge for the good of man: "Let empiricism once become associated with religion, as hitherto, through some strange misunderstanding, it has been associated with irreligion, and I believe that a new ea of religion as well as of philosophy will be ready to begin" (James, Hibbert Lectures, p. 314, quoted by Lowrie in his introduction to *Religion of a scientist,* Fechner, 1946, p. 71).

REFERENCES

ANAND, B. K., CHINA, G. S., and SINGH, B. Some aspects of electroencephalographic studies in Yogis. *Electroencephalography and Clinical Neurophysiology,* 1961, 13, 452-456.

BAGCHI, B. K. and WENGER, M. A. Electro-physiological correlates of some Yogi exercises. *Electroencephalography and Clinical Neurophysiology,* 1957, Supplement No. 7, 132-149.

BAILEY, P. Sigmund Freud: Scientific period (1873-1897). In J. Wolpe, A. Salter, and L. J. Reyna (Eds.), *The conditioning therapies.* New York: Holt, Rinehart and Winston, 1964. Pp. 83-95.

BARTER, J. P. *Toward subud.* London: Gollancz, 1967.

BEHANAN, K. T. *Yoga: A scientific evaluation.* New York: Dover, 1937.

BENOIT, H. *The supreme doctrine.* New York: Viking, 1955.

BORING, E. G. *The physical dimensions of consciousness.* New York: Dover, 1963.

BREGER, L. and MCGAUGH, J. L. Critique and reformulation of "learning theory" approaches to psychotherapy and neurosis. *Psychological Bulletin,* 1965, 63, 338-358.

BROSSE, T. A psychophysiological study of Yoga. *Main Currents in Modern Thought,* 1946, July, 77-84.

BROWN, N. O. *Love's body.* New York: Vintage, 1966.

BUCKE, R. M. *Cosmic consciousness.* New York: Dutton, 1923.

CLARK, W. H. The psychology of religious experience. *Psychology Today,* 1968, 1, 42-47.

DEIKMAN, A. J. Experimental meditation. *Journal of Nervous and Mental Disease,* 1963, 136, 329-343.

DEIKMAN, A. J. De-automatization and the mystic experience. *Psychiatry,* 1966a, 29, 324-338.

DEIKMAN, A. J. Implications of experimentally induced contemplative meditation. *Journal of Nervous and Mental Disease,* 1966b, 142, 101-116.

DEWAN, E. M. Communication by electroencephalography. *Air Force Cambridge Research Laboratories Reports,* 1964, Special Report No. 12, 1-7.

FARBEROW, N. L. (Ed.) *Taboo topics.* New York: Atherton Press, 1963.

FECHNER, G. *Religion of a scientist.* Selections edited and translated by Walter Lowrie. New York: Pantheon, 1946.

FINCH, J. K. *The story of engineering.* Garden City, New York: Doubleday, 1960.

FREUD, S. *The future of an illusion.* New York: Doubleday, 1957.

GOULDNER, A. Anti-minotaur: The myth of a value-free sociology. *Social Problems,* 1962, 9, 199-213.

HALL, W. W. *Observed illuminates.* London: C. W. Daniel Co., 1926.

HAPPOLD, F. C. *Mysticism: A study and an anthology.* Baltimore, Md.: Penguin, 1963.

HAPPOLD, F. C. *Religious faith and twentieth-century man.* Baltimore, Md.: Penguin, 1966.

HART, J. T. Autocontrol of EEG alpha. Paper presented at the Seventh Annual Meeting of the Society for Psychophysiological Research, San Diego, October 20-22, 1967.

HEDGEPETH, W. The non-drug turn-on hits campus. *Look,* 1968, Feb. 6.

HERRNSTEIN, R. J. and BORING, E. G. (Eds.) *A source book on the history of psychology.* Cambridge, Mass.: Harvard University Press, 1966, 599-604. (Excerpts taken from Titchener, E. G. *A textbook of psychology.* New York: Macmillan, 1910.)

HILGARD, E. *Hypnotic susceptibility.* New York: Harcourt, Brace & World, 1965.

HORN, P. A visit with India's high-powered new prophet. *Look,* 1968, Feb. 6, 64-66.

HUNT, J. McV. *Intelligence and experience.* New York: Ronald Press, 1961.

HUXLEY, A. *The devils of Loudun.* New York: Harper, 1952.

JAMES, W. *The varieties of religious experience.* New York: Mentor Books, 1958.

JONES, E. *The life and work of Sigmund Freud.* New York: Basic Books, 1955, Vol. 2.

JUNG, C. G. *Psychology and religion: West and East. Collected Works,* Vol. 11. New York: Pantheon Books, 1958.

KAMIYA, J. Conditioned discrimination of the EEG alpha rhythm in humans. Paper presented at the Western Psychological Association Meeting, San Francisco: 1962.

KAPLEAU, P. (Ed.) *The three pillars of Zen.* New York: Harper and Row, 1965.

KAPLAN, A. *The conduct of inquiry: Methodology for behavioral science.* San Francisco: Chandler, 1964.

KASAMATSU, A. and HIRAI, T. An electroencephalographic study on the Zen meditation (zazen). *Folia Psychiatrica et Neurologica Japonica,* 1966, 20, 315-336.

KASAMATSA, A., OKAMA, T., TAKENEKA, S., KOGA, E., IDEDA, K., and SUGIYAMA, H. The EEG of "Zen" and "Yoga" practitioners. *Electroencephalography and Clinical Neurophysiology,* 1957, Supplement No. 9, 51-52.

KUGLER, J. *Electroencephalography in hospital and general consulting practice.* New York: Elsevier, 1964.

LASKI, M. *Ecstasy: A study of some secular and religious experiences.* Bloomington, Indiana: Indiana University Press, 1961.

LONDON, P. *The modes and morals of psychotherapy.* New York: Holt, Rinehart, and Winston, 1964.

LONDON, P., HART, J. T., and LEIBOVITZ, M. EEG alpha rhythms and hypnotic susceptibility. *Nature,* 1968, 219, 71-72.

LONDON, P., HART, J. T., LEIBOVITZ, M., and McDEVITT, R. The psychophysiology of hypnotic susceptibility. In L. Chertoh (Ed.), *International symposium on psychophysiological mechanisms of hypnosis.* New York: Springer, 1969.

MASLOW, A. H. *Toward a psychology of being.* Princeton, New Jersey: D. Van Nostrand, 1962.

MASLOW, A. H. *Religion, values, and peak experiences.* Columbus, Ohio: Ohio State University Press, 1964.

MAUPIN, E. W. Zen Buddhism: A psychological review. *Journal of Consulting Psychology,* 1962, 26, 362-378.

MAUPIN, E. W. Individual differences in response to a Zen meditation exercise. *Journal of Consulting Psychology,* 1965, 29, 139-145.

MILLER, G., GALANTER, E., and PRIBRAM, K. *Plans and the structure of behavior.* New York: Holt and Co., 1960.

MOWRER, O. H. *The new group therapy.* Princeton, N. J.: D. Van Nostrand, 1964.

MULHOLLAND, T. Evaluation of attention and alertness with a stimulus-brain feedback loop. *Electroencephalography and Clinical Neurophysiology,* 1962, 14, 847-852.

MURPHY, G. and BALLOU, R. O. (Eds.) *William James on psychical research.* New York: Viking Press, 1963.

MURPHY, M. Esalen, where it's at. *Psychology Today,* 1967, 1, 34-41.

NICOLL, M. *The new man.* London: Vincent Stuart, 1950.

NICOLL, M. *The mark.* London: Vincent Stuart, 1954.

ONDA, A. Autogenic training and Zen. In W. Luthe (Eds.), *Autogenic training.* New York: Grune & Stratton, 1963, 251-258.

OUSPENSKY, P. D. *A new model of the universe.* New York: Knopf, 1961.

OUSPENSKY, P. D. *The psychology of man's possible evolution.* New York: Knopf, 1966.

PAHNKE, W. N. Drugs and mysticism. Unpublished doctoral dissertation, Harvard University, 1963.

POLANYI, M. *Personal knowledge.* Chicago: University of Chicago Press, 1958.

RIEFF, P. *Freud: The mind of the moralist.* New York: Doubleday, 1961.

RIEFF, P. *The triumph of the therapeutic.* New York: Harper and Row, 1966.

ROGERS, C. R. A therapist's view of the good life. *The Humanist,* 1957, 17, 291-300.

ROGERS, C. R. Toward a modern approach to values: The valuing process in the mature person. *Journal of Abnormal and Social Psychology,* 1964, 68, 160-167.

SCHULTZ, J. H. and LUTHE, W. *Autogenic training.* New York: Grune and Stratton, 1959.

SCHULTZ, W. *Joy: Expanding human awareness.* New York: Grove Press, 1967.

SKINNER, B. F. *Walden two.* New York: Macmillan, 1948.

SKINNER, B. F. A case history in scientific method. In S. Koch (Ed.), *Psychology: A study of a science.* New York: McGraw-Hill, 1959, 359-379, Vol. 2.

SOROKIN, P. A. (Ed.) *Forms and techniques of altruistic and spiritual growth.* Boston: Beacon Press, 1963.

SPINKS, G. S. *Psychology and religion.* Boston: Beacon Press, 1963.

STACE, W. T. *The teachings of the mystics.* New York: Mentor, 1960.

STERN, W. *General psychology from the personalistic standpoint.* New York: Macmillan, 1938.

SZASZ, T. S. *The myth of mental illness: Foundations of a theory of personal conduct.* New York: Hoeber-Harper, 1961.

UNDERHILL, E. *Mysticism: A study in the nature and and development of man's spiritual consciousness.* New York: Dutton, 1961.

WALLACE, J. An abilities conception of personality. *American Psychologist,* 1967, 21, 132-138.

WOOD, E. E. *Practical yoga.* Hollywood, Calif.: Wilshire Book Company, 1948.

Contributors

MICHAEL P. ANDRONICO attended Brown and Rutgers Universities and received his Ph.D. from the latter institution in 1963. His professional history includes appointments at the New Jersey State Reformatory, the E. R. Johnstone Training and Research Center for the Mentally Retarded, and the Children's Psychiatric Center at Eatontown, New Jersey. He is presently Chief Psychologist at the Hunterdon Medical Center and a Research Associate at the Psychological Clinic of Rutgers University. He has published several papers on the subjects of family dynamics and the utilization of significant figures in the treatment of patients.

G. T. BARRETT-LENNARD is Professor of Psychology at Waterloo University, Ontario, Canada. He was educated in Australia and received his doctorate at the University of Chicago. After spending a few years at the University of Alabama, Dr. Barrett-Lennard returned to Australia and spent several years at the University of New England. Upon his return to North America he went to Waterloo after a brief stay at Southern Illinois University. Dr. Barrett-Lennard's interests include the process of the therapeutic relationship and, more recently, the process of intensive group experiences and the development of workshops for mental health practitioners.

ALLEN E. BERGIN joined the faculty of Columbia Teachers College after receiving his Ph.D. degree from Stanford University and spending a year as a postdoctoral research fellow at the University of Wisconsin's Psychiatric Institute. During that year Dr. Bergin was associated with Carl Rogers' project on psychotherapy with schizophrenics. Since then his interests have continued to develop, and he lists some of them as psychotherapy research, development of multiphasic approach to therapeutic intervention, and research in self-regulation and self-control.

BETTY BERZON is a Research Associate at the Western Behavioral Sciences Institute, La Jolla, California, where she has been a staff member since 1959. She attended Stanford University and UCLA, and received an M.S. degree in Psychology from San Diego State College. Her primary interest centers on innovative uses of small groups for personal growth learning. She was Project Director of WBSI's effort to develop program materials for use by self-directed groups under a grant from the U.S. Vocational Rehabilitation Administration. Miss Berzon is author of a number of papers on small groups. She is also co-editor, with Dr.

Lawrence N. Solomon, of *The use of small groups in rehabilitation: New dimensions from research.*

DESMOND S. CARTWRIGHT received his doctorate in 1954 from the University of Chicago and is currently Professor of Psychology there. For more than a decade he has been a significant and prize-winning contributor in the areas of psychotherapy and juvenile delinquency research. In recent years Dr. Cartwright has become well known as a computer methodologist, thus aptly representing his own version of "new directions."

EUGENE T. GENDLIN was born in Vienna, Austria, came to this country in 1939, and received his doctorate from the University of Chicago in 1958. While there he studied under Richard McKeon in Philosophy and Carl Rogers in Psychology. Dr. Gendlin then went to the University of Wisconsin where he directed Dr. Rogers' research project on psychotherapy with hospitalized schizophrenics. Dr. Gendlin is now a member of the Psychology Department of the University of Chicago, and while directing a new program in Philosophical Psychology, is engaged in research on "focusing" on feeling in relation to outcome in psychotherapy. He is concerned with personality theory and personality change and is the author of *Experiencing and the creation of meaning* (The Free Press, 1962), an "experiential" philosophy and method relevant to the new trends in Psychology.

GERALD GOODMAN received his graduate degree in Clinical Psychology from the University of Chicago in 1962. He then joined the Institute of Human Development at the University of California, Berkeley. While there he developed his ideas about the use of nonprofessional clinical talent. Recently Dr. Goodman joined the Psychology faculty at the University of California, Los Angeles.

THOMAS GORDON is a practicing psychologist in Pasadena, California and the founder of the Parent Effectiveness Training program. He received his doctorate at the University of Chicago where he also served on the faculty from 1949 to 1954. He is the author of *Group-centered leadership* and has contributed chapters to Carl Rogers' *Client-centered therapy* and to *Psychotherapy and personality change,* edited by Rogers and Dymond. Dr. Gordon's research interests include communications, leadership, and parent-child relationships.

BERNARD G. GUERNEY, JR. received his Ph.D. degree from Pennsylvania State University in 1956. After working for a year as a psychologist in the Children's Services of Lafayette Clinic in Detroit, Michigan, he joined the faculty of Rutgers, The State University, where he is currently an Associate Professor of Psychology and Director of the Psychological Clinic. Dr. Guerney's articles, which have appeared in numerous professional journals, reflect his interests in interpersonal processes in general, and family interaction in particular, and in developing — and expanding the utilization of — psychotherapeutic procedures. With others, he has written or edited *Psychotherapy research: Selected readings* (Rand, McNally, 1966), *Families of the slums: An exploration of their structure and treatment* (Basic Books, 1967), and *Nonprofessionals as psychotherapeutic agents.*

LOUISE FISHER GUERNEY received her B.A. from Temple University in 1948, after which she was employed as a junior psychologist at the Newark State School in New York for three years. She then went to Pennsylvania State University, where she received her Ph.D. in 1956. Now the mother of three children, Dr. Guerney has worked part-time over the years as a clinical psychologist in the Head Start Program and as a Research Associate at the Psychological Clinic of Rutgers, The State University. With others, she has written articles in the area of psychotherapy for various psychological journals. This and the study of child rearing practices and their personality correlates represent her major interests.

JOSEPH HART has been a member of the faculty in Psychology at the University of California, Irvine, since he received his doctorate from Stanford University in 1965. During his career as a student he received several awards and honors, among which was first prize for the dissertation, "Recall, Recognition and the Memory-Monitoring Process," in the Fifth Annual American Institutes for Research Creative Talent Awards Program. As a "generalist" in Psychology Dr. Hart has published in diverse areas including the process of psychotherapy, visual perception, memory, and, most recently, autocontrol of brain waves and their relation to hypnosis. He leads workshops at various humanistic growth centers and, as Director of the Institute for Personal Development, is involved in developing approaches that integrate meditation, psychotherapy, and encounter techniques. He is currently working on a new book *Psychological studies of dreaming*.

DONALD J. KIESLER received his Ph.D. degree in Clinical Psychology from the University of Illinois in 1963. He was awarded a USPHS postdoctoral research fellowship with Carl Rogers' Psychotherapy Research Project at Madison, Wisconsin in 1963, and later assumed directorship of the Psychotherapy Research Group there. He was an Assistant Professor in Clinical Psychology at the University of Iowa from 1964 to 1967 and recently assumed new duties as an Associate Professor in the Department of Psychology at Emory University. His major interest is in the area of psychotherapy research, emphasizing the development of process measures as well as analog approaches to psychotherapy research.

WILLIAM L. KIRTNER received his Ph.D. degree from the University of Chicago in 1959. Since then he has served as Clinical and Research Psychologist at California Institute of Technology, Human Factors Scientist at Systems Development Corporation, and as Assistant Professor of Psychology at the University of Colorado. In 1964 Dr. Kirtner joined the faculty of Carleton College where he is still teaching. His primary interests are the analysis of language and other behavior, psychotherapy, and personality and social psychology theory.

NATHANIEL J. RASKIN majored in Psychology at City College of New York, received his M.A. degree in Clinical Psychology from Ohio State prior to World War II, and completed his doctorate at the University of Chicago following the war. Carl Rogers was his major professor at Chicago and Raskin's Ph.D. was the first such degree in Psychology awarded by Chicago. He is currently an Associate Professor of Neurology and Psychiatry and of Home Economics (Human Development) at Northwestern University. His research interests are focused presently on the study of different approaches to psychotherapy and of "true encounter" groups.

CARL R. ROGERS is too well known and his work too well documented to need or even allow brief description. He is the originator of client-centered therapy, which gives this book its title and its contents their substance. After long associations with Ohio State University, the University of Chicago, the University of Wisconsin, and the Western Behavioral Sciences Institute, Dr. Rogers and his colleagues recently established the Center for Studies of the Person in La Jolla, California. Here Rogers continues to make significant contributions to the development of Psychology as a science of the person as well as to the study of growth-producing interpersonal and intergroup relations. He is the only member of the American Psychological Association to have been the President and to have received both the Scientific Contribution Award and the American Board of Examiners in Profesional Psychology Award (ABEPP) for contribution to professional Psychology. In the language of the citation of the latter award, "Carl Rogers, wise and gifted student of the human psyche, has helped to shape the theory and practice of human relations at home and abroad."

JOHN M. SHLIEN began as a graduate student in Social Anthropology and Human Development but became interested in Carl Rogers and his school of thought from the standpoint of political democracy and the sociology of knowledge. After further study Dr. Shlien joined the staff of the Counseling Center at the University of Chicago and wrote his Ph.D. thesis on outcomes in time-limited therapy. He later served as Chairman of the Executive Committee of the Counseling Center and as Director of Clinical Training in the Department of Psychology. Dr. Shlien is presently Professor of Counseling Psychology and Education at Harvard University and is working in the areas of child development, children as therapeutic givers and receivers, physiological measures of outcome, and stages of moral development (with L. Kohlberg) in psychotherapy process.

LAWRENCE N. SOLOMON received his Ph.D. degree in Psychology from the Universiy of Illinois in 1954. He has taught at California Western University, University of California Extension, University of Louisville, George Washington University, and University of Virginia Extension. For two years he was Executive Secretary for the Committee on Psychology in National and International Affairs at the American Psychological Association Central Office in Washington, D.C. His present positions are Dean of the Intensive Study Division at United States International University and Associate Fellow at the Western Behavioral Sciences Institute. Dr. Solomon's research interests include human relations training, small group theory and practice, and development of programmed material for self-directed personal growth groups.

T. M. TOMLINSON received his Ph.D. degree in clinical psychology from the University of Wisconsin in 1962. Following five years with the Department of Psychology at the University of California, Los Angeles, he joined the Office of Economic Opportunity, Washington, D.C., as a Research Psychologist. Prior to the

1965 civil disorders in Los Angeles, Dr. Tomlinson had worked and published in the areas of personality change and psychotherapy. Since that time, however, he has devoted the major portion of his time to the study and analysis of racially based civil disorders and other race related social issues and to strategies for racial equalization. His future plans include continued study of urban problems, especially those growing out of racial conflict, and the creation of a program for training "social clinicians."

FERDINAND VAN DER VEEN received his Ph.D. degree from the University of Chicago in 1958. Following a postdoctoral fellowship at the Department of Psychiatry of the University of Wisconsin from 1958 to 1959, he joined the faculty in Psychology at the University of Kansas. Dr. van der Veen is currently Senior Research Associate at the Institute for Juvenile Research in Chicago and is also engaged in the private practice of psychotherapy. Present research interests center on the processes of therapy and psychological growth within the family group.

RICHARD E. WHITNEY is a doctoral candidate in Social Psychology at the University of California, Los Angeles. As an undergraduate he was director of the Tutorial Program at UCLA, and during this time he helped to develop a program of remedial education for disadvantaged school children which became a model for programs in universities across the country. During 1966-67 he spent a year as a Teaching Fellow at the Chinese University of Hong Kong. While there he studied the Chinese student riots, and out of that experience he is writing a number of papers dealing with cross-cultural determinants of attitude change.

FRED M. ZIMRING received both his Ph.D. in Clinical Psychology and his Doctor of Jurisprudence from the University of Chicago. Like many other graduates of Chicago, Dr. Zimring has been associated with the Counseling Center, but he now identifies himself as Dean of Students, Division of Social Sciences, and Assistant Professor of Psychology at the University of Chicago. He has worked closely with Eugene Gendlin in the development of the concept of experiencing. Among his current research interests Dr. Zimring lists problems of thinking and cognition together with a continuing involvement with psychotherapy theory and research.

Index

603

integration of therapies in, 60, 71-73, 79-80, 550-51
interpersonal relationships in, 73-77, 79-80, 83-84, 86-93
lead to new techniques, 547-50
outgrowth of client therapy, 544-50
process concept in, 77, 78-80, 87-93
steps in, 78-79, 87, 90
theory of, 70-80
Experiential response, 550
Explanatory orbit, 150n.
Explicit, 140-41
Explicit (meaning), 139-40
Eysenck, H. J.
criticize psychotherapy, 251, 261, 262, 263, 537
on learning theory, 446, 447-48

Facilitative behavior ratings
used in group therapy, 317, 323-34
Factor analysis, 42, 50, 51. *See also* Q-sort
Family Adjustment score, 401, 402
Family concept
defined, 389
role in adjustment and change, 400-03
Family Concept Q-sort, 400, 401, 402
Family Satisfaction score, 401, 402
Family therapy, 31. *See also* Client-centered family therapy
Fechner, G.
mysticism of, 581-82, 588-89
Feeling process, 134-38, 140-41, 141-52, 160-62, 163n. *See also* Experiencing
content mutation as aspect of, 172
defined, 134
in structure-bound experience, 164-68
self-propelled, defined, 151-52
Feelings
change in relation to, 195-96, 199
Felt concreteness, 60
in therapeutic terms, 87, 89
Felt experience
character of, 81-82
differentiations of, 71
emphasis on, 73, 77, 86, 90
in schizophrenics, 285
Felt meaning, 139, 140, 142-44, 146, 148, 149n., 150n., 160, 163n., 164, 168n., 169, 169n.
response to, in therapy, 545-50
Felt need (client), 38, 39, 43

Filial therapy
case illustration of, 382-85
future aims of, 386
historical roots of, 372-76
limitations to child in, 379-80, 384
method in, 377-79
parents in, 376-78, 382-84
training of, 380-81
process in, 384-85
research in, status of, 385-86
Focusing, 141-42, 149n.
direct reference in, 142-44
global application in, 146-47
referent movement in, 147-48
self-propelled feeling process in, 151-52
unfolding in, 144-46
Freud, Anna, 278
on play therapy, 373
Freud, Sigmund, 540
Freudian theory, 85. *See also* Psychoanalytic theory
change process in, 78, 79-80
ego in, 131-32
emotionally troubled child in, 374
man's nature in, 457, 552, 558, 573-74
moral ideal in, 572-74, 591
reconstituting response in, 157n.
religion in, 571-74
sampling in, 240-41
repression in, 131
unconscious in, 120-21, 122
values in, origin of, 455

Gendlin, E. T., 18
on experiencing, 11, 45
on experiential logic, 526
on experiential therapy, 59-60, 70-94, 500-01
on future of therapy, 544-62
research with schizophrenics of, 278, 280-91
theory of personality change of, 60, 129-73, 464-67
Genuineness, 10, 18, 19, 20, 26, 66, 73, 201, 264, 265, 281, 282, 289, 402, 449. *See also* Congruence
changed by schizophrenic encounter, 284-85
in facilitator of learning, 471-73, 477, 479, 482
measurement of, 191-94, 476
related to other therapist conditions, 192

Index